CHAMPIONS OF FREEDOM
Volume 18

AUSTRIAN ECONOMICS
A Reader

Richard M. Ebeling, Editor

Ronald L. Trowbridge, Executive Editor
Lissa Roche, General Editor

Hillsdale College Press
Hillsdale, Michigan 49242

Hillsdale College Press

Books by the Hillsdale College Press include the *Champions of Freedom* series on economics; *The Christian Vision* series; and other works.

CHAMPIONS OF FREEDOM:
AUSTRIAN ECONOMICS: A READER
© 1991 by Hillsdale College Press
Hillsdale, Michigan 49242

Printed in the United States

Second printing 1997
Library of Congress Catalog Card Number 90-084344
ISBN 9-916308-83-9

Contents

Foreword

For seventeen years, America's most distinguished scholars and active decision makers have met on the Hillsdale College campus to pay homage to one of the world's greatest champions of freedom, Austrian school economist Ludwig von Mises (1881–1973). Perhaps the College's proudest possession is Mises' personal library. Upon bequeathing the library to us, Professor Mises said he had done so because "Hillsdale, more than any other educational institution, most strongly represents the free market ideas to which I have given my life."

When the history of the twentieth century is written, the Mises' name will surely be remembered as that of the foremost economist of our age. Certainly the history of one period during this century ought to include his name writ large: the one in which we are now living, the one that will be forever remembered as the time when the Berlin Wall finally came crashing down. The man who took out the first brick was Ludwig von Mises. He did it with books such as *The Theory of Money and Credit, The Free and Prosperous Commonwealth, Omnipotent Government, Bureaucracy,* and *Human Action.*

Mises based his theory of economics on the supremacy of the individual. The rational, purposeful, day-to-day decisions of ordinary men and women are what constitute the market and are the basis of all human action. It was his understanding of the market as a process, against the background of continually changing conditions and limited individual knowledge, that set his theory so clearly apart from the rigid, mathematical attempts of other economists bent on devising "models" of equilibrium.

Few economists perceived so clearly the consequences of the ideas set in motion by the statist and collectivist mentality. He warned that the greatest danger to Western society would come with the increasing concentration of political and economic power in the hands of the state. He used the example of communism in the Soviet Union and Eastern Europe to point out that the peril was real indeed.

It was Mises who wrote so eloquently and forcefully that the state could never successfully control the market place any more than it could control the lives of men. In fact, Mises' testimony has convinced prominent Marxist-Leninist intellectuals to admit recently, "The world is run by human action, not by human design."

In this special eighteenth volume of the *Champions of Freedom* series, intended as a companion to Volume 17, *Austrian Economics: Perspectives on the Past and Prospects for the Future,* selected readings in the Austrian school, which Mises helped to found, are presented.

George Roche

Hillsdale College
Hillsdale, Michigan

Introduction

Richard M. Ebeling

The Austrian Economists and Their View of Economics

Economics studies human decision making under conditions of scarcity. Economics begins with the logic of individual choices. It then extends the analysis to the setting of the market, i.e., the arena in which individuals discover potential gains from trade amongst each other. It demonstrates the conditions under which trade may occur and the limits within which the terms of trade (i.e., prices) can fall, given the preferences of the potential traders and the resources at their disposal. And, finally, it attempts to specify the conditions under which equilibrium will prevail in and across markets.

Every field of study in economics—whether it be, e.g., monetary theory, international trade, the pricing of factors of production, financial intermediation, government intervention, and regulation—begins with and is dependent upon the core theory concerning the logic of individual choice and market interaction. Every implication and conclusion drawn in any corner of economic theory, therefore, is an extension and application of the core conceptions to the particular problems the economist is investigating. As a consequence, the assumptions built into those core conceptions are crucial, because they implicitly influence, to one degree or another, everything that follows. First principles, in other words, matter, and can matter a great deal.

The Austrian school of economics began in 1871, with the publication of *Grundsätze der Volkswirtschaftlehre* (*Principles of Economics*) by Carl Menger. He was joined in the 1880s and 1890s by two other economists who took up his ideas and developed them further, Eugen von Böhm-Bawerk and Friedrich von Wieser. Their contributions were in the areas of value, cost and price theory; the theory of capital and interest; and monetary theory. By the time of the First World War, the Austrian school had attained international status as one of the major approaches to both economic theory and economic policy.

In the years between the two world wars, the Austrian school continued to make important contributions to various areas of economics, especially in the areas of comparative economic systems, money and banking theory, the theory of market processes, and theory of government intervention. The major contributors in this period included Ludwig von Mises, Friedrich von Hayek, Fritz Machlup, Gottfried Haberler, Lionel Robbins, and Oskar Morgenstern.

Two events brought about the temporary decline of the Austrian school at this time. First, the rise of fascism and Nazism in central Europe led to the departure of many of the Austrians from their native land. Dispersed into a forced exile in either England or the United States, some of the Austrian economists became interested in other issues of economic theory or policy than those that had been of primary interest to most of the members of the school in earlier years. Second, the rise of Keynesian economics and the growing appeal of socialist central planning meant that the questions and issues the majority of economists were pursuing were different from those upon which the Austrians continued to focus.

The Austrian hiatus lasted until the 1970s. Two events brought about a renewed interest in and revival of the Austrian school. In the 1960s and early 1970s two economists who had studied with Ludwig von Mises in the 1950s, Murray N. Rothbard and Israel M. Kirzner, attracted a group of young economists to the Austrian approach. And in 1974, Friedrich A. Hayek won the Nobel Prize in economics. There soon emerged a new generation of "Austrian" economists, mostly in the United States.

Carl Menger, Böhm-Bawerk and Wieser are usually credited with being among the developers of the theory of marginal utility. And often books on the history of economic thought will limit mention of the Austrians of this early period to this contribution, and their applications of it, to the theories of cost, price, capital and interest. And if the Austrians of the interwar period are mentioned it is usually in terms of their writings about whether a centrally planned economy can efficiently allocate resources without market prices, and their work on a monetary theory of the business cycle.

These are indeed among their leading contributions to economics. But what is often missing in these discussions of the history of economic thought is any appreciation of the core conceptions upon which the Austrians built their work in the areas mentioned, the core conceptions that remain the essential building-blocks of the Austrian school of economics to the present.

Methodological Individualism

Beginning with Carl Menger, the Austrians have emphasized that all social and economic phenomena begin with and are, ultimately, the result of the actions and interactions of *individuals,* whose doings generate all the outcomes observed in the market. Any theory of market phenomena that cannot successfully trace its conclusions back to a logic of human choice and action is an incomplete and unsatisfactory theory. As a result, for the past half century, the Austrians have been particularly critical of most of macroeconomics. The Austrians have argued that analyzing economy-wide economic fluctuations in employment and output, and rises and falls in the general level of prices and wages in terms of statistical aggregates is the economic version of the grin without a cat. The statistical aggregates are the composite results of a multitude of individual market decisions. Unless one can successfully trace back those statistical residues of past actions to their origin in terms a coherent theory of individual choice, little of value has been explained; by "explained" we mean a convincing theory of the causal chains that have created those fluctuations in macoeconomic magnitudes. For most of the last fifty years, macroeconomists have generally failed in any such attempt.

Methodological Subjectivism

Market phenomena originate in the actions of individuals. But, contrary to the frequently used assumptions in the theory of perfect competition, market actors do not make their choices with perfect knowledge. Indeed, if actors had perfect knowledge there would be little meaning to the commonsensical notion of choice. Choice implies selection among alternatives, but where knowledge is perfect there is no real choice. The agent can only do what the future dictates, as revealed in his perfect knowledge of what present and future events require and, therefore, demands he do.

Nor does an alternative assumption of statistical probability of market outcomes solve the problem. Numerous, if not most, market outcomes have qualities and characteristics that make them historically "unique" and thus irreducible to homogeneous classes of events to which statistical methods may be applied. Furthermore, many if not most market decisions require the decision-maker to make a judgment concerning the specific next market turn of events if profits are to be made and losses avoided. Hence, knowing the probability of an outcome from a hypothetical series of events is insufficient for a wide range of choices that must be made in the market.

The Austrians, as a result, have tried to develop theory of human action and the market process that focuses upon the actor's point-of-view, rather than impose a set of hypothetical knowledge and informational assumptions upon the actor. Such assumptions may make the economic analyst's task easier for establishing determinate market outcomes, but they do not succeed in explaining how markets actually work, given that the actual actors in the market operate from a different perspective and with different knowledge than that which the economist may have endowed him for purposes of his theory. The Austrians have argued, therefore, that market phenomena must be analyzed within a theoretical framework constructed from the knowledge, intentions and expectations of the actors themselves. This notion of constructing economic theory from the actor's point-of-view is what they mean by methodological subjectivism.

The Unintended Consequences of Human Action and the "Laws" of Economics

If actors in the market and social arenas make choices and undertake actions with imperfect knowledge, this means that many of the outcomes and consequences of their choices and actions will have unintended elements and aspects. The Austrians argue that the imperfection and limited scope of human knowledge means that it is logically impossible to predict market and social events in their entirety. Nor can we know how actors will react to those future unanticipated outcomes that their own actions have helped generate. That cannot be known until those unintended consequences materialize and become part of the actors' knowledge, on the basis of which further choices and decisions will be made.

This insight has led the Austrians to argue that *the "laws" of economics are fundamentally logical relationships and not empirical relationships*. All that can be "predicted" are the formal and logical results and outcomes that necessarily follow from the constraint of scarcity, when studied under a variety of hypothetical and alternative settings. Another way of saying this is that the laws of economics are, "if this, then that" relationships. Informed judgments may be made by market actors concerning future changes in supply and demand, or "elasticities" of demand and supply, or rates of change of various factors or magnitudes over periods of time. But all attempts to discover empirically predictable economic relationships have been mere will-o-the-wisps. This inability to discover empirical laws of economics should have been, itself, predictable. Market phenomena arise from human actions and choices; human actions and choices arise from the knowledge, expectations, beliefs and preferences held by each individual; and individuals cannot know in the present what their knowledge, expectations, beliefs or preferences will be in the future; hence, the specific shape of future things to come in the market must always be inherently unpredictable.

Austrian Economics: A Reader

These have been, in general, the core conceptions upon which the Austrian Economists have constructed their theories of human action and the market process. The readings in this special Volume 18 in the *Champions of Freedom* series are meant to provide an overview of the Austrian approach in the context of many of the areas to which the Austrians have made contributions. It does not claim to be comprehensive. The limitations of space have prevented the inclusion of many important and, indeed, classic essays by the Austrians. But it is hoped that the selections at least offer a representative sampling of the richness of the Austrian contribution to economic theory and policy.

The first section, "The Austrian School—Historically Considered" offers overviews of the Austrian school and its relationship to the classical economists of the nineteenth century and twentieth century neoclassical economics.

The second section, "Philosophy and Method of the Austrian School," presents the philosophical and methodological underpinnings of the Austrian school. The contributions under this heading explain both the Austrian criticisms of essential elements in neoclassical economics and their alternative conception of how economic theory must be constructed if it is to fulfill its role in assisting in an understanding of market phenomena.

The third section, "The Austrian View of the Market Process," emphasizes the importance that the Austrian Economists have placed on the following ideas: the market is best viewed as a dynamic process of never-ending change; knowledge of the market is imperfect and divided among the participants in the social division of labor; prices are used not only as incentives for various types of actions, but as the primary method by which knowledge about changing market conditions is transmitted to every corner of the market; the entrepreneur is the central agent in a market economy; and market competition is a discovery process for finding out least-cost methods of production and the comparative advantages of each member of the social system of division of labor.

The fourth section, "The Austrian Theory of Capital and Interest," focuses on the importance of viewing a "capitalistic" economy as a time-using economy. Resources are used over time-horizons of various durations to more productively produce future streams of consumer goods. "Capital" is comprised of "produced means of production" used with land and labor in intertemporal processes of production. Time pervades all human activity and all human choices, and contain elements of "time preference," i.e., evaluations of present satisfactions versus future satisfactions. The market rates of interest are ultimately the reflection and result of the different time-valuations of the market participants discovering opportunities for intertemporal exchange.

The fifth section, "The Austrian Theory of Money and the Business Cycle," presents the Austrian theory of the origin of money as an example of a market institution that is the result of human action, but not of human design. The Austrian theory of the "non-neutrality of money" is explained, i.e., the process by which changes in the supply of money influence the price structure of an economy, setting in motion changes in the distribution of income and misallocations of resources among alternative uses. The theory of the non-neutrality of money is combined by the Austrians with their theory of capital and interest to demonstrate the process by which monetary changes can set in motion business cycles—booms and depressions. And the Austrian views on money and the business cycle are contrasted with alternative macroeconomic approaches.

Finally, in the sixth section, "Comparative Economic Systems—The Austrian Perspective," the Austrian analysis of alternative economic systems is presented. The Austrian critique of socialist central planning is contrasted with the workings of a free market economy, with the demonstration that the elimination of private property, competitive markets and prices under socialism makes a rational allocation of resources impossible. The selections in this section also explain what the Austrians see as the inherent problems and contradictions with all forms of government regulation and intervention in a market economy.

Hillsdale College and the Austrian Economic Tradition

Hillsdale College, as part of its dedication to the tradition of individual freedom and economic liberty in the western world, has been a major center for the study of Austrian economics for almost two decades. The College is the repository of the Ludwig von Mises Library and offers a two-semester course on Austrian economics as part of its academic program for students majoring in economics, political economy or business administration. Every spring, Hillsdale College is host to the Ludwig von Mises Lecture Series, which brings leading figures in academia and public policy to the campus to deliver lectures on a wide range of topics relating to economic policy and current affairs.

In April 1990, Hillsdale College, as part of its annual Ludwig von Mises Lecture Series, sponsored an expanded, international conference on Austrian economics. Many of the leading members of the Austrian school participated, delivering papers on almost every area in economics to which the Austrians have made contributions. This reader is meant to serve as a companion to the proceedings of that conference, published as Volume 17 in the *Champions of Freedom* series, under the title, *Austrian Economics: Perspectives on the Past and Prospects for the Future.*

It is hoped that this reader, besides offering a convenient, one-volume summary of the Austrian contribution to economic theory and policy, will also demonstrate that their view of man, society and economic order have a lasting and crucial significance for thinking about the problems of our own times and the decades to come. It is with this thought in mind that Hillsdale College offers this special volume to the public.

Richard M. Ebeling
Ludwig von Mises Chair
Hillsdale College

April 1991
Hillsdale, Michigan

Part I

The Austrian School—
Historically Considered

1

Austrian Economics—
An Annotated Bibliography:
The Austrian Economists

Richard M. Ebeling

Introductory Readings

Friedrich von Hayek, "Economic Thought: The Austrian School," in the *International Encyclopedia of the Social Sciences,* ed. by David Sills (New York: Macmillan Co., 1968), vol. 4, pp. 458–62.

Ludwig M. Lachmann, "The Significance of the Austrian School of Economics in the History of Ideas," in *Capital, Expectations and the Market Process,* ed. by Walter E. Grinder (Kansas City: Sheed Andrews and McMeel, 1977), pp. 45–64.

Ludwig von Mises, *The Historical Setting of the Austrian School of Economics* (New Rochelle: Arlington House, 1969).

Emil Kauder, *A History of Marginal Utility Theory* (Princeton University Press, 1965).

Henry Seager, "Economics at Berlin and Vienna," *Labor and Other Essays* (Freeport: Books for Libraries Press, 1968), pp. 1–29.

Reprinted from *The Humane Studies Review: A Research and Study Guide* 2 (1983):1, published by the Institute for Humane Studies.

In the history of economic thought various schools are distinguishable by the common core concepts or ideas that can be seen as binding the contributions of a group of writers into one tradition. In the case of the Austrian school this is exemplified by: a persistent adherence to methodological individualism and methodological subjectivism, and an emphasis on their application to a variety of economic problems. These applications have extended from the logic of human action and choice to the understanding of the spontaneous formation of market and social orders, and the processes of change, adjustment, and coordination in alternative institutional settings.

During the fifty years following 1870, the Austrian school economists focused upon a restatement of the theory of value in terms of the subjective valuations of market actors on the basis of the marginal principle. In opposition to the Labor Theory of Value of the Classical economists, they argued that value was not an intrinsic or objective quality embedded in an object, but rather value was bestowed upon an object by an evaluating mind. And, the Austrians said, it was an evaluation made at the "margin" of decision making, i.e., the importance in terms of utility of the next (last) unit of a good that could be obtained or would have to be given up in an act of choice and exchange. The Austrians spun out the wider implications of the marginal concept by applying the theory to the explanation of capital and interest, and wages and rent. While the Austrians shared the marginal concept with the other founders of neoclassical economics, William Stanley Jevons and Leon Walras, the Austrians' unique and distinctive twist was an emphasis on the wider aspects of a subjective approach, specifically the subjectivism of knowledge, perceptions and intention from the point-of-view of the market actors. This led the Austrians to an interest in *the market processes leading to an equilibrium* rather than a mere specification of the conditions requisite for a state of equilibrium to exist.

In the twenty years following World War I the Austrian economists continued their investigations into what has usually been called economic dynamics, by analyzing the role of time in economic processes; by applying the subjectivist-marginalist approach to monetary phenomena; by studying business cycles in terms of a microanalysis of sequential change, error, and adjustment in the wake of monetary disturbances; and through penetrating critiques of the meaning and significance of "equilibrium" in the body of economic theory.

During the thirty years following the 1936 publication of Keynes's *The General Theory,* however, the Austrian school and its approach were eclipsed by the new interest in macroeconomics. Rather than focusing on causal relationships connecting individual transactors and markets, the analysis was shifted to the study of statistically derived aggregate magnitudes, on the basis of which functional correlations were to be established for the purpose of both furthering theoretical understanding and assisting the implementation of stabilization policies. At the same time, microeconomic theory, under the influence of Walrasian and Paretian economics, was reduced to dry, mathematical formalism that returned a large portion of economic analysis to a study of *states of equilibrium* rather than *processes of markets.* In such an intellectual climate, the Austrian school was relegated by the economics profession to a small corner of the history of economic thought and was considered to represent an outdated stage of scientific development.

But over the last fifteen years doubts and uncertainties concerning the corpus of economics have resulted in a radical change in how the economics profession views the Austrian school. Having reached an analytical dead-end in their formulation of ever-more esoteric general equilibrium models, and experiencing growing concerns about the microeconomic foundations of a wobbly macroeconomics, a sizable number of economists has "rediscovered" the Austrian school. Furthermore, a new generation of Austrian school economists has made a conscious effort to pick up and advance the analytical strands that were severed during the Keynesian episode.

Historical Roots

A comprehensive history of the Austrian school and its members has yet to be written. The interested student, therefore, must draw from several sources to follow the school's evolution and development. Brief histories can be found in Friedrich von Wieser's "The Austrian School of Economics," in Henry Higgs, ed., *Palgraves Dictionary of Political Economy*, vol. I (London: Macmillan and Co., Ltd., 1926), pp. 814–18; and Friedrich von Hayek's "Economic Thought: The Austrian School," in David Sills, ed., *International Encyclopedia of the Social Sciences* (New York: Macmillan and Co., 1968), vol. 4, pp. 458–62.

The closest to a history of the Austrian school is Emil Kauder, *A History of Marginal Utility Theory* (Princeton University Press, 1965). Though far from comprehensive either in terms of content or interpretation, Kauder relates the Austrians to the development of utility theory over the centuries, discusses the specific contributions of the Austrians, and compares them with other marginalist schools in this century. Equally useful is R. S. Howey, *The Rise of the Marginal Utility School, 1870–1889* (Lawrence: University of Kansas Press, 1960); as the title suggests it covers only the earliest stages of the period and discusses the Austrians only in the context of the marginal concept, contrasting the Austrian formulation with that of others in the era. The Austrian chapters, however, contain a wealth of background material, though the author's interpretation and understanding of the Austrian position can at times be challenged. A fascinating account of life among the Austrians in the early 1890s was written by Henry Seager, who spent a semester at the University of Vienna in 1892–1893: "Economics at Berlin and Vienna," *Journal of Political Economy*, vol. I (March, 1893), pp. 236–62, reprinted in Seager, *Labor and Other Essays* [1931] (Freeport: Books for Libraries Press, 1968), pp. 1–29.

The particular social and intellectual environment in which the Austrian school arose in the Austro-Hungarian Empire is discussed by Ludwig von Mises in *The Historical Setting of the Austrian School of Economics* (New Rochelle: Arlington House, 1969). For the suggestion that socioeconomic position may have played a role in the emergence and form of the early Austrian school, see Erich Streissler, "Structural Economic Thought: On the Significance of the Austrian School Today," *Zeitschrift für Nationalökonomie*, Bd. 28 (1968), pp. 256–66. William M. Johnston held the view that Austrian sympathy for nonintervention in the market place originated with the impartiality which had been traditionally associated with the Josephenist bureaucracy, in "Economists as Bureaucrats," in *The Austrian Mind: An Intellectual and Social History, 1848–1938* (Berkeley: University of California Press, 1972), pp. 76–87. Nikolai Bukharin, on the other hand, accused the Austrian school of protecting the vested interests of parasitic rentiers in his *Economic Theory of the Leisure Class* (New York: Monthly Review Press, 1972).

The relationships between the Austrians and on one hand, the Classical economists who preceded them, and on the other, the mathematical economists of the contemporaneous Lausanne school, are concisely explained by Ludwig M. Lachmann in "The Significance of the Austrian school of economics in the History of Ideas," [1966] in *Capital, Expectations and the Market Process*, ed. by Walter E. Grinder (Kansas City: Sheed Andrews and McMeel, Inc., 1977), pp. 45–64.

There were important differences between the three marginalist co-founders. In particular, Menger placed a unique emphasis on the process of market adjustment rather than on the end-state equilibrium of that process. These differences are brought out by William Jaffé, in "Menger, Jevons and Walras De-Homogenized," *Economic Enquiry*, vol. 14 (December, 1976), pp. 511–24; and Erich Streissler, "To What Extent Was the Austrian School Marginalist?" in R. D. Colison, Black, A. W. Coats, and Craufurd D. W. Goodwin, eds., *The Marginalist Revolution in Economics, Interpretation and Evaluation* (Durham: Duke University Press, 1973), pp. 160–75.

Menger: The Founder

The Austrian school began with Carl Menger and the publication of his *Principles of Economics* [1871] (New York: New York University Press, 1981). This and the only other complete book he published, *Problems of Economics and Sociology* [1883] (Urbana: University of Illinois Press, 1963), have served as the seminal core from which all later developments of the school ultimately stem. How the young Menger, while a civil servant reporting on price movements, was led to the subjective theory of value by noticing the discrepancy between classical doctrine and the actual formation of prices is told by Friedrich von Wieser, "Carl Menger," *Palgraves Dictionary of Political Economy*, pp. 923–24.

Numerous essays have been written about Menger and his place in the history of economic thought. The ones most worthwhile consulting are: Friedrich von Hayek, "Carl Menger," *Economica* (1934), and reprinted as the introduction to the New York University Press edition of Menger's *Principles;* George Stigler, "The Economics of Carl Menger," *Journal of Political Economy*, vol. 45 (April, 1937), pp. 229–50, reprinted in *Production and Distribution Theories, The Formative Years* (New York: Macmillan Co., 1941), pp. 137–57; and Joseph A. Schumpeter, "Carl Menger, 1840–1921," in

Ten Great Economists (New York: Oxford University Press, 1951), pp. 80–90. For a less enthusiastic interpretation of Menger, see Frank H. Knight's "Introduction" to the first English edition of Menger's *Principles* (Glencoe: The Free Press, 1950), pp. 9–35. Henri-Simon Bloch, "Carl Menger: The Founder of the Austrian School," *Journal of Political Economy,* vol. 48 (June, 1940), pp. 428–33, emphasizes what he sees as the similarities between Menger, Jevons, and Walras as well as drawing attention to Menger's methodological writings. And Knut Wicksell, "Carl Menger" [1921] in *Selected Papers on Economic Theory,* Erik Lindahl, ed. (London: George Allen & Unwin, 1958), pp. 186–92, points out the revolutionary character of Menger's work.

Böhm-Bawerk and Wieser

If Menger was the founder of the school, its development and international recognition was due to the efforts of two young followers, Eugen von Böhm-Bawerk and Friedrich von Wieser. As students together they discovered Menger's *Principles* and immediately appreciated its importance.

Böhm-Bawerk's contribution centered on the careful working out of an Austrian theory of *Capital and Interest,* 3 vols. (South Holland: Libertarian Press, 1959). Embedded in volume two, *The Positive Theory of Capital,* is an elaborate and detailed discussion of the subjectivist basis of value and price, pp. 121–256. Also useful as background on the Austrians and their approach to value theory are Böhm-Bawerk's articles, "The Austrian Economists" [1891] and "The Ultimate Standard of Value" [1894] reprinted in *Shorter Classics of Böhm-Bawerk* (South Holland: Libertarian Press, 1962).

Joseph Schumpeter includes an extended and very complimentary evaluation of Böhm-Bawerk's works in *Ten Great Economists,* pp. 143–90. For a more critical discussion see George Stigler's *Production and Distribution Theories,* pp. 179–227. Böhm-Bawerk's participation in Austro-Hungarian public life is briefly discussed in Friedrich von Wieser's "Eugen von Böhm-Bawerk," *Palgraves Dictionary of Political Economy,* pp. 825–26. Böhm-Bawerk's policies as Minister of Finance of Austria at the turn of the century are explained in some detail by Alexander Gerschenkron in *An Economic Spurt That Failed* (Princeton: Princeton University Press, 1977), pp. 85–127, where the author focuses on what he sees as the detrimental consequences of Böhm-Bawerk's "fiscal conservativism."

Wieser's two principal works were *Natural Value* [1889] (New York: Augustus M. Kelley, 1971) and *Social Economics* [1914] (New York: Augustus M. Kelley, 1967), the latter being the only systematic treatise published by a member of the Austrian school before World War I. Wieser's two fundamental contributions were the concept of opportunity cost and the theory of imputation, i.e., the determination of the distributional shares of the factors of production. Wieser twice defended the Austrian approach to value, cost, and price in English; "The Austrian School and the Theory of Value," *Economic Journal,* vol. 1 (March, 1891), pp. 108–21, and "The Theory of Value," *Annals of the American Academy of Political and Social Science,* vol. 2 (March, 1892), pp. 24–52.

W. L. Valk contrasted Wieser's imputation theory with John Bates Clark's marginal productivity theory in *The Principles of Wages* (London: P. S. King & Son, Ltd., 1928). A critical analysis of Wieser's approach is offered in George Stigler, *Production and Distribution Theories,* pp. 158–78. For a more favorable interpretation see Wesley C. Mitchell, "Wieser's Theory of Social Economics," [1915] in *The Backward Art of Spending Money* [1937] (New York: Augustus M. Kelley, 1950), pp. 225–57. A summary of Wieser's life and work can be found in Friedrich A. Hayek, "Hayek on Wieser," [1926] in Henry William Spiegel, *The Development of*

Economic Thought (New York: John Wiley & Sons, Inc., 1952), pp. 555–67; Schumpeter, "Friedrich von Wieser, 1851–1926," in *Ten Great Economists,* pp. 298–301; and Oskar Morgenstern, "Friedrich von Wieser, 1851–1926," [1927] in *Selected Economic Writings of Oskar Morgenstern,* ed. by Andrew Schotter (New York: New York University Press, 1976), pp. 481–85. Also worth consulting is Hans Mayer, "Friedrich Freiherr von Wieser," *Neue Österreich Biographie,* Bd. 6 (Wien: Amalthea-Verlag, 1929), which contains a complete bibliography of Wieser's writings.

While Menger, Böhm-Bawerk, and Wieser are commonly regarded as the late nineteenth-century giants of the Austrian school, there were a number of minor figures as well. A brief summary of them and their works can be found in Howey's *The Rise of the Marginal Utility School, 1870–1889,* pp. 161–72. Amplifying Howey's discussion are reviews by Henry Seager of Eugen von Philippovich, *Grundriss der politischen Oekonomie* in *Annals of the American Academy of Political and Social Science,* vol. 4 (July, 1894), pp. 168–79; by Edmund J. James of Emil Sax, *Grundlegung der theoritschen Staatswirtschaft* in *Political Science Quarterly,* vol. 5 (March, 1890), pp. 166–69; and by Henry Raymond Mussey of Franz Cuhel, *Zur Theorie von den Bedürf-nissen* in *Political Science Quarterly,* vol. 24 (June, 1909), pp. 323–25.

Two excellent summaries of the Austrian theory of value, cost, and price as it was presented in the writings of these early Austrians can be found in James Bonar, "The Austrian Economists and Their View of Value," *Quarterly Journal of Economics,* vol. 3 (October, 1888), pp. 1–31; and William Smart, *An Introduction to the Theory of Value, Along the Lines of Menger, Wieser and Böhm-Bawerk* [1891] (New York: Augustus M. Kelley, 1965).

The Interwar Period

The Austrian school, while maintaining certain fundamental conceptions in common, broke into two branches in the interwar period. Some aspects of this division are discussed in an article critical of the Austrian approach in general by Alan R. Sweezy, "The Interpretation of Subjective Value Theory in the Writing of the Austrian Economists," *Review of Economic Studies,* vol. 1 (1934), pp. 176–85.

One branch of the Austrian school transformed economics into a formal analysis of the allocation of given means for the satisfaction of given ends which were ranked in order of importance. The basis for this formulation was Hans Mayer's psychological "Law of the Periodic Recurrence of Wants," and from this "law" an Austrian theory of consumption-period planning was constructed. The groundwork can be found in Mayer, "Untersuchung zu dem Grundgesetz der Wirtschaftlichen Wirtrechnung," *Zeitschrift für Volkswirtschaft und Sozialpolitik,* Bd. 2 (1922), pp. 1–23; and Mayer, Bedürfnis," *Handwörterbuch der Staatswissenschaften,* Be. 2 (Jena: Gustav Fischer, 1924), pp. 450–56; and recapitulated in Mayer, "Zur Frage der Rechenbarkeit des Subjektiven Wertes," in *Wirtschaftstheorie und Wirtschaftspolitik, Festschrift für Alfred Amonn,* ed. by Valentin F. Wagner and Fritz Marbach (Bern: Francke Verlag, 1953), pp. 57–78.

Mayer's approach was adopted by Leo Schönfeld in his *Grenznutzen und Wirtschaftrechnung* (Wien: Manz'sche Verlags-und Universitäts-Buchhandlung, 1924); summarized by Paul N. Rosenstein-Rodan, "Marginal Utility," [1927] *International Economic Papers,* vol. 10 (1960), pp. 82–83 and Rosenstein-Rodan, "The Role of Time in Economic Theory," *Economica,* vol. 1 (February, 1934), pp. 78–84; and extended by Oskar Morgenstern, "The Time Moment in Value Theory," [1935] in *Selected Economic Writings of Oskar Morgenstern,* pp. 151–67. On Hans Mayer, the reader should consult Alexander Mahr, "Hans Mayer—Leben und Werk," *Zeitschrift für Nationalökonomie,* Bd. 16 (March, 1956), pp. 3–16; and Wilhelm Weber, "Hans Mayer," *Handwörterbuch der Sozialwissenschaft,* Bd. 7 (Stuttgart: Gustav Fischer, 1961), pp. 364–65. On Schönfeld see Hans Mayer, "Leo Illy (Schönfeld)," *Zeitschrift für Nationalökonomie,* Bd. 14 (October, 1953), pp. 1–3.

The other branch of the Austrian school drew a sharp line between economics and psychology, viewing economics as a purely formal and logical analysis of action and choice. The nonpsychological formulation in Richard Strigl's *Die ökonomischen Kategorien und die Organisation der Wirtschaft* (Jena: Gustav Fischer, 1923) was, however, analogous to Mayer's, i.e., an analysis of the allocation of scarce given means among competing given ends, but in which the psychological state of the individual and the social and technological circumstances under which the allocation was made were "given" datum within which the ends-means framework applied. On Strigl, see, Friedrich von Hayek, "Richard von Strigl," *Economic Journal,* vol. 54 (June-September, 1945), pp. 284–86.

Ludwig von Mises

The leading and best-known member of this second branch of the Austrian school was Ludwig von Mises. Mises's formulation was of a more dynamic character, in that he adopted Max Weber's concept of "meaningful" behavior as purposeful or intentional conduct in which an individual initiated action on the basis of his *subjective* interpretation of circumstances. Rather than taking the ends and means as given, "purposeful conduct" was a broader concept that analyzed the logical process by which the individual constructed an ends-means framework within which economizing then occurred. This Misesian view emerged in a series of articles published as *Epistemological Problems of Economics* [1933] (New York: New York University Press, 1981) and was restated in a more complete and refined form in *Human Action, A Treatise on Economics* [1949] (Chicago: Contemporary Books, 3rd revised ed., 1966), *Theory and History* [1957]

(New Rochelle: Arlington House, 1969), and *The Ultimate Foundation of Economic Science* [1962] (Kansas City: Sheed Andrews and McMeel, 1978). Mises viewed his other writings on monetary theory, comparative economic systems, and the market process as "applications" of his concept of action. A complete bibliography of Mises's works can be found in Bettina Bien, *The Works of Ludwig von Mises* (Irvington: Foundation for Economic Education, 1969).

Mises explains his intellectual evolution in *Ludwig von Mises' Notes and Recollections* (South Holland: Libertarian Press, 1978), originally written in 1940 shortly after he arrived in the United States from Europe. A useful, though brief, summary of Mises's contributions can be found in Murray N. Rothbard, "The Essential Von Mises," an appendix in Mises, *Planning for Freedom* (South Holland: Libertarian Press, 4th ed., 1980), pp. 234–70. Mises's position vis-à-vis the development of economics as a science is analyzed by Israel M. Kirzner, *The Economic Point of View* [1960] (Kansas City: Sheed and Ward, Inc., 1976).

Extensive discussions of Mises's writings can also be found in several *Festschriften* in his honor: Mary Sennholz, ed., *On Freedom and Free Enterprise* (Princeton: D. Van Nostrand, Co., Inc., 1956); *Toward Liberty* (Menlo Park: Institute for Humane Studies, 1971); Lawrence S. Moss, ed., *The Economics of Ludwig von Mises* (Kansas City: Sheed and Ward, Inc., 1976); *Homage to Mises* (Hillsdale: Hillsdale College, 1981); "Ludwig von Mises—seine Ideen und seine Wirkung," *Wirtschaftpolitische Blätter*, Bd. 28 (Fall, 1981); Israel M. Kirzner, ed., *Method, Process and Austrian Economics* (Lexington: Lexington Books, 1982). Finally, a glimpse of the personal side of Mises can be found in Margit von Mises, *My Years with Ludwig von Mises* (New Rochelle: Arlington House, 1976).

In the Vienna of the 1920s and early 1930s, Mises's university and private seminars were the catalyst for a new generation of Austrian economists. Among them were such scholars as Gottfried Haberler, Friedrich von Hayek, Felix Kaufman, Fritz Machlup, Oskar Morgenstern, Paul N. Rosenstein-Rodan, Alfred Schütz and Richard von Strigl. The importance of the seminars is outlined in Gottfried Haberler, "Mises's Private Seminar," *Wirtschaftpolitische Blätter,* vol. 28 (Fall, 1981), pp. 121–26, also an earlier version reprinted in Mises's *Planning for Freedom,* pp. 276–78; and the contributions of Friedrich von Hayek and Fritz Machlup in *Tribute to Mises,* The Mont Pelerin Society (Kent: Quadrangle Publications, Ltd., 1974), pp. 2–7, 10–16.

Many of the strands of Mises's formulation of Austrian economics have been continued by his former student, the 1974 Nobel Laureate, Friedrich von Hayek. Hayek's voluminous and important contributions will be discussed in detail in later parts of this series. Summaries and evaluations of various aspects of Hayek's work are now available in Gerald P. O'Driscoll, *Economics as a Coordination Problem, The Contributions of Friedrich A. Hayek* (Kansas City: Sheed Andrews and McMeel, 1977); Norman P. Barry, *Hayek's Social and Economic Philosophy* (London: Macmillan Press, Ltd., 1979); G. L. S. Shackle, "F. A. Hayek, 1899- " in D. P. O'Brien and John R. Presley, ed., *Pioneers of Modern Economics* (Totowa: Barnes and Noble Books, 198a) pp. 234–61; and Fritz Machlup, ed., *Essays on Hayek* (New York: New York University Press, 1976). The particular contributions by other members of the interwar Austrian school will also be mentioned in the relevant sections of future segments of this bibliography.

The arrival of Keynesian economics eclipsed the Austrian school for almost three decades with only Ludwig von Mises, Friedrich von Hayek, and Ludwig M. Lachmann consciously continuing the tradition in their writings.

Ludwig M. Lachmann was a student of Hayek's at the London school of economics in the early 1930s; his Austrian approach is presented in a series of essays now collected as *Capital, Expectations and the Market Process,* ed. by Walter E.

Grinder (Kansas City: Sheed Andrews and McMeel, 1977) and in his book, *Capital and Its Structure* [1956] (Kansas City: Sheed Andrews and McMeel, 1978). For an intellectual biography of Lachmann, see the introduction to *Capital, Expectations and the Market Process* by Walter E. Grinder, pp. 3–24.

After World War II, a revival of the Austrian school emerged from Mises's seminar at New York University in the 1950s and 1960s, with the two most prominent figures being Israel M. Kirzner, *Market Theory and the Price System* (Princeton: D. Van Nostrand, Co., Inc., 1963) and *Competition and Entrepreneurship* (Chicago: University of Chicago Press, 1973), and Murray N. Rothbard, *Man, Economy and State*, 2 vols., [1962] (Los Angeles: Nash Publishing Co., 1970) and *Toward a Reconstruction of Utility and Welfare Economics* [1956] (New York: Center for Libertarian Studies, 1977).

The extent of the growing interest in the Austrian tradition is exemplified by a series of volumes that have appeared during the last decade devoted to exploring its various themes; among them, Sir John Hicks and Wilhelm Weber, ed., *Carl Menger and the Austrian School of Economics* (Oxford: Oxford University Press, 1973); Edwin G. Dolan, ed., *The Foundations of Modern Austrian Economics* (Kansas City: Sheed Andrews and McMeel, 1978); a series of articles on "Carl Menger and Austrian Economics," in the *Atlantic Economic Journal*, vol. VI, no. 3 (September, 1978); Mario J. Rizzo, ed., *Time, Uncertainty and Disequilibrium, Exploration of Austrian Themes* (Lexington: Lexington Books, 1979); Thomas C. Taylor, *The Fundamentals of Austrian Economics* (London: Adam Smith Institute, 1980); and Alex H. Shand, *Subjectivist Economics, The New Austrian School* (Exeter: The Pica Press, 1981).

The Significance of the Austrian School of Economics in the History of Ideas

Ludwig M. Lachmann

1

To speak of the spirit and its history in our age is a precarious undertaking. Even though one escapes the suspicion of having sat at the feet of a metaphysician such as Hegel, one still may face an indictment of "essentialism." Fortunately, the authors of this *Festschrift* need harbor no such fears. Neither the celebrant of this anniversary nor the readers of this journal will be in any doubt as to what is meant by the spirit of the Austrian school in economic theory.

It is almost a century since Menger wrote the *Grundsatze* and founded the Austrian school.[1] In this century there have been decades of triumph and decades of neglect. The favorable and unfavorable climate of the times has had

Reprinted from *Capital, Expectations, and the Market Process: Essays on the Theory of the Market Economy* by Ludwig M. Lachmann (Kansas City: Sheed Andrews and McMeel, Inc., 1911).

This essay, "Die geistesgeschichtliche Bedeutung der osterreichischen Schule in der Volkswirtschaftslehre," *Zeitschirft fur Natinalokonomie* 26 (February 1966): 152–67, was translated by Robert F. Ambacher of Millersville State College and Walter E. Grinder.

much to do with the successes and failures of the school. At the end of the first century of its existence, we may expect a number of critical assessments of its ideas and their development. It is not my intention, however, to deal with problems of the history of ideas in the narrower sense.

In what follows I shall attempt to indicate the cognitive aim, intellectual trend, and typical methodology of the Austrian school in the light of some of its major achievements, and to contrast them with those of other economic schools. I maintain that there is a characteristic and demonstrable "intellectual style" of the Austrian school and that this style is geared to the interpretation of cultural facts, as will have to be shown. This posture is of course in opposition to the currently dominant methodological monism of positivism, which proclaims that there is only one truly "scientific" mode of thought, namely, that of the modern natural sciences. In contrast, I shall attempt to show that the ideas and aims of the representatives of the Austrian school, perhaps unconsciously, were always directed not only toward the discovery of quantitative relationships among economic phenomena but also toward an *understanding* of the meaning of economic actions.

It is curious that two thinkers, so different in descent, temperament, and intellectual interests as Schumpeter and Sombart, agreed in their judgment of the work of the Austrian school at least insofar as they saw in the teachings of the Viennese an imperfect preliminary to the general equilibrium theory of the Lausanne school. Schumpeter's position followed naturally from his view that Walras's accomplishment represented the very apex of the history of economic thought. He ascribed to the "defective technique" of the Viennese their failure to ascend to the true height of Walras's accomplishment after having discovered the ladder.[2]

Sombart's aim, on the other hand, was apparently to be able to deny any intellectual affiliation with the Austrians. For him, they belong to "taxonomic economics" (*ord-nende Nationalokonomie*) but fare poorly compared with the Lausanners. "If there is to be any taxonomic economics, let it be Pareto's" appears to have been his verdict.[3] I believe that both were mistaken because they misunderstood the cognitive aim and intellectual trend of the Austrian school.

2

Characteristic of the trend of thinking of the Austrian school is, in our view, *Verstehen* (understanding), introduced as a method into the theoretical social sciences. This statement in no way diminishes the significance of the concept of marginal utility, but only indicates that in the creation of this fundamental concept the Austrians had predecessors like Dupuit and Gossen, as well as contemporaries like Jevons and Walras, who, however—as we shall see—developed their own methodologies.

On the other hand, *Verstehen* as a method in the social sciences has, as is well known, a long and glorious history. Not only in the interpretation of texts, as in theology, jurisprudence, and philology, but also in the interpretation of the meaning of human actions, as in all history, this method has always found application. There is, however, a significant difference between *understanding as historical method,* as it found its systematic expression, for example, in Droysen's *Historik,* and *understanding as a theoretical method,* that is, as a method for the interpretation of *typical courses of action with the aid of thought designs,* for example, economic plans.[4] The characteristic accomplishment of the Austrian school was, in our view, the gradual development of understanding as a method in the second sense. For them the thought design, the economic calculation or economic plan of the individual, always stands in the foreground of theoretical interest.

Before substantiating my thesis by contrasting the essential characteristics of Austrian thought with those of the classical and the Lausanne school, I must meet two obvious objections. It may seem that my interpretation of Austrian thinking cannot be reconciled with the methodological views of two thinkers like Menger and Mises.

One objection might be that in Menger's *Unter-suchungen*, for decades considered the methodological cate-chism of the school, understanding as a method of the theo-retical social sciences, and especially of economics, is never mentioned.[5] On the contrary, Menger declared again and again that the task of the social sciences, as of the natural sciences, is to find "exact laws." Sombart thus appears to be correct when he characterized the *Untersuchungen* as the "most significant methodological work dealing with eco-nomics in the manner of the natural sciences."[6]

We must, however, take into account the intellectual climate of the years in which Menger's work originated. In the first place, understanding as a method of theoretical culture study was scarcely known in 1883, the year in which both Dilthey's *Einleitung in die Geisteswissenschaften* [*Introduc-tion to the Social Sciences*] and Menger's *Untersuchungen* were published. Secondly, with the publication of Menger's work the *Methodenstreit* began. Menger, in particular, attacked the attempts of Schmoller and his friends to impose *historical understanding* on the theoretical social sciences, for exam-ple, economics, as the only legitimate method. Hence, one could hardly expect much sympathy from Menger for vari-ants of the same methodology still awaiting elucidation even if he had known them. But he did not.

Third, and probably most important, the real theoreti-cal work of the Austrian school had scarcely begun in 1883. Neither Wieser nor Böhm-Bawerk had appeared on the scene. Paradoxical as it may seem, the method defended by Menger in his *Untersuchungen* was neither his own nor the one followed by his disciples, but really that of the classical school. Mises correctly observed: "The transition from the classical to the modern system was not completed all at once, but gradually: it took considerable time until it became effective in all areas of economic thought, and a still longer time had to elapse before one became aware of the full significance of the completed change."[7] Hence I might say that what later on became the characteristic method of the school had scarcely made an impact in 1883.

Fourth, the day came when even Menger saw himself compelled to oppose the methods of the natural sciences in economics. In two letters to Walras, of June 1883 and February 1884, he insisted that we are dealing not only with quantitative relationships but also with the "essence" of economic phenomena. He also asked how with the aid of mathematics one could ascertain the essence, for example, of value, rent, or the entrepreneur's profit.[8] However, since mathematics is essential to the modern natural sciences, Menger's attack was directed just as much against the latter as against the former. And if it is permissible to equate the "comprehension of essence" with the "interpretation of meaning," we may conclude that Menger's intention in both letters was to defend the possibility of an economic theory designed to interpret meaning. It is of particular interest that both letters were written almost immediately after the completion of the *Untersuchungen*.

Another objection might be that Mises ascribed understanding as a method peculiar to the historical sciences, and that our formulation is incompatible with his distinction between *Begreifen* and *Verstehen*. The apparent contradiction, however, is purely verbal. Mises admitted explicitly: *"In itself, it would be conceivable to define as understanding any procedure directed toward the comprehension of the meaning of things,"* and that is precisely our standpoint. He continued, *"As things are today, we must resign ourselves to contemporary language usage. We want, therefore, within the procedure directed toward the comprehension of the meaning of things, a procedure of which the sciences of human conduct make use to separate 'Begreifen' and 'Verstehen.' 'Begreifen' seeks to comprehend the meaning of things by discursive thought; 'Verstehen' seeks the meaning through a total empathy with the total situation under consideration."*[9]

I do not believe that today's usage demands this distinction. It is nevertheless clear, I hope, that the method here ascribed to the Austrian school is the same as the one Mises labeled *"Begreifen."* This method, which aims at discovering the *meaning* of things, apparently conflicts with most methods used in and suitable to the natural sciences.

3

I shall now investigate in detail the characteristics peculiar to Austrian thinking. Let us first contrast it with that of the classical school. I shall, however, disregard Adam Smith, who is too firmly rooted in the eighteenth century for our problems to concern him. For to the mentality of his time natural law and the "natural economic order" were each "a piece of nature," and conceptual distinctions such as we shall have to make were completely foreign to it.

With Ricardo and his disciples it was different. They consciously emulated natural science. The cognitive aim was the ordering of economic processes in terms of quantities. Such theory could be called successful insofar as it was able to determine quantitative relationships. Typical of the classical intellectual style are three characteristics.

First, the central problem was the distribution of income among the three factors of production: labor, land, and capital. This distribution is determined by two "laws," which are regarded as empirical laws of nature (and they would be, if they really generally applied!), namely, the Malthusian law of population and the law of diminishing returns to land.

Secondly, the central concept: value. This is a concept

denoting "substance," which bears the typical traits of an older natural science. It is the measure of all economic things, as well as the fundamental norm of all exchange processes. But why exchange takes place at all is never discussed. In business the measure of all things is the monetary unit. The economist, knowing that the value of money fluctuates, distrusts this standard. Ricardo believed that he had found a measure free from this defect in the quantity of work necessary for the production of each good. Gradually, and almost without his noticing it, the measure became for him the substance of all economic processes, if not their cause. For us all that matters is that the classical "objective" theory of value is based on a concept denoting "substance."

Third, economic man appears in classical theory only in his capacity as a factor of production. This means not merely that the consumer is not an economic subject, but that *homo oeconomicus* is always a producer. It means, moreover, that the only transactions of economic interest are those one performs in one's capacity as a factor of production: as a worker, as a landowner, or as a capitalist. Within these three classes, all members are regarded as equal. This assumption of homogeneity of the factors of production has odd consequences for the realism of classical theory.[10] All capitalists, whether they invest wisely or unwisely, receive the average rate of profit on their invested capital. Malinvestments, capital losses, and bankruptcies do not exist. The assumed homogeneity of the factors of production makes it impossible to evaluate the success of any economic activity. Fundamentally, we cannot really speak of economic activity here. As in nature, people *react* to the current external conditions of their economic existence: they *do not act.*

It is only against this background of the classical thought that the specific accomplishment of the Austrian school becomes transparent. It can perhaps best be characterized in the following manner: Here, too, one strives to discover laws. But, no matter what Menger might originally have believed, the laws of catallactics are logical laws, *verites de raison*. From the law of marginal utility there gradually developed an economic calculus, that is, a "logic of choice." How this logic is related to reality, so that real processes can be interpreted with its help, is an important question and will be discussed later on.

The significance of the Austrian school in the history of ideas perhaps finds its most pregnant expression in the statement that here man *as an actor* stands at the center of economic events. Certainly, manifold quantitative economic relationships are also for the Austrian school in the first place the cognitive object of economic inquiry. But the determination of these quantitative relationships is not the ultimate objective. One does not stop there; for these relationships flow from acts of the mind that have to be "understood," that is, their origin, their significance, and their effects must be explained within the framework of our "common experience" of human action.

Also important for understanding the Austrian school is that here, in contrast to the classical school, men are viewed as *highly unequal.* Each one has different needs and abilities. The quantities and prices of goods sold in the market depend on these individual needs and abilities. This fact is exactly what the subjective theory of value stresses. Each economic agent through his action imprints his individuality on economic events. Man as a consumer cannot be squeezed into any homogeneous class. The same may be said of man as a producer. The concept of opportunity costs disrupts the homogeneity of the cost factors and broadens the area of subjectivity, which now also embraces the theory of production.

Finally, in the work of the Viennese school the classical concept of value undergoes a fundamental change. Value is no longer a "substance" inherent in goods. The central concept of Viennese theory is *evaluation,* an act of the mind. The value of a good now consists in a relationship to an appraising mind. Owing to the heterogeneity of needs, it is highly improbable that the same good will be given the same appraisal by different economic agents.[11] Out of the Ricardian concept of quasi-substance has emerged a concept of mental relationships.

4

My next task is to differentiate the specific characteristics of the Viennese school from those of the Lausanne school. It has been maintained that there are no fundamental differences between the two schools, that it is only a question of variations on the same theme, namely, of modern subjective value theory. I consider this view misleading and will attempt to show which fundamental differences do in fact exist here. Above all, this view ignores the fact that Austrian thinkers go far beyond the mere ordering of quantitative relationships, an activity much cultivated in Lausanne and elsewhere.

In the last eighty years, prominent Austrian thinkers in each generation have found it necessary to draw a dividing line between their mode of analysis and that of the school of Lausanne. I have already mentioned Menger's two letters to Walras. Almost three decades later Wieser himself was impelled to defend the "psychological" method adopted by him and his colleagues against the "mechanistic" method Schumpeter had borrowed from the Lausanners and his teacher Mach.[12] Twenty years later, H. Mayer attacked the "cognitive value of functional price theories" and subjected it to a sharp and thorough criticism.[13] And as late as 1948, Leo Illy, in a chapter in *Das Gesetz des Grenznultzens* [*The Law of Marginal Utility*],[14] rightly criticized the defects of certain price theories that merely order price phenomena without explaining them. So the differences existed, and they still do. It is for us to determine those characteristics of the Austrian style of thought to which formalistic analysis cannot do justice.

Now it is not to be denied that Austrian theorists have not always adroitly defended their position. The "occasional blunders and unfortunate formulations in the application of their method of research," which Hans Mayer justifiably criticized, have often impaired the effectiveness of their arguments.[15] For example, Wieser always spoke of the Austrian as the "psychological" school, although he admitted that "perhaps our method would be exposed to fewer misunderstandings, if one had called it not the psychological but the psychical, although this name as well would still be open to misunderstanding. Our object is, simply, the consciousness of economic man with its wealth of general experience, i.e., that experience which every practical man possesses and which, therefore, every theoretician as a practical man finds in himself, without the need first to acquire such experience by means of special scientific methods."[16] But Max Weber had already made clear, three years before Wieser, that the alleged "psychological" foundation of the Viennese theory was based on a misconception: "The rational theory of price formation not only has nothing to do with the concepts of experimental psychology, but has nothing to do with a psychology of any kind, which desires to be a 'science' going beyond everyday experience. . . . The theory of marginal utility and every other subjective value theory are not psychologically, but—if one desires a methodological term—'pragmatically' based, i.e., involve the use of the categories 'ends' and 'means.'"[17]

In other respects, too, the methodological defense of the Austrian school was not always successful. To speak of "the cause of value" is obviously questionable. One lays oneself open to the objection that the economic system constitutes a general nexus of relationships within which "causes" can only be ordered as a class and, as such, have to be dealt with as "data." The distinction between "genetic-causal" and "functional" price theories, which, as we shall see, positively strikes at the heart of the matter, met with the same objection.[18] The opponents maintained that, with a general interdependence of all quantities and prices, each individual quantity and price is, at the same time, the effect and cause of others. Against the distinction between "price formation theory" and "price change theory," the latter valid only within the framework of comparative statics, the argument was advanced that in disequilibrium the same forces must influence price, whether or not equilibrium existed before. In the timeless statics of the Lausanne theory this argument is certainly valid, but otherwise it is not.

The difference between the Vienna and the Lausanne school is already reflected in the assumptions made by both. Among these, the role of time is of special significance. It is certainly not overstating the case if we say that the real disagreement concerns, in the first place, the significance attributed to the element of time. Lausanne theory is meaningful within the framework of timeless statics; the world of the Austrian school, on the other hand, requires time for its full meaning. This is not just a matter of the level of abstraction; it is much more than that.

Austrian theory needs the dimension of time, since all human action is only possible in time. The Lausanne theory of equilibrium not only does not require time; it requires time's exclusion. From the very beginning, Edgeworth and Walras clearly saw that any passage of time before the state of equilibrium is reached renders that state itself indeterminate, since all data-changing events happening on the path to a state of equilibrium help to determine that state. Lausanne theory requires, then, that all transactions undertaken on the path to equilibrium can be nullified, whether by "recontract" or by other means. This is the essence of timeless statics. For the Austrians, however, it is exactly these transactions, undertaken in the course of time, that are their real objects of interest, since conscious human action is bound to plans, and all plans require a time dimension.

I described how, in the course of the development of the Austrian theory, a theory of economic calculus gradually unfolded as a corollary of the law of marginal utility. Economic plans depend on the economic calculations of each agent. The interplay of economic plans accounts for the market phenomena. Now, there is certainly a general nexus of all market phenomena, and the Austrians by no means denied this fact. However, they took relatively little interest in the forces that operate in this connection, since these could operate only in a timeless world, that is, in a world without change. What appeared to them much more urgent was to take into account the continual need, in a constantly changing world, to adapt economic plans to these changes. For in such a world a general condition of equilibrium cannot be achieved. We thus see why economic plans occupy a central place in Austrian theory, while the general nexus of market phenomena is neglected. One takes one's orientation from reality.

It might be held, however, that Lausanne theory also takes account of the economic plans of individuals since they enter into its system as "data." But the utility—and supply—functions in the work of Walras, and indifference curves in the work of Pareto, do not reflect real economic plans as we know them from our own experience. They must provide for every possible situation if the state of equilibrium is to be determinate. In fact they are comprehensive lists of alternative plans, comprehensive enough for unlimited application. Obviously, this requirement is quite beyond the capacity of the human mind. "No person will be in a position to indicate, truthfully and with mathematical accuracy, an infinite number of combinations of goods which would all be equally important to him. The expression 'experiment,' used here by Pareto, is completely unsuitable: we have here simply the figment of an experiment."[19]

For the general theory of equilibrium, such functions are certainly an essential logical foundation. The difference between a taxonomic (*ordnende*) and a *verstehende* economics becomes quite apparent here. What is a logical necessity for the former must be considered as an absurdity by the latter. Here, the two schools part company for good.[20]

The methodology borrowed from the natural sciences may eschew concern with the alien—and dangerous!— theme of the construction of economic plans. However, it can do so only by assuming that all conceivable plans are already "given" from the start!

Pareto saw much more clearly than his predecessor Walras that genuine economic plans do not really fit into the model of the Lausanne school, and that to use them as "data" one must first divest them of their nature as mental acts. This is the true meaning of the famous sentence: "*L'individu peut disparaitre, pourvu qu'il nous laisse cette photographie de ses gouts.*"[21] Here plainly man as economic agent does not stand at the center of economic life. This statement of course makes sense only in a timeless stationary world in which these photographs would retain permanent validity. Everyday human acts shape the real world anew. Accordingly, all attempts to attach a time dimension to the timeless theory of equilibrium and thus to make it "dynamic" must fail.

It is probably unnecessary to discuss in detail a criticism once marshalled against the Austrian school regarding the so-called "circle of economic determination." Viennese economists were charged with becoming entangled in circular reasoning since, on the one hand, market prices were derived from the valuations of the economic agents, and, on the other hand, the determination of these very valuations required prices already given. Illy showed that the reasoning in reality was not circular and that the criticism confused prices expected and prices actually paid.[22] Economics agents must certainly orient themselves to prices they expect, but they by no means have to be the prices then formed in the market. In the system of equations of the Lausanne school, it is of course impossible to distinguish between expected and paid prices. This is again a necessary consequence of timeless statics.

5

We saw that the methodology of the Austrian school evolved gradually, for a long time without the members of the school being aware of it. It sometimes happened that the methodological pronouncements of some of its most prominent members lacked programmatic validity—often even for the time in which they were expressed. This was true, for example, of Menger's *Untersuchungen*. Moreover, Menger, concerned with establishing "exact laws," never clearly distinguished between logical laws and empirical laws, between *verites de raison* and *verites de fait*.

As mentioned above, during its development marginal utility theory became a theory of economic calculus and of economic plans, and thereby a genuine "logic of choice." But as late as 1911, Wieser referred to "common experience" as the ultimate basis of economic knowledge. It is to Mises that we owe the clear formulation of the logic of choice. However, as regards the actual relevance of this logic to human action, it will be seen that common experience is still indispensable to us.

In Hayek's work are to be found penetrating discussions of the "scientistic" style of thought and its inadequacy for the problems of the social sciences,[23] but also the first indication of problems of economic theory lying beyond the pure logic of choice.[24] What matters here is, above all, the state of knowledge as a spring of human action and the process of its changes in time.

I now come to the main question of this section: how

can a system of pure logic, like that of the logic of choice, provide factual knowledge? The answer follows from the essence of my thesis: the distinction between logic and factual knowledge is justified in the realm of nature, where no meaning is directly accessible to us, and in which care must thus constantly be taken to distinguish between our concepts and reality. In the realm of human action it is different. Here such a distinction seems unjustified. On the one hand we are unable to verify or falsify our schemes of thought as hypotheses by predicting concrete events. Scientific tests are not available to us since they require a complete description of that concrete "starting position" in which the test is to take place. Every human action, however, depends on the state of knowledge of the actors. A verification test therefore would require an exhaustive description of the state of knowledge of all actors, also according to the mode of distribution—an obvious impossibility. Otherwise, however, the starting position is not exactly defined, and no real test is possible.

In economics this means that every concrete transaction depends, among other things, on the expectations of the participants. To test an economic theory *in concreto,* we must, then, be able, at the point of time of theory formulation, to predict the expectations of economic agents at the (future) point of time of the verification test. It is easy to see why the representatives of a taxonomic economics are eager to keep the problem of expectations at arm's length as far as possible.

For "understanding" in economics, on the other hand, some methods are available that, though closed to the natural sciences, lend themselves for interpreting human actions. The historian inquires into the meaning and significance of concrete actions of individuals and groups. This whole method is inapplicable in the natural sciences. The history of science shows that research is confined to the ordering of quantitative relationships. In the theoretical cultural sciences, on the other hand, the significance of typical courses of action is interpreted with the aid of schemes of thought, such as the logic of choice. The approach is justified by the fact that all human action, at least insofar as it is of scientific interest, is oriented to plans. Plans are logical constructs immanent to the course of action. A plan serves the economic agent as a guideline; he orients himself to it. The social sciences can thus use plans as means of interpretation. Actions certainly are events in space and time and, as such, are observable. But observation alone cannot reveal meaning; for this, methods of interpretation are needed.

Why exactly is the logic of choice the scheme needed for interpreting economic actions? The logic of choice is a "logic of success"; its categories are means and ends. Why should we opt for precisely this method in interpreting economic transactions? Common experience gives us the answer: in economic life most people seek success. The striving for success as the meaning of economic action warrants the validity of the logic of choice.

Thus Mises was correct when he asserted that only logic, and not experience, can warrant the validity of economic theories—as opposed to Wieser, who in his critique of Schumpeter invoked common experience.[25] And logic certainly is immanent in all human action. But this alone does not mean that the logic of success, which depends upon means and ends, is also the logic governing all action. Conceivably another kind of logic, one employing other categories, might be applicable here. In order to claim the validity of just this logic of success for economic life, we have to invoke common experience.

Finally we have to remember that, in a dynamic world there are economic problems that the logic of choice by itself cannot master. While it explains the designing of economic plans under given conditions, the revision of economic plans in the course of time, as well as the entire range of the problem of expectations, are outside the realm of logic. At best, we may say that in a stationary world economic plans will be adapted more and more to real conditions. It is exactly on this fact that the theory of general equilibrium of the Lausanne school rests.

6

I do not wish to conclude these observations without taking a brief look at the *future tasks of "verstehende,"* or *"interpretative," economics.*

Our main aim, naturally, must be to preserve and defend in all directions the methodological independence of the theoretical social sciences in general, and of economics in particular. This certainly does not mean that methods may never be borrowed from other disciplines. The relevant question, however, always is whether these methods, however successful they may be outside the realm of economics, are able to serve our purposes, namely, the interpretation of human action.

If we keep this question in mind, we shall continue the work of Menger under the altered circumstances of our own time. In this we need only follow precedents already given in the work of the Austrian school. According to one of its most perceptive thinkers, E. Schams, we must always distinguish, in accepting mathematical methods, between "the mathematical form of the the statement" (*ansetzendes Denken*) and the "material constants" to which it refers; only the uncritical acceptance of the latter into economic science is inadmissible.[26]

No doubt the task outlined here is not simple, especially in our time. In recent decades, especially in Anglo-Saxon countries, an unbelievable narrowing and impoverishment of the philosophical outlook has taken place. Today, innumerable economists everywhere, some in responsible positions, who have never learned of the existence of our problems, naively believe that the scientific method is the only legitimate one in all fields of knowledge.

How should we approach our task? First of all, we must continuously stress the inadequacy of the products of intellectual inquiry that ignores the meaning of actions. We must always be prepared to ask our opponents the following questions: Whence? By what means? To what end? When, for example, the designers of macroeconomic models present to us their creations, we may certainly admire their elegance: we may not, however, neglect to ask from which actions of the economic agents these models spring. We must also always ask what expectations guide these actions, and what would occur if these expectations were altered. When, moreover, such model builders attempt to include technical progress in their models, for example, in the form of a "technical progress function," they must be shown that they are attempting to grasp meaningful action by an intellectual method to which meaning is alien, and that a significant discussion of these interesting problems is thereby made impossible. But we must not rest content with criticism of a method of inquiry that defies meaning; we must show the fruitfulness of the *verstehende* method in its various applications. There are, we may show, alternatives to equilibrium analysis. Certainly, in the analysis of a state of disequilibrium, we cannot dispense with an account of the equilibrating forces, but that does not mean that we must describe in its entirety a state of equilibrium, which is never really attained, decorated with formulas and equations. We can save ourselves that endeavor. All that is important is that every state of disequilibrium presents possibilities for profitable activity—be it income, capital gains, or even only the avoidance of losses. Each disequilibrium stimulates alert minds, but by no means all minds, to profitable action, and this action will reduce the chances for further profit. That is all that may be said. The cumbersome pedantry of the usual market models, with their alleged "precision," is an obstacle rather than a help to understanding. What has happened to "perfect competition" should be enough of a warning.

Even outside the special field of economic theory, the need for the defense of the methods of inquiry specific to the cultural disciplines presents tasks that are as pressing as they are difficult. Here it is most important to put the methodological independence of the social sciences on a firm epistemological basis.

Since the Renaissance the theory of knowledge has taken its orientation almost exclusively from the methods of the natural sciences. For these sciences, which deal with apparently "meaningless" events, there is no alternative, in the absence of other criteria of comparison, but to attempt to make their theories and observable events agree in such a manner that predictions concerning these events may be made, and then "verified." With human activity, however, this is impossible, since every action depends on the state of knowledge of the agent *at the point in time of the action,* which is not predictable *at the point in time of the formulation of the theory.* What, then, must the social scientist do to distinguish useful from useless theories? Which criterion of valid knowledge are at his disposal?

Since we lack successful prediction as a means of evidence, we must of course devote special care to the validity of our theoretical assumptions. The Austrian school has always done so, as, for example, we saw above in the criticism of the Lausanne theory. Also, in the theoretical social sciences a gap between scheme of thought and reality may have a different significance than in the natural sciences. For their task is essentially the comparative study of schemes of the agents, on the one hand, and typical courses of action, on the other. Here the significant and meaningful character of both can serve as *tertium comparationis.* In such comparative studies deviations from the planned schedule are often more interesting than a smooth course proceeding according to plan would have been. An economic plan as an observed fact does not lose its significance for us when it fails. On the contrary, we owe to such a plan our criterion of success, which alone allows us to speak of failure. A coherent plan of action that no one applies often allows us to draw interesting conclusions concerning the character of the situation, including the expectations entertained by the agents.

In these reflections I have taken the economic plan of an individual as the prototype of the scheme of thought lying at the base of action, mainly on account of its central significance for economic theory of Austrian character. Economic agents orient themselves to plans. There is no parallel for this in the study of the physical world. But to what facts do the planners orient themselves when making their plans? Partly to natural data, and partly to the actual or expected actions of other people. But there also are certain superindividual schemes of thought, namely, *institutions,* to which the schemes of thought of the first order, the plans, must be oriented, and which serve therefore, to some extent, the coordination of individual plans. They constitute, we may say, "interpersonal orientation tables," schemes of thought of the second order. To them praxeology, for which until now the plan and its structure have understandably occupied the foreground of interest, will increasingly have to turn in time to come.

Notes

1. *Grundsatze der Volkswirtschaftslehre* [Foundations of Political Economy] (Vienna, 1871), 2nd ed. by Karl Menger, Jr. (1923); translated as *Principles of Economics* (Glencoe, IL, 1950).
2. J. A. Schumpeter, *History of Economic Analysis* (New York, 1954), p. 918. "They [the Austrians], too, found the ladder. Defective technique only prevented them from climbing to

the top of it. But they did climb as high as their technique permitted. In other words: we must see in the Jevons-Menger utility theory an embryonic theory of general equilibrium or, at all events, a particular form of the unifying principle that is at the bottom of any general-equilibrium system. Though they did not make it fully articulate, mainly because they did not understand the meaning of a set of simultaneous equations, and though they saw in marginal utility the essence of their innovation instead of seeing in it a heuristically useful methodological device, they are nonetheless, just like Walras, among the founding fathers of modern theory."

3. W. Sombart, *Die drei Nationalokonomien* (Munich, 1930), pp. 136–37. "The result of our investigations is clearly established. ... We could observe that the majority carried out its work with unclear and incomplete concepts of the essence of the scientific method. Only the relationists or functionalists, i.e., the adherents of the 'mathematical' school, have thought the problems through and arrived at a clear and consistent method. Every friend of lucid thought must therefore feel some sympathy for these economists. They alone, also, have earned the respected title of 'exact' researchers, which so many other adherents of the scientific method in economics have most unjustly arrogated to themselves." (The last sentence is, of course, a sideswipe at Menger.)

4. J. G. Droysen, "Historik," in *Vorlesungen uber die Methode der Sozialwissenschafter und der politischen Okonomie insbesondere.* [Inquiries into the Method of Social Sciences and Particularly Political Economy] (Leipzig, 1883); translated as *Problems of Economics and Sociology* (Urbana, IL, 1963).

5. Carl Menger, *Untersuchungen über die Methode der Sozialwissenschaften und der politischen Ökonomie insbesondere.* [*Inquiries into the Method of Social Sciences and Particularly Political Economy*] (Leipzig, 1883); translated as *Problems of Economics and Sociology* (Urbana, IL, 1963).

6. W. Sombart, op. cit., p. 159.

7. Ludwig von Mises, *Grundprobleme der Nationalokonomie* (Jena, 1933), p. 67n; translated as *Epistemological Problems of Economics* (Princeton, 1960).

8. W. Jaffe, "Unpublished Papers and Letters of Leon Walras," *Journal of Political Economy*, 1935, p. 200.
9. L. Mises, op. cit., p. 125.
10. Only for land is this not valid. Ricardo's rent theory rests on the heterogeneity of land.
11. H. Mayer, "Zur Frage der Rechenbarkeit des subjektiven Wertes," in *Festschrift fur Alfred Amonn* (Bern, 1953), p. 76, n. 6. "The exact conception of the process by itself and the feel for language should have made it clear that to speak of subjective values as thought they were a property of goods, is an elliptical and at bottom misleading way of expression: we are dealing with the process of evaluation, and this takes place not according to 'larger' or 'smaller,' but according to a higher or lower position within a hierarchy."
12. F. von Wieser, "Das Wesen und der Hauptinhalt der theoretischen Nationalokonomie," in *Gesammelte Abhandlungen* (Tubingen, 1929), pp. 10–34.
13. H. Mayer, "Der Erkenntniswert der Funktionellen Preistheorien," in *Die Wirtschaftstheorie der Gegenwart*, 2 vol. (Vienna, 1932) 2:147–239.
14. L. Illy, *Das Gesetz des Grenznutzens* (Vienna, 1948).
15. H. Mayer, loc. cit., p. 150.
16. F. von Wieser, loc. cit., p. 16.
17. M. Weber, "Die Grenznutzlehre und das psychophysisce Grundgesetz," in *Gesammelte Aufsatze zur Wissenschaftslehre*, 2nd ed., 1951, p. 396.
18. H. Mayer, loc. cit., p. 148.
19. A. Mahr, "Indifferenzkurven und Grenznutzenniveau," *Zeitschrift fur Nationalokonomie* 14 (1954): 325 SS.
20. Pareto saw very well how absurd it is to ask a poor peasant woman how many diamonds she would buy at a given price if she were a millionairess, but the logic of his system forced such assumptions upon him. Cf. V. Pareto, *Manuel d'Economie Politique*, 2nd ed. (Paris, 1927), p. 260.
21. V. Pareto, ibid., p. 170.
22. Leo Illy, *Das Gesetz des Grenznutzens* (Vienna, 1948), ch. 6, pp. 183–238.

23. F. A. Hayek, "Scientism and the Study of Society," *Economica* 9 (1942): 267; 10 (1943): 34 ff.; 11 (1944): 27 ff.

24. F. A. Hayek, "Economics and Knowledge," in *Individualism and Economic Order* (London, 1949), pp. 33–56.

25. L. Mises, loc. cit., pp. 21–22.

26. Cf. E. Schams, "Die zweite Nationalokonomie," *Archiv fur Sozialwissenschaft* 64 (1930): 453 ff.; and "Wirtschaftslogik," *Schmollers Jahrbuch* 58 (1934): 512 ff.

Part II

Philosophy and Method of the Austrian School

3

Austrian Economics—
An Annotated Bibliography:
Methodology of the Austrian School

Richard M. Ebeling

One of the distinctive features of the Austrian school of economics is its emphasis on the methodological foundations of the social sciences in general. Equally distinctive is the particular approach most members of the school have taken in their investigations. The two pillars of their approach have been methodological individualism and methodological subjectivism. Methodological individualism emphasizes that the essential building-blocks of economic and social analysis are the activities of the respective social and market participants, whose interactions generate the aggregate market and social outcomes. Methodological subjectivism draws attention to the fact that meaning and significance significance can be attached to those activities only in terms of an understanding and interpretation of the knowledge, intentions, and expectations of the actors themselves.

An implication of subjectivism is what Carl Menger and F. A. Hayek in particular saw as the pervasive presence of the *unintended consequences of human action*. The undertaking of many individual plans in a complex social order, in which each actor's knowledge and horizon is limited, sets the stage

3

Reprinted from *Humane Studies Review* 3 (1985):2, published by the Institute for Humane Studies at George Mason University.

for inevitable consequences that may be the result of human action but not of human design. One of the tasks of social and economic method and theory is to explain the emergence, formation, and evolution of the spontaneously generated social and market institutions that often coordinate economic and social activities independent of any single human plan.

The Austrian economists have also had significant diversity within their common viewpoint. This diversity concerns the source of knowledge in economic science. Ludwig von Mises considered economics to have its origin in a set of "a priori" axioms derived from logical reflection on the "essence of action." For Hayek, the field of knowledge requires "empirical elements" concerning the processes of human learning once we turn to problems of interpersonal activity. Fritz Machlup has argued for viewing economics as built on postulates selected as useful for the questions requiring solution through the construction of various "ideal types." Israel M. Kirzner has seen it as sufficient to emphasis the purposefulness of all human endeavor without having to delve further into any epistemological foundations. Murray N. Rothbard, on the other hand, has attempted to give Austrian economics an Aristotelian grounding. And most recently Mario Rizzo and Gerald P. O'Driscoll have attempted to use Henri Bergson's phenomenology of time and being as a basis for Austrian subjectivism.

But within this diversity has run and continues to run a common thread of emphasis on man as an intentional, creative being, an actor rather than a mere passive responder to given constraints and circumstances. The Austrian tradition has, therefore, always extended subjectivism beyond tastes and preferences to perspective, perception, and purposes, which are the ultimate engines of all social activity and processes.

Carl Menger

Practically every Austrian development in the past hundred years has its beginning in the writings of Carl Menger, methodology is no exception. In the introduction to his *Principles of Economics* [1871] (New York: New York University Press, 1981) we find a fervent argument for methodological individualism as a basis for economic theory and a strong attack against reducing social analysis to the methods of the natural sciences. And though never articulated explicitly, the exposition of the theory of value and price formation is grounded in a view of man as an active agent who plans, directs, and effects change on a basis of imperfect perceptions in an uncertain world.

In his *Problems of Economics and Sociology* [1883] (Urbana: University of Illinois Press, 1963), the question of the methods and aims of economics is taken up directly. Menger had two goals: to defend the applicability and universality of theory in all economic analysis against the relativist antitheoretical claims of some German historicists and to demonstrate how economic and social theory could explain the emergence of "institutions which serve the common welfare [that] came into being without a common will directed toward establishing them" (p. 146).

Menger's book was quickly criticized by one of the leaders of the German historical school, Gustav von Schmoller, who vehemently defended the "historical" method as *the* method for economic analysis. See Gustav von Schmoller, "Political Economy and Its Method," [1894] in *Introduction to Contemporary Civilization in the West,* prepared by the Contemporary Civilization Staff of Columbia College, Columbia University, vol. II (New York: Columbia University Press, 1946), pp. 514–24. Menger replied forcefully in a pamphlet on "The Errors of Historicism in German Economics." This set the stage for the long and bitter *Methodenstreit* of the last decades of the nineteenth century. Menger's views on the categories and organization of economic science can be found in his essay, "Toward a Systematic Classification of the Economic Sciences" [1889] in *Essays in European Economic Thought,* ed. by Louise Sommer (Princeton: D. Van Nostrand, Co., Inc., 1960), pp. 1–38.

The debate between Menger and Schmoller has been summarized in some detail, with extensive quotation, by Albion Small in "Later Phases of the Conflict Between the Historical and Austrian Schools." *Origins of Sociology* [1924] (New York: Russell & Russell, 1967), pp. 204–33. A good discussion can also be found in Samuel Bostaph, "The Methodological Debate Between Carl Menger and the German Historicists," *Atlantic Economic Journal* (September, 1978), pp. 3–16, which emphasizes the philosophical roots of the two schools.

Böhm-Bawerk and Wieser

Menger found loyal defenders among his followers. Eugen von Böhm-Bawerk insisted on the primacy of theory in tracing out economic causations and the categorizing of the facts of economic phenomena. See Böhm-Bawerk, "The Historical vs. the Deductive Method in Political Economy," in *Annals of the American Academy of Political and Social Science,* vol. I (1891), pp. 244–71.

Friedrich von Wieser, besides defending the "deductive method," also strongly argued in defense of the "introspective" source of economic knowledge, believing that it gave economics a stronger foundation than those found in the natural sciences. See Friedrich von Wieser, *Social Economics* [1914] (New York: Augustus M. Kelley, 1967), pp. 4, 8–9.

Ludwig von Mises

But it is in the writings of Ludwig von Mises that we find the most methodical exposition and defense of Austrian subjectivism after Menger's death in 1921. The thrust of Mises's writings on methodology can be seen as an attempt to establish an autonomous plane for economics that escapes the hazards of both historicism and positivism. His early essay on "Sociology and History" [1929] in *Epistemological Problems of Economics* [1933] (New York: New York University Press, 1981), pp. 68–129, is a criticism of Max Weber, in which Mises wishes to glean the insights that a subjectivist "action" framework offers without the excess weight of historical relativism. His 1930 essay on "Conception and Understanding," Ibid., pp. 130–45, tries to distinguish between conceptualization of the universal logic and categories of choice, distinct from time and place, and the understanding or interpretation of concrete manifestations of historical human actions. His essay, "On the Development of the Subjective Theory of Value," [1931] Ibid., pp. 146–66, attempts to demonstrate the "subjective" quality underlying the concepts and categories of all economic phenomena. And his essay, "The Task and Scope of the Science of Human Action" [1933] Ibid., pp. 1–67, tries to unify economic theory more rigorously on the basis of a concept of human action that incorporates all conscious, purposeful human behavior.

Mises's monumental work, *Human Action: A Treatise on Economics* [1949] (Chicago: Henry Regnery, 3rd rev. ed., 1966), pp. 1–142, however, most systematically defends what he calls "praxeology," the general science of human action. Besides restating his criticisms of historicism, he defends economics against positivism, arguing that the laws of economics are logical relationships, not empirical ones. The indeterminateness of human choice, depending as it does on volition, precludes the discovery of quantitative regularities along the lines of the natural sciences. Economics must instead construct its theorems from the inside out, through reflection on the formal logic of action and choice under alternative assumptions, which then serve as the schemas for intelligible organization and explanation of the historical sequences of human conduct.

Mises's later work, *Theory and History: An Interpretation of Social and Economic Evaluation* [1957] (New Rochelle: Arlington House, 1969), applies and extends his methodological outlook through critiques of determinism, materialism, scienticism, and historicism. It delineates more clearly the relationship between theory and historical analysis in his framework. *The Ultimate Foundation of Economic Science: An Essay on Method* [1962] (Kansas City: Sheed Andrews and McMeel, Inc., 1978) restates the "a priori" basis of praxeological reasoning, discusses the problem of human volition for social science and the nature of uncertainty in the real world, and criticizes several ositivist applications in economics.

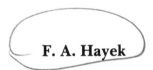

F. A. Hayek

Hayek's earliest writings on methods of economics can be found in the opening chapter of his *Monetary Theory and the Trade Cycle* [1929] (New York: Augustus M. Kelley, 1966), pp. 27–48, in which he discusses the relationship between economic theory and the use and application of statistical methods. In the essay opening the collection he edited under the title, *Collectivist Economic Planning* (London: George Routledge & Sons, Ltd., 1935), pp. 8–12, Hayek followed Wieser and Mises in distinguishing between the natural and social sciences on the basis of their sources of knowledge. He developed this theme in greater detail in *The Counter-Revolution of Science* [1952] (Indianapolis: Liberty Press, 1979). He emphasized that social theory relies primarily on the "composite method" by which it explains the emergence of "complex, composite phenomena from their elementary components" the activities of individual agents.

This has been the general theme for almost all of Hayek's writings on both methodology and social theory. The "composite method" has led him to emphasize that many social phenomena are "the results of human action but not of human design." See *Studies in Philosophy, Politics and Economics* (Chicago: The University of Chicago Press, 1967), pp. 96–105. The unintentional, complex quality of such phenomena also led Hayek to point out that the social scientist must be more modest in making his predictions. The most he can hope for is qualitative predictions of patterns and institutional forms, rather than precise quantitative determination of market outcomes. See his essays, "Degrees of Explanation," "The Theory of Complex Phenomena," and "Rules, Perception and Intelligibility," in Ibid., pp. 3–65. This analysis has also been his basis for continued criticism of what he calls social "constructivists." See his essays, "The Errors of Constructivism," "The Pretense of Knowledge," and "The Primacy of the Abstract" in *New Studies in Philosophy, Politics, Economics and the History of Ideas* (Chicago: The University of Chicago Press, 1978), pp. 3–49.

Oskar Morgenstern

In his 1928 volume, *Wirtschaftsprognose: eine Untersuchung ihrer Voraussetzungen und Moglichkeiten* (Wien: Julius Springer Verlag, 1928), Oskar Morgenstern expressed skepticism about quantitative prediction in economics on three grounds:

- the heterogeneity of the data and the smallness of "samples" make the application of probability theory extremely difficult, if not impossible, with, at the most, probability theory only enabling a prediction of "class" outcomes not the individual events;

- economic statistics hide both the behavioral qualities that underlie and generate the quantitative data and the interdependency of economic phenomena with social, cultural, and political events, and

- the possible influence of public forecasts on the decisions of the agents whose actions are being forecast leads to an infinite regress.

In his later work, *On the Accuracy of Economic Observations* (Princeton: Princeton University Press, 1963), Morgenstern reinforced his argument with an analysis of the ambiguities, crudeness, and frequent lack of compatibility of much "economic data" relative to the logical categories of economic theory.

An excellent "Austrian"-style analysis of the limits of quantitative economics can also be found in Leland B. Yeager, "Measurement as Scientific Method in Economics," *American Journal of Economics and Sociology* (July, 1957), pp. 337–46.

Fritz Machlup and Alfred Schutz

After Mises, Fritz Machlup is probably the Austrian who devoted the most care and time to methodological questions. In a series of essays concerned with the status and nature of the social sciences, Machlup, while not denying similarities in all scientific endeavors, drew special attention to the intentionalist quality of social phenomena in which the actor's subjective meanings were crucial elements to successful social analysis. See "On Comparisons Between Natural and Social Sciences," part five, in his collection *Methodology of Economics and Other Social Sciences* (New York: Academic Press, 1978), pp. 305–67.

The tool that Machlup considered particularly useful for such analysis was that of the "ideal type," a mental construct of human conduct under the constraints of certain specified circumstances, motivations, and states of knowledge, selected as appropriate for deriving implications of human action in alternative institutional and economic environments. See the essays in "On Ideal Types and the Interpretation of Reality" in Ibid., part 4, pp. 207–301. In his selection of methods Machlup was greatly influenced by his close friend Alfred Schutz who had tried to synthesize Husserl's phenomenology with Max Weber's "ideal type" construction and Austrian subjectivist economics. See Alfred Schutz, *The Phenomenology of the Social World* [1932] (Evanston: Northwestern University Press, 1967) and his *Collected Papers,* vol. I, "The Problem of Social Reality" (The Hague: Martinus Nijhoff, 1962), pp. 3–96.

Ludwig M. Lachmann

Ludwig M. Lachmann has, following the lead of Max Weber, also emphasized the significance of "understanding" (Verstehen) and "interpretation" of the subjectively meaningful act for social science. His slender volume, *The Legacy of Max Weber,* tries to reformulate the Weberian contribution along more Austrian lines in terms of the "planful" or "purposeful" act. He also attempts to blend Weber's and Menger's analyses of the function and evolution of social institutions as "nodal points" for interpersonal coordination. Lachmann has particularly emphasized the subjectivist quality of knowledge and expectations and their implications for economic theory and methods. See the essays in part II of his collection, *Capital Expectations and the Market Process,* ed. by Walter E. Grinder (Kansas City: Sheed, Andrews and McMeel, 1977) pp. 45–129, and "From Mises to Shackle: An Essay on Austrian Economics and the Kaleidic Society," *Journal of Economic Literature* (March, 1976), pp. 54–62.

Israel M. Kirzner and Murray N. Rothbard

The Misesian formulation of Austrian methodology has been rigorously defended and expounded by two of Mises's students, Israel M. Kirzner and Murray N. Rothbard. In *The Economic Point of View,* originally a dissertation written under Mises, Kirzner elaborates on the changing meanings of the subject matter of economics. In the last two chapters Kirzner discusses the emergence of economics as a science of economizing behavior, as influenced by Lionel Robbins's *Essay on the Nature and Significance of Economic Science* (itself influenced by the Austrian writings of the 1920s). Kirzner, however, contrasts the narrowness of the economizing point of view with the Misesian conception of human action and clarifies several of the ambiguities sometimes seen in Mises's own writings. He defends the praxeological perspective in "Rational Action and Economic Theory," *Journal of Political Economy* (August, 1962), pp. 380–85, and "What Economists Do," *Southern Economic Journal* (January, 1965), pp. 257–61. And in his "On the Method of Austrian Economics" in *The Foundations of Modern Austrian Economics,* ed. by Edwin G. Dolan (Kansas City: Sheed & Ward, Inc., 1976), pp. 40–51, he analyzes the implications of Austrian methodology with particular emphasis on human purposefulness and the indeterminacy in human decision making.

In 1951 Rothbard defended the praxeological perspective against the criticisms of G. J. Schuller. See "Mises' 'Human Action' Comment," *American Economic Review* (March, 1951), pp. 181–85, and "Praxeology: Reply to Mr. Schuller," *American Economic Review* (December, 1951), pp. 943–46. He restated the premises of the Misesian system in "In Defense of 'Extreme A Priorism,'" *Southern Economic Journal* (January, 1957), pp. 314–20. Rothbard's essays "The Mantle of Science" and "Praxeology as the Method of the Social Sciences," in *Individualism and the Philosophy of the Social Sciences* (San Francisco: Cato Institute, 1979) summarize several

Austrian arguments against "empirical" social sciences and explain the logic of praxeology. His contribution to the *Foundations of Modern Austrian Economics,* Ibid., pp. 19–39, titled "Praxeology: The Methodology of Austrian Economics," briefly discusses the intellectual tradition of praxeology and contrasts the Neo-Kantian and Aristotelian approaches for grounding its axioms.

The praxeological perspective has also recently received a particularly fair exposition and critique by a non-Austrian, Bruce J. Caldwell, in "Praxeology and Its Critics: An Appraisal," *History of Political Economy* (Fall, 1984), pp. 363–79.

New Directions in Austrian Methodology

Recently members of the "younger generation" of Austrians have attempted to extend the bounds of subjectivist methodology. In *The Economics of Time and Ignorance,* Gerald P. O'Driscoll and Mario J. Rizzo contrast static (or given-preference) subjectivism with dynamic (or changing knowledge and expectations) subjectivism. The latter draws its premise from the phenomenological writings of the French philosopher Henri Bergson. Their proposed tool of analysis for the study of acting man in an uncertain world is that of Schutzian ideal types.

A dynamic subjectivism that sees the inherent limits and tentativeness of knowledge and the problems this raises for understanding the process of social coordination seems to open new vistas for developments in Austrian methodology.

Introductory Readings

Lawrence H. White, *Methodology of the Austrian School* (Auburn: Mises Institute, 1984).

Murray N. Rothbard, *Individualism and the Philosophy of the Social Sciences* (Washington, D.C.: Cato Institute, 1979).

F. A. Hayek, "The Facts of the Social Sciences," in *Individualism and Economic Order* (Chicago: University of Chicago Press, 1948), pp. 57–76.

Ludwig von Mises, "Natural Science and Social Science," in *Journal of Social Philosophy & Jurisprudence* (April, 1942), pp. 240–53.

Israel M. Kirzner, *The Economic Point of View* (Kansas City: Sheed & Ward, Inc., 1976), pp. 146–85.

4

Excerpts from
Individualism and the Philosophy of the Social Sciences

Murray N. Rothbard

1. The Praxeological Method

During the past generation, a veritable revolution has taken place in the discipline of economics. I am referring not so much to the well-known Keynesian revolution, but to the quieter yet more profound revolution in the methodology of the discipline. This change has not occurred simply in the formal writings of the handful of conscious methodologists; it has spread, largely unnoticed, until it now permeates research and study in all parts of the field. Some effects of this methodological revolution are all too apparent. Let the nonspecialist in economics pick up a journal article or monograph today and contrast it with one of a generation ago, and the first thing that will strike him is the incomprehensibility of the modern product. The older work was written in ordinary language and, with moderate effort, was comprehensible to the layman; the current work is virtually all mathematics, algebraic or geometric. As one

Reprinted from "Praxeology as the Method of Economics" by Murray Rothbard in *Phenomenology and the Social Sciences*, vol. 2, edited by Maurice Natanson (Evanston: Northwestern University Press, 1973).

distinguished economist has lamented, "Economics nowadays often seems like a third-rate subbranch of mathematics," and one, he added, that the mathematician himself does not esteem very highly.

Of course, economics shares this accelerated mathematization with virtually every other field of knowledge, including history and literature. But, laboring under the common notion that it is a science with a special focus on *quantities,* economics has proceeded farther and faster than any of its sister disciplines down the mathematical and statistical road.

The emphasis on mathematics is a symptom of a deeper change in the discipline: the rapid adoption of what we may broadly call "positivism" as the guide for research and the criterion for the successful construction of economic theory. The growing influence of positivism has its source in the attempt of all social sciences to mimic the (allegedly) supremely successful science, physics. For social scientists, as for almost all intellectuals, physics has unfortunately all but replaced philosophy as the "queen of the sciences." In the hands of the positivists, philosophy has almost come to seem an elaborate running commentary on and explication of physics, too often serving as the handmaiden of that prestigious science. What positivists see as the methodology of physics has been elevated, at their hands, to be *the* scientific method, and any deviant approach has been barred from the status of science because it does not meet the rigorous positivist test.

At the risk of oversimplification, the positivist model of the scientific method may be summarized as follows:

Step 1. The scientist observes empirical regularities, or "laws," between variables.

Step 2. Hypothetical explanatory generalizations are constructed, from which the empirically observed laws can be deduced and thus "explained."

Step 3. Since competing hypotheses can be framed, each explaining the body of empirical laws, such "coherence" or consistent explanation is not enough; to validate the hypotheses, *other* deductions must be made from them, which must be "testable" by empirical observation.

Step 4. From the construction and testing of hypotheses, a wider and wider body of generalizations is developed; these can be discarded if empirical tests invalidate them, or be replaced by new explanations covering a still wider range of phenomena.

Since the number of variables is virtually infinite, the testing in Step 3, as well as much of the observation in Step 1, can only be done in "controlled experiments," in which all variables but the ones under study are held constant. Replicating the experimental conditions should then replicate the results.

Note that in this methodology we proceed from that which is known with *certainty*—the empirical regularities—up through even wider and more tentative hypotheses. It is this fact that leads the layman to believe erroneously that Newton "overthrew" his predecessors and was in his turn "overthrown" by Einstein. In fact, what happens is not so much substitution as the addition of more general explanations for a wider range of phenomena; the generalizations of a Newton or an Einstein *are* far more tentative than the fact that two molecules of hydrogen combine with one molecule of oxygen to produce water.

Now, I am not expert enough in the philosophy of science to challenge this positivist model of the methodology of physics, although my reading in the philosophy of nature leads me to suspect that it is highly inadequate.[1] My contention is rather that the wholesale and uncritical application of this model to economics in recent decades has led the entire discipline badly astray.

There is, however, unbeknownst to most present-day

economists, a competing methodological tradition. This tradition, the method of most of the older classical economists, has been called "praxeology" by Ludwig von Mises, its most eminent modern theorist and practitioner. Praxeology holds that in the social sciences where human beings and human choices are involved, Step 3 is impossible, since even in the most ambitious totalitarian society, it is impossible to hold *all* the variables constant. There *cannot* be controlled experiments when we confront the real world of human activity.

Let us take a recent example of a generally unwelcome economic phenomenon: the accelerated price inflation in the United States in the last few years. There are all manner of competing theoretical explanations for this, ranging from increases in the money supply to a sudden increase in greed on the part of the public or various segments thereof. There is no positivist-empirical way of deciding between these various theories; there is no way of confirming or disproving them by keeping all but one supposedly explanatory variable constant, and then changing that variable to see what happens to prices. In addition, there is the well-known social science analogue of the Heisenberg uncertainty principle: positivist science contains predictions, but how can predictions be tested when the very act of prediction itself changes the forces at work? Thus, economist A predicts a severe recession in six months; acting on this, the government takes measures to combat the supposedly imminent recession, the public and the stock market react, and so on. The recession then never takes place. Does that mean that the economist was basing his prediction on erroneous theories, or that the theories were correct but inappropriate to the actual data, *or* that he was "really" right but that prompt action forestalled the dreaded event? There is no way to decide.

One further example: Keynesian economists hold that depressions can be cured by massive doses of deficit spending by the government. The United States government engaged in large-scale deficit-spending to combat the depression in the late 1930s, but to no avail. The anti-Keynesians charge that this failure proves the incorrectness of Keynesian theory; the Keynesians reply that the doses were simply not massive enough, and that far greater deficits would have turned the tide. Again, there is no positivist-empirical way to decide between these competing claims.

Praxeologists share the contention of the impossibility of empirical testing with other critics of positivism, such as the institutionalists, who for this reason abandon economic theory altogether and confine themselves to purely empirical or institutional economic reportage. But the praxeologist does not despair; he turns instead to another methodology that *can* yield a correct body of economy theory. This methodology begins with the conviction that while the economist, unlike the physicist, cannot test his hypotheses in controlled experiments, he is, in another sense, in a *better* position than the physicist. For while the physicist is certain of his empirical laws but tentative and uncertain of his explanatory generalizations, the economist is in the opposite position. He begins, not with detailed, quantitative, empirical regularities, but with broad explanatory generalizations. These fundamental premises he knows with certainty; they have the status of apodictic axioms, on which he can build deductively with confidence. Beginning with the certain knowledge of the basic explanatory axiom A, he deduces the implications of A: B, C, and D. From these he deduces further implications, and so on. If he knows that A is true, and if A implies B, C, and D, then he knows with certainty that B, C, and D are true as well. The positivist, looking through the blinders imposed by his notion of physics, finds it impossible to understand how a science can possibly begin with the explanatory axioms and work downward to the more concrete empirical laws. He therefore dismisses the praxeological approach as "mythical" and "apriorist."

What are these axioms with which the economist can

so confidently begin? They are the existence, the nature, and the implications of human action. Individual human beings exist. Moreover, they do not simply "move," as do unmotivated atoms or molecules; they *act,* i.e., they have goals and they make choices of means to attain their goals. They order their values or ends in a hierarchy according to whether they attribute greater or lesser importance to them; and they have what they believe is technological knowledge to achieve their goals. All of this action must also take place through time and in a certain space. It is on this basic and evident axiom of human action that the entire structure of praxeological economic theory is built. We do not know, and may never know with certainty, the ultimate equation that will explain all electromagnetic and gravitational phenomena; but we *do* know that people act to achieve goals. And this knowledge is enough to elaborate the body of economic theory.[2]

There is considerable controversy over the empirical status of the praxeological axiom. Professor Mises, working within a Kantian philosophical framework, maintained that like the "laws of thought," the axiom is a priori to human experience and hence apodictically certain. This analysis has given rise to the designation of praxeology as "extreme apriorism." Most praxeologists, however, hold that the axiom is based squarely in empirical reality, which makes it no less certain than it is in Mises's formulation. If the axiom is empirically true, then the logical consequences built upon it must be empirically true as well. But this is not the sort of empiricism welcomed by the positivist, for it is based on universal reflective or inner experience, as well as on external physical experience. Thus, the knowledge that human beings have goals and act purposively to attain them rests, not simply on observing that human beings exist, but also on the introspective knowledge of what it means to be human possessed by each man, who then assents to this knowledge. While this sort of empiricism rests on broad knowl-

edge of human action, it is also prior to the complex historical events that economists attempt to explain.

Alfred Schutz pointed out and elaborated the complexity of the interaction between the individual and other persons, the "interpretive understanding" or *Verstehen,* upon
which this universal, prescientific knowledge rests. The
common-sense knowledge of the universality of motivated,
intentional human action, ignored by positivists as "unscientific," actually provides the indispensable groundwork on
which science itself must develop.[3] For Schutz this knowledge is empirical, "provided that we do not restrict this term
to sensory perceptions of objects and events in the outer
world but include the experiential form, by which common-
sense thinking in everyday life understands human actions
and their outcome in terms of their underlying motives and
goals."[4]

The nature of the evidence on which the praxeological
axiom rests is, moreover, fundamentally similar to that accepted by the self-proclaimed empiricists. To them, the
laboratory experiment is evidence because the sensory experience involved in it is available to each observer; the experience becomes "evident" to all. Logical proof is in this sense
similar; for the knowledge that B follows from A becomes
evident to all who care to follow the demonstration. In the
same way, the fact of human action and of purposive choice
also becomes evident to each person who bothers to contemplate it; it is just as evident as the direct sense experience of
the laboratory.

From this philosophical perspective, then, all disciplines
dealing with human beings—from philosophy to history,
psychology, and the social sciences—must take as their starting point the fact that humans engage in motivated, purposive action and are thus different from the unmotivated
atoms and stones that are the objects of the physical sciences. But where, then, does praxeology or economics differ
from the other disciplines that treat human beings? The

difference is that, to the praxeologist, economic *theory* (as distinct from applied economics, which will be treated below) deals, not with the content of human valuations, motivations, and choices, but with the formal fact *that* people engage in such motivated action. Other disciplines focus on the content of these values and actions. Thus, psychology asks how and why people adopt values and make choices; ethics deals with the problem of what values and choices they *should* adopt; technology explains how they should act in order to arrive at chosen ends; and history tries to explain the content of human motives and choices through recorded time. Of these disciplines, history is perhaps the most purely *verstehende,* for the historian is constantly attempting to describe, understand, and explain the motivations and choices of individual actors. Economic theory, on the other hand, is the least *verstehende,* for while it too begins with the axiom of purposive and intentional human action, the remainder of its elaborated structure consists of the deduced logical—and therefore true—implications of that primordial fact.

An example of the formal structure of economic theory is the well-known economic law, built up from the axiom of the existence of motivated human action, that if the demand for any product increases, given the existing supply, the price of that product will rise. This law holds regardless of the ethical or aesthetic status of the product, just as the law of gravity applies to objects regardless of their particular identity. The economic theorist is not interested in the content of what is being demanded, or in its ethical meaning—it may be guns or butter or even textbooks on philosophy. It is this universal, formal nature of economic law that has earned it among laymen the reputation of being cold, heartless, and excessively logical.

Having discussed the nature of the axiom on which the praxeological view of economics is grounded, we may now turn to examine the deductive process itself, the way in which the structure of economic laws is developed, the nature of those laws, and, finally, the ways in which the praxeological economist applies these economic laws to the social world.

One of the basic tools for the deduction of the logical implications of the axiom of human action is the use of the *Gedankenexperiment,* or "mental experiment." The *Gedankenexperiment* is the economic theorist's substitute for the natural scientist's controlled laboratory experiment. Since the relevant variables of the social world cannot actually be held constant, the economist holds them constant in his imagination. Using the tool of verbal logic, he mentally investigates the causal influence of one variable on another. The economist finds, for example, that the price of a product is determined by two variables, the demand for it and its supply at any given time. He then mentally holds the supply constant, and finds that an increase in demand—brought about by higher rankings of the product on the value scales of the public—will bring about an increase in price. Similarly, he finds, again using verbal deductive logic, that if these value scales, and therefore public demand, are mentally held constant, and the supply of the product increases, its price will fall. In short, economics arrives at *ceteris paribus* laws: *Given* the supply, the price will change in the same direction as demand; *given* the demand, price will change in the opposite direction from supply.

One important aspect of these economic laws must be pointed out: They are necessarily *qualitative*. The fact that human beings have goals and preferences, that they make choices to attain their goals, that all action must take place over time, all these are qualitative axioms. And since only the qualitative enters into the logical process from the real world, only the qualitative can emerge. One can only say, for example, that an increase in demand, given the supply, will raise the price; one *cannot* say that a 20 percent increase in demand will bring about a 25 percent increase in price.

The praxeologist must reject all attempts, no matter how fashionable, to erect a theory consisting of alleged quantitative laws. In an age that tries desperately to imitate prestigious physics, with its emphasis on mathematics and its quantitative laws, many social scientists, including many economists, have ignored this methodology because of this very insistence on the qualitative bounds of the discipline.

There is a basic reason for the quantity-quality dichotomy between the physical and the social sciences. The objects of physical science do not act; they do not choose, change their minds, and choose again. Their natures may therefore be investigated, and the investigations replicated indefinitely, with quantitative precision. But people do change their minds, and their actions, all the time; their behavior cannot be predicted with exact and therefore scientific precision. Among the many factors helping to determine the demand and the supply of butter, for example, are the valuations placed by each consumer on butter relative to all other products available, the availability of substitutes, the climate in the butter-producing areas, technological methods of producing butter (and margarine), the price of cattle feed, the supply of money in the country, the existence of prosperity or recession in the economy, and the public's expectations of the trend of general prices. Every one of these factors is subject to continuing and unpredictable change. Even if one mammoth equation could be discovered to "explain" all recorded prices of butter for the past 50 years, there is no guarantee, and not even the likelihood, that the equation would have anything to do with *next* month's price.

In fact, if empirical success is the test, it is surely noteworthy that all the determined efforts of quantitative economists, econometricians, and social scientists have not been able to find one single quantitative constant in human affairs. The mathematical laws in the physical sciences contain numerous constants; but the imitative method in the social sciences is proven vain by the fact that not a single constant has ever emerged. Moreover, despite the use of sophisticated econometric models and high-speed computers, the success rate of forecasting economic quantities has been dismal, even for the simplest of aggregates such as the Gross National Product, let alone for more difficult quantities; the record of GNP forecasting by economists has been poorer than a simple layman's extrapolation of recent trends.[5] In fact, the federal government has had notably poor success even in forecasting the one variable under its own absolute control—its *own* expenditure in the near future. Perhaps we will revise our critical opinion of econometric science if and when the econometricians prove themselves able to make flawless predictions of activity on the stock market—and make themselves vast fortunes in the process.

Except for the fact that they are not quantitative, however, the predictions of the praxeologist are precisely the same kind as those of the natural scientist. The latter, after all, is not a prophet or soothsayer; his successful prediction is not what *will* happen in the world, but what *would* happen if such and such should occur. The scientist can predict successfully that if hydrogen and oxygen are combined in proportions of two to one, the result will be water; but he has no way of predicting scientifically how many scientists in how many laboratories will perform this process at any given period in the future. In the same way, the praxeologist can say, with absolute certainty, that if the demand for butter increases, and the supply remains the same, the price of butter will rise; but he does not know whether the public's demand for butter will in fact rise or fall, let alone by how much it will change. Like the physical scientist, the economist is not a prophet, and it is unfortunate that the econometricians and quantitative economists should have so eagerly assumed this social role.[6]

The English economist John Jewkes suggests the properly limited role for economic forecasting, as well as for applied economics generally:

> I submit that economists cannot, without stepping outside their discipline, predict in the sense of telling us what will happen in the future. . . .
>
> In the most general sense, there is, indeed, no such thing as the *economic* future. There is only *the* future in which economic factors are bound together, inextricably and quite without hope of separate identification, with the whole universe of forces determining the course of events. . . . Anyone who proposes to look at it [the future] before the event must take as his province the whole of experience and knowledge. He must cease to behave as a specialist, which means that he must cease to behave as an economist. . . .
>
> The economist's claim to predictive authority must be false in that it leads to a palpable absurdity. If the economic future can, indeed, be described, why not also the scientific future, the political future, the social future, the future in each and every sense? Why should we not be able to plumb all the mysteries of future time?

What, then, is the praxeological view of the function of applied economics? The praxeologist contrasts, on the one hand, the body of qualitative, nomothetic laws developed by economic theory, and on the other, a myriad of unique, complex historical facts of both the past and the future. It is ironic that while the praxeologist is generally denounced by the positivist as an "extreme apriorist," he actually has a far more empirical attitude toward the facts of history. For the positivist is always attempting to compress complex historical facts into artificial molds, regarding them as homogeneous and therefore manipulable and predictable by mechanical, statistical, and quantitative operations in the attempt to find leads, lags, correlations, econometric relations, and "laws of history." This procrustean distortion is undertaken in the belief that the events of human history can be treated in the same mechanistic way as the movements of atoms or molecules—simple, unmotivated, homogeneous elements. The positivist thereby ignores the fact that while atoms and stones have no history, man, by virtue of his acts of conscious choice, creates a history. The praxeologist, in contrast, holds that each historical event is the highly complex result of a large number of causal forces, and, further, that it is unique and cannot be considered homogeneous to any other event. Obviously, there are similarities between events, but there is no perfect homogeneity and therefore no room for historical "laws" similar to the exact laws of physical science.

While accepting that there are no mechanical laws of history, however, the praxeologist holds that he can and must use his knowledge of other nomothetic sciences as part of his *verstehende* attempt to understand and explain the idiographic events of history. Let us suppose that the economic historian, or the student of applied economics, is attempting to explain a rapid rise in the price of wheat in a certain country during a certain period. He may bring many nomothetic sciences to bear: The sciences of agronomy and entomology may help reveal that an insect mentioned in the historical record was responsible for a drastic fall in wheat production; meteorological records may show that rainfall was insufficient; he may discover that during the period people's taste for bread increased, perhaps imitating a similar preference by the king; he may discover that the money supply was increasing, and learn from economic theory that an increase in the supply of money tends to raise prices in general, including therefore the price of wheat. And, finally, economic theory states that the price of wheat moves inversely with the supply and directly with the demand. The economic historian combines all of his scientific knowledge with his understanding of motives and choices to attempt to explain the complex historical phenomenon of the price of bread.

A similar procedure is followed in the study of such infinitely more complex historical problems as the causes of the French Revolution, where, again, the historian must blend his knowledge of causal theories in economics, military strategy, psychology, technology, and so on, with his understanding of the motives and choices of individual actors. While historians may well agree on the enumeration of all the relevant causal factors in the problem, they will differ on the weight to be attached to each factor. The evaluation of the relative importance of historical factors is an art, not a science, a matter of personal judgment, experience, and *verstehende* insight which will differ from one historian to another. In this sense, economic historians, like economists (and indeed other historians), can come to qualitative but not quantitative agreement.

For the praxeologist, forecasting is a task very similar to the work of the historian. The latter attempts to "predict" the events of the past by explaining their antecedent causes; similarly, the forecaster attempts to predict the events of the future on the basis of present and past events already known. He uses all his nomothetic knowledge, economic, political, military, psychological, and technological; but at best his work is an art rather than an exact science. Thus, some forecasters will inevitably be better than others, and the superior forecasters will make the more successful entrepreneurs, speculators, generals, and bettors on elections or football games.

The economic forecaster, as Professor Jewkes pointed out, is only looking at part of a tangled and complex social whole. To return to our original example, when he attempts to forecast the price of butter, he must take into consideration the qualitative economic law that price depends directly on demand and inversely on supply; it is then up to him, using knowledge and insight into general economic conditions as well as the specific economic, technological, political, and climatological conditions of the butter market, as well as the values people are likely to place on butter, to try to forecast the movements of the supply and demand of butter, and therefore its price, as accurately as possible. At best, he will have nothing like a perfect score, for he will run aground on the fact of free will altering values and choices, and the consequent impossibility of making exact predictions of the future.[8]

2. The Praxeological Tradition

The praxeological tradition has a long history in economic thought. We will indicate briefly the outstanding figures in the development of that tradition, especially since these economic methodologists and their views have been recently neglected by economists steeped in the positivist world view.

One of the first self-conscious methodologists in the history of economics was the early ninetheenth-century French economist Jean-Baptiste Say. In the lengthy introduction to his magnum opus, *A Treatise on Political Economy,* Say laments that people

> are too apt to suppose that absolute truth is confined to the mathematics and to the results of careful observation and experiment in the physical sciences; imagining that the moral and political sciences contain no invariable facts of indisputable truth, and therefore cannot be considered as genuine sciences, but merely hypothetical systems. . . .

Say could easily have been referring to the positivists of our day, whose methodology prevents them from recognizing that absolute truths can be arrived at in the social sciences, when grounded, as they are in praxeology, on broadly evident axioms. Say insists that the "general facts" underlying what he calls the "moral sciences" are undisputed and grounded on universal observation.

> Hence the advantage enjoyed by every one who, from distinct and accurate observation, can establish the existence of these general facts, demonstrate their connexion, and deduce their consequences. They as certainly proceed from the nature of things as the laws of the material world. We do not imagine them; they are results disclosed to us by judicious observation and analysis.... That can be admitted by every reflecting mind.

These general facts, according to Say, are "principles," and the science of

> political economy, in the same manner as the exact sciences, is composed of a few fundamental principles, and of a great number of corollaries or conclusions drawn from these principles. It is essential, therefore, for the advancement of this science that these principles should be strictly deduced from observation; the number of conclusions to be drawn from them may afterwards be either multiplied or diminished at the discretion of the inquirer, according to the object he proposes.[9]

Here Say has set forth another important point of the praxeological method: that the paths in which the economist works out the implications of the axioms and the elaborated system which results will be decided by his own interests and by the kind of historical facts he is examining. Thus, it is theoretically possible to deduce the theory of money even in an economy of primitive barter, where no money exists; but it is doubtful whether a primitive praxeologist would have bothered to do so.

Interestingly enough, Say at that early date saw the rise of the statistical and mathematical methods, and rebutted them from what can be described as a praxeological point of view. The difference between political economy and statistics is precisely the difference between political economy (or economic theory) and history. The former is based with certainty on universally observed and acknowledged general principles; therefore, "a perfect knowledge of the principles of political economy may be obtained, inasmuch as all the general facts which compose this science may be discovered." Upon these "undeniable general facts." "rigorous deductions" are built, and to that extent political economy "rests upon an immovable foundation." Statistics, on the other hand, only records the ever changing pattern of particular facts, statistics "like history, being a recital of facts, more or less uncertain and necessarily incomplete." Furthermore, Say anticipated the praxeologist's view of historical and statistical data as themselves complex facts needing to be explained. "The study of statistics may gratify curiosity, but it can never be productive of advantage when it does not indicate the origin and consequences of the facts it has collected; and by indicating their origin and consequences, it at once becomes the science of political economy." Elsewhere in the essay, Say scoffs at the gullibility of the public toward statistics: "Sometimes, moreover, a display of figures and calculations imposes upon them; as if numerical calculations alone could prove any thing, and as if any rule could be laid down, from which an inference could be drawn without the aid of sound reasoning."[10]

Say goes on to question sharply the value of mathematics in the construction of economic theory, once again referring back to the structure of the basic axioms, or general principles, for his argument. For political economy is concerned with men's values, and these values being "subject to the influence of the faculties, the wants and the desires of mankind, they are not susceptible of any rigorous appreciation, and cannot therefore furnish any data for absolute calculations. In political science, all that is essential is a knowledge of the connexion between causes and their consequences." Delving deeper into the then only embryonic use of the mathematical method in economics. Say points out that the laws of economics are strictly qualitative: "We may, for example, know that for any given year the price of wine will infallibly depend upon the quantity to be sold, compared with the extent of the demand." But "if we are desirous of submitting these two data to mathematical calculation," then it becomes impossible to arrive at precise quantitative forecasts of the innumerable, ever changing forces at work: the climate, the quantity of the harvest, the quality of the product, the stock of wine held over from the previous vintage, the amount of capital, the possibilities of export, the supply of substitute beverages, and the changeable tastes and values of the consumers.[11]

Say offers a highly perceptive insight into the nature and probable consequences of the application of mathematics to economics. He argues that the mathematical method, with its seeming exactitude, can only gravely distort the analysis of qualitative human action by stretching and oversimplifying the legitimate insights of economic principles:

> Such persons as have pretended to do it, have not been able to enunciate these questions into analytical language, without divesting them of their natural complication, by means of simplifications, and arbitrary suppressions, of which the consequences, not properly estimated, always essentially change the condition of the problem, and pervert all its results; so that no other inference can be deduced from such calculations than from formula arbitrarily assumed.[12]

In contrast to the physical sciences where the explanatory laws or general principles are always in the realm of the hypothetical, in praxeology it is fatal to introduce oversimplification and falsehood into the premises, for then the conclusions deduced from them will be irredeemably faulty as well.[13]

If mathematics and statistics do not provide the proper method for the political economist, what method is appropriate? The same course that he would pursue in his daily life. "He will examine the immediate elements of the proposed problem, and after having ascertained them with certainty ... will approximately value their mutual influences with the intuitive quickness of an enlightened understanding.... "[14] In short, the laws of the political economist are certain, but their blending and application to any given historical event is accomplished, not by pseudoquantitative or mathematical methods, which distort and oversimplify, but only by the use of *Verstehen,* "the intuitive quickness of an enlightened understanding."

The first economists to devote their attention specifically to methodology were three leading economists of mid-nineteenth-century Britain: John E. Cairnes, Nassau W. Senior, and John Stuart Mill. Cairnes and Senior, at least, may be considered as protopraxeologists. Cairnes, after agreeing with Mill that there can be no controlled experiments in the social sciences, adds that the latter have, however, a crucial advantage over the physical sciences. For, in the latter,

> *mankind have no direct knowledge of ultimate physical principles.* The law of gravitation and the laws of motion are among the best established and most certain of such principles; but what is the evidence on which they rest? We do not find them in our consciousness, by reflecting on what passes in our minds; nor can they be made apparent to our sense ... the proof of all such laws ultimately resolving itself into this, that, assuming them to exist, they account for the phenomena.

In contrast, however,

The economist starts with a knowledge of ultimate causes. He is already, at the outset of his enterprise, in the position which the physicist only attains after ages of laborious research. If any one doubt this, he has only to consider what the ultimate principles governing economic phenomena are ... : certain mental feelings and certain animal propensities in human beings; [and] the physical conditions under which production takes place.... For the discovery of such premises no elaborate process of induction is needed ... for this reason, that we have, or may have if we choose to turn our attention to the subject, direct knowledge of these causes in our consciousness of what passes in our own minds, and in the information which our senses convey ... to us of external facts. Every one who embarks in any industrial pursuit is conscious of the motives which actuate him in doing so. He knows that he does so from a desire, for whatever purpose, to possess himself of wealth; he knows that, according to his lights, he will proceed toward his end in the shortest way open to him....[15]

Cairnes goes on to point out that the economist uses the mental experiment as a replacement for the laboratory experiment of the physical scientist.

Cairnes demonstrates that deduced economic laws are "tendency," or "if-then," laws, and, moreover, that they are necessarily qualitative, and cannot admit of mathematical or quantitative expression. Thus, he too makes the point that it is impossible to determine precisely how much the price of wheat will rise in response to a drop in supply; for one thing, "it is evident that the disposition of people to sacrifice one kind of gratification to another—to sacrifice vanity to comfort, or decency to hunger—is not susceptible of precise measurement...."[16] In the preface to his second edition, two decades later in 1875, Cairnes reiterated his opposition to the growing application of the mathematical method to economics, which, in contrast to its use in the physical sciences, cannot produce new truths; "and unless it can be shown either that mental feelings admit of being expressed in precise quantitative forms, or, on the other hand, that economic phenomena do not depend upon mental feelings, I am unable to see how this conclusion can be avoided."[17]

Cairnes's older contemporary, Nassau Senior, was the most important praxeologist of that era. Before Senior, classical economists such as John Stuart Mill had placed the fundamental premises of economics on the shaky ground of being *hypotheses;* the major hypothesis was that all men act to obtain the maximum of material wealth. Since this is clearly not always true, Mill had to concede that economics was only a hypothetical and approximate science. Senior broadened the fundamental premise to include immaterial wealth or satisfaction, a complete, apodictic, and universally true principle based on insight into the goal-seeking nature of human action.

> In stating that every man desires to obtain additional wealth with as little sacrifice as possible, we must not be supposed to mean that everybody ... wishes for an indefinite quantity of everything.... What we mean to state is that no person feels his whole wants to be adequately supplied; that every person has some unsatisfied desires which he believes that additional wealth would gratify. The nature and urgency of each individual's wants are as various as the differences in individual character.[18]

In contrast to the physical sciences, Senior pointed out, economics and the other "mental sciences" draw their premises from the universal facts of human consciousness:

> The physical sciences being only secondarily conversant with mind, draw their premises almost exclusively from

observation or hypothesis. Those which treat only of
magnitude or number, ... the pure sciences, draw
them altogether from hypothesis.... They disregard almost entirely the phenomenon of consciousness....

On the other hand, the mental sciences and the
mental arts draw their premises principally from consciousness. The subjects with which they are chiefly
conversant are the workings of the human mind.[19]

These latter premises are "a very few general propositions,
which are the result of observation, or consciousness, and
which almost every man, as soon as he hears them, admits,
as familiar to his thought, or at least, as included in his
previous knowledge."[20]

During the 1870s and 1880s, classical economics was
supplanted by the neoclassical school. In this period the
praxeological method was carried on and further developed
by the Austrian school, founded by Carl Menger of the University of Vienna and continued by his two most eminent
disciples, Eugen von Böhm-Bawerk and Friedrich von Wieser. It was on the basis of their work that Böhm-Bawerk's
student, Ludwig von Mises, later founded praxeology as a
self-conscious and articulated methodology.[21] As it was outside the increasingly popular intellectual fashion of positivism and mathematics, however, the Austrian school has
been greatly neglected in recent years and dismissed as an
unsound approximation of the positivist-mathematical theory of the Lausanne school, founded by Leon Walras of
Lausanne and continued by the Italian economist and soci-
ologist Vilfredo Pareto.

A few followers or sympathetic observers, however,
have carried on investigations into the methodology of the
early Austrian school. Leland B. Yeager notes what we now
see as the typically praxeological view of the unique advantage of economic theory over the physical sciences: "While
the basic elements of theoretical interpretation in the natu-

ral sciences, such, he [Menger] says, as forces and atoms, cannot be observed directly, the elements of explanation in economics—human individuals and their strivings—are of a direct empirical nature." Furthermore, "The facts that economists induce from the behavior of themselves and other people serve as axioms from which a useful body of economic theory can be logically deduced, much as in geometry an impressive body of theorems can be deduced from a few axioms." In short, "Menger conceived of economic theory as a body of deductions from basic principles having a strong empirical foundation." Referring to the dominant positivist economists of our own day, Yeager adds perceptively,

> Not sharing ... Menger's understanding of how empirical content gets into so-called "armchair theory," many economists of our own day apparently regard theoretical and empirical work as two distinct fields. Manipulation of arbitrarily-assumed functional relationships is justified in the minds of such economists by the idea that empirical testing of theories against the real world comes afterward.[22]

Other writers have discovered links between the Austrian method and various strands of the *philosophia perennis.* Thus, Emil Kauder finds a close relationship between this method and Aristotelian philosophy, which was still influential in Austria at the end of the nineteenth century. Kauder points out that all the Austrians were "social ontologists," and that as such they believed in a structure of reality "both as a logical starting point and as a criterion of validity." He notes Mises's statement that economic laws are "ontological facts," and he characterizes as both ontological and Aristotelian the concern of Menger and his followers to uncover the "essences" of phenomena, rather than to treat superficial and complex economic quantities. Kauder also points out that for Menger and the Austrians, economic theory deals with types and typical relations, which provide knowledge that transcends the immediate, concrete case and is valid for all times and places. Concrete historical cases are thus the Aristotelian "matter" which contains potentialities, while the laws and types are the Aristotelian "forms" which actualize the potential. For the Austrians, and especially for Böhm-Bawerk, furthermore, causality and teleology were identical. In contrast to the functional-mutual determination approach of Walras and of contemporary economists, the Austrians traced the causes of economic phenomena back to the wants and choices of consumers. Wieser especially stressed the grounding of economic theory on the inner experience of the mind.[23]

Furthermore, Ludwig M. Lachmann, in contrasting the Austrian and Lausanne schools, shows that the Austrians were endeavoring to construct a "*verstehende* social science," the same ideal that Max Weber was later to uphold. Lachmann points out that the older Ricardian economists adopted the "objective" method of the natural sciences insofar as their major focus was upon the quantitative problem of income distribution. In their analysis, factors of production (land, labor, and capital goods) react mechanically to external economic changes. But, in contrast, "Austrian theory is 'subjective' also in the sense that individuals ... perform acts and lend the imprint of their individuality to the events on the market." As for the contrast between Austria and Lausanne,

> it is the contrast between those [Lausanne] who confine themselves to determining the appropriate magnitudes of the elements of a system (the conditions of equilibrium) and those [the Austrians] who try to explain events in terms of the mental acts of the individuals who fashion them. Most Austrian thinkers were dimly aware of this contrast, but before Hans Mayer, Mises and Hayek were unable to express it concisely. The validity

of the Lausanne model is limited to a stationary world. The background of the Austrian theory, by contrast, is a world of continuous change in which plans have to be conceived and continually revised.[24]

We may conclude this sketch of the history of the praxeological tradition in economics by treating an important but much neglected debate on economic methodology which occurred at the turn of the 20th century between Pareto and the philosopher Benedetto Croce. Croce, from his own highly developed praxeological position, opened the debate by chiding Pareto for having written that economic theory was a species of mechanics. Vigorously rejecting this view, Croce points out that a fact in mechanics is a mere fact, which requires no positive or negative comment; whereas words of approval or disapproval can appropriately be applied to an *economic* fact. The reason is that the true data of economics are not "physical things and objects, but actions. The physical object is merely the brute matter of an economic act.... "[25] Economic data, then, are acts of man, and these acts are the results of conscious choice.

In his lengthy reply, Pareto reiterates the similarity between economics and mechanics, and, like the positivists of today, defends unrealistic mechanistic assumptions as simple abstractions from reality, in the supposed manner of the natural sciences. Professing, in a typical positivist gambit, not to "understand" the concept of value, Pareto writes: "I see ... that you employ the term *value*.... I no longer use it as I do not know what it would convey to other people.... " The concept of value is vague and complex and not subject to measurement; therefore, "the equations of pure economics establish relations between quantities of things, hence objective relations, and not relations between more or less precise concepts of our minds."[26] Criticizing Croce's evident concentration on the essences of economic action, as exemplified in his insistence that "one ought to study not the things which are the result of actions but the actions themselves," Pareto complains that this method is an ancient scientific fallacy. "The ancients conjured up cosmogonies instead of studying astronomy, wondered about the principles of the elements water and fire ... , instead of studying chemistry. Ancient science wanted to proceed from the origin to the facts. Modern science starts from the facts and proceeds towards the origin at an extremely slow pace." Typically, Pareto sets forth the objectivist, positivist position by arguing from the analogy of the method of the natural sciences, thus completely begging the question of whether the methodologies of the natural and the social sciences should or should not be similar. Thus he concludes that "science proceeds by replacing the relationships between human concepts (which relationships are the first to occur to us) by relationships between things."[27]

Croce replies by criticizing Pareto's restriction of economics to measurable quantities as arbitrary; for what of those economic situations where the objects of action or exchange are not measurable? Croce suggests that it is Pareto who is really being metaphysical, while Croce is the true empiricist. For "your implied metaphysical postulate is ... this: that the facts of man's activity are of the same nature as physical facts; that in the one case as in the other we can only observe regularity and deduce consequences therefrom, without ever penetrating into the inner nature of the facts.... How would you defend this postulate of yours except by a metaphysical monism ... ?" In contrast, writes Croce, "I hold to experience. This testifies to me of the fundamental distinction between external and internal, between physical and mental, between mechanics and teleology, between passivity and activity.... " As for value, it is really a simple term wrapped up in human activity: "Value is observed immediately in ourselves, in our consciousness."[28]

In his rejoinder, Pareto begins with a typical example

of metaphysical obtuseness: He does *not* believe that "the facts of man's activity are of the same nature as physical facts" because he doesn't know what "nature" may be. He goes on to reiterate various examples from physical science to demonstrate the proper methodology for all disciplines. He wishes to follow the "masters of positive science" rather than mere philosophers. Pareto concludes with a concise summation of the differences between the two men and the two methodologies:

> We experimentalists ... accept hypotheses not for any intrinsic value they may have but only in so far as they yield deductions which are in harmony with the facts. You, considering the nature of things independently from the rest, establish a certain proposition A, and from it come down to the concrete facts B. We may accept proposition A, but only as a hypothesis, there-fore making not the slightest attempt to prove it.... Then we see what can be deduced from it. If those deductions agree with the facts we accept the hypothe-sis, for the time being of course, because we hold noth-ing as final or absolute.[29]

3. Methodological Individualism

Only an individual has a mind; only an individual can feel, see, sense, and perceive; only an individual can *act*. This primordial principle of "methodological individualism," central to Max Weber's social thought, must underlie praxeology as well as the other sciences of human action. It implies that such collective concepts as groups, nations, and states do not actually exist or act; they are only metaphorical constructs for describing the similar or concerted actions of individuals. there are, in short, no "governments" as such; there are only individuals acting in concert in a "govern-mental" manner. Max Weber puts it clearly:

These collectivists must be treated as solely the resultants and modes of organization of the particular acts of individual persons, since these alone can be treated as agents in a course of subjectively understandable action.... For sociological purposes ... there is no such thing as a collective personality which "acts." When reference is made in a sociological context to ... collectivities, what is meant is ... *only* a certain kind of development of actual or possible social actions of the individual persons.[30]

Ludwig von Mises points out that what differentiates purely individual action from that of individuals acting as members of a collective is the different *meaning* attached by the people involved.

It is the meaning which the acting individuals and all those who are touched by their action attribute to an action, that determines its character. It is the meaning that marks one action as the action of the state or of the municipality. The hangman, not the state, executes a criminal. It is the meaning of those concerned that discerns in the hangman's action an action of the state. A group of armed men occupies a place. It is the meaning of those concerned which imputes this occupation not to the officers and soldiers on the spot, but to their nation.[31]

In his important methodological work, Mises's disciple, F. A. Hayek, has demonstrated that the fallacy of treating collective constructs as directly perceived "social wholes" ("capitalism" "the nation," "the class") about which laws can be discovered stems from the objectivist-behaviorist insistence on treating men from the outside, as if they were stones, rather than attempting to understand their subjectively determined actions.

> It [the objectivist view] treats social phenomena not as something of which the human mind is a part and the principles of whose organization we can construct from the familiar parts, but as if they were objects directly perceived by us as wholes. . . .
>
> There is the rather vague idea that since "social phenomena" are to be the object of study, the obvious procedure is to start from the direct observation of these "social phenomena," where the existence in popular usage of such terms as "society" or "economy" is naively taken as evidence that there must be definite "objects" corresponding to them.[32]

Hayek adds that emphasis on the meaning of the individual act brings out that what of social complexes is directly known to us are only the parts and that the whole is never directly perceived but always reconstructed by an effort of our imagination."[33]

Alfred Schutz, the outstanding developer of the phenomenological method in the social sciences, has reminded us of the importance of going back "to the 'forgotten man' of the social sciences, to the actor in the social world whose doing and feeling lies at the bottom of the whole system. We, then, try to understand him in that doing and feeling and the state of mind which induced him to adopt specific attitudes towards his social environment." Schutz adds that "for a theory of action the subjective point of view must be retained in its fullest strength, in default of which such a theory loses its basic foundations, namely its reference to the social world of everyday life and experience." Lacking such a foundation, social science is likely to replace the "world of social reality" by a fictional nonexisting world constructed by the scientific observer. Or, as Schutz puts it succinctly: "I cannot understand a social thing without reducing it to human activity which has created it, and beyond it, without referring this human activity to the motives out of which it springs."[34]

Arnold W. Green has recently demonstrated how the use of invalid collective concepts has damaged the discipline of sociology. He notes the increasing use of "society" as an entity which thinks, feels, and acts, and, in recent years, has functioned as the perpetrator of all social ills. "Society," for example, and not the criminal, is often held to be responsible for all crime. In many quarters "society" is considered almost demonic, a "reified villain" which "may be attacked at will, blamed at random, derided and mocked with self-righteous fury, [and] may even be overturned by fiat or utopian yearning—and somehow, in some way, buses will still run on time." Green adds that "if on the other hand, society is viewed as people whose insecure social relationships are preserved only by the fealty paid their common store of moral rules, then the area of free choice available in which with impunity to demand, undermine, and wreck, is sharply restricted." Moreover, if we realize that "society" does not itself exist, but is made up only of individual people, then to say that "society is responsible for crime, and criminals are not responsible for crime, is to say that only those members of society who do not commit crime can be held responsible for crime. Nonsense this obvious can be circumvented only by conjuring up society as devil, as evil being apart from people and what they do."[35]

Economics has been rife with fallacies that arise when collective social metaphors are treated as if they were existent objects. Thus, during the era of the gold standard there was occasionally great alarm that "England" or "France" was in mortal danger becuase "it" was losing gold. What actually happened was that English*men* and French*men* were voluntarily shipping gold overseas and thus threatening the people who ran the banks of those countries with the necessity of meeting obligations to pay in gold which they could not possibly fulfill. But the use of the collective metaphor converted a grave problem of banking into a vague national crisis for which every citizen was somehow responsible.

Similarly, during the 1930s and 1940s many economists proclaimed that in contrast to debts owed overseas, the size of the domestic public debt was unimportant because "we only owe it to ourselves." The implication was that the collective national person owed "himself" money from one pocket to another. This explanation obscured the fact that it makes a substantial difference for every person whether he is a member of the "we" or the "ourselves."

Sometimes the collective concept is treated unabashedly as a biological organism. Thus, the popular concept of economic growth implies that every economy is somehow destined, in the manner of a living organism, to "grow" in some predetermined manner. The use of such analogical terms is an attempt to overlook or even negate individual will and consciousness in social and economic affairs. As Edith Penrose has written in a critique of the use of the "growth" concept in the study of business firms:

> Where explicit biological analogies crop up in economics they are drawn exclusively from that aspect of biology which deals with the unmotivated behavior of organisms.... We have no reason whatever for thinking that the growth pattern of a biological organism is *willed* by the organism itself. On the other hand, we have every reason for thinking that the growth of a firm is willed by those who make the decisions of the firm ... and the proof of this lies in the fact that no one can describe the development of any given firm ... except in terms of decisions taken by individual men.[36]

There is no better summary of the nature of praxeology and the role of economic theory in relation to concrete historical events than in Alfred Schutz's discussion of the economic methodology of Ludwig von Mises:

No economic act is conceivable without some reference to an economic actor, but the latter is absolutely anonymous; it is not you, nor I, nor an entrepreneur, nor even an "economic man" as such, but a pure universal "one." This is the reason why the propositions of theoretical economics have just that "universal validity" which gives them the ideality of the "and so forth" and "I can do it again." However, one can study the economic actor as such and try to find out what is going on in his mind; of course, one is not then engaged in theoretical economics but in economic history or economic sociology.... However, the statements of these sciences can claim no universal validity, for they deal either with the economic sentiments of particular historical individuals or with types of economic activity for which the economic acts in question are evidence....

In our view, pure economics is a perfect example of an objective meaning complex about subjective meaning-complexes, in other words, of an objective meaning-configuration stipulating the typical and invariant subjective experiences of anyone who acts within an economic framework .... Excluded from such a scheme would have to be any consideration of the uses to which the "goods" are to be put after they are acquired. But once we do turn our attention to the subjective meaning of a real individual person, leaving the anonymous "anyone" behind, then of course it makes sense to speak of behavior that is atypical.... To be sure, such behavior is irrelevant from the point of view of economics, and it is in this sense that economic principles are, in Mises' words, "not a statement of what usually happens, but of what necessarily must happen."[37]

Notes

1. On this, *see* Andrew G. Van Melsen, *The Philosophy of Nature* (Pittsburgh: Duquesne University Press, 1953).

2. Thus the fact that people must act to achieve their goals implies that there is a scarcity of means to attain them; otherwise the goals would already have been attained. Scarcity implies costs, which in a monetary system (developed much later in the logical elaboration) are reflected in prices, and so forth. For a consciously praxeological development of economic theory, *see* Ludwig von Mises, *Human Action* (New Haven: Yale University Press, 1949), and Murray N. Rothbard, *Man, Economy, and State,* 2nd ed. (Kansas City: Sheed Andrews and McMeel, 1970).

3. "It is ... not understandable that the same authors who are convinced that no verification is possible for the intelligence of other human beings have such confidence in the principles of verifiability itself, which can be realized only through cooperation with others by mutual control." Alfred Schutz, *Collected Papers,* vol. 2, *Studies in Social Theory,* ed. A. Brodersen (The Hague: Nijhoff, 1964), p. 4.

4. Alfred Schutz, *Collected Papers,* vol. 1, *The Problem of Social Reality,* ed. Maurice Natanson (The Hague: Nijhoff, 1962), p. 65; *see also* pp. 1–66, as well as Peter Winch, "Philosophical Bearings," and Maurice Natanson, "A Study in Philosophy and the Social Sciences," in *Philosophy of the Social Sciences: A Reader,* ed. Maurice Natanson (New York: Random House, 1963). On the importance of the common-sense, prescientific presuppositions of science from a slightly different philosphical perspective, *see* Van Melsen, *Philosophy of Nature,* pp. 6–29.

5. *See* Victor Zarnowitz, *An Appraisal of Short-Term Economic Forecasts* (New York: National Bureau of Economic Research, 1967). For a record of the problems of forecasting, *see* "Bad Year for Econometrics," *Business Week,* December 20, 1969, pp. 36–40.

6. The English economist P. T. Bauer properly distinguishes between scientific prediction and forecasting: "Prediction, in the sense of the assessment of the results of specified occur-

rences or conditions, must be distinguished from the forecasting of future events. Even if the prediction that the producers of a particular crop respond to a higher price by producing more is correct, this prediction does not enable us to forecast accurately next year's output (still less the harvest in the more distant future), which in the event will be affected by many factors besides changes in price." Peter T. Bauer, *Economic Analysis and Policy in Underdeveloped Countries* (Durham, N.C.: Duke University Press, 1957), pp. 10–11; *see also* pp. 28–32.

7. John Jewkes, "The Economist and Economic Change," in *Economics and Public Policy* (Washington, D.C.: Brookings Institution, 1955), pp. 82–83.

8. We may mention here the well-known refutation of the notion of predicting the future by Karl Popper, namely, that in order to predict the future, we would have to predict what knowledge we will possess in the future. But we cannot do so, for if we knew what our future knowledge would be, we would *already* be in possession of that knowledge at the present time. *See* Karl R. Popper, *The Poverty of Historicism* (New York: Harper & Row, 1964), pp. vi-viii.

9. Jean-Baptiste Say, *A Treatise on Political Economy*, trans. C.C. Biddle (New York: Kelley, 1964), pp. xxiv, xxv, xlv, xxvi.

10. Ibid., pp. xix-xx, li.

11. Ibid., pp. xxvi, xxvi n.

12. Ibid., p. xxvi n.

13. One of the most pernicious aspects of the current dominance of positivist methodology in economics has been precisely this injection of false premises into economic theory. The leading extreme positivist in economics, Milton Friedman, goes so far as to extol the use of admittedly false premises in the theory, since, according to Friedman, the *only* test of a theory is whether it predicts successfully. *See* Milton Friedman, "The Methodology of Positive Economics," in *Essays in Positive Economics* (Chicago: University of Chicago Press, 1953), pp. 3–46. Of the numerous critiques and discussions of the Friedman thesis, *see* in particular Eugene Rotwein, "On 'The Methodology of Positive Economics,'" *Quarterly Journal of Economics* 73 (November 1959):554–75; Paul A. Samuelson, "Discus-

sion," *American Economic Reivew, Papers and Proceedings* 53 (May 1963):231–36; Jack Meltz, "Friedman and Machlup on the Significance of Testing Economic Assumptions," *Journal of Political Economy* 73 (February 1965): 37–60.

14. Say, *Treatise on Political Economy*, p. xxvi n.

15. J. E. Cairnes, *The Character and Logical Method of Political Economy* (1857; 2nd ed., London: Macmillan, 1875, repr. 1888), pp. 83, 87–88 (italics Cairnes's). The emphasis of Cairnes and other classical economists on wealth as the goal of economic action has been modified by later praxeological economists to include all manner of psychological satisfactions, of which those stemming from material wealth are only a subset. A discussion similar to that of Cairnes can be found in F. A. Hayek, "The Nature and History of the Problem," in Hayek, ed., *Collectivist Economic Planning* (London: Routledge,

16. Cairnes, *Character and Logical Method*, p. 127.

17. Ibid., p. v.

18. Nassau William Senior, *An Outline of the Science of Political Economy* (1836; repr., New York: Kelley, n.d.), p. 27.

19. Marian Bowley, *Nassau Senior and Classical Economics* (New York: Kelley, 1949), p. 56.

20. Ibid., p. 43. *See also* p. 64, where Bowley points out the similarity between Senior's methodological views and the praxeology of Ludwig von Mises.

21. The outstanding example is Mises, *Human Action. See also* his *Theory and History* (New Haven: Yale University Press, 1957); *The Ultimate Foundation of Economic Science* (Kansas City: Sheed Andres and McMeel, 1978); and *Epistemological Problems of Economics* (Princeton, N.J.: Van Nostrand, 1960). *See also* F.A. Hayek, *The Counter- Revolution of Science* (Glencoe, IL: Free Press, 1955); Lionel Robbins, *An Essay on the Nature and Significance of Economic Science*, 2nd ed. (London: Macmillan, 1949); and Israel M. Kirzner, *The Economic Point of View*, 2nd ed. (Kansas City: Sheed Andrews and McMeel, 1976).

22. Leland B. Yeager, "The Methodology of Henry George and Carl Menger," *American Journal of Economics and Sociology* 13 (April 1954): 235, 238.

23. Emil Kauder, "Intellectual and Political Roots of the Older

Austrian School," *Zeitschrift fur Nationalokonomie* 17, no. 4 (1958):411–25.

24. English abstract of Ludwig M. Lachmann, "Die geistesges-chichtliche Bedeutung der osterreichischen Schule in der Volkwirtschaftslehre," *Zeitschrift fur Nationalokonomie* 26, nos. 1–3 (1966): 152-167, in *Journal of Economic Abstracts* 5 (September 1967):553–554. *See also* Lachmann, "Methodological Individualism and the Market Economy," in *Roads to Freedom: Essays in Honor of Friedrich A. von Hayek,* ed. E. Streissler (New York: Kelley, 1969), pp. 89–103; and Israel M. Kirzner, "Methodological Individualism, Market Equilibrium, and Market Process," *Il Politico* 32, no. 4 (December 1967):787–99.

25. Benedetto Croce, "On the Economic Principle: I" (1900), *International Economic Papers,* no. 3 (1953), pp. 173, 175. On Croce's views on economics, *see* Giorgio Tagliacozzo, "Croce and the Nature of Economic Science," *Quarterly Journal of Economics* 59 (May 1945):307–29. On the Croce-Pareto debate, *see* Kirzner, *Economic Point of View,* pp. 155–57. It is of interest that the Walrasian economist Joseph Schumpeter, in his only untranslated work, *Das Wesen und der Haupinhalt der theoretischen Nationalokonomie* (Leipzig: Duncker and Humblot, 1908), specifically declared that the economist must only treat changes in "economic quantities" as if they were caused automatically, without reference to the human beings who may have been involved in such changes. In that way, causality and purpose would be replaced in economic theory by functional, mathematical relationships. *See* Kirzner, *Economic Point of View,* pp. 68–70.

26. Vilfredo Pareto, "On the Economic Phenomenon" (1900), *International Economic Papers,* no. 3, p. 187.

27. Ibid., pp. 190, 196.

28. Croce, "On the Economic Principle: II" (1901), *International Economic Papers,* no. 3, pp. 198–99.

29. Pareto, "On the Economic Principle" (1901), *International Economic Papers,* no. 3, p. 206.

30. Max Weber, *The Theory of Social and Economic Organization* (Glencoe, IL: Free Press, 1957), quoted in Alfred Schutz, *The*

Phenomenology of the Social World (Evanston, IL: Northwestern University Press, 1967), p. 199. For an application of methodological individualism to foreign policy, *see* Parker T. Moon, *Imperialism and World Politics* (New York: Macmillan, 1930), p. 58. For a more general political application, *see* Frank Chodorov, "Society Are People," in *The Rise and Fall of Society* (New York: Devin-Adair, 1959), pp. 29–37.

31. Mises, *Human Action*, p. 42.
32. Hayek, *Counter-Revolution of Science*, pp. 53–54.
33. Ibid., p. 214.
34. Schutz, *Collected Papers* 2:7, 8, 10.
35. Arnold W. Green, "The Reified Villain," *Social Research* 35 (Winter 1968):656, 664. On the concept of "society," *see also* Mises, *Theory and History*, pp. 250 ff.
36. Edith Tilton Penrose, "Biological Analogies in the Theory of the Firm," *American Economic Review*, December 1952, p. 808.

Social Science and Natural Science

Ludwig von Mises

I

The foundations of the modern social sciences were laid in the eighteenth century. Up to this time we find history only. Of course, the writings of the historians are full of implications which purport to be valid for all human action irrespective of time and milieu, and even when they do not explicitly set forth such theses they necessarily base their grasp of the facts and their interpretation on assumptions of this type. But no attempt was made to clarify these tacit suppositions by special analysis.

On the other hand, the belief prevailed that in the field of human action no other criterion could be used than that of good and bad. If a policy did not attain its end, its failure was ascribed to the moral insufficiency of man or to the weakness of the government. With good men and strong governments everything was considered feasible.

Then in the eighteenth century came a radical change. The founders of political economy discovered regularity in the operation of the market. They discovered that to every

Reprinted from *Money, Method and the Market Process: Essays by Ludwig von Mises* edited by Richard M. Ebeling (Auburn, AL: Praxeology Press of the Ludwig von Mises Institute and Kluwer Academic Publishers, 1990). [Originally published in the *Journal of Social Philosophy and Jurisprudence* 7, no. 3 (April, 1942).]

state of the market a certain state of prices corresponded and that a tendency to restore this state made itself manifest whenever anything tried to alter it. This insight opened a new chapter in science. People came to realize with astonishment that human actions were open to investigation from other points of view than that of moral judgment. They were compelled to recognize a regularity which they compared to that with which they were already familiar in the field of the natural sciences.

Since the days of Cantillon, Hume, the Physiocrats and Adam Smith, economic theory has made continuous—although not steady—progress. In the course of this development it has become much more than a theory of market operations within the frame of a society based on private ownership of the means of production. It has for some time been a general theory of human action, of human choice and preference.

II

The elements of social cognition are abstract and not reducible to any concrete images that might be apprehended by the senses. To make them easier to visualize one likes to have recourse to metaphorical language. For some time the biological metaphors were very popular. There were writers who overworked this metaphor to ridiculous extremes. It will suffice to cite the name of Lilienfeld.[1]

Today the mechanistic metaphor is much more in use. The theoretical basis for its application is to be found in the positivist view of social science. Positivism blithely waved aside everything which history and economics taught. History, in its eyes, is simply no science; economics a special kind of metaphysics. In place of both, positivism postulates a social science which has to be built up by the experimental method as ideally applied in Newtonian physics. Economics has to be experimental, mathematical and quantitative. Its task is to measure, because science is measurement. Every statement must be open to verification by facts.

Every proposition of this positivist epistemology is wrong.

The social sciences in general and economics in particular cannot be based on experience in the sense in which this term is used by the natural sciences. Social experience is historical experience. Of course, every experience is the experience of something passed. But what distinguishes social experience from that which forms the basis of the natural sciences is that it is always the experience of a complexity of phenomena. The experience to which the natural sciences owe all their success is the experience of the experiment. In the experiments the different elements of change are observed in isolation. The control of the conditions of change provides the experimenter with the means of assigning to each effect its sufficient cause. Without regard to the philosophical problem involved he proceeds to amass "facts." These facts are the bricks which the scientist uses in constructing his theories. They constitute the only material at his disposal. His theory must not be in contradiction with these facts. They are the ultimate things.

The social sciences cannot make use of experiments. The experience with which they have to deal is the experience of complex phenomena. They are in the same position as acoustics would be if the only material of the scientist were the hearing of a concerto or the noise of a waterfall. It is nowadays fashionable to style the statistical bureaus laboratories. This is misleading. The material which statistics provides is historical, that means the outcome of a complexity of forces. The social sciences never enjoy the advantage of observing the consequences of a change in one element only, other conditions being equal.

It follows that the social sciences can never use experience to verify their statements. Every fact and every experience with which they have to deal is open to various interpretations. Of course, the experience of a complexity of phenomena can never prove or disprove a statement in the way in which an experiment proves or disproves. We do not have any historical experience whose import is judged identically by all people. There is no doubt that up to now in history only nations which have based their social order on private ownership of the means of production have reached a somewhat high stage of welfare and civilization. Nevertheless, nobody would consider this as an incontestable refutation of socialist theories. In the field of the natural sciences there are also differences of opinion concerning the interpretation of complex facts. But here freedom of explanation is limited by the necessity of not contradicting statements satisfactorily verified by experiments. In the interpretation of social facts no such limits exist. Everything could be asserted about them provided that we are not confined within the bounds of principles of whose logical nature we intend to speak later. Here, however, we already have to mention that every discussion concerning the meaning of historical experience imperceptibly passes over into a discussion of these principles without any further reference to experience. People may begin by discussing the lesson to be learnt from an import duty or from the Russian Soviet system; they will very quickly be discussing the general theory of interregional trade or the no less pure theory of socialism and capitalism.

The impossibility of experimenting means concomitantly the impossibility of measurement. The physicist has to deal with magnitudes and numerical relations, because he has the right to assume that certain invariable relations between physical properties subsist. The experiment provides him with the numerical value to be assigned to them. In human behavior there are no such constant relations, there is no standard which could be used as a measure and there are no experiments which could establish uniformities of this type.

What the statistician establishes in studying the relations between prices and supply or between supply and demand is of historical importance only. If he determines that a rise of 10 percent in the supply of potatoes in Atlantis in the years between 1920 and 1930 was followed by a fall in the price of potatoes by 8 percent, he does not say anything about what happened or may happen with a change in the supply of potatoes in another country or at another time. Such measurements as that of elasticity of demand cannot be compared with the physicist's measurement, e.g., specific density or weight of atoms. Of course, everybody realizes that the behavior of men concerning potatoes and every other commodity is variable. Different individuals value the same things in a different way, and the valuation changes even with the same individual with changing conditions. We cannot categorize individuals in classes which react in the same way, and we cannot determine the conditions which evoke the same reaction. Under these circumstances we have to realize that the statistical economist is an historian and not an experimenter. For the social sciences, statistics constitutes a method of historical research.

In every science the considerations which result in the formulation of an equation are of a nonmathematical character. The formulation of the equation has a practical importance because the constant relations which it includes are experimentally established and because it is possible to introduce specific known values in the function to determine those unknown. These equations thus lie at the basis of technological designing; they are not only the consummation of the theoretical analysis but also the starting point of practical work. But in economics, where there are no constant relations between magnitudes, the equations are void of practical application. Even if we could dispose of all qualms concerning their formulation we would still have to realize that they are without any practical use.

But the chief objection which must be raised to the

mathematical treatment of economic problems comes from another ground: it really does not deal with the actual operations of human actions but with a fictitious concept that the economist builds up for instrumental purposes. This is the concept of static equilibrium.

For the sake of grasping the consequences of change and the nature of profit in a market economy the economist constructs a fictitious system in which there is no change. Today is like yesterday and tomorrow will be like today. There is no uncertainty about the future, and activity therefore does not involve risk. But for the allowance to be made of interest, the sum of the prices of the complementary factors of production exactly equals the price of the product, which means there is no room left for profit. But this fictitious concept is not only unrealizable in actual life; it cannot even be consistently carried to its ultimate conclusions. The individuals in this fictitious world would not act, they would not have to make choices, they would just vegetate. It is true that economics, exactly because it cannot make experiments, is bound to apply this and other fictitious concepts of a similar type. But its use should be restricted to the purposes which it is designed to serve. The purpose of the concept of static equilibrium is the study of the nature of the relations between costs and prices and thereby of profits. Outside of this it is inapplicable, and occupation with it vain.

Now all that mathematics can do in the field of economic studies is to describe static equilibrium. The equations and the indifference curves deal with a fictitious state of things, which never exists anywhere. What they afford is a mathematical expression of the definition of static equilibrium. Because mathematical economists start from the prejudice that economics has to be treated in mathematical terms they consider the study of static equilibrium as the whole of economics. The purely instrumental character of this concept has been overshadowed by this preoccupation.

Of course, mathematics cannot tell us anything about

the way by which this static equilibrium could be reached. The mathematical determination of the difference between any actual state and the equilibrium state is not a substitute for the method by which the logical or nonmathematical economists let us conceive the nature of those human actions which necessarily would bring about equilibrium provided that no further change occurs in the data.

Occupation with static equilibrium is a misguided evasion of the study of the main economic problems. The pragmatic value of this equilibrium concept should not be underrated, but it is an instrument for the solution of one problem only. In any case the mathematical elaboration of static equilibrium is mere by-play in economics.

The case is similar with the use of curves. We may represent the price of a commodity as the point of intersection of two curves, the curve of demand and the curve of supply. But we have to realize that we do not know anything about the shape of these curves. We know *a posteriori* the prices, which we assume to be the points of intersection, but we do not know the form of the curve either in advance or for the past. The representation of the curves is therefore nothing more than a didactic means of rendering the theory graphic and hence more easily comprehensible.

The mathematical economist is prone to consider the price either as a measurement of value or as equivalent to the commodity. To this we have to say that prices are not measured in money but that they are the amount of money exchanged for a commodity. The price is not equivalent to the commodity. A purchase takes place only when the buyer values the commodity higher than the price, and the seller values it lower than the price. Nobody has the right to abstract from this fact and to assume an equivalence where there is a difference in valuation. When either one of the parties considers the price as the equivalent of the commodity no transaction takes place. In this sense we may say every transaction is for both parties a "bargain."

III

Physicists consider the objects of their study from without. They have no knowledge of what is going on in the interior, in the "soul," of a falling stone. But they have the opportunity to observe the falling of the stone in experiments and thereby to discover what they call the laws of falling. From the results of such experimental knowledge they build up their theories proceeding from the special to the more general, from the concrete to the more abstract.

Economics deals with human actions, not as it is sometimes said, with commodities, economic quantities or prices. We do not have the power to experiment with human actions. But we have, being human ourselves, a knowledge of what goes on within acting men. We know something about the meaning which acting men attach to their actions. We know why men wish to change the conditions of their lives. We know something about that uneasiness which is the ultimate incentive of the changes which they bring about. A perfectly satisfied man or a man who although unsatisfied did not see any means of improvement would not act at all.

Thus the economist is, as Cairnes says, at the outset of his researches already in possession of the ultimate principles governing the phenomena which form the subject of his study, whereas mankind has no direct knowledge of ultimate physical principles.[2] Herein lies the radical difference between the social sciences (moral sciences, *Geisteswissenschaften*) and the natural sciences. What makes natural science possible is the power to experiment; what makes social science possible is the power to grasp or to comprehend the meaning of human action.

We have to distinguish two quite different kinds of this comprehension of the meaning of action: we conceive and we understand.

We conceive the meaning of an action, that is to say, we take an action to be such. We see in the action the endeavor to reach a goal by the use of means. In conceiving the meaning of an action we consider it as a purposeful endeavor to reach some goal, but we do not regard the quality of the ends proposed and of the means applied. We conceive activity as such, its logical (praxeological) qualities and categories. All that we do in this conceiving is by deductive analysis to bring to light everything which is contained in the first principle of action and to apply it to different kinds of thinkable conditions. This study is the object of the theoretical science of human action (praxeology) and in particular of its hitherto most developed branch, economics (economic theory).

Economics therefore is not based on or derived (abstracted) from experience. It is a deductive system, starting from the insight into the principles of human reason and conduct. As a matter of fact, all our experience in the field of human action is based on and conditioned by the circumstance that we have this insight in our mind. Without this a priori knowledge and the theorems derived from it we could not at all realize what is going on in human activity. Our experience of human action and social life is predicated on praxeological and economic theory.

It is important to be aware of the fact that this procedure and method are not peculiar only to scientific investigation but are the mode of ordinary daily apprehension of social facts. These aprioristic principles and the deductions from them are applied not only by the professional economist but by everybody who deals with economic facts or problems. The layman does not proceed in a way significantly different from that of the scientist; only he sometimes is less critical, less scrupulous in examining every step in the chain of his deductions and therefore sometimes more subject to error. One need only observe any discussion on current economic problems to realize that its course turns very soon towards a consideration of abstract principles without any reference to experience. You cannot, for instance, discuss the Soviet system without falling back on the general principles both of capitalism and socialism. You cannot discuss a wage and hours bill without falling back on the general principles both of capitalism and socialism. You cannot discuss a wage and hours bill without falling back on the theory of wages, profits, interests and prices, that means the general theory of a market society. The "pure fact"—let us set aside the epistemological question whether there is such a thing—is open to different interpretations. These interpretations require elucidation by theoretical insight.

Economics is not only not derived from experience, it is even impossible to verify its theorems by appeal to experience. Every experience of a complex phenomenon, we must repeat, can be and is explained in different ways. The same facts, the same statistical figures are claimed as confirmations of contradictory theories.

It is instructive to compare the technique of dealing with experience in the social sciences with that in the natural sciences. We have many books on economics which, after having developed a theory, annex chapters in which an attempt is made to verify the theory developed by an appeal to the facts. This is not the way which the natural scientist takes. He starts from facts experimentally established and builds up his theory in using them. If his theory allows a deduction that predicts a state of affairs not yet discovered in experiments he describes what kind of experiment would be crucial for his theory; the theory seems to be verified if the result conforms to the prediction. This is something radically and significantly different from the approach taken by the social sciences.

To confront economic theory with reality we do not have to try to explain in a superficial way facts interpreted differently by other people so that they seem to verify our theory. This dubious procedure is not the way in which reasonable discussion can take place. What we have to do is this: we have to inquire whether the special conditions of action which we have implied in our reasoning correspond to those we find in the segment of reality under consideration. A theory of money (or rather of indirect exchange) is correct or not without reference to the question of whether the actual economic system under examination employs indirect exchange or only barter.

The method applied in these theoretical aprioristic considerations is the method of speculative constructions. The economist—and likewise the layman in his economic reasoning—builds up an image of a nonexistent state of things. The material for this construction is drawn from an insight into the conditions of human action. Whether the state of affairs which these speculative constructions depict corresponds or could correspond to reality is irrelevant for their instrumental efficiency. Even unrealizable constructions can render valuable service in giving us the opportunity to conceive what makes them unrealizable and in what respect they differ from reality. The speculative construction of a socialist community is indispensable for economic reasoning notwithstanding the question of whether such a society could or could not be realized.

One of the best known and most frequently applied speculative constructions is that of a state of static equilibrium mentioned above. We are fully aware that this state can never be realized. But we cannot study the implications of changes without considering a changeless world. No modern economist will deny that the application of this speculative concept has rendered invaluable service in elucidating the character of entrepreneur's profits and losses and the relation between costs and prices.

All our economic reasoning operates with these speculative concepts. It is true that the method has its dangers; it easily lends itself to errors. But we have to use it because it is the only method available. Of course, we have to be very careful in using it.

To the obvious question, how a purely logical deduction

from aprioristic principles can tell us anything about reality, we have to reply that both human thought and human action stem from the same root in that they are both products of the human mind. Correct results from our aprioristic reasoning are therefore not only logically irrefutable, but at the same time applicable with all their apodictic certainty to reality provided that the assumptions involved are given in reality. The only way to refuse a conclusion of economics is to demonstrate that it contains a logical fallacy. It is another question whether the results obtained apply to reality. This again can be decided only by the demonstration that the assumptions involved have or do not have any counterpart in the reality which we wish to explain.

The relation between historical experience—for every economic experience is historical in the sense that it is the experience of something past—and economic theory is therefore different from that generally assumed. Economic theory is not derived from experience. It is, on the contrary, the indispensable tool for the grasp of economic history. Economic history can neither prove nor disprove the teachings of economic theory. It is, on the contrary, economic theory which makes it possible for us to conceive the economic facts of the past.

IV

But to orient ourselves in the world of human actions we need to do more than merely conceive the meaning of human action. Both the acting man and the purely observing historian have not only to conceive the categories of action as economic theory does; they have besides to understand (*verstehen*) the meaning of human choice.

This understanding of the meaning of action is the specific method of historical research. The historian has to establish the facts as far as possible by the use of all the means

provided both by the theoretical sciences of human action—
praxeology and its hitherto most developed part, economics—and by the natural sciences. But then he has to go farther. He has to study the individual and unique conditions
of the case in question. *Individuum est ineffabile.* Individuality
is given to the historian, it is exactly that which cannot be
exhaustively explained or traced back to other entities. In
this sense individuality is irrational. The purpose of specific
understanding as applied by the historical disciplines is to
grasp the meaning of individuality by a psychological process. It establishes the fact that we face something individual. It fixes the valuations, the aims, the theories, the beliefs
and the errors, in a word, the total philosophy of the acting
individuals and the way in which they envisaged the conditions under which they had to act. It puts us into the milieu
of the action. Of course, this specific understanding cannot
be separated from the philosophy of the interpreter. That
degree of scientific objectivity which can be reached in the
natural sciences and in the aprioristic sciences of logic and
praxeology can never be attained by the moral or historical
sciences (*Geisteswissenschaften*) in the field of the specific understanding. You can understand in different ways. History
can be written from different points of view. The historians
may agree in everything that can be established in a rational
way and nevertheless widely disagree in their interpretations. History therefore has always to be rewritten. New phi-
losophies demand a new representation of the past.

The specific understanding of the historical sciences is
not an act of pure rationality. It is the recognition that reason has exhausted all its resources and that we can do nothing more than to try as well as we may to give an explanation
of something irrational which is resistant to exhaustive and
unique description. These are the tasks which the understanding has to fulfill. It is, notwithstanding, a logical tool
and should be used as such. It should never be abused for
the purpose of smuggling into the historical work obscuran-

ticism, mysticism and similar elements. It is not a free charter for nonsense.

It is necessary to emphasize this point because it sometimes happens that the abuses of a certain type of historicism are justified by an appeal to a wrongly interpreted "understanding." The reasoning of logic, praxeology and of the natural sciences can under no circumstances be invalidated by the understanding. However strong the evidence supplied by the historical sources may be, and however understandable a fact may be from the point of view of theories contemporaneous with it, if it does not fit into our rationale, we cannot accept it. The existence of witches and the practice of witchcraft are abundantly attested by legal proceedings; yet we will not accept it. Judgments of many tribunals are on record asserting that people have depreciated a country's currency by upsetting the balance of payments; yet we will not believe that such actions have such effects.

It is not the task of history to reproduce the past. An attempt to do so would be vain and would require a duplication not humanly possible. History is a representation of the past in terms of concepts. The specific concepts of historical research are type concepts. These types of the historical method can be built up only by the use of the specific understanding and they are meaningful only in the frame of the understanding to which they owe their existence. Therefore not every type-concept which is logically valid can be considered as useful for the purpose of understanding. A classification is valid in a logical sense if all the elements united in one class are characterized by a common feature. Classes do not exist in actuality, they are always a product of the mind which in observing things discovers likenesses and differences. It is another question whether a classification which is logically valid and based on sound considerations can be used for the explanation of given data. There is for instance no doubt that a type of class "fascism" which includes not only Italian fascism but also German Nazism, the

Spanish system of General Franco, the Hungarian system of Admiral Horthy and some other systems can be constructed in a logically valid way and that it can be contrasted to a type called "Bolshevism," which includes the Russian Bolshevism and the system of Bela Kun in Hungary and of the short Soviet episode of Munich. But whether this classification and the inference from it which sees the world of the last twenty years divided into the two parties, fascists and Bolsheviks, is the right way to understand present-day political conditions is open to question. You can understand this period of history in a quite different way by using other types. You may distinguish democracy and totalitarianism, and then let the type democracy include the western capitalist system and the type totalitarianism include both Bolshevism and what the other classification terms fascism. Whether you apply the first or the second typification depends on the whole mode in which you see things. The understanding decides upon the classification to be used, and not the classification upon the understanding.

The type-concepts of the historical or moral sciences (*Geisteswissenschaften*) are not statistical averages. Most of the features used for classification are not subject to numerical determination, and this alone renders it impossible to construct them as statistical averages. These type-concepts (in German one uses the term *Ideal-Typus* in order to distinguish them from the type-concepts of other sciences, especially of the biological ones) ought not to be confused with the praxeological concepts used for the conceiving of the categories of human action. For instance: the concept "entrepreneur" is used in economic theory to signify a specific function, that is the provision for an uncertain future. In this respect everybody has to some extent to be considered as an entrepreneur. Of course, it is not the task of this classification in economic theory to distinguish men, but to distinguish functions and to explain sources of profit or loss. Entrepreneur in this sense is the personification of the function which results in profit or loss. In economic history and in dealing with current economic problems the term "entrepreneur" signifies a class of men who are engaged in business but who may in many other respects differ so much that the general term entrepreneur seems to be meaningless and is used only with a special qualification, for instance big (medium-sized, small) business, "Wall Street," armaments business, German business, etc. The type entrepreneur as used in history and politics can never have the conceptual exactitude which the praxeological concept entrepreneur has. You never meet in life men who are nothing else than the personification of one function only.[3]

V

The preceding remarks justify the conclusion that there is a radical difference between the methods of the social sciences and those of the natural sciences. The social sciences owe their progress to the use of their particular methods and have to go further along the lines which the special character of their object require. They do not have to adopt the methods of the natural sciences.

It is a fallacy to recommend to the social sciences the use of mathematics and to believe that they could in this way be made more "exact." The application of mathematics does not render physics more exact or more certain. Let us quote Einstein's remark: "As far as mathematical propositions refer to reality they are not certain and as far as they are certain they do not refer to reality." It is different with praxeological propositions. These refer with all their exactitude and certainty to the reality of human action. The explanation of this phenomenon lies in the fact that both—the science of human action and human action itself—have a common root, i.e., human reason. It would be a mistake to assume that the quantitative approach could render them more exact. Every numerical expression is inexact because of the inherent limitations of human powers of measurement. For the rest we have to refer to what has been said above on the purely historical character of quantitative expressions in the field of the social sciences.

The reformers who wish to improve the social sciences by adopting the methods of the natural sciences sometimes try to justify their efforts by pointing to the backward state of the former. Nobody will deny that the social sciences and especially economics are far from being perfect. Every economist knows how much remains to be done. But two considerations must be kept in mind. First, the present unsatisfactory state of social and economic conditions has nothing to do with an alleged inadequacy in economic theory. If people do not use the teachings of economics as a guide for their policies they cannot blame the discipline for their own failure. Second, if it may some day be necessary to reform economic theory radically this change will not take its direction along the lines suggested by the present critics. The objections of these are thoroughly refuted forever.

Notes

1. Cf. for instance Paul von Lilienfeld, *La Pathologie Sociale* [Social Pathology] (Paris, 1896). ["When a government takes a loan from the House of Rothschild organic sociology conceives the process as follows: ... 'The House of Rothschild's operation, on such an occasion, is precisely similar to the action of a group of body cells which cooperate in the production of the blood necessary for nourishing the brain, in hope of being compensated by a reaction of the gray matter cells which they need to reactivate and to accumulate new energies,' Ibid., p. 104," in Ludwig von Mises, *Socialism*, J. Kahane, trans. (Indianapolis, IN: Liberty Classics, 1981), p. 257 n.—Ed.]

2. [John E. Cairnes, *The Character and Logical Method of Political*

Economics [1875] (New York: Augustus M. Kelley, 1965), pp. 89–97—Ed.]
3. For the sake of completeness we have to remark that there is a third use of the term entrepreneur in law which has to be carefully distinguished from the two mentioned above.

The Individualist and "Compositive" Method of the Social Sciences

Friedrich A. Hayek

At this point it becomes necessary briefly to interrupt the main argument in order to safeguard ourselves against a misconception which might arise from what has just been said. The stress which we have laid on the fact that in the social sciences our data or "facts" are themselves ideas or concepts must, of course, not be understood to mean that *all* the concepts with which we have to deal in the social sciences are of this character. There would be no room for any scientific work if this were so; and the social sciences no less than the natural sciences aim at revising the popular concepts which men have formed about the objects of their study, and at replacing them by more appropriate ones. The special difficulties of the social sciences, and much confusion about their character, derive precisely from the fact that in them ideas appear in two capacities, as it were, as part of their object and as ideas about that object. While in the natural sciences the contrast between the object of our study and our explanation of it coincides with the distinction between ideas and objective facts, in the social sciences it is necessary to draw a distinction between those ideas which

Reprinted from *The Counter-Revolution of Science: Studies on the Abuse of Reason* by Friedrich A. Hayek (Indianapolis: Liberty Press, 1980).

are *constitutive* of the phenomena we want to explain and the ideas which either we ourselves or the very people whose actions we have to explain may have formed *about* these phenomena and which are not the cause of, but theories about, the social structures.

This special difficulty of the social sciences is a result, not merely of the fact that we have to distinguish between the views held by the people which are the object of our study and our views about them, but also of the fact that the people who are our object themselves not only are motivated by ideas but also form ideas about the undesigned results of their actions—popular theories about the various social structures or formations which we share with them and which our study has to revise and improve. The danger of substituting "concepts" (or "theories") for the "facts" is by no means absent in the social sciences and failure to avoid it has exercised as detrimental an effect here as in the natural sciences;[1] but it appears on a different plane and is very inadequately expressed by the contrast between ideas and facts. The real contrast is between ideas which by being held by the people become the causes of a social phenomenon and the ideas which people form about that phenomenon. That these two classes of ideas are distinct (although in different contexts the distinction may have to be drawn differently)[2] can easily be shown. The changes in the opinions which people hold about a particular commodity and which we recognize as the cause of a change in the price of that commodity stand clearly in a different class from the ideas which the same people may have formed about the causes of the change in price or about the "nature of value" in general. Similarly, the beliefs and opinions which lead a number of people regularly to repeat certain acts, for example, to produce, sell, or buy certain quantities of commodities, are entirely different from the ideas they may have formed about the whole of the "society," or the "economic system," to which they belong and which the aggregate of all their actions constitutes. The first kind of opinions and beliefs is a condition of the existence of the "wholes" which would not exist without them; they are, as we have said, "constitutive," essential for the existence of the phenomenon which the people refer to as "society" or the "economic system," but which will exist irrespectively of the concepts which the people have formed about these wholes.

It is very important that we should carefully distinguish between the motivating or constitutive opinions on the one hand and the speculative or explanatory views which people have formed about the wholes; confusion between the two is a source of constant danger. Is it the ideas which the popular mind has formed about such collectives as society or the economic system, capitalism or imperialism, and other such collective entities, which the social scientist must regard as no more than provisional theories, popular abstractions, and which he must not mistake for facts? That he consistently refrains from treating these pseudo-entities as facts, and that he systematically starts from the concepts which guide individuals in their actions and not from the results of their theorizing about their actions, is the characteristic feature of that methodological individualism which is closely connected with the subjectivism of the social sciences. The scientistic approach, on the other hand, because it is afraid of starting from the subjective concepts determining individual actions, is, as we shall presently see, regularly led into the very mistake it attempts to avoid, namely of treating as facts those collectives which are no more than popular generalizations. Trying to avoid using as data the concepts held by individuals where they are clearly recognizable and explicitly introduced as what they are, people brought up in scientistic views frequently and naively accept the speculative concepts of popular usage as definite facts of the kind they are familiar with.

We shall have to discuss the nature of this collectivist

prejudice inherent in the scientistic approach more fully in a later section.

A few more remarks must be added about the specific theoretical method which corresponds to the systematic subjectivism and individualism of the social sciences. From the fact that it is the concepts and views held by individuals which are directly known to us and which form the elements from which we must build up, as it were, the more complex phenomena, follows another important difference between the method of the social disciplines and the natural sciences. While in the former it is the attitudes of individuals which are the familiar elements and by the combination of which we try to reproduce the complex phenomena, the results of individual actions, which are much less known—a procedure which often leads to the *discovery* of principles of structural coherence of the complex phenomena which had not been (and perhaps could not be) established by direct observation—the physical sciences necessarily begin with the complex phenomena of nature and work backward to infer the elements from which they are composed. The place where the human individual stands in the order of things brings it about that in one direction what he perceives are the comparatively complex phenomena which he analyzes, while in the other direction what are given to him are elements from which those more complex phenomena are composed that he cannot observe as wholes.[3] While the method of the natural sciences is in this sense, analytic, the method of the social sciences is better described as compositive[4] or synthetic. It is the so-called wholes, the groups of elements which are structurally connected, which we learn to single out from the totality of observed phenomena only as a result to our systematic fitting together of the elements with familiar properties, and which we build up or reconstruct from the known properties of the elements.

It is important to observe that in all this the various

types of individual beliefs or attitudes are not themselves the object of our explanation, but merely the elements from which we build up the structure of possible relationships between individuals. Insofar as we analyze individual thought in the social sciences the purpose is not to explain that thought but merely to distinguish the possible types of elements with which we shall have to reckon in the construction of different patterns of social relationships. It is a mistake, to which careless expressions by social scientists often give countenance, to believe that their aim is to *explain* conscious action. This, if it can be done at all, is a different task, the task of psychology. For the social sciences the types of conscious action are data[5] and all they have to do with regard to these data is to arrange them in such orderly fashion that they can be effectively used for their task.[6] The problems which they try to answer arise only insofar as the conscious action of many men produce undesigned results, insofar as regularities are observed which are not the result of anybody's design. If social phenomena showed no order except insofar as they were consciously designed, there would indeed be no room for theoretical sciences of society and there would be, as is often argued, only problems of psychology. It is only insofar as some sort of order arises as a result of individual action but without being designed by any individual that a problem is raised which demands a theoretical explanation. But although people dominated by the scientistic prejudice are often inclined to deny the existence of any such order (and thereby the existence of an object for theoretical sciences of society), few if any would be prepared to do so consistently: that at least language shows a definite order which is not the result of any conscious design can scarcely be questioned. The reason for the difficulty which the natural scientist experiences in admitting the existence of such an order in social phenomena is that these orders cannot be stated in physical terms, that if we define the elements in physical terms no such order is visible, and that the units which show an orderly arrangement do not (or at least need not) have any physical properties in common (except that men react to them in the "same" way—although the "sameness" of different people's reaction will again, as a rule, not be definable in physical terms). It is an order in which things behave in the same way because they mean the same thing to man. If, instead of regarding as alike and unlike what appears so to the acting man, we were to take for our units only what Science shows to be alike or unlike, we should probably find no recognizable order whatever in social phenomena—at least not till the natural sciences had completed their task of analyzing all natural phenomena into their ultimate constituents and psychology had also fully achieved the reverse task of explaining in all detail how the ultimate units of physical science come to appear to man just as they do, that is, how that apparatus of classification operates which our senses constitute.

It is only in the very simplest instances that it can be shown briefly and without any technical apparatus how the independent actions of individuals will produce an order which is no part of their intentions; and in those instances the explanation is usually so obvious that we never stop to examine the type of argument which leads us to it. The way in which footpaths are formed in a wild broken country is such an instance. At first everyone will seek for himself what seems to him the best path. But the fact that such a path has been used once is likely to make it easier to traverse and therefore more likely to be used again; and thus gradually more and more clearly defined tracks arise and come to be used to the exclusion of other possible ways. Human movements through the region come to conform to a definite pattern which, although the result of deliberate decisions of many people, has yet not been consciously designed by anyone. This explanation of how this happens is an elementary "theory" applicable to hundreds of particular historical instances; and it is not the observation of the actual growth of any particular track, and still less of many, from which this explanation derives its cogency, but from our general knowledge of how we and other people behave in the kind of situation in which the successive people find themselves who have to seek their way and who by the cumulative effect of their action create the path. It is the elements of the complex of events which are familiar to us from everyday experience, but it is only by a deliberate effort of directed thought that we come to see the necessary effects of the combination of such actions by many people. We "understand" the way in which the result we observe can be produced, although we may never be in a position to watch the whole process or to predict its precise course and result.

It makes no difference for our present purpose whether the process extends over a long period of time, as it does in such cases as the evolution of money or the formation of language, or whether it is a process which is constantly repeated anew, as in the case of the formation of prices or the direction of production under competition. The former instances raise theoretical (that is, generic) problems (as distinguished from the specifically historical problems in the precise sense which we shall have to define later) which are fundamentally similar to the problems raised by such recurring phenomena as the determination of prices. Although in the study of any particular instance of the evolution of an "institution" like money or the language the theoretical problem will frequently be so overlaid by the consideration of the particular circumstances involved (the properly historical task), this does not alter the fact that any explanation of a historical process involves assumptions about the kind of circumstances that can produce certain kinds of effects—assumptions which, where we have to deal with results which were not directly willed by somebody, can only be stated in the form of a generic scheme, in other words a theory.

The physicist who wishes to understand the problems of the social sciences with the help of an analogy from his own field would have to imagine a world in which he knew by direct observation the inside of the atoms and had neither the possibility of making experiments with lumps of matter nor the opportunity to observe more than the interactions of a comparatively few atoms during a limited period. From his knowledge of the different kinds of atoms he could build up models of all the various ways in which they could combine into larger units and make these models more and more closely reproduce all the features of the few instances in which he was able to observe more complex phenomena. But the laws of the macrocosm which he could derive from his knowledge of the microcosm would always remain "deductive"; they would, because of his limited knowledge of the data of the complex situation, scarcely ever enable him to predict the precise outcome of a particular situation; and he could never confirm them by controlled experiment—although they might be disproved by the observation of events which according to his theory are impossible.

In a sense some problems of theoretical astronomy are more similar to those of the social sciences than those of any of the experimental sciences. Yet there remain important differences. While the astronomer aims at knowing all the elements of which his universe is composed, the student of social phenomena cannot hope to know more than the types of elements from which his universe is made up. He will scarcely ever know even all of the elements of which it consists and he will certainly never know all the relevant properties of each of them. The inevitable imperfection of the human mind becomes here not only a basic datum about the object of explanation but, since it applies no less to the observer, also a limitation on what he can hope to accomplish in his attempt to explain the observed facts. The number of separate variables which in any particular social phenomenon will determine the result of a given change will as a rule be far too large for any human mind to master and manipulate them effectively.[7] In consequence our knowledge of the principle by which these phenomena are produced will rarely if ever enable us to predict the precise result of any concrete situation. While we can explain the principle on which certain phenomena are produced and can from this knowledge exclude the possibility of certain results, for example, of certain events occurring together, our knowledge will in a sense be only negative; that is, it will merely enable us to preclude certain results but not enable us to narrow the range of possibilities sufficiently so that only one remains.

The distinction between an explanation merely of the principle on which a phenomenon is produced and an explanation which enables us to predict the precise result is of great importance for the understanding of the theoretical methods of the social sciences. It arises, I believe, also elsewhere, for example, in biology and certainly in psychology. It is, however, somewhat unfamiliar and I know no place where it is adequately explained. The best illustration in the field of the social sciences is probably the general theory of prices as represented, for example, by the Walrasian or Paretian systems of equations. These systems show merely the principle of coherence between the prices of the various types of commodities of which the system is composed; but without knowledge of the numerical values of all the constants which occur in it and which we never do know, this does not enable us to predict the precise results which any particular change will have.[8] Apart from this particular case, a set of equations which shows merely the form of a system of relationships but does not give the values of the constants contained in it, is perhaps the best general illustration of an explanation merely of the principle on which any phenomenon is produced. This must suffice as a positive description of the characteristic problems of the social sciences. It will become clearer as we contrast in the following sections the specific procedure of the social sciences with the most characteristic aspects of the attempts to treat their object after the fashion of the natural sciences.

Notes

1. See the excellent discussions of the effects of conceptual realism *(Begriffsrealismus)* on economics in W. Eucken, *The Foundations of Economics* (London, 1950), pp. 51 *et seq.*
2. In some contexts concepts which by another social science are treated as mere theories to be revised and improved upon may have to be treated as data. One could, for example, conceive of a "science of politics" showing what kind of political action follows from the people holding certain views on the nature of society and for which these views would have to be treated as data. But while in man's actions toward social phenomena, that is, in explaining his political actions, we have to take his views about the constitution of society as given, we can on a different level of analysis investigate their truth or untruth. The fact that a particular society may believe that its institutions have been created by divine intervention we would have to accept as a fact in explaining the politics of that society; but it need not prevent us from showing that this view is probably false.
3. See Robbins, *An Essay on the Nature and Significance of Economic Science,* 2nd ed. (1935), p. 105; "In economics . . . the ultimate constituents of our fundamental generalizations are known to us by immediate acquaintance. In the natural sciences they are known only inferentially." Perhaps the following quotation from an earlier essay of my own *(Collectivist Economic Planning* [1935], p. 11) may help further to explain the statement in the text: "The position of man, midway between natural and social phenomena—of the one of which he is an effect and of the other a cause—brings it about that the essential basic facts which we need for the explanation are part of common experience, part of the stuff of our thinking. In the

social sciences it is the elements of the complex phenomena which are known to us beyond the possibility of dispute. In the natural sciences they can be at best surmised." See also C. Menger, *Untersuchungen über die Methoden der Sozialwissenschaften* (1883), p. 157 n: "Die letzten Elemente, auf welche die exacte theoretische Interpretation der Naturphänomene zurückgehen muss, sind 'Atome' und 'Kräfte.' Beide sind unempirischer Natur. Wir vermögen uns 'Atome' überhaupt nicht, und die Naturkräfte nur unter einem Bilde vorzusstellen, und verstehen wir in Wahrheit unter den letzteren lediglich die uns unbekannten Ursachen realer Bewegungen. Hieraus ergeben sich für die exacte Interpretation der Naturphänomene in letzter Linie ganz ausserordentliche Schwierigkeiten. Anders in den exacten Sozialwissenschaften. Hier sind die menschlichen *Individuen und ihre Bestrebungen,* die letzten Elemente unserer Analyse, empirischer Natur und die exacten theoretischen Sozialwissenschaften somit in grossem Vortheil gegenüber den exacten Naturwissenschaften, Die 'Grenzen des Naturerkennens' und die hieraus für das theoretische Verständnis der Naturphänomene such ergebenden Schwierigkeiten bestehen in Wahrheit nicht für die exacte Forschung auf dem Gebiete der Sozialerscheinungen. Wenn A. Comte die 'Gesellschaften' als reale Organismen, und zwar als Organismen komplicierterer Art, denn die natürlichen, auffasst und ihre theoretische Interpretation als das unvergleichlich komplicierte und schwierigere wissenschaftliche Problem bezeichnet, so findet er sich somit n einem schwaren Irrthume. Seine Theorie wäre nur gegenüber Sozialforschern richtig, welche den, mit Rücksicht auf den heutigen Zustand der theoretischen Naturwissenschaften, geradezu wahnwitzigen Gedanken fassen würden, die Gesellschaftsphänomene nicht in specifisch sozialwissenschaftlich, sondern in naturwissenschaftlich-atomistischer Weise interpretiren zu wollen."

4. I have borrowed the term *compositive* from a manuscript note of Carl Menger, who, in his personal annotated copy of Schmoller's review of his *Methoden der Sozialwissenschaften*

(*Jahrbuch für Gesetzgebung, etc.*, n.f. 7 [1883], p. 42), wrote it above the word *deductive* used by Schmoller. Since writing this I have noticed that Ernst Cassirer in his *Philosophie der Aufklärung* (1932, pp. 12, 25, 341) uses the term *compositive* in order to point out rightly that the procedure of the natural sciences presupposes the successive use of the "resolutive" and the "compositive" technique. This is useful and links up with the point that, since the elements are directly known to us in the social sciences, we can start here with the compositive procedure.

5. As Robbins (op. cit., p. 86) rightly says, economists in particular regard "the things which psychology studies as the data of their own deductions."

6. That this task absorbs a great part of the economist's energies should not deceive us about the fact that by itself this "pure logic of choice" (or "economic calculus") does not explain any facts, or at least does no more so by itself than does mathematics. For the precise relationship between the pure theory of the economic calculus and its use in the explanation of social phenomena. I again refer to my article "Economics and Knowledge" (*Economica* [February 1937]). It should perhaps be added that while economic theory might be very useful to the director of a completely planned system in helping him to see what he ought to do to achieve his ends, it would not help us to explain his actions—except insofar as he was actually guided by it.

7. Cf. M. R. Cohen, *Reason and Nature*, p. 356: "If, then, social phenomena depend upon more factors than we readily manipulate, even the doctrine of universal determinism will not guarantee an attainable expression of laws governing the specific phenomena of social life. Social phenomena, though determined, might not to a finite mind in limited time display any laws at all."

8. Pareto himself has clearly seen this. After stating the nature of the factors determining the prices in his system of equations, he adds (*Manuel d'économie politique*, 2nd ed. [1927], pp. 233–34): "It may be mentioned here that this determination

has by no means the purpose of arriving at a numerical calculation of prices. Let us make the most favorable assumptions for such a calculation; let us assume that we have triumphed over all the difficulties of finding the data of the problem and that we know the *ophélimités* of all the different commodities for each individual, and all the conditions of production of all the commodities, etc. This is already an absurd hypothesis to make. Yet it is not sufficient to make the solution of the problem possible. We have seen that in the case of 100 persons and 700 commodities there will be 70,699 conditions (actually a great number of circumstances which we have so far neglected will still increase that number); we shall, therefore, have to solve a system of 70,699 equations. This exceeds practically the power of algebraic analysis, and this is even more true if one contemplates the fabulous number of equations which one obtains for a population of forty million and several thousand commodities. In this case the roles would be changed: it would be not mathematics which would assist political economy, but political economy which would assist mathematics. In other words, if one really could know all these equations, the only means to solve them which is available to human powers is to observe the practical solution given by the market." Cf. also A. Cournot, *Researches into the Mathematical Principles of the Theory of Wealth* (1838), trans. N. T. Bacon (New York, 1927), p. 127, where he says that if in our equations we took the entire economic system into consideration, "this would surpass the powers of mathematical analysis and of our practical methods of calculation, even if the values of all the constants could be assigned to them numerically."

7

Excerpts from Human Society

Ludwig von Mises

I. Human Cooperation

Society is concerted action, cooperation.

Society is the outcome of conscious and purposeful behavior. This does not mean that individuals have concluded contracts by virtue of which they have founded human society. The actions which have brought about social cooperation and daily bring it about anew do not aim at anything else than cooperation and coadjuvancy with others for the attainment of definite singular ends. The total complex of the mutual relations created by such concerted actions is called society. It substitutes collaboration for the—at least conceivable—isolated life of individuals. Society is division of labor and combination of labor. In his capacity as an acting animal man becomes a social animal.

Individual man is born into a socially organized environment. In this sense alone we may accept the saying that society is—logically or historically—antecedent to the individual. In every other sense this dictum is either empty or nonsensical. The individual lives and acts within society. But

Reprinted from *Human Action: A Treatise on Economics, Part Two: Action Within the Framework of Society* by Ludwig von Mises (New Haven: Yale University Press, 1949.

society is nothing but the combination of individuals for cooperative effort. It exists nowhere else than in the actions of individual men. It is a delusion to search for it outside the actions of individuals. To speak of a society's autonomous and independent existence, of its life, its soul, and its actions is a metaphor which can easily lead to crass errors.

The questions whether society or the individual is to be considered as the ultimate end, and whether the interests of society should be subordinated to those of the individuals or the interests of the individuals to those of society are fruitless. Action is always action of individual men. The social or societal element is a certain orientation of the actions of individual men. The category *end* makes sense only when applied to action. Theology and the metaphysics of history may discuss the ends of society and the designs which God wants to realize with regard to society in the same way in which they discuss the purpose of all other parts of the created universe. For science, which is inseparable from reason, a tool manifestly unfit for the treatment of such problems, it would be hopeless to embark upon speculations concerning these matters.

Within the frame of social cooperation there can emerge between members of society feelings of sympathy and friendship and a sense of belonging together. These feelings are the source of man's most delightful and most sublime experiences. They are the most precious adornment of life; they lift the animal species man to the heights of a really human existence. However, they are not, as some have asserted, the agents that have brought about social relationships. They are fruits of social cooperation, they thrive only within its frame; they did not precede the establishment of social relations and are not the seed from which they spring.

The fundamental facts that brought about cooperation, society, and civilization and transformed the animal man into a human being are the facts that work performed under the division of labor is more productive than isolated work and that man's reason is capable of recognizing this truth. But for these facts men would have forever remained deadly foes of one another, irreconcilable rivals in their endeavors to secure a portion of the scarce supply of means of sustenance provided by nature. Each man would have been forced to view all other men as his enemies; his craving for the satisfaction of his own appetites would have brought him into an implacable conflict with all his neighbors. No sympathy could possibly develop under such a state of affairs.

Some sociologists have asserted that the original and elementary subjective fact in society is a "consciousness of kind."[1] Others maintain that there would be no social systems if there were no "sense of community or of belonging together."[2] One may agree, provided that these somewhat vague and ambiguous terms are correctly interpreted. We may call consciousness of kind, sense of community, or sense of belonging together the acknowledgment of the fact that all other human beings are potential collaborators in the struggle for survival because they are capable of recognizing the mutual benefits of cooperation, while the animals lack this faculty. However, we must not forget that the primary facts that bring about such consciousness or such a sense are the two mentioned above. In a hypothetical world in which the division of labor would not increase productivity, there would not be any society. There would not be any sentiments of benevolence and good will.

The principle of the division of labor is one of the great basic principles of cosmic becoming and evolutionary change. The biologists were right in borrowing the concept of the division of labor from social philosophy and in adapting it to their field of investigation. There is division of labor between the various parts of any living organism. There are, furthermore, organic entities composed of collaborating animal individuals; it is customary to call metaphorically such aggregations of the ants and bees "animal societies." But one must never forget that the characteristic feature of human society is purposeful cooperation; society is an outcome of human action, i.e., of a conscious aiming at the attainment of ends. No such element is present, as far as we can ascertain, in the processes which have resulted in the emergence of the structure-function systems of plant and animal bodies and in the operation of the societies of ants, bees, and hornets. Human society is an intellectual and spiritual phenomenon. It is the outcome of a purposeful utilization of a universal law determining cosmic becoming, viz., the higher productivity of the division of labor. As with every instance of action, the recognition of the laws of nature is put into the service of man's efforts to improve his conditions. . . .

3. The Division of Labor

The fundamental social phenomenon is the division of labor and its counterpart human cooperation.

Experience teaches man that cooperative action is more efficient and productive than isolated action of self-sufficient individuals. The natural conditions determining man's life and effort are such that the division of labor increases output per unit of labor expended. These natural facts are:

First: the innate inequality of men with regard to their ability to perform various kinds of labor. Second: the unequal distribution of the nature-given, nonhuman opportunities of production on the surface of the earth. One may as well consider these two facts as one and the same fact, namely, the manifoldness of nature which makes the universe a complex of infinite varieties. If the earth's surface were such that the physical conditions of production were the same at every point and if one man were as equal to all other men as is a circle to another with the same diameter in Euclidian geometry, division of labor would not offer any advantages for acting man.

There is still a third fact, viz., that there are undertakings whose accomplishment exceeds the forces of a single man and requires the joint effort of several. Some of them require an expenditure of labor which no single man can perform because his capacity to work is not great enough. Others again could be accomplished by individuals; but the time which they would have to devote to the work would be so long that the result would only be attained late and would not compensate for the labor expended. In both cases only joint effort makes it possible to attain the end sought.

If only this third condition were present, temporary cooperation between men would have certainly emerged. However, such transient alliances to cope with specific tasks which are beyond the strength of an individual would not have brought about lasting social cooperation. Undertakings which could be performed only in this way were not very numerous at the early stages of civilization. Moreover, all those concerned may not often agree that the performance in question is more useful and urgent than the accomplishment of other tasks which they could perform alone. The great human society enclosing all men in all of their activities did not originate from such occasional alliances. Society is much more than a passing alliance concluded for a definite purpose and ceasing as soon as its objective is realized, even if the partners are ready to renew it should an occasion present itself.

The increase in productivity brought about by the division of labor is obvious whenever the inequality of the participants is such that every individual or every piece of land is superior at least in one regard to the other individuals or pieces of land concerned. If A is fit to produce in 1 unit of time 6 p or 4 q and B only 2 p, but 8 q, they both, when working in isolation, will produce together 4 $p + 6$ q; when working under the division of labor, each of them producing only that commodity in whose production he is more efficient than his partner, they will produce 6 $p+8$ q. But what will happen, if A is more efficient than B not only in the production of p but also in the production of q?

This is the problem which Ricardo raised and solved immediately.

4. The Ricardian Law of Association

Ricardo expounded the law of association in order to demonstrate what the consequences of the division of labor are when an individual or a group, more efficient in every regard, cooperates with an individual or a group less efficient in every regard. He investigated the effects of trade between two areas, unequally endowed by nature, under the assumption that the products, but not the workers and the accumulated factors of future production (capital goods), can freely move from each area into the other. The division of labor between two such areas will, as Ricardo's law shows, increase the productivity of labor and is therefore advantageous to all concerned, even if the physical conditions of production for any commodity are more favorable in one of these two areas than in the other. It is advantageous for the better endowed area to concentrate its efforts upon the production of those commodities for which its superiority is greater, and to leave to the less endowed area the production of other goods in which its own superiority is less. The paradox that it is more advantageous to leave more favorable domestic conditions of production unused and to procure the commodities they could produce from areas in which conditions for their production are less favorable, is the outcome of the immobility of labor and capital, to which the more favorable places of production are inaccessible.

Ricardo was fully aware of the fact that his law of comparative cost, which he expounded mainly in order to deal with a special problem of international trade, is a particular instance of the more universal law of association.

If *A* is in such a way more efficient than *B* that he needs for the production of 1 unit of the commodity *p* 3 hours compared with *B's* 5, and for the production of 1 unit of *q* 2 hours compared with *B's* 4, then both will gain if *A* confines himself to producing *q* and leaves *B* to produce *p*. If each of them gives 60 hours to producing *p* and 60 hours to producing *q*, the result of *A's* labor is 20 *p*—30 *q;* of *B's,* 12 *p* + 15 *q;* and for both together, 32 *p* + 45 *q*. If, however, *A* confines himself to producing *q* alone, he produces 60 *q* in 120 hours, while *B*, if he confines himself to producing *p*, produces in the same time 24*p*. The result of their activities is then 24*p* + 60*q*, which, as *p* has for *A* a substitution ratio of 3/2*q* and for *B* one of 5/4*q*, signifies a larger output than 32*p* + 45 *q*. Therefore it is manifest that the division of labor brings advantages to all who take part in it. Collaboration of the more talented, more able, and more industrious with the less talented, less able, and less industrious results in benefit for both. The gains derived from the division of labor are always mutual.

The law of association makes us comprehend the tendencies which resulted in the progressive intensification of human cooperation. We conceive what incentive induced people not to consider themselves simply as rivals in a struggle for the appropriation of the limited supply of means of subsistence made available by nature. We realize what has impelled them and permanently impels them to consort with one another for the sake of cooperation. Every step forward on the way to a more developed mode of the division of labor serves the interests of all participants. In order to comprehend why man did not remain solitary, searching like the animals for food and shelter for himself only and at most also for his consort and his helpless infants, we do not need to have recourse to a miraculous interference of the Deity or to the empty hypostasis of an innate urge toward association. Neither are we forced to assume that the isolated individuals or primitive hordes one day pledged themselves by a contract to establish social bonds. The factor that brought about primitive society and daily works toward its progressive intensification is human action that is animated by the insight into the higher productivity of labor achieved under the division of labor.

Neither history nor ethnology nor any other branch of knowledge can provide a description of the evolution which has led from the packs and flocks of mankind's nonhuman ancestors to the primitive, yet already highly differentiated, societal groups about which information is provided in excavations, in the most ancient documents of history, and in the reports of explorers and travelers who have met savage tribes. The task with which science is faced in respect of the origins of society can only consist in the demonstration of those factors which can and must result in association and its progressive intensification. Praxeology solves the problem. If and as far as labor under the division of labor is more productive than isolated labor, and if and as far as man is able to realize this fact, human action itself tends toward cooperation and association; man becomes a social being not in sacrificing his own concerns for the sake of a mythical Moloch, society, but in aiming at an improvement in his own welfare. Experience teaches that this condition—higher productivity achieved under the division of labor—is present because its cause—the inborn inequality of men and the inequality in the geographical distribution of the natural factors of production—is real. Thus we are in a position to comprehend the course of social evolution.

6. The Individual Within Society

If praxeology speaks of the solitary individual, acting on his own behalf only and independent of fellow men, it does so for the sake of a better comprehension of the problems of social cooperation. We do not assert that such isolated autarkic human beings have ever lived and that the social stage of man's history was preceded by an age of independent individuals roaming like animals in search of food. The biological humanization of man's nonhuman ancestors and the emergence of the primitive social bonds were effected in the same process. Man appeared on the scene of earthly events as a social being. The isolated asocial man is a fictitious construction.

Seen from the point of view of the individual, society is the great means for the attainment of all his ends. The preservation of society is an essential condition of any plans an individual may want to realize by any action whatever. Even the refractory delinquent who fails to adjust his conduct to the requirements of life within the societal system of cooperation does not want to miss any of the advantages derived from the division of labor. He does not consciously aim at the destruction of society. He wants to lay his hands on a greater portion of the jointly produced wealth than the social order assigns to him. He would feel miserable if antisocial behavior were to become universal and its inevitable outcome, the return to primitive indigence, resulted.

It is illusory to maintain that individuals in renouncing the alleged blessings of a fabulous state of nature and entering into society have foregone some advantages and have a fair claim to be indemnified for what they have lost. The idea that anybody would have fared better under an asocial state of mankind and is wronged by the very existence of society is absurd. Thanks to the higher productivity of social cooperation the human species has multiplied far beyond the margin of subsistence offered by the conditions prevailing in ages with a rudimentary degree of the division of labor. Each man enjoys a standard of living much higher than that of his savage ancestors. The natural condition of man is extreme poverty and insecurity. It is romantic nonsense to lament the passing of the happy days of primitive barbarism. In a state of savagery the complainants would either not have reached the age of manhood, or if they had, they would have lacked the opportunities and amenities provided by civilization. Jean Jacques Rousseau and Frederick Engels, if they had lived in the primitive state which they describe with nostalgic yearning, would not have enjoyed the leisure required for their studies and for the writing of their books.

One of the privileges which society affords to the individual is the privilege of living in spite of sickness or physical disability. Sick animals are doomed. Their weakness handicaps them in their attempts to find food and to repel aggression on the part of other animals. Deaf, nearsighted, or crippled savages must perish. But such defects do not deprive a man of the opportunity to adjust himself to life in society. The majority of our contemporaries are afflicted with some bodily deficiencies which biology considers pathological. Our civilization is to a great extent the achievement of such men. The eliminative forces of natural selection are greatly reduced under social conditions. Hence some people say that civilization tends to deteriorate the hereditary qualities of the members of society.

Such judgments are reasonable if one looks at mankind with the eyes of a breeder intent upon raising a race of men equipped with certain qualities. But society is not a studfarm operated for the production of a definite type of men. There is no "natural" standard to establish what is desirable and what is undesirable in the biological evolution of man. Any standard chosen is arbitrary, purely subjective, in short a judgment of value. The terms racial improvement and racial degeneration are meaningless when not based on definite plans for the future of mankind.

It is true, civilized man is adjusted to life in society and not to that of a hunter in virgin forests.

Notes

1. F. H. Giddings, *The Principles of Sociology* (New York, 1926), p. 17.
2. R. M. MacIver, *Society* (New York, 1937), pp. 6–7.

8

The Results of Human Action but not of Human Design[1]

Friedrich A. Hayek

The belief in the superiority of deliberate design and planning over the spontaneous forces of society enters European thought explicitly only through the rationalist constructivism of Descartes. But it has its sources in a much older erroneous dichotomy which derives from the ancient Greeks and still forms the greatest obstacle to a proper understanding of the distinct task of both social theory and social policy. This is the misleading division of all phenomena into those which are "natural" and those which are "artificial."[2] Already the sophists of the fifth century B.C. had struggled with the problem and stated it as the false alternative that institutions and practices must be either due to nature (*physei*) or due to convention (*thesei* or *nomo*); and through Aristotle's adoption of this division it has become an integral part of European thought.

It is misleading, however, because those terms make it possible to include a large and distinct group of phenomena either under the one or the other of the two terms, according as to which of two possible definitions is adopted that

Reprinted from *Studies in Philosophy, Politics and Economics*, Chapter 6, by Friedrich A. Hayek (Chicago: The University of Chicago Press, 1967).

A French translation of this essay was published in: *Les Fomdements Philosophiques des Systemes Economiques*. Textes de Jacques Rueff et essais rediges en son honneur, Paris 1967.

were never clearly distinguished and are to the present day constantly confused. Those terms could be used to describe either the contrast between something which was independent of human action and something which was the result of human action, or to describe the contrast between something which had come about without, and something which had come about as a result of, human design. This double meaning made it possible to represent all those institutions which in the eighteenth century Adam Ferguson at last clearly singled out as due to human action but not to human design either as natural or as conventional according as one or the other of these distinctions was adopted. Most thinkers, however, appear to have been hardly aware that there were two different distinctions possible.

Neither the Greeks of the fifth century B.C. nor their successors for the next two thousand years developed a systematic social theory which explicitly dealt with those unintended consequences of human action or accounted for the manner in which an order or regularity could form itself among those actions which none of the acting persons had intended. It therefore never became clear that what was really required was a three-fold division which inserted between the phenomena which were natural in the sense that they were wholly independent of human action, and those which were artificial or conventional[3] in the sense that they were the product of human design, a distinct middle category comprising all those unintended patterns and regularities which we find to exist in human society and which it is the task of social theory to explain. We still suffer, however, from the lack of a generally accepted term to describe this class of phenomena; and to avoid continuing confusion it seems to be urgently necessary that one should be adopted. Unfortunately the most obvious term which should be available for that purpose, namely "social," has by a curious development come to mean almost the opposite of what is wanted: as a result of the personification of society, consequent on the very failure to recognize it as a spontaneous order, the word 'social' has come to be generally used to describe the aims of deliberate concerted action. And the new term "societal" which, conscious of the difficulty, some sociologists have attempted to introduce, appears to have small prospect of establishing itself to fill that urgent need.[4]

It is important to remember, however, that up to the appearance of modern social theory in the eighteenth century, the only generally understood term through which it could be expressed that certain observed regularities in human affairs were not the product of design was the term "natural." And, indeed, until the rationalist reinterpretation of the law of nature in the seventeenth century, the term "natural" was used to describe an orderliness or regularity that was not the product of deliberate human will. Together with "organism" it was one of the two terms generally understood to refer to the spontaneously grown in contrast to the invented or designed. Its use in this sense had been inherited from the stoic philosophy, had been revived in the twelfth century,[5] and it was finally under its flag that the late Spanish Schoolmen developed the foundations of the genesis and functioning of spontaneously formed social institutions.[6]

It was through asking how things would have developed if no deliberate acts of legislation had ever interfered that successively all the problems of social and particularly economic theory emerged. In the seventeenth century, however, this older natural law tradition was submerged by another and very different one, a view which in the spirit of the then rising constructivist rationalism interpreted the "natural" as the product of designing reason.[7] It was finally in reaction to this Cartesian rationalism that the British moral philosophers of the eighteenth century, starting from the theory of the common law as much as from that of the law of nature, built up a social theory which made the undesigned results of individual action its central object, and in particular provided a comprehensive theory of the spontaneous order of the market.

There can be little question that the author to whom more than to any other this "anti-rationalist" reaction is due was Bernard Mandeville.[8] But the full development comes only with Montesquieu[9] and particularly with David Hume,[10] Josiah Tucker, Adam Ferguson, and Adam Smith. The uncomprehending ridicule later poured on the latter's expression of the "invisible hand" by which "man is led to promote an end which was no part of his intention,"[11] however, once more submerged this profound insight into the object of all social theory, and it was not until a century later that Carl Menger at last resuscitated it in a form which now, yet another eighty years later, seems to have become widely accepted,[12] at least within the field of social theory proper.

There was perhaps some excuse for the revulsion against Smith's formula because he may have seemed to treat it as too obvious that the order which formed itself spontaneously was also the best order possible. His implied assumption, however, that the extensive division of labour of a complex society from which we all profited could only have been brought about by spontaneous ordering forces and not by design was largely justified. At any rate, neither Smith nor any other reputable author I know has ever maintained that there existed some original harmony of interests irrespective of those grown institutions. What they did maintain, and what one of Smith's contemporaries, indeed, expressed much more clearly than Smith himself ever did, was that institutions had developed by a process of the elimination of the less effective which did bring about a reconciliation of the divergent interests. Josiah Tucker's claim was not that "the universal mover of human nature, self love" always did receive, but that "it may receive such a direction in this case (as in all others) as to promote the public interest by those efforts it shall make towards pursuing its own."[13]

The point in this which was long not fully understood

until at last Carl Menger explained it clearly, was that the problem of the origin or formation and that of the manner of functioning of social institutions was essentially the same: the institutions did develop in a particular way because the co-ordination of the actions of the parts which they secured proved more effective than the alternative institutions with which they had competed and which they had displaced. The theory of evolution of traditions and habits which made the formation of spontaneous orders possible stands therefore in a close relation to the theory of evolution of the particular kinds of spontaneous orders which we call organisms, and has in fact provided the essential concepts on which the latter was built.[14]

But if in the theoretical social sciences these insights appear at last to have firmly established themselves, another branch of knowledge of much greater practical influence, jurisprudence, is still almost wholly unaffected by it. The philosophy dominant in this field, legal positivism, still clings to the essentially anthropomorphic view which regards all rules of justice as the product of deliberate invention or design, and even prides itself to have at last escaped from all influence of that "metaphysical" conception of "natural law" from the pursuit of which, as we have seen, all theoretical understanding of social phenomena springs. This may be accounted for by the fact that the natural law concept against which modern jurisprudence reacted was the perverted rationalist conception which interpreted the law of nature as the deductive constructions of "natural reason" rather than as the undesigned outcome of a process of growth in which the test of what is justice was not anybody's arbitrary will but compatibility with a whole system of inherited but partly inarticulated rules. Yet the fear of contamination by what was regarded as a metaphysical conception has not only driven legal theory into much more unscientific fictions, but these fictions have in effect deprived law of all that connection with justice which made it an intelligible instrument for the inducement of a spontaneous order.

The whole conception, however, that law is only what a legislator has willed and that the existence of law presupposes a previous articulation of the will of a legislator is both factually false and cannot even be consistently put into practice. Law is not only much older than legislation or even an organized state: the whole authority of the legislator and of the state derives from pre-existing conceptions of justice, and no system of articulated law can be applied except within a framework of generally recognized but often unarticulated rules of justice.[15] There never has been and there never can be a "gap-less" (*luckenlos*) system of formulated rules. Not only does all made law *aim* at justice and *not create* justice, not only has no made law ever succeeded in replacing all the already recognized rules of justice which it presupposes or even succeeded in dispensing with explicit references to such unarticulated conceptions of justice; but the whole process of development, change and interpretation of law would become wholly unintelligible if we closed our eyes to the existence of a framework of such unarticulated rules from which the articulated law receives its meaning.[16] The whole of this positivist conception of law derives from that factually untrue anthropomorphic interpretation of grown institutions as the product of design which we owe to constructivist rationalism.

The most serious effect of the dominance of that view has been that it leads necessarily to the destruction of all belief in a justice which can be found and not merely decreed by the will of a legislator. If law is wholly the product of deliberate design, whatever the designer decrees to be law is just by definition and unjust law becomes a contradiction in terms.[17] The will of the duly authorized legislator is then wholly unfettered and guided solely by his concrete interests. As the most consistent representative of contemporary legal positivism has put it, "From the point of view of rational cognition, there are only interests of human beings and hence conflicts of interests. The solution of these conflicts can be brought about either by satisfying one interest at the expense of another, or by a compromise between the conflicting interests."[18]

All that is proved by this argument, however, is that the approach of rationalist constructivism cannot arrive at any criterion of justice. If we realize that law is never wholly the product of design but is judged and tested within a framework of rules of justice which nobody has invented and which guided people's thinking and actions even before those rules were ever expressed in words, we obtain, though not a positive, yet still a negative criterion of justice which enables us, by progressively eliminating all rules which are incompatible with the rest of the system,[19] gradually to approach (though perhaps never to reach) absolute justice.[20] This means that those who endeavored to discover something "naturally" (i.e., undesignedly) given were nearer the truth and therefore more "scientific" than those who insisted that all law had been set ('posited') by the deliberate will of men. The task of applying the insight of social theory to the understanding of law has, however, yet to be accomplished, after a century of the dominance of positivism has almost entirely obliterated what had already been accomplished in this direction.

Because there has been a period in which those insights of social theory had begun to affect legal theory; Savigny and his older historical school, largely based on the conception of a grown order elaborated by the Scottish philosophers of the eighteenth century, continued their efforts in what we now call social anthropology and even appear to have been the main channel through which those ideas reached Carl Menger and made the revival of their conceptions possible.[21] That in this respect Savigny continued or resumed the aim of the older natural law theorists has been concealed by his rightly directing his argument against the rationalist natural law theories of the seventeenth and eighteenth centuries. But though he thereby helped to discredit that conception of natural law, his whole concern had been to discover how law had arisen largely without design, and even to demonstrate that it was impossible by design adequately to replace the outcome of such natural growth. The natural law which he opposed was not the natural law to be discovered but the natural law which was deductively derived from natural reason.

But if for the older historical school, though they spurned the word "natural," law and justice were still given objects to be discovered and explained, the whole idea of law as something objectively given was abandoned by positivism, according to which it was regarded as wholly the product of the deliberate will of the legislator. The positivists no longer understood that something might be objectively given although it was not part of material nature but a result of men's actions; and that law indeed could be an object for a science only in so far as at least part of it was given independently of any particular human will: it led to the paradox of a science which explicitly denied that it had an object.[22] Because, if 'there can be no law without a legislative act',[23] there may arise problems for psychology or sociology but not for a science of law.

The attitude found its expression in the slogan which governed the whole positivist period: that "what man has made he can also alter to suit his desires." This is, however, a complete *non sequitur* if "made" is understood to include what has arisen from man's actions without his design. This whole belief, of which legal positivism is but a particular form, is entirely a product of that Cartesian constructivism which must deny that there are rules of justice to be discovered because it has no room for anything which is "the result of human action but not of human design" and therefore no place for social theory. While on the whole we have now successfully expelled this influence from the theoretical sciences of society—and had to, to make them possible—the conceptions which today guide legal theory and legislation still belong almost wholly to this pre-scientific approach. And though it was French social scientists who earlier than others had clearly seen that from the famous *Discours de la Methode* "il etait sorti autant de deraison sociale et d'aberrations metaphysiques, d'abstractions et d'utopies, que de donnees positives, que s'il menait a Comte il avait aussi mene a Rousseau,"[24] it would seem at least to the outsider that in France, even more than elsewhere, law is still under its influence.

Supplementary Notes

Sten Gagner, *Studien zur Ideengeschichte der Gesetzgebung*, Uppsala 1960, pp. 208 and 242, shows that the terms "natural law" and "positive law" derive from the introduction by Gellius in the second century A.D. of the Latin adjectives *naturalis* and *positivus* to render the meaning of the Greek nouns *physis* and *thesis*. This indicates that the whole confusion involved in the dispute between legal positivism and the theories of the law of nature traces back directly to the false dichotomy here discussed, since it should be obvious that systems of legal rules (and therefore also the individual rules which have meaning only as part of such a system) belong to those cultural phenomena which are "the result of human action but not of human design." See on this also chapter 4 above.

Herr Christoph Eucken has drawn my attention to the fact that the contrast that is drawn in the opening sentence of Herodotus's *Histories* between what has arisen from [the actions of] men (*ta genomena ex anthropon*) and their great and astounding works (*erga megala kai thomasta*) suggests that he was more aware of the distinction here made than was true of many of the later ancient Greeks.

Notes

1. Adam Ferguson, *An Essay on the History of Civil Society,* London, 1767, p. 187: "Nations stumble upon establishments which are indeed the result of human action, but not the execution of any human design." Ferguson refers in this connection to the *Memoires du Cardinal de Retz,* presumably the reference (ed. Paris, 1820, vol. II, p. 497) to President de Bellievre's statement that Cromwell once told him that "on ne montait jamais si haut que quand on ne sait ou l'on va."

2. Cf. F. Heinimann, *Nomos und Physis,* Basel, 1945.

3. The ambiguity of the term "conventional," which may refer either to explicit agreement or to habitual practices and their results, has further contributed to enhance the confusion.

4. See F. Stuart Chapin, *Cultural Change,* New York, 1928 and M. Mandelbaum, "Societal Facts" in Patrick Gardiner, ed. *Theories of History,* London, 1959. The term "cultura," which social anthropologists have adopted as a technical term to describe these phenomena will hardly do for general usage, since most people would hesitate to include, e.g., cannibalism under "cultural" institutions.

5. Cf. particularly the account in Sten Gagner, *Studien zur Ideengeschichte der Gesetzgebwig,* Uppsala, 1960, pp. 225–40 of the work of Guillaume des Conches, especially the passage quoted on p. 231: "Et est positiva que est ab hominibus inventa.... Naturalis vero que nonest homine inventa." 6. See particularly Luis Molina, *De iustitia et iure,* Cologne, 1596–600, esp. tom. II, disp. 347, No. 3, where he says of natural price that "naturale dicitur, quoniam et ipsis rebus, seclusa quacumque humana lege eo decreto consurgit, dependetur tamen a multis circumstantiis, quibus variatur, atque ab hominum affectu, ac aestimatione, comparatione diversum usum, interdum pro solo hominum beneplacito et arbitrio." In an interesting but unpublished doctoral thesis of Harvard University, W. S. Joyce, *The Economics of Louis de Molina,* 1948 (p. 2 of the Appendix "Molina on Natural Law"), the author rightly says that "Molina explains that unlike positive law, natural law is "de objecto"—an untranslatable but very handy

scholastic term which means very much "in the nature of the case"—because from the very nature of the thing (*ex ipsamet natura rei*) it follows that, for the preservation of virtue or the avoiding of vice, that action should be commanded or forbidden, which the natural law commands or forbids. "Hence," Molina continues, "what is commanded or forbidden results from the nature of the case and not from the arbitrary will (*ex voluntate et libito*) of the legislator."

7. The change in the meaning of the concept of reason which this transition involves is clearly shown by a passage in John Locke's early *Essays on the Law of Nature* (ed. by W. von Leyden, Oxford, 1954, p. III) in which he explains that "By reason, however, I do not think is meant here that faculty of the understanding which forms trains of thought and deduces proofs, but certain definite principles of action from which spring all virtues and whatever is necessary for the proper moulding of morals." Cf. also Ibid., p. 149: "For right reason of this sort is nothing but the law of nature itself already known."

8. The basic idea is already contained in many passages of the original poems of 1705, especially: The worst of all the multitude Did something for the common good, but the fully developed conception occurs only in the second part of the prose commentary added more than twenty years later to *The Fable of the Best* (see ed. by F. B. Kaye, Oxford, 1924, Vol. II, esp. pp. 142, 287–88, and 349–50 and compare Chicki Nishiyama, *The Theory of Self-Love, An Essay in the Methodology of the Social Sciences, etc.*, Chicago Ph.D. thesis, June 1960— esp. for the relation of Mandeville's theories to Menger's).

9. On the influence of Mandeville on Montesquieu, see J. Dedicu, *Montesquieu et la Tradition Politique Anglaise*, Paris, 1909.

10. David Hume, *Works,* eds. T. H. Green and T .H. Grose, vol. I and II, *A Treatise on Human Nature*, vol. III and IV, *Essays, Moral, Political, and Literary*, esp. II, p. 296: "advantageous to the public though it be not intended for that purpose by the inventors"; also III, p. 99: "if the particular checks and controls, provided by the constitution ... made it not the interest,

even of bad men, to act for the public good"; as well as II, p. 289: "I learn to do a service to another without bearing him a real kindness"; and II, p. 195: "all these institutions arise merely from the necessity of human society." It is interesting to observe the terminological difficulties into which Hume is led because, as a result of his opposition to contemporary natural law doctrines, he has chosen to describe as "artifact," "artifice," and "artificial" precisely what the older natural law theorists had described as "natural," cf. esp. II, p. 258: "where an invention is obvious and absolutely necessary, it may as probably be said to be natural as anything that proceeds immediately from original principles; without the intervention of thought and reflection. Though the rules of justice be *artificial*, they are not *arbitrary*. Nor is the expression improper to call them *Laws of Nature;* if by natural we understand what is common to any species, or even if we confine it to mean what is inseparable from the species." Cf. my essay on "The Legal and Political Philosophy of David Hume." Professor Bruno Leoni has drawn my attention to the fact that Hume's use of "artificial" in this connection derives probably from Edward Coke's conception of law as "artificial reason" which is, of course, closer to the meaning the later scholastics had given to "natural" than to the usual meaning of "artificial."

11. Adam Smith, *An Inquiry into the Nature and Causes of the Wealth of Nations* (1776), Bk. IV, ii, ed. E. Cannan, London, 1904, vol. I, p. 421.

12. Carl Menger, *Untersuchungen uber die Methode der Socialwissenschaften und der Politischen Okonomie insbesondere,* Leipzig, 1883, p. 182: "die unbeabsichtigte Resultante individueller, d.i. individuellen Interessen verfolgender Bestrebungen der Volksglieder ... die unbeabsichtigte sociale Resultante individuell teleologischer Faktoren" (in the English translation of this work by F. J. Nock, ed. by L. Schneider, *Problems of Economics and Sociology,* Urbana, 1963, p. 158). The more recent revival of this conception seems to date from my own article on "Scientism and the Study of Society," *Economica,* N.S. IX/$_{35}$, August 1942, p. 276 (in the reprint in *The Counter-*

Revolution of Science, Glencoe, Ill., 1952, p. 25) where I argued that the aim of social studies is "to explain the unintended or undesigned results of many men." From this it appears to have been adopted by Karl Popper, "The Poverty of Historicism," *Economica,* N. S. XI/₃, August 1944, p. 122 (in the book edition, London, 1957, p. 65), where he speaks of "the undesigned results of human action" and adds in a note that "undesigned social institutions may emerge as *unintended consequences of rational actions*"; as well as in *The Open Society and its Enemies,* 4th ed., Princeton, 1963, vol. II, p. 93, where he speaks of "the indirect, the unintended and often the unwanted byproducts of such actions" (i.e., "conscious and intentional human actions"). (I cannot agree, however, with the statement, Ibid., p. 323, based on a suggestion of Karl Polanyi, that "it was Marx who first conceived social theory as the study of the *unwanted social repercussions of nearly all our actions.*" The idea was clearly expressed by Adam Ferguson and Adam Smith, to mention only the authors to whom Marx was unquestionably indebted.) The conception is also used (though perhaps not adopted) by Ernest Nagel, "Problems of Concept and Theory Formation in the Social Sciences," in *Science, Language and Human Rights* (American Philosophical Association, Eastern Division, vol. I), Philadelphia, 1952, p. 54, where he says that "social phenomena are indeed not generally the intended results of individual actions; nevertheless the central task of social science is the explanation of phenomena as the unintended outcome of springs of action." Similar though not identical is K. R. Merton's conception of "The unanticipated consequences of purposive social action" (see his article under that title in *American Sociological Review,* 1936, and the further discussion in *Social Theory and Social Structure,* rev. ed. Glencoe, IL, 1957, pp. 61–62).

13. Josiah Tucker, *The Elements of Commerce* (1756), reprinted in *Josiah Tucker: A Selection from his Economic and Political Writings,* ed. R. L. Schuyler, New York, 1931, p. 59. Cf. also my *Individualism and Economic Order,* London and Chicago, 1948, p. 7.

14. Carl Menger, *l.c.,* p. 88: "Dieses genetische Element ist untrennbar von der Idee theoretischer Wissenschaften"; also

C. Nishiyama, *l.c.* It is interesting to compare this with the insight from the biological field stressed by L. von Berta-lanffy, *Problems of Life,* New York, 1952, p. 134: "what are called structures are slow processes of long duration, functions are quick processes of short duration. If we say that a function such as a contraction of a muscle is performed by a structure, it means that a quick and short process-wave is superimposed on a long-lasting and slowly running wave."

15. Cf. Paulus (*Dig.* 50.17.I) "non ex regula ius sumatur, sed ex iure quod est regula fiat"; and Accursius (Gloss 9 to *Dig.* I.I.I.pr.) "Est autem ius a iustitia, sicut a matre sua, ergo prius fuit iustitia quam ius."

16. Cf. H. Kanotorowicz, *The Definition of Law,* ed. A.H. Campbell, London, 1958, p. 35: "The whole history of legal science, particularly the work of the Italian glossators and the German pandectists, would become unintelligible if law were to be considered as a body of commands of a sovereign."

17. Cf. T. Hobbes, *Leviathan,* Ch. 30, ed. M. Oakeshott, London, 1946, p. 227: "no law can be unjust."

18. Hans Kelsen, *What is Justice?*, University of California Press, 1960, pp. 21–22.

19. On the problem of comparability of the several rules as test, see now the interesting studies by Jurgen von Kempski, collected in *Recht und Politik,* Stuttgart, 1965, and his essay "Grundlegung zu einer Strukturtheorie des Rechts," *Abhandlungen der Geistes- und Sozialqissenschaftlichen Klasse der Akademie der Wissenschaften und der Literatur* in Mainz, Jg. 1961, No. 2.

20. The conception of a negative test of the justice of legal rules (essentially of the kind at which the legal philosophy of I. Kant aimed) which would enable us continuously to approach justice by eliminating all inconsistencies or incompatibilities from the whole body of rules of justice, of which at any one time a large part is always the common and undisputed possession of the members of a given civilization, is one of the central points of a book on which I am at present working.

21. For the channels through which the ideas of Burke (and through Burke, those of David Hume) appear to have

reached Savigny, see H. Ahrens, *Die Rechtsphilosophie oder das Naturrecht*, 4th ed. wien, 1854, p. 64. This book was probably also one of Carl Menger's first sources of information. On Savigny and his school, cf. also the acute observations of E. Ehrlich, *Juristische Logik*, Tubingen, 1918, p. 84: "Burke, Savigny und Puchta ... verstehen, was immer verkannt wird, unter Volk oder Nation dasselbe, was wir heute als Gesellschaft im Gegensatz zum Staate bezeichnen, allerdings in nationaler Begrenzung"; and Sir Frederick Pollock, *Oxford Lectures and Other Discourses*, London, 1890, pp. 41–42: "The doctrine of evolution is nothing else than the historical method applied to the facts of nature, the historical method is nothing else than the dectrine of evolution applied to human societies and institutions. When Charles Darwin created the philosophy of natural history ... , he was working in the same spirit and towards the same ends as the great publicists who, heeding his fields of labour as little as he heeded theirs, had laid in the patient study of historical facts the bases of a solid and rational philosophy of politics and law. Savigny, whom we do not yet know and honour enough, or our own Burke, whom we know and honour but cannot honour too much, were Darwinians before Darwin. In some measure the same may be said of the great Frenchman Montesquieu, whose unequal but illuminating genius was lost in a generation of formalists." The claim to have been "Darwinians before Darwin" was, however, first advanced by the theorists of language (see August Schleicher, *Die Darwinsche Theorie und die Sprachwissenschaft*, Weimar, 1869, and Max Muller, "Lectures on Mr. Darwin's Philosophy of Language," *Frazer's Magazine*, vol. VII, 1893, p. 662, from whom Pollock seems to have borrowed the phrase.

22. Cf. Leonard Nelson, *Rechtswissenschaft ohne Recht*, Leipzig, 1917.
23. John Austin, *Jurisprudence*, 3rd ed., London, 1872, p. 555.
24. Albert Sorel, "Comment j'ai lu la 'Reforme Sociale'," *Reforme Sociale*, ist November, 1906, p. 614, quoted by A. Schatz, *L'individualisme economique et sociale*, Paris, 1907, p. 41, which

together with H. Michel, *L'Idle de l'Etat,* 3rd ed., Paris, 1898, is most instructive on this influence of Cartesianism on French social thought.

9

Measurement as Scientific Method in Economics

Leland B. Yeager

I. Methodological Sermons

Time and again the cry goes up that economics has lagged behind the natural sciences and that it must adopt their methods, precise measurement in particular. This idea is epitomized in the former slogan of the Cowles Commission for Research in Economics—"Science is Measurement." It is reflected in Joseph Schumpeter's high admiration for statistical work, almost without regard to the results achieved.[1] It gets extreme emphasis in *Reconstruction of Economics,* a booklet by E. C. Harwood[2] distributed early in 1955 to members of the American Economic Association. Colonel Harwood uses terms like "Platonic idealism," "medieval scholasticism," "dialectical quest for certainty," "revelation," "intuition," "word magic," and "hypostatization and dialectical facility" in expressing his dismay at the backward and unscientific state of contemporary economics. Economists should wake up to the "Galilean revolution" and adopt "modern scientific method": quantitative measurement of change and study of the relations among changes. Harwood

Reprinted from the *American Journal of Economics and Sociology* 16:4 (July, 1957). The author thanks Mr. John C. Dawson for his painstaking and helpful arguments against the views expressed here.

scorns any "outmoded distinction" between the natural and social sciences purporting to justify differences in method.

II. Measurement in the Natural Sciences

Yet no number of epithets or references to Galileo can conjure away a real and important distinction. In the natural sciences, measurement is indeed important enough to suggest the slogan, "Science is Measurement." Let us see why. First, observation and experiment have forced belief in certain numerical laws and constants of nature. Some examples are the numerical relation among volume, pressure, and temperature of a gas, and constants such as Avogadro's number (the number of molecules in 22,400 liters of any gas at specified pressure and temperature), the mechanical equivalent of heat (foot-pounds per B.T.U.), the constant of universal gravitation, the velocity of light in a vacuum, Planck's elementary quantum of action, atomic weights and numbers, and the relative masses and charges of various subatomic "particles." Such constants were not merely invented; they forced themselves upon scientists through repeated agreement among results of all relevant measurements.[3] Thus the natural sciences do have things to measure—things other than transitory numerical facts of specific historical situations. A related point is that measurement in the natural sciences leads to inferences about conditions, including qualitative conditions, that are not directly observable. Measurement helps find "yes" or "no" answers. It yields clues needed to decide among rival hypotheses about qualitative aspects of nature.[4] This point can be made clear by reminding the reader of some well known examples:

Galileo was not content with the merely qualitative observation that bodies fall with increasing speed. He wanted to test the more definite hypothesis that speed goes on increasing in simple proportionality to time (which implies that the distance covered is proportional to the square of the elapsed time). Lacking instruments to measure the rapid motion of bodies in actual free fall, Galileo ingeniously "diluted" gravity by working with balls rolling down an inclined plane. His measurements were compatible with the hypothesis. Galileo thus discredited the Aristotelian concept of forces as that which produces velocity and arrived instead at the concept of force as that which produces acceleration. He inferred that a body in motion would continue moving in a straight line at a steady speed forever unless some force were opposing this motion.

Newton had the idea that the force holding astronomical bodies in their orbits was the same as the force of gravity at the earth's surface. This idea, expressed precisely in the inverse-square law of gravitation, found support in numerical observations (after a correct measurement of the earth's radius had become available). The law would predict the observational results already summarized in Kepler's laws of planetary motion. Other observational facts, such as the movement of the tides in their correlation with the position of the moon, could also be derived from it. Eventually Newton's law received further confirmation from measurements with a torsion balance of the gravitational attraction emanating from lead balls.

Count Rumford was intrigued by the hot shavings produced in boring brass cannon. The prevalent theory attributed the heat to the squeezing out of "caloric" from the brass. Rumford reasoned that if that were so, less "caloric" should remain in the shavings than in the same weight of solid brass. He measured whether a given weight of hot shavings had less ability to heat water than the same weight of solid brass at the same temperature. He found no difference. Rumford further noticed that a blunt borer would produce great heat with little removal of metal. The amount of heat developed seemed to depend more on the amount

of mechanical work done than on the amount of metal removed. Rumford set about making a crude measurement
of the proportionality between mechanical work and heat.
Later, Joule's more precise experiments on the dissipation
of mechanical energy by friction showed that the amount
of heat produced always bore the same quantitative relation
to the mechanical energy dissipated. As a result, heat came
to be recognized as a form of energy and not a substance.

Only precise weighing could have established the laws
of definite proportions and of multiple proportions: every
chemical compound always contains the same elements in
the same proportions by weight; and if two elements combine in more than one proportion, the quantities of one
element combining with a fixed quantity of the other are in
simple numerical proportion. These facts induced chemists
to adopt Dalton's atomic theory of matter.

Measurement of atomic weights was prerequisite to establishment of Mendeleyev's highly suggestive periodic system. An improved system became possible when Henry
Moseley measured the X-ray radiation frequencies of various elements and classified the elements in the order of
their frequencies. The successive frequencies appeared
to be arranged not haphazardly but in a step-like progression. Certain gaps in the series of "atomic numbers" (as Moseley called the positions in his table of frequencies) suggested missing elements. A formula devised by Moseley predicted the frequencies that the X-ray lines of the missing
elements should have and so led to spectroscopic detection
of these elements. The concept of a periodic table and the
systematic recurrence in it of elements with similar chemical
characteristics provided important clues in the study of
atomic structure.

In repeated breeding experiments, Mendel observed
that about one-fourth of the offspring of hybrid pea plants
showed the recessive trait (for example, green- rather than
yellow-seededness). Because he actually counted the num-

bers of offspring of each type, Mendel had reason to conceive of what are now called genes as carriers of hereditary traits. Current examples of how statistics can provide clues to cause-and-effect relations in the biological sciences are furnished by studies of the incidence of disease in city and country and among smokers and nonsmokers.

Before 1887, it had been common to postulate a motionless "ether" as carrier of light waves. It should, then, have been possible to detect the motion of the earth through the ether: a light beam sent in the direction of the earth's movement and reflected back should appear to travel a bit more slowly (relatively to the earth) than a beam sent transversely and reflected back. However, the famous Michelson-Morley experiment revealed no such difference in the speeds of the two beams. (Interference patterns showed whether the two speeds were the same; exact measurement entered into the design of the experiment.) This surprising negative result weakened the ether hypothesis and led Einstein to formulate his special theory of relativity.

On the basis of his general theory of relativity, Einstein predicted a definite slight degree of gravitational deflection of starlight beams grazing the sun's surface. Measurement by comparing star photographs taken during a solar eclipse with photographs of the same stars taken with the sun out of the way yielded results supporting Einstein's theory.

Einstein's general theory also implies a "slowing down of time" in intense gravitational fields. For example, an atom of sodium in an intense gravitational field should appear to vibrate more slowly and so emit a more reddish light than an atom of sodium on earth. This spectral shift would be too slight for detection ordinarily, but it was finally observed on the enormously dense companion star of Sirius. Einstein had previously said that absence of the predicted shift would render his theory untenable.

Astronomers had observed that Mercury did not revolve in its elliptical orbit with the regularity of the other planets: the orbit advances by 43 seconds of arc per century. This deviation could not be explained within the Newtonian theory but proved in agreement with the predictions of Einstein's more exact theory.

These last examples illustrate the importance of precision in measurement in the natural sciences. Very slight quantitative differences may be decisive on qualitative issues such as the validity of an entire theory. "Important advances in science are based on quantitative measurements only if the measured quantity is large as compared with possible systematic and accidental errors."[5]

III. The Contrast in Economics

In economics, no numerical constants occur.[6] Econometric parameters are vastly different from constants that force themselves on natural scientists in repeated experiments. When econometricians—or their statistical clerks— manage to get some numbers or other for the parameters postulated in theoretical equations, they are hardly blending observation and theory the way natural scientists do. Forcing statistics into a theoretical Procrustean bed is a far cry from experimental testing of theories.

People who believe in constants and dependable numerical relations in economics should be asked to name some (and it will not do merely to name relations that have held true fairly well on the average in particular countries during particular periods). Measurement of various elasticities, propensities, multipliers, monetary velocities, capital-output ratios, income-distribution parameters, and so forth is analogous not to measurement of the constant of universal gravitation or the mechanical equivalent of heat but rather to measurements at particular times of the flow of water in particular gutters, the temperature of particular electric light bulbs, the rainfall in particular localities, and the strain on particular bridges. Of course, measurements regarding human history may hold more interest than corresponding measurements of particular physical phenomena.

It might be argued that economic affairs can *in principle* be quantitatively described or predicted by stable functional relations, provided the functions include all relevant variables. However, everyone knows from personal experience that people's economic behavior depends on innumerable factors, including "noneconomic" factors for which no quantitative expression has been devised. Hence description of economic activity by stable functional relations would have to be merely one aspect of such description of the entire course of all human affairs.

A leading difference between the theoretical cores of economics and the natural sciences has to do with where empirical fact comes in. It comes in at the *beginning* of chains of deductive reasoning much more importantly in economics than in the natural sciences: " ... while at the world of nature we look from the outside, we look at the world of society from the inside; while, as far as nature is concerned, our concepts are about the facts and have to be adapted to the facts, in the world of society at least some of the most familiar concepts are the stuff from which that world is made."[7] In the natural sciences the underlying uniformities and structures—atoms, electrons, forces, gravitational fields, electromagnetic waves, and the like—cannot be observed directly. They are postulates whose legitimacy can only be inferred from the success of theories in coordinating what can be observed.[8] It is precisely because the postulates of theory cannot be confirmed directly that measurement has its great importance in the natural sciences. Instead of direct confirmation, consequences are logically or mathematically deduced from the postulates; and these deduced consequences are subjected to empirical check. The examples in section II above show why such a check typically involves measurement.[9]

Measurement plays a more modest role in economics. Often we cannot check economic theorems in the complex "real," or "macro," world because the effects of numerous influences are hopelessly intermingled. Fortunately, however, we can check economic theorems in another way—a way not available to natural scientists. We check the postulates directly. That is, we start the chains of deductive reasoning from dependable knowledge, as of the scarcity of productive resources in relation to practically unlimited human needs and wants, of the law of diminishing returns, and of human motives and wants and choices.[10] (For example: Other things being equal, people prefer more income to less. The more of some consumer good a person has beyond a certain amount, the less importance does he attach to still further units of it, relative to other goods.) Informing theories, we can sort out the influences of various factors on economic affairs because we know from personal experience how people react. We believe our economic theorems because they are logically implied by empirically verified postulates. Yet, disappointing though it may be to would-be imitators of the natural sciences, these postulates are qualitative rather than numerical truths.

Of course, the choice of empirical postulates about conditions of production and about human behavior involves abstraction. All theory, in the natural as well as social sciences, involves abstraction.[11] How, then, can economists be sure of having made the right abstractions or simplifications? For one things, the same direct knowledge of themselves and other people from which economists draw empirical postulates also gives them insight into how sensitively the conclusions of a particular piece of analysis depend on the simplifying assumptions used. For example, in analyzing the effects of a new excise tax, it should not be too hard to see whether businessmen's desire for profit or their desire for prestige is brought more directly into play. If, however, a particular theory could not be reconciled with observed "objective" phenomena, then economists would have to reconsider their simplifying assumptions. In any case, the fact remains that economists can draw on microempirical knowledge of a sort denied to natural scientists.

A further reason for emphasis in economics on empirical knowledge of human motives and choices lies in the very nature of scientific explanation. Science aims to order our experience, to reveal apparently unconnected observations as particular instances of a few wide principles, to deduce the greatest possible number of empirical facts from a few hypotheses or axioms.[12] To explain something meansto show how it exemplifies or results from principles so widely applicable or so familiar that we are intellectually satisfied, that we feel we "understand," and that our curiosity rests.[13] Explanation of a man's behavior means showing "that his motives are such as habitually inspire our own actions, or, in other words, that his motives are familiar to us."[14] Since economics is about human action, an explanation can hardly be intellectually satisfying unless it relates "objective" economic phenomena to human motives and choices; microempirical, introspective observations are among the facts to be integrated into the theoretical system.

Explanation, as described above, is correlated with ability to make predictions, understood as valid if-this-then-that propositions. (Neither in the natural sciences nor in economics does prediction, in general, mean foretelling the future.)

The above discussion admittedly allots an important role in economics to something that behaviorists scorn—introspection. But can introspection be banished completely from *any* field of knowledge? How can we avoid interpreting our sensations in the light of introspective experience? When we think we see a number indicated by a pointer on a dial, or when we think we are reading an article about a scientific experiment, how do we know that our sensations relate to an external world rather than to purely subjective fantasies? Surely introspection plays a part in our making this distinction. If introspection plays a more overt and important role in economics than in the natural sciences, may this not be due to the nature of the subject matter?

It is understandable that to people trained in the natural sciences, the method of economic theory may smack of Kantianism and its synthetic a priori. Such suspicions are strengthened by the unfortunate fact that *some* economists do try to generate knowledge from sterile definition-juggling and from arbitrary, nonempirical assumptions on which their conclusions sensitively depend. But economists who induce principles of human motives and choice from personal experience *are* using widely applicable empirical facts capable of supporting chains of deductive reasoning. Anthropomorphism, rightly scorned in the natural sciences as prescientific metaphysics, is justified in economics because economics is about human action.

IV. Measurement in Economics

To contrast the roles of measurement at the theoretical cores of economics and the natural sciences is not to scorn quantitative work in economics. Statistics is a powerful tool of research into economic history. Quantitative economic history of the very recent past may, with some risk, be projected for use in policy formation. Statistics can suggest fields for theoretical research (by pointing out, for example, the greater cyclical variability of capital-goods production than of consumer-goods production). Statistical and historical research may determine the presence or absence of the conditions to which particular theories relate. Statistical work may help in judging the relative strengths of opposing influences described by theory. For example, one strand of theory teaches that the risks of a fluctuating exchange rate hamper international trade; another strand teaches that a rate which always equilibrates supply and demand is more conducive to trade than a fixed and hence often disequilibrium rate. Which influence has been the stronger in particular experiences with fluctuating rates? Theory suggests that speculation may moderate exchange-rate fluctuations if speculators expect early reversals of rate movements; speculation may intensify fluctuations if speculators see movements as the start of continuing trends. Which behavior has predominated in a particular historical episode? Statistics may help answer questions like these. (Judging the relative strengths of influences already understood qualitatively is, however, hardly the role of measurement in the natural sciences. There, measurement is essential to provide clues about even the qualitative state of affairs.) From statistics economists may, with luck, even discover fairly dependable uniformities among similar historical situations. Finally, statistical and historical material can lend definiteness and expository strength to primarily theoretical discussions.

V. Different Methods for Different Subjects

This paper does not attack measurement in economics. It simply attacks naive exhortations to concentrate on gathering numbers. It shows why economists, who must be concerned with the behavior of people and not merely of things, can have little hope of finding stable numerical laws and constants (as distinguished from numerical facts of history). It shows how the essential function of measurement in the natural sciences is largely replaced in economics by direct empirical knowledge of the most generally applicable principles and concepts.

It is tyrannical—and shall we say unscientific?—to insist

on mechanically transplanting natural-science methods, narrowly conceived into a field where the subject matter is quite different. Paradoxically, those who are loudest in insisting on what they take to be "inductive" methods are most given to a priori methodological sermonizing and least willing to learn from experience what methods have been most fruitful in economics. The methods of a science must be appropriate to its own subject matter.[15] Economic theorists who know their jobs need not be intimidated by sermonizers trying to strut robed in the prestige of the natural sciences.

Notes

1. *History of Economic Analysis* (New York: Oxford University Press, 1954), pp. 211, 511, 519–26, 961–62, 1123–24, and *passim.* A few further examples should bring many more to the reader's mind: Jan Tinbergen, in *Econometric,* trans. by H. Rijken van Olst (Philadelphia: Blakiston, 1951), pp. 4–5, likens merely qualitative economics to the medieval stage of natural science. J. B. Condliffe, in *The Commerce of Nations*(New York: Norton, 1950), p. 673, prominently quotes a former natural scientist on "What the Social Scientist Can Learn from the Natural Scientist." Wassily W. Leontif, in "Input-Output Economics," (*Scientific American,* October, 1951), p. 15, makes an invidious contrast between deductive economics and quantitative physics.
2. Including papers by May Brotibeck and Richard S. Rudner (Great Barrington: American Institute for Economic Research, 1955).
3. Max Planck, *Scientific Autobiography and Other Papers,* trans. by Frank Gaynor (New York: Philosophical Library, 1949), pp. 172–73.
4. Cf. Morris R. Cohen and Ernest Nagel, *An Introduction to Logic and Scientific Method* (New York: Harcourt, Brace, 1934), p. 290; A. D'Abro, *The Evolution of Scientific Thought from Newton to Einstein* 2nd ed. (New York: Dover, 1950), pp. 439-40; A.

D'Abro, *The Rise of the New Physics*, 2 vol. (New York: Dover, 1951), vol. II, p. 478; Albert Einstein and Leopold Infeld, *The Evolution of Physics* (New York: Simon and Schuster, 1952), p. 291; Herbert Feigl, "The Scientific Outlook: Naturalism and Humanism," in Herbert Feigl and May Brodbeck, eds., *Readings in the Philosophy of Science* (New York: Appleton-Century-Crofts, 1953), p. 15; F. A. Hayek, *The Counter-Revolution of Science* (Glencoe, IL: Free Press, 1952), p. 23; Planck, op. cit., p. 110; and Hans Reichenbach, *The Rise of Scientific Philosophy*, Berkeley and Los Angeles, University of California Press, 1953, pp. 97–98.

5. James B. Conant, *On Understanding Science* (New York: New American Library, 1951), p. 99, where the quoted sentence is in italics.

6. This point has been much emphasized by Ludwig von Mises: see, for example, his *Human Action* (New Haven: Yale University Press, 1949), pp. 55–56, 118, 348–49.

7. F. A. Hayek, *Individualism and Economic Orde* (London: Rutledge & Kegan Paul, 1949), p. 76.

8. Cf. D'Abro, *Evolution*, op. cit., p. 431, and F. S. C. Northrop, *The Logic of the Sciences and the Humanities* (New YorK: Macmillan, 1949), pp. 106–7.

9. Cf. Hayek, *Counter-Revolution*, op. cit., pp. 50–51.

10. See the already cited works of Mises and Hayek; chapter XIII and pages 106–10 of Northrop's book; Lionel Robbins, *An Essay on the Nature and Significance of Economic Science*, 2nd ed.(London: Macmillan, 1948); Carl Menger, *Unterruchungen über die Methode der Socialwissenschaften und der Politischen Oekonomie insbesondere* (Leipzig: Duncher & Humblot, 1883); Henry George, *The Science of Political Economy* (New York: Schalkenback, 1941); and C. Weststrate, *Theorie van drie stelsels van socialeconomisch leven* (Leiden, Stenfert Kroese, 1948), pp. 20–44.

11. A corollary is that a theory is not to be tested according to the full descriptive accuracy of its assumptions. Cf. Milton Friedman, *Essays in Positive Economics* (University of Chicago Press, 1953), especially pp. 14–23.

12. Cf. Norman Campbell, *What is Science?* New York, Dover,

1952, p. 68; Albert Einstein, *Essays in Science,* trans. by Alan Harris; New York, Philosophical Library, 1934, p. 69.

13. Cf. Campbell, op. cit., pp. 77–79; Reichenbach, op. cit., pp. 6–7; R. E. Peierls, *The Laws of Nature* (New York: Scribner's, 1956), pp. 275–76, 278; P. W. Bridgman, *The Logic of Modern Physics* (New York: Macmillan, 1927), p. 37.

14. Campbell, op. cit., p. 77.

15. Northrop, op. cit., pp. 19, 273–74.

10

Praxeology and Econometrics: A Critique of Positivist Economics

Mario J. Rizzo

> The ultimate goal of a positive science is the develop-
> ment of a "theory" or "hypothesis" that yields valid and
> meaningful (i.e., not truistic) predictions about phe-
> nomena not yet observed.[1]

Although written a quarter of a century ago, Milton
Friedman's "The Methodology of Positive Economics" remains the immediate philosophical justification for much
of the contemporary approach to economics research. Nevertheless, the general points raised in that essay were not
new even at the time, but were an ingenious adaptation of
some of the positivist arguments of the 1930s, and the somewhat revisionist work of Sir Karl Popper.[2] Today, thoroughgoing positivism is clearly in retreat, if not already defeated,
in philosophical circles, but a variant of it remains quite
vibrant in many of the social sciences, particularly economics. It is the task of this essay to present a critique of "positive
economics" and, at least, some indications of a viable alternative.

Reprinted from *New Directions in Austrian Economics,* edited by Louis M. Spadaro
(Kansas City: Sheed Andrews and McMeel, Inc., 1976).

I. Prediction as the Goal

From the positivist epistemological viewpoint, is the opening quotation to be taken as an a priori or an empirical statement?

If a priori, then it is a statement about how we shall use the term "positive science" and is merely a linguistic stipulation. As such, one might equally well choose to stipulate some other meaning.

If empirical (i.e., a statement about what people have in fact considered positive science), then, of course, it does not express a necessary truth and *could* be otherwise. But then for a long time the Darwinian theory of evolution yielded no predictions and yet was considered scientifically acceptable.[3]

Furthermore, Friedman makes no attempt to survey what has been considered economic science to find out whether "prediction" has indeed been the defining characteristic. In fact, there are many theoretical frameworks which generate no testable predictions but are, nonetheless, considered part of economics. For example, it is frequently unclear what (predictive) relevance discussions on the existence and stability of equilibrium under many special assumptions (the empirical significance of which is unknown) have for a world which is never actually *in* equilibrium. Of course, one might claim that this is *bad* economics, and so the demarcation is really between "good" and "bad" science. There is, however, no escape here, for it merely leaves unanswered the question: Why is nonpredictive economics bad science?

Another possible escape might be to claim that, while nonpredictive theories may be scientific, they do not qualify as *positive* science. To this we are justified in merely replying: "So what?" What advantage is being claimed for positive science except that its ultimate goal is prediction? In that case, we are back where we started: Why *must* prediction be our goal?

The goal of prediction might well obscure what has in fact been considered a worthwhile aim of science: the explication and apprehension of *necessary* connections. Purely predictive "theory" is little more than a mnemonic device designed to relate *x* to *y*. But the *nature* of that relation may be unknown. The Babylonian astronomical forecasting techniques, which were merely trial-and-error arithmetic calculations, are an example of this kind of "black box" framework.[4] The principle of explanation remains unknown in the sense that the connection between the initial and marginal conditions (x_1, x_2, x, etc.) and the consequence (y) is not apprehended as necessary. The relation is characterized by an arbitrary givenness.

But while it may be true that prediction cannot be considered a *sufficient* attribute for "scientific" theory, it still might be a necessary one. However, we have already implicitly refuted this assertion by showing that within a positivist epistemological framework such necessity can be derived only from an essentially arbitrary prior stipulation.

II. Falsifiability as the Criterion of Meaning

The emphasis on prediction as *the* aim of science has its roots in a positivist criterion for the meaningfulness of a statement. To be meaningful, it has been said, a statement must be in a form such that it is *in principle* falsifiable by any observer.[5]

For example, let us take "the hypothesis that a substantial increase in the quantity of money within a relatively short period is accompanied by a substantial increase in prices."[6] Aside from problems concerning data availability and the skills of the particular investigator, is this hypothesis falsifiable? For now, let us say it is. Hence, the positivist would claim that this is a genuinely scientific statement. In fact, the meaning of a hypothesis is identified with the relevant test of its veracity. As Moritz Schlick tells us, "the meaning of a statement can be given only by indicating the way in which the truth of the statement is to be tested."[7] Of course, this cannot be literally true. If meaning is identified with the test, then what is being tested? But, if there is a meaning independent of the test, then the positivist criterion falls in on itself, and unfalsifiable statements can be meaningful. If we are not to take Schlick's statement literally, then it seems difficult to find any coherent interpretation of it.

But, of course, the whole concept of a unitary criterion for meaning is somewhat strange when viewed from within a positivist framework. Once again: Is the proposition a priori or empirical? A stipulated definition of "meaning" to include falsifiability is not in itself impressive: One could have stipulated otherwise. Viewed empirically, the criterion is immediately refuted by two thousand years of Western philosophy which claims that metaphysics and ontology are meaningful pursuits.

Aside from these issues, the falsifiability criterion loses much of its initial plausibility when the contradictory of a falsifiable statement is examined.[8] If we admit as falsifiable that all inflations are caused by increases in the money supply, then the contradictory,[9] some inflations are not caused by increases in the money supply, is *not* falsifiable. If the latter hypothesis is meant to apply to the future as well as to the past, one could always claim that the inflation not caused by money supply increases will appear if you just search long and hard enough. No example of money-supply-induced inflation refutes the proposition, and with a future, as well as a past, time horizon one has an *infinite* pool of inflations within which to search for the complete absence of nonmonetary inflations.

Consequently, the falsifiability criterion involves a major transformation in our system of logic: Although a given statement may be meaningful (or scientific), the negation of that statement is meaningless (or unscientific).[10]

A possible route of escape from this argument might appear to be the claim that while, strictly speaking, the statement that some inflations are not caused by increases in the money supply is not falsifiable, evidence could be accumulated which would render it more or less "probable." Alas, this is no escape either. The truth or falsity of any statement is not a random variable like tosses of a coin, and hence a frequential interpretation of the "probability" concept is impossible here. So the meaning of the term "probable" can only involve a *subjective* degree of belief. This amounts to a radical transformation of the whole positivist framework. The criterion now becomes: Any statement which could be rendered more or less "probable" by reference to empirical evidence is a meaningful statement. But then this is a psychological—rather than a logical—criterion. Any proposition for which our subjective degree of belief could be increased or decreased by "evidence" is meaningful. Worse still, what kinds of statements does this criterion exclude? Probably none. It would seem that human beings are not imaginative enough to conceive of propositions that have no relationship *at all* to the world. Hence, for any nontautologous (in the narrowest sense) statement, it is possible to find empirical "evidence" that has *some* bearing on its truth or falsity. Hence, all statements are meaningful. If this is so, the original intent of the positivist criterion crumbles.

Any statement of degree-of-belief probability does not fit comfortably within the positivist framework. Statements such as "that some inflations are not monetarily induced is 'probable'" are, of course, neither verifiable nor falsifiable in principle. More importantly, they do not carry with them any element of intersubjective testability (which was such an important goal). A stipulation that certain kinds of evidence will be interpreted as making a statement "probable" is no real solution. This makes the criterion of meaningfulness (or the demarcation between science and nonscience) purely conventional.

III. Critique of Econometrics[11]

Ceteris paribus prediction is prediction of "stylized facts": *x* leads to *y* *if* other factors are held constant. But since, in general, they aren't, we are not predicting a "real-world" event. Rather, we are predicting a hypothetical consequence.

To subject the hypothesis to potential falsification, we must control for the other relevant variables. Suppose we try to do this by using multiple regression analysis. Then:

1. How do we know when we have adequately controlled for extra-economic factors? (There is no a priori assurance that economic factors are the only ones that matter in a given situation.) This would require a theory of the interaction between economic and noneconomic variables. How do we go about subjecting this to falsifying tests?

2. How do we test the theory which enables us to determine the other economic factors that must be held constant in order to isolate the effect of *x*?

From the positivist framework the problem is crucial. How could we ever know that the (auxiliary) hypothesis, i.e., all other relevant factors have been held constant, has been falsified? We obviously cannot claim that it has been refuted if *x* does not result in *y* because it is *that* very relationship which is undergoing testing in the first place. It is clear that, unless we have additional hypotheses about the effects of each of the to-be-held-constant variables on *y*, we shall not be able to subject the crucial *ceteris paribus* clause to refutation. Furthermore, these auxiliary hypotheses (or perhaps a single hypothesis since it is their total effect with which we are concerned) must be independent of the central one in the sense that the falsification of the former must be independent of the falsification of the latter. Now, if we claim that we really don't care if the *ceteris paribus* clause is "true" because all that counts is the predictive ability of the central hypothesis, then we have gotten ourselves into a new quagmire. First, why have *ceteris paribus* clauses at all? Second, what are we falsifying if, in fact, *x* does not result in *y*? Certainly not the hypothesis as stated. Suppose the "evidence" fails to refute our hypothesis; then what have we corroborated? Again, not the original hypothesis because the apparent consistency of the data with the framework may be illusory, being entirely due to the "proper" variation of the factors which were supposed to be constant. Third, this whole viewpoint reinstates the "black box" approach to science and hence vitiates the aim of rational explanation.

It is quite possible to claim that, although the central hypothesis must be falsifiable in order to be meaningful or scientific, the *ceteris paribus* clause need not be. All that is needed in the latter case—it might be asserted—is a kind of educated judgment or *verstehen*. While this might be permissible within other epistemological frameworks, it will not be adequate to support the claims of positivism. If we can say that "all other relevant factors have been held constant" without falsifiability and still can be making a meaningful empirical statement, why can't we do the same in the case of "*x* causes *y*," the central hypothesis? If we can (which seems likely given the initial admission), then once again the criterion of positive science crumbles.

IV. Maximization

Under the influence of the "marginalist revolution," economics has become a discipline devoted in major part to the finding of functional maxima and minima. The individual consumer or producer is assumed to maximize or minimize something and, from this postulated behavior, testable implications are drawn. It is important to keep in mind that the maximization behavior itself is not subject to falsification, because it serves not as a substantive hypothesis but as a superstructure which gives rational coherence to the falsifiable implications.

Any particular instance of concrete behavior may be "explained" or rationalized in terms of maximization (or minimization) of some appropriate quantity (e.g., utility, wealth, etc.). since maximization is fundamentally a characteristic of intention (this the positivists won't admit), any concrete behavior may be viewed *as if* it were the maximization of *something*. This has serious implications.

Suppose we wish to test not the applicability of a specific economic hypothesis to a given area of human behavior (say, marriage), but, rather, the validity of viewing this kind of behavior as an instance of economic or maximizing activity per se. In other words, we don't care whether a particular maximizing model is appropriate, but we ask whether this is an example of maximizing behavior at all.

It might be claimed that this formulation of the problem makes no sense. After all, we are never testing economics or maximizing behavior as such, but only specific hypotheses of whatever kind. This, of course, misses the crucial point of the need to decide upon a research framework in advance of specific cases.

Is the statement "this is an example or instance of maximizing behavior" a meaningful and scientific one? Clearly not. Since the set of possible falsifiers is empty, any behavior can be "explained" in terms of maximizing something.[12] But the hypothesis, "this is an instance of maximizing sales," can be refuted by appropriate behavior, and so is a meaningful statement. This produces a curious paradox. The more general statement about maximization is meaningless (or unscientific), but the more particularized version of it constitutes a positive scientific hypothesis.

Some authors have tried to escape this problem by claiming that the (maximizing) framework *can* be refuted by comparison to an empirically richer and more general alternative framework. Indeed, Lakatos has gone so far as to say, "There is no falsification before the emergence of a better theory."[13] This means, in effect, that if two hypotheses—one maximizing and the other nonmaximizing—both equally well "explain" a particular case of economic behavior, then the one which is part of a more general approach, the specific applications of which have been corroborated in other cases, is to be preferred. This, however, introduces a subtle and important change in the falsifiability criterion. No longer is a statement meaningful or scientific by virtue of *its* empirical content but, rather, by the overall corroborated empirical content of other statements to which it is in some sense related. It is hard to recognize this as an epistemological criterion rather than as an aesthetic one.[14] Nevertheless, by some inexplicable train of thought, a statement becomes meaningful because of its relation to other similar statements which, having been corroborated, are themselves meaningful by virtue of their relation to, say, the former hypothesis. (Apparently, there is some kind of "simultaneous determination of meaning" argument underlying all of this.)

Let us look at this problem in a slightly different manner. The maximizing framework "proves" its worth, we might say, by predicting everything that the alternative framework does, plus a little more.[15] Hence, it acts, in a sense, as a falsifier of the alternative perspective.

This formulation does not seem very convincing. In

economics, at least, it would be surprising if, say, the maximizing framework predicted literally all of the facts predicted by the alternative. Normally, I suspect, the "better" framework would predict *some* of these facts, and some additional ones. Furthermore, competing frameworks frequently do not even ask the same questions. Why, then, should they be judged on whether they give the same answers (plus a little more)?

All this aside, it is hard to see why, from a purely positivist epistemological perspective, considerations of the framework's success in other particular instances should affect the meaningfulness or scientific character of a hypothesis in any given specific case.

V. Evidence

Until this point, we have implicitly considered as self-evident the answer to the question: "What shall count as evidence for and against a hypothesis?" How do we recognize a falsifying or corroborating result? The answer is, indeed, far from self-evident. In fact, this issue poses some crucial problems for the positivist approach, which, we shall contend, it is incapable of handling.

A hypothesis relates a variable x to a variable y, *ceteris paribus*. Let us assume that the *ceteris paribus* clause has been corroborated adequately; then what would amount to falsification of the hypothesis? To be more specific, hypothesize "that a substantial increase in the quantity of money ... is accompanied by a substantial increase in prices."[16] In order to test this statement, we must have some criteria by which we can relate the theoretical terms "money" and "prices" with their empirical counterparts. This is the crux of the problem.[17]

Something must point the way from theory to the relevant "facts"; we need what shall be called "referential statements." In our illustration, examples of referential statements might be: "The empirical counterpart of theoretical 'money' is M_1"; or, "by 'prices' is meant the consumer price index." The need for referential statements in applied economics is not restricted to the positivist variant of the science. What is peculiar to positivist economics, however, is a problem arising out of the epistemological status of such statements. If they are to be considered a priori, then (from a positivist viewpoint) we are merely talking about how we use words, and no link between the theoretical constructs and "empirical reality" is established. Then it must be established via falsifiable hypotheses. Yet this is an impossibility. (Referential statements make no predictions; they do not say, for example, that an increase in x results in an increase in y. Hence no predictions can be falsified.)

Now it is possible to recast the referential statements in such a way that they will be refutable: "If the criteria of applying the theoretical construct 'money' are, in fact, applied, then M_1 will be found to be the appropriate empirical counterpart." Clearly, this won't work because it requires that we know the criteria *prior* to the testing procedure which was to establish (or at least corroborate) these criteria in the first place.

Testing the referential statements is impossible unless we already know the criteria of applying the theoretical terms. If we already know these (in any meaningful way), then testing is unnecessary. But, from a positivist perspective, it is clearly impossible to have any meaningful knowledge about the real world which is given a priori.

One might attempt to obviate these difficulties by choosing empirical variables so as to present the particular hypothesis in its best light. (Choosing a definition of the money supply so as to best predict GNP is an example of this.) Unless one is attempting to insulate a hypothesis from refutation, there seems to be no clear reason for doing this. If empirical variables were chosen so as to present the hypothesis in its *worst* light, and it still remained unrefuted, would we not then have more fully corroborated it? In any event, the outcome of a potential test should not be the determining factor in whether it is performed.

VI. The Logical Character of Praxeology

The epistemological status of praxeology (which is identical to economics very broadly conceived) is a subject of considerable misunderstanding and confusion. Within a positivist framework the claims of praxeology make no sense. Knowledge is either a priori and certain but not pertaining to "reality," or it is empirical and uncertain but clearly embedded in the "real" world. An examination of the logical character of praxeology reveals these categories to be totally inappropriate. Praxeology claims to present knowledge which is at once both absolutely certain and empirical. This is the paradox which we shall have to explain.

Praxeological theorems or deductions are based upon the fundamental self-evident axiom, i.e., man acts or, what is the same, engages in purposeful behavior. The question at issue, then, is: In what precise sense is this axiom "self-evident," and what does it say about the world?

The action axiom is empirical in the sense that it is derived from inner experience or immediate introspection. It is *scientifically* empirical because it passes the intersubjectivity test: The experience is universal and hence, in principle, can be assented to by the observers and the observed alike. Hence, the fact that the axiom is based on introspection cannot open the praxeologist to the charge that his deductions are of a purely personal and unscientific character. We are dealing here with "universal inner experience."[18]

An attempt to deny the action axiom involves us in blatant self-contradiction. Denial consists of the use of means (arguments) to achieve ends (conclusions) and, hence, purposeful behavior. In addition, the assumption that men act is a necessary prerequisite for the existence of a scientific community. Arguments, attempts to convince other researchers of a different view, etc., are all fundamentally based on a conception of scientists themselves as engaging in purposeful behavior. To separate out the scientists, and say that while the observers engage in action and the observed do not, would seem to be an artificiality for which no support could be adduced.

While the action axiom is empirical and self-evident, it is, in a sense, also a priori.[19] That man acts is logically prior to any concrete manifestation of action. In fact, one must have a *concept* of action before one can even recognize action in the so-called real world. The action axiom is derived from absolutely certain inner experience but is a priori to historical phenomena. History, as a complex of human behavior, is analyzed and interpreted by use of praxeological theorems which are, in turn, derived from relatively simple experience.

Praxeology concerns the *form* of action *qua* action. Just because it is not about this specific action or that specific action does not mean that it concerns itself only with words. The category of action is about every action that has and will take place emptied of its specific means-ends content. As such, it is no less about "reality" than any generally recognized empirical statement. All statements about the world involve some degree of abstraction, so it is not the abstraction of praxeological deductions which is at issue. What may be of concern is that they are incapable of falsification. *In principle* the statement "man acts" cannot be falsified since we cannot conceive of the contrary. This is not because we are simply dealing with an arbitrary stipulated definition of "man" as an acting being. Rather, it is because our acquaintance with empirical man as acting is both so intimate and necessary that a purely reacting being would not be human in the only sense we can conceive. The concepts of purposeful behavior and man are linked so tightly not because of arbitrary definition, but because they are necessarily linked in empirical reality. Our language reflects something real, yet necessary.

Praxeology as applied to history (broadly viewed as to include current history) does not depend merely on deductions from the action axiom. It requires subsidiary assumptions derived empirically in order to delimit the scope of a praxeological system.[20] For example, we do not want to develop monetary theory in a world without money. Now, the subsidiary empirical assumptions are not self-evident or necessarily true like the action axiom. These assumptions could conceivably be otherwise, although they may be virtually certain (e.g., the existence of indirect exchange). Insofar as they are uncertain, so too is the applicability of the praxeological statements we can make using them.

To increase the quantitative definiteness of relationships in applied praxeology (economic history), we require increasing specificity of the subsidiary assumptions: These assumptions must become both more numerous and more precise. This, of course, results in conclusions which are no longer apodictically certain. In our terminology, we refer to applied praxeological theory as hypotheses (to indicate their tentative nature). Hence, while economic *theory* is immutable and necessary, economic *hypotheses* are changeable and could be otherwise. The view that economic *theory* is a body of tentative statements about the world (subject to refutation) is implicitly the position that knowledge of social reality is confined solely to historical knowledge.

VII. The Role of Econometrics

While it might appear as if econometrics has no role in the advancement of economic theory (defined as deductions from the action axiom), this is not quite accurate (although it may serve as a tolerable first approximation of the truth). Statistical regularities can be the starting point for a purely theoretical investigation, insofar as they raise questions to which the praxeologist addresses himself. But the connection here is more suggestive than logical.

The central role of econometrics is in the application of economic theory to the complex phenomena of history (current or past). There are two questions on which econometric work can shed light:

1. To what extent is a given (historical) instance of human behavior explicable by reference to purposeful activity, i.e., how much does a praxeological hypothesis explain?

2. What is the magnitude of the effect of x on the whole complex phenomenon, y, at some specific point in time?

With regard to the first question, it is important to understand that while man necessarily acts, it does not follow that he *always* acts, i.e., that he *never* engages in automatic response to stimuli or some other kind of nonpurposive behavior. To what extent is a given historical phenomenon the result of some blind emotion aiming at nothing? The answer to this cannot be given a priori.[21]

On the second question, it is important to keep in mind that praxeological reasoning per se cannot reveal quantitative relations (or even qualitative ones, when many conflicting forces are operative) in economic history. For this, statistical investigations are our only recourse. However, it is important *not* to interpret econometrically derived relations as great constants applicable to all situations at all times. These relations are not theoretical but merely historical. To extrapolate the latter to the former requires an inductive leap that we are not prepared to take.

In answering both of these questions, econometric evidence cannot, of course, give us the same certainty as praxeological reasoning. Answers in economic history must always be uncertain. Nevertheless, this is not the uncertainty of economic theory; rather, it is the uncertainty inherent in the application of a structure (involving the *form* of action) upon historicotemporal actions with specific content. The application of theory to history is not an exercise in deduction; it necessitates the use of judgment or understanding (*verstehen*) in defining the relevant variables and the appropriate means of measuring them.

A *caveat* is, however, in order. Econometrics ought to be only one tool in the apprehension of historical phenomena. Clearly, not all issues of interest are quantifiable. If we try to explain complex phenomena only by reference to quantifiable variables, then we are likely to be throwing away some information that we do, indeed, have. Another danger is that we shall begin to identify reality with statistical data when, in fact, it is just one aspect of reality, a particular transformation of more elementary experience. There is no reason whatever why a specific way of viewing history ought to be identified with history itself or, what is worse, with the whole of social reality.

VIII. Conclusions and Unresolved Questions

The purpose of this paper is primarily to present a critical analysis of "positive economics" and only secondarily to examine the praxeologic alternative. It is in the latter area that a great deal of work needs to be done. At this point, however, a number of concluding observations might be made:

1. A thoroughgoing positivist approach to economics cannot be consistently pursued. The positivist frame-

work creates certain problems that are insoluble from within that framework.

2. Although praxeology is concerned with action *qua* action, i.e., ahistorical and emptied of specific means-ends content, it is still about reality. The *form* of action is no less real than any of the other abstractions necessary in making generally recognized empirical judgments.

3. A crucial problem in praxeology is the epistemological nature of applied praxeology (economic history). How is the transition from theoretical constructs to empirical counterparts to be made? *Verstehen* is too vague an answer.

4. Does a praxeologist do economic history differently from a positive economist? If so, in what way?

In discussing some of the more philosophical issues of economics, it has been our intention to show that the day-to-day issues of explanation, hypothesizing, and testing do not go on in a philosophical vacuum. We do not have a choice as to whether we shall make methodological decisions. Our choice, rather, is whether we shall make them explicitly, examining the various implications and subtleties of meaning, or whether we shall make them implicitly, blind to everything but technique.

References

1. Milton Friedman, "The Methodology of Positive Economics," *Essays in Positive Economics* (Chicago, 1953), p. 7.
2. See especially Karl Popper, *Logik der Forschung* (Vienna, 1935). The English translation is Karl Popper, *The Logic of Scientific Discovery* (London, 1962). Other relevant works are Rudolf Carnap, *Philosophy and Logical Syntax* (London, 1935)

and A. J Ayer, *Language, Truth and Logic*, 2nd ed. (London, 1946).

3. Stephen Toulmin, *Foresight and Understanding: An Enquiry into the Aims of Science* (Bloomington, IN, 1961), p. 28.
4. Op. cit., p. 28.
5. Some philosophers, such as Popper, make this the criterion of science, and not meaningfulness. However, such a shift does not affect the main argument since we then must return to the question of why we define "science" the way we do. See section I above.
6. Friedman, p. 11.
7. Moritz Schlick, *Gesammelte Aufsätze, 1926–1936* (Vienna, 1938), p. 179 as cited in Brand Blanshard, *Reason and Analysis* (LaSalle, IL, 1964), p. 224.
8. Blanshard, p. 229.
9. The word "contradictory" is here used in its technical sense. Hence, the statement "no inflations are caused by increases in the money supply" is *not* the contradictory of the statement in the text. This is because if "no inflations are caused by increases in the money supply" is *false*, then *either* "some inflations are (not) caused. . . . " is true or "all inflations are caused. . . . " is true. "*A* and *O* are mutual contradictories, or negations: *A* is true if and only if *O* is false." On this see W. V. Quine, *Methods of Logic*, 3rd ed. (New York, 1972), p. 84.
10. Blanshard, p. 229.
11. The general conception of this and the next section is drawn from Martin Hollis and Edward Nell, *Rational Economic Man* (Cambridge, England, 1975), *passim*. However, in many cases the train of reasoning is different (the reader should beware of assuming that the same point is being made), while in others the argument is expanded.
12. In a somewhat different context, Friedman says, "If there is one hypothesis that is consistent with the available evidence, there are always an infinite number that are." Friedman, p. 9.
13. Imre Lakatos, "Falsification and the Methodology of Scientific Research Programmes," *Criticism and the Growth of Knowledge*, Imre Lakatos and Alan Musgrave, eds. (Cambridge, England, 1970), p. 119.

14. Friedman, pp. 10, 20.
15. Lakatos, p. 118.
16. Friedman, p. 11.
17. Much of what follows in this section is from Hollis and Nell, chapter 4. However, the reader should note that our referential statements are *not* the "criterial statements" of Hollis and Nell.
18. Murray N. Rothbard, "In Defense of 'Extreme Apriorism'," *Southern Economic Journal* (January 1957), p. 318.
19. Ludwig von Mises, *Human Action*, 3rd ed. (Chicago, 1966), chapter II.
20. Op. cit., pp. 64–66.
21. For some very preliminary observations on these issues, see Murray N. Rothbard, "Praxeology: Reply to Mr. Schuller," *American Economic Review* (December, 1951), p. 945.

11

The Theoretical Understanding of Those Social Phenomena which are not a Product of Agreement or of Positive Legislation, but are Unintended Results of Historical Development

Carl Menger

§1. That the acknowledgment of social phenomena as organic structures by no means excludes the striving for the exact (the atomistic) understanding of them

The theoretical understanding of *natural* organisms, too, can be twofold: an exact one (atomistic, chemical-physical) or an empirical-realistic one (collectivistic, specifically anatomical-physiological).—The exact understanding of natural organisms is not only desired in the natural sciences, but signifies an advance over the empirical-realistic understanding.—The exact understanding of social phenomena or of a part thereof can, accordingly, not be inadmissible because the phenomena concerned are viewed as so-called "social organisms."—The circumstance that the exact understanding of natural organisms and of their functions has been successful

Reprinted from *Investigations into the Method of the Social Sciences with Special Reference to Economics*, edited by Louis Schneider, translated by Francis J. Nock (New York and London: New York University Press, 1985), pp. 139–59.

only in part up to now does not prove that this goal is unattainable in respect to the so-called social organisms.—The theory that "organisms" are indivisible units and their functions are vital expressions of these these structures in their totality does not establish an objection to the exact (the atomistic!) orientation of theoretical research either in the realm of natural or of so-called social organisms.—The exact orientation of social research does not deny the real unity of social organisms; it seeks, rather, to explain their nature and origin in an exact way.—Just as little does it deny the justification for the empirical-realistic orientation of research in the realm of the above phenomena.

In the preceding chapter we dealt with the analogy between social phenomena and natural organisms, with the limits of its justification, and finally with the logical consequences resulting from this for the methodology of the social sciences. It turned out that this analogy is only a partial one and even in those respects in which it comes in question it is only a superficial one. Also, the understanding of those phenomena which do not point to a pragmatic origin, but are the result of "organic," i.e., unintended social development, can, accordingly, not be attained merely by way of analogy to natural organisms. Nor can it be attained by applying the points of view of physiology and anatomy to social research.

What remains for us now is to investigate how those problems for social research, *the solution of which is not attainable pragmatically according to the objective state of affairs* and was undertaken previously on the basis of the above analogy ("organically"), can be answered in a way adequate to the nature of social phenomena as well as to the special goals of theoretical research in the realm of the latter.

But before we go on to the examination of the pertinent

problems we should like to preface this with a few remarks of a general nature.

As we saw above, all theoretical understanding of phenomena can be the result of a double orientation of research, the *empirical-realistic* and the *exact*. This is true not only in general, but for each realm of phenomena in particular. The understanding of the social phenomena which point to an unintended or, if one prefers, to an "organic" origin, *indeed, even the understanding of natural organisms themselves*, can also be sought in the two above orientations of research. Only their combination can procure for us the deepest theoretical understanding of the phenomena considered here which is attainable in our age.

With this, of course, it is not stated that both kinds of theoretical understanding are *actually* attained in all realms of phenomena similarly. Nor is it stated that they can even definitely be designated as *attainable*, considering the present state of the theoretical sciences of the organic world. However, as a postulate of research the exact understanding of phenomena stands equally justified beside the realistic-empirical understanding in all realms of phenomena, in that of "organic social structures" no less than in that of natural organisms. It is possible that the exact analysis of natural organisms will never be *completely* successful and that realistic-empirical research, at least in certain respects, will always remain indispensable to theoretical understanding. It is possible that the physical-chemical (atomistic!) understanding of them will never attain *exclusive* dominance, simply for this reason. The empirical-realistic view of the organic world is a justified one at present. Perhaps it is one which along with the atomistic one will never lose its justification.

But only a person who is completely unfamiliar with the present state of theoretical research in the realm of natural organisms could draw the conclusion that the striving for the exact (atomistic) understanding of natural organisms is in general an unjustified one, or even an unscientific one. "Physiology," says Helmholtz, "in research into life processes, had to decide to take into account that natural forces adhere to laws without exception. It had to mean business in the pursuit of physical and chemical processes which take place within the organisms." And another outstanding scholar finds that the physical-chemical understanding of organic phenomena is really a measure for the development of the theoretical sciences of the organic world.

As has been said, the exact analysis of natural organisms has been only partly successful; it will perhaps never be *completely* successful. But it would mean being blind to the advances of the exact natural sciences if one refused to recognize the great things that have been accomplished already in the above respect or the successes of "atomism" in the realm of natural organisms, or if one wanted to designate as an unscientific aberration aspiration directed toward exact understanding of the organic world.

Even those who cling to the theory of the strict analogy of social phenomena and natural organisms cannot reject the atomistic orientation of research in the field of the social sciences. On the contrary, just those people who ceaselessly speak of this analogy ought logically to share the aspiration of the natural scientist to achieve exact (atomistic!) understanding of the organic world. They should be farthest removed from a one-sided estimation of the realistic-empirical orientation of research. Accordingly, the problem with which we plan to be occupied in this chapter may simply be designated as one of the "organic" world—the fact is thereby in no way changed that the exact understanding of the above social structures and their functions is a justified aim of theoretical research along with the empirical-realistic understanding. *The acknowledgment of a number of social phenomena as "organisms" is in no way in contradiction to the aspiration for exact (atomistic!) understanding of them.*

But what is to be said of the procedure of those who,

because exact understanding has been attained *only incompletely* in the realm of natural organisms, draw the conclusion that the desire for it is unjustified, even unscientific, in the realm of social phenomena, which really can be designated only figuratively as organisms? On the contrary, is it not clear that even when exact understanding of natural organisms is simply unattainable, or even inadequate in this realm of the empirical world, the same understanding would not at all be necessarily out of the question in the realm of social phenomena? Is it not clear, rather, that the question whether such understanding would be possible can never be answered except by an original investigation taking the nature of social phenomena directly into consideration? That it can never be answered by a superficial analogy?[1]

If the opinion has nonetheless found so many representatives in modern sociological literature that only the "organic" view, more correctly the "collectivist" view, is the justified one in the realm of social phenomena, or that it is the "higher" one as opposed to the exact one, the basis for this is a misunderstanding that will be refuted here briefly on account of its importance in principle.

A widespread objection to the exact solution of theoretical problems in the realm of social phenomena is derived from the circumstance that social structures, like natural organisms, are indivisible units; in respect to their parts they are higher units; their functions, however, are vital manifestations of the organic structures in their totality. Therefore the desire for an exact interpretation of their nature and their functions, the "atomistic" point of view in the theories of the organic world, means *a failure to recognize their unitary nature.*

We have already stressed that this view is by no means shared in the realm of natural research, since the exact interpretation of organic phenomena is numbered among the highest aims of modern natural research. At this point we should not like to neglect to supply the proof that this view is untenable in the field of social research, that it is, indeed, one which has an error in principle as its basis.

The sciences in their totality have the task of offering us the understanding of all realities; the theoretical sciences have especially that of offering the theoretical understanding of the real world. This, as is obvious, is also true of those theoretical sciences whose realm is the investigation of organisms. They could, however, fulfill this task only imperfectly if they were to leave unobserved the real unity of the phenomena discussed here, if they were to make us aware of these only as a juxtaposition of parts and not as a *whole*, and if they failed to make us aware of the functions of organisms as functions of organisms in their totality.

From the circumstance that organisms present themselves to us in each case as units and their functions as vital manifestations of them in their totality, it by no means follows that the exact orientation of research is in general inadequate for the realm of phenomena discussed here. It does not follow that *only* the realistic-empirical orientation of theoretical research is adequate for this group of phenomena. The actual consequence of the above circumstance for theoretical research in the realm of organisms is that it establishes a number of problems for exact research, and the solution of these cannot be avoided by exact research. These problems are the exact interpretation of the nature and origin of organisms (thought of as units) and the exact interpretation of their functions.

The exact orientation of research in the realm of the organic world does not thus deny the unity of organisms. It tries, rather, to explain the origin and the functions of these unified structures in an exact way, to explain how these "real unities" have come about and how they function.

This problem, which is one of the most advanced problems of modern natural research, is undertaken by the exact orientation of research in the realm of social phenomena also, and especially in the realm of those which are presented to us as the unintended product of historical development. Here, too, the failure to recognize the "unity" of social organisms. to the extent that it corresponds to real conditions, cannot come into question. What the exact orientation of research strives for is on the one hand the clarification of the special nature of the "unity" of those structures which are designated as social organisms. On the other, it strives for the exact explanation of their origin and their function. It does not give way to the illusion that this unity can be comprehended merely by analogy to natural organisms. Rather, it tries to establish its unified nature by direct investigation, by consideration of "social organisms." It is not content with wanting to understand the functions of the social structures discussed here by means of the above analogy. Instead, it strives for their exact understanding without any consideration of analogies, the inadmissibility of which it clarifies instead. It tries to achieve for the social sciences by direct investigation of social structures the same thing that the exact orientation of theoretical research in the realm of natural organisms strives for, the exact understanding of the so-called "social organisms" and their functions. It opposes the understanding of social structures on the basis of mere analogies, however, for *general, methodological* reasons, the same ones for which physiology, for example, had to reject the "politico-economical" understanding of human organisms as a principle of research. It rejects the opinion that theoretical problems which as yet have not been solved in the realm of natural research or which appear insoluble to our age are likewise to be characterized as insoluble a priori in the realm of social research. Rather, it investigates those problems without considering the results of physiology and anatomy, in the mere light of social structures themselves, just like physiology, which in its striving for the empirical or the exact understanding of natural organisms is not concerned with the results of social research. However, none of this is the result of the failure to recognize the unified nature of social organisms, but comes about for general methodological reasons.[1a]

The opinion that the unified nature of those social structures which are designated as "social organisms" excludes the exact (atomistic!) interpretation of them is thus a crude misunderstanding.

But in the following we will deal first with the exact understanding of "social organisms" and their functions, then with the realistic-empirical understanding of them.

§2. The various orientations of theoretical research which are the consequence of viewing social phenomena as "organic" structures

A portion of the social structures is of pragmatic origin and must thus be interpreted pragmatically.—Another portion is the unintended result of social development (of "organic" origin!) and the pragmatic interpretation of this is inadmissible.—The major problem of the theoretical interpretation of the origin of the social structures arising unintentionally ("organically").—The above problem and the most important problems of theoretical economics exhibit a close relationship.— Two other problems of the theoretical social sciences in general and of theoretical economics in particular, which come from the "organic" view of social phenomena: (a) the effort to understand the reciprocal conditioning of social phenomena; (b) the effort to understand social phenomena as functions and vital manifestations of society (or of economy, etc.) as an organic unit.—The striving for the exact (atomistic!) solution of the above problems and for the empirical-realistic (collectivistic, anatomical-physiological!) solution.— Plan of the presentation.

There are a number of social phenomena which are products of the agreement of members of society, or of positive legislation, results of the purposeful common activity of society thought of as a separate active subject. These are social phenomena, in connection with which there can properly be no thought of an "organic" origin in any admissible sense. Here the interpretation appropriate to the real state of affairs is the *pragmatic* one—the explanation of the nature and origin of social phenomena from the intentions, opinions, and available instrumentalities of human social unions or their rulers.

We interpret these phenomena *pragmatically* by investigating the aims which in the concrete case have guided the social unions, or their rulers, in the establishment and advancement of the social phenomena under discussion here. We investigate the aids which have been at their disposal in this case, the obstacles which have worked against the creation and development of those social structures, the way and manner in which the available aids were used for establishing them. We fulfill this task so much the more perfectly the more we examine the *ultimate* real aims of the active subjects on the one hand, and the most *original* means which they had at their command on the other, and the more we come to understand the social phenomena referring back to a pragmatic origin as links in a chain of regulations for the realization of the above aims. We make use of historical-pragmatic criticism of social phenomena of the above type when in each concrete case we test the real aims of the social unions or of their rulers by the needs of the social unions in question, when we test the application of the aids to social action, on the other hand, by the limitations of success (the fullest satisfaction possible of the social needs).

All this is true of those social phenomena which refer back to a pragmatic origin. Another portion of them, however, is not the result of agreement of members of society or of legislation, as we have already explained. Language, religion, law, even the state itself, and, to mention a few economic social phenomena, the phenomena of markets, of competition, of money, and numerous other social structures are already met with in epochs of history where we cannot properly speak of a purposeful activity of the community as such directed at establishing them. Nor can we speak of such activity on the part of the rulers. We are confronted here with the appearance of social institutions which to a high degree serve the welfare of society. Indeed, they are not infrequently of vital significance for the latter and yet are not the result of communal social activity. It is here that we meet a noteworthy, perhaps the most noteworthy, problem of the social sciences:

How can it be that institutions which serve the common welfare and are extremely significant for its development come into being without a common will[i] *directed toward establishing them?*

With this the problem is by no means exhausted of the theoretical interpretation of those social phenomena which do not refer back to a pragmatic origin in the above sense. There are a number of extremely significant social phenomena which are of "organic" origin in exactly the same sense as the previously characterized social structures. However, because they do not appear in their respective concrete forms as social "institutions" such as law, money markets, etc., they cannot be grouped in common as "organic structures" and interpreted accordingly.

Here we could point to a long series of phenomena of this kind. We intend, however, to set forth the above idea by an example that is so striking that it excludes any doubt of the meaning of what we plan to present here. We mean the example of the social prices of goods. As is well known, these are in individual cases completely or at least in part the result of positive social factors, e.g., prices under the sway of tax and wage laws, etc. But, as a rule, these are formed and changed free of any state influence directed toward regulating them, free of any social agreement, as unintended results of social movement. The same thing holds true of interest on capital, ground rents, speculative profits, etc.

What is the nature of all the above social phenomena—this is the question of importance for our science—and how can we arrive at a full understanding of their nature and their movement?

The remark is hardly needed that the problem of the origin of unintentionally created social structures and that of the formation of those economic phenomena that we have just mentioned exhibit an extremely close relationship. Law, language, the state, money, markets, all these social structures in their various empirical forms and in their constant change are to no small extent the unintended result of social development. The prices of goods, interest rates, ground rents, wages, and a thousand other phenomena of social life in general and of economy in particular exhibit exactly the same peculiarity. Also, understanding of them cannot be "pragmatic" in the cases considered here. It must be analogous to the understanding of unintentionally created social institutions. The solution of the most important problems of the theoretical social sciences in general and of theoretical economics in particular is thus closely connected with the question of theoretically understanding the origin and change of "organically" created social structures.

Here we must mention two more problems of the theoretical social sciences which likewise are rooted in the organic view of social phenomena.

It was already stressed above, where we talked of the analogy between natural organisms and the individual structures of social life in general and of economy in particular, that the observer of the latter is struck by an aggregate of institutions. Each one of these serves the normal function of the whole, conditions, and influences it, and in turn is conditioned and influenced by it in its normal nature and its normal function. Also in a number of social phenomena we meet with the appearance of the reciprocal conditioning of the whole and its normal functions and the parts, and vice versa. As a natural result of this fact we are met with a special orientation of social research which has the task of making us aware of this reciprocal conditioning of social phenomena.

In addition to the above-characterized orientation of theoretical social research another one closely related to that just presented could be designated as "organic." It is the one that tries to make us understand economic phenomena as functions, as vital manifestations of the whole of economy (the latter thought of as an organic unit!). It thus stands in a relationship, not to be discussed in any more detail, to certain problems of theoretical research in the realm of natural organisms.

All these orientations of research resulting from the organic view of society (or of economy) and the theoretical principles adequate for them can justly attract the interest of social philosophers. The empirical-realistic (the specifically physiological) orientations of research have most recently, however, been developed so comprehensively, especially in Germany, that we can properly dispense with a detailed presentation of them and confine ourselves to the *exact* interpretation of the so-called organic social structures. Thus, in the following we will deal with the striving for the exact understanding of unintentionally created social structures, both those which are commonly acknowledged to be "organisms" and those that have not had their "organic" character sufficiently stressed as yet. But we will preface the pertinent discussions with a survey of the chief attempts which have thus far been undertaken to solve the problems resulting from the organic view of social phenomena.

§3. The previous attempts to solve the problems resulting from the organic view of social phenomena

Pragmatism as a universal mode of explaining the origin and change of social phenomena.—Contradiction between it and the teaching of history.—The interpretation of the *origin* of unintentionally created social structures by characterizing them as "organic," as "original."—Aristotle's opinion.—The striving for the organic understanding of the *alterations* of social phenomena.—The conception of them as functions and vital manifestations of real social organisms (of society, of economy, etc.) in their totality.—The striving for the understanding of the reciprocal conditioning of social phenomena.—The physiological-anatomical orientation of social research.

The most obvious idea for arriving at understanding of social institutions, of their nature, and of their movement was to explain them as the result of human calculation aimed at their establishment and formation, to attribute them to agreement between people or to acts of positive legislation. This (pragmatic) approach was not adequate to real conditions and was thoroughly unhistorical. It still offered the advantage of interpreting from a common, easily understood point of view all social institutions, both those which are presented to us actually as the result of the common will of socially organized human beings and those in which such origin is not detectable. This is an advantage which will be underestimated by no one who is familiar with scientific works and knows the history of their development.

The contradiction to the facts of history in which the above merely formally satisfactory approach (stressing the exclusively *pragmatic* origin of the cause and change of social phenomena) stands brought it about nevertheless that a number of mostly meaningless attempts were undertaken in scientific investigations into the problem treated here. Along with the pragmatic, obviously one-sided mode of interpretation, and indeed, partially in direct opposition to it, there were attempts which document quite well the inadequacy of the previous "organic" views of social phenomena.

In this category belong above all the attempts of those who think that they have solved the problem involved merely by designating as "organic" the developmental process we are discussing. The process by which social structures originate without action of the common will may well be called "organic," but it must not be believed that even the smallest part of the noteworthy problem of the social sciences that we alluded to above has been solved by this image or by any mystic allusions attached to it.

Just as meaningless is another attempt to solve the problem discussed here. I mean the theory, which has attained widespread currency, that recognizes in social institutions something *original,* that is, not something that has developed, but an *original* product of the life of the people. This theory (which, incidentally, is also applied by a few of its adherents, for whom a unified principle means more than historical truth or the logic of things, by way of a peculiar mysticism to social institutions created by positive laws) indeed avoids the error of those who reduce all institutions to acts of positive common will. Still, it obviously offers us no solution of the problem discussed here, but evades it. The origin of a phenomenon is by no means explained by the assertion that it *was present from the very beginning* or that it *developed originally.* Aside from the question of the historical establishment of this theory, it involves a paradox with respect to every complicated phenomenon. Such a phenomenon must obviously have developed at some time from its simpler elements; a social phenomenon, at least in its most original form, must clearly have developed from individual factors.[2] The view here referred to is merely an analogy between the development of social institutions and that of natural organisms which is completely worthless for the purpose of solving our problem. It states, to be sure, that institutions are unintended creations of the human mind, but not *how* they came about. These attempts at interpretation are comparable to the procedure of a natural scientist who thinks he is solving the problem of the origin of natural organisms by alluding to their "originality," "natural growth," or their "primeval nature."

The previous attempts to interpret the *changes* of social phenomena as "organic processes" are no less inadmissible than the above theories which aim to solve "organically" the problem of the *origin* of unintentionally created social structures. There is hardly need to remark that the changes of social phenomena cannot be interpreted in a social-pragmatic way, insofar as they are not the intended result of the agreement of members of society or of positive legislation, but are the unintended product of social development. But it is just as obvious that not even the slightest insight into the nature and the laws of the movement of social phenomena can be gained either by the mere allusion to the "organic" or the "primeval" character of the processes under discussion, nor even by mere analogies between these and the transformations to be observed in natural organisms. The worthlessness of the above orientation of research is so clear that we do not care to add anything to what we have already said.

If this significant problem of the social sciences is truly to be solved, this cannot be done by way of superficial and, for the most part, inadmissible analogies.[3] It can be done, in any case, only by way of direct consideration of social phenomena, not "organically," "anatomically," or "physiologically," but only in a *specifically sociological* way. The road to this, however, is *theoretical* social research, the nature and main orientations of which (the exact and the empirical-realistic) we have characterized above.

We should further like to mention an orientation of social research at this point which is likewise in the sphere of the "organic" approach to social phenomena. We mean the striving to understand their *reciprocal conditioning*. This orientation of research has at its basis the idea of a "mutual causation" of social phenomena. The value of this idea for a deeper theoretical understanding of such phenomena, as we have already stated in another place,[4] is not entirely beyond question. Nonetheless, this approach is one so close to common understanding that it justly can claim the respect of social scientists, at least as long as the exact understanding of more complicated social phenomena has not yet been gained.

It would be an error to conceive of the above approach as the only justified one or even, as many want it, "*the* method" of the social sciences. It would be just as wrong, however, voluntarily to fail to recognize its significance and its usefulness for the theoretical understanding of social phenomena in general.[5]

The name that is applied to this orientation of research is a matter of terminology and thus without objective importance from the standpoint of methodology. But we still believe that it could, for lack of a better expression, be designated as "organic" or "physiological-anatomical," in consideration of a certain similarity, even if not a fully clarified one, to certain orientations of theoretical research in the realm of natural organisms. Only, it must be kept firmly in mind that the expressions here in question are merely symbolic and that really a specifically *sociological* orientation of theoretical research is designated by them which would have its objective justification even if sciences of natural organisms in general and anatomy and physiology in particular did not exist at all. Let the orientation be called "organic" or "physiological-anatomical"; it really is still a branch of the empirical-realistic orientation of theoretical social research.

§4. The exact (atomistic) understanding of the origin of those social structures which are the unintended result of social development

Introduction. Course of the presentation.—(a) The *origin* of *money:* The phenomenon of money.—Characteristics of it.—The theory that money originated through agreement or law.—Plato, Aristotle, the jurist Paulus.—Insufficiency of this theory.—Exact explanation of the origin of money.—(b) *The origin of a number of other social institutions:* The genesis of localities, of states.—The genesis of the division of labor, of markets.—Influence of legislation.—Exact explanation of the origin of the above social structures.—(c) *Concluding remarks:* General nature of the social-pragmatic origin of social phenomena and of their so-called "organic" origin: the contrast between these.—The methods for the exact understanding of the origin of "organically" created social structures and those for the solution of the main problems of exact economics are the same.

Introduction

In the preceding section I have presented the previous attempts to solve our problem and alluded to their insufficiency. If there is to be any question of a serious solution, it must be sought in other ways than the previous ones.

But I will first present the theory of the origin of the social structures under discussion here by way of a few examples, that of the genesis of money, of states, of markets, etc., and thus by the genesis of social institutions which serve social interests to a high degree and the first origins of which in the great majority of cases can in no way be traced back to positive laws or other expressions of intentional common will.

(a) The Origin of Money[6]

In the markets of nearly all nations which have advanced to the barter stage in their economic culture certain goods are gradually accepted in barter by everyone in return for wares brought to market. Initially, according to varying conditions, these are heads of cattle, hides, cowrie shells, cocoa beans, tea tiles, etc.; with advancing culture they are metals in the uncoined state, then in the coined state. They are, indeed, accepted even by people who have no immediate need for these goods or have already covered this need sufficiently. In a word, in trade markets certain wares emerge from the sphere of all the others and become means of barter, "money" in the broadest sense of the word. This is a phenomenon that from the beginning social philosophers have had the greatest difficulties in understanding. That in a market an item is readily turned over by its owner for another that seems more useful to him is a phenomenon which is clear to the meanest understanding. But that in a market anyone who offers goods for sale is ready to turn these over for a definite other item, that is, according to varying conditions, for cattle, cocoa beans, certain amounts by weight of copper or silver, even when he has no direct need for these goods or has completely satisfied his possible need for them, while he nevertheless rejects certain other goods under the same presupposition—this is a paradoxical procedure. It is so contradictory to the sense of the individual oriented simply to this own interest, that we must not be astonished when it seemed really mysterious even to so excellent a thinker as Savigny and its explanation by individual human interests appeared impossible to him.[7]

The problem which science has to solve here consists in the explanation of a *social* phenomenon, of a homogeneous way of acting on the part of the members of a community for which public motives are recognizable, but for which in the concrete case individual motives are hard to discern. The idea of tracing these back to an agreement or to a legislative act was fairly obvious, especially with respect to the later coin form of money. Plato thought money was "an *agreed-upon* token for barter,"[8] and Aristotle said that money came abut through *agreement,* not by nature, but by *law.*[9] The jurist Paulus[10] and with few exceptions the medieval theoreticians on coined money down to the economists of our day are of a similar opinion.[11]

It would be an error to reject the opinion as wrong in principle, for history actually offers us examples that certain wares have been declared money by law. To be sure, it must not be overlooked that in most of these cases the legal stipulation demonstrably had the purpose not so much of introducing a certain item as money, but rather the acknowledgment of an item which had already become money. Nonetheless, it is certain that the institution of money, like other social institutions, can be introduced by agreement or legislation, especially when new communities are formed from the elements of an old culture, e.g., in colonies. Moreover, there is no doubt that the future development of such institutions takes place as a rule in the latter way in times of higher economic culture. Therefore the above opinion has its partial justification.

It is otherwise with the understanding of the social institution discussed here when it can by no means be historically viewed as the result of legislative activity, that is, when we see that money developed from the economic conditions of a nation without such activity, "primevally," or, as others express it, "organically." Here the above, pragmatic approach is at any rate inadmissible, and the task of science is to make us understand the institution of money by presenting the process by which, as economic culture advances, a definite item or a number of items leaves the sphere of the remaining goods and becomes money, without express agreement of people and without legislative acts. This is to pose the question of how certain items turn into goods which are accepted by everyone in exchange for the goods offered for sale to him, even when he has no need for them.

The explanation of this phenomenon is given by the following considerations. As long as mere barter prevails in a nation economic individuals naturally first pursue one aim in their barterings. They exchange their excess only for goods for which they have an immediate need and reject those that they do not need at all or with which they are sufficiently supplied. For somebody who is bringing his excess to market to be able to get in exchange the goods he desires he must not only find somebody who needs his wares but also somebody who offers for sale the goods desired. This is the circumstance that presents so many obstacles to traffic when pure barter prevails and limits it to the narrowest confines.

In this state of affairs itself there lay a very effective means to do away with this untoward circumstance which is such a burden on the traffic in goods. Each individual could easily observe that there was a greater demand in the market for certain wares, namely those which fitted a very general need, than there was for others. Accordingly, among the competitors for these goods he more easily found those who offered for sale certain goods desired by him than if he went to market with less marketable wares. Thus everyone in a nomadic tribe knows from his own experience that, when he brings cattle to the market, he will more easily find among the many who try to get these goods by barter those who offer the goods he wants than if he brought another item that has only a small circle of takers. Thus every individual who brought to the market items of slight marketability in the above sense had the obvious idea of exchanging them not only for the goods he needed, but also, when these were not directly available, for others. These others were ones which he, to be sure, did not need at the moment, but which were more marketable than his. By this he did not, of course, directly attain the final goal of his planned economic operation (procuring by exchange the goods *he* needed!), but he approached it essentially. The economic interest of the economic individuals, therefore, with increased knowledge of their *individual* interests, without any agreement, without legislative compulsion, *even without any consideration of public interest,* leads them to turn over their wares for more marketable ones, even if they do not need the latter for their immediate consumer needs. Among the latter, however, as is readily evident, they again select those which are most easily and most economically suited to the function of a means of barter. Thus there appears before us under the powerful influence of custom the phenomenon to be observed everywhere with advancing economic culture that a certain number of goods are accepted in exchange by everybody. These are, with respect to time and place, the most marketable, the most easily transported, the most durable, the most easily divisible. They can, therefore, be exchanged for any other item. They are goods which our predecessors called *Geld*, from *gelten*, i.e., to perform, to "pay."ʲ

The great significance that *custom* has for the genesis of money is directly clear from the consideration of the just described process by which certain goods become money. The exchange of less marketable wares for those of greater marketability, durability, divisibility, etc., is in the interest of every *single* economic individual. But the actual closing of such an exchange operation presupposes the knowledge of this interest on the part of those economic subjects who for the sake of the above characteristics are to accept in barter for their wares an item which per se is perhaps utterly useless to them. This knowledge will never arise simultaneously with all members of a national group. Rather, at first only a number of economic subjects will recognize the advantage accruing to them. This happens because they accept in exchange other more marketable wares for their own where a direct barter of their wares for useful goods is not possible or is highly uncertain. This is an advantage *which is per se independent of the general acknowledgment of an item as money,* since such an exchange always and under all circumstances brings the economic individual considerably closer to *his* ultimate aim, the procuring of useful goods that *he* needs. But, as is well known, there is no better means to enlighten people about their economic interests than their perceiving the economic successes of those who put the right means to work for attaining them. Therefore it is also clear that nothing may have favored the genesis of money as much as the receiving of eminently marketable goods for all other goods, which had been practiced for quite a long time on the part of the most perspicacious and ablest economic subjects for their own economic advantage. Thus practice and custom have certainly contributed not a little to making the temporarily most marketable wares the ones which are received in exchange for their wares not only by many economic individuals, but ultimately by all.

Money, an institution serving the common good in the most outstanding sense of the word, can thus, as we saw, come into being legislatively, like other social institutions. But this is no more the only way than it is the most original way that money developed. This is rather to be sought in the process described above, the nature of which would be explained only imperfectly if we wanted to call it "organic," or if we wanted to designate money as something "primeval," "original," etc. It is clear, rather, that the origin of money can truly be brought to our full understanding only by our learning to understand the *social* institution discussed here as the unintended result, as the unplanned outcome of specifically *individual* efforts of members of a society.

(b) The Origin of a Number of Other Social Institutions in General and Economy in Particular

The question of the origin of a number of other social structures can be answered in a similar way. These likewise serve the common welfare, indeed, even cause it, without being regularly the result of an intention of society directed toward advancing this welfare.

The *development of new localities* takes place today only in the rarest cases because a number of people of different abilities and different professions unite with the intention of founding a locality and thereupon realize this intention by planning. To be sure, such a means of starting new settlements is not out of the question and has even been attested by experience. As a rule, however, new localities arise "unintentionally," i.e., by the mere activation of individual interests which of themselves lead to the above result furthering the common interest, i.e., without any intention really directed toward this. The first farmers who take possession of a territory, the first craftsman who settles in their midst, have as a rule only their *individual* interest in view. Likewise, the first innkeeper, the first shopkeeper, the first teacher, etc. With the increasing needs of the members of the society still other economic subjects find it advantageous to enter new professions in the gradually growing community or to practice the old ones in a more comprehensive way. Thus there gradually comes into being an economic organization which is to a high degree of benefit to the interests of the members of the community. Indeed, their normal existence finally could not be imagined without it. Yet this organization is by no means the result of the activation of the common will directed toward its establishment. This will is more likely to appear as a rule only in more advanced stages of development of communities, and it is more likely to produce, not the establishment, but the perfection of the "organically" created social structures.

A similar statement holds true for the *origin of the state.* No unprejudiced person can doubt that under favorable conditions the basis for a community capable of development can be laid by the agreement of a number of people with a territory at their disposal. Nor can it reasonably be doubted that from the natural conditions of power in the family new states capable of development could be established by individual rulers or groups of them, even without the agreement of all subjects of the new state. The theory, according to which that social structure which we call the state will simply arise "organically," is thus one-sided, at any rate. Just as erroneous, indeed to a still greater degree unhistorical, is the theory that all states originally came into being *by an agreement directed toward establishing them* or by the conscious activity of individual rulers or groups of rulers directed toward this aim. For it can scarcely be doubted that at least in the earliest epochs of human development states developed in the following way. Family heads joined by no political bond and living side by side came to have a state community and organization even if it was undeveloped at first. They did this without special agreement, merely because they progressively recognized their *individual* interests and endeavored to pursue them (by voluntary subjection of the weaker to the protection of the stronger, by the effective aid which neighbor gave to neighbor in those cases in which the latter was to be coerced under circumstances under which the remaining inhabitants of a territory also felt threatened in their welfare, etc.). Conscious agreement and power relationships of different kinds directed toward the goal of strengthening communities as such may actually have aided this process of state formation in particular cases. The correct recognition and the activation of the *individual* interests on the part of individual family heads living side by side have certainly in other cases led to state formation even without the above influences, indeed even without any consideration of the common interest by individuals. That social structure, too, which we call the state, has been the unintended result of efforts serving individual interests, at least in its most original forms.

In the same way it might be pointed out that other

social institutions, language, law,[12] morals, but especially numerous institutions of economy, have come into being without any express agreement, without legislative compulsion, even without any consideration of public interest, merely through the impulse of *individual* interests and as a result of the activation of these interests. The organization of the traffic in goods in markets which recur periodically and are held in definite localities, the organization of society by separation of professions and the division of labor, trade customs, etc., are nothing but institutions which most eminently serve the interests of the common good and whose origin seems at first glance to be based necessarily on agreement or state power. They are, however, not the result of agreement, contract, law, or special consideration of the public interest by individuals, but the result of efforts serving individual interests.

It is clear that legislative compulsion not infrequently encroaches upon this "organic" developmental process and thus accelerates or modifies the results. The unintended genesis of social phenomena may factually be the exclusively decisive genesis for the first beginnings of social formation. In the course of social development the purposeful encroachment of public powers on social conditions becomes more and more evident. Along with the "organically" created institutions there go those which are the result of purposeful social action. Institutions which came about organically find their continuation and reorganization by means of the purposeful activity of public powers applied to social aims. The present-day system of money and markets, present-day law, the modern state, etc., offer just as many examples of institutions which are presented to us as the result of the combined effectiveness of individually and socially teleological powers, or, in other words, of "organic" and "positive" factors.

(c) Concluding Remarks

We might ask now about the general nature of the process to which those social phenomena owe their origin which are not the result of socially teleological factors, but are the unintended result of social movement. This is a process, which in contrast to the genesis of social phenomena by way of positive legislation, can still be designated as "organic." The answer to the above question can scarcely be in doubt any longer.

The characteristic element in the socially teleological genesis of social phenomena is in the intention of society as such directed toward establishing these phenomena, under the circumstance that they are the intended result of the common will of society, thought of as an acting subject, or of its rulers. The social phenomena of "organic" origin, on the other hand, are characterized by the fact that they present themselves to us as the unintended result of individual efforts of members of society, i.e., of efforts in pursuit of individual interests. Accordingly, in contrast to the previously characterized social structures, they are, to be sure, the unintended social result of individually teleological factors.

But in the preceding we believe we have not only presented the true nature of that process to which a large part of social phenomena owe their origin, a nature which has up to now been characterized merely by vague analogies or by meaningless phrases. We believe we have also come to another result which is important for the methodology of the social sciences.

We already alluded above to the fact that a large number of the phenomena of economy which cannot usually be viewed as "organically" created "social structures," e.g., market prices, wages, interest rates, etc., have come into existence in exactly the same way as those social institutions which we mentioned in the preceding section.[13] For they, too, as a rule are not the result of socially teleological causes, but the unintended result of innumerable efforts of economic subjects pursuing *individual* interests. The theoretical understanding of them, the theoretical understanding of their nature and their movement can thus be attained in an exact manner only in the same way as the understanding of the above-mentioned social structures. That is, it can be attained by reducing them to their elements, to the *individual* factors of their causation, and by investigating the laws by which the complicated phenomena of human economy under discussion here are built up from these elements. This, however, as scarcely needs saying, is that method which we have characterized above[14] as the one adequate for the exact orientation of theoretical research in the realm of social phenomena in general. The methods for the exact understanding of the origin of the "organically" created social structures and those for the solution of the main problems of exact economics are by nature identical.

Notes

1. The ultimate elements to which the exact theoretical interpretation of natural phenomena must be reduced are "atoms" and "forces." Neither is of empirical nature. We cannot imagine "atoms" at all, and natural forces only by a representation, and by these we really understand merely unknown causes of real motions. From this there arise ultimately quite extraordinary difficulties for the exact interpretation of natural phenomena. It is otherwise in the exact social sciences. Here the human *individuals* and their *efforts,* the final elements of our analysis are of empirical nature, and thus the exact theoretical social sciences have a great advantage over the exact natural sciences. The "limits of knowledge of nature" and the difficulties resulting from this for the theoretical understanding of natural phenomena do not really exist for exact research in the realm of social phenomena.[h] When A. Comte conceives of "societies" as real organisms and to be sure as organisms of a more complicated nature than the natural ones and des-

ignates their theoretical interpretation as the incomparably more complicated and more difficult scientific problem, he exposes himself forthwith to a serious error. His theory would be correct only as against sociologists who might get the idea, which is really insane in the light of the present state of the theoretical natural sciences, of wanting to interpret social phenomena not in a specifically sociological way, but in the atomistic way of the natural sciences.

(h.) The view expressed in the last two sentences is an extremely interesting one in the history of social science. It is worth noting that Max Weber was later specifically critical of the type of "organicism" represented by Wilhelm Roscher, on the ground that it involved the view that the task of analyzing social "organisms" is more difficult than that of analyzing natural "organisms." Weber agrees with Menger that the task of the social sciences is in principle easier on account of the accessibility to them of the inner life of the individual human units of society. See Max Weber, *Gesammelte Aufsatze zur Wissenschaftslehre,* 2nd ed. (Tubingen: J. C. B. Mohr [Paul Siebeck], 19 1), p. 35, footnote 1. L.S.

1a. The "organic" view—more correctly, the "collectivist" view— of economy neither forms a contrast to the problems of theoretical political economy in general, nor does it comprise the totality of the tasks of the latter. It is nothing else than a part, a particular aspect of the science which teaches us to understand the phenomena of economy in theory. The acknowledgment of it is nothing which could nullify or in any way alter the concept of economics as a theoretical science. Also, the acknowledgment of the "organic" view of economy cannot change our science into either a historical or practical one, nor can it change it to a science of the mere "organic" understanding of human economy (to a mere "anatomy and physiology").

(i.) The words "common will" (*Gemeinwellen*) appear in boldface in the original. L.S.

2. Obviously Aristotle was unfamiliar with such nonsense, no matter how often he is alluded to as the founder of the theory that the state is something "original," that it is something

given with the existence of man itself. See Appendix VII: "The Opinion Ascribed to Aristotle That the State Is an Original Phenomenon Given Simultaneously with the Existence of Man."

3. See P. 131 ff.
4. See P. 132 ff.
5. It is here, too, that the works by A. Comte, H. Spencer, Schaffle, and Lilienfeld, which are excellent in their way, have really contributed essentially to a deepening of the theoretical understanding of social phenomena. This is furthermore the case even if we do not consider the analogies between natural organisms and structures of social life placed in the foreground of presentation by some of these authors.
6. Cf. my *Grundsatze der Volkswirthschaftslehre*, p. 250 ff., where the above theory is already presented.
7. Savigny, *Obligat.*, II, 406.
8. *De republica*, II, 12.
9. *Ethic, Nicom.*, V, 8.
10. *Dig. de contr. empt.*, Lib. 1, 18, 1.
11. Cf. the pertinent literature in my *Volkswirthschaftslehre*, p. 255 ff.

   (j.) *Geld* is the German word for "money"; it is a derivative of *gelten*, which, however, means "to compensate, to atone for." F.J.N.

   Compare Menger's own philological discussion of designations for money in his *Principles of Economics*, pp. 312–14. L. S.
12. See Appendix VIII: "The "Organic" Origin of Law and the Exact Understanding Thereof."
13. See p. 146 ff.
14. See p. 60 ff.

Part III

The Austrian View of the Market Process

12

Logical Catallactics versus Mathematical Catallactics

Ludwig von Mises

The problems of prices and costs have been treated also with mathematical methods. There have even been economists who held that the only appropriate method of dealing with economic problems is the mathematical method and who derided the logical economists as "literary" economists.

If this antagonism between the logical and the mathematical economists were merely a disagreement concerning the most adequate procedure to be applied in the study of economics, it would be superfluous to pay attention to it. The better method would prove its preeminence by bringing about better results. It may also be that different varieties of procedure are necessary for the solution of different problems and that for some of them one method is more useful than the other.

However, this is not a dispute about heuristic questions, but a controversy concerning the foundations of economics. The mathematical method must be rejected not only on account of its barrenness. It is an entirely vicious method, starting from false assumptions and leading to fallacious inferences. Its syllogisms are not only sterile; they divert the mind from the study of the real problems and distort the relations between the various phenomena.

Reprinted from *Human Action: A Treatise on Economics* by Ludwig von Mises (New Haven: Yale University Press, 1949), pp. 347–54.

The ideas and procedures of the mathematical economists are not uniform. There are three main currents of thought which must be dealt with separately.

The first variety is represented by the statisticians who aim at discovering economic laws from the study of economic experience. They aim to transform economics into a "quantitative" science. Their program is condensed in the motto of the Econometric Society: Science is measurement.

The fundamental error implied in this reasoning has been shown above.[1] Experience of economic history is always experience of complex phenomena. It can never convey knowledge of the kind the experimenter abstracts from a laboratory experiment. Statistics is a method for the presentation of historical facts concerning prices and other relevant data of human action. It is not economics and cannot produce economic theorems and theories. The statistics of prices is economic history. The insight that, *ceteris paribus,* an increase in demand must result in an increase in prices is not derived from experience. Nobody ever was or ever will be in a position to observe a change in one of the market data *ceteris paribus.* There is no such thing as quantitative economics. All economic quantities we know about are data of economic history. No reasonable man can contend that the relations between price and supply is in general, or in respect of certain commodities, constant. We know, on the contrary, that external phenomena affect different people in different ways, that the reactions of the same people to the same external events vary, and that it is not possible to assign individuals to classes of men reacting in the same way. This insight is a product of our aprioristic theory. It is true the empiricists reject this theory; they pretend that they aim to learn only from historical experience. However, they contradict their own principles as soon as they pass beyond the unadulterated recording of individual single prices and begin to construct series and to compute averages. A datum of experience and a statistical fact is only a price paid at a definite time and a definite place for a definite quantity of a certain commodity. The arrangement of various price data in groups and the computation of averages are guided by theoretical deliberations which are logically and temporally antecedent. The extent to which certain attending features and circumstantial contingencies of the price data concerned are taken or not taken into consideration depends on theoretical reasoning of the same kind. Nobody is so bold as to maintain that a rise of a percent in the supply of any commodity must always—in every country and at any time—result in a fall of b percent in its price. But as no quantitative economist ever ventured to define precisely on the ground of statistical experience the special conditions producing a definite deviation from the ratio $a::b$, the futility of his endeavors is manifest. Moreover, money is not a standard for the measurement of prices; it is a medium whose exchange ratio varies in the same way, although as a rule not with the same speed and to the same extent, in which the mutual exchange ratios of the vendible commodities and services vary.

There is hardly any need to dwell longer upon the exposure of the claims of quantitative economics. In spite of all the high-sounding pronouncements of its advocates, nothing has been done for the realization of its program. The late Henry Schultz devoted his research to the measurement of elasticities of demand for various commodities. Professor Paul H. Douglas has praised the outcome of Schultz's studies as "a work as necessary to help make economics a more or less exact science as was the determination of atomic weights for the development of chemistry."[2] The truth is that Schultz never embarked upon a determination of the elasticity of demand for any commodity as such; the data he relied upon were limited to certain geographical areas and historical periods. His results for a definite commodity, for instance potatoes, do not refer to potatoes in general, but to potatoes in the United States in the years from 1875 to 1929.[3] They are, at best, rather questionable and unsatisfactory contributions to various chapters of economic history. They are certainly not steps toward the realization of the confused and contradictory program of quantitative economics. It must be emphasized that the two other varieties of mathematical economics are fully aware of the futility of quantitative economics. For they have never ventured to make any magnitudes as found by the econometricians enter into their formulas and equations and thus to adapt them for the solution of particular problems. There is in the field of human action no means of dealing with future events other than that provided by understanding.

The second field treated by mathematical economists is that of the relation of prices and costs. In dealing with these problems the mathematical economists disregard the operation of the market process and moreover pretend to abstract from the use of money inherent in all economic calculations. However, as they speak of prices and costs in general and confront prices and costs, they tacitly imply the existence and the use of money. Prices are always money prices, and costs cannot be taken into account in economic calculation if not expressed in terms of money. If one does not resort to terms of money, costs are expressed in complex quantities of diverse goods and services to be expended for the procurement of a product. On the other hand prices—if this term is applicable at all to exchange ratios determined by barter—are the enumeration of quantities of various goods against which the "seller" can exchange a definite supply. The goods which are referred to in such "prices" are not the same to which the "costs" refer. A comparison of such prices in kind and costs in kind is not feasible. That the seller values the goods he gives away less than those he receives in exchange for them, that the seller and the buyer disagree with regard to the subjective valuation of the two goods exchanged, and that an entrepreneur embarks upon a project only if he expects to receive for the product goods that he values higher than those expended in their production, all this we know already on the ground of praxeological comprehension. It is this aprioristic knowledge that enables us to anticipate the conduct of an entrepreneur who is in a position to resort to economic calculation. But the mathematical economist deludes himself when he pretends to treat these problems in a more general way by omitting any reference to terms of money. It is vain to investigate instances of nonperfect divisibility of factors of production without reference to economic calculation in terms of money. Such a scrutiny can never go beyond the knowledge already available; namely that every entrepreneur is intent upon producing those articles the sale of which will bring him proceeds that he values higher than the total complex of goods expended in their production. But if there is no indirect exchange and if no medium of exchange is in common use, he can succeed, provided he has correctly anticipated the future state of the market, only if he is endowed with a superhuman intellect. He would have to take in at a glance all exchange ratios determined at the market in such a way as to assign in his deliberations precisely the place due to every good according to these ratios.

It cannot be denied that all investigations concerning the relation of prices and costs presuppose both the use of money and the market process. But the mathematical economists shut their eyes to this obvious fact. They formulate equations and draw curves which are supposed to describe reality. In fact they describe only a hypothetical and unrealizable state of affairs, in no way similar to the catallactic problems in question. They substitute algebraic symbols for the determinate terms of money as used in economic calculation and believe that this procedure renders their reasoning more scientific. They strongly impress the gullible layman. In fact they only confuse and muddle things which are satisfactorily dealt with in textbooks of commercial arithmetic and accountancy.

Some of these mathematicians have gone so far as to declare that economic calculation could be established on the basis of units of utility. They call their methods utility analysis. Their error is shared by the third variety of mathematical economics.

The characteristic mark of this third group is that they are openly and consciously intent upon solving catallactic problems without any reference to the market process. Their ideal is to construct an economic theory according to the pattern of mechanics. They again and again resort to analogies with classical mechanics which in their opinion is the unique and absolute model of scientific inquiry. There is no need to explain again why this analogy is superficial and misleading and in what respects purposive human action radically differs from motion, the subject matter of mechanics. It is enough to stress one point, viz., the practical significance of the differential equations in both fields.

The deliberations which result in the formulation of an equation are necessarily of a nonmathematical character. The formulation of the equation is the consummation of our knowledge; it does not directly enlarge our knowledge. Yet, in mechanics the equation can render very important practical services. As there exist constant relations between various mechanical elements and as these relations can be ascertained by experiments, it becomes possible to use equations for the solution of definite technological problems. Our modern industrial civilization is mainly an accomplishment of this utilization of the differential equations of physics. No such constant relations exist, however, between economic elements. The equations formulated by mathematical economics remain a useless piece of mental gymnastics and would remain so even if they were to express much more than they really do.

A sound economic deliberation must never forget these two fundamental principles of the theory of value: First, valuing that results in action always means preferring and setting aside; it never means equivalence. Second, there is no means of comparing the valuations of different individuals or the valuations of the same individuals at different instants other than by establishing whether or not they arrange the alternatives in question in the same order of preference.

In the imaginary construction of the evenly rotating economy all factors of production are employed in such a way that each of them renders the most valuable service. No thinkable and possible change could improve the state of satisfaction; no factor is employed for the satisfaction of a need *a* if this employment prevents the satisfaction of a need *b* that is considered more valuable than the satisfaction of *a*. It is, of course, possible to describe this imaginary state of the allocation of resources in differential equations and to visualize it graphically in curves. But such devices do not assert anything about the market process. They merely mark out an imaginary situation in which the market process would cease to operate. The mathematical economists disregard the whole theoretical elucidation of the market process and evasively amuse themselves with an auxiliary notion employed in its context and devoid of any sense when used outside of this context.

In physics we are faced with changes occurring in various sense phenomena. We discover a regularity in the sequence of these changes and these observations lead us to the construction of a science of physics. We know nothing about the ultimate forces actuating these changes. They are for the searching mind ultimately given and defy any further analysis. What we know from observation is the regular concatenation of various observable entities and attributes. It is this mutual interdependence of data that the physicist describes in differential equations.

In praxeology the first fact we know is that men are purposively intent upon bringing about some changes. It is this knowledge that integrates the subject matter of praxeology and differentiates it from the subject matter of the natural sciences. We know the forces behind the changes, and this aprioristic knowledge leads us to a cognition of the praxeological processes. The physicist does not know what electricity "is." He knows only phenomena attributed to something called electricity. But the economist knows what actuates the market process. It is only thanks to this knowledge that he is in a position to distinguish market phenomena from other phenomena and to describe the market process.

Now, the mathematical economist does not contribute anything to the elucidation of the market process. He merely describes an auxiliary makeshift employed by the logical economist as a limiting notion, the definition of a state of affairs in which there is no longer any action and the market process has come to a standstill. That is all he can say. What the logical economist sets forth in words when defining the imaginary constructions of the final state of rest and the evenly rotating economy and what the mathematical economist himself must describe in words before he embarks upon his mathematical work, is translated into algebraic symbols. A superficial analogy is spun out too long, that is all.

Both the logical and the mathematical economists assert that human action ultimately aims at the establishment of such a state of equilibrium and would reach it if all further changes in data were to cease. But the logical economist knows much more than that. He shows how the activities of enterprising men, the promoters and speculators, eager to profit from discrepancies in the price structure, tend toward eradicating such discrepancies and thereby also toward blotting out the sources of entrepreneurial profit and loss. He shows how this process would finally result in the establishment of the evenly rotating economy. This is the task of economic theory. The mathematical description of various states of equilibrium is mere play. The problem is the analysis of the market process.

A comparison of both methods of economic analysis makes us understand the meaning of the often raised request to enlarge the scope of economic science by the construction of a dynamic theory instead of the mere occupation with static problems. With regard to logical economics this postulate is devoid of any sense. Logical economics is essentially a theory of processes and changes. It resorts to the imaginary constructions of changelessness merely for the elucidation of the phenomena of change. But it is different with mathematical economics. Its equations and formula are limited to the description of states of equilibrium and nonacting. It cannot assert anything with regard to the formation of such states and their transformation into other states as long as it remains in the realm of mathematical procedures. As against mathematical economics the request for a dynamic theory is well substantiated. But there is no means for mathematical economics to comply with this request. The problems of process analysis, i.e., the only economic problems that matter, defy any mathematical approach. The introduction of time parameters into the equations is no solution. It does not even indicate the essential shortcomings of the mathematical method. The statements that every change involves time and that change is always in the temporal sequence are merely a way of expressing the fact that as far as there is rigidity and unchangeability there is no time. The main deficiency of mathematical economics is not the fact that it ignores the temporal sequence, but that it ignores the operation of the market process.

The mathematical method is at a loss to show how from a state of nonequilibrium those actions spring up which tend toward the establishment of equilibrium. It is, of course, possible to indicate the mathematical operations required for the transformation of the mathematical description of a definite state of nonequilibrium into the mathematical description of the state of equilibrium. But these mathematical operations by no means describe the market process actuated by the discrepancies in the price structure. The differential equations of mechanics are supposed to describe precisely the motions concerned at any instant of the time traveled through. The economic equations have no reference whatever to conditions as they really are in each instant of the time interval between the state of nonequilibrium and that of equilibrium. Only those entirely blinded by the prepossession that economics must be a pale replica of mechanics will underrate the weight of this objection. A very imperfect and superficial metaphor is not a substitute for the services rendered by logical economics.

In every chapter of catallactics the devastating consequences of the mathematical treatment of economics can be tested. It is enough to refer to two instances only. One is provided by the so-called equation of exchange, the mathematical economists' futile and misleading attempt to deal with changes in the purchasing power of money.[4] The second can be best expressed in referring to Professor Schumpeter's dictum according to which consumers in evaluating consumers' goods "*ipso facto* also evaluate the means of production which enter into the production of these goods."[5] It is hardly possible to construe the market process in a more erroneous way.

Economics is not about goods and services, it is about the actions of living men. Its goal is not to dwell upon imaginary constructions such as equilibrium. These constructions are only tools of reasoning. The sole task of economics is analysis of the actions of men, is the analysis of processes.

Notes

1. Cf. above, pp. 31, 55–56.
2. Cf. Paul H. Douglas in *Econometrica,* VII, 105.
3. Cf. Henry Schultz, *The Theory and Measurement of Demand* (University of Chicago Press, 1938), pp. 405–27.
4. Cf. below, p. 396.
5. Cf. Joseph A. Schumpeter, *Capitalism, Socialism and Democracy* (New York, 1942), p. 175. For a critique of this statement, cf. Hayek, "The Use of Knowledge in Society," *American Economic Review,* XXXV, 529–30.

13

Profit Management

Ludwig von Mises

1. The Operation of the Market Mechanism

Capitalism or market economy is that system of social cooperation and division of labor that is based on private ownership of the means of production. The material factors of production are owned by individual citizens, the capitalists and the landowners. The plants and the farms are operated by the entrepreneurs and the farmers, that is, by individuals or associations of individuals who either themselves own the capital and the soil or have borrowed or rented them from the owners. Free enterprise is the characteristic feature of capitalism. The objective of every enterpriser—whether businessman or farmer—is to make profit.

The capitalists, the enterprisers, and the farmers are instrumental in the conduct of economic affairs. They are at the helm and steer the ship. But they are not free to shape its course. They are not supreme, they are steersmen only, bound to obey unconditionally the captain's orders. The captain is the consumer.

Neither the capitalists nor the entrepreneurs nor the farmers determine what has to be produced. The consumers do that. The producers do not produce for their own

Reprinted from *Bureaucracy* by Ludwig von Mises (New Haven: Yale University Press, 1944).

consumption but for the market. They are intent on selling their products. If the consumers do not buy the goods offered to them, the businessman cannot recover the outlays made. He loses his money. If he fails to adjust his procedure to the wishes of the consumers he will very soon be removed from his eminent position at the helm. Other men who did better in satisfying the demand of the consumers replace him.

The real bosses, in the capitalist system of market economy, are the consumers. They, by their buying and by their abstention from buying, decide who should own the capital and run the plants. They determine what should be produced and in what quantity and quality. Their attitudes result either in profit or in loss for the enterpriser. They make poor men rich and rich men poor. They are no easy bosses. They are full of whims and fancies, changeable and unpredictable. They do not care a whit for past merit. As soon as something is offered to them that they like better or that is cheaper, they desert their old purveyors. With them nothing counts more than their own satisfaction. They bother neither about the vested interests of capitalists nor about the fate of the workers who lose their jobs if as consumers they no longer buy what they used to buy.

What does it mean when we say that the production of a certain commodity *A* does not pay? It is indicative of the fact that the consumers are not willing to pay the producers of *A* enough to cover the prices of the required factors of production, while at the same time other producers will find their incomes exceeding their costs of production. The demand of the consumers is instrumental in the allocation of various factors of production to the various branches of manufacturing consumers' goods. The consumers thus decide how much raw material and labor should be used for the manufacturing of *A* and how much for some other merchandise. It is therefore nonsensical to contrast production for profit and production for use. With the profit motive the enterpriser is compelled to supply the consumers with those goods which they are asking for most urgently. If the enterpriser were not forced to take the profit motive as his guide, he could produce more of A, in spite of the fact that the consumers prefer to get something else. The profit motive is precisely the factor that forces the businessman to provide in the most efficient way those commodities the consumers want to use.

Thus the capitalist system of production is an economic democracy in which every penny gives a right to vote. The consumers are the sovereign people. The capitalists, the entrepreneurs, and the farmers are the people's mandatories. If they do not obey, if they fail to produce, at the lowest possible cost, what the consumers are asking for, they lose their office. Their task is service to the consumer. Profit and loss are the instruments by means of which the consumers keep a tight rein on all business activities.

2. Economic Calculation

The preeminence of the capitalist system consists in the fact that it is the only system of social cooperation and division of labor which makes it possible to apply a method of reckoning and computation in planning new projects and appraising the usefulness of the operation of those plants, farms, and workshops already working. The impracticability of all schemes of socialism and central planning is to be seen in the impossibility of any kind of economic calculation under conditions in which there is no private ownership of the means of production and consequently no market prices for these factors.

The problem to be solved in the conduct of economic affairs is this: There are countless kinds of material factors of production, and within each class they differ from one another both with regard to their physical properties and to the places at which they are available. There are millions and millions of workers and they differ widely with regard to their ability to work. Technology provides us with information about numberless possibilities in regard to what could be achieved by using this supply of natural resources, capital goods, and manpower for the production of consumers' goods. Which of these potential procedures and plans are the most advantageous? Which should be carried out because they are apt to contribute most to the satisfaction of the most urgent needs? Which should be postponed or discarded because their execution would divert factors of production from other projects the execution of which would contribute more to the satisfaction of urgent needs?

It is obvious that these questions cannot be answered by some calculation in kind. One cannot make a variety of things enter into a calculus if there is no common denominator for them.

In the capitalist system all designing and planning is based on the market prices. Without them all the projects and blueprints of the engineers would be a mere academic pastime. They would demonstrate what could be done and how. But they would not be in a position to determine whether the realization of a certain project would really increase material well-being or whether it would not, by withdrawing scarce factors of production from other lines, jeopardize the satisfaction of more urgent needs, that is, of needs considered more urgent by the consumers. The guide of economic planning is the market price. The market prices alone can answer the question whether the execution of a project P will yield more than it costs, that is, whether it will be more useful than the execution of other conceivable plans which cannot be realized because the factors of production required are used for the performance of project P.

It has been frequently objected that this orientation of economic activity according to the profit motive, i.e., according to the yardstick of a surplus of yield over costs, leaves out of consideration the interests of the nation as a whole and takes account only of the selfish interests of individuals, different from and often even contrary to the national interests. This idea lies at the bottom of all totalitarian planning. Government control of business, it is claimed by the advocates of authoritarian management, looks after the nation's well-being, while free enterprise, driven by the sole aim of making profits, jeopardizes national interests.

The case is exemplified nowadays by citing the problem of synthetic rubber. Germany, under the rule of Nazi socialism, has developed the production of synthetic rubber, while Great Britain and the United States, under the supremacy of profit-seeking free enterprise, did not care about the unprofitable manufacture of such an expensive *ersatz*. Thus they neglected an important item of war preparedness and exposed their independence to a serious danger.

Nothing can be more spurious than this reasoning. Nobody ever asserted that the conduct of a war and preparing a nation's armed forces for the emergency of a war are a task that could or should be left to the activities of individual citizens. The defense of a nation's security and civilization against aggression on the part both of foreign foes and of domestic gangsters is the first duty of any government. If all men were pleasant and virtucus, if no one coveted what belongs to another, there would be no need for a government, for armies and navies, for policemen, for courts, and prisons. It is the government's business to make the provisions for war. No individual citizen and no group or class of citizens are to blame if the government fails in these endeavors. The guilt rests always with the government and consequently, in a democracy, with the majority of voters.

Germany armed for war. As the German General Staff knew that it would be impossible for warring Germany to import natural rubber, they decided to foster domestic production of synthetic rubber. There is no need to inquire whether or not the British and American military authorities were convinced that their countries, even in case of a new World War, would be in a position to rely upon the rubber plantations of Malaya and the Dutch Indies. At any rate they did not consider it necessary to pile up domestic stocks of natural rubber or to embark upon the production of synthetic rubber. Some American and British businessmen examined the progress of synthetic rubber production in Germany. But as the cost of the synthetic product was considerably higher than that of the natural product, they could not venture to imitate the example set by the Germans. No entrepreneur can invest money in a project which does not offer the prospect of profitability. It is precisely this fact that makes the consumers sovereign and forces the enterpriser to produce what the consumers are most urgently asking for. The consumers, that is, the American and the British public, were not ready to allow for synthetic rubber prices which would have rendered its production profitable. The cheapest way to provide rubber was for the Anglo-Saxon countries to produce other merchandise, for instance, motor cars and various machines, to sell these things abroad, and to import foreign natural rubber.

If it had been possible for the Governments of London and Washington to foresee the events of December 1941, and January and February 1942, they would have turned toward measures securing a domestic production of synthetic rubber. It is immaterial with regard to our problem which method they would have chosen for financing this part of defense expenditure. They could subsidize the plants concerned or they could raise, by means of tariffs, the domestic price of rubber to such a level that home production of synthetic rubber would have become profitable. At any rate the people would have been forced to pay for what was done.

If the government does not provide for a defense measure, no capitalist or entrepreneur can fill the gap. To reproach some chemical corporations for not having taken up production of synthetic rubber is no more sensible than to blame the motor industry for not, immediately after Hitler's rise to power, converting its plants into plane factories. Or it would be as justifiable to blame a scholar for having wasted his time writing a book on American history or philosophy instead of devoting all his efforts to training himself for his future functions in the Expeditionary Force. If the government fails in its task of equipping the nation to repel an attack, no individual citizen has any way open to remedy the evil but to criticize the authorities in addressing the sovereign—the voters—in speeches, articles, and books.[1]

Many doctors describe the ways in which their fellow citizens spend their money as utterly foolish and opposed to their real needs. People, they say, should change their diet, restrict their consumption of intoxicating beverages and tobacco, and employ their leisure time in a more reasonable manner. These doctors are probably right. But it is not the task of government to improve the behavior of its "subjects." Neither is it the task of businessmen. They are not the guardians of their customers. If the public prefers hard to soft drinks, the entrepreneurs have to yield to these wishes. He who wants to reform his countrymen must take recourse to persuasion. This alone is the democratic way of bringing about changes. If a man fails in his endeavors to convince other people of the soundness of his ideas, he should blame his own disabilities. He should not ask for a law, that is, for compulsion and coercion by the police.

The ultimate basis of economic calculation is the valuation of all consumers' goods on the part of all the people. It is true that these consumers are fallible and that their judgment is sometimes misguided. We may assume that they would appraise the various commodities differently if they were better instructed. However, as human nature is, we have no means of substituting the wisdom of an infallible authority for people's shallowness.

We do not assert that the market prices are to be considered as expressive of any perennial and absolute value. There are no such things as absolute values, independent of the subjective preferences of erring men. Judgments of value are the outcome of human arbitrariness. They reflect all the shortcomings and weaknesses of their authors. However, the only alternative to the determination of market prices by the choices of all consumers is the determination of values by the judgment of some small groups of men, no less liable to error and frustration than the majority, notwithstanding the fact that they are called "authority." No matter how the values of consumers' goods are determined, whether they are fixed by a dictatorial decision or by the choices of all consumers—the whole people—values are always relative, subjective, and human, never absolute, objective, and divine.

What must be realized is that within a market society organized on the basis of free enterprise and private ownership of the means of production the prices of consumers' goods are faithfully and closely reflected in the prices of the various factors required for their production. Thus it becomes feasible to discover by means of a precise calculation which of the indefinite multitude of thinkable processes of production are more advantageous and which less. "More advantageous" means in this connection: an employment of these factors of production in such a way that the production of the consumers' goods more urgently asked for by the consumers gets a priority over the production of commodities less urgently asked for by the consumers. Economic calculation makes it possible for business to adjust production to the demands of the consumers. On the other hand, under any variety of socialism, the central board of production management would not be in a position to engage in economic calculation. Where there are no markets and consequently no market prices for the factors of production, they cannot become elements of a calculation.

For a full understanding of the problems involved we must try to grasp the nature and the origin of profit.

Within a hypothetical system without any change there would not be any profits and losses at all. In such a stationary world, in which nothing new occurs and all economic conditions remain permanently the same, the total sum that a manufacturer must spend for the factors of production required would be equal to the price he gets for the product. The prices to be paid for the material factors of production, the wages and interest for the capital invested, would absorb the whole price of the product. Nothing would be left for profit. It is obvious that such a system would not have any need for entrepreneurs and no economic function for profits. As only those things are produced today which were produced yesterday, the day before yesterday, last year, and ten years ago, and as the same routine will go on forever, as no changes occur in the supply or demand either of consumers' or of producers' goods or in technical methods, as all prices are stable, there is no room left for any entrepreneurial activity.

But the actual world is a world of permanent change. Population figures, tastes, and wants, the supply of factors of production and technological methods are in a ceaseless flux. In such a state of affairs there is need for a continuous adjustment of production to the change in conditions. This is where the entrepreneur comes in.

Those eager to make profits are always looking for an opportunity. As soon as they discover that the relation of the prices of the factors of production to the anticipated prices of the products seem to offer such an opportunity, they step in. If their appraisal of all the elements involved was correct, they make a profit. But immediately the tendency toward a disappearance of such profits begins to take effect. As an outcome of the new projects inaugurated, the prices of the factors of production in question go up and, on the other hand, those of the products begin to drop. Profits are a permanent phenomenon only because there are always changes in market conditions and in methods of production. He who wants to make profits must be always on the watch for new opportunities. And in searching for profit, he adjusts production to the demands of the consuming public.

We can view the whole market of material factors of production and of labor as a public auction. The bidders are the entrepreneurs. Their highest bids are limited by their expectation of the prices the consumers will be ready to pay for the products. The co-bidders competing with them, whom they must outbid if they are not to go away empty-handed, are in the same situation. All these bidders are, as it were, acting as mandatories of the consumers. But each of them represents a different aspect of the consumers' wants, either another commodity or another way of producing the same commodity. The competition among the various entrepreneurs is essentially a competition among the various possibilities open to individuals to remove as far as possible their state of uneasiness by the acquisition of consumers' goods. The resolution of any man to buy a refrigerator and to postpone the purchase of a new car is a determining factor in the formation of the prices of cars and of refrigerators. The competition between the entrepreneurs reflects these prices of consumers' goods in the formation of the prices of the factors of production. The fact that the various wants of the individual, which conflict because of the inexorable scarcity of the factors of production, are represented on the market by various competing entrepreneurs results in prices for these factors that make economic calculation not only feasible but imperative. An entrepreneur who does not calculate, or disregards the result of the calculation, would very soon go bankrupt and be removed from his managerial function.

But within a socialist community in which there is only one manager there are neither prices of the factors of production nor economic calculation. To the entrepreneur of capitalist society a factor of production through its price sends out a warning: Don't touch me, I am earmarked for the satisfaction of another, more urgent need. But under socialism these factors of production are mute. They give no hint to the planner. Technology offers him a great variety of possible solutions for the same problem. Each of them requires the outlay of other kinds and quantities of various factors of production. But as the socialist manager cannot reduce them to a common denominator, he is not in a position to find out which of them is the most advantageous.

It is true that under socialism there would be neither discernible profits nor discernible losses. Where there is no calculation, there is no means of getting an answer to the question whether the projects planned or carried out were those best fitted to satisfy the most urgent needs; success and failure remain unrecognized in the dark. The advocates of socialism are badly mistaken in considering the absence of discernible profit and loss an excellent point. It is, on the contrary, the essential vice of any socialist management. It is not an advantage to be ignorant of whether or not what one is doing is a suitable means of attaining the ends sought. A socialist management would be like a man forced to spend his life blindfolded.

It has been objected that the market system is at any rate quite inappropriate under the conditions brought about by a great war. If the market mechanism were to be left alone, it would be impossible for the government to get all the equipment needed. The scarce factors of production required for the production of armaments would be wasted for civilian uses which, in a war, are to be considered as less important, even as luxury and waste. Thus it was imperative to resort to the system of government-established priorities and to create the necessary bureaucratic apparatus.

The error of this reasoning is that it does not realize that the necessity for giving the government full power to determine for what kinds of production the various raw materials should be used is not an outcome of the war but of the methods applied in financing the war expenditure.

If the whole amount of money needed for the conduct of the war had been collected by taxes and by borrowing from the public, everybody would have been forced to restrict his consumption drastically. With a money income (after taxes) much lower than before, the consumers would have stopped buying many goods they used to buy before the war. The manufacturers, precisely because they are driven by the profit motive, would have discontinued producing such civilian goods and would have shifted to the production of those goods which the government, now by virtue of the inflow of taxes the biggest buyer on the market, would be ready to buy.

However, a great part of the war expenditure is financed by an increase of currency in circulation and by borrowing from the commercial banks. On the other hand, under price control, it is illegal to raise commodity prices. With higher money incomes and with unchanged commodity prices people would not only not have restricted but have increased their buying of goods for their own consumption. To avoid this, it was necessary to take recourse to rationing and to government-imposed priorities. These measures were needed because previous government interference that paralyzed the operation of the market resulted in paradoxical and highly unsatisfactory conditions. Not the insufficiency of the market mechanism but the inadequacy of previous government meddling with market phenomena made the priority system unavoidable. In this as in many other instances the bureaucrats see in the failure of their preceding measures a proof that further inroads into the market system are necessary.

3. Management under the Profit System

All business transactions are examined by shrewdly calculating profit and loss. New projects are subject to a precise scrutiny of the chances they offer. Every step toward their realization is reflected in entries in the books and accounts. The profit-and-loss account shows whether or not the whole business, or any of its parts, was profitable. The figures of the ledger serve as a guide for the conduct of the whole business and of each of its divisions. Branches which do not pay are discontinued, those yielding profit are expanded. There cannot be any question of clinging to unprofitable lines of business if there is no prospect of rendering them profitable in a not-too-distant future.

The elaborate methods of modern bookkeeping, accountancy, and business statistics provide the enterpriser with a faithful image of all his operations. He is in a position to learn how successful or unsuccessful every one of his transactions was. With the aid of these statements he can check the activities of all departments of his concern no matter how large it may be. There is, to be sure, some amount of discretion in determining the distribution of overhead costs. But apart from this, the figures provide a faithful reflection of all that is going on in every branch or department. The books and the balance sheets are the conscience of business. They are also the businessman's compass.

The devices of bookkeeping and accountancy are so familiar to the businessman that he fails to observe what a marvelous instrument they are. It needed a great poet and writer to appreciate them at their true value. Goethe called bookkeeping by double-entry "one of the finest inventions of the human mind." By means of this, he observed, the businessman can at any time survey the general whole, without needing to perplex himself with the details.[2]

Goethe's characterization hit the core of the matter.

The virtue of commercial management lies precisely in the fact that it provides the manager with a method of surveying the whole and all its parts without being enmeshed in details and trifles.

The entrepreneur is in a position to separate the calculation of each part of his business in such a way that he can determine the role that it plays within his whole enterprise. For the public every firm or corporation is an undivided unity. But for the eye of its management it is composed of various sections, each of which is viewed as a separate entity and appreciated according to the share it contributes to the success of the whole enterprise. Within the system of business calculation each section represents an integral being, a hypothetical independent business as it were. It is assumed that this section "owns" a definite part of the whole capital employed in the enterprise, that it buys from other sections and sells to them, that it has its own expenses and its own revenues, that its dealings result either in a profit or a loss which is imputed to its own conduct of affairs as separate from the results achieved by the other sections. Thus the general manager of the whole enterprise can assign to each section's management a great deal of independence. There is no need for the general manager to bother about the minor details of each section's management. The managers of the various sections can have a free hand in the administration of their sections' "internal" affairs. The only directive that the general manager gives to the men whom he entrusts with the management of the various sections, departments, and branches is: Make as much profit as possible. And an examination of the accounts shows him how successful or unsuccessful they were in executing the directive.

In a large-scale enterprise many sections produce only parts or half-finished products which are not directly sold but are used by other sections in manufacturing the final product. This fact does not alter the conditions described.

The general manager compares the costs incurred by the production of such parts and half-finished products with the prices he would have to pay for them if he had to buy them from other plants. He is always confronted by the question: Does it pay to produce these things in our own workshops? Would it not be more satisfactory to buy them from other plants specializing in their production?

Thus within the framework of a profit-seeking enterprise responsibility can be divided. Every submanager is responsible for the working of his department. It is to his credit if the accounts show a profit, and it is to his disadvantage if they show a loss. His own selfish interests push him toward the utmost care and exertion in the conduct of his section's affairs. If he incurs losses, he will be their victim. He will be replaced by another man whom the general manager expects to be more successful, or the whole section will be discontinued. At any rate he will be discharged and lose his job. If he succeeds in making profits, he will see his income increased or at least he will not be in danger of losing it. Whether or not a departmental manager is entitled to a share in the profit of his department is not so important with regard to the personal interest he takes in the results of his department's dealings. His fate is at any rate closely connected with that of his department. In working for it, he works not only for his boss but also for himself.

It would be impracticable to restrict the discretion of such a responsible submanager by too much interference with detail. If he is efficient, such meddling would at best be superfluous, if not harmful by tying his hands. If he is inefficient, it would not render his activities more successful. It would only provide him with a lame excuse that the failure was caused by his superior's inappropriate instructions. The only instruction required is self-understood and does not need to be especially mentioned: seek profit. Moreover, most of the details can and must be left to the head of every department.

This system was instrumental in the evolution of modern business. Large-scale production in great production aggregates and the establishment of subsidiaries in distant parts of the country and in foreign countries, the department stores, and the chain stores are all built upon the principle of the subordinate managers' responsibility. This does not in any way limit the responsibility of the general manager. The subordinates are responsible only to him. They do not free him from the duty of finding the right man for every job.

If a New York firm establishes branch shops or plants in Los Angeles, in Buenos Aires, in Budapest, and in Calcutta, the chief manager establishes the auxiliary's relation to the head office or parental company only in fairly general terms. All minor questions are to be within the range of the local manager's duties. The auditing department of headquarters carefully inspects the branch's financial transactions and informs the general manager as soon as any irregularities appear. Precautions are taken to prevent irreparable waste of the capital invested in the branch, a squandering of the whole concern's good will and reputation and a collision between the branch's policy and that of headquarters. But a free hand is left to the local management in every other regard. It is practicable to place confidence in the chief of a subsidiary, a department, or a section because his interests and those of the whole concern coincide. If he were to spend too much for current operations or to neglect an opportunity for profitable transactions, he would imperil not only the concern's profits but his own position as well. He is not simply a hired clerk whose only duty is the conscientious accomplishment of an assigned, definite task. He is a businessman himself, a junior partner as it were of the entrepreneur, no matter what the contractual and financial terms of his employment are. He must to the best of his abilities contribute to the success of the firm with which he is connected.

Because this is so, there is no danger in leaving important decisions to his discretion. He will not waste money in the purchase of products and services. He will not hire incompetent assistants and workers; he will not discharge able collaborators in order to replace them by incompetent personal friends or relatives. His conduct is subject to the incorruptible judgment of an unbribable tribunal: the account of profit and loss. In business there is only one thing that matters: success. The unsuccessful department manager is doomed no matter whether the failure was caused by him or not, or whether it would have been possible for him to attain a more satisfactory result. An unprofitable branch of business—sooner or later—must be discontinued, and its manager loses his job.

The sovereignty of the consumers and the democratic operation of the market do not stop at the doors of a big business concern. They permeate all its departments and branches. Responsibility to the consumer is the lifeblood of business and enterprise in an unhampered market society. The profit motive through the instrumentality of which the entrepreneurs are driven to serve the consumers to the best of their ability is at the same time the first principle of any commercial and industrial aggregate's internal organization. It joins together utmost centralization of the whole concern with almost complete autonomy of the parts, it brings into agreement full responsibility of the central management with a high degree of interest and incentive of the subordinate managers of sections, departments, and auxiliaries. It gives to the system of free enterprise that versatility and adaptability which result in an unswerving tendency toward improvement.

4. Personnel Management under an Unhampered Labor Market

The staff of a modern large-scale enterprise sometimes includes many hundreds of thousands of clerks and workers. They form a highly differentiated body from the general manager or president down to the scrubwomen, messenger boys, and apprentices. The handling of such a huge body raises many problems. However, they can be solved.

No matter how big a concern may be, the central management deals only with sections, departments, branches, and subsidiaries, the role of which can be precisely determined from the evidence provided by the accounts and statistics. Of course, the accounts do not always demonstrate what may be wrong with a section. They show only that something is wrong, that it does not pay, and must be either reformed or discontinued. The sentences they pass are unappealable. They reveal each department's cash value. And it is cash value alone that matters on the market. The consumers are merciless. They never buy in order to benefit a less efficient producer and to protect him against the consequences of his failure to manage better. They want to be served as well as possible. And the working of the capitalist system forces the entrepreneur to obey the orders issued by the consumers. He does not have the power to distribute bounties at the expense of the consumers. He would waste his funds if he were to use his own money for such a purpose. He simply cannot pay anybody more than he can realize in selling the product.

The same relation that exists between the general manager and his immediate subordinates, the heads of the various sections, pervades the whole business hierarchy. Every section head values his immediate subordinates according to the same principle by which the chief manager values him, and the foreman applies similar methods in appraising his subordinates. The only difference is that under the simpler conditions of the lower units no elaborate accountancy schemes are required for the establishment of each man's cash value. It does not matter whether piece wages or hourly wages are paid. In the long run the worker can never get more than the consumer allows.

No man is infallible. It often happens that a superior errs in judging a subordinate. One of the qualifications required for any higher position is precisely the ability to judge people correctly. He who fails in this regard jeopardizes his chances of success. He hurts his own interests no less than those of the men whose efficiency he has underrated. Things being so, there is no need to look for special protection for the employees against arbitrariness on the part of their employers or their employer's mandatories. Arbitrariness in dealing with personnel is, under the unhampered profit system, an offense that strikes home to its author.

Under an unhampered market economy the appraisal of each individual's effort is detached from any personal considerations and can therefore be free both from bias and dislike. The market passes judgment on the products, not on the producers. The appraisal of the producer results automatically from the appraisal of his product. Each cooperator is valued according to the value of his contribution to the process of production of goods and services. Salaries and wages do not depend on arbitrary decisions. On the labor market every quantity and quality of work is prized to the amount the consumers are ready to pay for the products. It is not a favor on the part of the employer to pay wages and salaries, it is a business transaction, the purchase of a factor of production. The price of labor is a market phenomenon determined by the consumers' demands for goods and services. Virtually every employer is always in search of cheaper labor and every employee in search of a job with higher remuneration.

The very fact that labor is, under capitalism, a commodity and is bought and sold as a commodity makes the wage earner free from any personal dependence. Like the capitalists, the entrepreneurs, and the farmers, the wage earner depends on the arbitrariness of the consumers. But the consumers' choices do not concern the persons engaged in production; they concern things and not men. The employer is not in a position to indulge in favoritism or in prejudice with regard to personnel. As far as he does, the deed itself brings about its own penalty.

It is this fact, and not only constitutions and bills of rights, that makes the receivers of salaries and wages *within an unhampered capitalist system* free men. They are sovereign in their capacity as consumers, and as producers they are, like all other citizens, unconditionally subject to the law of the market. In selling a factor of production, namely, their toil and trouble, on the market at the market price to everybody who is ready to buy it, they do not jeopardize their own standing. They do not owe their employer thanks and subservience, they owe him a definite quantity of labor of a definite quality. The employer, on the other hand, is not in search of sympathetic men whom he likes but efficient workers who are worth the money he pays them.

This cool rationality and objectivity of capitalist relations is, of course, not realized to the same degree in the whole field of business. The nearer a man's function brings him to the consumers, the more personal factors interfere. In the service trades some role is played by sympathies and antipathies; relations are more "human." Stubborn doctrinaires and adamant baiters of capitalism are prepared to call this an advantage. In fact it curtails the businessman's and his employees' personal freedom. A small shopkeeper, a barber, an innkeeper, and an actor are not so free in expressing their political or religious convictions as the owner of a cotton mill or a worker in a steel plant.

But these facts do not invalidate the general characteristics of the market system. It is a system which automatically values every man according to the services he renders to the body of sovereign consumers, i.e., to his fellow men.

Notes

1. These observations do not imply any criticism of the prewar policies pursued by the British and American authorities. Only a man who had knowledge of the military events of 1941–1943 many years before they occurred would have the right to blame other people for their lack of foresight. Governments are not omniscient, as the planners would have us believe.
2. *Wilhelm Meister's Apprenticeship,* Book I, Chap. X.

14

The Use of Knowledge in Society

Friedrich A. Hayek

1

What is the problem we wish to solve when we try to construct a rational economic order? On certain familiar assumptions the answer is simple enough. *If* we possess all the relevant information, *if* we can start out from a given system of preferences, and *if* we command complete knowledge of available means, the problem which remains is purely one of logic. That is, the answer to the question of what is the best use of the available means is implicit in our assumptions. The conditions which the solution of this optimum problem must satisfy have been fully worked out and can be stated best in mathematical form: put at their briefest, they are that the marginal rates of substitution between any two commodities or factors must be the same in all their different uses.

This, however, is emphatically *not* the economic problem which society faces. And the economic calculus which we have developed to solve this logical problem, though an important step toward the solution of the economic problem of society, does not yet provide an answer to it. The reason for this is that the "data" from which the economic calculus

Reprinted from *Individualism and Economic Order* by Friedrich A. Hayek (Chicago: The University of Chicago Press, 1948).

starts are never for the whole society "given" to a single mind which could work out the implications and can never be so given.

The peculiar character of the problem of a rational economic order is determined precisely by the fact that the knowledge of the circumstances of which we must make use never exists in concentrated or integrated form but solely as the dispersed bits of incomplete and frequently contradictory knowledge which all the separate individuals possess. The economic problem of society is thus not merely a problem of how to allocate "given" resources—if "given" is taken to mean given to a single mind which deliberately solves the problem set by these "data." It is rather a problem of how to secure the best use of resources known to any of the members of society, for ends whose relative importance only these individuals know. Or, to put it briefly, it is a problem of the utilization of knowledge which is not given to anyone in its totality.

This character of the fundamental problem has, I am afraid, been obscured rather than illuminated by many of the recent refinements of economic theory, particularly by many of the uses made of mathematics. Though the problem with which I want primarily to deal in this paper is the problem of a rational economic organization, I shall in its course be led again and again to point to its close connections with certain methodological questions. Many of the points I wish to make are indeed conclusions toward which diverse paths of reasoning have unexpectedly converged. But, as I now see these problems, this is no accident. It seems to me that many of the current disputes with regard to both economic theory and economic policy have their common origin in a misconception about the nature of the economic problem of society. This misconception in turn is due to an erroneous transfer to social phenomena of the habits of thought we have developed in dealing with the phenomena of nature.

2

In ordinary language we describe by the word "planning" the complex of interrelated decisions about the allocation of our available resources. All economic activity is in this sense planning; and in any society in which many people collaborate, this planning, whoever does it, will in some measure have to be based on knowledge which, in the first instance, is not given to the planner but to somebody else, which somehow will have to be conveyed to the planner. The various ways in which the knowledge on which people base their plans is communicated to them is the crucial problem for any theory explaining the economic process, and the problem of what is the best way of utilizing knowledge initially dispersed among all the people is at least one of the main problems of economic policy—or of designing an efficient economic system.

The answer to this question is closely connected with that other question which arises here, that of *who* is to do the planning. It is about this question that all the dispute about "economic planning" centers. This is not a dispute about whether planning is to be done or not. It is a dispute as to whether planning is to be done centrally, by one authority for the whole economic system, or is to be divided among many individuals. Planning in the specific sense in which the term is used in contemporary controversy necessarily means central planning—direction of the whole economic system according to one unified plan. Competition, on the other hand, means decentralized planning by many separate persons. The halfway house between the two, about which many people talk but which few like when they see it, is the delegation of planning to organized industries, or, in other words, monopolies.

Which of these systems is likely to be more efficient depends mainly on the question under which of them we can expect that fuller use will be made of the existing knowledge. This, in turn, depends on whether we are more likely to succeed in putting at the disposal of a single central authority all the knowledge which ought to be used but which is initially dispersed among many different individuals, or in conveying to the individuals such additional knowledge as they need in order to enable them to dovetail their plans with those of others.

3

It will at once be evident that on this point the position will be different with respect to different kinds of knowledge. The answer to our question will therefore largely turn on the relative importance of the different kinds of knowledge: those more likely to be at the disposal of particular individuals and those which we should with greater confidence expect to find in the possession of an authority made up of suitably chosen experts. If it is today so widely assumed that the latter will be in a better position, this is because one kind of knowledge, namely, scientific knowledge, occupies now so prominent a place in public imagination that we tend to forget that it is not the only kind that is relevant. It may be admitted that, as far as scientific knowledge is concerned, a body of suitably chosen experts may be in the best position to command all the best knowledge available—though this is of course merely shifting the difficulty to the problem of selecting the experts. What I wish to point out is that, even assuming that this problem can be readily solved, it is only a small part of the wider problem.

Today it is almost heresy to suggest that scientific knowledge is not the sum of all knowledge. But a little reflection will show that there is beyond question a body of very important but unorganized knowledge which cannot possibly be called scientific in the sense of knowledge of general rules: the knowledge of the particular circum-

stances of time and place. It is with respect to this that practically every individual has some advantage over all others
because he possesses unique information of which beneficial
use might be made, but of which use can be made only if the
decisions depending on it are left to him or are made with
his active co-operation. We need to remember only how
much we have to learn in any occupation after we have
completed our theoretical training, how big a part of our
working life we spend learning particular jobs, and how
valuable an asset in all walks of life is knowledge of people,
of local conditions, and of special circumstances. To know
of and put to use a machine not fully employed, or somebody's skill which could be better utilized, or to be aware of
a surplus stock which can be drawn upon during an inter-
ruption of supplies, is socially quite as useful as the knowledge of better alternative techniques. The shipper who
earns his living from using otherwise empty or half-filled
journeys of tramp-steamers, or the estate agent whose whole
knowledge is almost exclusively one of temporary opportunities, or the *arbitrageur* who gains from local differences of
commodity prices—are all performing eminently useful
functions based on special knowledge of circumstances of
the fleeting moment not known to others.

It is a curious fact that this sort of knowledge should
today be generally regarded with a kind of contempt and
that anyone who by such knowledge gains an advantage
over somebody better equipped with theoretical or technical
knowledge is thought to have acted almost disreputably. To
gain an advantage from better knowledge of facilities of
communication or transport is sometimes regarded as almost dishonest, although it is quite as important that society
make use of the best opportunities in this respect as in using
the latest scientific discoveries. This prejudice has in a considerable measure affected the attitude toward commerce
in general compared with that toward production. Even
economists who regard themselves as definitely immune to

the crude materialist fallacies of the past constantly commit the same mistake where activities directed toward the acquisition of such practical knowledge are concerned—apparently because in their scheme of things all such knowledge is supposed to be "given." The common idea now seems to be that all such knowledge should as a matter of course be readily at the command of everybody, and the reproach of irrationality leveled against the existing economic order is frequently based on the fact that it is not so available. This view disregards the fact that the method by which such knowledge can be made as widely available as possible is precisely the problem to which we have to find an answer.

4

If it is fashionable today to minimize the importance of the knowledge of the particular circumstances of time and place, this is closely connected with the smaller importance which is now attached to change as such. Indeed, there are few points on which the assumptions made (usually only implicitly) by the "planners" differ from those of their opponents as much as with regard to the significance and frequency of changes which will make substantial alterations of production plans necessary. Of course, if detailed economic plans could be laid down for fairly long periods in advance and then closely adhered to, so that no further economic decisions of importance would be required, the task of drawing up a comprehensive plan governing all economic activity would be much less formidable.

It is, perhaps, worth stressing that economic problems arise always and only in consequence of change. As long as things continue as before, or at least as they were expected to, there arise no new problems requiring a decision, no need to form a new plan. The belief that changes, or at least day-to-day adjustments, have become less important in modern times implies the contention that economic problems also have become less important. This belief in the decreasing importance of change is, for that reason, usually held by the same people who argue that the importance of economic considerations has been driven into the background by the growing importance of technological knowledge.

It is true that, with the elaborate apparatus of modern production, economic decisions are required only at long intervals, as when a new factory is to be erected or a new process to be introduced? Is it true that, once a plant has been built, the rest is all more or less mechanical, determined by the character of the plant, and leaving little to be changed in adapting to the ever changing circumstances of the moment?

The fairly widespread belief in the affirmative is not, as far as I can ascertain, borne out by the practical experience of the businessman. In a competitive industry at any rate—and such an industry alone can serve as a test—the task of keeping cost from rising requires constant struggle, absorbing a great part of the energy of the manager. How easy it is for an inefficient manager to dissipate the differentials on which profitability rests and that it is possible, with the same technical facilities, to produce with a great variety of costs are among the commonplaces of business experience which do not seem to be equally familiar in the study of the economist. The very strength of the desire, constantly voiced by producers and engineers, to be allowed to proceed untrammeled by considerations of money costs, is eloquent testimony to the extent to which these factors enter into their daily work.

One reason why economists are increasingly apt to forget about the constant small changes which make up the whole economic picture is probably their growing preoccupation with statistical aggregates, which show a very much greater stability than the movements of the detail. The comparative stability of the aggregates cannot, however, be accounted for—as the statisticians occasionally seem to be inclined to do—by the "law of large numbers" or the mutual compensation of random changes. The number of elements with which we have to deal is not large enough for such accidental forces to produce stability. The continuous flow of goods and services is maintained by constant deliberate adjustments, by new dispositions made every day in the light of circumstances not known the day before, by B stepping in at once when A fails to deliver. Even the large and highly mechanized plant keeps going largely because of an environment upon which it can draw for all sorts of unexpected needs: tiles for its roof, stationery or its forms, and all the thousand and one kinds of equipment in which it cannot be self-contained and which the plans for the operation of the plant require to be readily available in the market.

This is, perhaps, also the point where I should briefly mention the fact that the sort of knowledge with which I have been concerned is knowledge of the kind which by its nature cannot enter into statistics and therefore cannot be conveyed to any central authority in statistical form. The statistics which such a central authority would have to use would have to be arrived at precisely by abstracting from minor differences between the things, by lumping together, as resources of one kind, items which differ as regards location, quality, and other particulars, in a way which may be very significant for the specific decision. It follows from this that central planning based on statistical information by its nature cannot take direct account of these circumstances of time and place and that the central planner will have to find some way or other in which the decisions depending on them can be left to the "man on the spot."

5

If we can agree that the economic problem of society is mainly one of rapid adaptation to changes in the particular circumstances of time and place, it would seem to follow that the ultimate decisions must be left to the people who are familiar with these circumstances, who know directly of the relevant changes and of the resources immediately available to meet them. We cannot expect that this problem will be solved by first communicating all this knowledge to a central board which, after integrating all knowledge, issues its orders. We must solve it by some form of decentralization. But this answers only part of our problem. We need decentralization because only thus can we insure that the knowledge of the particular circumstances of time and place will be promptly used. But the "man on the spot" cannot decide solely on the basis of his limited but intimate knowledge of the facts of his immediate surroundings. There still remains the problem of communicating to him such further information as he needs to fit his decisions into the whole pattern of changes of the larger economic system.

How much knowledge does he need to do so successfully? Which of the events which happen beyond the horizon of his immediate knowledge are of relevance to his immediate decision, and how much of them need he know?

There is hardly anything that happens anywhere in the world that *might* not have an effect on the decision he ought to make. But he need not know of these events as such, nor of *all* their effects. It does not matter for him *why* at the particular moment more screws of one size than of another are wanted, *why* paper bags are more readily available than canvas bags, or *why* skilled labor, or particular machine tools, have for the moment become more difficult to obtain. All that is significant for him is *how much more or less* difficult to procure they have become compared with other things with which he is also concerned, or how much more or less urgently wanted are the alternative things he produces or uses. It is always a question of the relative importance of the particular things with which he is concerned, and the causes which alter their relative importance are of no interest to him beyond the effect on those concrete things of his own environment.

It is in this connection that what I have called the "economic calculus" (or the Pure Logic of Choice) helps us, at least by analogy, to see how this problem can be solved, and in fact is being solved, by the price system. Even the single controlling mind, in possession of all the data for some small, self-contained economic system, would not—every time some small adjustment in the allocation of resources had to be made—go explicitly through all the relations between ends and means which might possibly be affected. It is indeed the great contribution of the Pure Logic of Choice that it has demonstrated conclusively that even such a single mind could solve this kind of problem only by constructing and constantly using rates of equivalence (or "values," or "marginal rates of substitution"), that is, by attaching to each kind of scarce resource a numerical index which cannot be derived from any property possessed by that particular thing, but which reflects, or in which is condensed, its significance in view of the whole means-end structure. In any small change he will have to consider only these quantitative indices (or "values") in which all the relevant information is concentrated; and, by adjusting the quantities one by one, he can appropriately rearrange his dispositions without having to solve the whole puzzle *ab initio* or without needing at any stage to survey it at once in all its ramifications.

Fundamentally, in a system in which the knowledge of the relevant facts is dispersed among many people, prices can act to coordinate the separate actions of different people in the same way as subjective values help the individual to coordinate the parts of his plan. It is worth contemplating for a moment a very simple and commonplace instance of the action of the price system to see what precisely it accomplishes. Assume that somewhere in the world a new opportunity for the use of some raw material, say, tin, has arisen, or that one of the sources of supply of tin has been eliminated. It does not matter for our purpose—and it is significant that it does not matter—which of these two causes has made tin more scarce. All that the users of tin need to know is that some of the tin they used to consume is now more profitably employed elsewhere and that, in consequence, they must economize tin. There is no need for the great majority of them even to know where the more urgent need has arisen, or in favor of what other needs they ought to husband the supply. If only some of them know directly of the new demand, and switch resources over to it, and if the people who are aware of the new gap thus created in turn fill it from still other sources, the effect will rapidly spread throughout the whole economic system and influence not only all the uses of tin but also those of its substitutes and the substitutes of these substitutes, the supply of all the things made of tin, and their substitutes, and so on; and all his without the great majority of those instrumental in bringing about these substitutions knowing anything at all about the original cause of these changes. The whole acts as one market, not because any of its members survey the whole field, but because their limited individual fields of vision sufficiently overlap so that through many intermediaries the relevant information is communicated to all. The mere fact that there is one price for any commodity—or rather that local prices are connected in a manner determined by the cost of transport, etc.—brings about the solution which (it is just conceptually possible) might have been arrived at by one single mind possessing all the information which is in fact dispersed among all the people involved in the process.

6

We must look at the price system as such a mechanism for communicating information if we want to understand its real function—a function which, of course, it fulfills less perfectly as prices grow more rigid. (Even when quoted prices have become quite rigid, however, the forces which would operate through changes in price still operate to a considerable extent through changes in the other terms of the contract.) The most significant fact about this system is the economy of knowledge with which it operates, or how little the individual participants need to know in order to be able to take the right action. In abbreviated form, by a kind of symbol, only the most essential information is passed on and passed on only to those concerned. It is more than a metaphor to describe the price system as a kind of machinery for registering change, or a system of telecommunications which enables individual producers to watch merely the movement of a few pointers, as an engineer might watch the hands of a few dials, in order to adjust their activities to changes of which they may never know more than is reflected in the price movement.

Of course, these adjustments are probably never "perfect" in the sense in which the economist conceives of them in his equilibrium analysis. But I fear that our theoretical habits of approaching the problem with the assumption of more or less perfect knowledge on the part of almost everyone has made us somewhat blind to the true function of the price mechanism and led us to apply rather misleading standards in judging its efficiency. The marvel is that in a case like that of a scarcity of one raw material, without an order being issued, without more than perhaps a handful of people knowing the cause, tens of thousands of people whose identity could not be ascertained by months of investigation, are made to use the material or its products more sparingly; that is, they move in the right direction. This is enough of a marvel even if, in a constantly changing world, not all will hit it off so perfectly that their profit rates will always be maintained at the same even or "normal" level.

I have deliberately used the word "marvel" to shock the reader out of the complacency with which we often take the working of this mechanism for granted. I am convinced that if it were the result of deliberate human design, and if the people guided by the price changes understood that their decisions have significance far beyond their immediate aim, this mechanism would have been acclaimed as one of the greatest triumphs of the human mind. Its misfortune is the double one that it is not the product of human design and that the people guided by it usually do not know why they are made to do what they do. But those who clamor for "conscious direction"—and who cannot believe that anything which has evolved without design (and even without our understanding it) should solve problems which we should not be able to solve consciously—should remember this: The problem is precisely how to extend the span of our utilization of resources beyond the span of the control of any one mind; and, therefore, how to dispense with the need of conscious control and how to provide inducements which will make the individuals do the desirable things without anyone having to tell them what to do.

The problem which we meet here is by no means peculiar to economics but arises in connection with nearly all truly social phenomena, with language and with most of our cultural inheritance, and constitutes really the central theoretical problem of all social science. As Alfred Whitehead has said in another connection, "It is a profoundly erroneous truism, repeated by all copy-books and by eminent people when they are making speeches, that we should cultivate the habit of thinking what we are doing. The precise opposite is the case. Civilization advances by extending the number of important operations which we can perform without thinking about them." This is of profound significance in the social field. We make constant use of formulas, symbols, and rules whose meaning we do not understand and through the use of which we avail ourselves of the assistance of knowledge which individually we do not possess. We have developed these practices and institutions by building upon habits and institutions which have proved successful in their own sphere and which have in turn become the foundation of the civilization we have built up.

The price system is just one of those formations which man has learned to use (though he is still very far from having learned to make the best use of it) after he had stumbled upon it without understanding it. Through it not only a division of labor but also a coordinated utilization of resources based on an equally divided knowledge has become possible. The people who like to deride any suggestion that this may be so usually distort the argument by insinuating that it asserts that by some miracle just the sort of system has spontaneously grown up which is best suited to modern civilization. It is the other way round: man has been able to develop that division of labor on which our civilization is based because he happened to stumble upon a method which made it possible. Had he not done so, he might still have developed some other, altogether different, type of civilization, something like the "state" of the termite ants, or some other altogether unimaginable type. All that we can say is that nobody has yet succeeded in designing an alternative system in which certain features of the existing one can be preserved which are dear even to those who most violently assail it—such as particularly the extent to which the individual can choose his pursuits and consequently freely use his own knowledge and skill.

7

It is in many ways fortunate that the dispute about the indispensability of the price system for any rational calculation in a complex society is now no longer conducted entirely between camps holding different political views. The thesis that without the price system we could not preserve a society based on such extensive division of labor as ours was greeted with a howl of derision when it was first advanced by Von Mises twenty-five years ago. Today the difficulties which some still find in accepting it are no longer mainly political, and this makes for an atmosphere much more conducive to reasonable discussion. When we find Leon Trotsky arguing that "economic accounting is unthinkable without market relations"; when Professor Oscar Lange promises Professor von Mises a statue in the marble halls of the future Central Planning Board; and when Professor Abba P. Lerner rediscovers Adam Smith and emphasizes that the essential utility of the price system consists in inducing the individual, while seeking his own interest, to do what is in the general interest, the differences can indeed no longer be ascribed to political prejudice. The remaining dissent seems clearly to be due to purely intellectual, and more particularly methodological, differences.

A recent statement by Joseph Schumpeter in his *Capitalism, Socialism, and Democracy* provides a clear illustration of one of the methodological differences which I have in mind. Its author is pre-eminent among those economists who approach economic phenomena in the light of a certain branch of positivism. To him these phenomena accordingly appear as objectively given quantities of commodities impinging directly upon each other, almost, it would seem, without any intervention of human minds. Only against this background can I account for the following (to me startling) pronouncement. Professor Schumpeter argues that the possibility of a rational calculation in the absence of markets for the factors of production follows for the theorist "from the elementary proposition that consumers in evaluating ('demanding') consumers' goods *ipso facto* also evaluate the means of production which enter into the production of these goods."[1]

Taken literally, this statement is simply untrue. The consumers do nothing of the kind. What Professor Schumpeter's "*ipso facto*" presumably means is that the valuation of the factors of production is implied in, or follows necessarily from, the valuation of consumers' goods. But this, too, is not correct. Implication is a logical relationship which can be meaningfully asserted only if propositions simultaneously present to one and the same mind. It is evident, however, that the values of the factors of production do not depend solely on the valuation of the consumers' goods but also on the conditions of supply of the various factors of production. Only to a mind to which all these facts were simultaneously known would the answer necessarily follow from the facts given to it. The practical problem, however, arises precisely because these facts are never so given to a single mind, and because, in consequence, it is necessary that in the solution of the problem knowledge should be used that is dispersed among many people.

The problem is thus in no way solved if we can show that all the facts, *if* they were known to a single mind (as we hypothetically assume them to be given to the observing economist), would uniquely determine the solution; instead we must show how a solution is produced by the interactions of people each of whom possesses only partial knowledge. To assume all the knowledge to be given to a single mind in the same manner in which we assume it to be given to us as the explaining economists is to assume the problem away and to disregard everything that is important and significant in the real world.

That an economist of Professor Schumpeter's standing should thus have fallen into a trap which the ambiguity of the term "datum" sets to the unwary can hardly be explained as a simple error. It suggests rather that there is something fundamentally wrong with an approach which habitually disregards an essential part of the phenomena with which we have to deal: the unavoidable imperfection of man's knowledge and the consequent need for a process by which knowledge is constantly communicated and acquired. Any approach, such as that of much of mathematical economics with its simultaneous equations, which in effect starts from the assumption that people's *knowledge* corresponds with the objective *facts* of the situation, systematically leaves out what is our main task to explain. I am far from denying that in our system equilibrium analysis has a useful function to perform. But when it comes to the point where it misleads some of our leading thinkers into believing that the situation which it describes has direct relevance to the solution of practical problems, it is high time that we remember that it does not deal with the social process at all and that it is no more than a useful preliminary to the study of the main problem.

Note

1. *Capitalism, Socialism and Democracy* (New York: Harper & Bros., 1942), p. 175. Professor Schumpeter is, I believe, also the original author of the myth that Pareto and Barone have "solved" the problem of socialist calculation. What they, and many others, did was merely to state the conditions which a rational allocation of resources would have to satisfy and to point out that these were essentially the same as the conditions of equilibrium of a competitive market. This is something altogether different from showing how the allocation of resources satisfying these conditions can be found in practice. Pareto himself (from whom Barone has taken practically everything he has to say), far from claiming to have solved the practical problem, in fact explicitly denies that it can be solved without the help of the market. See his *Manuel d'economie pure* (2nd ed., 1927), pp. 233–34. The relevant passage is quoted in an English translation at the beginning of my article on "Socialist Calculation: The Competitive 'Solution,'" in *Economica*, VIII, No. 26 (new ser., 1940), 125; reprinted below as chapter viii.

15

The Meaning of Competition

Friedrich A. Hayek

1

There are signs of increasing awareness among economists that what they have been discussing in recent years
under the name of "competition" is not the same thing as
what is thus called in ordinary language. But, although
there have been some valiant attempts to bring discussion
back to earth and to direct attention to the problems of real
life, notably by J.M. Clark and F. Machlup,[1] the general view
seems still to regard the conception of competition currently
employed by economists as the significant one and to treat
that of the businessman as an abuse. It appears to be generally held that the so-called theory of "perfect competition"
provides the appropriate model for judging the effectiveness of competition in real life and that, to the extent that
real competition differs from that model, it is undesirable
and even harmful.

For this attitude there seems to me to exist very little
justification. I shall attempt to show that what the theory of
perfect competition discusses has little claim to be called
"competition" at all and that its conclusions are of little use

Reprinted from *Individualism and Economic Order* by Friedrich A. Hayek (Chicago: The University of Chicago Press, 1980). This essay reproduces the substance of the Stafford Little Lecture delivered at Princeton University on May
20, 1946.

as guides to policy. The reason for this seems to me to be that this theory throughout assumes that state of affairs already to exist which, according to the truer view of the older theory, the process of competition tends to bring about (or to approximate) and that, if the state of affairs assumed by the theory of perfect competition ever existed, it would not only deprive of their scope all the activities which the verb "to compete" describes but would make them virtually impossible.

If all this affected only the use of the word "competition," it would not matter a great deal. But it seems almost as if economists by this peculiar use of language were deceiving themselves into the belief that, in discussing "competition," they are saying something about the nature and significance of the process by which the state of affairs is brought about which they merely assume to exist. In fact, this moving force of economic life is left almost altogether undiscussed.

I do not wish to discuss here at any length the reasons which have led the theory of competition into this curious state. As I have suggested elsewhere in this volume,[2] the tautological method which is appropriate and indispensable for the analysis of individual action seems in this instance to have been illegitimately extended to problems in which we have to deal with a social process in which the decisions of many individuals influence one another and necessarily succeed one another in time. The economic calculus (or the Pure Logic of Choice) which deals with the first kind of problems consist of an apparatus of classification of possible human attitudes and provides us with a technique for describing the interrelations of the different parts of a single plan. Its conclusions are implicit in its assumptions: the desires and the knowledge of the facts, which are assumed to be simultaneously present to a single mind, determine a unique solution. The relations discussed in this type of analysis are logical relations, concerned solely with the conclusions which follow for the mind of the planning individual from the given premises.

When we deal, however, with a situation in which a number of persons are attempting to work out their separate plans, we can no longer assume that the data are the same for all the planning minds. The problem becomes one of how the "data" of the different individuals on which they base their plans are adjusted to the objective facts of their environment (which includes the actions of the other people). Although in the solution of this type of problem we still must make use of our technique for rapidly working out the implications of a given set of data, we have now to deal not only with several separate sets of data of the different persons but also—and this is even more important—with a process which necessarily involves continuous changes in the data for the different individuals. As I have suggested before, the causal factor enters here in the form of the acquisition of new knowledge by the different individuals or of changes in their data brought about by the contacts between them.

The relevance of this for my present problem will appear when it is recalled that the modern theory of competition deals almost exclusively with a state of what is called "competitive equilibrium" in which it is assumed that the data for the different individuals are fully adjusted to each other, while the problem which requires explanation is the nature of the process by which the data are thus adjusted. In other words, the description of competitive equilibrium does not even attempt to say that, if we find such and such conditions, such and such consequences will follow, but confines itself to defining conditions in which its conclusions are already implicitly contained and which may conceivably exist but of which it does not tell us how they can ever be brought about. Or, to anticipate our main conclusion in a brief statement, competition is by its nature a dynamic process whose essential characteristics are assumed away by the assumptions underlying static analysis.

2

That the modern theory of competitive equilibrium *assumes* the situation to exist which a true explanation ought to account for as the effect of the competitive process is best shown by examining the familiar list of conditions found in any modern textbook. Most of these conditions, incidentally, not only underlie the analysis of "perfect" competition but are equally assumed in the discussion of the various "imperfect" or "monopolistic" markets, which throughout assume certain unrealistic "perfections."[3] For our immediate purpose, however, the theory of perfect competition will be the most instructive case to examine.

While different authors may state the list of essential conditions of perfect competition differently, the following is probably more than sufficiently comprehensive for our purpose, because, as we shall see, those conditions are not really independent of each other. According to the generally accepted view, perfect competition presupposes:

1. A homogeneous commodity offered and demanded by a large number of relatively small sellers or buyers, none of whom expects to exercise by his action a perceptible influence on price.

2. Free entry into the market and absence of other restraints on the movement of prices and resources.

3. Complete knowledge of the relevant factors on the part of all participants in the market.

We shall not ask at this stage precisely for what these conditions are required or what is implied if they are assumed to be given. But we must inquire a little further about their meaning, and in this respect it is the third condition which is the critical and obscure one. The standard can evidently not be perfect knowledge of everything affecting the market on the part of every person taking part in it. I shall here not go into the familiar paradox of the paralyzing effect really perfect knowledge and foresight would have on all action.[4] It will be obvious also that nothing is solved when we assume everybody to know everything and that the real problem is rather how it can be brought about that as much of the available knowledge as possible is used. This raises for a competitive society the question, not how we can "find" the people who know best, but rather what institutional arrangements are necessary in order that the unknown persons who have knowledge specially suited to a particular task are most likely to be attracted to that task. But we must inquire a little further what sort of knowledge it is that is supposed to be in possession of the parties of the market.

If we consider the market for some kind of finished consumption goods and start with the position of its producers or sellers, we shall find, first, that they are assumed to know the lowest cost at which the commodity can be produced. Yet this knowledge which is assumed to be given to begin with is one of the main points where it is only through the process of competition that the facts will be discovered. This appears to me one of the most important of the points where the starting-point of the theory of competitive equilibrium assumes away the main task which only the process of competition can solve. The position is somewhat similar with respect to the second point on which the producers are assumed to be fully informed: the wishes and desires of the consumers, including the kinds of goods and services which they demand and the prices they are willing to pay. These cannot properly be regarded as given facts but ought rather to be regarded as problems to be solved by the process of competition.

The same situation exists on the side of the consumers or buyers. Again the knowledge they are supposed to possess in a state of competitive equilibrium cannot be legitimately assumed to be at their command before the process of competition starts. Their knowledge of the alternatives before them is the result of what happens on the market, of such activities as advertising, etc.; and the whole organization of the market serves mainly the need of spreading the information on which the buyer is to act.

The peculiar nature of the assumptions from which the theory of competitive equilibrium starts stands out very clearly if we ask which of the activities that are commonly designated by the verb "to compete" would still be possible if those conditions were all satisfied. Perhaps it is worth recalling that, according to Dr. Johnson, competition is "the action of endeavoring to gain what another endeavors to gain at the same time." Now, how many of the devices adopted in ordinary life to that end would still be open to a seller in a market in which so-called "perfect competition" prevails? I believe that the answer is exactly none. Advertising, undercutting, and improving ("differentiating") the goods or services produced are all excluded by definition— "perfect" competition means indeed the absence of all competitive activities.

Especially remarkable in this connection is the explicit and complete exclusion from the theory of perfect competition of all personal relationships existing between the parties.[5] In actual life the fact that our inadequate knowledge of the available commodities or services is made up for by our experience with the persons or firms supplying them— that competition is in a large measure competition for reputation or good will—is one of the most important facts which enables us to solve our daily problems. The function of competition is here precisely to teach us *who* will serve us well: which grocer or travel agency, which department store or hotel, which doctor or solicitor, we can expect to provide the most satisfactory solution for whatever particular personal problem we may have to face. Evidently in all these fields competition may be very intense, just because the services of the different persons or firms will never be exactly alike, and it will be owing to this competition that we are in a position to be served as well as we are. The reasons competition in this field is described as imperfect have indeed nothing to do with the competitive character of the activities of these people; it lies in the nature of the commodities or services themselves. If no two doctors are perfectly alike, this does not mean that the competition between them is less intense but merely that any degree of competition between them will not produce exactly those results which it would if their services were exactly alike. This is not a purely verbal point. The talk about the defects or competition when we are in fact talking about the necessary difference between commodities and services conceals a very real confusion and leads on occasion to absurd conclusions.

While on a first glance the assumption concerning the perfect knowledge possessed by the parties may seem the most startling and artificial of all those on which the theory of perfect competition is based, it may in fact be no more than a consequence of, and in part even justified by, another of the presuppositions on which it is founded. If, indeed, we start by assuming that a large number of people are producing the same commodity and command the same objective facilities and opportunities for doing so, then indeed it might be made plausible (although this has, to my knowledge, never been attempted) that they will in time all be led to know most of the facts relevant for judging the market of that commodity. Not only will each producer by his experience learn the same facts as every other but also he will thus come to know what his fellows know and in consequence the elasticity of the demand for his own product. The condition where different manufacturers produce the identical product under identical conditions is in fact the most favorable for producing that state of knowledge among them which perfect competition requires. Perhaps this means no more than that the commodities can be identical in the sense in which it is alone relevant for our understanding human action only if people hold the same views about them, although it should also be possible to state a set of physical conditions which is favorable to all those who are concerned with a set of closely interrelated activities learning the facts relevant for their decisions.

However that be, it will be clear that the facts will not always be as favorable to this result as they are when many people are at least in a position to produce the same article. The conception of the economic system as divisible into distinct markets for separate commodities is after all very largely the product of the imagination of the economist and certainly is not the rule in the field of manufacture and of personal services, to which the discussion about competition so largely refers. In fact, it need hardly be said, no products of two producers are ever exactly alike, even if it were only because, as they leave his plant, they must be at different places. These differences are part of the facts which create our economic problem, and it is little help to answer it on the assumption that they are absent.

The belief in the advantages of perfect competition frequently leads enthusiasts even to argue that a more advantageous use of resources would be achieved if the existing variety of products were reduced by *compulsory* standardization. Now, there is undoubtedly much to be said in many fields for assisting standardization by agreed recommendations or standards which are to apply unless different requirements are explicitly stipulated in contracts. But this is something very different from the demands of those who believe that the variety of people's tastes should be disregarded and the constant experimentation with improvements should be suppressed in order to obtain the advantages of perfect competition. It would clearly not be an improvement to build all houses exactly alike in order to create a perfect market for houses, and the same is true of most other fields where differences between the individual products prevent competition from ever being perfect.

3

We shall probably learn more about the nature and significance of the competitive process if for a while we forget about the artificial assumptions underlying the theory of perfect competition and ask whether competition would be any less important if, for example, no two commodities were ever exactly alike. If it were not for the difficulty of the analysis of such a situation, it would be well worth while to consider in some detail the case where the different commodities could not be readily classed into distinct groups, but where we had to deal with a continuous range of close substitutes, every unit somewhat different from the other but without any marked break in the continuous range. The result of the analysis of competition in such a situation might in many respects be more relevant to the conditions of real life than those of the analysis of competition in a single industry producing a homogeneous commodity sharply differentiated from all others. Or, if the case where no two commodities are exactly alike be thought to be too extreme, we might at least turn to the case where no two producers produce exactly the same commodity, as is the rule not only with all personal services but also in the markets of many manufactured commodities, such as the markets for books or musical instruments.

For our present purpose I need not attempt anything like a complete analysis of such kinds of markets but shall merely ask what would be the role of competition in them. Although the result would, of course, within fairly wide margins be indeterminate, the market would still bring about a set of prices at which each commodity sold just cheap enough to outbid its potential close substitutes—and this in itself is no small thing when we consider the unsurmountable difficulties of discovering even such a system of prices by any other method except that of trial and error in the market, with the individual participants gradually learning the relevant circumstances. It is true, of course, that in such a market correspondence between prices and marginal costs is to be expected only to the degree that elasticities of demand for the individual commodities approach the conditions assumed by the theory of perfect competition or that elasticities of substitution between the different commodities approach infinity. But the point is that in this case this standard of perfection as something desirable or to be aimed at is wholly irrelevant. The basis of comparison, on the grounds of which the achievement of competition ought to be judged, cannot be a situation which is different from the objective facts and which cannot be brought about by any known means. It ought to be the situation as it would exist if competition were prevented from operating. Not the approach to an unachievable and meaningless ideal but the improvement upon the conditions that would exist without competition should be the test.

In such a situation how would conditions differ, if competition were "free" in the traditional sense, from those which would exist if, for example, only people licensed by authority were allowed to produce particular things, or prices were fixed by authority, or both? Clearly there would be not only no likelihood that the different things would be produced by those who knew best how to do it and therefore could do it at lowest cost but also no likelihood that all those things would be produced at all which, if the consumers had the choice, they would like best. There would be little relationship between actual prices and the lowest cost at which somebody would be able to produce these commodities; indeed, the alternatives between which both producers and consumers would be in a position to choose, their data, would be altogether different from what they would be under competition.

The real problem in all this is not whether we will get *given* commodities or services at *given* marginal costs but mainly by what commodities and services the needs of the people can be most cheaply satisfied. The solution of the economic problem of society is in this respect always a voyage of exploration into the unknown, an attempt to discover new ways of doing things better than they have been done before. This must always remain so as long as there are any economic problems to be solved at all, because all economic problems are created by unforeseen changes which require adaptation. Only what we have not foreseen and provided for requires new decisions. If no such adaptations were required, if at any moment we knew that all change had stopped and things would forever go on exactly as they are now, there would be no more questions of the use of resources to be solved.

A person who possesses the exclusive knowledge or skill which enables him to reduce the cost of production of a commodity by 50 percent still renders an enormous service to society if he enters its production and reduces its price by only 25 percent—not only through that price reduction but also through his additional saving of cost. But it is only through competition that we can assume that these possible savings of cost will be achieved. Even if in each instance prices were only just low enough to keep out producers which do not enjoy these or other equivalent advantages, so that each commodity were produced as cheaply as possible, though many may be sold at prices considerably above costs, this would probably be a result which could not be achieved by any other method than that of letting competition operate.

4

That in conditions of real life the position even of any two producers is hardly ever the same is due to facts which the theory of perfect competition eliminates by its concentration on a long-term equilibrium which in an ever changing world can never be reached. At any given moment the equipment of a particular firm is always largely determined by historical accident, and the problem is that it should make the best use of the given equipment (including the acquired capacities of the members of its staff) and not what it should do if it were given unlimited time to adjust itself to constant conditions. For the problem of the best use of the given durable but exhaustible resources the long-term equilibrium price with which a theory discussing "perfect" competition must be concerned is not only not relevant; the conclusions concerning policy to which preoccupation with this model leads are highly misleading and even dangerous. The idea that under "perfect" competition prices should be equal to long-run costs often leads to the approval of such antisocial practices as the demand for an "orderly competition" which will secure a fair return on capital and for the destruction of excess capacity. Enthusiasm for perfect competition in theory and the support of monopoly in practice are indeed surprisingly often found to live together.

That is, however, only one of the many points on which the neglect of the time element makes the theoretical picture of perfect competition so entirely remote from all that is relevant to an understanding of the process of competition. If we think of it, as we ought to, as a succession of events, it becomes even more obvious that in real life there will at any moment be as a rule only one producer who can manufacture a given article at the lowest cost and who may in fact sell below the cost of his next successful competitor, but who, while still trying to extend his market, will often be overtaken by somebody else, who in turn will be prevented from capturing the whole market by yet another, and so on. Such a market would clearly never be in a state of perfect competition, yet competition in it might not only be as intense as possible but would also be the essential factor in bringing about the fact that the article in question is supplied at any moment to the consumer as cheaply as this can be done by any known method.

When we compare an "imperfect" market like this with a relatively "perfect" market as that of, say, grain, we shall now be in a better position to bring out the distinction which has been underlying this whole discussion—the distinction between the underlying objective facts of a situation which cannot be altered by human activity and the nature of the competitive activities by which men adjust themselves to the situation. Where, as in the latter case, we have a highly organized market of a fully standardized commodity produced by many producers, there is little need or scope for competitive activities because the situation is such that the conditions which these activities might bring about are already satisfied to begin with. The best ways of producing the commodity, its character and uses, are most of the time known to nearly the same degree to all members of the market. The knowledge of any important change spreads so rapidly and the adaptation to it is so soon effected that we usually simply disregard what happens during these short transition periods and confine ourselves to comparing the two states of near-equilibrium which exist before and after them. But it is during this short and neglected interval that the forces of competition operate and become visible, and it is the events during this interval which we must study if we are to "explain" the equilibrium which follows it.

It is only in a market where adaptation is slow compared with the rate of change that the process of competition is in continuous operation. And though the reason why adaptation is slow *may* be that competition is weak, e.g., because there are special obstacles to entry into the trade, or because of some other factors of the character of natural monopolies, slow adaptation does by no means necessarily mean weak competition. When the variety of near-substitutes is great and rapidly changing, where it takes a long time to find out about the relative merits of the available alternatives, or where the need for a whole class of goods or services occurs only discontinuously at irregular intervals, the adjustment must be slow even if competition is strong and active.

The confusion between the objective facts of the situation and the character of the human responses to it tends to conceal from us the important fact that competition is the more important the more complex or "imperfect" are the objective conditions in which it has to operate. Indeed, far from competition being beneficial only when it is "perfect," I am inclined to argue that the need for competition is nowhere greater than in fields in which the nature of the commodities or services makes it impossible that it ever should create a perfect market in the theoretical sense. The inevitable actual imperfections of competition are as little an argument against competition as the difficulties of achieving a perfect solution of any other task are an argument against attempting to solve it at all, or as little as imperfect health is an argument against health.

In conditions where we can never have many people offering the same homogeneous product or service, because of the ever changing character of our needs and our knowledge, or of the infinite variety of human skills and capacities, the ideal state cannot be one requiring an identical character of large numbers of such products and services. The economic problem is a problem of making the best use of what resources we have, and not one of what we should do if the situation were different from what it actually is. There is no sense in talking of a use of resources "as if" a perfect market existed, if this means that the resources would have to be different from what they are, or in discussing what somebody with perfect knowledge would do if our task must be to make the best use of the knowledge the existing people have.

5

The argument in favor of competition does not rest on the conditions that would exist if it were perfect. Although, where the objective facts would make it possible for competition to approach perfection, this would also secure the most effective use of resources, and, although there is therefore every case for removing human obstacles to competition, this does not mean that competition does not also bring about as effective a use of resources as can be brought about by any known means where in the nature of the case it must be imperfect. Even where free entry will secure no more than that at any one moment all the goods and services for which there would be an effective demand if they were available are in fact produced at the least current[6] expenditure of resources at which, in the given historical situation, they can be produced, even though the price the consumer is made to pay for them is considerably higher and only just below the cost of the next best way in which his need could be satisfied, this, I submit, is more than we can expect from any other known system. The decisive point is still the elementary one that it is most unlikely that, without artificial obstacles which government activity either creates or can remove, any commodity or service will for any length of time be available only at a price at which outsiders could expect a more than normal profit if they entered the field.

The practical lesson of all this, I think, is that we should worry much less about whether competition in a given case is perfect and worry much more whether there is competition at all. What our theoretical models of separate industries conceal is that in practice a much bigger gulf divides competition from no competition than perfect from imperfect competition. Yet the current tendency in discussion is to be intolerant about the imperfections and to be silent about the prevention of competition. We can probably still learn more about the real significance of competition by studying the results which regularly occur where competition is deliberately suppressed than by concentrating on the shortcomings of actual competition compared with an ideal which is irrelevant for the given facts. I say advisedly "where competition is deliberately suppressed" and not merely "where it is absent," because its main effects are usually operating, even if more slowly, so long as it is not outright suppressed with the assistance or the tolerance of the state. The evils which experience has shown to be the regular consequence of a suppression of competition are on a different plane from those which the imperfections of competition may cause. Much more serious than the fact that prices may not correspond to marginal cost is the fact that, with an intrenched monopoly, costs are likely to be much higher than is necessary. A monopoly based on superior efficiency, on the other hand, does comparatively little harm so long as it is assured that it will disappear as soon as anyone else becomes more efficient in providing satisfaction to the consumers.

In conclusion I want for a moment to go back to the point from which I started and restate the most important conclusion in a more general form. Competition is essentially a process of the formation of opinion: by spreading information, it creates the unity and coherence of the economic system which we presuppose when we think of it as one market. It creates the views people have about what is best and cheapest, and it is because of it that people know at least as much about possibilities and opportunities as they in fact do. It is thus a process which involves a continuous change in the data and whose significance must therefore be completely missed by any theory which treats these data as constant.

Notes

1. J. M. Clark, "Toward a Concept of Workable Competition," *American Economic Review,* vol. XXX (June, 1940); F. Machlup, "Competition, Pliopoly, and Profit," *Economica,* vol. IX (new ser.; February and May, 1942).
2. See the second and fourth chapters.
3. Particularly the assumptions that *at all times* a uniform price must rule for a given commodity throughout the market and that sellers know the shape of the demand curve.
4. See O. Morgenstern, "Vollkommene Voraussicht und wirtschaftliches Gleichgewicht," *Zeitschrift fur Nationalokonomie,* vol. VI (1935).
5. Cf. G. J. Stigler, *The Theory of Price* (1946), p. 24: "Economic relationships are never perfectly competitive if they involve any personal relationships between economic units" (see also *ibid.,* p. 226).
6. "Current" cost in this connection excludes all true bygones but includes, of course, "user cost."

16
Cost and Choice—
Austrian vs. Conventional Views

E. C. Pasour, Jr.

The relationship between product prices and production costs is front page news today. President Carter assured farmers during the 1976 presidential campaign that his administration would raise farm prices sufficiently high to cover production costs. A year later there were farmer demonstrations in the President's home town and throughout the country, protesting the unfavorable relationship between farm prices and production costs.

There is also widespread sentiment for setting prices of electricity, oil, natural gas and other energy sources on the basis of production costs. Government intervention to base prices on cost requires that costs be calculated. Politicians and most economists (except for members of the Austrian school) have assumed that costs relevant to production decisions, can, in fact, be determined. Little attention has been given by conventional economists, politicians, and the public-at-large, however, to problems the outside observer faces in determining costs of any production process. This paper demonstrates that choice-influencing costs are inherently subjective and not subject to objective measurement, and stresses the implications for economic regulation and efficiency measurements of real world economic activity.

Reprinted from *Journal of Libertarian Studies* 2:4 (1978), pp. 327–36.

The primary purpose of this paper is to contrast Austrian and conventional concepts of cost. Cost in the logic-of-choice context of conventional neoclassical economic theory is contrasted with subjective cost relevant to individual decision making. The Austrian subjectivist concept of cost is shown to be sound as it relates to individual choice. The limitations of objective estimates of "cost" when used as a normative standard in evaluating observed market behavior are stressed. Implications of the findings are related to a number of policy issues and problems involving cost.

The Nature of Costs

Austrian (and virtually all other) economists define cost in terms of opportunity cost. The opportunity cost of any decision represents the value of opportunities foregone as a result of the decision made. Cost involves the conscious sacrifice of an available opportunity by the decision-maker. The cost of a vacation trip, for example, is the value placed by the decision-maker on the boat, refrigerator, or other alternatives which must be foregone if the trip is taken.

Opportunity cost stresses the relationship between the act of choice by the decision-maker and opportunities foregone. "Costs are equal to the value attached to the satisfaction which one must forego in order to attain the end aimed at."[1] This cost as it influences choice is based on the decision-makers' anticipations and cannot be discovered by another person. That is, no one else is capable of accurately assessing the value of the sacrificed alternative by the decision-maker. Thus, as recognized and emphasized by the Austrians, the opportunity cost of any activity is inherently subjective.

A recognition that cost is subjective has profound implications for the economic analyst. Since cost is experienced by the decision-maker at the moment of choice, it means that there is no way for outsiders to objectively measure the costs which are relevant to decisions actually made. Thus, the definition of cost in terms of opportunities foregone, though accepted by conventional and Austrian economists, is consistent only with the basic subjectivist approach of the Austrians.

Conventional neoclassical theorists implicitly assume that cost is objective, i.e., that the cost of production can be determined by outside observers. The market price of the resources used in production is typically taken in neoclassical theory to be an estimate of opportunity cost. The "cost" of producing corn, for example, is obtained by adding together the market values of land, labor, fertilizer and other inputs required to produce a bushel of corn.

The *ex ante* planning process, however, inevitably involves subjective judgment by the entrepreneur. Summing up production outlays is an objective procedure but does not provide the relevant cost of production which influences entrepreneurial behavior. The market price of an input may differ considerably from its opportunity cost to the entrepreneur, as illustrated by the following example. Consider the cost to be imputed to (say) land in producing corn. The cost of land in corn is the value of opportunities foregone by using land for corn instead of using land in its best alternative use. Cost by its very nature, however, involves choice, and choice cannot be predetermined and still remain choice.[2] The cost of similar land in corn may well be quite different for Jones and Smith. Jones, for example, may anticipate a return to land of $30 per acre when using the land for soybeans (the best alternative use). Smith, on the other hand, being more optimistic about future soybean yields or prices, may anticipate a return of $50 per acre for Jones and $50 per acre for Smith, even though Jones and Smith pay the same rental price for land.

This example illustrates the fact that cost of land (and other inputs) as it influences the entrepreneurial decision (choice) is inherently subjective. It explains why Jones may be observed to plant corn and Smith soybeans even though a conventional enterprise budget of costs and returns might show the same cost for each producer. Such budgets typically assume that yields and prices are given. In reality, of course, the entrepreneur must estimate both yields and prices. Production decisions are based on opportunity costs which exist only in the mind of the decision-maker. Since choice is among thoughts or things imagined, there is no way for an outside observer to determine these subjective evaluations.[3]

Consider a second illustration of why the *ex ante* planning process under uncertainty involves subjective judgment by the entrepreneur as well as a capacity for arithmetical calculations. Expectations concerning future demand and cost conditions affect the decision of whether to continue to operate with present plant, machinery, and equipment or whether to make major adjustments in the productive facility. Expectations determine expected depreciation (including obsolescence) and, consequently, determine allowances for interest and depreciation. Here again, there is no way for the outside observer to determine the relevant costs which influence entrepreneurial choice. The depreciation and interest cost estimates by outside observers must be based on historical costs or on the observer's estimate of opportunity costs, which may bear little or no relationship to opportunity costs as perceived by the entrepreneur.[4]

Hayek stresses the point that anticipating future changes is an entrepreneurial function and necessarily subjective. "In no sense can costs during any period be said to depend solely on prices during that period ... in fact, almost every real world decision concerning how to produce depends at least in part on the views held about the future."[5]

As shown later, the fact that expectations are subjective poses seemingly insurmountable problems for economic analysis of entrepreneurial choices.

In neoclassical economic theory, revenues and costs are assumed to be known. The major emphasis is placed on the logic of maximizing profits subject to given costs and returns. Given these data, profit maximization is an objective procedure.[6] The Austrian subjectivist approach, on the other hand, stresses the fact that such data should not, in fact, be assumed to be given to the decision-maker. In reality, a key function of the entrepreneur is to estimate prospective costs and returns in choosing between alternative production plans or strategies.[7] Alchian has shown that profit maximization loses meaning as a guide in choosing among alternative courses of action under conditions of uncertainty.[8]

There is no hard and fast distinction between the Austrian and conventional neoclassical economists on the cost issue. In fact, some economists not usually identified with the Austrian school are more in the Austrian subjectivist tradition than in the conventional neo-Marshallian objectivist tradition on the cost issue. James Buchanan and Ronald Coase are good examples. Buchanan, along with G. F. Thirlby, recently edited a book which defends the subjectivist view of cost.[9] The book presents a collection of articles mainly by economists identified at some time with the London School of Economics (Lionel Robbins, F. A. Hayek, R. S. Edwards, G. F. Thirlby and Jack Wiseman). One of the articles is by R. H. Coase.

Coase's article consists of a shortened version of a series of articles which he wrote for *The Accountant* (a British publication) in 1938. In these articles, Coase clearly illustrates the problems posed to the accountant by the subjectivist nature of cost. Cost to the decision-maker involves an *ex ante* evaluation of uncertain future outcomes. Since the future is always uncertain, the evaluation of future outcomes will vary from person to person and will be influenced by numerous factors including the attitude toward risk. The result is that cost as it influences choice loses its objective content. As

Coase states,

> There is no one decision which can be considered to maximize profits independently of the attitude of risk taking of the business man. A further point is that the correctness of the decision cannot be determined by subsequent events. If a businessman undertakes to do something which entails certain risk, he considers that the chance of gain is worth the risk he runs, and whether he succeeds or fails has no relevance to his preference.[10]

Although the subjective nature of cost emerges clearly in his early work, Coase does not appear to have pursued the implications of this work as it relates to empirical applications of neoclassical price theory.

Implications

The distinction between the objective and subjective views of cost has a number of implications both theoretical and empirical.

Methodology

Cost theory in economic texts is handled quite differently by the Austrian school when contrasted with the conventional neoclassical school of economics. Since cost as it influences choice is inherently subjective, little use is made of cost curves in economic texts written by the neo-Austrians. Rothbard, in his *magnum opus, Man, Economy and State*, justifies this difference in approach between Austrians and other economists as follows:

> It may be noted that, in this work, there is none of that plethora and tangle of "cost curves" which fill the hori-

zon of almost every recent neoclassical work in economics. This omission has been deliberate, since it is our contention that the cost curves are at best redundant (thus violating the simplicity principle of Occam's Razor), and at worst misleading and erroneous.[11]

The Austrians take the same methodological approach to cost theory as they take toward economic theory in general. The Austrians stress the logical theory of economic choice and deny the value of empirical testing of economic hypotheses. As Kirzner states in explaining the approach of Mises and other latter-day Austrians:

> ... empirical confirmation of the theorems obtained by abstract knowledge is neither possible nor necessary. It is not possible, because there are no constants in the realm of human actions; it is therefore impossible to investigate the consequences of changes in one variable with assurance that no disturbance is at the same time being caused by changes in other variables. On the other hand, confirmation of economic theorems is not necessary because the theorems themselves describe relationships logically implied by hypothesized conditions. The validity of these relationships can be tested by examining the reasoning employed to establish them.[12]

There is a fundamental difference of opinion between Austrian and conventional economists concerning prediction and hypothesis testing. A general discussion of these differences as reflected in Kirzner's comments is beyond the purview of this study. However, in the context of the topic of this paper it seems clear that there is no way for an outside observer to test hypotheses related to opportunity cost, since only the decision-maker is able to evaluate sacrificed opportunities.

Consider, for instance, the example of an outside observer who wishes to test the hypothesis that the cost for Jones of commuting by bus is lower than his cost of commuting by car. The analyst has no way to determine the relevant costs, the sacrificed opportunities, associated with a particular mode of travel. What, for example, is the value placed on flexibility, on time spent travelling, etc.? When the economic analyst arbitrarily assigns values to these variables, there is no reason to expect them to correspond with the actual opportunity cost experienced by the decision-maker. Thus, the result of such an analysis is not valid for normative purposes. It is invalid to conclude from such an analysis that the driver could reduce cost by changing his mode of travel.

In the conventional neoclassical theory of the firm, emphasis is placed on the logic of profit-maximizing behavior by the firm, assuming that information on costs and returns is given. Stress is placed on the relationship between marginal and average cost curves and product demand under equilibrium conditions.

A problem usually not explicitly recognized, arises in conventional cost theory when resources are specialized. Most conventional theory texts deal with a world of unspecialized resources. In the real world, however, land, labor, productive facilities, and entrepreneurship are specialized and differ between firms. The price theory book by Friedman is one of the few texts to point out the problem posed by specialized resources to conventional cost analysis.

> The existence of specialized resources ... makes it impossible to define the average cost of a particular firm for different hypothetical outputs independently of demand.... Take the copper mine of the preceding paragraph: its cost curve cannot be computed without knowledge of the royalty or rent that must be paid to owners of the mine, if the firm does not itself own it, or imputed as royalty or rent, if the firm does. But the

royalty is clearly dependent on the price at which copper sells on the market and is determined in such a way as to make average cost tend to equal price.... The equality of price to average cost ... is forced on the firm by the operation of the capital market or the market determining rents for specialized resources.[13]

The specific implications of specialized resources are further considered in a later section. In spite of the explicit recognition of problems posed to conventional cost theory by specialized resources in Friedman's text, there is no recognition of the problems involved in obtaining the cost data which lie behind cost curves.

Problems associated with the subjectivity of cost do not arise as long as concern is limited to the *logic* of choice, and much of conventional economic theory is concerned with this logic. The logic of choice, as it relates to cost, for example, instructs the decision-maker on which outlays are relevant for current decisions and which are "fixed costs." The rule, "let bygones be bygones," is often difficult to apply in making real world choices. "Instructing the decision-maker as to how he should choose may produce 'better' choices as evaluated by his own standards."[14] Thus, the logic of choice as it applies to cost can be treated independently of the process of determining cost.

In many cases, historical data can provide useful information to the entrepreneur in assessing future conditions. Today, there are private firms which specialize in providing cost estimates and (other) outlook information based on historical economic data. It should be clear, however, that operations research and econometric studies at most can provide useful information to the entrepreneur. The data provided will be interpreted in different ways by different entrepreneurs and do nothing to reduce the subjective nature of the entrepreneurial function.

The use of objective cost estimates poses no problem as

long as they are considered to be *data* for use by the entrepreneur and not as choice-influencing costs. A serious problem arises in neoclassical theory, however, when objective
"cost" estimates made by external observers are used for
normative purposes and are assumed to represent the costs
appropriate to current decision making, i.e., to the theory
of choice. As shown by the above example relating to land
cost in producing copper, there is no reason to expect a
direct relationship between the objective cost estimates of
neoclassical theory and the costs relevant to the act of
choice.[15]

The examples discussed below demonstrate how common it is to use objective cost estimates in a choice context
(for normative purposes), viz. in determining "optimum"
price and output levels and for evaluating the efficiency of
firm and household decisions. The Austrian criticism of the
use of cost and return estimates by outside observers for
normative purposes appears to be unassailable. The results
are not valid because the costs relevant to the act of choice
in any economic decision are subjective. That is, outside
observers cannot obtain objective cost estimates which are
appropriate to the moment of choice. The inappropriate-
ness of using objective cost estimates as though these estimates were costs appropriate to the act of choice will be
discussed in three different contexts.[16]

Economic Regulation

A considerable amount of attention is devoted to the
problem of monitoring firm costs in regulating public utilities and other "natural monopolies." State utility commissions are active throughout the U.S. estimating the cost of
providing electricity, telephone services, etc., to be used as
a basis for rate setting. This activity presumes that the
government regulator has an objective basis for setting
prices based on costs which would prevail under competitive
conditions.

An appreciation of the nature of the role of the entrepreneur is necessary to understand the problems faced by regulators in setting prices. In the case of public utilities, regulatory commissions attempt to insure that these "natural monopolies" charge a competitive price (or rate of return) as determined by production costs. Since choice-influencing costs are subjective and incurred at the moment of choice, cost as it influences entrepreneurial behavior cannot be obtained from the firms' accounting "cost" records. Attempts to force utilities (or other "natural monopolies") to set price equal to cost can be no more than hollow appeals.[17] Production decisions, as stressed by Hayek, hinge on views held about the future as well as current conditions, and there is no reason to expect the regulator's view to coincide with that of the entrepreneur. Thus, there is no objective procedure by which the regulator can determine whether prices should be increased or decreased if prices are to be based on "costs."

A closely related point concerns the nature of the market. The market, as Hayek stressed, is not merely an alternative way of discovering costs and prices which are capable of being determined by central direction. Competitive costs can only be determined by having competition. Yet, much economic regulation assumes that competitive costs can be determined through the regulatory process.

In view of these problems in measuring cost, it should not come as a surprise when economic studies find the effect of regulatory commissions on utility rates to be negligible. Stigler and Friedland, for example, in a pioneering study were unable to find any significant effect of the regulation of electrical utilities on utility rates.[18] Perhaps the apparent lack of effect of regulatory commissions in holding down rates in such cases is fortunate for the consumer. There is no reason to expect that the effect of holding down current rates (thereby curtailing future supply below the level of an unregulated public utility) will redound to the benefit of the public. It seems just as likely that the effects will be similar to those of current price controls on oil and natural gas. These controls reduced the production and supply of these products below the level dictated by the market, causing, or at least exacerbating, the shortage during the winter of 1976–1977.

The subjective nature of cost poses the same problems for all other regulatory agencies which are charged with setting prices in "the public interest." In some cases, however, the problem differs slightly from the case of utilities. In the case of milk (and other commodities produced under government price supports), the price is *deliberately set above* the competitive level. In the case of price supports for milk and other agricultural products, minimum wages, etc., where price is deliberately raised above the market level, the lack of any objective basis in setting price is even more apparent than in the case of public utilities where the avowed purpose is to set price on the basis of cost. When the price is not set at the competitive level, the problem of determining the appropriate price is the same as that faced by Aristotle and others who sought the "just price."

The example of milk and other agricultural products where price is deliberately raised above the market level illustrates another important point. When price is set above the market level by government fiat, increases in produce price will be capitalized into specialized input prices through competitive market forces so that production outlays will rise to meet returns. In the Austrian terminology, it is milk prices which determine milk costs and not production costs which determine milk prices. Consequently, attempts to set price based on production outlays (as proposed by Candidate Carter) are meaningless in the case of all production involving specialized resources since an increase in product price will be capitalized into increased production outlays. Under these conditions, the best estimate of cost is product price!

The phenomenon of input prices rising in response to changes in product price has also been observed in the case of farm real estate in recent years. Consider the effect of the price explosion of agricultural products in 1973 on the price of land. Farm real estate values in the U.S. have, on the average, more than doubled since 1972. Increases in land prices, however, are not responsible for high food prices. Instead, the expectation of high farm product prices in the future are responsible for high farm real estate prices. Lower farm product prices in 1977 dampened future expectations and reduced agricultural land prices in some states.

Assessing Economic Efficiency

The correctness of entrepreneurial decisions made under uncertain conditions, as Coase pointed out 40 years ago, cannot be determined by the outcome of subsequent events. Yet, the economics literature is replete with examples purporting to measure economic inefficiencies. The sources of inefficiency identified are definitional, however, and not related to the only appropriate norm for measuring efficiency, viz., the goal of the decision-maker. Efficiency, meaningfully defined, means that the decision-maker has no preferred alternative at the time the decision is made, given the circumstances.[19] When the subjective nature of choice is recognized, it becomes clear that it is impossible for the outside observer to identify any action or choice as inefficient or irrational in terms of the costs and benefits experienced by the decision-maker at the moment of choice.[20]

Empirical studies which compare the costs and benefits of regulatory agencies, for example, can never establish that such agencies are inefficient in a planning or choice sense. The costs and returns relevant to choice are those related to the expectations and goals of the entrepreneur when the program was initiated. These data, of course, are subjective, and not available *ex post* to economic analysts. If the expected gains and costs at the moment of choice could be fully specified, the regulatory agency would appear rational or efficient.

Recent studies have shown the FDA, FCC, FTC, and ICC and other regulatory agencies to be contrary to purpose and ineffectual as perceived by the empiricist using historical data.[21] This does not mean, however, that they are inefficient in the planning or choice sense since, as Coase stresses, correctness of decisions made under uncertain conditions cannot be determined *ex post,* i.e., by subsequent events.

Even though an outside observer can never establish that an action of a particular firm is inefficient based on a measurement of costs and returns which motivate choice, the economic analyst is not completely helpless in evaluating the degree to which the entrepreneur is successful. In a world of uncertainty, the relationship between purposive behavior and success is likely to be ambiguous. Success may be due to chance rather than to superior motivation or foresight. Alchian has proposed survival as a criterion for evaluating firm success.[22] This means that success should be judged on results rather than on motivation. In a market economy, realized positive "profits" may be taken as the criterion by which successful and surviving firms are selected. If monetary losses are large enough, the firm will be driven out of business regardless of its goals. As indicated above, success in some cases is accidental while in others it is due to entrepreneurial astuteness. Regardless of the reason for success, however, survival of the firm is achieved by those whose actions are most appropriate in terms of adapting to market conditions.

What is the process by which traits associated with success are acquired by firms? Trial and error is likely to play an important role since the firm must always operate in a climate of uncertainty. In addition, whenever successful firms are observed, we might expect that the elements common to success will be copied by competitors in their quest for success. In explaining past results (success), the economist may be able to determine the attributes which were important to survival, even though individual participants were not aware of them.[23] This does not imply that purposive behavior is absent from reality. It does mean that the economist can select the most successful firms and predict the effects of higher taxes, wage rates, etc. under market conditions without assuming that participants are aware of and act according to their cost and revenue curves.

The ability of the economist to identify firms on the basis of success is largely negated under a regime of economic regulation. Under government regulation, "profits" do not determine firm survival since prices can be raised or taxes can be used to cover losses. Thus, there is no presumption that surviving firms are efficient in terms of meeting the market test. It is significant that most goods and services provided through the government sector are sold at a price which requires a government subsidy.

Although survival provides a criterion for identifying the most successful firms, identification of the traits associated with success will always be tentative. Firms differ in an almost infinite variety of ways, including differences in size, location, capital facilities, and management, and it is not generally possible to select traits which are necessary for survival. At one time, for example, economists placed a great deal of emphasis on determining the "optimum size" firm. However, since a range of firm sizes persists over time, there is no reason to think that there is *an* optimum size of firm.

Alchian realizes that it will not be easy for economists to determine the more viable types of economic interrelationships.[24] Similar difficulties are faced in isolating the effects of economic regulation.

Economic Regulation:
Why Hope Springs Eternal

Machan points out that empirical cost and benefit studies can never discredit attempts at regulation:

> Empirical objections to a particular proposal for regulation cannot in themselves invalidate the *general* course of conduct. So what if studies demonstrate that this particular effort of such and such a regulatory agency has not worked? The *next one might*. Especially if we change some features of the policy in what appear to be significant ways.[25]

Machan's point is closely related to the *ex ante* versus *ex post* distinction noted above. The relevant costs and benefits in evaluating any decision are those appropriate to the decision at the moment of choice. The fact that there is a discrepancy between the net benefits anticipated when the decision was made and those realized when the program was implemented doesn't mean that the original decision was "bad." To so conclude would be to judge a decision on the basis of subsequent events.

The astuteness of a decision must be based on *ex ante* data, i.e., on the expected costs and benefits at the time the decision was made. As Machan indicates, the fact that one type of regulation is generally agreed to be counterproductive doesn't necessarily lead to the expectation that other types of regulation will also be counter-productive or unfavorable in the sense of its anticipated cost-benefit ratio. Why? "Better regulation" is always a possibility. The lack of effectiveness of Nixon-era price controls, for example, was attributed by J. K. Galbraith (and others) to the fact that the people in charge weren't sufficiently dedicated to the concept of price controls. For Ralph Nader and many people in the "consumerist" movement, the basic problem with government regulation lies in laxity, ineptitude, or venality by the regulators. In this view, the ICC, CAB, and other regulatory agencies can achieve their objective by placing better people in charge.

There are almost an infinite number of similar arguments which might be used to lead people to think that new regulation will be more effective than current regulation. The effectiveness of regulation might be improved by moving it from the federal to the local or state level, i.e., by moving it "closer to the people." Or, it might be improved by moving it from the local or state level to the federal level to avoid the corruption of local and state politicians, to standardize the level of service among wealthy and poor states, etc. The administration of regulatory agencies might be improved by increased "consumer" representation, by eliminating "petty rules," by allowing for a greater diversity of consumer tastes, by "sunset" features in legislation, by a new Consumer Advocacy Agency, etc.

Since government regulation can vary in an almost infinite number of ways, it seems unlikely that empirical cost and benefit studies of existing regulation will ever discredit the concept of government regulation. At the same time that the Carter Administration professes dissatisfaction with airline regulation, for example, it is waging the "moral equivalent of war" to regulate further energy and medical care. The failure of past government regulation to achieve stated goals appears to have little or no influence on the momentum to regulate further currently unregulated areas.

Summary and Conclusions

Cost is defined in terms of sacrificed alternatives by both Austrian and conventional neoclassical economists. The latter group holds that cost can be measured by an outside observer, while the former group stresses the fact that only the decision-maker is able to assess the value of the sacrificed alternative. This paper has attempted to demonstrate that the distinction between the Austrian and conventional views of cost is important and greatly influences the way the economist's role is viewed. In conventional neoclassical theory, the role of the entrepreneur is minimized, as emphasis is placed on the allocation of *given* means among *known* alternative ends. The Austrian approach stresses the fact that information about means and ends is not given to the entrepreneur, but that the entrepreneur's success hinges on how effectively he gains control of and uses resources in a world permeated with uncertainty.

Can the conventional and Austrian approaches to cost be reconciled? No problems arise in conventional economic theory so long as the task of cost theory is viewed in terms of the logic of choice. That is, there is no problem so long as cost theory is viewed as a system of logic by which the decision-maker can make "better choices." The problem arises when attempts are made to estimate costs which influence entrepreneurial choice.[26]

A recognition of the fact that choice-influencing costs cannot be objectively measured by outside observers places a new perspective on efforts by government to set prices on the basis of cost in the case of farm prices, petroleum prices, hospital prices, utility prices, etc. A recognition of this fact also makes it clear that government regulatory agencies cannot base prices on costs which motivate entrepreneurial behavior. So long as this basic subjective nature of cost is not realized, central planners, public policy makers, consumer interests, and other groups will continue to demand of government regulation that which it cannot provide, viz. cost data relevant in setting utility rates and product prices. Objective "cost" data and cost estimates are often useful to the entrepreneur. It should not be forgotten, however, that objective "cost" estimates are not the costs which influence individual choice and, hence, cannot be used for normative purposes.

Notes

An earlier version of this paper was presented at a seminar in the Department of Agricultural Economics, University of Kentucky, Lexington, Kentucky on January 21, 1977. The author wishes to thank Gerald P. O'Driscoll and Garry F. Vocke for helpful suggestions in revising the paper.

1. Ludwig von Mises, *Human Action* (Chicago: Henry Regnery Co., 1966), p. 97. Rothbard, closely identified with the "subjectivist economics" of the Austrian school, also stresses the subjective nature of cost. "In the first place, it must be stressed that these costs are subjective and cannot be precisely determined by outside observers or be gauged *ex post* by observing accountants." Murray Rothbard, *Man, Economy and State* (Los Angeles: Nash Pub. Co., 1970), p. 291.
2. J. M. Buchanan, "Is Economics the Science of Choice?" in *Roads to Freedom— Essays in Honour of Friedrich A. von Hayek,* ed. E. Streissler (New York: Augustus M. Kelley, 1969).
3. "Choice is necessarily amongst thoughts, amongst things imagined. For when experience is actual and proceeding, outside the realm of ideas, it is unique and already chosen." G. L. S. Shackle, *Epistemics and Economics: A Critique of Economic Doctrines* (Cambridge: Cambridge University Press, 1972), p. 130.
4. Shackle clearly demonstrates the relationship between cost and the entrepreneur's expectations. "The material possessions, the equipment of the business or of the economic society as a whole, would have no more value than the most casual objects and features of the scene, were they not embraced in a technology, an organization, a policy and, at any moment, a plan of action specified as to the persons whose interests it is to serve or whose orders or desires it is to satisfy, and as to

its location and its timing .... The 'facts' at best are like a few pieces of coloured stone or glass intended for a mosaic as a whole from the suggestions offered by these few disconnected fragments. A slight, accidental re-arrangement of the scattered fragments can reveal new possibility...." Shackle, *Epistemics*, p. 428.

5. F. A. Hayek, *Individualism and Economic Order* (Chicago: University of Chicago Press, 1974), p. 198.

6. Shackle points out that there is no place for choice in this approach. "In economics of the accepted Western, maximizing kind we are confronted with a basic contradiction: men are choosers, they choose the best, each for himself; what is the best can always be known to each person, either by merely consulting his own tastes or by applying the techniques of engineering or, where knowledge lacks a *simple* precision, by applying statistical techniques which turn ignorance of the particular into knowledge of the aggregate. ... And so we have men in this situation: what is 'the best' for him is known to him uniquely and for certain; how to attain it is dictated by circumstances, and can be inferred from them. What, then, is left for him to do in the way of choosing?" G. L. S. Shackle, *Decision, Order, and Time in Human Affairs* (2nd ed., Cambridge: Cambridge University Press, 1969), p. 272.

7. Israel M. Kirzner, *Competition and Entrepreneurship* (Chicago: The University of Chicago Press, 1973).

8. "Under uncertainty, by definition, each action that may be chosen is identified with a distribution of potential outcomes, not with a unique outcome.... It is worth emphasis that each possible action has a *distribution* of potential outcomes, only one of which will materialize if the action is taken, and that one outcome cannot be foreseen. Essentially, the task is converted into making a decision (selecting an action) whose potential outcome *distribution* is preferable, that is, choosing the action with the optimum *distribution*, since there is no such thing as a maximizing distribution." A. A. Alchian, "Uncertainty—Evolution and Economic Theory," *Journal of Political Economy*, 58 (June, 1950), p. 212.

9. J. M. Buchanan and G. F. Thirlby, eds., *L.S.E. Essays on Cost* (London: Weidenfeld and Nicholson, 1973).

10. Ibid., pp. 104–5.

11. Rothbard, *Man, Economy and State*, p. 529.

12. I. Kirzner, "Divergent Approaches in Libertarian Economic Thought," *Intercollegiate Review* (January-February, 1967), p. 107.

13. Milton Friedman, *Price Theory* (Chicago: Aldine, 1976), p. 147.

14. " ... the logic reduces to the economic principle, the simple requirement that returns to like units of outlay or input must be equalized at the margin in order to secure a maximum of output.... If a potential chooser is made aware of the principle in its full import, he will weigh alternatives more carefully, he will think in marginal terms, he will make evaluations of opportunity costs, and finally, he will search more diligently for genuine alternatives. The norms for choice can be meaningfully discussed, even if the specific implementation takes place only in the internal calculus of the decision-maker." Buchanan, "Is Economics the Science of Choice?" pp. 48–49.

15. J. M. Buchanan, *Cost and Choice* (Chicago: Markham Pub. Co., 1969), p. 35.

16. "The false step is taken when the explicitly objectified payoff structure that is postulated for use in the abstract theory of economic behavior is translated into direct guidelines for the explicit manipulation of choice alternatives. This procedure must assume that the actual *choice-maker* in the real world *behaves* strictly as the pure economic man of the theorist's model." Buchanan, "Is Economics the Science of Choice?" p. 60. Moorhouse makes the point in a slightly different way, " ... social phenomena are inherently subjective. Men act according to their *perception* of relevant data. Subjective evaluation of external stimuli, though unobservable and hence, nonquantifiable, are part and parcel of the phenomena economists wish to explain." John C. Moorhouse, "The Mechanistic Foundations of Economic Analysis," *Reason Papers* No. 4 (Winter, 1978), p. 65.

17. E. C. Pasour, "Regulation's Fatal Flaw," 10 *Reason* (October 1978), pp. 26–30.

18. G. J. Stigler and Claire Friedland, "What Can Regulators Regulate? The Case of Electricity," *Journal of Law and Economics* (October, 1962).

19. E. C. Pasour, Jr. and J. B. Bullock, "Implications of Uncertainty for the Measurement of Efficiency," *Am. Journal of Ag. Econ.*, vol. 57, no. 2 (May, 1975), pp. 335–39.

20. "Human action is necessarily always rational. . . . The ultimate end of action is always the satisfaction of some desires of the acting man. . . . It is a fact that human reason is not infallible and that man very often errs in selecting and applying means. An action unsuited to the end sought falls short of expectation. It is contrary to purpose, but it is rational, i.e., the outcome of a reasonable—although faulty—deliberation and an attempt—although an ineffectual attempt—to attain a definite goal." Ludwig von Mises, *Human Action* (Chicago: Henry Regnery Co., 1966), pp. 19-20.

21. A good discussion of the problems of a number of present government regulatory agencies is presented in *The Crisis of the Regulatory Commissions*, ed. Paul W. MacAvoy (New York: W. W. Norton & Co., 1970).

22. Alchian is not advocating "scientism," i.e., that economists emulate the procedures of the natural sciences. Instead, he seeks to increase an understanding of the precise role and nature of purposive behavior in the presence of uncertainty and incomplete information. Hayek's comments on "prediction and control" in biology apply even more strongly in economics and the social sciences. "The theoretical understanding of the growth and functioning of organisms can only, in the rarest of instances, be turned into specific predictions of what will happen in a particular case because we can hardly ever ascertain all the facts which will contribute to determine the outcome." F. A. Hayek, *Studies in Philosophy, Politics and Economics*, pp. 33–34.

23. "It is not even necessary to suppose that each firm acts as if it possessed the conventional diagrams and knew the analytical principles employed by economists in deriving optimum

and equilibrium conditions.... The fact that an economist deals with human beings does not *automatically* warrant imparting to these humans the great degree of foresight and motivations which the economist may require for his customary analysis as an outside observer or 'oracle'" Alchian, "Uncertainty," p. 216.

24. "The undiscerning person who sees survivors corresponding to changes in environment claims to have evidence for the 'Lysenko' doctrine. In truth, all he may have is evidence for the doctrine that the environment, by competitive conditions, selects the most viable of the various phenotypic characteristics for perpetuation. Economists should beware of economic 'Lysenkoism'," ibid., p. 215.

25. Tibor Machan, "Costs and Virtue, the Debate on Planning," *National Review* (June 11, 1976).

26. "The failure of economists to recognize that the sense data upon which individuals actually choose in either market or political choice structures are dimensionally distinct from any data that can be objectively called upon by external observers led directly to the methodological chaos that currently exists." Buchanan, "Is Economics the Science of Choice?" p. 64.

17

The Primacy of Entrepreneurial Discovery

Israel M. Kirzner

I. Introduction

An economically successful society is one whose members pursue the "right" set of coordinated actions. The "ideal" economic organization for a society consists, therefore, of the pattern of institutions and incentives that will promote the pursuit of the "correct" set of actions by its members. Economic theory has, in general terms, been able to enunciate the conditions to be fulfilled if a set of actions is to be "correct." These optimality conditions are, not surprisingly, governed basically by the available resources and technological possibilities, on the one hand, and, on the other, by the pattern of consumers' tastes. The "economic problem" faced by society is then often viewed as being somehow to ensure that the various economic agents in society indeed undertake those actions that will, altogether, satisfy the conditions for optimality. While this formulation is in some respects not quite satisfactory, it will serve reasonably well in introducing our discussion of the role of entrepreneurial discovery.

Reprinted from *The Prime Mover of Progress: The Entrepreneur in Capitalism and Socialism* (London: The Institute of Economic Affairs, 1980).

II. Patterns of Economic Organization

In theory there exists a variety of possible patterns of economic organization for society, ranging from completely centralized decision-making at one extreme, through an array of "mixed" systems, to pure laissez-faire. Several related observations may be made.

First, *all* these possible systems of economic organization involve making *decisions*—with greater or lesser degree of decentralization.

Second, these decisions will necessarily involve an *entrepreneurial element*—regardless of the degree of decentralization sought.

Third, one dimension along which the effectiveness of each of the alternative patterns of societal economic organization will need to be assessed, will therefore be that of measuring the *success with which entrepreneurial activity can be evoked in that pattern of organization.*

These observations call for some elaboration.

(i) The Entrepreneurial Element in Decisions

We have asserted that decisions necessarily involve an entrepreneurial element. What do we mean by the "entrepreneurial element" in decision?

The *non* entrepreneurial element in decisions is easy to pin down. In most textbooks of microeconomics, this non-entrepreneurial element is often made to appear the *only* element in decision-making. The nonentrepreneurial element in decision-making consists of the task of calculation. A decision-maker is, in this context, seen as seeking to achieve an array of goals (or to "maximize" some goal or utility function) with the scarce resources available. In seeking to arrive at the optimal decision, the decision-maker must therefore calculate the solution to what, in the jargon of economics, is called a "constrained maximization problem."[1] Correct decision-making, in this nonentrepreneurial sense, means correct calculation; faulty decision-making is equivalent to mistakes in arithmetic.

This nonentrepreneurial aspect does not have to assume initial omniscience; it is entirely possible for the incompletely informed decision-maker to calculate (i.e., to decide) how much knowledge to acquire.[2] But this nonentrepreneurial aspect does presume, at least, that the decision-maker has a clear perception of the scope of his ignorance, and of how this ignorance can be reduced; in a sense he knows precisely what it is that he does not know. And it is here that we can recognize the scope for the other element in decision-making, the entrepreneurial element.

For the truth is that the calculative aspect is far from being the most obvious and most important element in decisions. When a wrong decision has been made, the error is unlikely to have been a mistake in calculation. It is far more likely to have resulted from an erroneous assessment of the situation—in being over-optimistic about the availability of means, or about the outcomes to be expected of given actions; in pessimistically under-estimating the means at one's disposal, or the results to be expected from specific courses of action. Making the "right" decision, therefore, calls for far more than the correct mathematical calculation; it calls for a shrewd and wise assessment of the realities (both present and future) within the context of which the decision must be taken. It is with this aspect of decision that we will be dealing in analyzing the entrepreneurial element in subsequent discussion.

No matter how centralized or decentralized a decision making system may be, its decision-makers will regret their decisions if the entrepreneurship embodied in these decisions is of poor quality. Whatever the institutional context, a correct decision calls for reading the situation correctly; it calls for recognizing the true possibilities and for refusing to be deluded into seeing possibilities where none exist; it requires that true possibilities should not be overlooked, but that true limitations not be overlooked either. It is therefore our contention that alternative systems of economic organizations have to be appraised, in part, with an eye to the respective success with which they can evoke entrepreneurship of high quality.

(ii) Entrepreneurship in Received Economic Theory

It is by now fairly well recognized that standard economic theory has developed along lines that virtually exclude the entrepreneurial role. This has largely been a result of the tendencies, long dominant in neoclassical economics, to exclude all elements of unexpected change, to focus attention almost exclusively on equilibrium states of affairs, and to treat individual decisions as immune from the hazards of error.[3]

As Frank Knight of Chicago explained many years ago, in a world from which the troublesome demon of unexpected change has been exorcised, it is not difficult to imagine away any need for entrepreneurship.[4] In such a world we can reasonably expect decision-makers, given sufficient time, to have come somehow to perceive the world correctly. To decide, in such a world, involves nothing more than to perform those calculations which we have described as constituting the nonentrepreneurial element in decision-making.

In a world of unchanging certainty, where the future unfolding of events is anticipated with assurance and accuracy, selecting the optimal course of action is not a task which challenges the entrepreneurial qualities of vision, daring, and determination. Indeed, it is difficult to imagine how such a world could ever fail to be in anything but a state of optimality. To be sure, such a world must be envisaged as bounded by resource scarcities. But it is difficult to imagine how anyone in such a world—given these resource limitations, and given the accepted structure of ownership—can ascribe any perceived short-comings to faulty decision-making. Such an imaginary world is not paradise, but it can hardly fail to be the closest to paradise imaginable within the given limitations of supply and the given institutional framework.

When this theoretical framework is uncritically adopted, it becomes easy to fall into the error of tackling economic problems with nonentrepreneurial analytical tools. It becomes natural to assume that the correct decisions are being made, from the viewpoint of the relevant decision-makers; that the problems encountered are to be attributed to inadequate resources or to a faulty institutional structure. What is overlooked, in such treatments, is the possibility that a great deal of want and misery are the result of nothing less mundane than *sheer error* on the part of decision-makers, that is, of decisions made that, from the decision-maker's *own* point of view, are suboptimal. That such errors may and do occur requires us to recognize scope for entrepreneurial error, for decisions made with faulty assessments of the facts of the world, future as well as present, upon which the decision is to impinge.

Certainly, in a perspective which simply assumes that decision-makers, under all circumstances, regardless of institutional environment, inevitably and unerringly find their way to the correct decisions—there is little point in inquiring into the circumstances that are most conducive to alert, entrepreneurially successful decision-making. It is fundamental insight upon which, I believe, the proceedings of today's Colloquium are being conducted, that simply to assume correct decision-making is to beg far too large a fraction of the essential question confronting us. We begin, in other words, with a healthy awareness that the world is very far from being the best of all possible worlds—even from being the best of those worlds possible with available resources, and within existing institutional environments.

It is from this beginning that we are led to appreciate the primordial importance of our question: What institutional circumstances or arrangements, which system of economic and political institutions, can be expected most successfully to evoke those qualities of entrepreneurial alertness upon which the quest for optimality in decision-making necessarily depends?

(iii) Entrepreneurship as a Scarce Resource

It might perhaps be argued that, important as the quality of entrepreneurship undoubtedly is, it does not involve any really new considerations beyond those usually taken into account in studying the conditions for optimality. All that has been established in the preceding pages, it may be held, is merely that we must bear in mind the need for a special resource, entrepreneurship, which has often been incorrectly taken for granted. Instead of viewing entrepreneurship as exercised flawlessly, tirelessly, and universally, we must begin to recognize that It is a scarce, valuable resource of which our economic models had better begin to take careful account. But all this, it may perhaps be maintained, does not justify our demand that we transcend the standard maximizing model of decision-making. All that has to be done, it may be contended, is to incorporate into our list of required resources the flow of required entrepreneurial services, and to ensure that available stocks of such service flows be used optimally. Social optimality, it may be contended, will now be judged within a broader framework in which there is recognition of both the demand for, and availability of, the service of entrepreneurial vision.

More particularly, in respect of the question we have described as primordial, it may be objected that it is fundamentally inappropriate to inquire into the comparative effectiveness of alternative institutional frameworks, for the evocation of entrepreneurship. It will be objected that, since entrepreneurship is a resource no different, for pure theory, from other resources, any comparison among alternative social economic systems must begin with the assumption of some *given,* initial stock of that resource. It will not do to begin a comparison between different economic systems by suggesting that the very pattern of institutional arrangement may have important implications for the initial size of a particular stock of resource. Different economic systems may certainly differ in the efficiency with which they deploy and allocate given resource supplies; but, it may be argued, if we postulate some given supply of a particular resource in one economic system, there can be no objection in principle to supposing any other system to begin with exactly the same supply of that resource.

Our response to this line of argument (and thus our defence of the validity of the central question to be addressed here) rests on the insight that entrepreneurship cannot usefully be treated simply as a resource, similar in principle to the other resources available to an economic system.

III. The Primacy of Entrepreneurship

What is important is to insist that entrepreneurial alertness differs in fundamental respects from the resources ordinarily discussed in decision-making. These differences will justify our contention that there may be important differences between different economic systems in respect of their success in harnessing entrepreneurial alertness for making error-free decisions.

A cardinal quality of a potential resource, in the economists' analysis of decisions, is that the decision-maker can deploy it, if he so chooses, in specific processes geared toward the achievement of specified goals. What the decision-maker has to decide is whether to deploy a particular resource, how and in what quantity to deploy it. He must decide whether to use it at all, whether to use it for one purpose or for another. The quality of entrepreneurial alertness cannot be discussed in these terms.

Entrepreneurial Alertness is not a Conventional Economic Resource

If an entrepreneur's discovery of a lucrative arbitrage opportunity galvanizes him into immediate action to capture the perceived gain, it will not do to describe the situation as one in which the entrepreneur has "decided" to use his alertness in order to capture this gain. He has not "deployed" his hunch for a specific purpose; *rather, his hunch has propelled him to make his entrepreneurial purchase and sale.* The entrepreneur never sees his hunches as potential inputs about which he must decide whether or not they are to be used. To decide *not* to use a hunch means—if it means anything at all—that a businessman realizes that he has no hunch (or that his hunch is that it will be best to be inactive for the time being). If one has become sufficiently alerted to the existence of an opportunity—i.e., if one has become sufficiently convinced regarding the facts of a situation—it becomes virtually impossible to imagine *not* taking advantage of the opportunity so discovered.

Entrepreneurship is thus not something to be deliberately introduced into a potential production process; it is, instead, something primordial to the very idea of a potential production process awaiting possible implementation. Entrepreneurial alertness is not an ingredient *to be deployed* in decision-making; it is rather something in which *the decision itself is embedded* and without which it would be unthinkable.

It is true that *knowledge* (e.g., in the sense of technical expertise) may be deployed. A person may certainly decide that it does not pay to use his knowledge in a specific manner. Or he may decide that it does pay to use it. Here knowledge is a resource at the disposal of the entrepreneur. He is conscious of his knowledge as something to be used or not. But this refers only to knowledge of how to achieve specific goals, not knowledge of whether or not it is worthwhile to attempt to achieve a goal altogether. A distinguishing feature of entrepreneurial insight consists precisely in the absence of self-awareness by its possessor that he does possess it. A would-be entrepreneur may agonize over whether or not to embark on a particular venture. His trauma arises not from deciding whether or not to use his entrepreneurial vision; it stems from his unsureness of what he "sees."

Entrepreneurial Opportunity may be Blocked by Lack of a Resource but not of Insight

Again, it is integral to a necessary resource (in the usual sense) that a decision-maker may feel its lack. A decision-maker may say: "I have all the ingredients necessary to produce ice-cream, except sugar." The opportunity to achieve a particular goal is blocked only by lack of some necessary resource. But it is absurd to imagine a decision-maker saying (on a commercial venture about the profitability of which he is profoundly skeptical) that he sees a profitable opportunity the exploitation of which is blocked only by lack of entrepreneurial insight. It would be absurd because this entrepreneur is (correctly or otherwise) convinced that he does *not* see any profitable opportunity in this venture at all.

To repeat what was stated earlier, all this does not apply to *technical* knowledge which an entrepreneur may know exists and which he knows he lacks. It is certainly possible for a decision-maker to say: "I have all the ingredients for ice-cream, but I lack the relevant recipe." He may know that a recipe exists, and that it is a good one, without knowing what it is. But for a man to refrain from a particular productive venture because he is not convinced that it is sound—

even if it turns out that he was wrong—is not to refrain from it because he has been unable to lay hands on the appropriate vision; it is to refrain because he is convinced (rightly or wrongly) that, with respect to this venture, the *best entrepreneurial alertness finds nothing to be seen.*

Entrepreneurial Alertness is not a Potential Stock Available to Society

It is because of this inherent *primacy* of entrepreneurial alertness and vision (as contrasted with deployable resources)[5] that we cannot avoid the question to be addressed in this paper—the varying degrees of success with which alternative economic systems can inspire entrepreneurial alertness. We do not view the *potential* stock of entrepreneurial alertness in a society as some quantity "available to be used by society." (Were this the case one could proceed to inquire how different systems variously succeed in most effectively using this uniformly *given* stock.) Instead we recognize the quality of entrepreneurial alertness as something which *somehow emerges into view at the precise moment when decisions have to be made.* As we shall see (VII), this opens up the important possibility that the institutional framework within which decisions are made may itself vitally affect the alertness out of which those decisions emerge.

IV. The Cost of Entrepreneurship

This line of argument points to a further related insight: *entrepreneurship is costless.* In using any quantity of a scarce resource (in the usual sense of that term) the decision-maker is always viewed as choosing between alternative goals to which the scarce resource might be applied. The goal foregone is the cost of using the resource for its present purpose. In the case of entrepreneurial alertness, however, a decision-maker never considers whether to apply some given potential alertness to the discovery of opportunity A or opportunity B. As already argued, the opportunities (or any one of them) are either perceived or they are not perceived; alertness is not something about which a decision can be made *not* to deploy it. (In this we distinguish sharply between pure alertness, on the one hand, and "deployable" scarce inputs that may be useful in decision-making, e.g., time, technical knowledge, managerial expertise, on the other.) To recognize that opportunity A exists need not preclude simultaneously recognizing that opportunity B exists.

Conversely, to fail to recognize that opportunity A exists cannot be explained in terms of the high cost of so recognizing it; if opportunity A has not been recognized, the failure represents some shortcoming in entrepreneurial alertness, not the outcome of a decision to deploy it for the discovery of other opportunities.

Faulty Entrepreneurship means Alertness Remains Untapped

That in the real world we encounter innumerable instances of faulty and inadequate entrepreneurship must be interpreted, therefore, not as evidence of the absolute scarcity of entrepreneurial alertness (with the existing stock of it having been applied elsewhere), but as evidence that the alertness costlessly available has somehow remained latent and untapped. The central question then looms even more significantly than ever: What institutional frameworks are best suited to tap the reservoir of entrepreneurial alertness which is certainly present—in potentially inexhaustible supply—among the members of society?

V. The Qualities of Entrepreneurship—
The Uncharted Frontier

Although, as Ludwig von Mises pointed out long ago,[6] *all* individual action is entrepreneurial, and although we have described entrepreneurial alertness as in principle inexhaustible, we have also been careful to notice that potential alertness may be (and so often is) untapped and inert. We know, certainly, that individuals display vastly different degrees of entrepreneurial alertness. Some are quick to spot as yet unnoticed opportunities, others notice only the opportunities revealed by the discoveries of others. In some societies, in some climates, among some groups, it appears that entrepreneurial alertness is keener than in others. Studies of economic development have come to recognize that the qualities called for in successful entrepreneurship are not uniformly distributed, and certainly do not appear to be in infinite supply.

It would certainly be desirable to be able to identify with precision those human qualities, personal and psychological, which are to be credited with successful entrepreneurial alertness, drive and initiative. It would be most valuable to be able to study the short-run and long-run impact upon the development of these "entrepreneurial" qualities, of alternative social, economic and institutional frameworks. It would be important to know, for example, if a comfortable sense of security discourages the noticing of new opportunities. If "independence" or "economic freedom" encourages entrepreneurial drive and initiative, this would be significant information. Likewise, does "competition" encourage alertness to new opportunities?

Research on Psychological Aspects Desirable

Up to the present, little systematic work appears to have been done on these questions. Observations made are likely

to be based on "common sense" or on anecdotal foundations. It is certainly necessary to go beyond this elementary
stage. Indeed, an important frontier of knowledge, largely
unexplored, appears to consist of those aspects of psychology such as temperament, thirst for adventure, ambition
and imagination that are likely to throw light on the development of the qualities of entrepreneurship, and on the
ways in which alternative institutional arrangements may
affect such development. It is to be expected and very much
to be desired that research should proceed on this frontier
during the years ahead.

Applied entrepreneurial theorists should look to this
research with considerable interest; it is to be hoped that
their own needs and interests will help to define the directions along which this research proceeds and to formulate
the questions it seeks to answer.

My tentative observations here will suggest that a number of important general statements can be made even before we enjoy the systematic knowledge anticipated to
emerge from research into the psychology of entrepreneurship.

VI. The Incentive for Entrepreneurial Discovery

Were entrepreneurship a scarce resource in the usual
sense, economists would have no difficulty in spelling out,
at least in general terms, the kinds of incentives capable of
coaxing out the desired quantity of entrepreneurial discovery. Potential entrepreneurs would have to be offered re-
wards that more than offset the costs of exercising entrepreneurship. This, after all, is how economists understand the
role of incentives; this is how the price system is perceived
to offer, *via* the resource market, the incentives required to
stimulate resource supply and to allocate it among alternative uses. But the special aspects of entrepreneurship render

this kind of incentive system inappropriate to entrepreneurial alertness and discovery.

Since entrepreneurship is costless (no incentive at all is needed, in principle, to activate entrepreneurial vision), and since on the other hand entrepreneurial vision is not uniformly and continuously "switched on" to take advantage of all opportunities, we are very much concerned to identify what it is that *does* "switch on" entrepreneurial vision and discovery.

With scarce resources in the usual sense, it is meaningful to talk of the kind of incentive needed to be "offered" to owners to stimulate supply. We can imagine, that is, that some entrepreneur already has a fairly clear picture of the results to be obtained from deploying the relevant resource in some particular line of production. We can then talk of whether or not it is worthwhile for him to offer the resource price required to overcome the cost of supplying the resource. The point is that the notion of a needed incentive, in this usual sense, presupposes the clear perception, even before the deployment of the service, of its usefulness in production.

As has already been emphasized, such a perception is ruled out by definition in the case of entrepreneurial alertness. No one "hires" or "offers incentives" to the entrepreneur. To hire an "entrepreneur" *is to be an entrepreneur*— simply shifting the problem back to the incentives that might galvanize *this* latter entrepreneur into action. It cannot be sufficiently emphasized that

(a) until an opportunity *has* been discovered, no one knows how much to offer as an incentive for its discovery;

(b) once the opportunity has been discovered, it is no longer relevant to inquire into the springs of entrepreneurship—since it will already have been exercises.

The Promise of Pure Gain
is Entrepreneurial Incentive

There seems one statement which, however, can be made about the incentives required to excite entrepreneurial alertness. it is a statement which sees such incentives as having little in common with the character of and role for incentives in the usual sense. It can be stated with considerable confidence *that human beings tend to notice that which it is in their interest to notice.* Human beings notice "opportunities" rather than "situations." They notice, that is, concatenations of events, realized or prospective, which offer *pure gain.* It is not the abstract *concatenation* of these events which evokes notice; it is the circumstance that these events offer the promise of pure *gain*—broadly understood to include fame, power, prestige, even the opportunity so serve a cause or to help other individuals.

Two individuals walk through the same city block teeming with hundreds of people in a variety of garbs, with shops of different kinds advertising signs for many goods, buildings of different architectural styles. Each of these individuals will notice a different set of items out of these countless impressions impinging on his senses. What is noticed by the one is not what is noticed by the other. The difference will not merely be one of chance. It is a difference that can be ascribed, in part, to the *interests* of the two individuals. Each tends to notice that which is of interest *to him.*

A difference between the price of apples traded in one part of the market and the price of apples traded in another part may pass unnoticed. It is less likely to pass unnoticed it if constitutes a phenomenon of interest to its potential discoverer. A concatenation of possible events (in this case the possible purchase of apples at a lower price, to be followed by their sale at a higher price) may not be noticed at all unless the potential discovered stands to gain from the price differential. *In order to "switch on" the alertness of a potential discoverer to socially significant opportunities, they must offer gain to the potential discoverer himself.* This kind of incentive—the incentive that somehow converts a socially desirable opportunity into a personally gainful one—is not needed to ensure pursuit of that opportunity *after* its discovery. Once the socially desirable opportunity has been perceived, individuals may be persuaded (or threatened) to act on that opportunity simply by suitable choice of reward (or punishment). The kind of incentive here under discussion is that required to reveal opportunities that have *until now been perceived by no one at all.*

VII. Performance of Alternative Economic Systems Under Entrepreneurial Incentive

How do alternative social-economic systems appear likely to perform in terms of this kind of incentive? We will consider: (a) a free market economy; (b) a centralized (socialist) economic system; (c) a regulated market economy. Our concern is solely with the comparative scope they hold for entrepreneurial incentives.

(a) Entrepreneurship in the Free Market

The free market is characterized most distinctively, for our purpose, *by freedom of entrepreneurial entry.* Given some accepted system of property rights, individual participants are free to enter into mutually beneficial trades with each other. Production decisions involve judgments about buying inputs on factor markets in order to sell output in product markets. Market prices, therefore, guide the decisions which determine the allocation of society's resources among alternative lines of output. Were the market to have attained full equilibrium, it may, under specific assumptions, be described as having attained an optimal allocation of resources.[7] But (especially in view of ambiguities surrounding the interpretation of "social optimum," and of the possibility that not all the specific assumptions will be fulfilled in practice), this is *not* the interesting proposition—even were it reasonable to view the free market economy as in continuous equilibrium.

What is important about the market economy is that unexploited opportunities for reallocating resources from one (low-market-valued) use to another of higher value offer the opportunity for pure entrepreneurial gain. A misallocation of resources occurs because, so far, market participants have not noticed the price discrepancy involved. This price discrepancy presents itself as an opportunity to be exploited by its discoverer. *The most impressive aspect of the market system is the tendency for such opportunities to be discovered.*

The Discovery Process of the Market

It is in a sense similar to this that Hayek has referred to the competitive market process as a "discovery procedure."[8] The essence is not that market prices offer spontaneously developed "signals" able faultlessly to coordinate millions of independently made decisions. (This would occur only in equilibrium; in disequilibrium the prices which prevail would *not* so perfectly coordinate decisions.) It is rather that the disequilibrium situation—in which prices do not offer the correct signals—is one which offers entrepreneurs the required incentives for the discrepancies to be noticed and corrected. In the course of this entrepreneurial process, new products may be introduced, new qualities of existing products may be developed, new methods of production may be ventured, new forms of industrial organization, financing, marketing or tackling risk may be developed. All the ceaseless churning and agitation of the market is to be understood as the consequence of the never-ending discovery process of which the market consists.

(b) Entrepreneurship in the Socialized Economy

Little work has been done on the analysis of entrepreneurship in fully socialized societies. The great debate on economic calculation under socialism carried on between the two world wars, in many respects revolved precisely around this issue, but was couched in terms which unfortunately permitted the central importance of this issue to be overlooked. The attempts by Oskar Lange (of Poland) and others to show how a socialist system could be set up that would permit decentralized decisions by managers of socialist enterprises on the basis of centrally promulgated "prices," along the same lines as the price system under the free market, unfortunately completely overlooked the entrepreneurial character of the price system.

Lange relied on the so-called "parametric function" of prices, i.e., on that aspect of prices which permits each decision-maker to treat them as equilibrium prices to which he must passively adjust himself.[9] But in this view of the market (and hence of the possibility of a socialist "price" system), Lange failed to recognize that the distinctive aspect of the market is the manner in which prices *exchange*, i.e., that market prices are in fact treated nonparametrically. It is one thing to imagine that socialist managers can be motivated to obey rules on the basis of centrally promulgated "prices"; it is quite another to take it for granted that the *non*parametric function of price (in which, that is, price is *not* being treated as a datum but subject to change by individual market participants), a function which depends entirely on entrepreneurial discovery of *new* opportunities for pure profit, can be simulated in a system from which the private entrepreneurial function is completely absent.

Alertness by "Price" Planners and Plant Managers

Under a Lange-type system, alertness would be called for at a number of levels. Officials deciding on the "price" structure must do so by what they know about the performance of the economy under earlier "price" structures, and by what they anticipate to be the pattern of consumer demand and of resource supply in the period ahead. In promulgating a list of "prices" it is necessary to determine, first of all, the list of commodities and of resource services for which "prices" are to be set. The construction of this list requires an enormous volume of entrepreneurial alertness on the part of these officials. After all, some products should not be produced at all; others very definitely ought to be produced, but officials may be quite ignorant of them or of their urgency. This will, of course, be more particularly likely to be true of new and innovative products and product qualities. But it could occur with any product whatever.

Again, the Lange system would call for alertness by socialist plant managers. They would have to identify sources of resource supply; they would have to notice technological possibilities that may not hitherto have been known, or which, given the old price structure, may not have been economic. They would have to notice the need for and possibility of any number of changes (innovative or otherwise) which changed patterns of tastes, for example, might make worthwhile. There is certainly nothing in Lange's own description of his system to suggest how this might be ensured.

Will Available Options be Noticed? How?

The question which the entrepreneurial theorist must ask is not whether, given available known options, the relevant socialist official is operating under an incentive system that will make it personally gainful for him to select the optimal course of action for society. Our question is rather whether there is any assurance that relevant options will in practice be noticed as being available. What might motivate an official to notice an opportunity not yet adopted (but which it might be highly valuable to pursue)? It will not do to suggest that some higher official arrange matters so that, when the (lower) official does notice the opportunity, he can personally benefit by its adoption. This merely passes our question up the line: What might motivate this higher official to notice the opportunity?—and even to notice its worthwhileness *after* it has been brought to his attention?

We will, for the present, ignore the question of how a newly discovered valuable social opportunity is revealed, even after the event, as having been such. Our question will confine itself to asking how it might be ensured that such social opportunities constitute at the same time privately gainful opportunities for their potential discoverers. It is doubtful in the extreme if ideals such as benevolence or patriotism can be relied upon, in general, to enable a potential discoverer to identify his own personal interest with that of the discovery of an opportunity for a desirable reallocation of resources for society.

We might imagine, of course, a system in which there is not merely decentralization of decision making, in the Lange sense, but also freedom for socialist managers to buy and sell on behalf of the state (when discrepancies among socialist "prices" might have been discovered) and to retain for themselves some fraction of the price-differential. if such trading is restricted to those who are already socialist managers, we will have to examine the mechanism of selection of managers to see whether it indeed ensures that those with entrepreneurial skills tend to become socialist managers (since the socialist state would not be permitting others to "prove" their entrepreneurial skills in this way). On the other hand, if entrepreneurial trading is to be open for all (raising, let us, of course, note, the obvious question of access to society's capital to be risked in such ventures), then clearly we have moved closer and closer toward a "mixed" capitalist system in which private entrepreneurs might be free to seek profits within a system of state-controlled prices (a regulated system which will be briefly considered below).

Individual Decision-Makers Cannot Profit
under "Market" Socialist Schemes

We may talk of various schemes for "market" socialism along Lange lines, in which some decisions are left to lower-ranking officials to be made on the basis of centrally designed systems of "prices." No matter how extensive the degree of decentralization thus achieved, however, a critical condition for the socialist quality of the system appears to be that neither at the level of the central design of "prices," nor of individual-manager decisions made on the basis of these "prices," may decisions be made primarily in order that the decision-taker can profit personally from errors discovered. Those responsible for designing the system of socialist "prices" are clearly not participants in any entrepreneurial market; their function is to impose "prices" upon the socialist "market."

To imagine that in this socialist "market," freedom of entry for private profit-making entrepreneurial activity is to be permitted, is surely to compromise fatally the definition of a socialist economic system. But without such freedom of entrepreneurial entry market-socialism has a fatal flaw: It has not succeeded in identifying any way by which errors, whether of omission or commission, can be systematically avoided by decision-makers. It has not identified any way by which the discovery and avoidance of error redounds directly to the personal benefit of the discoverer. It has not identified how the unsuspectedly inefficient socialist venture might reveal itself to a socialist decision-maker in advance as a threat to his own well-being; it has not identified how the currently undreamed-of venture, of critical benefit to society, might reveal itself to a socialist planner as one offering him personal gain.

Incentives to Socialist Managers Deny Essential Role of Entrepreneurial Discovery

We do not deny the possibility of arranging incentives to socialist managers to produce more, or to produce with a smaller labor force, or lower energy consumption. Nor do we even deny the possibility of offering incentives that will reward innovation. Incentives can certainly be structured to reward inventors and innovators of new products and new production techniques. Recent extensive study of innovation in the Soviet Union has, for example, confirmed the significant vitality of the innovative process there (although the process lags more or less behind that in capitalist economics).[10] But to reward managers for meeting or exceeding target output quantities presupposes that *it is already known* that more of these outputs is urgently required by society; to reward managers for introducing a new product is to presume that *it is already known* that this particular new product—or else that *any* new product—is socially more important (taking into account the resources required for its production) than the product it replaces; to reward managers for introducing innovative methods of production is to presume that *it is already known* that the additional inputs called for by the new technique are less costly to society than those the technique avoids—or else that *any* change in production technique must be an improvement over those currently employed.

That these matters may already be known is in many instances entirely plausible. But if they *are* assumed already known, we are simply assuming away the need for entrepreneurial discovery. The task is to ensure the discovery—by someone, somewhere, who possesses power to set things into motion—of which products (existing or new) should be produced (and in what quantities), the urgency of which the currently conventional wisdom has *failed* to recognize. The problem is to identify techniques of production the usefulness of which has up until now *not* been perceived. Not all innovation is socially desirable; not all expansion of lies of output is socially desirable. what is required is an incentive system to convince decision makers that when they discover opportunities which others will deny to exist, they (the discoverers) will be the gainers.

Thus far, in all the discussion of varieties of socialism, of incentive systems and planning theories, we have not seen *this* problem addressed. Nor is it at all apparent how, without fundamentally compromising the essential defining criteria for socialism, it can be solved.

(c) Entrepreneurship in the Regulated Market Economy[11]

Most societies in the modern world have allowed their economic systems to follow the pattern neither of pure socialism nor of pure capitalism. They consist of market economies that have been circumscribed more or less extensive systems of state intervention. Convinced that the unhampered market will generate undesirable price structures, or undesirable arrays of output qualities, working conditions, or other undesirables, the state intervened, replacing the laissez-faire market by the regulated market. Price ceilings and price and wage floors, transfer of income, imposed safety standards, child labor laws, zoning laws, prohibited industrial integration, prohibited competition, imposed health warnings, compulsory old-age pensions, and prohibited drugs, are among the countless controls that possible well-meaning public officials impose. What is the role of entrepreneurial discovery in the regulated market?

Genuine—But Inhibited—Entrepreneurial Incentive

Despite the controls, regulations and interventions, there exist, in such systems, genuine markets for both re-source services and consumer products. Although the prices which emerge in regulated markets may have been more or less drastically distorted in the regulatory process, they are (except for directly controlled prices) nonetheless market prices. To the extent that entrepreneurial entry remains free, discrepancies in these prices provide the incentives for entrepreneurs to capture pure profit, leading to a process of entrepreneurial competition acting at all times to modify the existing price structure.

Nevertheless, it is not difficult to perceive the many ways in which entrepreneurial discovery may come to be inhibited or redirected under regulatory constraints. And regulation arises new and important questions concerning the way in which the agents of the state (whether legislators or officials in other stages of regulation and its enforcement) come to notice where opportunities for supposedly benefi-cial regulation may exist. Let us take up these latter ques-tions first.

Knowledge and Discovery Absent in Price Setting
And Resource Allocation

Government regulation takes the general form of im-posed price floors, price ceilings, mandated quality specifi-cations, and similar measures. We will assume that the hope surrounding such governmental impositions is that they will confine market activities to desired channels and at desired levels. But it is by no means clear how officials will know what prices to set, or if their earlier decisions have been in error. It is not clear how officials will *discover* those opportu-nities for improving the allocation of resources (which, after all, we can hardly assume to be automatically known at the outset of a regulatory endeavor). The regulator's estimates of the prices consumers are prepared to pay, or of the prices resource owners are prepared to accept, are not *profit-motivated* estimates. But estimates of market demand conditions, or of market supply conditions, that are not profit-motivated cannot reflect the powerful, discovery inspiring incentives of the entrepreneurial quest for profit.

It is further not clear how it can be ensured that government officials who perceive market conditions more accurately than others will tend systematically to replace less competent regulators. It is not clear what proxy for entrepreneurial profit and loss there might be that could inspire officials to see personal gain for themselves in successful discovery. What regulators know (or believe they know) at a given moment is presumably only partly correct. No systematic process seems available through which regulators might come to discover that which they have not known, especially since they have not known that they enjoy less than complete awareness of relevant situations. *If they do not know what they do not know, how will they know what remains to be discovered?*

Quite apart from the question of entrepreneurship required to engage in regulation believed to be desirable, we must, in the context of the regulated market economy, also consider the impact of regulation upon the pattern and direction of entrepreneurial discovery in the market place. There is a serious likelihood that regulator constraints may bar the discovery of pure profit opportunities (and thus of possibilities for socially beneficial resource re-allocation).

Damaging Effects of Regulatory Controls and Price Ceilings

A good deal of regulation consists in creating *barriers to entry*. Tariffs, licensing requirements, labor legislation, airline regulation and bank regulation, for example, do not merely limit numbers in particular markets. These kinds of regulatory activity tend to bar entry to entrepreneurs who believe they have discovered profit opportunities in barred areas of the market. Such barriers may, by removing the personal gain which entrepreneurs might have reaped by their discoveries, bring it about that *some opportunities may simply not be discovered by anyone*. An entrepreneur who knows that he will not be able to enter the banking business may simply not notice opportunities in the banking field that might otherwise have seemed obvious to him; those who are already in banking, and who have failed to see these opportunities, may continue to overlook them. Protection from entrepreneurial competition does not provide any spur to entrepreneurial discovery.

Imposed price ceilings may, similarly, not merely generate dis-coordination in the markets for existing goods and services (as is, of course, well recognized in the theory of price controls), they may inhibit the discovery of wholly new opportunities. A price ceiling does not merely block the upper reaches of a given supply curve—further increases in supply to meet demand. It may also inhibit the discovery of as yet unsuspected sources of supply (which in the absence of the ceiling might have shifted the entire supply curve to the right—made supplies marketable at lower prices—as these sources came to be discovered), or of wholly unknown new products.

The imposition of price ceilings, which has switched off the lure of pure profits in this way, is not accompanied, as far as can be seen, by any device that might, in some alternative manner, lead a potential discoverer to associate a discovery with his own personal gain.

VIII. Conclusion

Our discussion has focussed attention on a neglected aspect of economic decision making, the urgency for incentives for the "entrepreneurial" discovery of what opportunities exist for economic action. Pursuing this point further, we have pointed to the need for critical assessment, within any economic system of organization, of the way in which the system permits the potential discoverers to identify their own personal interest with the successful discovery of socially desirable opportunities for change. In the briefest possible framework, we have considered aspects of the socialist system, and of the regulated market economy, in contrast to the laissez-faire market system.

A great deal of work is waiting to be done in the economics of entrepreneurship. It has been my purpose to emphasize the enormous stake which society—under whatever economic system it may operate—holds in the successful pursuit of such research.

Notes

1. I.e., the problem of achieving maximum desirable results without overstepping the constraints imposed by the limited resources available.

    This emphasis on maximization is to be traced to the influence of Lord Robbins, *The Nature and Significance of Economic Science* (London: Macmillan, 193).

2. The literature on the economics of search proceeds on this basis. The classic article is G. J. Stigler, "The Economics of Information," *Journal of Political Economy* (June, 1961), pp. 213–25.

3. An elaboration of this theme is in the author's *Competition and Entrepreneurship* (Chicago and London: University of Chicago Press, 1973), Chapters 1–3.

4. F. H. Knight, *Risk, Uncertainty and Profit* (Boston: Houghton Mifflin, 1921).

5. A fuller discussion of this insight is in the author's *Perception, Opportunity, and Profit* (Chicago and London: University of Chicago Press, 1979), Chapters 9, 10.

6. In *Human Action* (New Haven: Yale University Press, 1949), p. 253
7. A complete discussion of this central theorem of welfare economics is in W. J. Baumol, *Economic Theory and Operations Analysis*, 4th ed. (Englewood Cliffs, NJ: Prentice-Hall, 1977), Chapter 221.
8. F. A. Hayek, "Competition as a Discover Procedure," in *New Studies in Philosophy, Politics, Economics and the History of ideas* (Chicago and London: University of Chicago Press and Routledge & Kegan Paul, 1978).
9. Oskar Lange, "On the Economic Theory of Socialism," in Lange and Fred. M. Taylor, *On the Economic Theory of Socialism,"ed.* Benjamin E. Lippincott (New York: McGraw-Hill, 1964,) p. 70. The initial statement by Mises, demonstrating the problems in socialist economic calculation, was "Die Wirtschaftsrechnung in sozialistischen Gemeinwesen," *Archiv für Sozialwissenschaften und Sozialpolitik* (April, 1920), translated in Friedrich A. Hayek (ed.), *Collectivist Economic Planning* (London: Routledge & Kegan Paul, 1935). Hayek's own response to Lange is contained in his *Individualism and Economic Order* London: Routledge & Kegan Paul, 1949).
10. Joseph S. Berliner, *The Innovation Decision in Soviet Industry* (Cambridge, MA: The MIT Press, 1976).
11. Further discussion of this theme is in the author's *The Perils of Regulation: A Market-Process Approach*, Occasional Paper of the Law and Economics Center of the University of Miami School of Law, 1978.

Bibliography

Armentano, Dominic T. "Resource Allocation Problems Under Socialism," in *Theory of Economic Systems: Capitalism, Socialism, Corporatism*, ed.William P. Snavely. Columbus, OH: Merrill, 1969.

Hayek, Friedrich A., ed. 1935. *Collectivist Economic Planning*. London: Routledge and Kegan Paul, 1935.

———. "Competition as a Discovery Procedure." In *New Studies in Philosophy, Politics, Economics and the History of Ideas.* Chicago: University of Chicago Press, 1978.

————."Economics and Knowledge." *Economica* 4 (February, 1937): 33–54; reprinted in *Individualism and Economic Order.*

————. *Individualism and Economic Order.* Chicago: University of Chicago Press, 1948.

————. "The Meaning of Competition." In *Individualism and Economic Order.*

————. "The New Confusion About 'Planning,'" *Morgan Guarantee Survey.* January, 1976.

————, ed. "The Nature and History of the Problem." In *Collectivist economic Planning;* reprinted as "Socialist Calculation I: The Nature and History of the Problem." In *Individualism and Economic Order.*

————, ed. "The Present State of the Debate." In *Collectivist Economic Planning;* reprinted as "Socialist Calculation II: The State of the Debate (1935)." In. *Individualism and Economic Order.*

————. "Socialist Calculation: The Competitive 'Solution.'" *Economica* 7 (May 1940): 125–49; reprinted as "Socialist Calculation III: The Competitive 'Solution.'" In *Individualism and Economic Order.*

————. "The Use of Knowledge in Society." *American Economic Review* 35 (September, 1945): 419–30; reprinted in *Individualism and Economic Order.*

Hoff, Trygve J. B. *Economic Calculation in the Socialist Society.*Translated by M. A. Michael. London and Edinburg: Hodge, 1949.

Kirzner, Israel M. *Competition and Entrepreneurship.* Chicago: University of Chicago Press, 1973.

————. *Perception, Opportunity, and Profit.* Chicago: University of Chicago Press, 1979.

Lange, Oskar. "On the Economic Theory of Socialism." In Oskar Lange and Fred M. Taylor, *On the Economic Theory of Socialism.* Edited by Benjamin E. Lippincott. New York: McGraw-Hill, 1964.

Littlechild, Stephen C. *The Fallacy of the Mixed Economy: An "Austrian" Critique of Economic Thinking and Policy.* Hobart paper; 80, Institute of Economic Affairs, London, 1978.

Mises, Ludwig von. "Die Wirschaftsrechnung im sozialistischen Gemeinwesen." *Archiv für Sozialwissenschaften und Sozialpolitik* (April, 1920); reprinted in F. A. Hayek, ed., *Collectivist Economic Planning* (1935), pp. 87–130.

———. Human Action: *A Treatise on Economics*. New Haven: Yale University Press, 1949.

Rothbard, Murray N. "Ludwig von Mises and Economic Calculation Under Socialism." In Lawrence S. Moss, ed., *The Economics of Ludwig von Mises*. Kansas City: Sheed and Ward, 1976.

Part IV

The Austrian Theory
of Capital and Interest

18

Excerpts from
Capital and Interest
Volume II: Positive Theory of Capital

Eugen von Böhm-Bawerk

The Nature of Capital*

The ultimate goal of all production is to provide things with which to satisfy our wants, that is to say, consumers' goods or "goods of first order," as I have called them elsewhere.[1] The road to the preparation of such goods is already familiar to us in a general way. We combine our natural powers with the powers of the external world in such an association that through operation of the laws of nature the origination of the desired material must necessarily result. But within the framework of the process, here outlined in extremely general terms, there is an important variation possible, to which we have not yet directed our attention. We have not noted the directness or indirectness of the road that lies between the expending of the human labour we contribute and the genesis of he desired material good. We may, on the one hand, contribute our labor at a point only a brief distance short of our destination on that road. Then our labor is the last link needed for the immediate comple-

Reprinted from *Capital and Interest, Volume II: Positive Theory of Capital* by Eugen von Böhm-Bawerk (South Holland, IL: Libertarian Press, 1959).
*Chapter II of Book I: *Concept and Nature of Capital*.

338 *Austrian Economics: A Reader*

tion of the chain of conditions prerequisite to origination of the good, and the production of the good is the *direct* consequence of the expenditure of our labor. But we may, on the other hand, deliberately choose a roundabout road. In that case our labor comes into immediate combination only with more remote causative factors in the origination of the good; and the combination now yields, not the desired good itself, but only a less remote causative factor. The latter must itself be combined with still further suitable materials and forces until finally—perhaps only after several, or even after numerous intermediate steps—there is produced the finished means of satisfying the want.

The nature and the implications of this variation are best illustrated by a few examples. I feel it is both necessary and permissible to elaborate upon them at some length, inasmuch as they are calculated to represent, to a considerable extent, proof of one of the most fundamental propositions of our theory.

A farmer needs and desires drinking water. There is a spring at some distance from his house. In order to meet his requirements he may follow any one of several procedures. He may go to the spring and drink from his cupped hands. That is the most direct way. Satisfaction is the immediate consequence of his expenditure of labor. But it is inconvenient, for our farmer must travel the distance to the spring as often during the day as he feels thirsty. Moreover it is inadequate, for this method never enables him to gather and store any considerable quantity such as is required for a variety of purposes. Then there is a second possibility. The farmer can hollow out a section of log, fashioning it into a bucket, and in it he can carry a full day's supply of water to his house all at once. The advantage is obvious, but to gain it he must go a considerable distance on a roundabout course. It takes a whole day's carving to hollow out the pail; to do the carving it is necessary first to fell a tree; to do the felling, he must first procure or make himself an axe, and so forth. Finally, there is a third possibility for our farmer. Instead of felling one tree, he fells a number of them, hollows out the trunks of all of them, constructs a pipe line from them, and through it conducts an abundant stream of spring water right to his house. Clearly, the roundabout road from expenditure of labor to attainment of water has become considerably longer, but to make up for it, the road has led to a far more successful result. Now our farmer is entirely relieved of the task of plying his weary way from house to spring burdened with the heavy bucket, and yet he has at all times a copious supply of absolutely fresh water right in the house.

Here is another example. I need quarried stone to build a dwelling, and a nearby cliffside offers stone of excellent quality. But how am I to get hold of some? The first method is to tug and pull with my bare hands until I break off whatever can be loosened by that method. It is the most direct way, but also the least productive. A second method is for me to attempt to procure some iron, fashion a chisel and a hammer and to belabor the hard rock with them. That is a roundabout road, but one which, as everyone knows, leads to a considerably better result. Then there is a third way. I get hold of some iron, make a hammer and chisel, but use them only to drive holes into the cliffside. I next devote my efforts to procuring charcoal, sulphur and saltpeter and then to mixing gunpowder. Thereupon I pour the powder into the holes I bored before, and the ensuing explosion splits the rock. This is a still more roundabout road, but one which experience has shown to be at least as far superior to the second as the second is to the first.

And now for a third example. I am nearsighted and wish to procure spectacles. For the purpose I require ground lenses and a steel frame. But nature offers me only siliceous earth and iron ore. How can I change these substances into the ones I need? No matter how hard I try, it is impossible for me to make lenses out of the siliceous earth directly, and it is just as much out of the question to make a steel frame directly from the iron ore. The straight direct path of production is barred. No help for it, I must pursue the roundabout road. And it is an extremely roundabout road indeed, with a multitude of way stations. I must procure both siliceous earth and fuel, I must build a glassworks where my silica is fused into glass, and then by means of one apparatus after another I must purify, must work and must cool the glass. When it is cold I can, by using still another set of carefully prepared and ingenious instruments, grind it down into the particular shape of lens that is adapted to my myopic eye. Similarly, I have to utilize a blast furnace to melt down the iron ore, then convert the pig iron into steel and out of that steel make my frame. These are all processes that cannot be performed without a long series of tools and buildings, and these in turn demand a great amount of preliminary work. Thus by an extremely long roundabout course I attain the desired goal.

The lesson to be drawn from all these examples is quite clear. It is to the effect that roundabout methods are more fruitful than direct methods in the production of consumers' goods. And as a matter of fact, this greater fruitfulness manifests itself in two ways. Whenever a consumers' good can be produced either by direct or by indirect methods, superiority of the latter is demonstrated by the fact that the indirect method either turns out a greater quantity of product with the same quantity of labor or the same quantity of product with a smaller quantity of labor. In addition, the superiority appears in the fact that some consumers' goods cannot be produced at all, except by indirect methods. Here we might say the indirect is so much the better way that it is often the only way!

We have, then, the proposition that the adoption of roundabout methods of production leads to greater returns from the production process. In affirming that proposition we are enunciating one of the most important and most fundamental tenets of the whole theory of production. It should be distinctly stated at this point, that its basis is furnished by the experience of practical life, and by nothing else. Economic theory does not prove it, and it cannot prove *a priori*, that this must be so. Yet the experience gained in the technique of production in every field is unanimous in its dictum: "That is the way things are!" And that suffices. It does so all the more, since the empirical facts on which it is based are universally recognized and are familiar to us all.[2]

But why are things that way? The economist could decline to answer that question, were he so inclined. For while it is a fact that production methods having their inception in very remote processes regularly turn out a greater quantity of product, this is a purely technical fact. And the economist does not make it a practice to go into the explanation of technique. There are, for instance such technical facts as the greater fertility of tropical climes as compared with polar zones, the greater durability of coins made of alloys as compared with pure metals, the greater serviceableness of superhighways as compared with ordinary roads. But they are technical facts which the economist takes into account, though his science is not particularly called upon to explain them. However, in the present instance we have one of those cases which confront the economist with the pressing necessity of transcending, in his own interest, the limits of the purely economic, in order to verify his own premises. If the naked fact is once exposed in all the sobriety and clarity of physical science, then economic science will be barred from indulging in fancies and fallacies concerning it. And it must be admitted that in the past there has been no dearth in economic theory of the temptation or the desire to do just that. For such reasons I think it will be of particular value in this case to reveal the causes underlying the empirical law, sufficiently attested though it be without that. And after what has been said concerning the nature of production, it should not be too difficult to do.

All the problems of production are reducible in the last analysis to that of transferring and combining matter. We have to know how to put together the right materials at the right time, so that their combined powers can turn out the desired result of production. But we already know that the materials offered by nature are so very, very often either too massive or too delicate for the human hand which is at once so weak and so grossly inept. We are as incapable of overcoming the cohesiveness of the granite cliff from which we wish to derive building material, as we are of combining carbon and nitrogen, hydrogen and oxygen, phosphorus and potassium and the like, to form a single grain of wheat. But what is denied our own powers is quite feasible for other forces, namely, the forces of nature herself. There are natural forces which can perform prodigies of strength infinitely beyond human capacity, and there are other natural forces which, in the world of minutiae are capable of contacts of incredible delicacy. If we could succeed in enlisting these potent forces as our allies in the task of production, we could extend the limits of our capacity enormously. And we do succeed.

Success is ours provided that it is easier for us to control the matter in which the helpful power resides, than it is to command the matter which we wish to transform into the desired good itself. Fortunately, this condition very frequently obtains. Our soft weak hand cannot overcome the power of cohesion possessed by the granite cliff. But the hard sharp steel of the crowbar can. And it is fortunately an easy matter for us to control the crowbar as well as the sledge that drives it. We do not have the ability to gather atoms of phosphorus and potassium from the ground, of carbon and oxygen from the atmosphere and combine them to form a grain of wheat. But the principles of organic chemistry can be put in play by the forces within the seed-kernel of wheat to initiate the magical process of growth, while for us it is ridiculously easy to place the seed in the bosom of the earth, the one place where it can carry out its mysterious function.

Now it must be admitted that we are often unable to control directly the matter in which the helping power resides. In that case we enlist a second form of matter which must help us against the helper, in the same way in which that helper was originally conscripted. That is to say, it must do for us what we cannot do for ourselves. Thus a second auxiliary material force endows us with dominion over the bearer of the first force. We wish, for example, to lead water from the spring to the house. Wooden pipes would perform our will and force the water into the prescribed channel, but our hand does not possess the power to force the tree to take the shape of a pipe. We seek an auxiliary natural force and find it in the axe and the auger. Their help procures the pipes for us and the pipes procure us the water. And what takes place in these examples with the aid of one or two intermediate members can be attained with equal or greater success by using five or ten or twenty such members. Just as we control the immediate material of the good through one auxiliary force and the latter through a second, so we can control the second through a third, the third through a fourth, and so on. We need but continue the progression to include causative factors increasingly remote from the ultimate product we are seeking, until such time as we finally reach that causative factor in the series over which we can easily exercise control by virtue of our own natural powers. Therein lies the true significance of the adoption of circuitous methods of production, and the reason for the success with which those methods are crowned. Every "detour" denotes the conscription of an auxiliary power that is more potent or more clever than the human hand; everything that lengthens the roundabout road signifies an increase in the number of the auxiliary forces that enter man's service, and means the shifting of part of the burden of production from the shoulders of human labor, which is scarce and costly, to those of the natural forces, which are available in prodigal profusion.

And now it is high time to put explicitly into words a thought which has been for some time clamoring for expression, and the imminence of which the reader has doubtless sensed. This method of production which wisely follows an indirect course is nothing more nor less than what the economist calls *capitalist* production.[3] Similarly, we might describe the production methods that proceed directly to their goal by sheer barehanded strength as noncapitalist production, that is to say, production without benefit of capital. *Capital is nothing but the sum total of intermediate products which come into existence at the individual stages of the roundabout course of progression.*

The Capitalist Production Process*

We have already presented[4] in its general outlines a sketch of the process of capitalist production. Some features of it still require more detailed treatment. I shall recapitulate briefly the points already presented and interpolate the new matter at the appropriate places.

All human production has as its object the acquisition of consumption goods. The origination of the latter is dependent upon conditions imposed by the laws of nature. If we are to fulfill those conditions, we must attempt to effect such combinations of active forces that, by the operation of the laws of nature, the inevitable result is a product which has the substance and the form we desire. Let us consider somewhat more closely the powers which are available for man to combine productively in this manner. They comprise two constituents of vastly different magnitude; the

---

*Excerpted from Chapter II of Book II: *Capital as Tool of Production.*

first is the enormous mass of powers which nature manifests spontaneously year in and year out, the second is the much scantier array of natural powers with which the human organism is endowed.

The natural world in which man lives is endowed with multitudinous powers that are never in abeyance for a single moment. Gravity holds our ball of earth together, and holds all things firmly to it, it causes the rain to fall, the streams and rivers to flow into the ocean, the tides to rise and fall, it is unceasingly at work all over the surface of the globe, manifest as stress, weight and pressure. The sun sheds light and warmth upon the globe and thereby sets in motion untold mechanical and chemical reactions. Of these the process of vegetation is probably the one which is most conspicuous in our eyes, both by reason of its mysterious magic and because of its enormous importance for man's well-being. Unnumbered and innumerable are the molecular, electrical and chemical reactions and counterreactions which take place incessantly between every particle of matter and its neighbors. This abundance of manifestations of power which nature pours forth in an unbroken stream and without any contributory activity by man may be regarded as one branch of man's endowment of productive power. Let us call this exceedingly valuable branch his *natural endowment.* It is an inexhaustible treasure from which man may draw as much as he will and can. To be sure, only the smallest part of that treasure has as yet been brought to light. Most of the manifestations of nature's powers are still being dissipated in combinations which, from man's teleological viewpoint, appear useless or even harmful. The enormous kinetic energy of the rising and ebbing tides, of the streams and waterfalls, of the air currents, the colossal electrical, magnetic and gravitational forces that slumber in the bowels of the earth—all are employed only to a tiny fraction of their capacity. Other powers of the earth, such as its vegetational potency, are exploited to a greater degree, but still far short of maximum. The progress that is made each year in agricultural science means more than a constant improvement in our yield per acre, for it suggests that the limit of our possibilities in that direction still lies far ahead of us.

It is a well-known fact that the realization of these natural treasures is accomplished only through recourse to the second branch of our endowment of natural powers. We call upon our personal forces for the performance of labor, and effect a skillful combination with the most suitable natural processes. And thus all our achievements in the field of production are the result of two elemental productive powers and only two. Those two are nature and labor. That is one of the truly infallible ideas of the theory of production. The human race is confronted with an abundance of natural processes and adds to them its own activities. What nature does and what man adds constitute the twin fountainheads from which flow all our goods. There is no other spring. There is no possibility of a third elemental source.

These two elements account for everything which, from the *technical viewpoint,* is accomplished in the production process. *From the economic viewpoint,* however, it is necessary to make further significant distinctions. There is a broad stream of natural phenomena which feeds the reservoir where are stored all the productive combinations available to man, but only a part of that stream claims our *economic* interest. That part is composed of those useful manifestations of nature which are supplied only in limited or scanty amount. There is of course no lack, *per se,* either of material or of forces. Carbon and nitrogen, oxygen and hydrogen, indeed most of the "elements" are no less abundant than are the electrical, chemical, magnetic or gravitational forces. But certain spontaneously produced combinations of those elements can very well be relatively rare, especially in a form that is adaptable to the satisfaction of man's wants. There are for instance plants that can be utilized, water that can be harnessed, ground that can be tilled, minerals that can be worked. Rare gifts and forces of nature of that kind acquire true *economic* significance. If we are not to play the part of simpletons, we must treat them in accordance with economic principles. Superabundant technical elements of production like air and water and sunlight may be used or squandered as we will, and still we suffer no loss in the proceeds of our production. But the rare technical elements call for husbandry, frugality, complete utilization. Within the compass of man's broader *technical* endowment they constitute his specifically *economic* natural endowment. And since all, or nearly all rare gifts and powers of nature are linked to the soil, we shall be safe from appreciable error if we designate all examples of this economic natural endowment by the term *land, or uses of land.*[5]

Man's expenditures of labor constitute the complement to the uses of land. Virtually all human labor is economic in character. This is partly due to the fact that in proportion to the extensive labor that our wants require, our energies are so scantily meted out that even maximum industriousness will not suffice to fill our need for goods completely, let alone superabundantly. And it is partly due to the feelings of vexation and laboriousness which are connected with the exerting of our powers, at least beyond a certain point.[6] These feelings admonish us to a husbanding and economizing of our efforts.

Nature and labor are thus the *technical* elements of production, land and labor are its *economic* elements. These two, like the talents which the good and faithful servant "put to the exchangers," are put out by man at usury with the fruitful and prodigally abundant free forces of nature. Only land and labor are of economic import for production, since the technically requisite cooperation of the free forces of nature is unquestioningly and gratuitously supplied. Anyone who has the disposition of the necessary land and labor can achieve the desired economic product. Anyone who lacks them must also go without the product. He who possesses a double quantity or a half quantity will, if the techniques of production remain uniform, achieve a double quantity or a half quantity of the product. They are the only elements of production with which economics is concerned and with which it must reckon. In short, *land and labor are the elemental economic powers of production.*[7]

How does man make use of these primary productive forces? In answering this question we return to follow familiar paths for a little way.

There are two ways for man to fashion consumption goods out of those productive elements. One way is to combine the productive economic forces with each other or with the activities of free forces of nature in such a way that the desired consumption good is an immediate result of the combination. For instance, he gathers shellfish thrown up by the tides on the shore. The other way is to tread a roundabout path by first producing another good from those elements and then subsequently and with its help producing the desired good. For example, he constructs a boat and some nets and then with the help of these implements he takes up fishing as a calling. We are already aware that direct production is what might be termed "capitalless," or better perhaps, "noncapitalist" production and that indirect production is another name for capitalist production. And we also know that the intermediate products which come into existence as a result of the roundabout methods of indirect production represent social capital.

There are two concomitants of the adoption of the capitalist methods of production, both of them as characteristic as they are fraught with consequences. One is advantageous, the other disadvantageous. We are already familiar with the advantage. With an equal expenditure of the two originary productive forces,[8] labor and valuable forces of nature, it is possible by well-chosen roundabout capitalist methods to produce more or better goods than would have been possible by the direct noncapitalist method. It is a truism well corroborated by empirical evidence.[9]

The explanation lies in the fact that skillfully chosen circuitous methods tap the stupendous treasure of natural forces for fresh auxiliary powers, the activity of which is beneficial to the process of production. It is this well-known fact which is usually alluded to by those who use the term "productivity of capital." But this very term reads an interpretation into the facts which will be subjected to examination in the succeeding chapter.

The disadvantage which attends the capitalist method of production consists in a *sacrifice of time.* Capitalist roundaboutness is productive but time consuming. It yields more or better consumption goods, but not until a later time. This is another proposition that, like the earlier one, constitutes one of the essential pillars of the whole doctrine of capital. Even the function of capital as a means of acquisition, as a source of income, is largely based upon it, as we shall see in due time. I shall therefore take it upon myself to make careful efforts to establish its correctness. It becomes my duty to defend this proposition against the numerous objections and misunderstandings which it may encounter and which it actually has already encountered since publication of the first edition of this work. And yet I am loath to delay unduly the present concise description of the facts involved in the production process. In place of making an extended interpolation at this point, I shall for the nonce anticipate only so much of a full explanation as I consider indispensable for the understanding of the facts. And the description of those facts will then follow without delay.

Exceptional cases may occur, in which a roundabout method is not only *better* but also *quicker.* Let us take the case of an attempt to gather apples from a tall tree. The object will probably be accomplished sooner by first cutting a pole from another tree with which to knock down the apples than by climbing the tree and plucking each apple by hand.

But that is not the rule. In an overwhelming majority of cases, the adoption of circuitous methods imposes conditions that require us to wait for a time and sometimes for a very long time indeed, before we obtain possession of the product in consumable form. It is not necessary to cite examples, as these will doubtless occur spontaneously and in great number to the reader. Let me point out instead, that the loss of time which is ordinarily connected with roundabout capitalist methods of production constitutes the only basis for the much discussed and much deprecated dependence of the worker upon the capitalist. I say "capitalist" only because the situation is different with respect to the landowner. If circuitous capitalist methods brought results as quickly as direct noncapitalist production, there would be nothing to prevent the workers from employing the roundabout methods from beginning to end on their own account. They would still, of course, be dependent on the landowners who would be in a position to deny access to the uses of land, and such access is indispensable at the start. But their dependence on the capitalist would be over. However, the workers cannot wait until the circuitous path that begins with the obtaining of raw materials and the making of tools finally leads to its destination—consumption goods in ready-to-use form. That is the one reason why they continue to be dependent on those who already possess a finished store of the so-called intermediate products, in a word, on the capitalists.[10]

It goes without saying that it is no refutation of our proposition to content that, with the help of *previously finished* capital objects, a given product can be produced more quickly than by the direct "capitalless" method. This sort of refutation might be exemplified by the argument that a tailor needs only one day to turn out a coat with the help of a sewing machine, whereas it will require three days without that capital object. But it is obvious that the sewing by machine is only a portion—and indeed the smallest portion—of the circuitous capitalist path. The principal length of that path is covered by the making of the sewing machine. And it is equally apparent that the traversing of the entire length of the path requires a great deal more than three days.

Up to this point we have contrasted capitalist production, as an undivided whole, with completely noncapitalist production. But that is only a partial recognition of the facts. For even within the whole system of capitalist production there are gradations of "capitalism" and their number is, to be truthful, infinite. For the attainment of a consumption good can be reached by roundabout paths of widely varying length. Intermediate products can be made which make it possible to acquire a particular consumption good at the end of a month; other intermediate products may not accomplish the result in less than a year or 10 years or 100 years. The question then arises, what influences these differences of degree have upon the product.

On the whole it may be said that not only is the first step on the roundabout way of production accompanied by an increase in technical productivity, but every succeeding increase in the length of the way is marked by a concomitant augmentation of productivity. However, each step by which the way is lengthened is marked by a proportionately smaller technical improvement. This observation, too, is based on experience, and only on experience. Its message simply has to be accepted as an empirical aspect of the technique of production, but the reader can easily check on its accuracy, if he will but follow in thought the way that leads to the production of any consumption good. Firewood can very easily be obtained by simply gathering up dry twigs or breaking off small branches. A short circuitous path of production leads to the making and using of a stone axe. A longer path leads to the digging of iron ore, the gathering of the fuel and tools needed for smelting, the production of iron from the ore, of steel from the iron, and finally from the steel a well-sharpened axe. To go into it at greater length we might mention that the mining requires ingenious machinery and rolling stock, the smelting calls for efficient blast furnaces, the shaping and sharpening of the axe necessitate the building of special machinery. Going still further back we see that these machines in turn call for other factories and machinery, and so on. No one is likely to doubt that each of these two roundabout methods enhances the productivity of the total production process. In other words, that each unit of product—in this case, each cord of firewood—is obtained with a smaller total expenditure of direct and indirect labor. And it is equally certain the impression will be gained, that the first two circuitous steps, the use of a stone axe and the later use of a steel axe, must have been far more revolutionary in the woodcutting industry than any later improvements, however advantageous these might be.

If necessary, that impression can be corroborated by a calculation that may be regarded as tantamount to evidence. Let us suppose for example, that a worker can gather two cords of firewood in a day with his bare hands. But with a stone axe which it takes three days to make, he can raise his two cords a day to 10. The three-day indirect method in the production process therefore brings about an increase in product of eight cords per day. Now it is possible that doubling the circuitousness to six days (by more careful fashioning of the axe, let us say) may further raise the increase in product to 16 cords a day. But we can begin to be skeptical of the possibility that tripling the roundaboutness to nine days will triple the increase in product to 24. And we can be quite certain of the result of increasing it a thousandfold. This might be the case, for instance, if we sank a shaft in order to mine ore which could not produce a steel axe until some years had passed. Certainly that would not augment the increase in product to a thousandfold, which would involve the almost unthinkable supposition that a *single* worker in a *single* day should turn out 8,000 cords of wood!

No! At a certain and probably not very remote point along the line the increase in product will, though existent, be proportionately less than the increase in production time.

Of course, in such cases no exact figure can be determined, either for the point at which the proportionate productiveness of further extensions of the roundaboutness begins to fall off, or for the magnitude of the increase in product which may be attributed to any specific lengthening of the circuitous way. The figures vary according to the technical conditions prevailing in each area of production, and at every stage in productional skill. Every new invention modifies the figures. The invention of gunpowder opened up possibilities which had not existed the instant before. The huntsman's potential productivity was, perhaps, doubled, while the quarryman was greeted with the prospect of a hundredfold increase in productiveness.[11]

Nevertheless, one thing that can be stated with a reasonable degree of certainty is the proposition previously formulated, namely, that as a general rule a wisely selected extension of the roundabout way of production does result in an increase in the magnitude of the product. It can be confidently maintained that there is no area of production which could not materially increase its product over the result obtained by its present method. It would require no new invention, simply the intercalation of some familiar capitalist intermediate factor, such as an engine here, a well-devised transmission there, an ingenious regearing, a blast mechanism, a lever, a governor or the like. How far the majority of our agricultural and industrial plants lag behind the most progressive model establishments in their own fields! And even the latter, in all probability, fall just as far short of the ideal of truly perfected equipment.[12]

Economic science long ago observed and recognized two facts. One is, that a lengthening of the roundabout methods of production results in an increased quantity of the product; the other is that this increase begins to fall off at a certain point. It must be conceded that these facts have, for the most part, been stated differently and couched in the jargon borrowed from one version or another of the "productivity theory." The most impartial formulation is from the pen of Thünen. He showed that where new capital is constantly added, the most recently added installment, while it does affect an increase in the product of labor, does so in constantly decreasing proportion.[13] This furnished the factual basis of the well-known doctrine he himself erected. It reads to the effect that the rate of interest is determined by the productiveness of the last installment of capital which is employed in the least productive enterprise. And in the wake of his doctrine his factual pronouncements found recognition in the widest circles.[14] Only, in conformity with the economic fashion of the time, they were forcibly fitted into the form of conception and the form of statement current among proponents of the productivity theory. And that opened the door to highly vexatious misapprehensions and misinterpretations.[15] In accordance with the terms of the task which this chapter imposes upon me, I have taken it upon myself to restate the facts here in all their naked simplicity.

It is self-evident that capitalist production of consumption goods, even though it is carried on circuitously and in stages, nevertheless constitutes a cohesive, unified process of production. Both the labor which produces the intermediate products and which, with Rodbertus,[16] we shall call *indirect labor,* and the labor which produces the desired consumption good from and with the help of the intermediate products, contribute alike to the production of that consumption good. The obtaining of wood results not only from the labor of felling trees, but also from that of the smith who makes the axe, of the carpenter who carves the haft, of the miner who digs the ore from which the steel is derived, of the foundryman who smelts the ore. Our modern system of specialized occupations does, of course, give the intrinsically unified process of production the extrinsic appearance of a heterogeneous mass of apparently independent units. But the theorist who makes any pretensions to understanding the economic workings of the production process in all its vital relationships must not be deceived by appearances. His mind must restore the unity of the production process which has had its true picture obscured by the division of labor.[17]

And now it is my hope that I need fear no misapprehension of misinterpretation of my general summary. I should like to conclude by compressing the general picture of the capitalist process of production into the following succinct statement.

All consumption goods which man produces come into existence through the cooperation of human powers with the forces of nature, which are in part of economic character, in part free natural powers. Man can produce the consumption goods he desires through those elemental productive powers. He does so either directly, or indirectly through the agency of intermediate products which are called capital goods. The indirect method entails a sacrifice of time but gains the advantage of an increase in the quantity of the product. Successive prolongations of the roundabout method of production yield further quantitative increases though in diminishing proportion.[18]

The Theory of The Formation of Capital*

In economic science there are three theories current concerning the formation of capital. One ascribes the origination of capital to saving, another to production, the third to both factors. The third is probably the most widely held, and it is the correct one. The difficulty is to amplify the

*Chapter V of Book II: *Capital as Tool of Production.*

correct formula beyond the dimensions it usually attains and to imbue it with a content that is clearer and truer to life than is generally the case.[19]

In order to begin with the simplest conceivable instance, let us imagine a recluse carrying on his economy completely devoid of capital, somewhat after the manner of a Robinson Crusoe cast ashore on a solitary island and entirely without resources of any kind. Since he is without capital, he must at first gain his sustenance in the most primitive manner, let us say by the gathering of wild fruits and berries. What must now take place in order that he may gain possession of his first capital, let us say a bow and some arrows?

Let our initial step be to test the first theory.

Is saving enough to give birth to capital? Certainly not. Our Robinson Crusoe can save and scrimp as he will with his fruit and berries, the most he can do is to amass a treasure of stored up consumption goods. But it certainly will not gain for him a single bow or arrow. It is quite obvious that those must be *produced.* Does production then suffice for the origination of capital, and is the second theory therefore correct? No more than the first. To be sure, once the point has been attained of starting the production of capital goods, then the formation of capital is as good as achieved. But before that period *is* attained something else has to be done that is by no means a matter of course. Productive forces have to be liberated for the proposed formation of capital and the only way to do that is by saving. Let us see why that is so.

The entire sum of originary productive forces at Crusoe's daily disposal—aside from gifts of nature—is a day's labor which we shall assume to be a 10-hour workday. We shall assume also that the wild fruits in Crusoe's area grow so sparsely that it takes a full 10-hour workday for him to gather enough fruit for the barest sustenance. In such case any formation of capital is obviously out of the question. It is vain to advise Crusoe to get ahead with his production of a bow and arrows. Producing requires time and strength, and all the time and the strength that he possesses is required in full for the immediate task of eking out an existence. "Producing" is a long way off unless something can be done about it. And what that something is, will become readily apparent if we may be permitted to vary the assumed facts of our illustration just a little.

Let us assume that the fruit harvest increases enough to enable our castaway to gather the subsistence minimum in nine hours a day, and enough in 10 hours to furnish him with adequate sustenance for complete health and vigor. It is quite clear that Crusoe now has a choice between two lines of conduct. One alternative is to utilize the opportunity offered him of obtaining a completely adequate food supply, and to consume each day the fruits gathered by a full 10 hours' work. In that case it is plain as a pikestaff that he still has neither time nor strength left to make a bow and arrows. The other alternative is to restrict himself to the subsistence minimum that can be garnered in nine hours, even though the productive forces available to him place an adequate food supply within his grasp. In that event—but only in that event—he has a tenth hour open in which he can make hunting equipment for future use. Let us put that into general terms. Before there can be any real formation of capital, the productive forces necessary to its production must be *saved up* at the expense of the enjoyment of the moment.

There is one particular error which is very easy to make at this point, and I hope, by anticipating it, to prevent it. It should be expressly noted that the "expense of the enjoyment of the moment" need not always entail downright privation. In the foregoing example, if Crusoe's labor were somewhat more productive his two alternatives might be altered. Instead of "bare subsistence minimum" and "adequate supply," the choice offered might be between "adequate supply" and "bounteous fare." It is not a matter of the

absolute magnitude of the minimal claims to enjoyment of
the moment, but of their relative magnitude in comparison
with "income." I use that word because it seems the briefest
and the most widely understood term to convey my meaning, and despite the fact that economic science unfortunately has not yet defined the term with sufficient exact-
ness.[20] The essential point is, that the current endowment
of productive forces be not devoted entirely to the enjoyment of the "moment"—the present period—so that a portion of them may be reserved for the service of a future
period. Behavior of that kind must unquestionably be called
a genuine saving of productive forces.

I say saving up of *productive forces,* for it is these and not
the capital goods themselves which are saved up. This is the
important point and one which must be sharply emphasized
because prevalent opinion has given it too little attention.
We are *saving of* consumption goods, thereby *saving up* productive forces and thus can in the end use the latter in order
to *produce* capital goods.[21] Only by exception are capital
goods themselves occasionally the direct object of saving.
This situation occurs in the case of goods which are by nature adapted to use in two ways. Such articles as grain, for
instance, can be used as food or as seed, in other words as a
consumption good or a production good. Withdrawal of
such goods from use for consumption purposes does constitute a direct saving of the material from which capital is
formed. To complete the act of forming capital it is of
course necessary to complement the negative factor of saving with the positive factor of devoting the thing saved to a
productive purpose or, in other words, to endow it with the
status of an intermediate product. The same conditions that
govern the initial formation of capital also apply to every
subsequent increase in the existing stock of capital. This can
be easily demonstrated. Let us assume that our Crusoe has
continued throughout one month to consume each day only
as much fruit as he could gather in nine hours and has

devoted the tenth hour of each day to making hunting equipment. As a result of this total of 30 hours' activity he has a bow and some arrows and the possibility of obtaining his subsistence with far greater ease and in much greater abundance than before. But of course his desires go beyond that. He wants comfortable clothing, a dwelling and all sorts of devices that minister to his comfort. All that requires a previous supply of appropriate intermediate products, namely tools, an axe, nails, braces and the like. Let us again put the question as to what conditions must be fulfilled, if Crusoe is to gain possession of these new capitals.

No question could be easier to answer. One possibility open to him is to utilize the improvement in his conditions, effected by his possession of bow and arrows, for nothing more than a heightened enjoyment of the life of the moment—in other words, he can spend all the time available to him for labor on consumption for the present, that is to say, on hunting, fruit-gathering and resting in indolence. If he chooses that possibility he not only cannot acquire new capital, but will lose the old. For his weapons of the chase will not last forever. In a month let us say, his arrows will be spent and his bow worn out.

He must choose another possibility if he is to preserve his capital at its previous level. He must devote at least one hour of his daily allotment of 10 working hours to the rehabilitation of his working equipment and may not spend more than a daily maximum of nine hours on hunting and fruit-gathering. If we express that idea in terms of universal validity it will run as follows. In order to preserve capital *in statu quo ante* a certain quantity of the productive forces of the current period must be assigned to the service of the future. And that quantity must be at least equal to the total product of the productive forces of prior periods which is consumed during the current period.[22] Or let us put it still another way. *Consumption during the current period of the yield of all current and prior productive forces combined, must not exceed the total products that can be derived from the productive forces which accrue afresh in the current period.*

The third possibility is an increase in the store of capital, and that possibility obviously demands that a still greater proportion of the current period's productive forces be withheld from consumption in the present and assigned to the future. Crusoe wants to be able to produce the capital objects requisite for the satisfaction of his increased desires in a liberated remnant of his 10 working hours per day. If he is to do so, he must devote *one* hour to the rehabilitation of his equipment, and *less than nine hours* to gathering fruit and shooting game. Couched in general terms that reads as follows. *Consumption during the current period must be curtailed to such a degree that he uses up only a total product (of all current and prior productive forces combined) which is exceeded by the product that can be derived from the productive forces which accrue afresh in that same period.* Or to express it with extreme brevity, *productive forces must be saved up.*

That is all very clear and simple; it is even a bit too simple for our purpose. Robinson Crusoe settings and hypothetical primitive conditions serve well enough to clarify the simplest, most typical fundamental features, to teach the skeleton, as it were, of the whole structure of economic processes. And I hope that the foregoing "Robinsonade" has been serviceable in that respect. But such hypotheses do not, of course, adequately convey the picture of the peculiar and highly developed forms with which the skeleton is clothed when it becomes the living actuality of a modern economy. It is just at this point that it becomes my great concern to imbue the abstract formula with representational and conceptual data that are vividly concrete and true to life. Our theater of operations must be transferred from Crusoe's lonely island to the center of the bustling economic life of a nation of many million souls.

Let us imagine a community of 10 million able-bodied workers. Its annual allotment of productive forces therefore amounts to 10 million labor-years. In order to present the problem without presenting unnecessarily complicated figures, I shall ignore the currently available uses of land. Its hitherto accumulated stock of capital we shall assume to represent the fruits of 30 million labor-years (plus, of course, the corresponding quantity of uses of land), which during prior economic years have been invested in intermediate products. Let us examine the structure of this stock of capital more closely.

Every capital is by nature composed of a mass of intermediate products, all of which have as their common goal, to mature into means of enjoyment, that is to say, into consumption goods. They reach that goal through a continuation of the production process in the course of which they themselves come into existence. They are all, as it were, en route to the destination of maturity for consumption. But the roads that lead them there will vary. That is in part due to the circumstance that different areas of production have circuitous paths of production which vary in length. Mining or railroad building goes a far more circuitous road than wood carving. But it is also due in part to the fact that the goods which comprise at a given moment the total amount of the community's capital are located at very different points along the respective production roads. Some intermediate products have just set out upon a very long roundabout path such as, for instance, a boring machine that is destined to dig a mine shaft. Others are midway to the goal and still others are close to the terminus of the "long trail" of production they must cover, such as bolts of cloth which are about to be made up into suits and overcoats. The inventory of capital constitutes, so to speak, a cross section of the many processes of production which are of varying length and which began at different times. It therefore cuts across them at very widely differing stages of development. We might compare it to the census which is a cross section through the paths of human life and which encounters and which arrests the individual members of society at widely varying ages and stages.

With respect to the varying remoteness from readiness for consumption, the composite mass of capital adapts itself to a highly appropriate scheme of presentation as a number of concentric annual rings each representing a yearly class, or what might be termed a "maturity class." The outermost annual ring (*see Fig. 1*) embraces those parts of the capital which will become finished consumption goods within the following year, the second outermost ring represents the capitals which will mature into consumption goods in the second year and so on. In a community where capitalist production is not yet strongly developed, the inner rings will shrink in rapidly progressive proportion (*see Fig. 2*). This is because in such a community lengthy circuitous processes of production, which come to fruition only after a period of many years, are rarely and sparingly adopted. In rich and well-developed economies, on the other hand, a considerable number of well-developed circles can be distinguished, and of these the inner rings will have an area or content that is relatively smaller, to be sure, but by no means inconsiderable.

Representation of the maturity classes by concentric circles is particularly appropriate because that picture provides a felicitous method of helping us to visualize the relative magnitudes of those classes. The outermost of the concentric rings has the greatest area, and the areas of the succeeding rings diminish gradually. In exactly the same way the greatest proportion of the total capital of a community will at all times consist of the first maturity class, the goods that are at a point in the production process closest to completion. Similarly, the increasingly remote maturity classes will represent a progressively diminishing proportion of the community's capital. There are two reasons for this. The first is that in the various areas of production roundabout

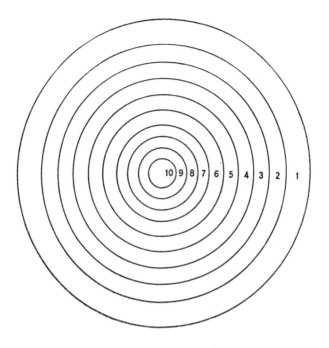

Figure 1

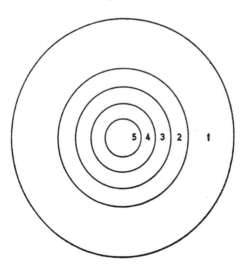

Figure 2

methods of production are adopted which vary in length by reason of their varying technical nature. In some, the entire production process from the initial preparatory operations to the production of the final product ready for consumption, is completed within the course of a single year. In others, two, three or five years are required; in only a few do production periods measure 10, 20, and 30 years. As a result, the highest maturity classes (those most remote from maturity) draw their membership from only a few areas of production. Intermediate products in a stage, let us say, that assigns them to the tenth maturity class can come only from areas of production where the production period lasts at least 10 years. The lower maturity classes *do* draw their membership from these last-mentioned areas of production (since the intermediate products must pass successively through the classes closer to maturation); but they also draw from the areas of production where the duration of the production period is shorter. Thus the quantity of intermediate products becomes greater as progress is made toward the first maturity class. In that class every area of production, without exception, is represented. But a second circumstance works in the same direction. The maturation of intermediate products into consumption goods necessitates a constant addition of current productive forces. At each stage of the production process new labor is added to the intermediate products handed on from the preceding stage, and they are then in turn delivered over to the succeeding stage. At one stage, the intermediate product wool is transformed by the addition of labor into yarn; in a later stage labor is again added to transform it into the intermediate product cloth, and so on. The natural consequence is that within each production area the amount of capital invested increases with every forward step to a succeeding stage of production, that is to say, with every forward step to a lower maturity class. For that reason the lower maturity classes do not only comprise representatives from more numerous areas of production, as set forth in the preceding paragraph, but the membership has fattened on relatively larger amounts of capital. That makes the lower classes exceed the upper classes in two respects—their membership is more numerous and more weighty, the first class taking complete precedence.[23]

Let us now set down in figures these relations which are present in our example. In order to make the situation easier to grasp at a glance I shall assume that the total amount of capital in our community is composed of only 10 annual rings. If that total capital embodies labor-years in the amount of 30 millions (again ignoring the invested uses of land, for the sake of simplicity) then we can assume some such distribution of the maturity classes as follows:

Maturity Class No.	*Contains intermediate products embodying labor years to the number*
1	6 millions
2	5 "
3	4 "
4	3.5 "
5	3 "
6	2.5 "
7	2 "
8	1.7 "
9	1.3 "
10	1 "

Each year, in the normal course of events, the outermost annual ring is completely severed from the total amount of capital, and is converted into consumption goods which serve to satisfy the wants of the community. Each of the inner rings receives the addition of new labor, and this both advances it one stage in the production process, and also increases its mass; as a result each ring advances to the next succeeding maturity class. Thus the first class becomes consumption goods, the second becomes the first class, the third becomes the second, and so on.

There now arises a question that is important for our topic. What use is our economy to make of the originary productive forces which accrue to it afresh in the current year? In other words, how is it to utilize the 10 million labor-years which the current year makes available? (Once more in the interest of simplicity, we ignore uses of land.) The question is really "two-headed." What is the procedure if we wish just to preserve the amount of capital in its previous magnitude? What must be done, if there is to be an increase of capital?

Both questions are easily answered.

To preserve its capital *in statu quo,* the economy must not expend more than 4 million labor-years in *present production.* For the sake of brevity. I shall use that term to designate all those acts of production which have in common the characteristic that the productive forces which manifest themselves in those acts achieve their full mission (i.e., produce consumption goods) within the same economic period. This applies to two kinds of productive acts. In part, and principally, it applies to the performance of those concluding labors which are required to transform goods of the first capital ring into consumption goods. Examples of this kind of act are the labor of the farmer, the miller, the baker, the cobbler, the tailor, etc. But it applies also in part to those labors which are concerned in production processes of such short duration that they are initiated and concluded within a single economic period.

The other 6 million labor-years must be devoted to restoring the quantitative and qualitative level of the stock of capital, which has been reduced through the abscission of the first annual ring. This makes it necessary to promote the other nine annual rings by adding to each the quota of labor which will advance it one stage nearer maturity. It also becomes necessary to recreate a tenth class which is now completely lacking. The magnitude of these additions can be precisely determined. What was hitherto the second class, in which but 5 million labor-years were embodied, requires an addition of 1 million labor-years to attain

Class No.	In order to equal previous Class No.	Must have added to it labor-years in the amount of
2	1	1.0 million
3	2	1.0 + "
4	3	0.5 "
5	4	0.5 "
6	5	0.5 "
7	6	0.5 "
8	7	0.3 "
9	8	0.4 "
10	9	0.3 "
Entirely new tenth class requires		1.0 "
making a total of		6.0 "

equality with the former first class with its 6 million labor-years. The complete table presents the foregoing appearance.

Let it be explicitly and pointedly stated that it is by no means a matter of indifference where and in which maturity classes the 6 million labor-years are expended. Suppose, for instance, that consideration were centered on the expenditure of a total of 6 million labor-years for the creation of intermediate products without regard to the distribution indicated above. If the whole 6 million were expended in turning out intermediate products of, say, the first class—products attaining maturity for consumption one year later—this would result in a twofold disadvantage. In the first place, those intermediate products which had as yet advanced only as far as the higher maturity classes would come to a standstill. In the second place, the shorter, less circuitous methods of production are, as we have already learned, less productive. It is true that 6 million labor-years, all invested in a one-year indirect production process, would still mean that the present would be transferring to the future the same quantity of *productive forces*. But the thing of prime importance is, that by doing so the present would be subjected to the defect of lesser productiveness and thus would deliver to the future a smaller quantity of products than it had itself acquired for consumption from the past. The annual production of the succeeding year would necessarily diminish, and the total capital, instead of being maintained, would be impaired.

Now let us proceed to the matter of an increase of capital. It is quite apparent that the community must renounce a portion of those enjoyments it could have allowed itself under an arrangement calling for maintenance of the *status quo*. In other words, it must liberate a part of the productive forces at its disposition from the service of the present and assign it to the service of the future—it must make *a saving* which it devotes to additional future production. The saving of productive forces can be effected in several ways. One is to expend a smaller proportion of current productive forces—say 3 million labor-years instead of 4 million—on "present production" while the quotas assigned to other years remain the same. A second way is to have made provision for saving in advance and to have organized the total capital in such a way that the annual ring attaining maturity in the present year be smaller in amount—say 5 million labor-years instead of 6. The result would be that preservation of capital would require only 5 million labor-years. If under those circumstances only 4 million of the annually accruing 10 million allotment still are expended on present production, then there is a remainder of one million available for the formation of new capital. A third way is also open. It is conceivable that in the last moment disposition of capital is altered in such a way that less of it reaches the stage of maturity for consumption than had been originally intended. It is a well-known fact that many goods admit of several methods of utilization. That makes it possible to take goods which have reached maturity or which stand on its threshold, and to retard their consumption by one or several stages. Grain need not be milled for food purposes, but can be used or even stored for planting as seed, or it can be used in the distillery. Fuel can be used to fire blast furnaces rather than restaurant kitchens, iron can be used for building machinery rather than park railings, and so on. If it is possible by that kind of change in disposition of capital, to reduce the quantity of it maturing in the present year from 6 to 5 million labor-years, then there is again, after 4 million are devoted to present production, a remainder of 1 million labor-years available for the formation of new capital.

Of these three methods, the second is probably applied most frequently in practical life and the first most infrequently. At any rate, they have one important feature in common. That is the fact that in the current period the consumable product of only 9 million labor-years is actually consumed, while in the same period 10 million such labor-years accrue afresh. In other words there is a saving of 1 million labor-years out of the current productive endowment.[24]

So far we have discussed the formation of a nation's capital as if that nation were carrying on a unified economy governed by a single will. Of course that is not the case. We therefore still have to show how, under the actual system of diversified and multiple control of our economy, the dispositions which lead to the formation of capital are actually carried out. And it still remains to be proven, whether those dispositions presuppose "saving" as I maintained above. It is a just contention that generalizations must be demonstrably valid, not for the present and historically factual organization of society, but also for every such organization of it. I shall therefore consider, in this present investigation, not only the existing economic organization which is predominantly individualist in character, but also an economic form that is certainly conceivable—the socialist system of economy. And I shall begin with the latter because it represents a form which is, for the purposes of our problem, by far the simpler.

In a socialist state, where private capital and private enterprise have been abolished and the entire national production is under the organizational control of the state, the formation of capital and the necessary antecedent saving up of productive forces would likewise be matters under state control. Such control would take the simple form of assigning the national labor forces to capital-forming, long-range production, in a ratio that would exceed the ratio in which the consumable products of such past production become available for present consumption. It would be a simple matter of employing a relatively large number of workers in mines, at railroad building, flood control, manufacturing machinery and the like, while relatively few would be assigned to working in vineyards, raising silkworms, manufacturing lace, brewing beer or weaving cloth. Through pressure from above the nation would thus be compelled to save through the simple device of so controlling national production as to make a relatively small amount of consumption goods available for the nation's population—a smaller amount than that which could be annually produced and consumed, if only the maintenance of the previous level of the capital were the desideratum. The excess of productive forces so liberated would then be invested in roundabout production.

The procedure is somewhat more complicated in an individualistically organized society such as is represented

by the actual conditions prevailing today. And yet its underlying principles can be recognized. Here the prime factor
in the control over the assignment of the annually accruing
productive forces and over the direction given to the national production is the entrepreneur. But he does not exercise this control as his own desires dictate. On the contrary,
he is subject to the influence exerted by the prices of products. Where lively demand promises profitable prices, the
entrepreneur expands his production; where diminishing
demand no longer keeps pace with the supply and certain
goods no longer command sufficiently profitable prices, the
entrepreneur restricts production of those kinds of goods.
Expansion and restriction of supply continue to alternate
until for the individual classes of merchandise a balance has
been established between production and demand. In the
last analysis, then, it is not the entrepreneur who determines
the direction the national production shall take, but the consumer—the "public." Everything depends on what "Mr.
Public" wants to spend his income for.

Now the income of a nation is, in the long run, identical
with the yield of its production. One annual ring of its income coincides approximately with the yield from one annual ring of its productive forces.[25] Suppose that every individual member of a nation were to use up the exact amount
of his yearly income in the form of consumption goods. In
that case a demand for consumption goods would develop
that would so influence the fluctuation of prices as to induce
the entrepreneur to guide production along a line that
would each year result in having the yield of an entire annual ring of productive forces assume the form of consumption goods. If the annual allotment of a nation amounts to
10 million labor-years and the corresponding uses of land,
and if that nation desires to and does consume its entire
year's income in the form of consumption goods, then it is
necessary for the yield of a full 10 million labor-years, plus

the corresponding uses of land, to be converted annually into consumption goods. In that event there are no productive forces available for an increase of capital, and that nation can do no more than preserve its capital *in statu quo ante.*

If, on the other hand, each individual consumes, on the average, only three-quarters of his income and saves the other quarter, then obviously there will be a falling off in the desire to buy consumption goods and in the demand for them.Only three-quarters as great a quantity of consumption goods as in the preceding case will become the subject of demand and of sale. If the entrepreneurs were nevertheless to continue for a time to follow the previous disposition of production and go on bringing consumption goods to market at the rate of a full 10 million labor-years annually, the oversupply would soon depress the prices of those goods, render them unprofitable and hence induce the entrepreneurs to adjust their production to the changed demand. They will see to it that in one year only the product of 7.5 million labor-years is converted into consumption goods, be it through maturation of the first annual ring or be it through additional present production.[26] The remaining 2.5 million labor-years left over from the current annual allotment can be used for increasing capital. *And it will be so used.* For an economically advanced nation does not engage in hoarding, but invests its savings. It buys securities, it deposits its money at interest in savings banks or commercial banks, puts it out on loan, etc. In this way it is added to the nation's productive credit, increases the producer's purchasing power for productive purposes, and so becomes the cause of an increase in the demand for production goods, which is to say intermediate products. And that demand is, in the last analysis, what induces the managers of business enterprises to invest available productive forces in desired intermediate products.

We can therefore perceive a real connection between saving and the formation of capital. If not a single individual saves, then the nation as a whole cannot build up capital because the great conversion to use of consumption goods forces producers through the medium of price so to apply productive forces that the product of a whole year's allotment of productive forces is supplied and consumed in the form of consumption goods. As a result no productive forces are left over for an increase of capital. But if individuals do save, then the change in demand, once more through the agency of price, forces the entrepreneurs into a changed disposition of productive forces. In that case fewer productive powers are enlisted during the course of the year for the service of the present as consumption goods, and there is a correspondingly greater quantity of productive forces tied up in the transitional stage of intermediate products. In other words, there is an increase in capital, which redounds to the benefit of an enhanced enjoyment of consumption goods in the future.[27]

There is also a third possibility. Individuals may, on the average, consume *more* than their income; instead of saving, they may squander their stock of wealth. According to our theory that would necessarily lead to a diminution of the nation's capital. And that is in actual fact the case. It comes about by the following steps. Where squandering is the rule, more than the year's income of the nation is advanced to the stage of conversion to use in the form of consumption goods. That is to say, more than the product of one annual ring of productive forces is so consumed. Production yields to the demand, under the pressure of price. Suppose for instance, that the previous disposition was such, that the first maturity class of the stock of capital was intended to mature in the current year with 6 million labor-years, and that out of the 10 million comprising the labor allotment of the current year, 4 million were intended to be employed in present production and the remaining 6 in replacing capital consumed. But we must now further suppose that the extravagance of the citizens causes a demand for consumption goods in the amount of the product of 12 million labor-years. In that case the entrepreneurs will act somewhat as follows. Perhaps instead of investing 4 million of the current allotment in present production, they will invest 5 million labor-years. That covers 1 million of the increased demand. At the same time a change is made in the disposition of those goods whose nature permits of employing them in several ways. Thus possibly the product of another million labor-years may be diverted from higher maturity classes and promoted to the first class, which is to say converted to the first class, which is to say converted to the use and enjoyment in the current period. That covers the other million of the whole additional requirement. The economy does now, in truth, receive the desired products of 12 million labor-years,[28] and it enjoys the consumption of them. But it does so at the expense of the totality of capital which becomes impaired by 2 million labor-years by virtue of the inadequate replacement.[29]

Perhaps I have already used too many words to prove a truth so obvious that people who think along simple and unscholarly lines would never have doubted it anyhow. Every child knows that a capital good, such as a hammer, must be produced if it is to come into existence. And any straight-thinking man is also quite ready to concede that a stock of capital cannot be increased if the entire available income is constantly converted to enjoyment as consumption goods—if, in other words, nothing is saved. It was reserved for the hairsplitting perspicuity of scholarly theorists to cast the first doubts upon these simple truths. Things could hardly have come to that sorry pass if there had been less desire to launch didactic formulae on the formation of capitals, and more attempts to visualize the whole process of forming capital in terms of plastic objectivity. Herein lies the chief, perhaps almost the only difficulty that invests this and many other economic doctrines. And I should like to add that here, too, lies the reason why so many abstract deductions have been discredited and gone astray. It is not the method that deserves to be discredited, but the people who misapply it. Now downright blunders in reasoning are extremely rare on the part of profound thinkers. The error must therefore lie in the fact that these theorists failed to project before their inner eye a sufficiently factual image of the conditions and events which they took as the presuppositions on which to base their deductive reasonings. Or at the very least they did not have the ability to retain the picture with sufficient vividness throughout the entire course of their deductions. The image before the mind's eye became blurred or obliterated, and instead of clinging to the picture, they clutch the frame which is all that remains—they hold to *words*. Instead of reasoning deductively from the essence of the things concerned, they slip imperceptibly into a most dangerous and treacherous course of action—they engage in dialectics and bandy hollow words. That error is one that I would avoid at any cost. Even if I fail to steer my ship between the reefs of exegesis unscathed by all reproach, I would rather suffer reproach twice over for the sins of prolixity and excessive detail, than once for that of empty dialecticism.

I should like to supplement my positive presentation with some brief observations concerning the most important of the objections that have been raised to it. Two seem to me to be particularly deserving of attention. One of them is to the effect that most capital goods are by nature not adapted to immediate enjoyment. It therefore does not represent even the slightest measure of sacrifice to refrain from deriving from them an enjoyment which they are in any case incapable of affording. Consequently it is ridiculous to speak of the "nonconsumption" of steam engines and land improvements, of roofing tiles and lumps of ore, as if it were an act of saving or renunciation.[30]

This sounds to me like a rather cheap argument, though one that should be effective against anyone who formulates the theory of saving incorrectly or superficially. But it proves nothing against the genuine intent of the theory. For who could wish to interpret the theory of savings so clumsily as to think that finished capital goods would have to be saved in the concrete form in which they actually appear? If there is any such person, he must submit to the retort that the iron machines could not be eaten![31] But that is not the meaning of any thoughtful representatives of that theory. All that they maintain is that capital cannot be originated or increased without saving, and that saving is just as essential a condition for the formation of capital as is labor. And that is literally true. Of course it is true that the machines themselves are not saved but built. But in order that they might be built it was first necessary to withhold the necessary productive forces from use in the making of present consumption goods. And thus they are saved in the truest sense of the word.[32]

Perhaps it may serve to help resolve this difference if I observe that the concept of saving does not by any means necessarily imply any sacrificial or morally meritorious behavior.[33] Saving *can* involve sacrifice and meritorious action, but it does not necessarily do so. The man who has only a small income will concededly not be able to lay aside something of the little he has without appreciable deprivation and the display of vigorous self-control. But the man with an annual income of a million who is content to live on only a half million while he lays aside the other half million, need perform no heroic act of renunciation. The formation of capital requires only that the saving be a *factual reality* and any moral admixture of sacrifice or merit is a matter of complete indifference so far as the result is concerned. It follows then that the genuineness of the theoretical necessity of "saving" for the formation of capital, cannot by any means be exploited as a justification on moral or social grounds of any and every receipt of interest. This is just one more instance of the great mischief that has been done by a coalescing of the theoretical and the social problems of interest. I have had occasion to condemn this practice before.[34] One group of economists perceived the theoretical truth that saving is a condition precedent of the formation of capital but combined with it the erroneous moral judgment that interest is justified by "meritorious renunciation." The other party correctly realized that this justification does not apply with such universality, and then fell a victim to the same error of combining both problems, by letting the rejection of the erroneous social conclusion mislead them into denial of the scientifically valid premise as well. A proper differentiation will perhaps help to set both parties aright. Let us concede to Rodbertus and Lassalle without ado that saving need not be an act of moral heroism, and hence also no adequate social justification for interest. But let us demand in return the admission that the objective fact of saving is a prerequisite for the formation of capital.

A second group of objectors emphasized the fact that in order to be able to accumulate a capital, man *must first acquire more* than he needs. From that they conclude that it is really the productivity of labor, and hence industriousness to which the origination of capital is due, and not thriftiness. Rodbertus develops his point in great detail. He points out that in the primitive stages of economic development "an isolated economizing individual has no time to produce a tool because he is constantly forced to live from hand to mouth." In such a situation, says Rodbertus, the fault is to be ascribed solely to the inadequately productive character of the individual's labor. But if that productivity is subsequently enhanced so that, say, eight hour's labor suffice for procuring the daily necessaries for subsistence, then "out of the working hours which he previously had to devote entirely to procuring the bare necessaries of daily subsistence, he now has some time left over for other work; and it is this *additional labor* which he is now in a position to devote to the production of a tool." And from this observation—in itself quite correct—Rodbertus draws the conclusion that it is "only the increase in the productivity of his labor, and *not any saving* that makes possible the origination of this first capital."[35] Kleinwächter gives the same basic idea much more drastic expression when he says, "If a man deposits a part, say the half, of his earned income in the savings bank, the man is *merely industrious*. He could, for instance, earn a meager subsistence by working only four hours a day, and then devote every afternoon to recuperation or recreation. Instead of that the man works eight hours a day and regularly deposits in the savings bank what he earns in the afternoon."[36]

I believe this objection can be very easily refuted. It simply is not true that the man is "merely industrious." He is both industrious and thrifty. Were he merely industrious, he would each day spend for immediate enjoyment not only his morning's earnings, but also those of his afternoon's labor. The reason he does not do so is because he is also thrifty. I gladly concede several points. I concede that greater industriousness, which yields a product well in excess of necessary requirements, greatly facilitates saving; I concede just as readily that greater productivity of labor does the same; and I also concede that in the absence of earning, saving and formation of capital as well are a sheer impossibility. Conversely, however, I demand that it be conceded that the greatest possible earnings cannot lead to the formation of capital unless some part of the earnings is withheld from present enjoyment—unless, in other words, it is saved. Production and saving constitute equally indispensable conditions of the formation of capital. The only thing that made it possible to deny the cooperative contribution of either one of them was the dialectical bias which has unfortunately played far too large a part in the doctrine of capital.[37]

Does not that statement plunge me into contradiction with the proposition I so vigorously defended in the preceding chapter? I maintained there that all goods, and hence capital goods too, consist of two elements, *not including saving*, for the two elements are nature and labor.[38] No, there is certainly no contradiction here. Nothing is further from my thoughts than to follow the example of Senior[39] and attempt to claim that saving constitutes a third factor of production arrayed beside nature and labor. It does not stand *beside* them, but in the background behind them. Its participation in the production work to be accomplished is not in the nature of performing a part of the work which is peculiarly its own province. Instead, its function is to see to it that the productive forces nature and labor, which, in any event, must perform the entire work of production themselves, shall not direct their efforts toward any goal but production, that is to say, shall produce capital goods and not consumption goods. To put it briefly, saving does not belong among the *means* of production but among the *motives* which determine the *direction* that production shall take. For that reason there is no inconsistency between the statement that nature and labor are the only genuine productive forces and the further statement that if capital is to originate, certain physical dispositions must first be present as a result of which a portion of the attainable immediate enjoyment is forgone, or in other words a "saving" is determined upon.

The objection that will probably be made at this point is that saving is a "nonconsumption" and hence something negative, and that a pure negation is incapable of producing anything.[40] I have the feeling that there is more dialecticism than truth in that argument. But is it correct at all, that saving is something purely negative? How is it then, that so many persons find saving so egregiously difficult and onerous, although nothing is easier than a "pure absence of action?" In truth, saving is a psychological act, and very often, though not always, a very onerous psychological act born of lengthy deliberation and the opposition between conflicting motives. Concededly it is not an act which results in production, and to that extent the representatives of the dialectical argument presented above are quite right when they urge it against those theorists who are intent upon earmarking it as a third factor of production. But this purely psychological act does suffice to perform effectively the part I have assigned to saving in the process of forming capital. That part is to exert an influence on the direction taken by production.

No matter what the situation may be with respect to a "pure negation," in no event may we be permitted to allow considerations of dialecticism to deter us from establishing scientific facts. And there is one such important fact which must be all the more emphatically pointed out, for the very reason that it has been disputed. It is the fact that progress in the formation of capital stands in a causal relationship to the expansion of claims to consumption goods on the part of individuals or of whole communities. It is possible for an individual or a nation so far to expand present claims to consumption goods on the part of individuals or of whole communities. It is possible for an individual or a nation so far to expand present claims to consumption goods as to exhaust within the current period the entire extent of the enjoyments which the income for the current period makes possible. In such case there can be neither any formation of new capital, nor any increase in the capital already on hand. And this fact can be expressed in words which not only are correct and accurate, but which will be conceded, by all but those who are themselves captiously inclined, to be entirely free from captiousness. Those words might read: "Saving is an indispensable condition precedent of the formation of capital."[41]

Notes

1. In my *Rechte und Verhältnisse vom Standpunkte der volkswirtschaftlichen Güterlehre*, p. 101, in which I was following the terminology used by Menger in his *Grundsatze der Volkswirtschaftslehre*, p. 8 ff.

2. I was confident that the facts I have cited speak so strongly for themselves as to be certain to carry conviction. That confidence proves, however, not to have been entirely justified. Since the publication of my first edition, in which I first made these statements, there have been all sorts of doubts and objections levelled at this very point. The fact that they did arise induced me some years ago to discuss the point at length. I did so in the first of my three treatises entitled "Einige strittige Fragen der Kaptialstheorie" (Vienna, 1899). For the same reason I shall revert to the subject on a suitable occasion and in greater detail later in this volume.

3. The expression "capitalist production" is widely used in two different sense. one of these signifies a method of production which makes use of concrete capital, such as raw materials, tools, machinery and the like. The other signifies production which is engage din for the account and under the control of private entrepreneur capitalists. These two meanings do not by any means need to coincide. My own use of the expression is always in the first of these two sense.

4. In Book I, Chap. II of this volume.

5. In sparsely populated regions it is, of course, possible for land, or at least certain uses of it, to be superabundant and hence a free good. An example of such a use might be timber. But my observations refer, by a perfect understandable preference, to conditions obtaining in our modern economy. Under those conditions, land—other than waste land—is always an *economic* good, as are also the uses of land.

6. On the common experience that "as labor is prolonged the effort becomes, as a rule, more and more painful," see Gossen's *Entwicklung der Gesetz des menschlichen Verkehrs*, 1854, as also Jevons, *Theory of Political Economy*, 2nd ed., p. 185 ff.

7. This principle is, to my mind, clearly and incontrovertibly patent from the facts, but it is a principle that Rodbertus gave evidence he profoundly misunderstood, when he emphatically maintained and reiterated that labor is the only orginary force with which man economizes. That invalidates his conclusion that all goods can be conceived of, economically speaking, only as products of labor. (*Zur Erkenntnis unserer staatswirtschaftlichen Zustände,* Theorem I; *Zur Erklu der heutigen Kreditnot des Grundbesitzes,* 2nd ed., p. 160; *Zur Beleuchtung der sozialen Frage,* p. 69.) Nowadays to allow a fertile field to lie fallow, or some mine or source of water power to go unused— in short, to fail to put valuable uses of land to economic use— is behavior that is just as inimical to our economic welfare as is the uneconomic squandering of labor.

8. I use this as the more correct term to supplant the word "labor" which I used by itself in Book I, Chapter II in order to avoid long-winded explanations.

9. I do not believe that the dissidence of any of my critics begins as early as this point. The strictures that became "audible" after the appearance of my first edition were directed principally against the relation between the quantitative increase in surplus product and the *temporal* extent of the roundabout methods of production. This is a matter discussed in the pages immediately to follow.

10. The manner in which Rodbertus describes the economic effects of adopting circuitous production methods is highly characteristic. For he chooses his example from the very minority of cases in which the roundabout way "leads more quickly to the goal" (*Das Kapital,* p. 236). For in this case, as in all others, he is consistent in simply consigning to obscurity all the *economic* factors that help to explain the phenomenon of interest. And the loss of time consequent upon execution of the more productive roundabout methods of production is of paramount importance in this connection. Rodbertus's purpose is to satisfy his own bias and lay the origination of income from capital at the door of private property rights as constituted under existing law. But the institution of private property would not in itself cause the workers any embarrass-

ment, and they could easily evade the capitalists' "toll gates" if it were not for that troublesome time interval between the beginning and the end of roundabout capitalist production methods. That is the thing that makes it impossible for the workers to adopt those methods on their own account.

11. The essence of so-called inventions lies, in general, in the discovery of new and more productive methods of production. frequently, and in all likelihood usually, the new way is more circuitous than the old, for utilization of the invention requires the preparation of a particularly large number of intermediate products. This is what is ordinarily described as "a heavy investment of capital." Extreme examples are the machine foundry and railroad industries. Frequently, however, a fortunate invention may uncover a method of production that is not only better, but *shorter*. Such an invention was the production of dyestuffs by chemical processes instead of form vegetable sources. No matter how involved the chemical process may be, it is certainly far more direct and rapid than any process which must wait on the long span of vegetable growth. My Essays I and II in the third volume (*Further Essays on Capital and Interest*) of this work will contain a more detailed treatment of this subject.

12. At this point the dissentient question may be raised, "Why is there not complete exploitation of the opportunity which current technical knowledge affords for increasing the technical output?" The answer most commonly heard is "Lack of capital." This reply avers that with the limited capital at our disposal only the most highly remunerative among the many profitable opportunities can be turned to account, the multitude of less rewarding, though still worthwhile possibilities must be forgone. This explanation is not entirely accurate, but it is at least correct in the main. We can therefore rest content with it until such time as we shall achieve complete understanding of the situation in connection with our examination of another topic.

13. *Der isolierte Staat*, 3rd ed., Part II, Sec. I, p. 97 *et seq.;* see particularly the table on his p. 101 and the reprint of the last preceding edition (*Sammlung sozialwissenschaftlicher Meister*,

vol. XIII) 2nd ed., Jena 1921, Part II, p. 50 ff. (with especial attention to the table on p. 407).

14. E.G., in Roscher's *Grundlagen*, Sec. 183, Mangoldt's *Volkswirtschaftslehre*, 1868, p. 432 f., Mithoff in Schönberg's *Handbuch*, 2nd ed., p. 663 and in many other places.

15. Especially the error of confusing two kinds of productivity. The first of these is the "physical productivity" or "technical productivity" that manifests itself in the fact that the number of products that can be produced with the help of capital is greater than that producible without capital. The other productivity—a fruit of biased thinking—is an ostensible power on the apt of capital to produce more value than it possesses itself. Cf. my *History and Critique of Interest Theories*, (Chap. VII, opening paragraphs of Section 1, p. 74 ff.; opening paragraphs of Section 3, p. 78 f.).

16. *Das Kapital*, p. 346 ff.

17. In relatively recent times, J. B. Clark depicted the inner workings of the production process in an economy organized on the basis of the division of labor. (See his *Distribution of Wealth*, 1899, *passim*.) He presents the picture with well nigh unsurpassable vividness and plasticity. It is a pleasure to avail myself of this opportunity to express my respect and admiration for the scientific accomplishments of this excellent writer. Those feelings are unaffected by the fact that I have felt constrained to oppose him vigorously on certain individual points.—I feel that the activity of Cassel, quite on the contrary, represents a regrettable retrogression in the art of economic analysis. He reverts to the practice of giving prominence, for purpose of scientific discussion, to the individual portions of the production process. He thinks of each stage in the process of production, as it is carried on under the system of divided labor, as an independent "process of production'l and the duration of that stage, or that partial process is for Cassel the "period of production," corresponding to the respective "process." He considers a unified view to be superfluous, at least with respect to the problem of interest because, says Cassel, his approach to the subject is the only

one "that has any significant bearing on the problem of interest." (*The Nature and Necessity of Interest*, p. 123 ff.).

18. The first table set forth in the text above applies to a production process in which one single tool is employed which itself took 10 years to produce, such as an axe of Bessemer steel. The second table applies to a production in which not only the axe but also a number of other capitalist tools, auxiliary devices and auxiliary materials were used, the origination of which does not date back further than 10 years. The comparison of the two tables illustrates clearly how the capitalist character of the process can be materially heightened without lengthening the absolute length of the production period. It is necessary only to make a change in the ratio of early-stage workers and finishing-stage workers. The total production period remains 10 years, no matter whether the ratio of finishing-stage workers to early-stage workers is 10 to one or one to 10. But in the former case the workers of the completion-stage would be very scantily supplied with tools, materials, etc., in the latter case they would be very generously supplied. The second instance is therefore of a far more highly capitalist nature.

19. The controversy over the part played by saving in the formation of capital is almost as old as economics itself, and began with the promulgation of the savings theory. Although the theory was hinted at by the physiocrats it remained for Adam Smith to formulate it effectively by giving us the frequently quoted proposition, "Parsimony and not industry is the immediate cause of the increase of capital." (*Wealth of Nations*, Book II, Chap. III) Backed by the authority of Adam Smith the theory for a time practically had the field to itself, and although it subsequently suffered a great loss in popularity, it still numbers among its supporters some economists of note. These include John Stuart Mill with his "Capital is the Result of Saving" (*Principles of Political Economy*, Book I, Chap. V., Sec. 4); Roscher and his "capitals arise principally through saving" (*Grundlagen*, Sec. 45); and Francis Walker who said "it arises solely out of saving. It stands always for self-denial and

abstinence" (*Political Economy*, 2nd ed., New York, p. 66). But the savings theory also encountered early opposition. The earliest probably came from Lauderdale (*Inquiry*, 1804, Chap. IV). Then after quite an interval came the socialists including Rodbertus, who in *Das Kapital*, (p. 240 ff. and 267 f.), made such statements as "The capital of the individual is like that of nations in that it originates and increases *only through labor and not through saving*"; Lassalle (*Kapital und Arbeit*, p. 64 ff.) and Marx (*Das Kapital*, 2nd ed., vol. I, p. 619 ff.). In more recent times numerous writers of other schools have joined the opposition some more and some less sharp and pronounced in their hostility. See Gide's *Principes* I, p. 167 ff., also Bostedo's "The Function of Saving" in the *Annals of the American Academy*, vol. XVII, 1901, p. 95 ff.; the antagonism is less marked in Kleinwächter (Schönberg's *Handbuch*, 2nd ed., p. 213 ff.) and in R. Meyer's *Das Wesen des Einkommens*, 1887, p. 213 ff. Wagner in his *Grundlegung*, 2nd ed., Sec. 290 ff., and very recently in his *Grundriss der theoretischen Sozialökonomie*, 1907, Sec. 39, is more conciliatory. Cohn's *Grundlegung der Nationalökonomie*, 1885, Sec. 257 ff. is somewhat vague and nebulous in his opposition. Nevertheless, the opinion which assigned to saving a share in the formation of capital retained an unmistakable ascendancy, although the modern representatives of that view limit the share quite correctly and emphasize explicitly that saving alone is not enough. There must also be "labor" or "devotion to production" or other additional factors. It is probable that such as the opinion of many an earlier adherent of the saving theory, but that it was left unmentioned because its obviousness would presumably have made the mention of it superfluous. Compare also B. Rau's *Volkswirtschaftslehre*, 8th ed., vol. I, Sec. 133, as well as Ricca-Salerno's *Sulla Teoria del Capitale*, Chap. IV, p. 118, where he says, "Il capitale deve la sua origne all'industria e al risparmio." See also Cossa, *Elementi*, 8th ed., p. 39, and many others. For a general view of the whole controversy see the excellent survey and presentation of Spiethoff in his *Lehre vom Kapitale*, pp. 32–41.

20. On the many divergent and contradictory versions of the

concept of income, compare R. Meyer, *Das Wesen des Einkommens*, 1887, particularly pp. 1–27. I am deliberately avoiding any discussion of the controversy over the concept of income, for in spite of the merits of Meyer's work, I do not consider that it by any means settles the dispute conclusively. Wherever I use the term income in the pages that follow, I do not mean it in Meyer's sense of the word, but rather in a sense that approximately coincides with its meaning in everyday ordinary speech. I have already indicated (Book I, Chap. III) that I have many more objections to the treatment of the income concept in Irving Fisher's most recent monograph entitled *The Nature of Capital and Income*, 1906.

21. Accordingly, Adam Smith's statement "Parsimony and not industry is the immediate cause of the increase of capital" must be corrected by restating it in reverse. The *immediate* cause of the origination of capital goods is production, its *mediate* cause a saving which preceded the production.

22. Only in the event that the technique of producing the particular capital objects has improved in the meantime, will it be sufficient to assign to the future a smaller amount of productive forces. Let us suppose, for instance, that Crusoe has learned to fashion in 15 hours the same weapons which had in the beginning required 30 hours. In that case he will, of course, need to work only a half hour daily to maintain the previous level of capital, that is to say, to renew his hunting equipment. He can then devote nine and one-half hours to the immediate provision of a more generous standard of living, without suffering nay deterioration in his economic position.

23. Durable productive goods dispense their utility bit by bit over the course of several years. The several parts of their use content, since they are spread over the various annual rings to which their renditions of service belong, confer on those goods simultaneous membership in various maturity classes.

24. If the current year has seen sufficient improvement in the technique of production to enable the nation to replace the consumption of a capital of 6 million labor years by the expenditure of 5 million labor years, then the *figures* in our

example would be somewhat altered, but the *principle* would remain the same. For the maintenance of the status quo, with respect to capital is then possible if 5 million labor years are applied to present-period production, and if total consumption goods in the amount of 11 million labor years is consumed. (See Note 4 of this chapter.) An increase in the formation of capital will require the renunciation of some part of such enjoyment of consumption goods as would be possible in nothing were attempted beyond maintenance of capital *in statu quo*. The same idea may be expressed in different words by saying that capital is increased when part of the "income" that *could be* consumed without impairing the principal stock of capital, is not so consumed, but is instead, saved. Moreover, in the absence of further technical advances, and after the passage of a few years during which the capital produced by the old methods is completely utilized, the previous numerical relationship will be re-established. That relationship provided that the status quo is maintained when, in one period, there is consumption of the proceeds (in the from of consumption goods) derived from a quantity of productive forces exactly equal to the amount of such forces which becomes newly available in that same period.

25. I have neither the time nor the desire to go into subtle distinctions, though there is no lack of material for them. The comments in R. Meyer (op. cit., p. 5 ff., and p. 84 ff.) on the relation between national product and national income I find interesting even though I am not in complete agreement with all of them. See also the treatise by Lexis entitled "Über gewisse Wertgesamtheiten und deren Beziehungen zum Geldwert," (*Tübinger Zeitschrift*, 44th year, 2nd number, p. 221 ff.), where in like manner the annual "consumption sum," "production sum" and "primary income sum" are all treated as beings "quantitatively approximately equal" magnitudes.

26. A change in the disposition is, as we have already seen, considerably facilitated by the high degree of adaptability possessed by many forms of capital goods. See foregoing, p. 110 f.

27. In his "The Function of Saving," appearing in the *Annals of the American Academy*, vol. XVII (1901) p. 95 ff., Bostedo has presented views and conclusions on this subject which, to my mind, do not fit the case at all well. Cf. my reply on p. 454 ff. of the same publication.

28. That is to say, 6 million from the original amount of the first maturity class, 1 million from the addition to that class by alteration of disposition, and 5 million from the current labor endowment.

29. The stock of capital originally amounted to the proceeds of 30 million labor years; it suffers a diminution of 7 million through consumption of the current year and experiences an accretion of only 5 million to take their place; the result is a shrinkage from 30 to 28 million labor years.

30. This is couched in especially drastic terms by the writers of the socialist school. See, for instance, Lassalle, *Kapital und Arbeit*, p. 69 ff., and Rodbertus, *Das Kapital*, p. 271. The same doctrine is put into somewhat milder language by Wagner in his *Grundlegung*, 2nd ed., p. 600, where he distinguishes goods in which the quality of capital is inherent and those in which it is not. The former, he says, can at least not be the *direct* object of saving. A similar position is taken by Kleinwächter (Schönberg's *Handbuch*, 1st ed., p. 178).

31. Lassalle, op. cit.

32. In the second edition of Schönberg's *Handbuch* (p. 214), Kleinwächter's position becomes a great deal more like my own in that he accepts this point with respect to one principal group of capital goods at least—tools of production. He agrees that the making of *tools* of production "always involves to a certain extent the renunciation of an immediate enjoyment" because the materials which are used for the making of tools of production, could have been used for making consumption goods of one kind or another. There can be no objection, says Kleinwächter, to designate that sort of renunciation "saving." That does not apply, he says, to the raw materials of production. Things like raw wool, stones and lime cannot be consumed directly in any way, and hence cannot be saved. Economically speaking, they can be regarded

only as products of labor and not as results of saving. In this argument, Kleinwächter is not consistent. In the case of the tools, he very correctly refuses to be misled by the impossibility of consuming the finished tools and gives his attention to the fact that it would have been possible, by means of the materials from which the tools were made, to produce and enjoy a consumption good. And because he recognizes that situation, he accepts and affirms the matter of saving. If he had adhered faithfully to this line of reasoning with respect to the materials of production, he could not have failed to perceive that the same productive powers that were utilized to quarry the stone of which to build a house, or to calcine limestone in order to obtain mortar, could have been employed in the direct acquisition of consumption goods. It would, for example, have been just as possible to hunt game or catch fish. And so in this instance, for the same reason and in the same manner as apply in the case of tools, saving plays a part.

33. Cf. foregoing, p. 103

34. See vol. I, *History and Critique of Interest Theories,* p. 2 ff.

35. *Das Kapital,* p. 242 f.

36. Kleinwächter in the *second* edition of Schönberg's *Handbuch,* p. 215.

37. A drastic illustration of the statement above can be found in the remarks of Rodbertus which have been mentioned before. On p. 242 he is still content to admit that when work is insufficiently productive, no saving and hence no formation of capital is possible. He draws from that the perfectly correct conclusion that "*one other factor* than saving must necessarily be involved." He thereby assigns to saving its rightful place as a factor in the formation of capital which, while necessary, is not sufficient in and by itself. Not until he reaches p. 243 does the fact that a certain degree of productivity on the part of labor is *also* indispensable, suffer a dialectic transmutation by which an increase in the productivity of labor becomes exaggerated into the *sole* requisite for the formation of capital, so that saving becomes *not at all* necessary. In spite of my pointing this out in my first edition, Kleinwächter adheres to

his former position in all essential respects in his more recent utterances on the subject. One example is his *Lehrbuch der Nationalökonomie* 1902, p. 136 ff. His only concession with respect to the criticism I raised is a slight emendation in the wording of his text which is to my mind inadequate. Nor do I consider that Gide's position is an iota more tenable when he seeks to satisfy criticism by taking refuge in a purely dialectical turn of phrase. His point of departure is the idea that every formation of capital presupposes an excess of goods produced over goods consumed. But this excess, according to Gide, may arise in two ways. Either "production can exceed wants" or consumption can be "reduced below the level of wants" to a painful and onerous degree (*péniblement*). Only the latter, says Gide, would deserve the name of "saving"; fortunately, however, the former alternative is far more frequent and, historically speaking, the only one that has ever resulted in the formation of capital (*Principes,* 9th ed., p. 134). I think Gide has taken a current vernacular phrase too literally. It is true that the phrase "production exceeds requirements" is a phrase that frequently trips from the tongue, but never in the strict and literal sense in which Gide cites it as one of his alternatives. For the production of economics goods to attain a copiousness that would literally overtop the needs of economizing mankind, completely satisfy all requirements and still leave a surplus—that is entirely impossible in actual practice. Goods on hand in such profusion would cease to be *economic* goods, and they would no longer be produced. Even when production is extremely plenteous, people who lay aside capital are unable to satisfy their wants down to the last extreme. Every laying aside of capital takes place at the expense of a failure to satisfy some want, be it never so unimportant. All actual formation of capital thus results, in a manner quite in conflict with Gide's opinion. It is the second alternative which holds true, namely, the "depressing of consumption below the level of wants," there being only a difference in the degree of importance attaching to those wants which, by reason of that depressing, fail to find satisfaction at the time. But, as has often been pointed out, the element

Gide cites by his *péniblement,* the presence or the magnitude of any "sacrifice" has absolutely no bearing whatever on the objective fact of saving. Indeed, saving is much more frequently the result of a wise, economically calculated estimation of advantageousness, than it is an inclination to make a sacrifice. And that is just as true of the indigent savers as it is of wealthy hoarders of treasure!

38. Lauderdale long ago expressed a similar objection to the saving theory. See his *Inquiry,* p. 207 f., p. 272.

39. *Political Economy,* 3rd ed., p. 57 ff. Senior distinguishes three "agents" or "instruments of production," "labor," "natural agents" and "abstinence."

40. Marx, *Das Kapital,* vol. I, 2nd ed., p. 619, footnote: "The lay economist has never given consideration to the simple circumstance that every human action can be thought of as an 'abstinence' from its opposite. Eating is an abstinence from fasting, to walk is to abstain from standing, to loaf is to abstain from working, to work is to abstain from loafing, and so on. The gentleman would do well to ponder Spinoza's 'determinatio est negatio.'" Gide, *Principes d'Economie Politique,* p. 168: "Un acte purement négatif, une abstention ne saurait produire quoi que ce soit .... Sans doute on peut dire que si ces richesses avaient été consommées au fur et à mesure qu'elles ont pris naissance, elles n'existeraient pas à cette heure, et qu'en conséquence l'épargne les a fair naitre une seconde fois. Mais à ce compte, il faudrait dire qu'on produit une chose toutes les fois qu'on s'abstient d'y toucher et la non destruction devrait être classée parmi les causes de la production, ce qui serait une singulière logique."

41. I will not deny, a priori, that it might be possible to conceive isolated subtle examples of capital, especially social capital, which originated without actual "saving." But I maintain all the more emphatically that in the vast majority of cases of the formation of social capital "saving" plays a part in the manner I have indicated.

19

The Function of Saving

L. G. Bostedo

Böhm-Bawerk, in his "Positive Theory of Capital," makes saving the primary factor in the formation of capital. I shall endeavor to show that he uses the term "saving" ambiguously, and that by so doing he reaches a false conclusion as to the function of "saving" in its proper and generally understood sense, although his conclusion is sound as regards a certain limited sense of the word.

He says (page 102): "The essential thing is that the current endowment of productive powers should not be entirely claimed for the immediate consumption of the current period, but that a portion of this endowment should be retained for the service of a future period. But such a retention will undoubtedly be called a real saving of productive powers. A saving of *productive powers,* be it noted; for productive powers, and not the goods which constitute capital, are the immediate object of saving. This is an important point, which must be strongly emphasized because, in the current view, too little consideration is given to it. Man saves consumption goods, his means of enjoyment; he thus *saves*

Reprinted from *Annals of the American Academy of Political and Social Science* (January, 1900).

[Bostedo's remarks represent a proto-Keynesian rebuttal of Böhm-Bawerk's preceding chapter on capital and interest. In the chapter following Bostedo's, Böhm-Bawerk replies.]

productive powers, and with these finally he can *produce* capital."

Again (page 122): "It is not my intention to do as Senior did, and try to make Saving a third factor in production along with Nature and Labor ... It does not share with them in the work of production in such a way that any part of the same is due to it solely and peculiarly; it only effects that the productive powers, nature and labor, which in any case must do the *whole* work of production, are directed straight to this and no other goal—the production of capital and not of consumption goods. In a word, it has its place, not among the *means* of production, but among the *motives* of production—the motives which decide the *direction* of production."

If all that is implied by the term *saving* is that it changes the *direction* of production, very little if any fault can be found with what I have so far quoted. That capital must be *produced* is a self-evident proposition. That durable capital cannot be produced if all producers expend their energies upon what Professor Böhm-Bawerk calls "present time production" (that is, goods that can be made quickly for immediate consumption) is another self-evident proposition. If the whole working population spends all its time plucking flowers, no lathes and steam engines will be made; but the entire population would pluck flowers only in the event of the wants of the entire population being limited to flowers. Whenever the wants become varied and a portion of the population demands articles that can be produced in sufficient quantities only by means of lathes and steam engines, then lathes and steam engines (capital) will come into existence. Now if the term *saving* is to be applied only to the motives which, with a varied demand, cause certain producers to make capital, then little if any fault can be found with the contention, and also very little, if any, importance attaches to it. But he uses the term in a wholly different sense, which other sense is the generally understood one. On page 115 he says, "If every individual in the community were to consume exactly his year's income in the form of consumption goods, there would arise a demand for consumption goods which, through the agency of prices, would induce the undertakers so to regulate production that, in each year, the return of a whole year's circle of productive powers would take the form of consumption goods ... In this case there is no productive power left to dispose of in increasing capital, and capital only remains as it was.

If, on the other hand, each individual consumes, on the average, only three-quarters of his income, and saves the rest, obviously the wish to buy, and the demand for, consumption goods will fall. Only three-fourths of the former consumption goods will find demand and sale."

It should be here noted that Professor Böhm-Bawerk supposes a very unnatural case. It is hardly conceivable that in any real society all of the members would save at the same time. Any assumption, however, is legitimate if due caution be exercised in drawing conclusions. He proceeds, "If the undertakers, however, were for some time to continue the old dispositions of production, and bring to market consumption goods to the amount of ten million labor-years (the assumed total amount before saving commenced) the over-supply would very soon press down the price, business would become unremunerative, and the pressure of loss would compel the undertakers to adapt their production to the changed circumstances of demand."

Professor Böhm-Bawerk sees clearly the effect of demand being reduced one-fourth. Undertakers would have to curtail their production. It is now time to ask how it would be possible for all the members of the community to save at the same time. What would they do with their savings? It is true all the members of a community might *hoard* at the same time, but the author is not talking about hoarding—he elsewhere (page 125) carefully distinguishes between hoarding and saving. We thus see that his assumption of all the members of the community saving one-fourth is not only unnatural but impossible. The effect of attempting it would be the curtailment of production one-fourth, but no saving could be effected if production and consumption both fell one-fourth.

Professor Böhm-Bawerk continues: "They will now provide that, in one year, only the produce of seven and one-half million labor-years is transformed into consumption goods, ... and the two and one-half millions which remain of the current year's endowment may and will be spent in the increasing of capital."

Here is where the Professor becomes unconsciously switched from the track and henceforth goes wide astray. He draws a wholly unwarranted conclusion in stating that two and one-half millions will be spent in the increasing of capital. It is difficult to see how he could fall into this error after having done so much to show us that capital is unfinished goods. He has himself shown us that demand for consumption goods calls capital into existence. I wish to emphasize what he has taught us—we cannot put too much emphasis upon it; *demand for consumption goods is an absolutely indispensable condition for the calling into existence of capital.* Now, where, in the Professor's assumed case is the *demand* for two and one-half millions of new capital? He has assumed that all of the people have *curtailed their demand* for consumption goods one-fourth. That would throw out of use one-fourth of the capital formerly employed. All of the people are to save one-fourth, whence then comes the demand for additional capital? He attempts to explain this as follows (pp. 115–126): "I say, 'will be spent,' for an economically advanced people does not hoard, but puts out what it saves—in the purchase of valuable paper, in deposits in a bank or savings bank, in loan securities, etc. In these ways the amount saved becomes part of the productive credit; it increases the purchasing power of producers for productive purposes; it is thus the cause of an extra demand for means of production or intermediate products; and this, in the last resort, induces those who have the regulation of undertakings to invest the productive powers at their disposal in these intermediate products."

This explanation is very confused. He sees the necessity of a *demand* for the two and one-half millions of new capital and is thus led to say "that which is" saved will be spent; but under the assumed conditions the only way they could be saved would be by hoarding, as the assumption was that all of the members of the community had curtailed their demand one-fourth. How could they invest in valuable paper in a community where all of the members have curtailed their expenditures one-fourth. How could they invest in valuable paper in a community where all of the members have curtailed their expenditures one-fourth? How could they invest in valuable paper in a community where all of the members have curtailed their expenditures one-fourth? People who have curtailed their expenditures do not then become borrowers. If the members of the community all put their savings in a bank or savings bank, that would be hoarding, under the assumed conditions; for the bank could not loan these deposits to a community, the members of which had all curtailed their expenditures one-fourth. Granted the purchasing power of producers for productive purposes would be increased, but such producers do not increase the production in a community where the demand has just had a uniform shrinkage of one-fourth. It is strange that Professor Böhm-Bawerk could reason out to his satisfaction how a shrinkage of demand could induce undertakers to invest the productive powers at their disposal in intermediate products as he states. Intermediate products to become what products? By whom demanded? According to the assumption, we at first had an annual production and consumption of 10,000,000, then all the members of the community reduced their demand one-fourth, thus requiring only seven and one-half millions. The capital, or intermediate products for the seven and one-half millions was already in existence, and besides the capitalists have on hand two and one-half millions of idle capital. Where is their inducement to produce new capital under those conditions?

Professor Böhm-Bawerk, on page 117, says "to every simple man it is obvious that no stock of capital can be made, or can increase if men regularly consume their whole available income, if, in other words, they do not save. It was reserved for the sharp and subtle wits of learned theorists to suggest the first doubt about it."

I ask whether the Professor has not himself fallen into the same kind of subtle theorizing that he here criticizes, in his confused argument, to try to prove that sane men would borrow money and build factories and machinery as a result of a sudden resolve on the part of all the members of the community to curtail their purchases 25 per cent.

This error led Professor Böhm-Bawerk to the conclusion stated as follows (p. 116):

"We see, therefore, as a fact, an intimate connection between saving and formation of capital. If no individual saves, the people, as a whole, cannot accumulate capital, because the great consumpt of consumption goods forces the producers, by the impulse of prices, so to employ the productive powers that, every year, the produce of a whole year's endowment is demanded and used up in the shape of consumption goods, and no productive powers are left free for the increasing of capital. But if individuals save, the altered demand, again through the impulse of prices, compels the undertakers to dispose of the productive powers differently; fewer powers are put, each year, at the service of the present, and thereby is increased the amount of those productive powers whose produce will be found in suspense as intermediate products; in other words, the economical capital will be increased with a view to an increased consumption in the future."

This is wholly wrong. The fact is that "Saving," as the

term is commonly understood, has no influence whatever upon the formation of capital. The amount of capital brought into existence is determined wholly by the demand for consumption goods immediately, and by the conditions which determine the general purchasing power. Any condition that raises the general purchasing power, and therefore the demand for goods, will call into existence as an incident to the production of the goods more capital. Any condition that decreases the general purchasing power, and therefore the demand for goods, will throw capital out of use and curtail its production. As the amount of capital is determined by the extent of the demand, so is the kind of capital determined by the nature of the goods demanded. If the demand for flowers, fruit and other goods of a short production period predominates, then the capital for producing goods of this kind will come into existence. If the demand for travel predominates, then more durable capital such as railroads, steamships and hotels will be produced.

What then is the real function of saving? The object of saving in the vast majority of cases is to provide a fund or income for future use, usually for the late period of life. What one saves is purchasing power, or in other words due bills upon the community's stock of goods. In actual society, instead of all people saving at the same time, as in the assumed case, some are saving and others are consuming without producing, or consuming more than they produce. Those who save lend their surplus purchasing power to those who cannot at the time save. In the case of children, invalids and some other nonproducers, the purchasing power is *given* instead of loaned. In either case the purchasing power (leaving hoarding out of account) is simply transferred from the savers to other members of the community, who demand the goods that the savers might have demanded. In an ideal society free from legal monopolies, saving would not curtail demand in the least; neither would it increase demand in the least. It therefore would have no effect upon the formation of capital. Suppose that nobody saved in expectation of retiring from business voluntarily or otherwise. Suppose that all the members of the community produced all their lives, and all their lives lived up to their income. This would be the plainest possible case of a complete demand for everything produced; and if all legal monopolies could be abolished, the greatest possible amount of wealth would be produced, and the maximum amount of capital would come into existence and remain permanently. The amount of capital could not be increased one iota by such a people changing their habits in the direction of saving for future use. The only effect would be that the purchasing power of the savers would be transferred temporarily to others, in time to be returned to the savers or their heirs.

20

The Function of Saving

E. von Böhm-Bawerk

Under the above title Mr. Bostedo has criticized, in the January number of the ANNALS,[2] some views which I expressed in my work, "The Positive Theory of Capital," in regard to the influence of saving on the formation of capital. While I advanced and illustrated by means of various examples the opinion, that an increase in the capital of a community can only take place in consequence of a balance of saving over spending on the part of its members, Mr. Bostedo arrives at an exactly opposite conclusion, namely, that "saving, as the term is commonly understood, has no influence whatever on the formation of capital."

My surest vindication would consist, I have no doubt, in asking the reader to study point by point, the detailed exposition of this subject in my "Positive Theory."[3] The solution of a problem of this nature can only be presented by creating in the reader's imagination, in place of a superficial view of the surface money phenomena which present themselves to every-day observation, a complete and at the same time plastic picture of the actual relations of modern industrial society. Such a complete picture I have tried to sketch in my "Positive Theory," and I cannot, for obvious reasons, repeat the undertaking in these pages. I must rather content

Reprinted from the *Annals of the American Academy of Political and Social Science* (May, 1901).

myself with commenting upon the particular points and difficulties which Mr. Bostedo raises in his criticism.

Mr. Bostedo accuses me, in substance, of having committed three errors: Of having made an ambiguous use of the word "saving," of having chosen an "unnatural" and therefore inadmissible illustration for the development of my doctrine, and of having fallen into a logical blunder in the course of this development.

First, he maintains that I have characterized indifferently two quite distinct conceptions as "saving." Sometimes I have designated by this term the motives which determine the direction of production—and, in this sense my theory in regard to the influence of saving upon the formation of capital, though indeed correct, is of slight importance—sometimes, however, I have employed the term for an altogether different purpose, denoting thereby what everybody understands by "saving"—and in this usual sense my theory is false.

In reply I wish merely to insist that I have not confused two conceptions of "saving" in my writings, but that I have merely endeavored to analyze completely one conception and to present to the reader an all-around picture of the "saving" process. To put the matter more concretely, that which "everybody understands as saving" has first of all its negative side, that is, the nonconsuming of a portion of income, or, in terms applicable to our money-using society, the not-spending of a portion of the money annually received. This negative aspect of saving is the one which is made most prominent in every-day speech, and is often the only one considered, since comparatively few people follow the sums of money saved further than to the receiving window of a bank or trust company. But here the positive part of the saving process only just begins, to complete itself quite out of the range of vision of the person who saves, whose action has nevertheless given the impulse to the whole movement: the bank collects the savings of its depositors and places them at the disposal of the business community in one form or another—through advances on mortgages, loans to railroads and other corporations in exchange for their bonds, accommodations to business managers, etc.— for use in the furtherance of productive enterprises, which but for such aid either could not be prosecuted at all or not with the same efficiency. If those who save had refrained from so doing and instead had lived more luxuriously, that is, bought and consumed more or finer foods, wines, clothing and other pleasure-affording goods, they would, through their increased demand for these commodities, have stimulated their production; conversely, as a result of their saving portions of their incomes and depositing them in banks, they give an impulse to production in the direction of increasing the output of productive appliances, of railroads, factories, machines, etc. Whether I am accurate in this analysis of the effect of saving will appear in connection with my discussion of the third of the above criticisms. At this point I wish merely to insist that my theory does not involve two different conceptions of saving, but that the saving which acts as impulse or motive in giving direction to production is exactly the same "saving as it is commonly understood." I simply direct attention to the other side of the process, to the positive consequences of the negative first step, which is the not-consuming.

Turning to the second point, Mr. Bostedo declares, that the illustration by means of which I try to make clear the influence of saving on the formation of capital, "supposes a very unnatural case." I had, merely by way of illustration, assumed that "each individual in the community consumes, on the average, only three-quarters of his income and saves the rest." If Mr. Bostedo means by his criticism that it is quite improbable that in any large community every individual, without a single exception, should save from his income at the same time and in the same proportion, he is undoubtedly right. but, as a matter of fact, as my introductory phrase, "on the average," indicates, I do not lay the slightest weight upon the details of my illustration, and even if I did, the mere *improbability* of the case assumed would not in the least invalidate it as an aid in the exposition of a general principle. Indeed, I would like, here, to venture the paradoxical assertion that good illustrations which are to serve in the elucidation of complex phenomena, must always involve a large measure of improbability. This is because good examples must always be simple, comprehensive and striking, and must accordingly depart widely from the confused and undifferentiated facts of real life. I believe that Hume's classic example, that every person in the country on rising in the morning finds a gold piece in his pocket, will be admitted to be more improbable than the one I employed, and that Mr. Bostedo's own assumption, with which his criticism concludes, "that all the members of the community produced all their lives and all their lives lived up to their incomes," is, from the point of view of actual conditions, certainly no more probable than mine.

But—and this brings us to the third criticism, which touches at once the most important and most interesting point in the controversy—my illustration is characterized as not merely "unnatural" but even as "impossible," and the explanation built upon it is described as both "confused and contradictory."

The "impossibility" of my assumption, Mr. Bostedo undertakes to prove by means of the following syllogism: When all of the members of a community simultaneously save one-quarter of their incomes, they thereby reduce by one-quarter their demand for consumption goods. The lessened demand compels producers to curtail production correspondingly. But if production shrinks along with consumption, then obviously there can be no outlet for savings; the realization of the assumed saving of one-quarter of the community's income is thus shown to be impossible.

I suspect that this syllogism will arouse in the minds of

most readers the suspicion that altogether too much has been proved. For if it were true, then not only would the simultaneous saving of one-fourth of the community's income be impossible, but all real saving would be impossible. If every attempt to curtail consumption must actually result in an immediate and proportionate curtailment of production, then indeed no addition to the accumulated wealth of society could ever result from saving. Particular individuals might save portions of their incomes, but only on condition that other individuals in the same community consumed in excess of theirs; as a whole society could never lay aside portions of its social income, and the accumulations which certain nations like the French or Dutch have made in consequence of their greater average thrift in comparison with such peoples as the Spaniards or the Turks, must, however universal such phenomena may appear, be described as sheer illusion. I believe that Mr. Bostedo is really disposed to cling to this opinion with all its consequences; at any rate, his concluding statements seem to me to harmonize with this view, for he says with special emphasis that every saving is only a transfer of purchasing power from the savers *to other members* of the community. I am even more confident, however, that most readers will refuse to accept this analysis as one corresponding with their experience, and will conclude rather that there is something wrong with a chain of reasoning which leads to such an improbable conclusion.

The fault in the reasoning is indeed not far to seek. It is that one of the premises, the one which asserts that a curtailment of "consumption for immediate enjoyment" must involve also a curtailment of production, is erroneous. The truth is that a curtailment of consumption involves, not a curtailment of production generally, but only, through the action of the law of supply and demand, a curtailment in certain branches. If in consequence of saving, a smaller quantity of costly food, wine and lace is bought and consumed, less of these things will *subsequently*—and I wish to emphasize this word—be produced. There will not, however, be a smaller production of goods generally, because the lessened output of goods ready for immediate consumption may and will be offset by an increased production of "intermediate" or capital goods.

This last proposition is just what Mr. Bostedo refuses in express terms to admit. In defending his position he adds to his first syllogism a second designed especially to prove that this assumption of mine is incorrect and, moreover, that it is inconsistent with the premises upon which my own theory rests.

His argument is essentially as follows: Production is universally called forth and guided by demand. This is true, even of the production of capital, since capital consists, according to my own theory as quoted by Mr. Bostedo, simply of unfinished goods. These are demanded, it goes without saying, only when and in so far as the finished or consumption goods expected to be made from them are demanded. It follows that, at last analysis, the production of capital goods is also called forth and guided only by demand for consumption goods. If, now, in consequence of universal saving, the demand for consumption goods is reduced by one-quarter, then it is not apparent how it can be possible for more capital goods than formerly to be demanded and produced. For who would have any inducement to producing an additional quantity of unfinished goods when the demand for finished goods, instead of becoming greater, has actually become less? What kinds of products are to be made from the increased supply of unfinished goods? Who is to buy them?

This reasoning of my honored critic is certainly presented with great dialectical skill. It has, however, one weak point. There is lacking from one of his premises a single but very important word. Mr. Bostedo assumes and represents me as assuming in my illustration, that saving signifies necessarily a curtailment in the demand for consumption goods. "He had assumed," he says, referring to me, "that all the people have curtailed their demand for consumption goods one-fourth." Here he has omitted the little word "present." The man who saves curtails his demand for *present* consumption goods but by no means his desire for pleasure-affording goods generally. This is a proposition which, under a slightly different title, has already been repeatedly and, I believe, conclusively discussed in our science both by the older writers and in contemporary literature. Economists are to-day completely agreed, I think, that the "abstinence," connected with saving is no true abstinence, that is, no final renunciation of pleasure-affording goods, but, as Professor Macvane happily described it, a mere "waiting." The person who saves is not willing to hand over his savings without return, but requires that they be given back at some future time, usually indeed with interest, either to himself or to his heirs. Through saving not a single particle of the demand for goods is extinguished outright, but, as J. B. Say showed in a masterly way more than one hundred years ago in his famous theory of the "vent or demand for products" (*des débouchés*),[4] the demand for goods, the wish for means of enjoyment is, under whatever circumstances men are found, insatiable. A person may have enough or even too much of a particular kind of goods at a particular time, but not of goods in general nor for all time. This doctrine applies particularly to saving. For the principal motive of those who save is precisely to provide for their own futures or for the futures of their heirs. This means nothing else than that they wish to secure and make certain their command over the means to the satisfaction of their future needs, that is over consumption goods at a future time. In other words, those who save curtail their demand for consumption goods in the present merely to increase proportionately their demand for consumption goods in the future.

But if this is true—and I believe that Mr. Bostedo himself has no other conception of the nature of saving since he also, towards the end of his communication, recognizes that those who save expect a future return either to themselves or to their heirs, that they therefore do not "renounce" but merely "wait"—then the occasion for a curtailment of production—as Mr. Bostedo describes the matter— is absent, since the demand for goods generally has not become smaller. There is, however, it is true, occasion for a change in the direction of production as I should describe it; for if fewer consumption goods are demanded at the moment and more in the future, and production is not to outrun the demand—as both of us assume—the productive powers must be so disposed that fewer consumption goods will be produced at the moment and proportionally more will come to maturity in the future. The principal way to effect this result is to invest the productive forces, land and labor, in more extended or roundabout processes of production, or to produce in larger quantity than before "intermediate products," from which, at a later period, goods ready for consumption may issue—in other words to increase the production of capital goods.

When Crusoe on his island saves up a store of provisions in order to gain time for the fashioning of better weapons, with which he hopes later to secure a much larger quantity of provisions, these relations are all clearly discernible. It is obvious that Crusoe's saving is no renunciation, but simply a waiting, not a decision not to consume at all, but simply a decision not to consume yet; that furthermore there is no lack of stimulus to the production of capital goods nor of demand for the consumption goods subsequently to be produced by their aid.

In a complex industrial society with a highly differentiated division of labor the relations are the same, though they are not quite so easy to understand. One difficulty in the latter case is connected with the fact that the varieties of consumption goods to be demanded and the periods of time when they will be demanded, either by the person who saves or by his heirs, is not usually predetermined. The person who saves has in his hand, as it were,—and I think Mr. Bostedo's opinion coincides closely with this view—an order calling for future means of enjoyment in general, which he may have filled, exactly as he pleases in this or that kind of consumption goods, dwelling houses, clothes, equipages, wines, etc., and which he may present for partial or complete satisfaction whenever he pleases, or even cause to be renewed again. From this circumstance results, it is not to be denied, a certain complexity from the point of view of production. But Mr. Bostedo appears to me not only to exaggerate the degree of this complexity, but to altogether misunderstand its real nature. While it is usually not possible to designate in advance the kinds of consumption goods towards which the demand of those who save will be directed, Mr. Bostedo assumes without more ado that such a demand, which is to serve as a stimulus and motive to further production, will be altogether absent. Such an assumption is just as indefensible as would be the assumption of a banker, who has received deposits and issued in exchange therefor certificates payable on demand in whatever form of currency the depositor may prefer, that he has no deposit liabilities whatever, and therefore is under no necessity of making provision to redeem these certificates of deposit by setting aside a reserve of means of payment. To be sure it is uncertain in just what form of currency or at just what time the deposit will be demanded, but that *it will be* demanded is certain. In exactly the same way it is certain that those who save will not merely not forego their claim to goods in the future, but that sometime they will assert it as regards both capital and interest, and that they will then draw out such goods as they choose in such quantity as they choose, up to the limit fixed by the amount of their claim, and that production may and must take into account this future demand.

But how can production take account of a demand

whose direction is not yet known? This difficulty appears at first thought to be very great, but as a matter of fact it is not at all serious and in any event it is no different and no greater than analogous difficulties with which every system of production depending upon the division of labor must reckon quite aside from the phenomenon of saving. The difficulty is not very serious because, in accordance with the law of large numbers, particular idiosyncrasies and whims to a certain extent offset and compensate each other. The case of depositors in a bank serves here again as a good illustration. Each separate depositor may draw out the whole or a part of his deposit, whenever he chooses, but if the banker has a large number of depositors experience teaches that all of them will never want their deposits at once, but that the withdrawals will obey, more or less perfectly, a regular rule, and, in consequence of this fact, as is well known, bankers need to keep as a reserve in ready money only a small proportion of their demand liabilities and may invest the remainder in their business. It is exactly the same way in the case of saving. Here, too, production may count on having only a certain proportion of the claims to capital and interest presented as demands for consumption goods in each productive period and on having the remainder prolonged as titles to ownership over intermediate products or capital goods. Production, consciously or unconsciously adjusts itself to the situation, when, as must be the case in every capitalistically organized community, matters are so ordered that in each period a certain quantity of goods ready for consumption is turned out, while a greater stock of goods in the form of capital remains over for the service of future periods.

But, one may ask, to what kinds of consumption goods shall production be directed when it is not known in what kinds of goods those who save may decide to have their claims discharged? The answer is very simple: those directing production know this no better, but also no worse of the special demand of those who save than they know it of the demand of consumers generally. A highly complex, capitalistic and subdivided system of production does not wait usually for wants to assert themselves before providing for them, it has to anticipate them some time in advance. Its knowledge of the amount, the time and the direction of the demand for consumption goods does not rest on positive information, but can only be acquired by a process of testing, guessing or experimenting. Production may indeed make serious mistakes in this connection and when it does so it atones for them through the familiar agency of crises. Usually, however, it feels its way, drawing inferences for the future from the experience of the past, without serious mishap, although sometimes little mistakes are with difficulty corrected by a hasty rearrangement of the misapplied productive forces. Such readjustments are materially facilitated, as I was at pains to show at length in my "Positive Theory," by the great mobility of many intermediate products.

Moreover, the law of large number acts here again as a balancing and compensating agency. It is, indeed, highly improbable that all of those who save will liquidate their counter claims in exactly the same kinds of consumption goods. It is much more probable that their claims to pleasure-affording goods will divide themselves between the different branches of production in the same proportion that has already determined the direction of previous productive processes, or at any rate that they will not depart suddenly and violently from the standard so set. The compensating effect of the law of large numbers is further re-enforced by the fact that the demand for consumption goods arising from the counter claims of those who have saved constitutes no isolated influence but is fused with the other demands for consumption goods of all the other classes in industrial society into one great composite demand.

Finally, one further consideration, whose influence Mr. Bostedo appears to me to have ignored without the least justification, must not be overlooked. This is the increased efficiency which production acquires in consequence of the prolongation of the period of production made possible through saving. With or without an increasing demand on the part of the public, every individual producer is striving to improve his methods of production, since in this way he may get ahead of his competitors and secure for himself a larger share of the market. If, now, the opportunity is presented to business managers through the offer of the savings of others, to improve their productive appliances, no one need feel any anxiety that they will not be glad to embrace such a chance and that the "inducement to a greater investment of capital," which Mr. Bostedo fails to discover, will not be present. And if the technical improvement once works out its effects in the shape of more efficient production and cheaper products, no one need again be concerned lest the cheapening shall fail to call forth new strata of demand, nor lest the all around increase in the supply of products shall fail to lead on the other hand to a proportionate increase in sales in the sense of Say's famous theory of "vent or demand for products."

It is thus, in my opinion, that the phenomena connected with saving are interrelated. The matter presents itself to me otherwise than to Mr. Bostedo, but not, I hope, because my view is less comprehensive or more superficial.

Mr. Bostedo appears to me to leave a serious gap in his explanation of the formation of capital, when he decides to disregard entirely the part which saving plays in the process and to rely exclusively upon the ability of capital goods to come into existence of themselves so soon as the demand for consumption goods directs itself towards those in whose production the capital goods required play a useful role. For he overlooks here the fact that all kinds of pleasures and pleasure-affording goods may be created in a great variety of different ways; grain, the most universal necessity of life, may be produced either by so-called "intensive," long-period culture with correspondingly more capital; and one may travel either on a mule's back, in a sedan chair, by carriage, by automobile or by railway. When a nation acquires a taste for travel, it cannot unfortunately place the slightest reliance on the ability of lines of railway to spring up spontaneously out of the ground, but if it wishes to construct them with its own resources, it must have previously saved the needed sums out of its income, and if this has not been done, it must call in the aid of the savings of other nations; but for the savings of the English and the French, Egypt would not to the end of time have built the Suez Canal.

Notes

1. Translated from the German by the Editor.
2. Vol. xvii, pp. 95–99.
3. Pp. 100–18 in the English version.
4. *"Traitë a ëconomie politique,"* Bk. I, Chap. XV.

21

Time Preference

Murray N. Rothbard

Time preference is the insight that people prefer "present goods" (goods available for use at present) to "future goods" (present expectations of goods becoming available at some date in the future), and that the social rate of time preference, the result of the interactions of individual time preference schedules, will determine and be equal to the pure rate of interest in a society. The economy is pervaded by a time market for present as against future goods, not only in the market for loans (in which creditors trade present money for the right to receive money in the future), but also as a "natural rate" in all processes of production. For capitalists pay out present money to buy or rent land, capital goods, and raw materials, and to hire labor (as well as buying labor outright in a system of slavery), thereby purchasing expectations of future revenue from the eventual sales of product. Long-run profit rates and rates of return on capital are therefore forms of interest rate. As businessmen seek to gain profits and avoid losses, the economy will tend toward a general equilibrium, in which all interest rates and rates of return will be equal, and hence there will be no pure entrepreneurial profits or losses.

In centuries of wrestling with the vexed question of the justification of interest, the Catholic scholastic philosophers

Reprinted from *Capital Theory*, edited by John Eatwell, Murray Milgate and Peter Newman (New York: W. W. Norton & Company, 1990).

arrived at highly sophisticated explanations and justifications of return on capital, including risk and the opportunity cost of profit foregone. But they had extreme difficulty with the interest on a riskless loan, and hence denounced all such interest as sinful and usurious.

Some of the later scholastics, however, in their more favorable view of usury, began to approach a time preference explanation of interest. During a comprehensive demolition of the standard arguments for the prohibition of usury in his *Treatise on Contracts* (1499). Conrad Summenhart (1465–1511), theologian at the University of Tübingen, used time preference to justify the purchase of a discounted debt, even if the debt be newly created. When someone pays $100 for the right to obtain $110 at a future date, the buyer (lender) doesn't profit usuriously from the loan because both he and the seller (borrower) value the future $110 as being worth $100 at the present time (Noonan, 1957).

A half-century later, the distinguished Dominican canon lawyer and monetary theorist at the University of Salamanca, Martin de Azpilcueta Navarrus (1493–1586) clearly set forth the concept of time preference, but failed to apply it to a defence of usury. In his *Commentary on Usury* (1556), Azpilcueta pointed out that a present good, such as money, will naturally be worth more on the market than future goods, that is, claims to money in the future. As Azpilcueta put it:

> a claim on something is worth less than the thing itself, and ... it is plain that that which is not usable for a year is less valuable than something of the same quality which is usable at once (Gordon, 1975, p. 215).

At about the same time, the Italian humanist and politician Gian Francesco Lottini da Volterra, in his handbook of advice to princes, *Arredimenti cirili* (1574), discovered time preference. Unfortunately, Lottini also inaugurated the tradition of moralistically deploring time preference as an overestimation of a present that can be grasped immediately by the senses (Kauder, 1965, pp. 19–22).

Two centuries later, the Neopolitan abbé, Ferdinando Galiani (1728–1787) revived the rudiments of time-preference in his *Della Moneta* (1751) (Monroe, 1924), Galiani pointed out that just as the exchange rate of two currencies equates the value of a present and a spatially distant money, so the rate of interest equates present with future, or temporally distant, money. What is being equated is not physical properties, but subjective values in the minds of individuals.

These scattered hints scarcely prepare one for the remarkable development of a full-scale time preference theory of interest by the French statesman, Anne Robert Jacques Turgot (1727–1781), who, in a relatively few hastily written contributions, anticipated almost completely the later Austrian theory of capital and interest (Turgot, 1977). In the course of a paper defending usury, Turgot asked: why are borrowers willing to pay an interest premium for the use of money? The focus should not be on the amount of metal repaid but on the usefulness of the money to the lender and borrower. In particular, Turgot compares the "difference in usefulness which exists at the date of borrowing between a sum currently owned and an equal sum which is to be received at a distant date," and notes the well-known motto, "a bird in the hand is better than two in the bush." Since the sum of money owned now "is preferable to the assurance of receiving a similar sum in one or several years' time," returning the same principal means that the lender "gives the money and receives only an assurance." Therefore, interest compensates for this difference in value by a sum proportionate to the length of the delay. Turgot added that what must be compared in a loan transaction is not the value of money lent with the value repaid, but rather the "value of the *promise* of a sum of money compared to the value of money available now" (Turgot, 1977, pp. 158–59).

In addition, Turgot was apparently the first to arrive

at the concept of *capitalization,* a corollary to time preference, which holds that the present capital value of any durable good will tend to equal the sum of its expected annual
rents, or returns, discounted by the market rate of time
preference, or rate of interest.

Turgot also pioneered in analyzing the relations between the quantity of money and interest rates. If an increased supply of money goes to low time preference
people, then the increased proportion of savings to consumption lowers time preference and hence interest rates
fall while prices rise. But if an increased quantity goes into
the hands of high time preference people, the opposite
would happen and interest rates would rise along with
prices. Generally, over recent centuries, he noted, the spirit
of thrift has been growing in Europe and hence time preference rates and interest rates have tended to fall.

One of the notable injustices in the historiography of
economic thought was Böhm-Bawerk's brusque dismissal in
1884 of Turgot's anticipation of his own time-preference
theory of interest as merely a "land fructification theory"
(Böhm-Bawerk, 1, 1959). Partly this dismissal stemmed
from Böhm's methodology of clearing the ground for his
own positive theory of interest by demolishing, and hence
sometimes doing injustice to, his own forerunners (Wicksell,
1911, p. 177). The unfairness is particularly glaring in the
case of Turgot, because we now know that in 1876, only
eight years before the publication of his history of theories
of interest. Böhm-Bawerk wrote a glowing tribute to Turgot's theory of interest in an as yet unpublished paper in
Karl Knies's seminar at the University of Heidelberg (Turgot, 1977, pp. xxix-xxx).

In the course of his demolition of the Ricardo-James
Mill labor theory of value on behalf of a subjective utility
theory, Samuel Bailey (1825) clearly set forth the concept
of time preference. Rebutting Mill's statement that time, as
a "mere abstract word," could not add to value, Bailey de-

clared that "we generally prefer a present pleasure or enjoyment to a distant one," and therefore prefer present goods to waiting for goods to arrive in the future. Bailey, however, did not go on to apply his insight to interest.

In the mid-1830s, the Irish economist Samuel Mountifort Longfield worked out the later Austrian theory of capital as performing the service for workers of supplying money at present instead of waiting for the future when the product will be sold. In turn the capitalist receives from the workers a time discount from their productivity. As Longfield put it, the capitalist

> pays the wages immediately, and in return receives the value of [the worker's] labour.... [which] is greater than the wages of that labour. The difference is the profit made by the capitalist for his advances ... as it were, the discount which the laborer pays for prompt payment (Longfield, 1834).

The "pre-Austrian" time analysis of capital and interest was most fully worked out, in the same year 1834, by the Scottish and Canadian eccentric John Rae (1786–1872). In the course of attempting an anti-Smithian defence of the protective tariff, Rae, in his *Some New Principles on the Subject of Political Economy* (1834), developed the Böhm-Bawerkian time analysis of capital, pointing out that investment lengthens the time involved in the processes of production. Rae noted that the capitalist must weigh the greater productivity of longer production processes against waiting for them to come to fruition. Capitalists will sacrifice present money for a greater return in the future, the difference—the interest return—reflecting the social rate of time preference. Rae saw that people's time preference rates reflect their cultural and psychological willingness to take a shorter or longer view of the future. His moral preferences were clearly with the low time preference thrifty as against the high time preference people who suffer from a "defect of the imagination. Rae's analysis had little impact on economics until resurrected at the turn of the twentieth century, whereupon it was generously hailed in the later editions of Böhm-Bawerk's history of interest theories (Böhm-Bawerk, I, 1959).

Time preference, as a concept and as a foundation for the explanation of interest, has been an outstanding feature of the Austrian school of economics. Its founder, Carl Menger (1840–1921), enunciated the concept of time preference in 1871, pointing out that satisfying the immediate needs of life and health are necessarily prerequisites for satisfying more remote future needs. In addition, Menger declared, "all experience teaches that we humans consider a present pleasure, or one expected in the near future, more important than one of the same intensity, which is not expected to occur until some more distant time" (Wicksell, 1924, p. 195; Menger, 1871, pp. 153–54). But Menger never extended time preference from his value theory to a theory of interest; and when his follower Böhm-Bawerk did so, he peevishly deleted this discussion from the second edition of his *Principles of Economics* (Wicksell, 1924, pp. 195–56).

Böhm-Bawerk's *Capital and Interest* (1884) is the *locus classicus* of the time preference theory of interest. In his first, historical volume, he demolished all other theories, in particular the productivity theory of interest; but five years later, in his *Positive Theory of Capital* (1889), Böhm brought back the productivity theory in an attempt to combine it with a time preference explanation of interest (Böhm-Bawerk, I, II, 1959). In his "three grounds" for the explanation of interest, time preference constituted two, and the greater productivity of longer processes of production the third, Böhm ironically placing greatest importance upon the third ground. Influenced strongly by Böhm-Bawerk, Irving

Fisher increasingly took the same path of stressing the marginal productivity of capital as the main determinant of interest (Fisher, 1907, 1930).

With the work of Böhm-Bawerk and Fisher, the modern theory of interest was set squarely on the path of placing time preference in a subordinate role in the explanation of interest: determining only the rate of consumer loans, and the supply of consumer savings, while the alleged productivity of capital determines the more important demand for loans and for savings. Hence, modern interest theory fails to integrate interest on consumer loans and producer's returns into a coherent explanation.

In contrast, Frank A. Fetter, building on Böhm-Bawerk, completely discarded productivity as an explanation of interest and constructed an integrated theory of value and distribution in which interest is determined solely by time preference, while marginal productivity determines the "rental prices" of the factors of production (Fetter, 1915, 1977). In his outstanding critique of Böhm-Bawerk, Fetter pointed out a fundamental error of the third ground in trying to explain the return on capital as "present goods" earning a return for their productivity in the future; instead, capital goods are *future* goods, since they are only valuable in the expectation of being used to produce goods that will be sold to the consumer at a future date (Fetter, 1902). One way of seeing the fallacy of a productivity explanation of interest is to look at the typical practice of any current microeconomics text: after explaining marginal productivity as determining the demand curve for factors with wage rates on the y-axis, the textbook airily shifts to interest rates on the y-axis to illustrate the marginal productivity determination of interest. But the analog on the y-axis should not be interest, which is a ratio and not a price, but rather the *rental price* (price per unit time) of a capital good. Thus, interest remains totally unexplained. In short, as Fetter pointed out, marginal productivity determines rental prices, and time preference determines the rate of interest, while the capital value of a factor of production is the expected sum of future rents from a durable factor discounted by the rate of time preference or interest.

The leading economist adopting Fetter's pure time preference view of interest was Ludwig von Mises, in his *Human Action* (Mises, 1949). Mises amended the theory, in two important ways. First, he rid the concept of its moralistic tone which had been continued by Böhm-Bawerk, implicitly criticizing people for "under"-estimating the future. Mises made clear that a positive time preference rate is an essential attribute of human nature. Secondly, and as a corollary, whereas Fetter believed that people could have either positive or negative rates of time preference. Mises demonstrated that a positive rate is deductible from the fact of human action, since by the very nature of a goal or an end people wish to achieve that goal as soon as possible.

Bibliography

Bailey, S. 1825. *A Critical Dissertation on the Nature, Measure, and Causes of Value*. New York: Augustus M. Kelley, 1967.

Böhm-Bawerk, E. von. 1884–1889. *Kapital und Kapitalzins. Zweite Abteilung: Positive Theorie des Kapitales*, 4th ed. Trans. by G. D. Huncke as *Capital and Interest*, Vols I and II. South Holland, IL: Libertarian Press, 1959.

Fetter, F. A. 1902. "The 'Roundabout process' in the interest theory," *Quarterly Journal of Economics* 17, November, 163–80. Reprinted in F. A. Fetter, *Capital, Interest and Rent: Essays in the Theory of Distribution*, ed. M. Rothbard, Kansas City: Sheed Andrews and McMeel, 1977.

Fetter, F. A. 1915. *Economic Principles*, vol I. New York: The Century Co.

Fetter, F. A. 1977. *Capital, Interest, and Rent: Essays in the Theory of Distribution*, ed. M. Rothbard. Kansas City: Sheed Andrews and McMeel.

Fisher, I. 1907. *The Rate of Interest.* New York: Macmillan.

Fisher, I. 1930. *The Theory of Interest,* New York: Kelley & Millman, 1954.

Gordon, B. 1975. *Economic Analysis Before Adam Smith: Hesiod to Lessius.* New York: Barnes & Noble.

Kauder, E. 1965. *A History of Marginal Utility Theory.* Princeton: Princeton University Press.

Longfield, S. M. 1971. *The Economic Writings of Mountifort Longfield,* ed. R. D. C. Black. Clifton, NH: Augustus M. Kelley.

Menger, C. 1871. *Principles of Economics,* ed. J. Dingwall and B. Hoselitz. Glencoe, IL: Free Press, 1950.

Mises, L. von. 1949. *Human Action: a Treatise on Economics,* 3rd rev. ed. Chicago: Regnery, 1966.

Monroe, A., ed. 1924. *Early Economic Thought.* Cambridge, MA: Harvard University Press.

Noonan, J. T., Jr. 1957. *The Scholastic Analysis of Usury.* Cambridge, MA: Harvard University Press.

Rae, J. 1834. *Some New Principles on the Subject of Political Economy.* In *John Rae: Political Economist,* ed. R. W. James. Toronto: University of Toronto Press, 1965.

Turgot, A. R .J. 1977. *The Economics of A. R. J. Turgot,* ed. P. D. Groenewegen. The Hague: Martinus Nijhoff.

Wicksell, K. 1911. "Böhm-Bawerk's theory of interest." In K. Wicksell, *Selected Papers on Economic Theory,* ed. E. Lindahl. Cambridge, MA: Harvard University Press, 1958.

Wicksell, K. 1924. "The new edition of Menger's *Grundsatze.*" In K. Wicksell, *Selected Papers on Economic Theory,* ed. E. Lindahl. Cambridge, MA: Harvard University Press, 1958.

22

Excerpts from

Interest

Vernon A. Mund

The Early Use of the Term "Interest"

The word "interest" is derived from the Latin word *interesse* which means to be between, or in an equivalent sense, the interval. According to Roman law a debtor who failed to repay his loan on the due date was forced to pay also an extra sum for the time between the due date and the date of actual payment. The extra payment for this interval was called *interesse* and was intended to compensate the creditor for damage caused by the delay. The regular charge for a money loan was called *usura* or usury, and the common practice was to pay usury on a monthly basis. The practice of borrowing and lending was widespread in the Roman Empire.

During the Middle Ages the Church disapproved the taking of usury and even forbade its members to charge usury on a money loan. At that time there was little commercial activity and most of the loans were made to people in distress who needed money for a personal use, such as sickness, a death in the family, the need for food and so on. In forbidding usury, therefore, the Churchmen stated that the

Reprinted from *Economic Principles and Problems, Third Edition,* Volume II, edited by Walter E. Spahr (New York: Farrar & Rinehart, Inc., 1936).

more fortunate should not take advantage of a brother's need. Following the doctrine of Aristotle, they reasoned further that money was barren and could not in itself yield a fruit or payment. They failed to see that among merchants money was really borrowed to buy goods and services from which an income could be obtained.

The Change in the Meaning of Interest

Upon the basis of the Roman law, however, the Churchmen usually held that if a creditor actually suffered loss, because of the debtor's failure to pay on the due date, a charge of interest (*interesse*) for the delay was permissible. Upon the basis of this proviso, a considerable business in lending money developed with the growth of trade and commerce after the eleventh century. Loans were made for short periods to come due at times when it was not likely that the borrower could pay. In view of the default, creditors would claim that they were damaged and would demand *interesse* from the due date to the date of actual payment. Gradually the civilian and Church authorities came to tolerate these practices, and by the middle of the sixteenth century a regular payment for money loans at prescribed rates was pretty generally permitted, although still looked upon with suspicion and dislike outside commercial circles. This payment was quite generally called interest, and the word "usury" came to be employed to designate only an exorbitant rate of interest.

The Typical or Usual Preference of Individuals is for Present Uses, Goods, and Enjoyments

The essential nature of borrowing—the transaction for which interest is paid—is the obtaining of general purchasing power now and the postponement of payment to a later date. When a principal sum ($100) is borrowed now, a larger sum (say $105 or $110) is returned a year later. Why can lenders obtain this surplus? How can borrowers afford to pay it? In answering these questions we must consider, first of all, the way in which people evaluate goods in point of time.

Time-preference—In general, people prefer present goods to an equal amount of like future goods. In the morning the *present desire* for breakfast is greater than the *present desire* for a breakfast a year from now. If a person has his choice of accepting a dollar now or a year later, he usually would take it now. The present desire for a new automobile now is greater than the present desire for one next season. In these and innumerable other instances, a person expresses a preference for present goods and present uses of goods rather than for an equal amount of future goods and uses. But sometimes the reverse is the case. The preference which an individual has for things at one time rather than at another is called *time-preference.*

Reasons for the Usual Preference of Individuals for Present Uses, Goods, and Enjoyments

The typical preference which people have for present goods or uses arises, first, from man's physiological nature. Man's present appetites and needs for food, drink, shelter, and so on, are real, insistent, and constantly demand immediate satisfaction. As the saying goes, "A man must live." Even when man's elemental needs are met, he still desires sustenance of a better quality. In addition, he desires other types of goods and services, and these desires are almost without limit. It is difficult for people to discipline themselves to forego the present satisfaction of a desire. A concern for the future, in fact, comes only after much training and with the development of foresight and will power.

A second reason for the usual preference for present goods is the prevailing hope among people that the future will have an adequate or a better provision. Many people think and hope that "the future will take care of itself," that someday they will "strike it lucky," and that in time "their ship will come in." Such attitudes cause people to put a high value on the present use of goods. The present is all-important and they are willing "to trust to luck" for the future. Students, young doctors, and others beginning professional careers place a high valuation on present goods and much prefer to have goods now rather than in the future when they expect to be earning a good income.

A third reason for the preference for present goods over future goods is the uncertainty of the future. There is, first of all, the uncertainty of life itself. The philosophy of "Eat, drink, and be merry, for tomorrow we die" expresses the fact that a person's life is certain only for the present moment. One often hears the opinion expressed that the present should be enjoyed from day to day without waiting for the year or month which is to be "taken off" sometime in the future.

The uncertainty of whether or not future goods will be forthcoming also causes people to prefer present goods. The old proverb "A bird in the hand is worth two in the bush" expresses this feeling. The future is distant and dim, and many things may occur which will prevent the actual realization of a future good or income. A common remark is that "a person cannot make plans very far in advance." Present goods are the most certain and in most cases people prefer present goods to an equal amount of future goods.

In Some Instances Future Goods are Preferred

Although the usual preference is for present goods, it may be that in some specific instances individuals prefer to have things in the future. The present desire for food after a meal, for example, is less than the present desire for the food for a future time. Fruit and nuts in the fall are worth less than they will be worth during the winter months. One may also postpone the use of a certain amount of money when one believes it will bring him more satisfaction if spent later. It is only in a minority of cases, however, that future goods are preferred to an equal amount of present goods. The typical or usual preference of individuals is for present goods and enjoyments.

Differences in the Degree of Time-Preference

The preference of an individual for present goods may vary from one period to another. A man dying of thirst on a desert would give the whole future for a glass of water. Sickness, death, robbery, and other mishaps send people to the "loan sharks" even though they are forced to pay an interest rate of several hundred percent. During the "banking holiday" in March, 1933, the Associated Press reported the case of "one traveling man who needed $5 cash to get out of town quickly. He even offered to sell a $45 company check for that amount."

At any one time, different people have different degrees of time-preference. Some individuals fulfill promptly their various duties and are thrifty and prudent in their use of present goods. On the other hand, some people value the present too highly to make repairs, mend clothing, prepare their lessons, and so on. It is an old proverb that "a stitch in time saves nine"; and the decision to spend nine times as much labor in the future as would be required now, indicates a very high preference for present goods or enjoyments.

In general, an individual's degree of time-preference

varies with his present desire for goods and services and their relative plenty or scarcity. This relationship, however, is always modified by the personal characteristics of the individual—his intelligence, training, habit, and foresight.

Time-Preference is Expressed as a Rate

As a result of time-preference, present goods usually have more *value* than an equal amount of future goods. An individual's time-preference (for the present) can be measured by observing the extra units which must be added to a given future sum to make it equivalent in value to a like present sum. If a present sum $100 is preferred to an equal sum a year later, and the future sum must be increased to $110 to offset the preference, we say that the preference for the present amount is measured by $10. The *rate* of time-preference is the ratio of the extra number of future units to the present sum. In many cases, a person may not be conscious of the fact that he is employing a rate of time-preference in his comparisons of the present and the future. He may know only that he has a preference for present goods and that he would be willing to pay $105 one year hence for $100 now, or that he would forego the use of $100 now in order to receive a payment of $105 a year from now. Each such comparison by an individual, however, involves a rate of time-preference.

Future Goods and Incomes are Given a Discounted Present Price

As people usually place a premium upon *present* direct goods and *present* purchasing power as compared with an equal amount of *future* goods or purchasing power, so conversely the future value of goods and incomes is discounted in the present price. Thus, if \$100 will be the worth of a good a year hence, an individual with a time-preference rate of 5 percent evaluates the good now at \$95.24. The present worth (\$94.24) must be less than the future sum (\$100) to make it equivalent in value because a premium or surplus value is placed on present goods and purchasing power.

The discounted future price (present worth) is a sum which will amount to the future income in a given time at the given rate of time-preference. If we use the formula $P(I + r) = F$, we find that \$95.24 X 1.05 = \$100.[1] The placing of a present value on a future sum is just the reverse of this accumulation, and the formula for determining the present worth of a sum one year hence is $P = F/(I + r)$ in which F is the future sum, r is the rate of time-preference, and P is the present worth. If the future income consists of a sum at the end of one year, and a second sum at the end of two years, the present worth formula is $P = \{F/(I + r)\} + \{F/(I + r)^2\}$. Each additional annual income is given a present worth by dividing its amount by $(I + r)^n$, the exponent n representing the number of years in the future when the income will occur. If the annual income is expected to continue forever, the formula is $P = a/r$, in which a is the annual income and r is the rate of time-preference.

If an individual's rate of time-preference is high, he will place a low present worth on a future income; if an individual's rate is low, on the other hand, he will put a relatively high present worth on a future income. For example, a farm which is expected to yield a net income of \$100 a year forever will be given a present valuation of \$1,000 if one's rate of time-preference is 10 percent $\{(P = a/r)$ or \$1000 = (\$100/.10)\}$. If one's rate of time-preference, however, is 4 percent, the present worth will be \$2,500.

A Typical Rate of Time-Premium Comes to Prevail in a Community

Since an owner having a high rate of time-preference will place a low present worth on his farm ($1,000 in the above illustration), it is evident that he could very easily sell the good to a prospective buyer having a lower rate of time-preference. The farm at a price below $2,500 would be "cheap" to the person with a low time-preference, and bargaining by the two individuals may result in a price of $2,000, which involves a time-premium rate of 5 percent. The rate of *time-premium* is the market rate (price) resulting from buyers' and sellers' individual rates of time-preference (subjective valuations).

Through countless purchases and sales of present and future goods and incomes in regular markets, a prevailing rate (price) of time-premium is established in the community, and future incomes are capitalized upon the basis of this rate. The process of placing a present worth upon a future sum or series of incomes is called *capitalization,* and the value so expressed is capital. Individuals who have rates of time-preference higher than the market rate will tend to bring their rates in line by selling some of their future goods and incomes. Individuals with lower rates of time-preference, on the other hand, are able to obtain the market rate of time-premium on their present purchasing power and need not take less.

These principles of time-preference adjustment are illustrated in Figure XXXIX. The annual net income from a durable good of a given type is assumed to be $100 and it is expected that this income will continue forever. Owners with high rates of time-preference will be the sellers of durable goods because they are very eager for present goods. People with low rates of time-preference, on the other hand, will enter the market as buyers of durable goods, for the high future incomes are more attractive than their present

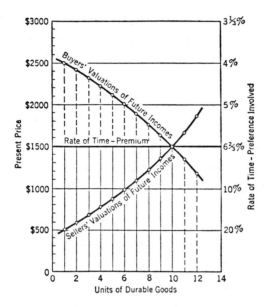

Figure XXXIX

The annual net income for each unit of a given grade of land is assumed to be $100. With careful maintenance the land is expected to yield this income forever. It may be noted that every possible price is a capitalized price and involves a rate of time-preference. Competition in bidding will result in a market price of $1,500 per unit of land and at this figure time-preference rates will be equalized at $6^{2}/3$ percent.

goods or funds. Competition among buyers and sellers in a given market will result in an equilibrium rate of time-premium, and all sales of the durable goods will be made upon this basis. In terms of Figure XXXIX the market rate of time-premium is $6^{2}/3$ percent, for that is the rate which will equate demand and supply.

The market rate of time-premium is always a plus rate because it is an expression of the general premium on present purchasing power which pervades the whole system of prices. The typical or usual preference of individuals is for present goods and enjoyments, and in the buying and selling of durable goods, future money incomes, and so on, this preference brings about a general premium on present purchasing power.

The Present Prices of All Durable Goods, Whether Direct or Indirect, and of All Future Monetary Incomes are Discounted Prices of Future Uses

Similar adjustments of time-preference rates will occur in the commodity markets for all types of durable and indirect goods. The price of a factory, an office building, a machine, a private dwelling, a piano, and so on, is a capitalized price, which reflects the prevailing rate of time-premium. Indirect goods which may be kept for use at a future date likewise have present prices which are based upon their future values discounted upon the basis of the prevailing rate of time-premium less the cost of conserving them. In this category are such things as wheat used for making flour, newly made cheese, whiskey in bond, apples in storage, and raw materials generally.

Also in the markets where securities bearing future money incomes are bought and sold, the prevailing rate of time-premium will operate. A ten-year 4 percent bond for $1,000 will yield nine annual incomes of $40 and an income on the tenth year of $1,040. A share of stock paying dividends, on the other hand, has no maturity, and may yield an income perpetually. If the bond which yields $40 a year for nine years and $1,040 at the end of a tenth year sells now for more than $1,000, one knows that the rate of time-premium involved is less than 4 percent. On the other hand, if the rate of time-premium in the market is higher than the rate of interest specified on a bond, the future incomes discounted at the higher market rate will give a present price less than $1,000. In a true market the nominal par price of a security is of no significance in its valuation, but its annual income is. Fundamentally, the present price of all securities is based upon a capitalization of the expected future incomes.

The Risk Element

Although a general net rate of time-premium tends to pervade the price system of a community, the actual gross time-premium rate in particular markets varies with the risk that the future income will not be forthcoming, or will be forthcoming only in reduced amount. If the security of the future income is somewhat hazardous, there will be fewer buyers and buying valuations will be lower. The resulting discounted prices, therefore, will be relatively low in comparison with the expected incomes, and this fact indicates that an addition for risk has been made to the prevailing rate of time-premium. The stock of mining concerns, oil well royalties, and farms in drouth or frost areas, for example, are generally capitalized at very high rates of time-premium, and the resulting prices reflect the considerable risk of investing money in these ventures. Over a period of time, the buyer may obtain more or less than the prevailing rate of time-premium, depending upon whether or not the future incomes have been forthcoming. In general, however, the losses tend to cancel the gains, so that buyers of stocks, bonds, and so on, promising large returns get little, if any, more than the prevailing net rate of time-premium on their investments, and frequently lose their whole investment.

The Capitalization of "Riskless" Incomes

Two series of future money incomes which long have been looked upon as involving the very minimum of risk are those in the British consols and French *rentes.* These securities have been issued by the national governments of England and France and promise to pay interest perpetually. Although the coupon rate on the consols may be as low as $2^1/2$ percent and the rate on the *rentes* 3 percent, each security has a price based upon the rates of time-premium prevailing each day in the English and French markets.

The annual income on these securities is a fixed amount, and the rate of time-premium at which each income is capitalized is revealed by calculating the percentage that the income is of the market price. The rates at which these perpetual incomes were capitalized over a period of thirty-three years are shown in Figure XL. The average time-premium rate at which British consols were capitalized during this period is 3.80 percent; and the average rate at which the *rentes* were capitalized is 4.09 percent. The time-premium rates at which these two types of income are capitalized are usually looked upon as representing the prevailing time-premium rates in the English and French markets.

An interesting aspect of the time-premium rates shown in Figure XL is their relative stability over a period of years. Historical evidence indicates that since earliest times a rate of time-premium has been involved in the relative valuations which people place on present and future incomes. Throughout history, moreover, there has been a distinct trend of time-premium rates upwards or downwards; and at no time have the rates fallen below the levels now prevailing. All the evidence available seems to indicate that time-preference is, and has been, a universal psychological characteristic of all people.

Some Conclusions as to Time-Preference

So far, we have been studying the part played by time in the evaluation of goods. We have seen that usually people

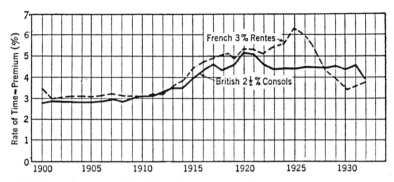

Based upon data from David F. Jordan, *Investments* (Prentice-Hall, Inc., New York, 1934), p. 9.

Figure XL
The prevailing rates of time-premium at which British consols and French *rentes* have been capitalized.

prefer present goods to an equal amount of future goods and that this involves an individual time-preference rate. Through countless purchases and sales of present and future goods and incomes in regular markets there is established a rate of time-premium which tends to prevail throughout the community. Future goods, uses, and incomes are capitalized upon the basis of this rate and normally bear a present price less than the future value of the uses and incomes. The price of a suit or dress, for example, is the present worth of its whole series of future uses. The price the tailor, in turn, pays for the woolen cloth is a discounted price based upon the expected price of the suit. The price the cloth manufacturer pays for wool, in turn, is based upon the present worth of the cloth. Since sheep will grow fleeces of wool for many years, their price (aside from their value as mutton) is based upon a capitalization of the expected future annual incomes from the sale of wool. And finally, the price of the land used for raising sheep is a capitalization of its future uses, or rents, estimated as continuing forever. In this way the prevailing rate of time-premium permeates the entire price system; every price, except the price of a perishable good with a present, direct use, is a capitalized price.

The Form and Use of Savings

In some cases, savings may be made in kind. A farmer, for example, may increase his flock of chickens by retaining each year some of the young pullets. Nowadays, however, most incomes are money incomes and savings are almost invariably made in money form. Only in rare instances are money savings hoarded. A miser may get pleasure from looking at his store of coins, and immigrants have buried gold, silver, and paper currency in the ground in a tin box because of their distrust of banking institutions. In most cases, however, savers of money desire the uses of goods which money will buy or the income which it will yield upon careful investment. As a result, money savings are constantly being spent and invested.

Money savings may be spent by individuals for direct durable goods such as a piano, a radio, a home, and so on, or they may be used to buy indirect goods such as a farm, a factory, a business enterprise, new equipment, or raw materials, for use in a business enterprise. A large part of money savings is deposited in the various banking institutions which we have already analyzed,[2] and through these agencies the savings become available as money loans to borrowers. A saver may also buy insurance policies, bonds, notes, and mortgages, or make direct money loans to individuals.

The Meaning of Credit and Interest

The transaction for which interest is paid is a credit transaction. *Credit may be defined as the obtaining of present goods or purchasing power and the postponement of payment to a later date.* The word "credit" is derived from the Latin word *creditum,* meaning a loan, or a debt. *Creditum* in turn is derived from the Latin *credo* which means to trust, or place confidence in a person or thing. It is apparent that a lender will give up present goods or purchasing power only when he has faith in a borrower's intention and ability to give payment at some future time. The phrase "use your credit" literally means "use your credit rating with a lender." If a lender has faith in one's ability to give payment in the future, he will be willing to make a loan or entrust present goods to that person.

We may define interest as *the price paid for credit or the obtaining of something now and the postponement of payment to a later date.* Interest is a contractual payment and when its amount is not specified, the rate of premium on the principal is assumed to be the customary rate or the rate specified by law. The amount of money loaned or debt incurred is called the *principal* and the ratio of *interest* ($10) to the principal ($100) is called *the rate of interest* (10 percent). Payments of interest are usually made at the end of various stipulated periods of time until the loan or debt is repaid.

The actual amount of interest which a borrower pays is called *gross interest* because it usually includes a payment for things other than the time element, or pure credit. Thus, gross interest contains a payment for the lender's cost of making, administering, and collecting the loan. A second element in gross interest arises from the risk that the principal or interest will not be returned. After an allowance has been made for the cost and risk, the remainder is called *net interest.* As we shall see presently, the rate of net interest is a reflection, in the loan markets, of the rate of time-premium which prevails in the community and is embodied in the existing system of prices.

Although interest is normally paid at the end of a stipulated period of time, commercial banks commonly charge interest in advance. The charging of interest in advance is called bankers' "discount." When a person borrows $100 at a bank, for example, the banker may deduct the interest at 10 percent ($10) at once, and the customer will get only $90. In this case the loan is really only $90 and one year later the borrower will repay $100 or $10 for a loan of $90. Inasmuch as 10 percent on $90, the amount of the loan, would be only $9, bankers' discount really involves a rate of interest actually greater than the nominal rate.

Borrowers' Valuations for Money Loans

Borrowers who want a money loan to buy perishable goods for their own direct use (or for the direct use of their dependents) may be forced to pay a rate of interest based upon their latent individual rates of time-preference. Inasmuch as most of these borrowers have very inadequate security, there is really no open, competitive market to which they can go to bargain for present funds. Instead, each loan is usually negotiated separately. As a result, the rates of interest on loans to necessitous and spendthrift borrowers are often much higher than the prevailing rate of time-premium and the cost and risk involved in making the loans.

Most of the borrowing today is done in regular markets by borrowers with approved security. A comparatively few of these borrowers want money loans to buy specific direct durable goods, but the bulk of the borrowers want to obtain a complex of goods for use in productive activity. How can borrowers with approved security afford to pay interest? Why must they pay interest? The prices of durable goods and indirect goods, we have seen, are their discounted future prices. When the expected returns of present goods appear in the future, they will, unless the goods have been imprudently chosen, ordinarily be greater than their present prices. It is this fact which enables a borrower to repay his money loan with a surplus (interest) in the future.

The Prospect of Profits Leads Enterprisers to Borrow

An enterpriser, of course, borrows money for use in a business activity in which he hopes to make a profit. It is the opportunity to buy goods at discounted prices, however, which enables an enterpriser to pay interest. A person, for example, can pay interest on a money loan made in the fall to put apples in storage because the present price of the apples is the discounted amount of their price next spring. When the apples are sold in the spring (assuming no unusual change in demand), the income received will be sufficient to pay not only the storage charges and the loan, but also interest. If the enterpriser is skillful in marketing his product or in buying "low valued" goods—namely, those which are capitalized at a price less than that reflecting the prevailing rate of time-premium—he will have a larger profit.

A similar relation exists between the present prices of dwelling houses, farms, factories, mines, machines, raw materials, and similar things, and the incomes which those goods will yield up to the time the loan is repaid. If a machine will last two years and yield a net income of $1,000 per year, its present worth, assuming a time-premium rate of 6 percent, is $1,833.40 $\{P = (\$1,000/(1.06)) + (\$1,000/(1.06)^2\}$,whereas the future incomes will be $2,000. If the future incomes were not discounted, an enterpriser could not afford to repay his money loan with a surplus, or interest. The present prices of indirect and durable goods, however, are discounted prices, and a borrower can afford to pay interest because of the difference in the present worth of such goods and the worth of their products when they mature.

We have seen that individuals may have very different rates of time-preference but that with countless purchases and sales a typical market rate tends to prevail. Those who borrow money to buy durable and indirect goods play an important part in the equalizing of the time-premium rates which exist in the various commodity markets. Business enterprisers seek out those goods which are "low valued"—that is, capitalized at a high rate of time-premium—and transfer them to markets where the usual rate prevails (where the price is higher). In order to buy such "low valued" goods, some borrowers may be able to pay an interest rate higher than the prevailing rate of time-premium. Many borrowers, on the other hand, buy goods capitalized at the prevailing rates because they think they can change them, transport them, store them, and so on, and by their skill obtain more than the expected returns. Various factors will account for the presence or absence of profits when the future incomes mature. The surplus income (as compared with the present price) with which we are concerned in the study of interest, however, is that surplus which exists because of the discount for time. The prices of durable and indirect goods are discounted prices and the maximum rate of interest which a borrower can afford to pay is based upon the rate of time-premium at which the goods he wants to buy are capitalized.

Factors which Influence Lenders' Valuations

When a person lends a sum of money, he foregoes the opportunity of using it to buy goods at their present capitalized prices. Instead of lending the present purchasing power, a lender could buy durable goods, such as land, a business enterprise, or a dwelling; perishable goods in storage, such as apples, potatoes, or whiskey in bond; or a money income, such as royalties or bonds. In each of these cases, the present price represents a capitalization of the future incomes at the prevailing rate of time-premium; and for a present sum invested in one of these goods or incomes a lender could get a rate of time-premium on his money. Lenders, therefore, will base their valuation of money loans upon the prevailing rate of time-premium at which durable goods and money incomes are capitalized.

In making loans, lenders will also take into account the risk of the loan, and the cost of making, administering, and collecting it. The risk and cost involved in making a loan to the Federal government, for example, are the very minimum and the rate of interest on United States bonds reflects closely the prevailing net rate of time-premium. When money is loaned to a farmer on a real estate mortgage, on the other hand, the lender assumes the somewhat greater risk that the farmer may be unable to repay the loan, and in addition he assumes the expense and trouble of making the loan and collecting the interest and principal. The desire and ability of lenders to assume these extra risks and duties determine in large measure the type of loans they make. There are thus various money markets with various prevailing premium rates.

The rates of interest charged by commercial banks and other lending institutions also reflect the prevailing rate of time-premium at which goods are capitalized. If such lending agencies charge borrowers more than the prevailing rate of time-premium, plus an allowance for risk and expense, they will accumulate a surplus of loanable funds; and if the rate charged is less, due to a temporary surplus of funds, the competition of borrowers, in time, will force up the rate. To the extent that the law permits, banks can also invest in bonds, warrants, and similar money incomes and obtain a rate of time-premium on their present funds. The difference between the rate of interest which banks pay savers and the rate which they charge borrowers results from the ready payment and greater safety which banks offer savers, and also from the fact that banks assume the cost of making, administering, and collecting loans.

When present goods are sold on credit, the seller foregoes the opportunity to use the money due him. Thus, a person may buy a farm for $12,000, pay $4,000 in cash, and give a note secured by a mortgage on the land for $8,000. The seller, in this instance, would want a rate of interest on the note because he foregoes the opportunity to buy with the purchase price other goods or money incomes at capitalized prices. Similarly, when merchandise, automobiles, and similar things are sold on credit, the seller foregoes the use of the money which is invested in the goods; and consequently he must pay interest upon funds borrowed to finance new purchases. Sales of goods on a credit basis usually involve considerable risk, for buyers rarely pledge any special collateral. If the goods sold are pledged as security, moreover, there is the possibility that they will be misused and have little repossession value. Considerable expense is also involved in sending bills, making collections, and so on. As a result of these extra expense items, the rate of interest involved in credit sales is usually high.

The Determination of a Rate of Interest

When there are several competing borrowers and lenders in a given credit market, the various rates of time-preference unite and form a curve of borrowers' (buyers') valuations and a curve of lenders' (sellers') valuations (see Figure XLI). The maximum amount of interest which borrowers can afford to pay is based upon the estimated rate of time-premium involved in the prices of goods which they expect to buy. Lenders, on the other hand, are parting with money which could have been used to buy goods at discounted prices; and their valuations are based upon the alternative uses for the present purchasing power. The valuations of

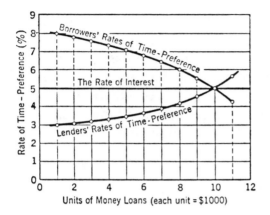

Figure XLI

This figure illustrates the various latent rates of time-preference which borrowers and lenders may place on a money loan (or the getting of present goods) and a postponement of repayment until one year later. The rate of 5 percent establishes a equilibrium between demand and supply and becomes the contractual rate of interest for credit transactions in the given market.

lenders are also influenced by the quality of the security which borrowers present and by the probable cost of making and collecting the loan. In a given credit market for a certain class of borrowers, the security offered by borrowers tends to be approximately the same, and anyone who cannot meet the usual standards is denied credit. The various valuations of borrowers and lenders are brought into conformity by competition and an equilibrium rate of interest results. This rate (5 percent in Figure XLI) becomes the contractual rate of interest at which all money loans to a certain class of borrowers tend to be made.

The rate of interest which prevails in a market is, superficially viewed, a price which is paid for the use of money, but the "use of money" is to buy goods at present prices which are less than future prices. In essence, interest is a payment for the right to obtain something now and to repay at a later date. The amount which a borrower can afford to pay, and must pay, for credit is governed by the rate of time-premium at which the future incomes of the goods he expects to buy are capitalized, that is, discounted. Thus, the net rate of interest reflects and indicates, in the money loan market, the rate of time-premium which prevails in the community.

Notes

1. See the preceding chapter, pp. 173–74, for a derivation of the formulas used in this paragraph.
2. See vol. I, Chaps, X, XIII, XXIII, XXIV.

23

Complementarity and Substitution in the Theory of Capital

Ludwig M. Lachmann

1

Complementarity, introduced into economic dynamics by Professor Hicks in 1939,[1] has since given rise to a host of bewildering and intricate problems. Soon Dr. Lange, in defending the Hicksian view of complementarity against overt criticism by Professor Machlup,[2] had to warn us against confusing the effects of complementarity with those of a "sympathetic shift in demand."[3] But a few years later the same Dr. Lange relegated complementarity to a scornful footnote.[4] For this he was promptly taken to task by Mr. Harrod, who told us that "in the context of the enquiry, in which we are interested in changes of the prices not of highly specific factors, but of widely employed factors or categories of factors . . . the co-operant attribute predominates."[5] Mr. Harrod also expressed the view that "factors may be co-operant or alternative to one another. The latter attribute belongs to factors that are very specific. Thus if tool B becomes cheaper it may lead entrepreneurs to have

Reprinted from *Capital, Expectations, and the Market Process* by Ludwig M. Lachmann, edited by Walter E. Grinder (Kansas City: Sheed Andrews and McMeel, Inc., 1976).

no further use for tool A (which does roughly the same job)."[6] This view plainly contradicts Professor Hicks's statement that "there is a tendency for factors jointly employed in the same firm to be complementary."[7] There is thus good reason to believe that this is a field in which the wise walk warily.

We may start by recognizing with Professor Hicks that goods subject to "sympathetic shifts in demand" will probably be also complementary goods, that "companionable commodities will very usually be complements."[8] Where the cause of a dynamic change lies on the demand side, the effects of complementarity and companionableness may therefore be almost impossible to disentangle. It follows that if it is our aim to study the effects of complementarity on dynamic change, it will be better to choose as our standard model a case in which the change originates on the supply side. This method we shall adopt in the latter part of this paper.

Next, we have to realize that the traditional treatment of factor complementarity in economic theory has been quite unduly narrow. The standard case discussed is here, of course, the labor-land-capital relationship in the distribution of incomes, Mr. Harrod's "widely employed categories of factors." But what precisely is our criterion of classification of these categories? And why cannot complementarity exist within each category? In this paper we shall endeavor to show that it is in the theory of capital that the concept of complementarity proves a most powerful lamp to throw light into some notoriously dark corners.

2

To reduce that heterogeneous assortment of buses, blast furnaces, telephone kiosks and hotel-room carpets that we call Capital to an intelligible order, to exhibit the design of the pattern into which all of these have to fit, is the chief task of the theory of capital. This is usually done by representing capital as a "stock" or "fund" the component parts of which are units of money value. Our heterogeneous assortment is thus converted into a homogeneous aggregate by using Money value as a common denominator. As Professor Hayek has shown, this becomes impossible under conditions of dynamic change likely to cause relative value changes.

In a homogeneous aggregate each unit is a perfect substitute for every other unit, as drops of water are in a lake. Once we abandon the notion of capital as homogeneous, we should therefore be prepared to find less substitutability and more complementarity. There now emerges, at the opposite pole, a conception of capital as a *structure*, in which each capital good has a definite function and in which all such goods are complements. It goes without saying that these two concepts of capital, one as a homogeneous fund, each unit being a perfect substitute for every other unit, the other as a complex structure, in which each unit is a complement to every other unit, are to be regarded as *ideal types*, pure equilibrium concepts neither of which can be found in actual experience.

In reality we should expect individual capital instruments to be substitutes for some, and complements to some other instruments. Each locomotive, we may surmise, is complementary to a number of wagons, but at the same time a more or less perfect substitute for every other locomotive. If this is so, the next question we have to ask is whether, over the field of capital as a whole, complementarity or substitutability is the dominant relationship; or, more precisely, under what conditions we may expect one or the other to predominate. Mr. Harrod believes that among capital instruments substitutability prevails. But we should require further evidence. Enthusiasts of econometrics may well have a dreamy vision of new playgrounds to conquer and new toys to hug, for is this not precisely the kind of situation in which the harassed theorist has to "appeal to the facts"? But a little further reflection shows that here, as so often, "the facts" refuse to give a simple answer to our question.

The view that factor complementarity and substitutability are alternative modes of the relationship between factors *in the same situation* rests on a fallacy. There are too many instances of change, of which labor-saving invention is the most familiar, where complements are suddenly turned into substitutes; or, even more intriguingly, in which capital (our supposedly homogeneous stock?) is split into two parts one of which becomes a substitute for, while the other remains a complement to, labor. There are also cases where both relations appear to exist side by side. If a firm has four delivery vans, each delivering goods in a quarter of the town, are they complements or substitutes? According to Professor Hicks they are the former, as "factors jointly employed in the same firm"; according to Mr. Harrod they are bound to be the latter ("doing roughly the same job:). But are they not really both? Furthermore, while locomotives may be substitutes, and locomotives and wagons complements, from the point of view of the time table, the production plan for the railway system as a whole, all trains are complements. But if trains are complements, how can locomotives be substitutes?

These examples go to show that factor complementarity and substitutability are not exclusive alternatives. Factor complementarity and substitution are phenomena belonging to different provinces of the realm of action. Complementarity is a property of means employed for the same end, or a group of consistent ends. All the means jointly employed for the same end, or such ends, are necessarily complements. Factor complementarity presupposes a *plan* within the framework of which each factor has a function. It is therefore only with respect to a given plan that we can meaningfully speak of factor complementarity. Factors are complements insofar as they fit into a production plan and participate in a productive process.

Substitution, on the other hand, is a phenomenon of change the need for which arises whenever something has gone wrong with a prior plan. Substitutability indicates the ease with which a factor can be turned into an element of an existing plan.[9] A change in plan is possible without a change of end. The importance of substitutability lies in that it is usually possible to pursue the same end (output) with a different combination of factors. The importance of complementarity lies in that "technical rigidity" (invariability of the mode of complementarity) may often make it necessary to change the end rather than the means; an existing combination of factors is used to produce a different output.

The change in question must be possible but not predictable. If it were predictable there would be no need for substitution. We should take it into account in drawing up our plan. Here, as elsewhere in the theory of action, predictable change is indistinguishable from any other known element of the situation. The designer of a motor-car is as unlikely to forget the lamps as the mudguard.

A production plan involving a large number of factors and with a complex complementarity pattern is particularly vulnerable in case any of them breaks down. We safeguard ourselves against such occurrences by keeping a reserve stock of perfect substitutes for the operating factors (spare parts). We diminish its necessary size by devices calculated to increase substitutability, like the standardization of equipment. Where the complementarity pattern of the plan is complex, a high degree of substitutability between operating factors and factors held in reserve may be required to keep it going. We have to provide for many minor changes in order to prevent a major one.

We now understand why the locomotives in our example gave us so much trouble. In saying that each locomotive is complementary to so and so many wagons we think of a given production plan (time table). In saying that each is a more or less perfect substitute for every other we are, as it were, turning our mind to an entirely different situation, one in which our original production plan with its allocation of locomotives to trains has been modified. In the first case we think of a given situation, in the second of a change in the situation.

This is not to say, of course, that every change will turn all complements into substitutes. Most factor complementarities, to be sure, can stand up to a number of changes, some of them, like the one mentioned, may outlast almost any change. Our point is merely that every major change is bound to upset some plans and disrupt some complementarities. On the other hand, it is impossible to speak of substitutable factors without defining the kind of change we wish to provide for. One cannot help feeling that the plant bred in the rarefied atmosphere of a static world with a given system of wants, does not stand up very well to the rough climate of a dynamic world which we cannot but study in terms of plans, but in which failure and revision of plans is an every-day occurrence.

It is now clear why factors jointly employed in the same firm tend to be complementary: they are all means to the same end, elements of the same plan. Unity of management here ensures consistency of action.

3

We shall now extend the scope of our analysis from the individual enterprise and its production plan to the economic system as a whole. Shall we now find factor complementarity throughout the system? At first sight one might think that here, where factors are employed, not in one production plan but in many, there can be little or no complementarity. But further reflection shows that this need not be so. A firm, carrying out a plan extending over a period of time, is during that period in equilibrium, as equilibrium means essentially consistency of a number of acts by different individuals, or the same individual. We may now imagine an economic system in equilibrium in the sense that the acts of all individuals, producers and consumers, are consistent with each other, hence so are all production plans. The stationary state is the simplest type of such a system, but generally foreseen change will not affect the essence of the matter. In such an economic system in equilibrium, complementarity will exist between all factors in the system in precisely the same way as in each firm. For where the production plans of all firms fit into a coherent whole, they may, of course, be regarded as elements of one large plan constituted by this whole.

Let us now assume that an unforeseen change throws our system into disequilibrium. Substitution of factors ensues. It is important to realize that while factor substitution destroys one set of complementary relations, another will be created, though possibly of a different mode. If the factor substituted is a perfect substitute for the factor displaced, nothing further need be done. We fit the spare part into the machine, and it continues to run as before. But if the factor substituted is not a perfect substitute, there may have to be an adjustment of other factors. In the former case the new factor merely joins an existing combination, in the latter the *coefficients of production*,[10] the proportions in which the various factors are combined, will have to be altered. A change in the coefficients of production in one firm will, of course, have repercussions throughout the economic system and entail further acts of substitution in other firms. A sequence of changes will permeate the system, affecting prices, output and coefficients of production. But however many subsequent acts of substitution our first act may entail, as long as factors are used together in productive processes there will always be factor complementarity.

What we have said so far about complementarity and substitution applies to factors in general. Now, capital resources are more sensitive to unforeseen change than are either labor or permanent resources, and this marks them out for special treatment. Capital goods are products of the human mind, artefacts, produced in accordance with a plan. Capital gains and losses as effective tests of such plans will therefore affect decisions concerning capital production in a sense in which wage fluctuations, in general, do not affect the birth-rate.

Every capital instrument is designed for a purpose. Where it is highly specific, this purpose is identical with a certain kind of (anticipated) use. Where it is "versatile,"[11] it may cover a wide range of uses. But in any case it is planned for *some* kind of use, and failure to succeed in any of them as reflected in loss of earning power will result in revision of plan. At the moment at which a new machine is installed in a factory, one production plan impinges upon another. If the second plan, in which our machine is in use, fails, there will be repercussions on the first kind of plan: fewer such machines will be produced.

4

We have seen that if capital is to be regarded as a homogeneous aggregate, all its constituent elements have to be perfect substitutes. But the complementarity of capital resources (plant, equipment, working capital) is a fact of experience. Hence, if we are to take account of it, we have to give up the "aggregative" conception of capital in favour of a structural conception. But if capital is to be regarded as a structure, what determines its shape? We have to allow for the heterogeneity of different capital resources which now have different functions. But what determines the character of these functions?

The shape of the capital structure is determined by the network of production plans. Each production plan utilizes a given combination of factors. The proportions in which factors enter a combination, the coefficients of production, express the mode of factor complementarity in it. More particularly, the proportions in which the various capital resources enter it express the mode of capital complementarity in it, what we shall call the *capital coefficients*. The capital coefficients in each combination are thus the ultimate determinants of the capital structure, at least in equilibrium. In disequilibrium the degree of consistency between plans is a modifying factor.

Strictly speaking, of course, a capital structure in our sense can only exist in equilibrium, where all plans are consistent with each other, and the network of plans displays the firm outline of a clear and distinguishable pattern. But in dynamic reality this structure is in a state of continuous transformation. As production plans prove inconsistent and fail, the outline of our pattern becomes inevitably blurred. Plans have to be revised, new combinations formed, old combinations disintegrate, even those which persist have to undergo an often drastic modification of their factoral composition.[12] In reality the coefficients of production are ever changing. Every day the network of production plans is torn, every day it is mended anew. Under these circumstances we shall find some, at least temporarily, unutilized capital resources while others are scarce. In any case, in the world of our daily experience all unexpected change entails more or less extensive capital regrouping.[13]

The theory of capital has therefore every reason to occupy itself with the network of production plans. It is readily seen how failure of plans affects investment decisions and how, broadly speaking, complementarity serves as an amplifier of *internal* capital change. These phenomena of internal capital change the theory of capital neglects at its peril. Unfortunately, scant attention is paid to them in most of the economic thought of our time,[14] which, as regards capital change, seems almost exclusively preoccupied with problems of investment, i.e., problems of *external* capital change. Interrelations between internal and external changes are almost completely ignored.[15]

We now must pause for a moment and contemplate our results against the background of traditional capital theory. We have tried to show that a theory of capital based on a notion of homogeneity is bound to miss our problem entirely. It is to a structural conception of capital that we have to look for encouragement and inspiration. But in the sphere of human action Structure implies Function, and Function, where a number of factors is involved, implies co-ordination and complementarity.

Such a structural conception of capital is to be found in the system of Böhm-Bawerk. Contrary to what appears to be a widely held view, Böhm-Bawerk's chief contribution to the theory of capital was not the introduction of *time,* but of *complementarity over time.* Here, to be sure, the "stock of real capital" becomes a flow, but not a homogeneous flow. Its elements, the individual capital goods, are not, like drops of water, perfect substitutes, but each has its place in the flow. If it is true that Böhm-Bawerk's "stock of intermediate products" is essentially a wage fund in motion, we must remember that its different elements move at different speeds.

Hides, leather, and shoes in wholesale stocks, are not just physically similar goods at different points of time, but *products* at different stages of processing. And "processing" requires the existence of a production plan in which complementary factors come into operation in accordance with a time schedule. Time is relevant here as the dimension of processing, the medium of complementarity. Thus, what really matters is not time, but complementarity over time. On the other hand, under the stationary conditions characteristic of Böhm-Bawerk's system all capital instruments in

existence at the same point of time are necessarily complements. Thus, whatever their position in time, all capital instruments are linked together by complementarity.[16]

We may say that within the realm of capital complementarity is an all-pervasive fact, at least as long as equilibrium is maintained.

If we regard capital as a complex structure the pattern
of which is determined by the proportions in which the various capital resources co-operate in productive processes, it
follows that all capital change, including new investment, is
bound to modify the structure. Under these circumstances
it is difficult to see how there could be "widening," or even
"deepening" of capital. As Professor Hayek has shown,
"widening," i.e., the multiplication of existing equipment, is,
for the whole economic system, impossible in the absence
of unused resources, while it is possible in some industries
at the expense of other industries. "For the economic system
as a whole the first of these alternatives is possible only if
there is a labor reserve available. But in any particular industry the required additional labor may be attracted from
another industry."[17]

Now, as we shall see in the next section, the existence
of unemployed labor and unutilized resources is very important for the dynamics of capital, because they provide
potential complements for the new productive combinations. But in their absence there can be no capital change
which leaves coefficients of production unaffected. "Widening" of capital in some industries must be accompanied by
disintegration of existing factor combinations elsewhere.
The contrary impression is evidently due to the habit of
confining our attention in matters of capital to what happens in a few expanding industries. The notion of capital
"widening" is apparently an empirical generalization of the
well-known fact that the accumulation of capital as a rule
takes the form of successive growth of new industries, and
that at each moment a few expanding industries appear to

bear the brunt of it. We may accept this empirical generalization, but the impression that we may safely neglect what happens elsewhere, is nevertheless mistaken. Furthermore, even capital "deepening" is bound to modify not only the coefficients of production as far as labor and capital are concerned, but the capital coefficients. It is hard to imagine cases in which the proportion of capital assets to other factors increases while relative proportions of plant, machinery, tools, raw materials, etc., remain constant.

In other words, there can be no major change which leaves the existing structure and composition of capital intact. All such change tends to create situations in which there is too much of some capital assets and too little of others. In this fact lies the ultimate reason for that instability of the "capitalistic" economy which so many deplore and so few understand.

5

We shall now test the efficiency of the analytical tools we have forged by applying them to a problem which in recent years has become a focus of economic controversy, viz., the effect of the accumulation of capital on profits and the inducement to invest. According to a powerful school of thought this effect is bound to be depressing. As more and more capital is accumulated, investment opportunities gradually become exhausted and the rate of profit declines. "*Other things being equal, the marginal efficiency of capital will be lower the greater the amount of capital goods already possessed.*" (Author's italics.)[18] We shall endeavor to show that the accumulation of capital gives rise to processes which make it impossible for "other things" to remain equal. On the other hand, Professor Hayek has pointed out that there are cases in which investment actually raises the demand for capital.[19] An obvious example would be a copper mine in Central

Africa in which we could not even begin to sink capital without having first built a railway from the coast.

It is clear that the issue hinges on complementarity and substitution. The "depressionists" evidently regard capital as a homogeneous aggregate; each unit of capital is a perfect substitute for every other unit, and accumulation means essentially an addition of further units to a preexisting homogeneous stock. It is equally evident that Professor Hayek's view is based on complementarity. The "investment that raises the demand for capital" is investment in capital goods complementary to those to be constructed later.

The question now confronting us is, which of the two rival influences, the stimulating influence of complementarity or the depressing effect of substitutability, will on balance prevail within the economic system. At first sight it might be thought that, as complementarity is all-pervasive while substitution will probably be confined to a few expanding industries in which new capital goods are installed, the former influence will prevail. But this would be a premature conclusion based on an unwarranted use of *ceteris paribus* assumptions. For the effect of new capital assets on the capital structure is not confined to those sectors in which they are installed and their immediate neighborhood. By its effect on the coefficients of production, the breaking-up of existing combinations, and the formation of new ones, the accumulation of capital affects the whole economic system. But its *modus operandi* is gradual, depends in each case on the composition of the factor combinations affected, and is certainly very different from that usually assumed in capital theories based on the notion of homogeneity. We shall illustrate it by an example.

Let us assume that there is an increase of capital in the film[20] industry. More cameras, studio equipment, etc., are produced and installed. The greater number of films produced makes it necessary to have more cinemas[24] (complements). As film rentals fall cinema earnings rise. To the extent to which there is unemployed labor and unutilized resources new cinemas will be built. But this may be possible only within fairly narrow limits. The typical location of cinemas is in the central sector of urban areas where as a rule there are no empty spaces. Any considerable rise in cinema earnings, together probably with some decline in the demand for other forms of entertainment,[22] *will thus* cause existing capital equipment to be turned over to new uses. Theaters, ice rinks, dance halls, will be converted into cinemas. Existing factor combinations, house-cum-theatre, house-cum-ice rink, etc., will disintegrate. But while rents earned on such buildings will increase, considerable capital losses will be suffered on theatrical settings and costumes, freezing equipment, and musical instruments. In fact, unless these can be sold to somebody able to fit them into a new combination, they may altogether lose their capital character and become scrap. On the other hand, owners of "free" capital instruments complementary to them are now able to get them at "bargain prices" permitting large capital gains.

The accumulation of capital will therefore have what we may term a "chain reaction" effect. The initial change entails a sequence of subsequent changes as the final result of which the structure of capital becomes modified. The new capital instruments cause the disintegration of existing combinations, increase the earning power of elements complementary to them, and set free those for which they are substitutes. The latter will either lose their capital character or have to seek out other complements, new partners with whom to enter into new combinations. For this they depend on the existence of, at least temporarily, "free," i.e., unutilized capital goods, or on the breaking-up of other existing combinations. But the disintegration of the latter, by setting free some elements, would again create the same problem. The process will continue until all discarded factors have either found their way to the scrap-heap, or found "free" partners, or found owners willing to wait and hold them until a complement turns up.

This conclusion incidentally throws new light on the vexed problem of "excess capacity." We now realize that in a world of dynamic change unused resources have two functions. Firstly, they act as shock-absorbers when combinations disintegrate. Secondly, their existence provides an inducement to invest in those capital goods which are complementary to them.

We may therefore conclude that the production of new capital instruments will have different effects on the earnings of different existing capital resources. Those to which they are complements will earn more, those for which they are substitutes will earn less and often nothing at all. To ask what is the effect of the accumulation of capital on "the" rate of profit is to ask a meaningless question, since one of its main effects is to make rates of profit diverge. If in equilibrium it is possible to speak of "a" rate of profit, the accumulation of capital will destroy such equilibrium.

6

We may now briefly survey the chief results of our enquiry.

Our first result, and the most general, is the inadequacy of static equilibrium methods in the theory of capital which clearly emerges as an eminently dynamic discipline. The concept of complementarity, which originated in a static three-commodity world, with a given system of wants, does not stand up well to its transplantation into the sphere of dynamics, and is not very well suited to the kind of plan analysis appropriate in this sphere.[23] At any rate, factor complementarity and product complementarity cannot be treated on the same level.

Secondly, it is useless to treat capital change as quantitative change in one factor under *ceteris paribus* conditions, when it is plain that at least some *cetera* will not remain *paria*. What is really needed is a new type of sequence analysis which enables us to follow up, sector by sector, the chain of changes set in motion by the impact of the original change. We may add that this applies at least as much to technical progress as to the accumulation of capital.

Thirdly, *internal capital change*, the regrouping of existing capital resources in response to unforeseen change, emerges as by far the most important topic of capital theory, although in present-day economic thought it is almost completely ignored. Undue preoccupation with mere *external* capital change, like investment, preferably in quantifiable money value terms, in the discussion of which internal repercussions are neglected, is seen to lead us nowhere. Furthermore, the question of the effect of the accumulation of capital on "the" rate of profit and the inducement to invest now appears as a meaningless question. Some profits will rise, some will fall. Unforeseen change always engenders capital gains and losses. It remains a question of some interest, to what extent the expectation of such gains and losses influences the inducement to invest. But in any case the installing of new capital instruments cannot meaningfully be regarded as "growth" of anything concrete or measurable. For it is bound to entail the, at least partial, destruction of some existing capital values.

Finally, if all this is important for the theory of capital, it is of equal, if not greater, importance to the theory of industrial fluctuations. Perhaps the concept of net investment pure and simple, as chief motor of economic change, has by now yielded us all that it is ever likely to yield. Between 1900 and 1915 economists like Cassel, Spiethoff, and Professor Robertson, basing their conclusions, not on alleged "psychological laws," but on a study of the actual events of the time, laid the foundations of a theory which takes account of intersectional maladjustment as a result of disproportionate growth of different groups of capital resources. The overinvestment theories currently in fashion are now seen to be fallacious. But what are we to substitute for them? This problem of factor substitution in economic theory will, if we may hazard a guess, occupy economists for many a day to come.

Notes

Reprinted from *Economica* 14 (May, 1947).

1. In the realm of statics the theory of marginal productivity is, of course, a set of variations on this theme. In dynamics, on the other hand, most of Professor Hayek's work implies complementarity of different capital resources. What constituted the novelty was the explicit introduction of complementarity into dynamics.
2. "Professor Hicks' Statics," *Quarterly Journal of Economics* 54 (February, 1940): 277–97.
3. Oscar Lange, "Complementarity and Interrelations of Shifts in Demand," *Review of Economic Studies* 8 (October, 1940): 58-63.
4. *Price Flexibility and Employment*, 1944, p. 9n.
5. R. F. Harrod, "Review of Oscar Lange's *Price Flexibility and Employment*," *Economic Journal* 56 (March, 1946): 102–7.
6. Ibid.
7. *Value and Capital*, p. 98. Cf. also J. R. Hicks, *Théorie mathématique de la valeur* (Paris: Hermann & Lie, 1937), p. 49.
8. "The Interrelations of Shifts in Demand," *Review of Economic Studies* 12 (1944): 73.
9. The factor in question may have to be taken out of another plan, or may be temporarily unemployed, or may be newly created for the purpose.
10. Walras's "coefficients de fabrication." Cf. his *Éléments d'économie politique pure*, éd. défin., 1926, pp. 211–12.
11. The term is due to Dr. G. L. Shackle. Cf. F. A. Hayek, *Pure*

Theory of Capital (London: Routledge & Kegan Paul, 1941), p. 251n.

12. The revision of plans is the function of the entrepreneur, the carrying out of existing plans is the function of the manager.

13. Some economic and financial aspects of capital regrouping are discussed in "Finance Capitalism?" *Economica 11* (May, 1944): 64–73.

14. Professor Hayek's work is, of course, the outstanding exception.

15. For example: "The prices of *existing* [author's italics] assets will always adjust themselves to changes in expectation concerning the prospective value of money. The significance of such changes in expectation lies in their effect on the readiness to produce *new* [author's italics] assets through their reaction on the marginal efficiency of capital." J. M. Keynes, *General Theory of Employment, Interest, and Money* (New York: Harcourt, Brace & World, 1936), p. 142. In other words, changes in expectations have no significance for the regrouping of existing capital assets.

16. Böhm-Bawerk's "third ground," the higher productivity of roundabout processes, lends itself easily to interpretation in terms of complementarity over time.

17. *The Pure Theory of Capital,* p. 286.

18. J. R. Hicks, "Mr. Keynes' Theory of Employment," *Economic Journal* 46 (June, 1936): 249.

19. "Investment That Raises the Demand for Capital," *Review of Economic Statistics* 19 (November 1937): 174–77. (Now reprinted in F. A. Hayek, *Profits, Interest, and Investment* [London: G. Routledge & Sons, 1939], pp. 73–82.)

20. It is not necessary to assume that the film industry is the only expanding industry. But we have accepted the empirical generalization that at each moment current accumulation is likely to show itself prominently in a few expanding industries. What we wish to rule out, and would regard as highly unrealistic, is an increase of capital in all industries in the same proportions.

21. We assume that total demand increases *pari passu* with total supply. It is, of course, possible to deduce the depressing

effect of accumulation merely from the postulate that total demand falls short of total supply, as "the marginal propensity to consume is always less than one." But there is no reason to believe that this is necessarily so. Cf. A. F. Burns, *Economic Research and the Keynesian Thinking of Our Times* (26th Annual Report of the Nat. Bureau of Economic Research, June, 1946, pp. 18–19).

22. That total demand increases *pari passu* with total supply does not entail that this will be so in every market.

23. In this respect, the discovery of the fact that "sympathetic shifts," i.e., dynamic demand changes, are liable to throw our whole system into indeterminacy, should have served us as a warning.

24
Ludwig von Mises and the Theory of Capital and Interest

Israel M. Kirzner

Students of Misesian economics often agree that the theory of capital and interest occupies a central and characteristically Austrian position in the general Misesian system. That is the reason Frank H. Knight, in his lengthy and critical review article of the first complete exposition of that system,[1] chose to concentrate on "the theory of capital and interest" after deciding to confine his review to "some one main problem which at once is peculiarly central in the structure of theory, and on which [his] disagreement with the author reaches down to basic premises and methods."[2] In that article Knight identified Mises as the foremost exponent of the Austrian position on capital and interest. In a 1945 article Friedrich A. Hayek also alluded to Mises as the most thoroughgoing among the Austrians on these problems.[3]

And yet, in his published works, Mises appears to have devoted little attention to the theories of capital and interest until relatively late in his career. His influence on these matters was largely confined to his oral teaching and seminar discussions. As late as 1941 (presumably without having seen Mises's *Nationalökonomie*, published in 1940), Hayek re-

---

Reprinted from *The Economics of Ludwig von Mises*, edited by Laurence S. Moss (Kansas City: Sheed and Ward, Inc., 1976).

marked in his *Pure Theory of Capital* that, while Mises's "published work deals mainly with the more complex problems that only arise beyond the point at which [this book] ends," Mises had nonetheless "suggested some of the angles from which the more abstract problem is approached [in this book]."[4]

Apart from a 1931 *Festschrift* paper on inconvertible capital,[5] Mises's published work on capital and interest prior to 1940 is confined (apart from casual *obiter dicta*) to a few brief pages in his *Socialism.*[6] On the other hand, there is an intriguing, somewhat cryptic footnote in the second (1924) edition of his *Theory of Money and Credit.*[7] It makes clear that since 1912 Mises (1) had given much critical thought to the theory of interest, (2) now considered Eugen von Böhm-Bawerk, while "the first to clear the way that leads to understanding of the problem," nonetheless to have presented a theory that was *not* satisfactory, and (3) hoped to publish "in the not-too-distant future" his own special study of the problem. It is certainly unfortunate that Mises never published such a study and that we are forced to rely on a relatively meager collection of scattered remarks in his larger works in order to understand what he considered unsatisfactory about Böhm-Bawerk's position. Fortunately, while his later works do not include a detailed critical discussion of Böhm-Bawerk's writings, they do provide us with a complete theoretical treatment of the problems of capital and interest, thereby justifying Knight's claim that the theory of capital and interest occupies a central position in the Misesian system. In what follows I shall first summarize Mises's own views on the problems of capital and interest and then discuss the extent to which his views differed from those of Böhm-Bawerk and Knight. In so doing we shall discover that Mises's later position is, as was noted by both Knight and Hayek, characteristically and consistently Austrian.

1. Mises on Capital and on Interest

Mises's views on capital and on interest may be conveniently summarized as follows:

a. Interest is *not* the specific income derived from using capital goods;[8] nor is it "the price paid for the services of capital."[9] Instead, interest expressed the universal ("categorial") phenomenon of time preference and will therefore inevitably emerge also in a pure exchange economy without production.

b. Since production takes time, the market prices of factors of production (which tend to reflect the market prices of the consumer goods they produce) are themselves subject to considerations of time preference. Thus the market in a production economy generates interest as the excess *value* of produced goods over the appropriately discounted values of the relevant factors of production.

c. The concept of *capital* (as well as of its correlative *income*) is strictly a tool for economic calculation and hence has meaning only in the context of a market in which monetary calculation is meaningful. Thus, capital is properly defined as the (subjectively perceived) monetary value of the owner's equity in the assets of a particular business unit. *Capital* is therefore to be sharply distinguished from *capital goods*.

d. *Capital goods* are produced factors of production; they are "intermediary stations on the way leading from the very beginning of production to its final goal, the turning out of consumers' goods."[10]

e. It is decidedly *not* useful to define *capital* as the totality of capital goods. Nor does the concept of a *totality* of capital goods provide any insight into the productive process.

f. Capital goods are the results of earlier (i.e., higher) stages of production and therefore are not factors of production in their own right apart from the factors employed in their production. Capital goods have no productive power of their own that cannot be attributed to these earlier productive factors.

In his discussions about capital and interest, Mises did not, to any extent, name the specific authors with whom he took issue. As Knight observed (with respect to the entire volume that he was reviewing) Mises's exposition of capital and interest "is highly controversial in substance, and in tone, though the argument is directed toward positions, with very little debate or *Auseinandersetzung* with named authors."[11]

The hints that Mises himself gave, together with a careful comparison of Mises's own stated views with those of other capital theorists, enable us to understand how his views relate to the more widely known theories of capital and interest against which he was rebelling. Such an understanding is of the utmost importance in order to fully appreciate Mises's contribution. In the following analysis I shall indicate the points of disagreement between Mises and the two major contesting approaches of his time on the issue of capital and interest. I shall consider the Böhm-Bawerkian tradition first and then move on to review the [John Bates] Clark-Knight point of view.

2. Mises and the Böhm-Bawerkian Theory

We have already seen that, as early as 1924, Mises had indicated dissatisfaction with Böhm-Bawerk's theory. This may come as a surprise to those who—quite mistakenly— believe that the Austrian position on most questions of economic theory, and especially on the theory of capital and interest, is a monolithic one. The truth of the matter is that, while the suggestive brilliance of Böhm-Bawerk's contribution won international recognition as typifying the work of the Austrian school, it was by no means acceptable to other leading representatives of that school. It is by now well known, as reported by Joseph A. Schumpeter, that Carl Menger considered Böhm-Bawerk's theory of capital and interest to have been "one of the greatest errors ever committed."[12] Referring specifically not only to Menger but also to Friedrich von Wieser and Schumpeter himself, Hayek remarked that those "commonly regarded as the leaders of the 'Austrian school' of economics" did not accept Böhm-Bawerk's views.[13] So we should not be overly surprised at Mises's disagreement with his own mentor's teachings.

Mises's disagreements with the Böhm-Bawerkian theory reflect a consistent theme. Mises was concerned with distilling Böhm-Bawerk's basic ideas from the nonsubjective, technical, and empirical garb in which they had been presented. Mises tried to show that Böhm-Bawerk's basic ideas flowed smoothly out of his own praxeological approach, or, in other words, that they could be cast in a strictly subjectivist mold. Knight (correctly) characterized Mises as taking an extreme Austrian position on interest by refusing to attribute any explanatory role to the objective, or physical, conditions governing production in a capital-using world. As the Austrian theory of value depends on utility considerations, with no recognition accorded objective costs, so, too, Knight explained, the Misesian theory of interest depends entirely on subjective time preference, with no influence attributed to physical productivity.[14] One is reminded of Hayek's penetrating comment concerning the nature of Mises's contribution to economics. Remarking that "it is probably no exaggeration to say that every important advance in economic theory during the last hundred years was a further step in the consistent application of subjectivism,"[15] Hayek cited Mises as the economist who most consistently carried out this subjectivist development: "Probably all the characteristic features of his theories ... follow

directly ... from this central position."[16] More specifically,
Mises's theory of capital and interest is in disagreement with
Böhm-Bawerk's on the following points:

a. On the role of time: Mises, while paying tribute to the
"imperishable merits" of Böhm-Bawerk's seminal role in the
development of the time-preference theory, sharply criticized the epistemological perspective from which Böhm-
Bawerk viewed time as entering the analysis. For Böhm-
Bawerk time preference is an empirical regularity observed
through casual psychological observation. Instead, Mises
saw time preference as a "definite categorial element ...
operative in every instance of action."[17] In Mises's view,
Böhm-Bawerk's theory failed to do justice to the universality
and inevitability of the phenomenon of time preference. In
addition, Mises took Böhm-Bawerk to task for not recognizing that time should enter analysis only in the *ex ante* sense.
The role that time "plays in action consists entirely in the
choices acting man makes between periods of production
of different length. The length of time expended in the
past for the production of capital goods available today does
not count at all.... The 'average period of production' is
an empty concept."[18] It may be remarked that here Mises
identified a source of perennial confusion concerning the
role of time in the Austrian theory. Many of the criticisms
leveled by Knight and others against the Austrian theory are
irrelevant when the theory is cast explicitly in terms of the
time-conscious, *forward-looking decisions* made by producers
and consumers.[19]

b. On the role of productivity: As already mentioned,
Mises sharply deplored the concessions Böhm-Bawerk
made to the productivity theorists. To Mises it was both
unfortunate and inexplicable that Böhm-Bawerk, who in his
critical history of interest doctrines had "so brilliantly refuted" the productivity approach, himself fell, to some extent, into the same kinds of error in his *Positive Theory.*

There is some disagreement in the literature on the degree to which Böhm-Bawerk in fact allowed productivity considerations to enter his theory. The issue goes back at least to Frank A. Fetter's remark in 1902 that it "has been a surprise to many students of Böhm-Bawerk to find that he has presented a theory, the most prominent feature of which is the technical productiveness of roundabout processes. His criticism of the productivity theories of interest has been of such a nature as to lead to the belief that he utterly rejected them. ... [But] it appears from Böhm-Bawerk's later statement that he does not object to the productivity theory as a partial, but as an exclusive, explanation of interest."[20] Much later Schumpeter insisted that productivity plays only a subsidiary role in what is in fact wholly a time-preference theory.[21] It is of some interest to note that when Böhm-Bawerk considered the alternative roles for productivity in a time-conscious theory, he came out squarely for an interpretation that placed productivity and "impatience" on the same level.[22] Böhm-Bawerk made it very clear that he was not willing to identify his position with that of Fetter, who espoused a time-preference theory of interest without any mention of productivity considerations. Böhm-Bawerk remarked that "Fetter himself espouses a [theory which] places him on the outermost wing of the purely 'psychological' interest theorists—'psychological' as opposed to 'technical.' He moves into a position far more extreme than the one I occupy.... "[23]

Certainly Mises offered a theory of interest fully as "extreme" as the one developed by Fetter. Later we shall consider Mises's denial that capital productivity has any role in interest theory.

c. On the definition of capital: Böhm-Bawerk defined capital as the aggregate of intermediate products (i.e., of produced means of production)[24] and in so doing was criticized by Menger.[25] Menger sought "to rehabilitate the abstract concept of capital as the money value of the property devoted to acquisitive purposes against the Smithian concept of the 'produced means of production.'"[26] As early as his work on *Socialism* (1923), Mises emphatically endorsed the Mengerian definition.[27] In *Human Action* he pursued the question even more thoroughly though without making it explicit that he was objecting to Böhm-Bawerk's definition. Economists, Mises maintained, fall into the error of defining capital as *real capital*—an aggregate of physical things. This is not only an "empty" concept but also one that has been responsible for serious errors in the various uses to which the concept of capital has been applied.

Mises's refusal to accept the notion of capital as an aggregate of produced means of production expressed his consistent Austrian emphasis on forward-looking decision making. Menger had already argued that "the historical origin of a commodity is irrelevant from an economic point of view."[28] (Later Knight and Hayek were to claim that emphasis on the historical origins of produced means of production is a residual of the older cost-of-production perspectives and inconsistent with the valuable insight that bygones are bygones.[29]) Thus, Mises's rejection of Böhm-Bawerk's definition reflects a thoroughgoing subjective point of view.

In addition, Mises's unhappiness with the Böhm-Bawerkian notion of capital is due to his characteristically Austrian skepticism toward economic aggregates. As Mises wrote, "[The] totality of the produced factors of production is merely an enumeration of physical quantities of thousands and thousands of various goods. Such an inventory is of no use to acting. It is a description of a part of the universe in terms of technology and topography and has no reference whatever to the problems raised by the endeavors to improve human well-being."[30] Lachmann suggested that a similar objection to the questionable practice of economic aggregation may have been the reason for Menger's own sharp disagreement with Böhm-Bawerk's theory.[31]

In place of the Böhm-Bawerkian notion of capital,

Mises took over Menger's definition of the term. Thus, in *Human Action*, Mises emphasized at great length that the measurement of capital has significance only for the role it plays in economic calculation. The term denotes, therefore, an accounting concept and depends for its measurement upon a system of market prices: Mises explained that "the capital concept is operative as far as men in their actions let themselves be guided by capital accounting."[32] At another place Mises wrote: "Capital is the sum of the money equivalent of all assets minus the sum of the money equivalent of all liabilities as dedicated at a definite date to the conduct of the operations of a definite business unit."[33] It follows, in Mises's words, that capital "is inescapably linked with capitalism, the market economy. It is a mere shadow in economic systems in which there is no market exchange and no money prices of goods of all orders."[34] We shall return to several implications of Mises's substitution of the Mengerian capital concept for Böhm-Bawerk's definition.

3. Mises and the Clark-Knight Tradition

If Mises's writings on capital and interest diverge from Böhm-Bawerk's theory, they certainly imply a total rejection of the principal alternative to that tradition, the approach developed in the writings of both Clark and Knight. The Clark-Knight concept of capital and the productivity theory of interest came under sharp attack in Mises's major (later) works. As we have mentioned, Knight's review article of Mises's *Nationalökonomie* consisted almost entirely of an attack on Mises's theory of capital and interest, coupled with a restatement and clarification of his [Knight's] own position. By enumerating Mises's various objections to the Clark-Knight view, we acquire, at the same time, a more complete understanding of Mises's disagreement with Böhm-Bawerk. The reason is that the Knightian theory of interest is, as

Knight proclaimed, completely opposed to the "absolute Austrianism" of Mises's approach. And what Mises found objectionable in Böhm-Bawerk's theory were, again, just those points in it which he saw as incompatible with a consistently Austrian perspective. So that it is entirely understandable why Mises's position with regard to Böhm-Bawerk's theory is clarified by his criticisms of Clark's and Knight's views. We may group Mises's objections to the Clark-Knight position as follows:

a. The Clark-Knight concept of capital: Mises had little patience with the notion of capital as a self-perpetuating fund, which he (and others) declared to be sheer mysticism.[35] "An existence," Mises wrote, "has been attributed to 'capital,' independent of the capital goods in which it is embodied. Capital, it is said, reproduces itself and thus provides for its own maintenance. . . . All this is nonsense."[36]

It is easy to see how foreign the notion of the "automatic maintenance of capital" must have appeared to Mises. An approach that concentrates analytical attention—as Austrian economics does—on the purposive and deliberate decisions of individual human beings when accounting for all social economic phenomena must treat the notion of capital as a spontaneously growing plant as not merely factually incorrect but simply absurd.[37] Moreover Mises sensed that such Knightian ideas can lead men to quite dangerous mistakes in public policy, when they ignore the institutional framework and incentive system needed to encourage those deliberate decisions necessary for maintaining the capital stock and enhancing its continued growth.[38]

The Misesian critique of the Clark-Knight view and his endorsement of the Mengerian capital concept suggest what Mises might have said about Hicks's recent classification of the views of economists concerning the aggregate of productive assets as being either "fundist" or "materialist."[39] Mises would have rejected a fundism that, by submerging the separate physical capital goods, ends up concentrating on some supposed quality apart from the goods themselves. He would have argued that the recognition of the time-conscious plans of producers does not require that we submerge the individualities of these goods into, say, a notion such as the average period of production. And, as we have seen, he rejected out of hand the Clarkian view—in Hicks's opinion a "materialist" view—that, by abstracting from the multiperiod plans needed to generate output with capital goods, sees these goods spontaneously generating perpetual flows of net income. In fact, Mises would argue, the entire fundist-materialist debate is predicated on the quite unfortunate practice of directing attention to the aggregate of physical goods. The only useful purpose for a capital concept consists strictly in its accounting role as a tool for economic calculation—a role enormously important for the efficient operation of a productive economy. It was, Mises would insist, Böhm-Bawerk's failure to see all this (and his willingness to accept the basis for a fundist-materialist debate) that lent credence to a Clark-Knight view of the real-capital concept, which implied the mythology of a kind of fundism ("perpetual capital") that Böhm-Bawerk himself did *not* accept. In rejecting Böhm-Bawerk's definition of capital in favor of the Mengerian definition, Mises rendered the Hicksian classification inapplicable to his own work.

b. Trees and fruit: Mises's adoption of Menger's concept of capital made it possible for him to avoid the pitfalls in interest theory that stem from the *capital-income* dichotomy. In everyday lay experience the ownership of capital provides assurance of a steady income. As soon as capital is identified as some aggregate of factors of production, it becomes tempting to ascribe the steady income that capital ownership makes possible as somehow expressing the *productivity* of these factors. This has always been the starting point for productivity theories of interest. Knight's permanent-fund-of-capital view of physical capital is simply a variant of those theories that view interest as net income generated perpetually by the productivity of the abstract capital temporarily embodied in particular lumps of physical capital. The capital stock, in this view, is a permanent tree that spontaneously and continuously produces fruit (interest).[40] Mises was explicit in concluding that this erroneous view of interest results from defining capital as an aggregate of produced factors of production. "The worst outgrowth of the use of the mythical notion of real capital was that economists began to speculate about a spurious problem called the productivity of (real) capital." It was such speculation, Mises made clear, that is responsible for the "blunder" of explaining "interest as an income derived from the productivity of capital."[41]

The Mengerian concept of capital as an accounting tool enables us to steer clear of such blunders. The accounting concept comes into play only as reflecting a particular motive that calculating human beings display: "The calculating mind of the actor draws a boundary line between the consumer's goods which he plans to employ for the immediate satisfaction of his wants and the goods … which he plans to employ for providing by further acting, for the satisfaction of future wants."[42] There is no implication whatsoever that the flow of income thus achieved for consumption purposes—through the careful deployment of capital—is the automatic fruit of the productivity of capital.

c. The structure of the productive process: Perhaps at the core of Mises's rejection of the Clark-Knight productivity theory of interest lies his wholehearted support of the Mengerian insight that the productive process consists of deploying goods of higher order toward the production of goods of lower order. "It is possible to think of the producers' goods as arranged in orders according to their proximity to the consumers' good for whose production they can be used. Those producers' goods which are the nearest to the production of a consumers' good are ranged in the second order, and accordingly those, which are used for the production of goods of the second order, in the third order and so on."[43] The purpose of such a scheme of classification is to demonstrate "how the valuation and the prices of the goods of higher orders are dependent on the valuation and the prices of the goods of lower orders produced by their expenditure."[44] This fundamental approach to the pricing of productive factors is able, Mises explained, to lay aside the reasoning of the productivity theorists. *The prices of capital goods must reflect the services expected from their future employment.*[45] In the absence of time preference the price of a piece of land (or of a capital good)—that is, the price in terms of consumer goods—would equal the undiscounted sum of the marginal values of the future services attributed to it. The productive capacity of a factor cannot (without time preference) account for a flow of interest income on its market value. The phenomenon of interest arises because, as a result of time preference, factor prices reflect only the *discounted* values of their services. "As production goes on, the factors of production are transformed or ripen into present goods of a higher value."[46] For Mises, the important economic characteristic of capital goods is not merely that they can be employed in future production, but that the relationship they bear to their future products is one of higher-order goods to goods of lower order. It is this factor that vitiates the productivity theory.

Knight's refusal to grant merit to this reasoning must be seen as a consequence of rejecting Menger's position that factors of production are really *higher-order* goods. "Perhaps the most serious defect in Menger's economic system ... is his view of production as a process of converting goods of higher order into goods of lower order."[47] Because of Knightian view of the productive process emphasizes the repetitive "circular flow" of economic activity while denying the paramount importance of a *structural order* linked to final consumer demand, it is possible to simply ignore the Austrian critique of the productivity theory of interest. In essence, this is what Knight did.

4. Mises, Capitalists and Entrepreneurship

One final observation concerning Mises's theory of capital and interest is in order. At all times Mises stressed what he termed the "integration of catallactic functions" that takes place in the real world. Real-world capitalists, Mises constantly reminds us, must of necessity—like landowners, laborers, and consumers—be also *entrepreneurs.* "A capitalist [besides investing funds] is always also virtually an entrepreneur and speculator. He always runs the chance of losing his funds."[48] It follows that "interest stipulated and paid in loans includes not only originary interest but also entrepreneurial profit."[49]

In other words, entrepreneurship exists in capital-using production processes, not only in the usual sense that an entrepreneur-producer borrows or otherwise assembles capital as part of his entrepreneurial function, but also in the more subtle sense that the capitalists themselves, in lending their capital to entrepreneur-producers, are necessarily acting "entrepreneurially." While this does not prevent us from analytically isolating the pure capitalist and pure entrepreneurial functions, it does mean that in the real world originary interest and entrepreneurial profit are never found in isolation from one another.

Notes

1. Ludwig von Mises, *Nationalökonomie: Theorie des Handelns und Wirtschaftens* (Geneva: Editions Union, 1940).
2. Frank H. Knight, "Professor Mises and the Theory of Capital," *Economica* 8 (November, 1941): 410.

3. Friedrich A. Hayek, "Time-Preference and Productivity: A Reconsideration," *Economica* 12 (February, 1945): 22.
4. Friedrich A. Hayek, *Pure Theory of Capital* (London: Routledge & Kegan Paul, 1941), p. 45.
5. Ludwig von Mises, "Das festangelegte Kapital," in *Economische Opstelen: Aangeboden aan Prof. Dr. C.A. Verrijn Stuart* (Haarlem: De Erven F. Bohn N.V., 1931), pp. 214–28; also in *Epistemological Problems of Economics,* trans. George Reisman (Princeton: D. Van Nostrand, 1960), pp. 217–310. For bibliographical information on Mises's works I am indebted to Bettina Bien [Greaves], *The Works of Ludwig von Mises* (Irvington-on-Hudson, NY: Foundation for Economic Education, 1969).
6. Ludwig von Mises, *Socialism: An Economic and Sociological Analysis* (New Haven: Yale University Press, 1959), pp. 142–43.
7. Ludwig von Mises. *The Theory of Money and Credit* (New Haven: Yale University Press, 1959), p. 339, and esp. p. 24.
8. Ludwig von Mises, *Human Action: A Treatise on Economics* (Chicago: Henry Regnery, 1966), p. 524.
9. Ibid., p. 526.
10. Ibid., p. 493.
11. Knight, "Professor Mises," p. 409.
12. See Joseph A. Schumpeter, *History of Economic Analysis* (New York: Oxford University Press, 1954), p. 847. See also Erich Streissler and W. Weber, "The Menger Tradition," in *Carl Menger and the Austrian School of Economics,* ed. J. R. Hicks (Oxford: Clarendon Press, 1973), p. 231.
13. Hayek, *Pure Theory of Capital,* p. 46n. For Hayek's criticisms of Böhm-Bawerk's work, see ibid., pp. 414–23. A critique of Böhm-Bawerk by an "Austrian" theorist may be found in Ludwig M. Lachmann, *Capital and Its Structure* (London: London School of Economics and Political Science, 1956). 14. Knight, "Professor Mises," pp. 422.
15. Friedrich A. Hayek, *The Counter- Revolution of Science: Studies on the Abuse of Reason* (Glencoe, IL: Free Press, 1955), p. 31.
16. Ibid., p. 210, note 24.
17. Mises, *Human Action,* p. 488. See also Ludwig von Mises, *Epis-*

temological Problems of Economics, trans. George Reisman (Princeton: D. Van Nostrand, 1960), p. 31.

18. Mises, *Human Action,* pp. 499–89.
19. See Israel M. Kirzner, *An Essay on Capital*(New York: Augustus Kelly, 1966), pp. 79, 99.
20. Frank A. Fetter, "The 'Roundabout Process' in the Interest Theory," *Quarterly Journal of Economics* 17 (November, 1902): 177.
21. Schumpeter, *History of Economic Analysis,* pp. 931–32.
22. Eugen von Böhm-Bawerk, *History and Critique of Interest Theories,* vol. 1, *Capital and Interest,* trans. George D. Huncke and Hans F. Sennholz South Holland, IL: Libertarian Press, 1959), p. 482, note 112.
23. Ibid., p. 476, note 14.
24. Ibid., pp. 14, 32.
25. Carl Menger, "Zur Theorie des Kapitlas," (Conrad's) *Jahrbucher fur Nationalökonomie und Statistik* (Jena: Gustav Fischer Verlag, 1888), 17.
26. Friedrich A. Hayek, "Carl Menger," in *Grundsätze der Volkswirtschaftslehre,* Scarce Tracts in Economics and Political Science, 1934), p. xxvi.
27. Mises, *Socialism,* pp. 123, 142.
28. Hayek, "Carl Menger," p. xxvi.
29. Hayek, *Pure Theory of Capital,* p. 89.
30. Mises, *Human Action,* p. 263.
31. More precisely Lachmann suggested that Menger was objecting to the notion of the homogenization of capital (Ludwig M. Lachmann, "Sir John Hicks as Neo-Austrian," *South African Journal of Economics* 41 [September, 1973] 205).
32. Mises, *Human Action,* p. 515.
33. Ibid., p. 262.
34. Ludwig von Mises, *Human Action: A Treatise on Economics,* 2nd ed. rev. (New Haven: Yale University Press, 1963), p. 515. [In the 1966 edition the second line of this quotation is omitted.—Ed.]
35. For a listing of writers who have ascribed "mysticism" or "mythology" to the Clark-Knight concept of capital, see Kirzner, *An Essay on Capital,* p. 59.

36. Mises, *Human Action*, p. 515.
37. As Knight did in his well-known "Crusonia Plant" example (Frank H. Knight, "Diminishing Returns from Investment," *Journal of Political Economy* 52 [March, 1944]: 29).
38. Mises, *Human Action*, p. 844.
39. See John R. Hicks, "Capital Controversies: Ancient and Modern," *American Economic Review* 64 (May, 1974): 308–10. According to Hicks, "fundists" are those who see capital as something apart from the physical goods of which it happens to consist at a particular time. The "materialists" are those who refuse to see capital in any sense other than the physical goods that make it up. Hicks's terminology here is quite unfortunate and may lead to a misunderstanding of his own thesis. From what has been said in the text, it would seem that Clark and Knight are what Hicks meant when he spoke of "fundists." It turns out, however, that Hicks classified them as "materialists"! The Austrian school (which is vehemently opposed to the Clark-Knight notion of capital as a self-perpetuating fund) turns out, in Hick's classification, to be "fundist" because it viewed the stock of capital goods in terms of the multiperiod future plans in which they enter. The Clark-Knight notion of capital as a fund is therefore quite different from the Austrian notion of a fund. Clearly, in the Clark-Knight view, capital goods are not the representatives of *plans* for future production processes but rather permanent sources of automatic income flow.
40. See note 37 above.
41. Mises, *Human Action*, p. 263.
42. Ibid., p. 260.
43. Ibid., p. 94.
44. Ibid.
45. Ibid., p. 263–64.
46. Ibid., p. 525.
47. Frank H. Knight, "Introduction," in Carl Menger, *Principles of Economics*, trans. James Dingwall and Bert F. Hoselitz (Glencoe, IL: Free Press, 1950), p. 25.
48. Mises, *Human Action*, p. 253.
49. Ibid., p. 536.

Part V

The Austrian Theory of Money
and the Business Cycle

25

On the Origin of Money

Carl Menger

I. Introduction

There is a phenomenon which has from of old and in
a peculiar degree attracted the attention of social philosophers and practical economists, the fact of certain commodities (these being in advanced civilizations coined pieces of
gold and silver, together subsequently with documents representing those coins) becoming universally acceptable media of exchange. It is obvious even to the most ordinary
intelligence, that a commodity should be given up by its
owner in exchange for another more useful to him. But that
every economic unit in a nation should be ready to exchange
his goods for little metal disks apparently useless as such,
or for documents representing the latter, is a procedure so
opposed to the ordinary course of things, that we cannot
well wonder if even a distinguished thinker like Savigny
finds it downright "mysterious."

It must not be supposed that the *form* of coin, or document, employed as current-money, constitutes the enigma
in this phenomenon. We may look away from these forms
and go back to earlier stages of economic development, or
indeed to what still obtains in countries here and there,
where we find the precious metals in an uncoined state serv-

Reprinted from *The Economic Journal* (June, 1892).

ing as the medium of exchange, and even certain other commodities, cattle, skins, cubes of tea, slabs of salt, cowrieshells, etc.; still we are confronted by this phenomenon, still we have to explain why it is that the economic man is ready to accept a certain kind of commodity, *even if he does not need it, or if his need of it is already supplied,* in exchange for all the goods he has brought to market, while it is none the less what he needs that he consults in the first instance, with respect to the goods he intends to acquire in the course of his transactions.

And hence there runs, from the first essays of reflective contemplation in social phenomena down to our own times, an uninterrupted chain of disquisition upon the nature and specific qualities of money in its relations to all that constitutes traffic. Philosophers, jurists, and historians, as well as economists, and even naturalists and mathematicians, have dealt with this notable problem, and there is no civilized people that has not furnished its quota to the abundant literature thereon. What is the nature of those little disks or documents, which in themselves seem to serve no useful purpose, and which nevertheless, in contradiction to the rest of experience, pass from one hand to another in exchange for the most useful commodities, nay, for which everyone is so eagerly bent on surrendering his wares? Is money an organic member in the world of commodities, or is it an economic anomaly? Are we to refer its commercial currency and its value in trade to the same causes conditioning those of other goods, or are they the distinct product of convention and authority?

II. Attempts at Solution Hitherto

Thus far it can hardly be claimed for the results of investigation into the problem above stated, that they are commensurate either with the great development in historic research generally, or with the outlay of time and intellect expanded in efforts at solution. The enigmatic phenomenon of money is even at this day without an explanation that satisfies; nor is there yet agreement on the most fundamental questions of its nature and functions. Even at this day we have no satisfactory theory of money.

The idea which lay first to hand for an explanation of the specific function of money as a universal current medium of exchange, was to refer it to a general convention, or a legal dispensation. The problem, which science has here to solve, consists in giving an explanation of a general, homogeneous course of action pursued by human beings when engaged in traffic, which, taken concretely, makes unquestionably for the common interest, and yet which seems to conflict with the nearest and immediate interests of contracting individuals. Under such circumstances what could lie more contiguous than the notion of referring the foregoing procedure to causes lying outside the sphere of individual considerations? To assume that certain commodities, the precious metals in particular, had been exalted into the medium of exchange by general convention or law, in the interest of the commonweal, solved the difficulty, and solved it apparently the more easily and naturally inasmuch as the shape of the coins seemed to be a token of state regulation. Such in fact is the opinion of Plato, Aristotle, and the Roman jurists, closely followed by the mediaval writers. Even the more modern developments in the theory of money have not in substance got beyond this standpoint.[1]

Tested more closely, the assumption underlying this theory gave room to grave doubts. An event of such high and universal significance and of notoriety so inevitable, as the establishment by law or convention of a universal medium of exchange, would certainly have been retained in the memory of man, the more certainly inasmuch as it would have had to be performed in a great number of places. Yet no historical monument gives us trustworthy tidings of any transactions either conferring distinct recognition on media of exchange already in use, of referring to their adoption by peoples of comparatively recent culture, much less testifying to an initiation of the earliest ages of economic civilization in the use of money.

And in fact the majority of theorists on this subject do not stop at the explanation of money as stated above. The peculiar adaptability of the precious metals for purposes of currency and coining was noticed by Aristotle, Xenophon, and Pliny, and to a far greater extent by John Law, Adam Smith and his disciples, media of exchange, in their special qualifications. Nevertheless it is clear that the choice of the precious metals by law and convention, even if made in consequence of their peculiar adaptability for monetary purposes, presupposes the pragmatic origin of money, and selection of those metals, and that presupposition is unhistorical. Nor do even the theorists above mentioned honestly face the problem that is to be solved, to wit, the explaining how it has come to pass that certain commodities (the precious metals at certain stages of culture) should be promoted amongst the mass of all other commodities, and accepted as the generally acknowledged media of exchange. It is a question concerning not only the origin but also the nature of money and its position in relation to all other commodities.

III. The Problem of the Genesis of a Medium of Exchange

In primitive traffic the economic man is awaking but very gradually to an understanding of the economic advantages to be gained by exploitation of existing opportunities of exchange. His aims are directed first and foremost, in accordance with the simplicity of all primitive culture, only at what lies first to hand. And only in that proportion does the value in use of the commodities he seeks to acquire, come into account in his bargaining. Under such conditions each man is intent to get by way of exchange just such goods as he directly needs, and to reject those of which he has no need at all, or with which he is already sufficiently provided. It is clear then, that in these circumstances the number of bargains actually concluded must lie within very narrow limits. Consider how seldom it is the case, that a commodity owned by somebody is of less value in use than another commodity owned by somebody else! And for the latter just the opposite relation is the case. But how much more seldom does it happen that these two bodies meet! Think, indeed, of the peculiar difficulties obstructing the immediate barter of goods in those cases, where supply and demand do not quantitatively coincide: where, e.g., an indivisible commodity is to be exchanged for a variety of goods in the possession of different persons, or indeed for such commodities as are only in demand at different times and can be supplied only by different persons! Even in the relatively simple and so often recurring case, where an economic unit, A, requires a commodity possessed by B, and B requires one possessed by C, while C wants one that is owned by A—even here, under a rule of mere barter, the exchange of the goods in question would as a rule be of necessity left undone.

These difficulties would have proved absolutely insurmountable obstacles to the progress of traffic, and at the same time to the production of goods not commanding a regular sale, had there not lain a remedy in the very nature of things, to wit, *the different degrees of saleabiences (Absatzfähigkeit) of commodities.* The difference existing in this respect between articles of commerce is of the highest degree of significance for the theory of money, and of the market in general. And the failure to turn it adequately to account in explaining the phenomena of trade, constitutes not only as such a lamentable breach in our science, but also one of the essential causes of the backward state of monetary theory. *The theory of money necessarily presupposes a theory of the saleableness of goods.* If we grasp this, we shall be able to understand how the almost unlimited saleableness of money is only a special case,—presenting only a difference of degree—of a generic phenomenon of economic life—namely, the difference in the saleableness of commodities in general.

IV. Commodities as More or Less Saleable

It is an error in economics, as prevalent as it is patent, that all commodities, at a definite point of time and in a given market, may be assumed to stand to each other in a definite relation of exchange, in other words, may be mutually exchanged in definite quantities at will. It is not true that in any given market 10 cwt. of one article = 2 cwt. of another = 3 lbs. of a third article, and so on. The most cursory observation of market-phenomena teaches us that it does not lie within our power, when we have bought an article for a certain price, to sell it again forthwith at that same price. If we but try to dispose of an article of clothing, a book, or a work of art, which we have just purchased, in the very same market, even though it be at once, before the same juncture of conditions has altered, we shall easily convince ourselves of the fallaciousness of such an assumption. The price at which any one can at pleasure buy a commodity at a given market and a given point of time, and the price at which he can dispose of the same at pleasure, are two essentially different magnitudes.

This holds good of wholesale as well as retail prices. Even such marketable goods as corn, cotton, pig-iron, cannot be voluntarily disposed of for the price at which we have purchased them. Commerce and speculation would be the simplest things in the world, if the theory of the "objective equivalent in goods" were correct, if it were actually true, that in a given market and at a given moment commodities could be mutually converted at will in definite quantitative relations—could, in short, at a certain price be as easily disposed of as acquired. At any rate there is no such thing as a general saleableness of wares in this sense. The truth is, that even in the best organized markets, while we may be able to purchase when and what we like at a definite price, viz.: the *purchasing price,* we can only dispose of it again when and as we like at a loss, viz.: at the *selling price.*[2]

The loss experienced by anyone who is compelled to dispose of an article at a definite moment, as compared with the current purchasing prices, is a highly variable quantity, as a glance at trade and at markets of specific commodities will show. If corn or cotton is to be disposed of at an organized market, the seller will be in a position to do so in practically any quantity, at any time he pleases, at the current price, or at most with a loss of only a few pence on the total sum. If it be a question of disposing, in larger quantities, of cloth or silk-stuffs at will, the seller will regularly have to content himself with a considerable percentage of diminution in the price. Far worse is the case of one who at a certain point of time has to get rid of astronomical instruments, anatomical preparations, Sanskrit writings, and such hardly marketable articles!

If we call any goods or wares *more or less saleable,* according to the greater or less facility with which they can be disposed of at a market at any convenient time at current purchasing prices or with less or more diminution of the same, we can see by what has been said, that an obvious difference exists in this connection between commodities. Nevertheless, and in spite of its great practical significance, it cannot be said that this phenomenon has been much taken into account in economic science. The reason of this is in part the circumstance, that investigation into the phenomena of price has been directed almost exclusively to the *quantities* of the commodities exchanged, and not as well to the greater or less *facility* with which wares may be disposed of at normal prices. In part also the reason is the thorough-going abstract method by which the saleableness of goods has been treated, without due regard to all the circumstances of the case.

The man who goes to market with his wares intends as a rule to dispose of them, by no means at any price whatever, but at such as corresponds to the greater economic situation. If we are going to inquire into the different degrees of saleableness in goods so as to show its bearing upon practical life, we can only do so by consulting the greater or less facility with which they may be disposed of at prices corresponding to the general economic situation, that is, at *economic* prices.[3] A commodity is more or less saleable according as we are able, with more or less prospect of success, to dispose of it at prices corresponding to the general economic situation, at *economic* prices.

The *interval of time*, moreover, within which the disposal of a commodity at the economic price may be reckoned on, is of great significance in an inquiry into its degree of saleableness. It matters not whether the demand for a commodity be slight, or whether on other grounds its saleableness be small; if its owner can only bide his time, he will finally and in the long run be able to dispose of it at economic prices. Since, however, this condition is often absent in the actual course of business, there arises for practical purposes an important difference between those commodities, on the one hand, which we expect to dispose of at any given time at economic, or at least approximately economic, prices, and such goods, on the other hand, respecting which we have no such prospect, or at least not in the same degree, and to dispose of which at economic prices the owner foresees it will be necessary to wait for a longer or shorter period, or else to put up with a more or less sensible abatement in the price.

Again, account must be taken of the *quantitative* factor in the saleableness of commodities. Some commodities, in consequence of the development of markets and speculation, are able at any time to find a sale in practically any quantity at economic, or approximately economic, prices. Other commodities can only find a sale at economic prices in smaller quantities, commensurate with the gradual growth of an effective demand, fetching a relatively reduced price in the case of a greater supply.

V. Concerning the Causes of the Different Degrees of Saleableness in Commodities

The degree to which a commodity is found by experience to command a sale, at a given market, at any time, at prices corresponding to the economic situation (economic prices), depends upon the following circumstances.

1. Upon the number of persons who are still in want of the commodity in question, and upon the extent and intensity of that want, which is unsupplied, or is constantly recurring.

2. Upon the purchasing power of those persons.

3. Upon the available quantity of the commodity in relation to the yet unsupplied (total) want of it.

4. Upon the divisibility of the commodity, and any other ways in which it may be adjusted to the needs of individual customers.

5. Upon the development of the market, and of speculation in particular. And finally,

6. Upon the number and nature of the limitations imposed politically and socially upon exchange and consumption with respect to the commodity in question.

We may proceed, in the same way in which we considered the degree of the saleableness in commodities at definite markets and definite points of time, to set out the *spatial and temporal limits* of their saleableness. In these respects also we observe in our markets some commodities, the saleableness of which is almost unlimited by place or time, and others the sale of which is more or less limited.

The *spatial* limits of the saleableness of commodities are mainly conditioned—

a. By the degree to which the want of the commodities is distributed in space.

b. By the degree to which the goods lend themselves to transport, and the cost of transport incurred in proportion to their value.

c. By the extent to which the means of transport and of commerce generally are developed with respect to different classes of commodities.

d. By the local extension of organized markets and their intercommunication by "arbitrage."

e. By the differences in the restrictions imposed upon commercial intercommunication with respect to different goods, in interlocal and, in particular, in international trade.

The time-limits to the saleableness of commodities are mainly conditioned—

(1) By permanence in the need of them (their independence of fluctuation in the same).

(2) Their durability, i.e., their suitableness for preservation.

(3) The cost of preserving and storing them.

(4) The rate of interest.

(5) The periodicity of a market for the same.

(6) The development of speculation and in particular of time-bargains in connection with the same.

(7) The restrictions imposed politically and socially on their being transferred from one period of time to another.

All these circumstances, on which depend the different degrees of, and the different local and temporal limits to, the saleableness of commodities, explain why it is that certain commodities can be disposed of with ease and certainty in definite markets, i.e., within local and temporal limits, at any time and in practically any quantities, at prices corre-

sponding to the general economic situation, while the saleableness of other commodities is confined within narrow
spatial, and again, temporal, limits; and even within these
the disposal of the commodities in question is difficult, and,
in so far as the demand cannot be waited for, is not to be
brought about without a more or less sensible diminution
in price.

VI. On the Genesis of Media of Exchange[4]

It has long been the subject of universal remark in centers of exchange, that for certain commodities there existed
a greater, more constant, and more effective demand than
for other commodities less desirable in certain respects, the
former being such as correspond to a want on the part of
those able and willing to traffic, which is at once universal
and, by reason of the relative scarcity of the goods in question, always imperfectly satisfied. And further, that the person who wishes to acquire certain definite goods in exchange for his own is in a more favorable position, if he
brings commodities of this kind to market, than if he visits
the markets with goods which cannot display such advantages, or at least not in the same degree. Thus equipped he
has the prospect of acquiring such goods as he finally wishes
to obtain, not only with greater ease and security, but also,
by reason of the steadier and more prevailing demand for
his own commodities, at prices corresponding to the general
economic situation—at economic prices. Under these circumstances, when any one has brought goods not highly
saleable to market, the idea uppermost in his mind is to
exchange them, not only for such as he happens to be in
need of, but, if this cannot be effected directly, for other
goods also, which, while he did not want them himself, were
nevertheless more saleable than his own. By so doing he
certainly does not attain at once the final object of his traf-

ficking, to wit, the acquisition of goods needful to *himself.*
Yet he draws nearer to that object. By the devious way of a
mediate exchange, he gains the prospect of accomplishing
his purpose more surely and economically than if he had
confined himself to direct exchange. Now in point of fact
this seems everywhere to have been the ease. Men have been
led, with increasing knowledge of their individual interests,
each by his own economic interests, without convention,
without legal compulsion, nay, even without any regard to
the common interest, to exchange goods destined for exchange (their "wares") for other goods equally destined for
exchange, but more saleable.

With the extension of traffic in space and with the expansion over ever longer intervals of time of prevision for
satisfying material needs, each individual would learn, from
his own economic interests, to take good heed that he bar-
tered his less saleable goods for those special commodities
which displayed, beside the attraction of being highly saleable in the particular locality, a wide range of saleableness
both in time and place. These wares would be qualified by
their costliness, easy transportability, and fitness for preservation (in connection with the circumstance of their corresponding to a steady and widely distributed demand), to
ensure to the possessor a power, not only "here" and "now,"
but as nearly as possible unlimited in space and time generally, over all other market-goods at economic prices.

And so it has come to pass, that as man became increasingly conversant with these economic advantages, mainly
by an insight become traditional, and by the habit of economic action, those commodities, which relatively to both
space and time are most saleable, have in every market become the wares, which it is not only in the interest of every
one to accept in exchange for his own less saleable goods,
but which also are those he actually does readily accept. And
their superior saleableness depends only upon the relatively
inferior saleableness of every other kind of commodity, by

which alone they have been able to become *generally* acceptable media of exchange.

It is obvious how highly significant a factor is habit in
the genesis of such generally serviceable means of exchange.
It lies in the economic interests of each trafficking individual to exchange less saleable for more saleable commodities.
But the willing acceptance of the medium of exchange presupposes already a knowledge of these interests on the part
of those economic subjects who are expected to accept in
exchange for their wares a commodity which in and by itself
is perhaps entirely useless to them. It is certain that this
knowledge never arises in every part of a nation at the same
time. It is only in the first instance a limited number of
economic subjects who will recognize the advantage in such
procedure, an advantage which, in and by itself, is independent of the general recognition of a commodity as a medium
of exchange, inasmuch as such an exchange, always and
under all circumstances, brings the economic unit a good
deal nearer to his goal, to the acquisition of useful things of
which he really stands in need. But it is admitted, that there
is no better method of enlightening any one about his economic interests than that he perceive the economic success
of those who use the right means to secure their own. Hence
it is also clear that nothing may have been so favorable to
the genesis of a medium of exchange as the acceptance, on
the part of the most discerning and capable economic subjects, for their own economic gain, and over a considerable
period of time, of eminently saleable goods in preference
to all others. In this way practice and habit have certainly
contributed not a little to cause goods, which were most
saleable at any time, to be accepted not only by many, but
finally by all, economic subjects in exchange for their less
saleable goods: and not only so, but to be accepted from the
first with the intention of exchanging them away again.
Goods which had thus become generally acceptable media
of exchange were called by the Germans *Geld,* from *gelten,*

i.e., to pay, to perform, while other nations derived their designation for money mainly from the substance used,[5] the shape of the coin,[6] or even from certain kinds of coin.[7]

It is not impossible for media of exchange, serving as they do the commonweal in the most emphatic sense of the word, to be instituted also by way of legislation, like other social institutions. But this is neither the only, nor the primary mode in which money has taken its origin. This is much more to be traced in the process depicted above, notwithstanding the nature of that process would be but very incompletely explained if we were to call it "organic," or denote money as something "primordial," of "primaval growth," and so forth. Putting aside assumptions which are historically unsound, we can only come fully to understand the origin of money by learning to view the establishment of the social procedure, with which we are dealing, as the spontaneous outcome, the unpremeditated resultant, of particular, individual efforts of the members of a society who have little by little worked their way to a discrimination of the different degrees of saleableness in commodities.[8]

VII. The Process of Differentiation Between Commodities Which Have Become Media of Exchange and the Rest

When the relatively most saleable commodities have become "money," the event has in the first place the effect of substantially increasing their originally high saleableness. Every economic subject bringing less saleable wares to market, to acquire goods of another sort, has thenceforth a stronger interest in converting what he has in the first instance into the wares which have become money. For such persons, by the exchange of their less saleable wares for those which as money are most saleable, attain not merely, as heretofore, a higher probability, but the certainty, of being able to acquire forthwith equivalent quantities of every other kind of commodity to be had in the market. And their control over these depends simply upon their pleasure and their choice. *Pecunian habens, habet omnem rem quem vult habere.*

On the other hand, he who brings other wares than money to market, finds himself at a disadvantage more or less. To gain the same command over what the market affords, he must first convert his exchangeable goods into money. The nature of his economic disability is shown by the fact of his being compelled to overcome a difficulty before he can attain his purpose, which difficulty does not exist for, i.e., has already been overcome by, the man who owns a stock of money.

This has all the greater significance for practical life, inasmuch as to overcome this difficulty does not lie unconditionally within reach of him who brings less saleable goods to market, but depends in part upon circumstances over which the individual bargainer has no control. The less saleable are his wares, the more certainly will he have either to suffer the penalty in the economic price, or to content himself with awaiting the moment, when it will be possible for him to effect a conversion at economic prices. He who is desirous, in an era of monetary economy, to exchange goods of any kind whatever, which are not money, for other goods supplied in the market, cannot be certain of attaining this result at once, or within any predetermined interval of time, at economic prices. And the less saleable are the goods brought by an economic subject to market, the more unfavorably, for his own purposes, will his economic position compare with the position of those who bring money to market. Consider, e.g., the owner of a stock of surgical instruments, who is obliged through sudden distress, or through pressure from creditors, to convert it into money. The prices which it will fetch will be highly accidental, nay, the goods being of such limited saleableness, they will be fairly incalculable. And this holds good of all kinds of conversions which in respect of time are compulsory sales.[9] Other is his case who wants at a market to convert the commodity, which has become *money*, forthwith into other goods supplied at that market. He will accomplish his purpose, not only with certainty, but usually also at a price corresponding to the general economic situation. Nay, the habit of economic action has made us so sure of being able to procure in return for money any goods on the market, whenever we wish, at prices corresponding to the economic situation, that we are for the most part unconscious of how many purchases we daily propose to make, which, with respect to our wants and the time of concluding them, are compulsory purchases. Compulsory sales, on the other hand, in consequence of the economic disadvantage which they commonly involve, force themselves upon the attention of the parties implicated in unmistakable fashion. What therefore constitutes the peculiarity of a commodity which has become money is, that the possession of it procures for us at any time, i.e., at any moment we think fit, assured control over every commodity to be had on the market, and this usually at prices adjusted to the economic situation of the moment: the control, on the other hand, conferred by other kinds of commodities over market goods is, in respect of time, and in part of price as well, uncertain, relatively if not absolutely.

Thus the effect produced by such goods as are relatively most saleable becoming money is an increasing differentiation between their degree of saleableness and that of all other goods. And this difference in saleableness ceases to be altogether gradual, and must be regarded in a certain aspect as something absolute. The practice of every-day life, as well as jurisprudence, which closely adheres for the most part to the notions prevalent in every-day life, distinguish two categories in the wherewithal of traffic—goods which have become money and goods which have not. And the ground of this distinction, we find, lies essentially in that difference in the saleableness of commodities set forth above—a difference so significant for practical life and which comes to be further emphasized by intervention of the state. This distinction, moreover, finds expression in language in the difference of meaning attaching to "money" and "wares," to "purchase" and "exchange." But it also affords the chief explanation of that superiority of the buyer over the seller, which has found manifold consideration, yet has hitherto been left inadequately explained.

VIII. How the Precious Metals Became Money

The commodities, which under given local and time relations are most saleable, have become money among the same nations at different times, and among different nations at the same time, and they are diverse in kind. The reason why the *precious metals* have become the generally current medium of exchange among here and there a nation prior to its appearance in history, and in the sequel among all peoples of advanced economic civilization, is because their saleableness is far and away superior to that of all other commodities, and at the same time because they are found to be specially qualified for the concomitant and subsidiary functions of money.

There is no center of population, which has not in the very beginnings of civilization come keenly to desire and eagerly to covet the precious metals, in primitive times for their utility and peculiar beauty as in themselves ornamental, subsequently as the choicest materials for plastic and architectural decoration, and especially for ornaments and vessels of every kind. In spite of their natural scarcity, they are well distributed geographically, and, in proportion to most other metals, are easy to extract and elaborate. Further, the ratio of the available quantity of the precious met-

als to the total requirement is so small, that the number of
those whose need of them is unsupplied, or at least insufficiently supplied, together with the extent of this unsupplied
need, is always relatively large—larger more or less than in
the case of other more important, though more abundantly
available, commodities. Again, the class of persons who wish
to acquire the precious metals, is, by reason of the kind of
wants which by these are satisfied, such as quite specially to
include those members of the community who can most
efficaciously barter; and thus the desire for the precious
metals is as a rule more effective. Nevertheless the limits of
the effective desire for the precious metals extend also to
those strata of population who can less effectively barter,
by reason of the great divisibility of the precious metals, and
the enjoyment procured by the expenditure of even very
small quantities of them in individual economy. Besides this
there are the wide limits in time and space of the saleableness of the precious metals; a consequence, on the one
hand, of the almost unlimited distribution in space of the
need of them, together with their low cost of transport as
compared with their value, and, on the other hand, of their
unlimited durability and the relatively slight cost of hoarding them. In no national economy which has advanced beyond the first stages of development are there any commodities, the saleableness of which is so little restricted in
such a number of respects—personally, quantitatively, spatially, and temporally—as the precious metals. It cannot be
doubted that, long before they had become the generally
acknowledged media of exchange, they were, amongst very
many peoples, meeting a positive and effective demand at
all times and places, and practically in any quantity that
found its way to market.

Hence arose a circumstance, which necessarily became
of special import for their becoming money. For any one
under those conditions, having any of the precious metals
at his disposal, there was not only the reasonable prospect

of his being able to convert them in all markets at any time and practically in all quantities, but also—and this is after all the criterion of saleableness—the prospect of converting them at prices corresponding at any time to the general economic situation, *at economic prices.* The proportionately strong, persistent, and omnipresent desire on the part of the most effective bargainers has gone farther to exclude prices of the moment, of emergency, of accident, in the case of the precious metals, than in the case of any other goods whatever, especially since these, by reason of their costliness, durability, and easy preservation, had become the most popular vehicle for hoarding as well as the goods most highly favoured in commerce.

Under such circumstances it became the leading idea in the minds of the more intelligent bargainers, and then, as the situation came to be more generally understood, in the mind of every one, that the stock of goods destined to be exchanged for other goods must in the first instance be laid out in precious metals, or must be converted into them, even if the agent in question did not directly need them, or had already supplied his wants in that direction. But in and by this function, the precious metals are already constituted generally current media of exchange. In other words, they hereby function as commodities for which every one seeks to exchange his market-goods, not, as a rule, in order to consumption but entirely because of their special saleableness, in the intention of exchanging them subsequently for other goods directly profitable to him. No accident, nor the consequence of state compulsion, nor voluntary convention of traders effected this. It was the just apprehending of their individual self-interest which brought it to pass, that all the more economically advanced nations accepted the precious metals as money as soon as a sufficient supply of them had been collected and introduced into commerce. The advance from less to more costly money-stuffs depends upon analogous causes.

This development was materially helped forward by the ratio of exchange between the precious metals and other commodities undergoing smaller fluctuations, more or less, than that existing between most other goods,—a stability which is due to the peculiar circumstances attending the production, consumption, and exchange of the precious metals, and is thus connected with the so-called intrinsic grounds determining their exchange value. It constitutes yet another reason why each man, in the first instance (i.e., till he invests in goods directly useful to him), should lay in his available exchange-stock in precious metals, or convert it into the latter. Moreover the *homogeneity* of the precious metals, and the consequent facility with which they can serve as *res fungibiles* in relations of obligation, have led to forms of contract by which traffic has been rendered more easy; this too has materially promoted the saleableness of the precious metals, and thereby their adoption as money. Finally the precious metals, in consequence of the peculiarity of their *colour,* their *ring,* and partly also of their *specific gravity,* are with some practice not difficult to recognize, and through their taking a durable stamp can be easily controlled as to quality and weight; this too has materially contributed to raise their saleableness and to forward the adoption and diffusion of them as money.

IX. Influence of the Sovereign Power

Money has not been generated by law. In its origin it is a social, and not a state-institution. Sanction by the authority of the state is a notion alien to it. On the other hand, however, by state recognition and state regulation, this social institution of money has been perfected and adjusted to the manifold and varying needs of an evolving commerce, just as customary rights have been perfected and adjusted by statute law. Treated originally by weight, like other commodities, the precious metals have by degrees attained as coins a shape by which their intrinsically high saleableness has experienced a material increase. The fixing of a coinage so as to include all grades of value (*Wertstufen*), and the establishment and maintenance of coined pieces so as to win public confidence and, as far as is possible, to forestall risk concerning their genuineness, weight, and fineness, and above all the ensuring their circulation in general, have been everywhere recognized as important functions of state administration.

The difficulties experienced in the commerce and modes of payment of any country from the competing action of the several commodities serving as currency, and further the circumstance, that concurrent standards induce a manifold insecurity in trade, and render necessary various conversions of the circulating media, have led to the legal recognition of certain commodities as money (to legal standards). And where more than one commodity has been acquiesced in, or admitted, as the legal form of payment, law or some system of appraisement has fixed a definite ratio of value amongst them.

All these measures nevertheless have not first made money of the precious metals, but have only perfected them in their function as money.

Notes

1. *Cf.* Roscher, *System der Volkswirthschaft*, I. 116; my *Grundsätze der Volkswirtschaftslehre*, 1871, p. 255, *et seq.;* M. Block, *Les Progres de la Science economique depuis A. Smith*, 1890, II., p. 59, *et seq.*
2. We must make a distinction between the higher purchasing prices for which the buyer is rendered liable through the wish to purchase at a definite point of time, and the (lower) selling prices, which he, who is obliged to get rid of goods within a definite period, must content himself withal. The smaller the

difference between the buying and selling prices of an article, the more saleable it usually proves to be.

3. The height of saleableness in a commodity is not revealed by the fact that it may be disposed of at any price whatever, including such as result from distress or accident. In this sense all commodities are pretty well equally saleable. A high rate of saleableness in a commodity consists in the fact that it may at every moment be easily and surely disposed of at a price corresponding to, or at least not discrepant from, the general economic situation—at the economic, or approximately economic, price. The price of a commodity may be denoted as *uneconomic* on two grounds: (1) in consequence of error, ignorance, caprice, and so forth; (2) in consequence of the circumstance that only a part of the supply is available to the demand, the rest for some reason or other being withheld, and the price in consequence not commensurate with the actually existing economic situation.

4. *Cf.* my article on "Money" in the *Handwörterbuch der Staatswissenschaften* (Dictionary of Social Science), Jeus, 1891, iii, p. 730 *et seq.*

5. The Hebrew *Keseph,* the Greek ἀργυριον, the Latin *argentum,* the French *argent,* &c.

6. The English *money,* the Spanish *moneda,* the Portuguese *moeda,* the French *monnaie,* the Hebrew *maoth,* the Arabic *gulus,* the Greek νόμισμα, &c.

7. The Italian *danaro,* the Russian *dengi,* the Polish *pienondze,* the Bohemian and Elavonian *penise,* the Danish *penge,* the Swedish *penningar,* the Magyar *penx,* &c. (i.e., *denare = Pfennige = penny*).

8. *Cf.* on this point my *Grundsotze der Volkswirtschaftslehrn,* 1871, p. 250 *et seq.*

9. Herein lies the explanation of the circumstance why compulsory sales, and cases of distraint in particular, involve as a rule the economic ruin of the person upon whose estate they are carried out, and that in a greater degree the less the goods in question are saleable. Correct discernment of the uneconomic character of these processes will necessarily lead to a reform in the available legal mechanism.

26

The Non-Neutrality of Money

Ludwig von Mises

The monetary economists of the sixteenth and seventeenth centuries succeeded in dissipating the popular fallacies concerning an alleged stability of money. The old error disappeared, but a new one originated, the illusion of money's neutrality.

Of course, classical economics did its best to dispose of these mistakes. David Hume, the founder of British Political Economy, and John Stuart Mill, the last in the line of classical economists, both dealt with the problem in a masterful way. And then we should not forget Cairnes, who in his essay on the course of depreciation paved the way for a realistic view of the issue involved.[1]

Notwithstanding these first steps towards a more correct grasp, modern economists incorporated the fallacy of money neutrality into their system of thought.

The reasoning of modern marginal utility economics begins from the assumption of a state of pure barter. The mechanism of exchanging commodities and of market transactions is considered on the supposition that direct exchange alone prevails. The economists depict a purely hypothetical entity, a market without indirect exchange, without a medium of exchange, without money. There is no doubt

---

Reprinted from *Money, Method and the Market Process*, edited by Richard M. Ebeling (Auburn, AL: Praxeology Press of the Ludwig von Mises Institute and Kluwer Academic Publishers, 1990).

that this method is the only possible one, that the elimination of money is necessary and that we cannot do without this concept of a market with direct exchange only. But we have to realize that it is a hypothetical concept which has no counterpart in reality. The actual market is necessarily a market of indirect exchange and money transactions.

From this assumption of a market without money, the fallacious ideal of neutral money is derived. The economists were so fond of the tool which this hypothetical concept provided that they overestimated the extent of its applicability. They began to believe that all problems of catallactics could be analyzed by means of this fictitious concept. In accordance with this view, they considered that the main work of economic analysis was the study of direct exchange. After that all that was left was to introduce the monetary terms into the formulas obtained. But this was, in their eyes, a work of only secondary importance, because, as they were convinced, the introduction of monetary terms did not affect the substantial operation of the mechanism they had described. The functioning of the market mechanism as demonstrated by the concept of pure barter was not affected by monetary factors.

Of course, the economists knew that the exchange ratio between money and commodities was subject to change. But they believed—and this is exactly the essence of the fallacy of money's neutrality—that these changes in purchasing power were brought about simultaneously in the whole market and that they affected all commodities to the same extent. The most striking expression of this point of view is to be found in the current metaphorical use of the term "level" in reference to prices. Changes in the supply or demand of money—other things remaining equal—make all prices and wages simultaneously rise or fall. The purchasing power of the monetary unit changes, but the relations among the prices of individual commodities remain the same.

Of course, economists have developed for more than a

hundred years the method of index numbers in order to measure changes in purchasing power in a world where the ratios between the prices of individual commodities are in continuous transition. But in doing so, they did not give up the assumption that the consequences of a change in the supply or demand of money were a proportional and simultaneous modification of prices. The method of index numbers was designed to provide them with a means of distinguishing between the consequences of those changes in prices which take their origins from the side of the demand for or supply of individual commodities and those which start from the side of demand for or supply of money.

The erroneous assumption of money neutrality is at the root of all endeavors to establish the formula of a so-called equation of exchange. In dealing with such an equation the mathematical economist assumes that something—one of the elements of the equation—changes and that corresponding changes in the other values must needs follow. These elements of the equation are not items in the individual's economy, but items of the whole economic system, and consequently the changes occur not with individuals but with the whole economic system, with the *Volkswirtschaft* as a whole. Proceeding thus, the economists apply unawares for the treatment of monetary problems a method radically different from the modern catallactic method. They revert to the old manner of reasoning which doomed to failure the work of older economists. In those early days philosophers dealt in their speculations with universal concepts, such as mankind and other generic notions. They asked: What is the value of gold or of iron, that is: value in general, for all times and for all people, and again gold or iron in general, all the gold or iron available or even not yet mined. They could not succeed in this way; they discovered only alleged autinomies which were insoluble for them.

All the successful achievements of modern economic theory have to be ascribed to the fact that we have learned to proceed in a different way. We realize that individuals acting in the market are never presented with the choice between all the gold existing and all the iron existing. They do not have to decide whether gold or iron is more useful for mankind as a whole, but they have to choose between two limited quantities both of which they can not have together. They decide which of these two alternatives is more favorable for them under the conditions and at the moment when they make their decision. These acts of choice performed by individuals faced with alternatives are the ultimate causes of the exchange ratios established in the market. We have to direct our attention to these acts of choice and are not at all interested in the metaphysical and purely academic, nay, vain question of which commodity in general appears more useful in the eyes of a superhuman intelligence surveying earthly conditions from a transcendental point of view.

Monetary problems are economic problems and have to be dealt with in the same way as all other economic problems. The monetary economist does not have to deal with universal entities like volume of trade meaning total volume of trade or quantity of money meaning all the money current in the whole economic system. Still less can he make use of the nebulous metaphor "velocity of circulation." He has to realize that the demand for money arises from the preferences of individuals within a market society. Because everybody wishes to have a certain amount of cash, sometimes more, sometimes less, there is a demand for money. Money is never simply in the economic system, in the *Volkswirtschaft,* money is never simply circulating. All the money available is always in the cash holding of somebody. Every piece of money may one day—sometimes oftener, sometimes more seldom—pass from one man's cash holding to another man's. But at every moment it is owned by somebody and is a part of his cash holdings. The decisions of individuals regarding the magnitude of their cash holdings constitute the ultimate factor in the formation of purchasing power.

Changes in the quantity of money and in the demand for money for cash holding do not occur in the economic system as a whole if they do not occur in the households of individuals. These changes in the households of individuals never occur for all individuals at the same time and to the same degree and they therefore never affect their judgments of value to the same extent and at the same time. It is exactly the merit of Hume and Mill that they tried to construct a hypothetical case where the changes in the supply of money could affect all individuals in such a way that the prices of all commodities would rise or fall at the same time and in the same proportion. The failure of their attempts provided a negative proof, and modern economics has added to this the positive proof that the prices of different commodities are not influenced at the same time and to the same extent. The oversimple formula both of the old quantity theory and of contemporary mathematical economists according to which prices, that is all prices, rise or fall in the proportion of the increase or decrease in the quantity of money, is disproved.

To simplify and to shorten our analysis let us look at the case of inflation only. The additional quantity of money does not find its way at first into the pockets of all individuals; not every individual of those benefited first gets the same amount and not every individual reacts to the same additional quantity in the same way. Those first benefited— in the case of gold, the owners of the mines, in the case of government paper money, the treasury—now have greater cash holdings and they are now in a position to offer more money on the market for goods and services they wish to buy. The additional amount of money offered by them on the market makes prices and wages go up. But not all the prices and wages rise, and those which do rise do not rise to the same degree. If the additional money is spent for military purposes, the prices of some commodities only and the wages of only some kinds of labor rise, others remain unchanged or may even temporarily fall. They may fall because there are now on the market some groups of men whose incomes have not risen but who nevertheless are obliged to pay more for some commodities, namely for those asked by the men first benefited by the inflation. Thus, price changes which are the result of the inflation start with some commodities and services only, and are diffused more or less slowly from one group to the others. It takes time till the additional quantity of money has exhausted all its price changing possibilities. But even in the end the different commodities are not affected to the same extent. The process of progressive depreciation has changed the income and the wealth of the different social groups. As long as this depreciation is still going on, as long as the additional quantity of money has not yet exhausted all its possibilities of influencing prices, as long as there are still prices left unchanged at all or not yet changed to the extent that they will be, there are in the community some groups favored and some at a disadvantage. Those selling the commodities or services whose prices rise first are in a position to sell at the new higher prices and to buy what they want to buy at the old still unchanged prices. On the other hand, those who sell commodities or services whose prices remain for some time unchanged are selling at the old prices whereas they already have to buy at the new higher prices. The former are making a specific gain, they are profiteers, the latter are losing, they are the losers, out of whose pockets the extra-gains of the profiteers must come. As long as the inflation is in progress, there is a perpetual shift in income and wealth from some social group, to other social groups. When all price consequences of the inflation are consummated, a transfer of wealth between social groups has taken place. The result is that there is in the economic system a new dispersion of wealth and income and in this new social order the wants of individuals are satisfied to different relative degrees, than formerly. Prices in this new order can not simply be a multiple of the previous prices.

The social consequences of a change in the purchasing power of money are twofold: first, as money is the standard of deferred payments, the relations between creditors and debtors is changed. Second, as the changes in purchasing power do not affect all prices and wages at the same moment and to the same extent, there is a shift of wealth and income between different social groups. It was one of the errors of all proposals to stabilize purchasing power that they did not take into account this second consequence. We may say that economic theory in general did not pay enough attention to this matter. As far as it did, it principally considered it only in reference to the reaction of a change in a country's currency on its foreign trade. But this is only a special application of a problem which has a much wider scope.

What is fundamental for economic theory is that there is no constant relation between changes in the quantity of money and in prices. Changes in the supply of money affect individual prices and wages in different ways. The metaphorical use of the term price level is misleading.

The erroneous opinion to the contrary was based on a consideration which may be represented thus: let us think of two absolutely independent systems of static equilibrium A and B. Both are in every respect alike except that to the total quantity of money (M) in A and to every individual cash holding (m) in A there correspond in B a total quantity of Mn and individual cash holdings mn. On these assumptions of course all the prices and wages in B are n times those in A. But they are exactly thus because these are our hypothetical assumptions. But nobody can devise a way by which the system *A* can be transformed into the system *B*. Of course it is impermissible to operate with static equilibrium if we wish to approach a dynamic problem.

Setting aside all qualms about the use of the terms dynamic and static, I wish to say: money is necessarily a dynamic agent and it was a mistake to deal with monetary problems in a static way.

Of course there is no room left for money in a concept of static equilibrium. In forming the concept of a static society we assume that no changes are taking place. Everything is going on in the same old manner. Today is like yesterday and tomorrow will be like today. But under these conditions nobody needs a cash holding. Cash holding is necessary only when the individual does not know what situation he will have to face in an uncertain future. If everybody knows when and what he will have to buy, he does not need a private cash holding and can entrust all his money to the central bank as time deposits due on the dates and in the amounts necessary for his future payments. As everybody would proceed in the same way, the central bank does not need any reserves to meet its obligations. Of course, the total amount which it has to pay out to the buyers every day exactly balances the amount which it receives as deposits from the sellers. If we assume that in this world of static equilibrium once, before the equilibrium was attained, there was metallic currency only, let us say gold, we have to assume that with the gradual approach towards conditions of equilibrium the citizens deposited more and more of their gold and that the bank, which had no need for it, sold the gold to jewelers and others for industrial consumption. With the advent of equilibrium there is no more metallic money, there is in fact no more money at all, but an unsubstantial and immaterial clearing system, which cannot be considered as money in the ordinary sense. It is rather an unrealizable and even unthinkable system of accounting, a numeraire as some economists believed ideal money ought to be. This, if it could be called money, would be neutral money. But we should never forget, that the state of equilibrium is purely hypothetical, that this concept is nothing but a tool for our mental work. Not being able to make experiments, the social sciences have to forge such tools. But we must be very careful in their use. We have to be aware that the state of static equilibrium can never be attained in real life. Still more important is the fact, that in this hypothetical state the individual does not make choices, does not act and does not have to decide between incompatible alternatives. Life in this hypothetical state is therefore robbed of its essential element. In constructing this hypothetical state we want merely to understand the incentives of action, which always implies change, by conceiving conditions, in which no action takes place. But a changeless world would be a dead world. We do not just have to deal with death, but with life, action, and change. In a living world there is no room for neutrality of money.

Money, of course, is a dynamic factor and as such cannot be discussed in terms of static equilibrium.

Let me now briefly point out some of the major conclusions derived from an insight into the non-neutrality of money.

First we have to realize that the abandonment of the fallacious concept of neutral money destroys the last stronghold of the advocates of quantitative economics. For a very long time eminent economists have believed that it will be possible one day to replace qualitative economics by quantitative economics. What renders these hopes vain, is the fact, that in economic quantities we never have any constant ratios among magnitudes. What the economist discovers when he studies relations between demand and prices is not comparable with the work of the natural scientist who determines by experiments in his laboratory constant relations, e.g., the specific gravity of different substances. What the economist determines is of historical value only; he is in his statistical work a historian, but not an experimenter. The work of the late lamented Henry Schultz[2] was economic history; what we learn from his research is what happened with some commodities in a limited period of the past in the United States and Canada. It tells us nothing about what happened with the same commodities elsewhere or in another period or what will happen in the future.

But there still has remained the belief that it is different with money. I may cite, for example, Professor Fisher's book on the *Purchasing Power of Money,* which is founded on the assumption that the purchasing power of the monetary unit changes in inverse proportion to the quantity of money.[3] I think that this assumption is arbitrary and fallacious.

The second conclusion which we have to draw is the futility of all endeavors to make money stable in purchasing power. It is beyond the scope of my short address to explain the advantages of a sound money policy and the disadvantages of both inflation and deflation. But we should not confuse the political concept of sound money with the theoretical concept of stable money. I do not wish to discuss the inner contradictions of this stability concept. From the point of view of the present subject it is more important to emphasize that all proposals for stabilization, apart from other deficiencies, are based on the idea of money's neutrality. They all suggest methods to undo changes in purchasing power already effected if there has been an inflation they wish to deflate to the same extent and vice versa. They do not realize that by this procedure they do not undo the social consequences of the first change, but simply add to it the social consequences of a new change. If a man has been hurt by being run over by an automobile, it is no remedy to let the car go back over him in the opposition direction.

The popularity of all schemes for stabilization invites us to a philosophical consideration. It is a general weakness of the human mind to regard the state of rest and absence of change as more perfect than the state of motion. The absolute, that old phantom of misguided philosophical speculation, is still with us; its modern name is stability. But stability, e.g., absence of change, is, we have to repeat, absence of life.

The third conclusion which we may draw is the futility of the distinction between statics and dynamics and between short-run and long-run economics. The way in which we have to study monetary changes provides us with the best evidence that every correct economic consideration has to be dynamic and that static concepts are only instrumental. And at the same time we have to realize that all correct economic theorizing is a gradual progress from short-run to long-run effects.

But the most important value of the theory of money's dynamism is its use for the development of the monetary theory of the trade cycle. The old British Currency-Theory was already in a restricted sense a monetary explanation of the cycle. It studied the consequences of credit expansion on the assumption only that there is credit expansion in one country whereas in the rest of the world things are left unchanged. This seemed to be enough for the explanation of the business cycle in Great Britain in the first half of the nineteenth century. But the explanation of an external drain does not provide an answer to the question what may happen in a completely isolated country or in the case of a simultaneous credit expansion all over the world. But only the answer to this second question is important, if we have to consider the proposals for eliminating the cyclical changes either by loosening the international ties of the national economy or by making credit expansion international in the way the Bretton Woods Agreements[4] provide. It is the boast of the monetary theory of the trade cycle that it provides us with a satisfactory answer to these and to some other serious problems.

I do not wish to infringe more upon your time and so I wish only to add some remarks on the treatment of the problem by certain younger economists. I myself am not responsible for the term "neutral money." I have developed a theory of the changes in purchasing power and its social consequences. I have demonstrated that money acts as a dynamic agent and that the assumption that the changes in purchasing power are inversely proportional to the changes in the relation of demand for to the supply of money is fallacious. The term "neutral money" was coined by later authors.[5] I do not wish to consider the question of whether it was a happy choice. But in any case I must protest against the belief that it has to be a goal of monetary policy to make money neutral and that it is the duty of the economists to determine a method of doing so. I wish to emphasize that in a living and changing world, in a world of action, there is no room left for a neutral money. Money is non-neutral or it does not exist.

Notes

[This essay was delivered as a lecture to a group in Paris in 1938 and again to the New York City Economics Club in 1945 and previously unpublished—Ed.]

1. David Hume, "On Money," in *Writings on Economics,* Eugene Rotwein, ed. (University of Wisconsin Press, Madison, 1970), pp. 33–46; John Stuart Mill, *Principles of Political Economy,* Sir William Ashley, ed. (1909), bk. 3, chap. 8; John E. Cairnes, *Essays in Political Economy* (London: MacMillan, 1973), pp. 1–65.
2. In his treatise *Theory and Measurement of Demand* (Chicago: University of Chicago Press, 1938) he set forth his crop theory of cycles.
3. Irving Fisher, *The Purchasing Power of Money,* 2nd ed. (New York: Macmillan, 1920), p. 157, "there is no possible escape from the conclusion that a change in the quantity of money

(M) must normally cause a proportional change in the price level."

4. The Bretton Woods agreement in 1945 established an international gold exchange standard that valued the dollar at 1/35th of an ounce of gold.

5. F. A. Hayek, *Prices and Production*, 2nd ed. (New York: Augustus M. Kelley, 1935), pp. 31 and 129–31.

27

Can Price Stabilization Help?

M. A. Abrams

There is today a considerable body of reputable opinion that is convinced that such distortions of the structure of production and dislocations of economic life as we have described can be avoided by manipulations of the supply of money so as to produce a stable price-level. They urge that a rising price level provides producers, since they are largely borrowers, with windfall profits and the result is an unhealthy stimulation of production; and, conversely, a falling price level imposes unmerited losses on producers who then reduce production. Such adventitious gains and losses, and consequently booms and depressions, it is urged, can be eliminated by increasing the supply of money when prices are falling and decreasing the supply when prices are rising; the objective is to ensure that the dollar or the pound shall always be able to buy the same complex of goods and services.

On this side of the Atlantic the influential advocates of this policy include among economists Prof. Gustav Cassel, Sir Josiah Stamp, Sir Basil Blackett and Prof. Bellerby, while in the United States the answers received to a questionnaire sent out in 1927 to 281 professional economists showed that 252 "consider stabilisation of the price level to be a matter

Reprinted from *Money and a Changing Civilisation* by M. A. Abrams (London: John Lane The Bodley Head Ltd., 1934).

of major importance."¹ Prof. Irving Fisher has devoted the greater part of his abundant energy to propagating this doctrine in the belief that "when we really get stable units of money we shall have the greatest economic boon of all time"; and the present monetary advisers of President Roosevelt have organized the whole resources of the country in a spectacular attempt to construct a "rubber" or compensated dollar. Their work is inspired by the same chain of reasoning that led Prof. Fisher on the eve of this depression to write:² "Our prosperity has been looked on with pride by natives and with envy by foreigners, and almost as many explanations of it have been given as there have been onlookers. American genius, and inventiveness, capitalism, labor efficiency, horse power, the mechanization of industry, democracy, prohibition—all these have been mentioned as factors in our prosperity—but the cause which is probably the most important of all, that is, stable money since 1921— approximately stable—has been all but overlooked. But it is no mere coincidence. I believe that, of the ten periods in our history since 1849—the tenth (1922–1928) has been unprecedented in prosperity and unprecedented in stability."³

Side by side with these economists there stands an equally impressive host of business men and politicians. The *Midland Bank Review* of June-July 1927 wrote: "History has shown that apart perhaps from wars and religious intolerance no single factor has been more productive of misery and misfortune than the high degree of variability in the general price level. This may sound like an extravagant statement, but so far from being of the nature of demagogic outburst, it is clearly demonstrable from the course of events in various countries ever since money became an important element in the life of civilized communities. A stable price level is a thing to be desired, second only to international and domestic peace."

The famous memorandum on economic policy signed by one hundred of England's leading industrialists in May

1928, declared: "We believe that a more stable system of currency credit and a means of stabilizing the price level are prerequisite to the restoration of prosperity of the great basic industries of the country."[4]

On the other side of the Atlantic similar pronouncements have been issued by Chambers of Commerce and Merchants Associations, by bankers like the late Paul M. Warburg and by the editor of the *Saturday Evening Post*, and regularly and frequently bills have been introduced in Congress to provide that Federal Reserve Banks should: "Establish from time to time, subject to review and determination of the Federal Reserve Board, a rate of discount to be charged by such banks for each class of paper, which shall be made with a view to accommodating commerce and promoting a stable price level for commodities in general. All of the powers of the Federal Reserve system shall be used for promoting stability in the price-level."[5]

What is the worth of these opinions? I believe that it can be shown, firstly, that those who foresee an approximation to economic paradise as the result of a stable price-level have failed to suggest convincingly any efficient mechanism for attaining this stability; and, secondly, that even if such stability were achieved either by accident or design it would aggravate rather than eliminate industrial fluctuations. The price stability which Prof. Fisher and his allies[6] have in mind is a mistaken policy except perhaps in a stationary economy; it will produce all the evils of inflation in a progressive economy and all the evils of deflation in a decaying economy; in short, it will generate all the disorders that they are convinced it will abolish, and therefore their precepts are based on an inadequate diagnosis of the relation between money and the trade cycle.

First, we have no reason to be anything but extremely skeptical about the value and reliability of any of the existing methods of measuring changes in the price level. In the opinion of J. M. Keynes, one of the world's acknowledged experts on the subject, "there is at present a most serious lack of satisfactory index numbers of Purchasing Power.... An index number of the purchasing power of money should include, directly or indirectly once and once only, all the items which enter into final consumption (as distinct from an intermediate productive process) in proportion to the amount of their money-income which the consuming public devote to them. Since it would be a matter of great complexity to compile a completely comprehensive index on these lines, we should be satisfied in practice with an index which covered a large and representative part of total consumption. But we have not at present even this."[7]

Next, which price-level are we to adopt as our guide? In nearly all countries today there is to be found a bewildering collection of price index numbers, both governmental and private. Some of them are concerned merely with retail prices, or the cost of living, others refer to wholesale prices, and recently, Mr. Carl Snyder on behalf of the Federal Reserve Bank of New York has produced a composite index number that takes account of retail prices, wholesale prices and the level of wages. Which of these is to be regarded as *the* price level that must be stabilized? And certainly a choice is necessary because the movements of these various indices are not always either parallel or even in the same direction. For example, in England during the three years from 1923 to 1925 the Ministry of Labor's index number of the cost of living rose slightly but steadily from 169 to 170 to 171. During the same three years the Board of Trade's index number of wholesale prices jumped from 158.9 in 1923 to 166.2 in 1924 and slumped again to 159.1 in 1925. Similarly, in the United States, from 1925 to 1927 the cost of living index number declined by barely 2 percent; the Bureau of Labor's index number of wholesale prices declined about 12 percent; while Mr. Snyder's index showed hardly any fall at all.

Clearly, it is at least ambiguous to talk about stabilizing *the* price level; there are many of them, and we must ask the stabilizers to choose carefully which one they intend to stabilize, otherwise the result will certainly be chaos. Thus, accepting for the moment the stabilizers' somewhat naive views as to the simple way that changes in the supply of money affect the price level, if the financial authorities of this country had decided to stabilize the cost of living in 1924 and 1925 by decreasing the supply of money they would have increased the considerable fall in wholesale prices over those two years; and conversely, if they had chosen to stabilize the value of the Pound Sterling spent on wholesale commodities by increasing the supply of money there would have been a substantial fall in the value of the Pound spent on buying consumption goods. How do the stabilizers propose to solve this dilemma? So far the bulk of them have not even noticed its existence. The central fallacy of the stabilizers, in fact, springs from their inability to see that there are essentially different price levels. The key to the understanding of the part played by money in influencing production is the realization that money can be spent either on consumption goods or on producers' goods, and that these two classes of goods are competitors for the available supply of purchasing power.

Next, even if we have a general price level and an index number that truly reflects changes in the purchasing power of money, how can this price level be kept stable? Changes in the cost of living have been and are likely to be frequent and substantial. What facilities have the government and the banks for changing quickly and considerably the amount of money spent by consumers? The stream of money in circulation consists of bank money and currency. Bank-money is used primarily by business people so that if the banks increase or decrease the amount of credit they are issuing the main result will be to increase or decrease expenditure on intermediate goods, and to leave, at least in the short-run, the amount of money spent on consumption goods unaltered. So that we can expect little help from the banks in stabilizing the "general" purchasing power of money. But what about the government? The government does indeed hand over money at frequent intervals to consumers in the form of salaries for civil servants and other employees, pensions for the old and disabled, and relief for the poor and unemployed. Can these sums, which admittedly are spent largely on consumption goods, be altered from week to week? Quite apart from the disorganizing effect upon public finance, it is almost undeniable that neither the general public nor the recipients of government money would tolerate such manipulations. Why, at a time when the index number threatens to rise should civil servants and the unemployed be singled out to suffer income cuts? And why, when prices are about to fall should this minority alone benefit by increased purchasing power?[8]

Next, the stabilizers are, for the most part, convinced that the price-level can be influenced rapidly by appropriate changes in the open market operations of the central bank and thus by the amount of credit made available by the other banks. But recent American experience suggests that during a period of sharply falling prices and depression even a gigantic expansion of the reserves of commercial banks will not bring about rising commodity prices. The truth is that "the quantity of bank credit outstanding is ... only one factor in the determination of the price level. Equally important is the willingness of the community to hold a larger or smaller part of its available resources in the comparatively unproductive form of cash and bank balances. The greater the demand for till and pocket money and bank balances as a form of saving, the larger the amount of credit that must be outstanding to support a given price level. These demands are affected by changes in population, by the growth of the use of cheques, by the multiplication or consolidation of individual business units, by changes in the banks' requirements as to average balances, and above all (so far as short period changes are concerned) by anticipated changes in the level of prices. When prices are moving up or are expected to move up, depositors prefer to carry small balances and keep their funds invested; when falling prices are anticipated bank balances are deemed better investments than commodities or securities."[9] The lesson seems to be that an effective stabilisation of any price-level must involve a considerable amount of interference, not only with the supply of money, but also with the demand for it. Very few stabilizers are prepared to permit the government to decide when and how the ordinary man is to spend his money, and those who would permit this are wasting their time in striving after a stabilized price level; for the simple reason that as soon as the government controls the spending of the citizens' money and consequently controls the employment of the factors of production, money as we know it ceases to exist, and to talk then of changes in the price level affecting production becomes an anachronism.

Finally, there are still some stabilizers who do not realize that price stabilisation is completely incompatible with the maintenance of any international monetary standard and with stable exchange rates between different countries. The world has had since 1931 an excellent opportunity to learn what happens when governments decide to abandon an international standard and to let exchange rates fluctuate in order to stabilize internal price levels. Comparing the world's international trade in 1930 and 1932 we find a fall in the value of the total of over 52 percent;[10] this fall has increased during 1933. Another year or two of wildly uncertain exchange rates and world economic co-operation—the fruit of centuries of economic progress—will be abolished. Almost simultaneously with President Roosevelt's decision to restore American prices to their 1926 level by depressing the value of the dollar in terms of all other currencies, America's competitors decided to place further restrictions on international trade. Unless the world grows tired of this insanity very soon, it will become a collection of poverty-stricken isolated economies where the Dane refuses to drive any car that was not made in Denmark, the Englishman refuses to drink any but English wine, the Frenchman refuses to use medical instruments not made in France, the American refuses to read books not written by an American; the people of Iceland will start growing wheat, and Brazil will abandon all its industries that are dependent on imported coal. Only if the price stabilizers are prepared to push national isolation to these lengths, only if they are prepared to cut their country off completely from international trade does their policy become workable. Given international trade and a world monetary standard (whether it is the gold standard or any other standard does not matter), money will flow in and flow out of a country with no regard to the stabilisation of prices.[11]

These, however, are not the most serious deficiencies in the equipment of the price stabilizers. Even if we grant them an isolated state, an adequate method of measuring the general price level, and the means to regulate this price level delicately and fairly quickly, there remains, and this is of decisive importance, their inability to appreciate the effects of changes in the supply of money upon the structure of production.

In an economically progressive community, that is, one where the real costs of production per unit are falling and output per head is increasing,[12] any additions to the supply of money in order to prevent falling prices will be hidden inflation; and in a retrogressive community, that is, one where output per head is diminishing and real costs of production are rising,[13] any contraction of the supply of money in order to prevent rising prices will be hidden deflation. Inflation and deflation can occur just as well behind a stable price level as when the price level is rising and falling.

Since the experience of the nineteenth and twentieth centuries has been almost entirely with economically progressive communities our argument will approximate closely enough to reality if we deal merely with a state of affairs where output per head is increasing. If we start from an equilibrium position there are only two ways in which such progress can be made; either by an increase in the supply of savings so that the available stock of labor and natural resources can be used in a more roundabout way in the production of consumption goods, and every extension of the period of production, as we already know, leads to a larger ultimate output; or economic progress can be made by improvements in the community's stock of knowledge applied to the utilization of the available factors of production. In real life, of course, both causes, additional savings and inventions are often at work simultaneously; for purposes of analysis, however, we must separate them.

Let us take first the results of increased saving. We have seen that if a community decides to save a larger proportion of its income the result will be to lower the equilibrium rate of interest and to make possible a more roundabout and therefore a more productive utilization of the original factors of production. In the new equilibrium the price level of consumption goods is lower and the supply of consumption goods has increased in a greater proportion than the total amount of money spent on them has fallen. Figure ii[14] expresses the new conditions; let us turn back to it for a moment and suppose that a government of price-stabilizers are faced with the situation shown there. Their index number of the cost of living will record a considerable fall, and since they regard such a fall partly as the prelude to, and partly as an indication of dislocation, they will at once move to correct it. The increased saving meant that the proportionate expenditure of the community's money as between consumption goods and intermediate goods changed from 40:80 to 30:90, so that to "correct" this position, that is, to make a Pound spent on consumption goods go as far as it did before, the stabilizers must provide consumers with an additional £15 to spend; when they do this the figures return to the old ratio that existed before any additional saving took place and become £45:£90.

But when this correction is effected the whole of the benefit of the increased saving is destroyed. Once more only two-thirds of the community's purchasing power is spent on the production of future goods, and the roundaboutness of the process of production must be reduced to its old structure of four stages, that is, no more productive use is made of society's stock of labor and natural resources in spite of the increased willingness to save.

Now let us turn to the other form of economic progress—improvements in technical knowledge. From the entrepreneur's point of view the essence of an invention is that it reduces his costs of production; from the consumer's point of view the important consideration is that such a reduction in the producer's costs must sooner or later be passed on in the form of reduced selling prices. The entrepreneur who is responsible for introducing the invention finds that as long as selling prices are not reduced he makes on each unit he sells a bigger margin of profit than before. These exceptionally high profits will either induce him to expand production so as to make larger total profits, or else they will attract new rivals with similar ambitions. In any case, the total output will be enlarged, and the selling price will tend to fall to the point where there is no undue margin of profit left even on the reduced costs.

If the improved knowledge is introduced into the island where the community's money is divided into proportions of £40 spent on consumption goods and £80 spent on intermediate goods there does not result, if the supply of money remains constant, any change in the structure of production. The only difference is that the £40 spent on consumption goods is able to buy a larger quantity since the price per unit of these goods has fallen. But as soon as the index number registers this the stabilizers will at once prepare for action. The consumer will not be allowed to enjoy the lower prices at which entrepreneurs are ready and able to sell; instead, more money will be rushed into circulation. In the hands of consumers this will mean that a larger proportion of the community's purchasing power will be devoted to buying consumption goods. Accordingly, the structure of production will be shortened, so that the improvements in knowledge will be applied to a less roundabout process of production and will probably yield an output no larger than when the old stock of knowledge was applied in a more roundabout process.

Thus, in the case where a fall in prices due to increased saving is corrected by additional money for consumers the result is to prevent any extension of the roundaboutness of production; and where a fall in prices due to improved knowledge is corrected by additional money the result is to force a transition to less roundabout methods. In both cases the fruits of progress are rejected because of a determination to deep prices stable. Moreover, in both cases the correction of the attempted advances has involved the abandonment of some of the higher stages of production where certainly some of the factors used are highly specialized and these will therefore become unemployed as a result of the transition.

We have taken it for granted so far that the stabilizers in seeking to raise a falling index number constructed largely on the prices of consumption goods will adopt the remedy of providing consumers with more money to spend. They may not, however, be so logical, and may attempt to raise the falling prices of consumption goods by giving more money to entrepreneurs. Such action, as we already know, will cause a shift in the employment of the factors of production to more roundabout methods of production. If we start from an equilibrium position entrepreneurs will only be induced to take up additional loans at less than the equilibrium rate of interest; that is, there will be an unjustifiable increase in the construction of capital goods. This will proceed while the general price level remains approximately stable, and so the stabilizers will be able to deny that any inflation is taking place. Hidden inflation of this sort probably occurred on a large scale during the post-war decade when technical progress was advancing rapidly.[15] Its effects are just as inevitably a depression as when inflation shows itself in a rising general price level.

Notes

1. Irving Fisher, *The Money Illusion*, London, 1928, p. 201.
2. Op. cit., p. 136.
3. In fact, the price stability perceived by Prof. Fisher has been declared to be an hallucination of the author of *The Money Illusion*. Mr. Walter W. Stewart, ex-director of research for the Federal Reserve Board, stated: "There is no period during the last quarter century, except the war period when prices have fluctuated over so wide a range as from 1922 to 1926." This has been substantiated by the analysis of Prof. Wesley C. Mitchell in *Recent Economic Changes in the United States*. A good deal depends, of course, on which price level we are looking at.
4. Recent annual conferences of the Labour Party have demanded that "the average level of prices shall remain as nearly as possible constant, so that the pound shall buy roughly the same basketful of goods today, next month, next year and ten years hence."
5. Mr. C. O. Hardy, of the Brookings Institution, Washington, D.C., quotes this preamble in his *Credit Policies of the Federal Reserve System*, Washington, 1932. It is, I am sure, no exaggeration to say of this book that no more penetrating or clearer analysis and history of the Federal Reserve System has yet appeared.
6. The bill referred to above was actively supported by Profs. Cassel, John R. Commons, James H. Rogers and J. W. Jenks.
7. J. M. Keynes, *A Treatise on Money*, vol. I, p. 57, London, 1930.

8. To be effective, of course, the increased purchasing power of civil servants, etc., must come from a creation of new currency. If it comes from additional taxation, then the gains of the civil servants are exactly offset by the losses of tax-payers.

9. Hardy, op. cit., p. 220. Presumably even when the price level is stabilized, the price of securities will fluctuate and therefore people will vary their bank balances.

10. League of Nations: World Economic Survey 1932–33, p. 210, Geneva, 1933. Part of this fall is due to a fall in the prices at which commodities were bought and sold, but this explains less than half the decrease.

11. The reasons for this are developed in the section dealing with the gold standard.

12. Economic progress may be defined shortly as the process of satisfying more wants with a given effort.

13. For example, because natural resources are becoming exhausted.

14. On p. 28.

15. It seems likely that a not inconsiderable part of the technological unemployment that we have heard so much about recently was caused by the fact that employers were induced to displace labor by capital goods because of the artificially low rate of interest. Many of the inventions adopted were not commercial propositions as soon as an equilibrium rate of interest was charged. Any attempt to offset the additional money given to employers by insisting that consumers by given extra money in the form of higher wages would clearly have encouraged employers to adopt even more labor-saving inventions.

28

Intertemporal Coordination and the Invisible Hand: An Austrian Perspective on the Keynesian Vision

Roger W. Garrison

I. Introduction

This article offers a critical evaluation of Keynes's *General Theory* from an Austrian[1] perspective. Although many— if not most—of today's macroeconomists share with the Austrians a dissatisfaction with the current state of macroeconomics, the Austrians are in a unique position to identify the roots of this dissatisfaction. Critical intertemporal market forces working within the capital goods sector were emphasized in the Austrian vision and totally ignored in the Keynesian vision. This sharp contrast provides a fruitful basis for comparison and evaluation. The Keynesian theme of macroeconomic discoordination, which is based on a highly aggregative treatment of the capital goods sector, can be evaluated in the light of the Austrian theme of macroeconomic coordination, which is based on a disaggregated capital-goods sector. The comparison serves to highlight a central deficiency of the Keynesian vision in a way that suggests how the deficiency might be remedied.

Reprinted from *History of Political Economy* 17:2 (1985).

II. The Relevance of the Austrian Perspective

From Adam Smith on it is possible to judge theories— or at least to categorize them—on the basis of the use they make of the "invisible hand." This familiar metaphor, of course, is just a way of recognizing that the coordination of economic activities is not to be directly attributed to the intention of any individual or group of individuals. It is instead the "result of human action but not of human design."[2] Economic problems are coordination problems, and economic theories are explanations of how the invisible hand solves these problems or why—in particular circumstances—it fails to solve them.

The problem of *intertemporal* coordination is of special significance in economic theory. Whether addressed explicitly in terms of the allocation of goods over time or implicitly in terms of the determination of the level of investment spending, the intertemporal-coordination problem looms large in theories dealing with capital and with macroeconomic phenomena. Various explanations of macro maladies often hinge on the various ways in which the invisible hand can fail to achieve an intertemporal coordination of economic activity. Such coordination failures underlie a number of different macroeconomic phenomena, such as overinvestment, malinvestment, liquidity crises, and cyclical unemployment.

In the context of macroeconomics, the problem of intertemporal coordination is treated most directly by the theorists of the Austrian school. The level of aggregation in Austrian macroeconomic theory is chosen so as to give full play to the relevant market forces—most usually by allowing for a disaggregated capital sector whose constituent parts make up an alterable structure of production.[3] Because of its explicit attention to this particular aspect of the coordination problem and its relatively low level of aggregation. Austrian theory provides a useful framework for the evaluation of other theories that make use of various economy-wide aggregates. Increasing the level of aggregation in some particular way always means concealing a market process of some particular kind. The consequences of adopting different aggregation schemes can be spelled out in terms of the Austrian view. Competing theories can be compared on the basis of the market processes that each overlooks, and anomalous implications of a particular theory can be traced to the absence (due to aggregation) of some critical market process. By the nature of things, it is difficult to tell just where and how the invisible hand disappears, but by adopting an Austrian approach, we can identify the crucial market processes that have been lost from view, and stipulate the theoretical modifications required to account for the intertemporal allocation of resources.

Evaluating macroeconomic theories in terms of the market processes that are overlooked because of the level of aggregation is not new to the Austrian tradition. Nor is it an entirely new approach to understanding Keynes. F. A. Hayek observed at the earliest opportunity that "Mr. Keynes's aggregates conceal the most fundamental mechanisms of change."[4] This statement is taken from Hayek's detailed critique of *A Treatise on Money*. But the critique was largely ignored by both Keynes and his followers, and both schools pressed on in their own separate directions. Hayek continued the development of a theory of the capital structure in order to explain how the market copes with the problem of intertemporal coordination: Keynes increased the level of aggregation in his later formulations and was led to conclude that the economy lacks the ability to achieve intertemporal coordination. The present article can be seen as an attempt to extend the Hayekian critique of Keynes's *Treatise* to his more influential *General Theory*.[5]

III. Intertemporal Coordination in the
Austrian Vision

Attention to the problem of intertemporal coordination in the Austrian tradition is as old as the tradition itself. Carl Menger, in his *Principles of Economics,* allowed for the working out of intertemporal market forces when he conceived of various "orders" of capital goods.[6] "Goods of the first order" are consumer goods; "goods of the second order" are capital goods, once removed in time from the emergence of the corresponding consumer good; and goods of the third, fourth, and higher orders are defined accordingly. In effect, Menger conceived of an economy in which the capital-goods sector is disaggregated and in which the individual subsectors differ from one another in terms of their temporal relationships to the eventual emergence of consumer goods. The capital goods that make up a given subsector have a value that reflects both their contribution to the production of the consumer good and, as Böhm-Bawerk was later to emphasize, the remoteness in time from the consumer good.

This vision of the capital structure served as a backdrop for Ludwig von Mises's *The Theory of Money and Credit.*[7] Drawing from Knut Wicksell, Mises recognized that a policy-induced credit expansion would be accompanied by a temporarily and artificially low rate of interest. The distortion of the interest rate would in turn lead to a misallocation of resources: too many capital goods of the higher orders, too few consumer goods and capital goods of the lower orders. Credit policy could disrupt the market processes that otherwise would (might?) achieve intertemporal coordination.

It was left to Hayek to specify just how this market process might work—just how the invisible hand might coordinate intertemporally—and to indicate just how monetary disturbances could interfere with such a market process. These tasks were undertaken in *Prices and Production,* where Hayekian triangles, as they came to be called, were employed to represent the economy's structure of production.[8] An individual triangle represents the intertemporal allocation of resources under the assumptions that intertemporal preferences are given and that monetary disturbances are absent. One leg of the triangle represents the time dimension of the structure of production—the time that separates the employment of capital goods[9] with the emergence of the corresponding consumer goods, the other leg represents the value of the consumer goods. The triangle is divided into a number of slices parallel to the value dimension in order to account for the vertical, or intertemporal, disaggregation of the capital-goods sector. Each slice represents a particular "stage of production," or in Mengerian terms, a particular order of capital goods. The hypotenuse of the Hayekian triangle represents the general relationship between time and capital value: the more (less) remote the stage of production from the emergence of consumer goods, the lower (higher) the value of the capital goods which make up that stage. In equilibrium the value differentials between the various stages of production reflect the equilibrium rate of interest.

An equilibrium structure of production can be upset by an exogenous change in intertemporal consumption preferences. A shift in intertemporal preferences towards the more remote future leads to an increase in current savings and a fall in the market rate of interest. This lower rate of interest has implications for the relative values of the capital goods that make up the various stages of production: the capital goods in the early stages will increase systematically in value relative to the capital goods in the later stages—for the same reason that a lower interest rate increases the value of a consol relative to a Treasury Bill.

Corresponding profit differentials will lead entrepreneurs to bring about the appropriate quantity adjustments, which have the collective result of a new structure of production that matches the new intertemporal preferences. Achieving the new equilibrium does require that entrepreneurial activity not be systematically perverse, but this requirement applies to any theory of economic coordination that relies on the invisible hand.[10] By contrast, systematic perversity was virtually guaranteed in the Keynesian vision when Keynes theorized in terms of *total* profits instead of profit *differentials*. Obscuring the differentials with the totals, in fact, was the very basis of Hayek's critical remark cited above. On the issue of intertemporal coordination, Keynes—even in the *Treatise*—simply failed to bring the invisible hand into view.

Hayek's theory of the business cycle—of intertemporal *dis*coordination—is no more than a corollary to his theory of intertemporal coordination.[11] A policy-induced fall in the rate of interest will create the same profit differentials among the stages of production as a market-induced fall. Entrepreneurs will be led, as if by an invisible hand, to restructure the capital sector only to discover in time that real saving (as opposed to bank credit) is insufficient to allow for the completion of the restructuring. For Hayek, this policy-induced intertemporal discoordination is the essence of the business cycle.[12]

In the Austrian vision the capital sector serves as the focus for the analysis of intertemporal coordination. The Hayekian structure of production illustrates and conceptually isolates the relevant intertemporal relationships. By disaggregating the capital sector, Hayek has shown how the invisible hand can bring about intertemporal coordination and how bank policy can cause this same coordinating mechanism to yield perverse results. This capsulization of the Austrian vision serves as the basis for the following critical assessment of the corresponding Keynesian vision.

IV. Intertemporal Relationships in the Keynesian Vision

An Austrian perspective on Keynes can serve to draw attention to the lack of capital theory in Keynes's writings and point out the consequences of ignoring the market processes that give rise to a capital structure. That his theory lacked a satisfactory treatment of capital is explicitly affirmed by Keynes himself.[13] What Keynes denied—implicitly in *The General Theory* and explicitly in his reply to Hayek's critique of the *Treatise*—was that a satisfactory theory of capital is a prerequisite for dealing with the problem of intertemporal discoordination.[14]

The capsulization of the Austrian vision served to identify the market processes that were concealed by Keynes. The remaining task is one of sifting through *The General Theory* to find remarks that are germane to the problem of intertemporal coordination. The objective of this exercise is not to save Keynes from himself, but to emphasize the importance of a comprehensive theory of capital in this regard. In lieu of a positive theory of capital, we must look for remarks about the way in which the present and the future are linked. These remarks, scattered throughout the book, focus mostly on what Keynes perceived as an absence of intertemporal links rather than on his perception of the links that do, even in his own judgment, actually exist. Nonetheless, a compilation of the relevant passages yields a consistent and revealing view of intertemporal relationships in the Keynesian vision.

Keynes never treats intertemporal preferences by themselves as a parameter, or exogenous variable.[15] That is, no change in the *actual* intertemporal pattern of consumption is ever attributed to or associated with a change in the preferred pattern. Implicitly, the preferred pattern is assumed to be a constant rate of consumption over time. This characterization of the Keynesian vision is consistent with

Axel Leijonhufvud's understanding that for Keynes, "pref-erence functions defined for alternative time paths of con-sumption are assumed to exhibit a considerable degree of intertemporal complementarity."[16] By equating present sav-ing with future consumption, we can see this complemen-tary relationship in Keynes's discussion of the consumption function: "If saving is the pill and consumption is the jam, the extra jam has to be proportioned to the size of the addi-tional pill" (Keynes, *GT*, 117f.) Intertemporal preferences do not change autonomously, and hence they cannot cause changes in the rate of interest or in other relative prices. Nor do changes in the rate of interest have any effect on preferred consumption patterns. The absence of any such relationship is "suggested by experience," according to Keynes (Ibid., 94). Again, Leijonhufvud's understanding is supportive. "Keynes regards the substitution effect of inter-est changes as 'open to a good deal of doubt,' as 'secondary and relatively unimportant.'—a phrase which in his works means, in effect, that the relationship is ruled out of consid-eration" (Leijonhufvud, 106).

Having established that Keynes regards intertemporal consumption preferences as neither the cause nor the effect of a market process, we turn our attention to his treatment of the time element in production. To make the most direct comparison of Keynes's treatment of production time with its Austrian counterpart, we can consider his remarks on the notion of 'roundaboutness.' This summary term was used by Böhm-Bawerk and subsequent Austrian writers to char-acterize the allocation of resources among the various stages of production: an increase in roundaboutness, for instance, means an allocation of resources away from the relatively late stages of production and towards the relatively early stages. The relevant remarks are confined to the first two sections of Keynes's chapter of sundry observations (*GT*, 210–17) where he gives us some insights into why he consid-ers Böhm-Bawerk's analysis to be useless. Clearly, the intended effect of Keynes's remarks is to trivialize the notion of roundaboutness and to ridicule those who focus attention on this particular aspect of the production process. The fact that this term is used by the Austrian theorists in their discussions of the time element in the production process and the ever-critical problem of coordinating production plans with intertemporal preferences appears to have escaped him. For Keynes the degree of roundaboutness is just one of a nearly infinite number of aspects that characterize the production process. Analystically, this aspect is no more significant, according to Keynes, than the "smelliness" (Ibid., 215) of the process.[17]

If intertemporal consumption preferences are assumed not to change and the degree of roundaboutness is considered to be a trivial aspect of the production process, the link between the present and the future must be sought elsewhere in Keynes's theory. Of his three "independent variables," which he takes to be "the propensity to consume, the schedule of the marginal efficiency of capital and the rate of interest."[18] It is reasonable to look for an intertemporal link in the latter two. But Keynes makes it quite clear that the rate of interest constitutes no part of the link when he states that "the rate of interest is, virtually, a *current* phenomenon" (Ibid., 145–46). In a footnote he explains that the word "virtually" is inserted to admit of some intertemporal consideration, such as the effect of expectations about the future interest rate. Keynes's critics, though, have pointed out that these expectations are the *only* consideration in his theory of interest.[19] Thus, the interest rate may be a fully intertemporal rather than a current phenomenon, but even if it is, it does not serve to link anything except present and future values of itself.

Recognizing the bootstrap nature of Keynes's interest theory does help explain why he persistently lists the interest rate—rather than the schedule of liquidity preferences—as an independent variable. It also suggests that the link between the present and the future must be sought in the one remaining independent variable, the marginal efficiency of capital. Indeed this is the variable that, in Keynes's own view, contains the primary, if not the only, link. He warns against attempting to reduce the marginal efficiency of capital to the same status as the interest rate on the grounds that this approach would "cut [us] off from taking any direct account of the influence of the future in our analysis of the existing equilibrium" (Keynes, *GT*, 146). This link consists, of course, of expectations about the yield and hence the demand price of capital goods. Significantly, Keynes used a single variable, the marginal efficiency of capital, to gauge the value of capital goods. The Austrian theorists, by comparison, distinguished between the different stages of production and associated a demand price with each stage. It is precisely at this point in *The General Theory* that Keynes's propensity to aggregate conceals critical market processes. More specifically, by adopting a single measure of the yield on capital, Keynes lost sight of the market processes associated with changes in the relative prices of capital goods in different stages of production—and thereby lost sight of the possibility that the invisible hand can achieve intertemporal coordination.

V. Intertemporal Discoordination and the Role of Expectations

The reader of *The General Theory* might expect that after identifying the marginal efficiency of capital as the dominant intertemporal link, Keynes would seek to establish the conditions under which the present and the future would most successfully be linked, that is, the conditions under which (present) investment plans and (future) consumption plans would tend to be coordinated. Keynes might be expected to ask the obvious question: Under what conditions would expectations generally be right? As Hayek has pointed out, it is only after we establish how an economy could conceivably work right that we are in a position to ask what could go wrong.[20] But for Keynes the possibility that expectations could serve, under any conditions, to coordinate investment and consumption plans is simply out of the question. Although expectations (about the yield on capital goods) constitute a link between the present and the future, they do not constitute a coordinating link. Expectations are portrayed sometimes as autonomous and hence only correct by chance, sometimes as distinctly perverse; but there is never a hint about even the *possibility* of coordinating or equilibrating expectations. There is no market process that equilibrates *the* price of capital goods.[21]

Keynes's denial of the existence of a (coordinating) intertemporal link is not difficult to substantiate. He criticized the orthodoxy for "fallaciously supposing that there is a nexus which unites decisions to abstain from present consumption with decisions to provide for future consumption" (Keynes, *GT*, 21) And ruling out the invisible hand, he held that it is only "by accident or design" that current investment is consistent with the level of consumption spending (Ibid., 28). On the question of just how the expectations that constitute the (noncoordinating) intertemporal link are formulated, Keynes appears to be of two minds. On the one hand, he regards investment decisions as fundamentally irrational and therefore independent of consumers' preferences: "the marginal efficiency of capital [is] determined ... by the uncontrollable and disobedient psychology of the business world" (Ibid., 317). This remark is taken from his discussion of the trade cycle, but the idea that investment decisions are basically irrational transcends his view of cyclical variations in output. He makes a similar remark in his discussion of long-term expectations: "Most, probably, of our decisions to do something positive, the full consequences of which will be drawn out over many days to come, can only be a result of animal spirits—of a spontaneous urge to action rather than inaction" (Ibid., 161). Also, in connection with his discussion of "Incentives to Liquidity," he writes of the "fickle and highly unstable marginal efficiency of capital" (Ibid., 204).

On the other hand, Keynes sees a definite relationship between consumption decisions and investment decisions. After casting animal spirits in a key role, he does warn against concluding that "everything depends on waves of 'irrational psychology'" (Ibid., 161), but from Keynes's alternative treatment we cannot avoid concluding that to the extent that investment decisions are related to consumption decisions, they are related in a perverse manner. This perversity shows up quite clearly in one of his more homely discussions of consumption plans: "An act of individual saving means—so to speak—a decision not to have dinner today. But it does *not* necessitate a decision to have dinner or to buy a pair of boots a week hence or a year hence or to consume any specified thing at any specified date" (Ibid., 210). It is true, of course, that there is more uncertainty about future consumption than about present consumption and hence a greater role for expectations. Keynes goes on, though, to suggest that the uncertainty about the nature and timing of the future consumption activity made possible by the act of saving is equivalent, in expectations, to the total absence of that future consumption: "the expectation of future consumption is so largely based on current experience of present consumption that the reduction of the latter is likely to depress the former" (Ibid.). As far as Keynes's capitalist-entrepreneur is concerned, the decision not to have dinner today means—so to speak—a decision not to have dinner tomorrow either. In Keynes's formulation, if there are individuals who do decide to consume less now *in order* to be able to consume more in the future, their actions are doomed to be misinterpreted by the capitalist-entrepre-

neur: "every weakening in the propensity to consume regarded as a permanent habit must weaken the demand for
capital as well as the demand for consumption" (Ibid., 106).
And in the Keynesian vision every weakening *is* so regarded.

That Keynes does not allow for even the possibility of
coordinating expectations is evidenced in two ways. He
imagines two alternative arrangements in which things
might be different, that is, in which expectations would not
lead to perverse results. One alternative arrangement involves investment decisions; the other involves consumption
decisions. What is important to note is that Keynes is not
spelling out the conditions under which expectations would
tend to be correct; he is spelling out conditions under which
the role of expectations is all but eliminated. When he focuses on investment decisions, he does not ask how the market for capital goods could work correctly; he simply laments the emergence of an organized capital market. He
points out: "Decisions to invest in private business of the old
fashion type were ... decisions largely irrevocable, not only
for the community as a whole, but also for the individual"
(Ibid., 150). Once such a decision was made, changes in
expectations were simply inconsequential and hence irrelevant—but not so after the emergence of organized capital
markets. Investment decisions are now continuously influenced by "mass psychology" and the "fetish of liquidity."
These are the factors that cause Keynes to equate the capital
market to a casino and to treat investment as "a game of
Snap, of Old Maid, of Musical Chairs" (Ibid., 155–56). Such
spectacles "moved [Keynes] toward the conclusion that to
make the purchase of an investment permanent and indis-
soluble, like marriage, except by reason of death or other
grave cause, might be a useful remedy for our contemporary evils" (Ibid., 160). Keynes does not seek to formulate
policy that might improve the quality of expectations or to
give expectations more leeway in his theory, as by introduc-

ing multiple categories of capital goods; he seeks to eliminate the investor's opportunity to act on the basis of his expectations.

The elimination of the role of expectations could also be accomplished by restricting the actions of consumers. "If savings consisted not merely in abstaining from present consumption but in placing simultaneously a specific order for future consumption, the effect [on investment decisions] might indeed be different" (Ibid., 210). No doubt it would, and if the Black Jack dealer were to announce in advance the order in which the cards are arranged, the player would be in a better position to decide whether to 'stay' or 'take a hit.' Again, expectations that coordinate investment decisions with not-yet-announced consumption plans are simply out of consideration. Intertemporal coordination, in Keynes's view, requires that the role of expectations be eliminated.

Prospects for eliminating the play of expectations are considered once more when Keynes discusses the relationship between money and expectations. The notion of an intertemporal link in this connection is made very explicit: *"the importance of money essentially flows from its being a link between the present and the future"* (Ibid., 293; emphasis original). This statement does not belie Keynes's earlier remarks about the importance of the marginal efficiency of capital. The marginal efficiency of capital is determined by expectations which, in turn, are calculated in terms of money. Money and the marginal efficiency of capital are not seen as alternative links but as integral parts of a chain—a chain no stronger than its weakest link. In no sense, then, is money seen as a coordinating link. At best money could permit an accurate expression of irrational or perverse expectations; at worst it could add distortions of its own. It even occurs to Keynes that if there were no money, there would be no effective means of expressing and hence giving play to expectations. The discussion is ended, though, by

Keynes pointing out (lamenting?) that "We cannot get rid of money even by abolishing gold and silver and legal tender instruments" (Ibid., 294). The possibility that money is part of a coordinating mechanism is never given serious consideration; the focus instead is on the prospects for abolishing or otherwise rendering ineffective this discoordinating intertemporal link.[22]

VI. A Summary Assessment

The Austrian perspective on Keynes can be summarized in terms of the theoretical prerequisites for analyzing the problem of intertemporal coordination. Israel Kirzner makes the most concise statement of these prerequisites:

> if we wish to understand the course of economic events over time, including those events that are the outcome of multiperiod plans, we must be prepared to deal with these plans in the way in which they are constructed. Our analytical apparatus must be able to handle decisions in which it is contemplated to sacrifice inputs today *in order* to obtain output tomorrow; and our explanation of states of affairs and chains of events in the real world must be able to trace them back to such multiperiod plans [emphasis original].[23]

This passage can be seen as setting the research agenda for many of the modern contributions in the Austrian tradition.[24] But dealing with intertemporal relationships in this way is precisely what Keynesian theory is unable to do. The level of aggregation will not permit it. The Keynesian vision does not allow for changes in the preferred intertemporal consumption pattern. Such changes as do occur are bound to be either ignored or misinterpreted by the capitalist-entrepreneurs. There is no possibility that investors will correctly expect that individuals have decided to consume less now in order to be able to consume more in the future and will have correct expectations about what in particular these individuals will want to consume. In other words, there is no *conceivable* market mechanism in the Keynesian vision by which changes in intertemporal consumption preferences could be successfully translated into investment decisions. Indeed, the intertemporal characteristics of investment corresponding to the intertemporal characteristics of the preferred consumption pattern—as might be described in terms of roundaboutness—are simply dropped from consideration. As a result, the intertemporal market processes that give rise to these characteristics are concealed by Keynes's theory, and the dominant theme of intertemporal *dis*coordination emerges by default.

I gratefully acknowledge comments on earlier drafts from Don Bellante, Don Boudreaux, and Leland B. Yeager of Auburn University, and three anonymous referees.

Notes

1. The label "Austrian," like most such labels in the history of ideas, has come to mean different things to different people. In the present article it is used to refer to a strand of thought that can be traced from Menger to Mises to Hayek. The focus is on Hayek, since he was a contemporary of Keynes. And the particular ideas singled out for special attention are those "Austrian" ideas that form the clearest counterpart to the Keynesian vision.
2. F. A. Hayek. 'The results of human action but not of human design,' in Hayek, *Studies in Philosophy, Politics and Economics* (Chicago, 1967), 96–107. Hayek drew this title from the writings of Adam Ferguson.
3. The structure of production is the major focus, for instance, in F. A. Hayek, *Prices and Production* (1931; New York, 1967).
4. F. A. Hayek, "Reflections on the pure theory of money," *Economica* 33 (August, 1931): 227.

5. An account of why Hayek himself did not produce such a critique is contained in F. A. Hayek, *A Tiger by the Tail* (London, 1972), 100. In short, Keynes had responded to Hayek's painstaking critique of the *Treatise* by attacking Hayek's *Prices and Production* and indicating that he (Keynes) had changed his mind in any event and no longer held the views that Hayek was challenging. This response did not encourage Hayek to write a similar critique of *The General Theory*.

6. Carl Menger, *Principles of Economics*, trans. James Dingwall and Bert F. Hoselitz, with an introduction by Frank Knight (Glencoe, IL, 1950), 58–67. Basing the present discussion on Menger's treatment of the capital sector rather than on Böhm-Bawerk's allows us to focus on the essential intertemporal market forces without getting embroiled in the conceptual difficulties inherent in Böhm-Bawerk's "average period of production." The inattention to these well-recognized difficulties is intended to suggest that the Hayekian insights do not depend upon any precise quantification of the dimensions of the capital sector. For an elaboration of the development of Austrian capital theory and its importance as the underpinnings of the macroeconomic relationships introduced by Mises and developed by Hayek, see Gerald P. O'Driscoll, Jr., and Mario J. Rizzo. *The Economics of Time and Ignorance* (Oxford, 1985), 160–87.

7. Ludwig von Mises, *The Theory of Money and Credit*, trans. H. E. Batson (New Haven, 1953), 339–66.

8. Hayek, *Prices and Production*, 32–54.

9. For simplicity Hayek formulates these relationships in terms of the application of the "original means of production"—by which he means land and labor. But once these means are applied, the immediate results are capital goods—which serve as the focus of the present exposition (Ibid., 36–43).

10. Those critics of the Austrian school who demand a 'proof' that the invisible hand can achieve economic coordination are bound to be disappointed. The acceptance or rejection of the notion that invisible hand processes create a spontaneous order (both atemporally and intertemporally) defines alternative paradigms in economic thought. And paradigms, as such,

are not subject to 'proof.' Ultimately, the willingness to rely on the invisible hand rests on a belief that profit opportunities will be discovered and acted upon by entrepreneurs. For a reinforcement of this belief, see Israel M. Kirzner, *Perception, Opportunity, and Profit* (Chicago, 1979). I am indebted to an anonymous referee for reminding me that there are some members of the Austrian school who reject the idea that market mechanisms can achieve intertemporal coordination. Ludwig Lachmann, following Shackle, holds that there is no tendency toward equilibrium in the market for long-term capital assets. Ludwig M. Lachmann, "From Mises to Shackle: an essay on Austrian economics and the kaleidic society," *Journal of Economic Literature*, 14.1 (March 1976):54–65. shackle, of course, bases his interpretation of Keynes on the absence of this crucial equilibrating tendency. G. L. S. Shackle, *Keynesian Kaleidics* (Edinburgh, 1974). From a policy perspective, the question of a 'proof' of the presence or the absence of an invisible hand that can achieve an intertemporal equilibrium gives way to the question of which set of institutions (the market or the government) is the more likely to facilitate the intertemporal coordination of economic activity. Recasting the issue in this way suggests that the burden of proof—at least for economists who associate themselves with the Classical Liberal tradition—shifts to those who advocate government policies aimed at increasing the degree of intertemporal coordination.

11. Hayek, *Prices and Production*, 36–43. This relationship between Hayek's capital theory and his trade-cycle theory can be seen by comparing pp. 36–54 with 54–68. The sharpest contrast between Keynes and Hayek is achieved by taking Keynes to believe that the interest rate is affected solely by changes in liquidity preferences and Hayek to believe that the interest rate is affected solely by changes in time preferences. Both theorists, of course, recognized that the interest rate can be affected by more than one thing. An anonymous referee has pointed out that Hayek made some concessions to Keynes by recognizing the effect of changes in liquidity preferences

on the rate of interest. See F. A. Hayek, *The Pure Theory of Capital* (Chicago, 1941). The referee cites chapter 26 of this volume, in which Hayek puts the liquidity-preference issue into perspective and then warns against undue attention to this factor (Ibid., 359). Also see Ibid., 397–410. Several years before the publication of *The General Theory*, Hayek suggested, in effect, that considerations of both liquidity preferences and time preferences should be taken into account if the General Theory of interest is to be advanced. See Hayek, "The present state and immediate prospects of the study of industrial fluctuations," in Hayek, *Profits, Interest and Investment* (Clifton, N.J., 1975), 177. Undoubtedly, it was Keynes's undue attention to liquidity preferences that caused Hayek to downplay this consideration in his own analysis.

12. This view is reinforced by Fritz Machlup, whose summary statement draws from Hayek's own overview: "The fundamental thesis of Hayek's theory of the business cycle is that *monetary* factors *cause* the cycle but *real* phenomena *constitute* it." See Fritz Machlup. "'Hayek's Contribution to Economics," in Machlup, ed., *Essays on Hayek* (Hillsdale, MI, 1976), 23.

13. John Maynard Keynes, "The Pure Theory of Money: A Reply to Dr. Hayek," *Economica* 33 (November, 1931): 394.

14. Ibid., 395.

15. The phrase "by themselves" is an important qualifier. Generally, Keynes chose to deal with an exogenous change in liquidity preferences that implicitly involved a change in time preferences as well. These complex preference changes lie at the root of the non-neutrality propositions in Keynes's monetary theory.

16. Axel Leijonhufvud, *On Keynesian Economics and the Economics of Keynes* (New York, 1968), 196.

17. The categorization of smelliness and roundaboutness as just two of a nearly infinite number of characteristics is especially puzzling in view of Keynes's earlier remark that "the social objective of skilled investment is to defeat the dark forces of *time* and ignorance which envelop our future" (Ibid., 155; emphasis added).

18. Keynes persistently lists the rate of interest rather than the schedule of liquidity preferences as the third independent variable (Ibid., 184, 245, 260).
19. The "interest rate is what it is because it is expected to be other than what it is." Dennis H. Robertson, "Alternative Theories of the Rate of Interest," *Economic Journal* 47 (September, 1937):433.
20. F. A. Hayek, "Economics and Knowledge," in *Individualism and Economic Order* (Chicago, 1948), 34.
21. This claim is not intended to deny that Keynes allowed for a current supply price and a current demand price of capital goods and hence a market-clearing price for capital goods in each period. What Keynesian theory lacks is a sequence of market-clearing prices that are consistent with intertemporal equilibrium.
22. Reinforcing this view is Keynes's support for monetary reformers like Silvio Gesell: "Those reformers, who look for a remedy by creating artificial carrying-costs for money through the device of requiring legal-tender currency to be periodically stamped at a prescribed cost in order to retain its quality as money, or in analogous ways, have been on the right track; and the practical value of their proposals deserves consideration" (Ibid., 234).
23. Israel M. Kirzner, *An Essay on Capital* (New York, 1966), 80.
24. Noteworthy contributions include Gerald P. O'Driscoll, Jr., and Mario J. Rizzo, *The Economics of Time and Ignorance* (Oxford, 1985); Gerald P. O'Driscoll, Jr., *Economics as a Coordination Problem* (Kansas City, MO, 1977); Don Bellante, "A Subjectivist Essay on Modern Labor Economics," *Managerial and Decision Economics.* December 1983, 234–43; and Peter Lewin, "Perspectives on the Costs of Inflation," *Southern Economic Journal* 48.3 (January, 1983): 627–41.

Part VI

Comparative Economic Systems— The Austrian Perspective

29

Capitalism versus Socialism

Ludwig von Mises

I

Most of our contemporaries are highly critical of what they call "the unequal distribution of wealth." As they see it, justice would require a state of affairs under which nobody enjoys what are to be considered superfluous luxuries as long as other people lack things necessary for the preservation of life, health, and cheerfulness. The ideal condition of mankind, they pretend, would be an equal distribution of all consumers' goods available. As the most practical method to achieve this end, they advocate the radical expropriation of all material factors of production and the conduct of all production activities by society, that is to say, by the social apparatus of coercion and compulsion, commonly called government or state.

The supporters of this program of socialism or communism reject the economic system of capitalism for a number of reasons. Their critique emphasizes the alleged fact that the system as such is not only unjust, a violation of the perennial God-given natural law, but also inherently inefficient and thus the ultimate cause of all the misery and poverty

Reprinted from *Money, Method, and the Market Process*, edited by Richard M. Ebeling (Aubrun, AL: Praxeology Press of the Ludwig von Mises Institute and Kluwer Academic Publishers, 1990).

that plague mankind. Once the wicked institution of private ownership of the material factors of production will have been replaced by public ownership, human conditions will become blissful. Everybody will receive what he needs. All that separates mankind from this perfect state of earthly affairs is the unfairness in the distribution of wealth.

The essential viciousness of this method of dealing with the fundamental problems of mankind's material and spiritual welfare is to be seen in its preoccupation with the concept of distribution. As these authors and doctrinaires see it, the economic and social problem is to give to everybody his due, his fair share in the endowment that God or nature has destined for the use of all men. They do not see that poverty is "the primitive condition of the human race."[1] They do not realize that all that enables man to elevate his standard of living above the level of the animals is the fruit of his planned activity. Man's economic task is not the distribution of gifts dispensed by a benevolent donor, but production. He tries to alter the state of his environment in such a way that conditions become more favorable to the preservation and development of his vital forces. He works.

Precisely, say the superficial among the critics of social conditions. Labor and nothing but labor brings forth all the goods the utilization of which elevates the condition of men above the level of the animals. As all products are the output of labor, only those who labor should have the right to enjoy them.

This may sound rather plausible as far as it refers to the conditions and circumstances of some fabulous nonhuman beings. But it turns into the most fateful of all popular delusions when applied to homo sapiens. Man's eminence manifests itself in his being fully aware of the flux of time. Man lives consciously in a changing universe: he distinguishes, sooner and later, between past, present,[2] and future: he makes plans to influence the future state of affairs and tries to convert these plans into fact. Conscious planning for the future is the specifically human characteristic. Timely provision for future wants is what distinguishes human action from the hunting drives of beasts and of savages. Premeditation, early attention to future needs, leads to production for deferred consumption, to the intercalation of time between exertion and the enjoyment of its outcome, to the adoption of what Böhm-Bawerk called round-about methods of production. To the nature-given factors of production, man-made factors are added by the deferment of consumption. Man's material environment and his style of life ar radically transformed. There emerges what is called human civilization.

This civilization is not an achievement of kings, generals or other *Führers*. Neither is it the result of the labors of "common" men. It is the fruit of the cooperation of two types of men of those whose saving, i.e., deferment of consumption, makes entering upon time-absorbing, round-about methods of production possible, and of those who know how to direct the application of such methods. Without saving and successful endeavors to use the accumulated savings wisely, there cannot be any question of a standard of living worthy of the qualification human.

Simple saving, that is, the abstention from immediate consumption in order to make more abundant consumption at a later date possible, is not a specifically human contrivance. There are also animals that practice it. Driven by instinctive urges, some species of animals are also committed to what we would have to call capitalistic saving if it were done in full consciousness if its effects. But man alone has elevated intentional deferment of consumption to a fundamental principle of action. He abstains temporally from consumption in order to enjoy later the continuous services of appliances that could not have been produced without such a postponement.

Saving is always the abstention from some kind of immediate consumption for the sake of making an increase or improvement in later consumption possible. It is saving that accumulates capital, dissaving that makes the available supply of capital shrink. In acting, man chooses between increasing his competence by additional saving or reducing the amount of his capital by keeping his consumption above the rate correct accountancy considers as his income.

Additional saving as well as the nonconsumption of already previously accumulated savings are never "automatic," but always the result of an intentional abstention from instantaneous consumption. In abstaining from instantaneous consumption, the saver expects to be fully rewarded either by keeping something for later consumption or by acquiring the *property* of a capital good.

Where there is no saving, no capital goods come into existence. And there is no saving without purpose. A man defers consumption for the sake of an improvement of later conditions. He may want to improve his own conditions or those of definite other people. He does not abstain from consumption simply for the pleasure of somebody unknown.

There cannot be any such thing as a capital good that is not owned by a definite owner. Capital goods come into existence as the property of the individual or the group of individuals who were in the position to consume definite things but abstained from this consumption for the sake of later utilization. The way in which capital goods come into existence as private property determines the institutions of the capitalistic system.

Of course, today's heirs of the capitalistic civilization also construct the scheme of a world-embracing social body that forces every human being to submit meekly to all its orders. In such a socialist universe everything will be planned by the supreme authority and to the individual "comrades" no other sphere of action will be left than unconditional surrender to the will of their masters. The comrades will drudge, but all the yield of their endeavors will be at the disposal of the high authority. Such is the ideal of socialism or communism, nowadays also called planning. The individual comrade will enjoy what the supreme authority assigns to him for his consumption and enjoyment. Everything else, all material factors of production, will be owned by the authority.

Such is the alternative. Mankind has to choose: on the one side—private property in the material factors of production. Then the demand of the consumers on the market determines what has to be produced, of what quality, and in what quantity. On the other side—all the material factors of production are owned by the central authority and thus every individual entirely depends on its will and has to obey its orders. This authority alone determines what has to be produced and what and how much each comrade should be permitted to use or consume.

If one does not permit individuals to keep as their property the things produced for temporally deferred utilization, one removes any incentive to create such things and thus makes it impossible for acting man to raise his condition above the level of nonhuman animals. Thus the anti-property (i.e., socialist or communist) authors had to construct the design of a society in which all men are forced to obey unconditionally the orders issued from a central authority, from the great god called state, society, or mankind.

II

The social meaning and the economic function of private property have been widely misunderstood and misinterpreted because people confuse conditions of the market economy with those of the militaristic systems vaguely labeled feudalism. The feudal lord was a conqueror or a conqueror's accomplice. He was anxious to deprive all those who did not belong to his own cluster of any opportunity to make a living otherwise than by humbly serving him or one of his class comrades. All the land—and this means in a primitive society virtually all the material factors of production—was owned by members of the proprietary caste and to the others, to those disdainfully called the "villains," nothing was left but unconditional surrender to the armed hereditary nobility. Those not belonging to this aristocracy were serfs or slaves, they had to obey and to drudge while the products of their toil were consumed by their master.

The eminence of the inhabitants of Europe and their descendants who have settled in other continents consists in the fact that they have abolished this system and substituted for it a state of freedom and civic rights for every human being. It was a long and slow evolution, again and again interrupted by reactionary episodes, and great parts of our globe ar even today only superficially affected by it. At the end of the eighteenth century the triumphal progress of this new social system was accelerated. Its most spectacular manifestation in the moral and intellectual sphere is known as the Enlightenment, its political and constitutional reforms as the liberal movement, while its economic and social effects are commonly referred to as the Industrial Revolution and the emergence of modern capitalism.

The historians dealing with the various phases of this up-to-now most momentous and weighty period of mankind's evolution tend to confine their investigations to special aspects of the course of affairs. They mostly neglect to show how the events in the various fields of human activity were connected with one another and determined by the same ideological and material factors. Unimportant detail sometimes engrosses their attention and prevents them from seeing the most consequential facts in the right light.

The most unfortunate outcome of this methodological confusion is to be seen in the current fateful misinterpretation of the recent political and economic developments of the civilized nations.

The great liberal movement of the eighteenth and nineteenth centuries aimed at the abolition of the rule of hereditary princes and aristocracies and the establishment of the rule of elected representatives of the people. All kinds of slavery and serfdom ought to be abolished. All members of the nation should enjoy the full rights and privileges of citizenship. The laws and the practice of the administrative officers should not discriminate between the citizens.

This liberal revolutionary program clashed very soon with another program that was derived from the postulates of old communist sects. These sects, many of them inspired by religious ideas, had advocated confiscation and redistribution of land or some other forms of egalitarianism and of primitive communism. Now their successors proclaimed that a fully satisfactory state of human conditions could be attained only where all material factors of production are owned and operated by "society," and the fruits of economic endeavors are evenly distributed among all human beings.

Most of these communist[3] authors and revolutionaries were convinced that what they were aiming at was not only fully compatible with the customary program of the friends of representative government and freedom for all, but was its logical continuation, the very completion of all endeavors to give to mankind perfect happiness. Public opinion was by and large prepared to endorse this interpretation. As it was usual to call the adversaries of the liberal[4] demand for representative government the parties of the "right" and the liberal groups the parties of the "left," the communist (and later also the socialist) groups were considered as "more to the left" than the liberals. Popular opinion began to believe that while the liberal parties represent only the selfish class interests of the "exploiting" bourgeoisie, the socialist parties were fighting for the true interests of the immense majority, the proletariat.

But while these reformers were merely talking and drafting spurious plans for political action, one of the greatest and most beneficial events of mankind's history was going on—the Industrial Revolution. Its new business principle—that transformed human affairs more radically than any religious, ethical, legal, or technological innovation had done before—was mass production destined for consumption by the masses, not merely for consumption by members of the well-to-do classes. This new principle was not invented by statesmen and politicians: it was for a long time even not noticed by the members of the aristocracy, the gentry, and the urban patricians. Yet, it was the very beginning of a new and better age of human affairs when some people in Hanoverian England started to import cotton from the American colonies: some took charge of its transformation to cotton goods for customers of modest income; while still others exported such goods to the Baltic ports to have them ultimately exchanged against corn that, brought to England, appeased the hunger of starving paupers.

The characteristic feature of capitalism is the traders' unconditional dependence upon the market, that is, upon the best possible and cheapest satisfaction of the most urgent demand on the part of the consumers. For every kind of production human labor is required as a factor of production. But labor as such, however masterfully and conscientiously performed, is nothing but a waste of time, material, and human effort if it is not employed for the production of those goods and services that at the instant of their being ready for use or consumption will best satisfy in the cheapest possible way the most urgent demand of the public.

The market is the prototype of what are called democratic institutions. Supreme power is vested in the buyers, and vendors succeed only by satisfying in the best possible way the wants of the buyers. Private ownership of the factors of production forces the owners—enterprisers—to serve the consumers. Eminent economists have called the market a democracy in which every penny gives a right to vote.

III

Both the political or constitutional democracy and the economic or market democracy are administered according to the decisions of the majority. The consumers, by their buying or abstention from buying, are as supreme in the market as the citizens through their voting in plebiscites or in the election of officers are supreme in the conduct of the affairs of state. Representative government and the market economy are the product of the same evolutionary process, they condition one another, and it would seem today that they are disappearing together in the great reactionary counter-revolution of our age.

Yet, reference to this striking homogeneousness must not prevent us from realizing that, as an instrument of giving expression to the genuine wants and interests of the individuals, the economic democracy of the market is by far superior to the political democracy of representative government. As a rule it is easier to choose between the alternatives which are open to a purchaser than to make a decision in matters of state and "high" politics. The average housewife may be very clever in acquiring the things she needs to feed and to clothe her children. But she may be less fit in electing the officers called to handle matters of foreign policy and military preparedness.

Then there is another important difference. In the market not only the wants and wishes of the majority are taken into account but also those of minorities, provided they are not entirely insignificant in numbers. The book trade publishes for the general reader, but also for small groups of experts in various fields. The garment trades are not only supplying clothing for people of normal size, but also merchandise for the use of abnormal customers. But in the political sphere only the will of the majority counts, and the minority is forced to accept what they may detest for rather serious reasons.

In the market economy, the buyers determine with every penny spent the direction of the production processes and thereby the essential features of all business activities. The consumers assign to everybody his position and function in the economic organism. The owners of the material factors of production are virtually mandatories or trustees of the consumers, revocably appointed by a daily repeated election. If they fail in their attempts to serve the consumers in the best possible and cheapest way, they suffer losses and, if they do not reform in time, lose their property.

Feudal property was acquired either by conquest or by a conqueror's favor. Once acquired, it could be enjoyed forever by the owner and his heirs. But capitalistic property must be acquired again and again by utilizing it for serving the consumers in the best possible way. Every owner of material factors of production is forced to adjust the services he renders to the best possible satisfaction of the continually changing demand of the consumers. A man may start his business career as the heir of a large fortune. But this does not necessarily help him in his competition with newcomers. The adjustment of an existing railroad system to the new situation created by the emergence of motor cars, trucks, and airplanes was a more difficult problem than many of the tasks that had to be solved by enterprises newly started.

The fact that made the capitalistic methods of the conduct of business emerge and flourish is precisely the excellence of the services it renders to the masses. Nothing characterizes the fabulous improvement in the standard of living of the many better than the quantitative role that the entertainment industries play in modern business.

Capitalism has radically transformed all human affairs. Population figures have multiplied. In the few countries where neither the policies of the governments nor obstinate preservation of traditional ways on the part of the citizens put insurmountable obstacles in the way of capitalistic entrepreneurship, the living conditions of the immense majority of people have improved spectacularly. Implements never known before or considered as extravagant luxuries are now customarily available to the average man. The general standard of education and of material and spiritual well-being is improving from year to year.

All this is not an achievement of governments or of any charitable measures. More often than not it is precisely governmental action that frustrates beneficial developments which the regular operation of capitalistic institutions tends to bring about.

Let us look upon one special case. In the precapitalistic ages, saving and thereby the betterment of one's economic condition was really possible, apart from professional money-lenders (bankers), only to people who owned a farm or a shop. They could invest savings in an improvement or expansion of their property. Other people, the propertyless proletarians, could save only by hiding a few coins in a corner they considered as safe. Capitalism made the accumulation of some capital through saving accessible to everybody. Life insurance institutions, savings banks, and bonds give the opportunity of saving and earning interest to the masses of people with modest incomes, and these people make ample use of it. On the loan markets of the advanced countries, the funds provided by the numerous classes of such people play an important role. They could be an important factor in making the operation of the capitalistic system familiar to those who are not themselves employed in the financial conduct of business affairs. And first of all—they could more and more improve the economic and social standing of the many.

But unfortunately the policies of practically all nations sabotage this evolution in the most disgraceful manner. The governments of the United States, Great Britain, France, and Germany, not to speak of most of the smaller nations, were or are still committed to the most radical inflationist policies. While continually talking about their solicitude for the common man, they have without shame, again and again through government-made inflation, robbed the people who have taken out insurance policies, who are working under pension plans, who own bonds or savings deposits.

IV

The authors who in Western Europe at the end of the eighteenth century and in the first decades of the nineteenth century developed plans for the establishment of socialism were not familiar with the 2 social ideas and conditions in Central Europe. They did not pay any attention to the *Wohlfahrtsstaat*, the welfare-state of the German monarchical governments of the eighteenth century. Neither did they read the classical book of German socialism, Fichte's *Geschlossener Handelsstaat*, published in the year 1800. When much later—in the last decades of the nineteenth century—the nations of the West, first among them England, embarked upon the Fabian methods of a temperate progress toward socialism, they did not raise the question why continental governments whom they despised as backward and absolutist had long before already adopted the allegedly new and progressive principles of social reform.

But the German socialists of the second part of the nineteenth century could not avoid dealing with this problem. They had to face the policies of Bismarck, the man of whom the pro-socialist *Encyclopaedia of the Social Sciences* says that he was "with reason regarded as the foremost exponent of state socialism in his day."[5] Lassalle toyed with the idea to further the cause of socialism by cooperation with this most "reactionary" paladin of the Hohenzollern. But Lassalle's premature death put an end to such plans and, very soon, also to the activities of the socialist group of which he had been the chief. Under the leadership of the disciples of Marx, the German socialist party turned to radical opposition to the Kaiser's regime. They voted in the Reichstag against all bills suggested by the government. Of course, being a minority party, their votes could not prevent the Reichstag's approval of various pro-labor laws, among them those establishing the famous social security system. Only in one case could they prevent the creation of a government-supported socialization measure, viz., the establishment of a governmental tobacco monopoly. But all the other nationalization and municipalization measures of the Bismarck age were adopted in spite of the passionate opposition of the socialist party. And the nationalization policy of the German Reich that, thanks to the victories of its armies, in those years enjoyed all over the world an unprecedented prestige was adopted by many nations of Eastern and Southern Europe.

In vain did the German socialist doctrinaires try to explain and to justify the manifest contradiction between their fanatical advocacy of socialism and their stubborn opposition to all nationalization measures put into effect.[6] But notwithstanding the support the nationalization and municipalization policy of the authorities got from self-styled conservative and Christian parties, it very soon lost its popularity with the rulers as well as with those ruled. The nationalized industries were rather poorly operated under the management of the administrators appointed by the authorities. The services they had to render to the customers became highly unsatisfactory, and the fees they charged were more and more increased. And, worst of all, the financial results of the management of public servants were deplorable. The deficits of these outfits were a heavy burden on the national treasuries and forced again and again an increase in taxation. At the beginning of the twentieth century, one could no longer deny the obvious fact that the public authorities had scandalously failed in their attempts to administer the various business organizations they had acquired in the conduct of their "state socialism."

Such were conditions when the outcome of the first World War made the socialist parties paramount in Central and Eastern Europe and also considerably strengthened their influence in Western Europe. There was in those years in Europe practically no serious opposition to most radical pro-socialist plans.

The German revolutionary government was formed in 1918 by members of the Marxian social-democratic party. It had no less power than the Russian government of Lenin and, like the Russian leader, it considered socialism as the only reasonable and possible solution to all political and economic problems. But it was also fully familiar with the fact that the nationalization measures adopted by the Imperial Reich before the war had brought unsatisfactory financial results and rather poor service and also that the socialist measures resorted to in the years of the war had been unsuccessful. Socialism was in their opinion the great panacea, but it seemed that nobody knew what it really meant and how to bring it about properly. Thus, the victorious socialist leaders did what all governments do when they do not know what to do. They appointed a committee of professors and other people considered to be experts. For more than fifty years the Marxians had fanatically advocated socialization as the focal point of their program, as the nostrum to heal all earthly evils and to lead mankind forward into the new garden of Eden. Now they had seized power and all of the people expected that they would redeem their promise.

Now they had to socialize. But at once they had to confess that they did not know what to do and they were asking professors what socialization meant and how it could be put into practice.

It was the greatest intellectual fiasco history has ever known and it put in the eyes of all reasonable people an inglorious end to all the teachings of Marx and hosts of lesser-known utopians.

Neither was the fate of the socialist ideas and plans in the West of Europe better than in the country of Marx. The members of the Fabian Society were no less perplexed than their continental friends. Like these, they too were fully convinced that capitalism was stone dead forever and that henceforth socialism alone would rule all nations. But they too had to admit that they had no plan of action. The flamboyantly advertised scheme of Guild Socialism was, as all people had to admit very soon, simply nonsense. It quietly disappeared from the British political scene.

But, of course, the intellectual debacle of socialism and especially of Marxism in the West did not affect conditions in the East, Russia and other Eastern countries of Europe and China turned to all-round nationalization. For them, neither the critical refutation of the Marxian and other socialist doctrines nor the failure of all nationalization experiments meant anything. Marxism became the quasi-religion of the backward nations which were anxious to get the machines and, first of all, the deadly weapons developed in the West, but which abhorred the philosophy that had brought about the West's social and scientific achievements.

The Eastern political doctrine asking for immediate full socialization of all spheres of life and the pitiless extermination of all opponents gets rather sympathetic support on the part of many parties and influential politicians in the Western countries. "Building bridges to the communist sector of the world" is a task rather prevalent with many governments of the West. It is fashionable with some snobbish people to praise the unlimited despotism of Russia and China. And, worst of all, out of the taxes collected from the revenues of private business some governments, first of all that of the United States, are paying enormous subsidies to governments that have to face tremendous deficits precisely because they have nationalized many enterprises, especially railroads, post, telegraph and telephone service, and many others.

In the fully industrialized parts of our globe, in the countries of Western and Central Europe and North America, the system of private enterprise not merely survives, but continually improves and expands the services it renders. The statesmen, the bureaucrats, and the politicians look askance upon business. Most of the journalists, the writers of fiction, and the university teachers are propagating various brands of socialism. The rising generation is imbued with socialism in the schools. Only very rarely does one hear a voice criticizing socialist ideas, plans, and actions.

But socialism is for the peoples of the industrial world no longer a living force. There is no longer any question of nationalizing further branches of business.[7]

None of the many governments sympathizing with the socialist philosophy dares today seriously to suggest further measures of nationalization. On the contrary. For example, the American government as well as every reasonable American would have reason to be glad if the new Administration[8] could get rid of the Post Office with its proverbial inefficiency and its fantastic deficit.

Socialism started in the age of Saint-Simon as an attempt to give articulation to the ripeness of Caucasian man's Western civilization. It tried to preserve this aspect when it later looked upon colonialism and imperialism as its main targets. Today it is the rallying cry of the East, of the Russians and the Chinese, who reject the West's ideology, but eagerly try to copy its technology.

Notes

[Reprinted from *The Intercollegiate Review* 5 (Spring 1969)—Ed.]

1. Jeremy Bentham, "Principles of the Civil Code," vol. 1, in *Works*, J. Bowring, ed. (London: Simpkin, Marshall, 1843), p. 309.
2. About the praxeological concept of "present," see *Human Action*, 3rd ed. (Chicago: Henry Regnery, 1966), pp. 100 f.
3. The term "socialism," was fashioned only many decades later and did not come into general use before the 1850s.
4. "Liberal" is here used in its nineteenth-century meaning that still prevails in European usage. In America "liberal" is nowadays used by and large as synonymous with socialism or "moderate" socialism.
5. See W.H. Dawson, "Births," in *Encyclopaedia of the Social Sciences*, vol. 2 (New York: Macmillan, 1930), p. 573.
6. About the lame excuses of Frederick Engels and Karl Kautsky, see my book *Socialism*, J. Kahane, trans. (New Haven, CT: Yale University Press, 1951), pp. 240 ff.
7. The British Labor cabinet paid homage to its party ideology in dealing with the steel industry. But everybody knows that this is merely a facade to conceal a little the great failure of all that the various British left-wing parties were aiming at for many decades.
8. [This was the first administration of Richard Nixon; he was elected president in 1968—Ed.]

30

Excerpts from
The Free and Prosperous Commonwealth: Socialism and Interventionism
Ludwig von Mises

4. The Impracticability of Socialism

People are wont to consider socialism impracticable because they think that men lack the moral qualities demanded by a socialist society. It is feared that under socialism most men will not exhibit the same zeal in the performance of the duties and tasks assigned to them that they bring to their daily work in a social order based on private ownership of the means of production. In a capitalist society, every individual knows that the fruit of his labor is his own to enjoy, that his income increases or decreases according as the output of his labor is greater or smaller. In a socialist society, every individual will think that less depends on the efficiency of his own labor, since a fixed portion of the total output is due him in any case and the amount of the latter cannot be appreciably diminished by the loss resulting from the laziness of any one man. If, as is to be feared, such a conviction should become general, the

Reprinted from *The Free and Prosperous Commonwealth* by Ludwig von Mises (Princeton, NJ: D. Van Nostrand Company, Inc., 1962).

productivity of labor in a socialist community would drop considerably.

The objection thus raised against socialism is completely sound, but it does not get to the heart of the matter. Were it possible in a socialist community to ascertain the output of the labor of every individual comrade with the same precision with which this is accomplished for each worker by means of economic calculation in the capitalist system, the practicability of socialism would not be dependent on the good will of every individual. Society would be in a position, at least within certain limits, to determine the share of the total output to be allotted to each worker on the basis of the extent of his contribution to production. What renders socialism impracticable is precisely the fact that calculation of this kind is impossible in a socialist society.

In the capitalist system, the calculation of profitability constitutes a guide that indicates to the individual whether the enterprise he is operating ought, under the given circumstances, to be in operation at all and whether it is being run in the most efficient possible way, i.e., at the least cost in factors of production. If an undertaking proves unprofitable, this means that the raw materials, half-finished goods, and labor that are needed in it are employed by other enterprises for an end that, from the standpoint of the consumers, is more urgent and more important, or for the same end, but in a more economical manner (i.e., with a smaller expenditure of capital and labor). When, for instance, hand weaving came to be unprofitable, this signified that the capital and labor employed in weaving by machine yield a greater output and that it is consequently uneconomical to adhere to a method of production in which the same input of capital and labor yields a smaller output.

If a new enterprise is being planned, one can calculate in advance whether it can be made profitable at all and in what way. If, for example, one has the intention of constructing a railroad line, one can, by estimating the traffic to be expected and its ability to pay the freight rates, calculate whether it pays to invest capital and labor in such an undertaking. If the result of this calculation shows that the projected railroad promises no profit, this is tantamount to saying that there is other, more urgent employment for the capital and the labor that the construction of the railroad would require; the world is not yet rich enough to be able to afford such an expenditure. But it is not only when the question arises whether or not a given undertaking is to be begun at all that the calculation of value and profitability is decisive; it controls every single step that the entrepreneur takes in the conduct of his business.

Capitalist economic calculation, which alone makes rational production possible, is based on monetary calculation. Only because the prices of all goods and services in the market can be expressed in terms of money is it possible for them, in spite of their heterogeneity, to enter into a calculation involving homogeneous units of measurement. In a socialist society, where all the means of production are owned by the community, and where, consequently, there is no market and no exchange of productive goods and services, there can also be no money prices for goods and services of higher order. Such a social system would thus, of necessity, be lacking in the means for the rational management of business enterprises, viz., economic calculation. For economic calculation cannot take place in the absence of a common denominator to which all the heterogeneous goods and services can be reduced.

Let us consider a quite simple case. For the construction of a railroad from A to B several routes are conceivable. Let us suppose that a mountain stands between A and B. The railroad can be made to run over the mountain, around the mountain, or, by way of a tunnel, through the mountain. In a capitalist society, it is a very easy matter to compute which line will prove the most profitable. One ascertains the cost involved in constructing each of the three lines and the differences in operating costs necessarily incurred by the anticipated traffic on each. From these quantities it is not difficult to determine which stretch of road will be the most profitable. A socialist society could not make such calculations. For it would have no possible way of reducing to a uniform standard of measurement all the heterogeneous quantities and qualities of goods and services that here come into consideration. In the face of the ordinary, everyday problems which the management of an economy presents, a socialist society would stand helpless, for it would have no possible way of keeping its accounts.

The prosperity that has made it possible for many more people to inhabit the earth today than in the precapitalist era is due solely to the capitalist method of lengthy chains of production, which necessarily requires monetary calculation. This is impossible under socialism. In vain have socialist writers labored to demonstrate how one could still manage even without monetary and price calculation. All their efforts in this respect have met with failure.

The leadership of a socialist society would thus be confronted by a problem that it could not possibly solve. It would not be able to decide which of the innumerable possible modes of procedure is the most rational. The resulting chaos in the economy would culminate quickly and irresistibly in universal impoverishment and a retrogression to the primitive conditions under which our ancestors once lived.

The socialist ideal, carried to its logical conclusion, would eventuate in a social order in which all the means of production were owned by the people as a whole. Production would be completely in the hands of the government, the center of power in society. It alone would determine what was to be produced and how, and in what way goods ready for consumption were to be distributed. It makes little difference whether we imagine this socialist state of the future as democratically constituted or otherwise. Even a democratic socialist state would necessarily constitute a tightly organized bureaucracy in which everyone, apart from the highest officials, though he might very well, in his capacity as a voter, have participated in some fashion in framing the directives issued by the central authority, would be in the subservient position of an administrator bound to carry them out obediently.

A socialist state of this kind is not comparable to the state enterprises, no matter how vast their scale, that we have seen developing in the last decades in Europe, especially in Germany and Russia. The latter all flourish *side by side with* private ownership of the means of production. They engage in commercial transactions with enterprises that capitalists own and manage, and they receive various stimuli from these enterprises that invigorate their own operation. State railroads, for instance, are provided by their suppliers, the manufacturers of locomotives, coaches, signal installations, and other equipment, with apparatus that has proved successful elsewhere in the operation of privately owned railroads. Thence they receive the incentive to institute innovations in order to keep up with the progress in technology and in methods of business management that is taking place all around them.

It is a matter of common knowledge that national and municipal enterprises have, on the whole, failed, that they are expensive and inefficient, and that they have to be subsidized out of tax funds just to maintain themselves in operation. Of course, where a public enterprise occupies a monopolistic position—as is, for instance, generally the case with municipal transportation facilities and electric light and power plants—the bad consequences of inefficiency need not always express themselves in visible financial failure. Under certain circumstances it may be possible to conceal it by making use of the opportunity open to the monopolist of raising the price of his products and services high enough to render these enterprises, in spite of their uneconomic management, still profitable. The lower productivity of the socialist method of production merely manifests itself differently here and is not so easily recognized as otherwise; essentially, however, the case remains the same.

But none of these experiments in the socialist management of enterprises can afford us any basis for judging what it would mean if the socialist ideal of the communal ownership of *all* means of production were to be realized. In the socialist society of the future, which will leave no room whatsoever for the free activity of private enterprises operating side by side with those owned and controlled by the state, the central planning board will lack entirely the gauge provided for the whole economy by the market and market prices. In the market, where all goods and services come to be traded, exchange ratios, expressed in money prices, may be determined for everything bought and sold. In a social order based on private property, it thus becomes possible to resort to monetary calculation in checking on the result of all economic activities. The social productivity of every economic transaction may be tested by the methods of bookkeeping and cost accounting. It yet remains to be shown that public enterprises are unable to make use of cost accounting in the same way as private enterprises do. Nevertheless, monetary calculation does give even governmental and communal enterprises some basis for judging the success or failure of their management. In a completely socialist economic system, this would be quite impossible, for in the absence of private ownership of the means of production, there could be no exchange of capital goods in the market and consequently neither money prices nor monetary calculation. The general management of a purely socialist society will therefore have no means of reducing to a common denominator the costs of production of all the heterogeneous commodities that it plans to produce.

Nor can this be achieved by setting expenditures in kind against savings in kind. One cannot calculate if it is not possible to reduce to a common medium of expression hours of labor of various grades, iron, coal, building materials of every kind, machines, and all the other things needed in the operation and management of different enterprises. Calculation is possible only when one is able to reduce to monetary terms all the goods under consideration. Of course, monetary calculation has its imperfections and deficiencies, but we have nothing better to put in its place. It suffices for the practical purposes of life as long as the monetary system is sound. If we were to renounce monetary calculation, every economic computation would become absolutely impossible.

This is the decisive objection that economics raises against the possibility of a socialist society. It must forgo the intellectual division of labor that consists in the cooperation of all entrepreneurs, landowners, and workers as producers and consumers in the formation of market prices. But without it, rationality, i.e., the possibility of economic calculation, is unthinkable.

5. Interventionism

The socialist ideal is now beginning to lose more and more of its adherents. The penetrating economic and sociological investigations of the problems of socialism that have shown it to be impracticable have not remained without effect, and the failures in which socialist experiments everywhere have ended have disconcerted even its most enthusiastic supporters. Gradually people are once more beginning to realize that society cannot do without private property. Yet the hostile criticism to which the system of private ownership of the means of production has been subjected for decades has left behind such a strong prejudice against the capitalist system that, in spite of their knowledge of the inadequacy and impracticability of socialism, people cannot make up their minds to admit openly that they must return to liberal views on the question of property. To be sure, it is conceded that socialism, the communal ownership of the means of production, is altogether, or at least for the present, impracticable. But, on the other hand, it is asserted that unhampered private ownership of the means of production is also an evil. Thus people want to create a third way, a form of society standing midway between private ownership of the means of production, on the one hand, and communal ownership of the means of production, on the other. Private property will be permitted to exist, but the ways in which the means of production are employed by the entrepreneurs, capitalists, and landowners will be regulated, guided, and controlled by authoritarian decrees and prohibitions. In this way, one forms the conceptual image of a regulated market, of a capitalism circumscribed by authoritarian rules, of private property shorn of its allegedly harmful concomitant features by the intervention of the authorities.

One can best acquire an insight into the meaning and nature of this system by considering a few examples of the consequences of government interference. The crucial acts of intervention with which we have to deal aim at fixing the prices of goods and services at a height different from what the unhampered market would have determined.

In the case of prices formed on the unhampered market, or which would have been formed in the absence of interference on the part of the authorities, the costs of production are covered by the proceeds. If a lower price is decreed by the government, the proceeds will fall short of the costs. Merchants and manufacturers will, therefore, unless the storage of the goods involved would cause them to deteriorate rapidly in value, withhold their merchandise from the market in the hope of more favorable times, perhaps in the expectation that the government order will soon be rescinded. If the authorities do not want the goods concerned to disappear altogether from the market as a result of their interference, they cannot limit themselves to fixing the price; they must at the same time also decree that all stocks on hand be sold at the prescribed price.

But even this does not suffice. At the price determined on the unhampered market, supply and demand would have coincided. Now, because the price was fixed lower by government decree, the demand has increased while the supply has remained unchanged. The stocks on hand are not sufficient to satisfy fully all who are prepared to pay the prescribed price. A part of the demand will remain unsatisfied. The mechanism of the market, which otherwise tends to equalize supply and demand by means of price fluctuations, no longer operates. Now people who would have been prepared to pay the price prescribed by the authorities must leave the market with empty hands. Those who were on line earlier or who were in a position to exploit some personal connection with the sellers have already acquired the whole stock; the others have to go unprovided. If the government wishes to avoid this consequence of its intervention, which runs counter to its intentions, it must add rationing to price control and compulsory sale: a governmental regulation must determine how much of a commodity may be supplied to each individual applicant at the prescribed price.

But once the supplies already on hand at the moment of the government's intervention are exhausted, an incomparably more difficult problem arises. Since production is no longer profitable if the goods are to be sold at the price fixed by the government, it will be reduced or entirely suspended. If the government wishes to have production continue, it must compel the manufacturers to produce, and, to this end, it must also fix the prices of raw materials and half-finished goods and the wages of labor. Its decrees to this effect, however, cannot be limited to only the one or the few branches of production that the authorities wish to regulate because they deem their products especially important. They must encompass all branches of production.

They must regulate the price of all commodities and all wages. In short, they must extend their control over the conduct of all entrepreneurs, capitalists, landowners, and workers. If some branches of production are left free, capital and labor will flow into these, and the government will fail to attain the goal that it wished to achieve by its first act of intervention. But the object of the authorities is that there should be an abundance of production in precisely that branch of industry which, because of the importance they attach to its products, they have especially singled out for regulation. It runs altogether counter to their design that precisely in consequence of their intervention this branch of production should be neglected.

It is therefore clearly evident that an attempt on the part of the government to interfere with the operation of the economic system based on private ownership of the means of production fails of the goal that its authors wished to achieve by means of it. It is, from the point of view of its authors, not only futile, but downright contrary to purpose, because it enormously augments the very "evil" that it was supposed to combat. Before the price controls were decreed, the commodity was, in the opinion of the government, too expensive; now it disappears from the market altogether. This, however, is not the result aimed at by the government, which wanted to make the commodity accessible to the consumer at a cheaper price. On the contrary: from its viewpoint, the absence of the commodity, the impossibility of securing it, must appear as by far the greater evil. In this sense one can say of the intervention of the authorities that it is futile and contrary to the purpose that it was intended to serve, and of the system of economic policy that attempts to operate by means of such acts of intervention that it is impracticable and unthinkable, that it contradicts economic logic.

If the government will not set things right again by desisting from its interference, i.e., by rescinding the price controls, then it must follow up the first step with others. To the prohibition against asking any price higher than the prescribed one it must add not only measures to compel the sale of all stocks on hand under a system of enforced rationing, but price ceilings on goods of higher order, wage controls, and, ultimately, compulsory labor for entrepreneurs and workers. And these regulations cannot be limited to one or a few branches of production, but must encompass them all. There is simply no other choice than this: either to abstain from interference in the free play of the market, or to delegate the entire management of production and distribution to the government. Either capitalism or socialism: there exists no middle way.

The mechanism of the series of events just described is well known to all who have witnessed the attempts of governments in time of war and during periods of inflation to fix prices by fiat. Everyone knows nowadays that government price controls had no other result than the disappearance from the market of the goods concerned. Wherever the government resorts to the fixing of prices, the result is always the same. When, for instance, the government fixes a ceiling on residential rents, a housing shortage immediately ensues. In Austria, the Social Democratic Party has virtually abolished residential rent. The consequence is that in the city of Vienna, for example, in spite of the fact that the population has declined considerably since the beginning of the World War and that several thousand new houses have been constructed by the municipality in the meantime, many thousands of persons are unable to find accommodations.

Let us take still another example: the fixing of minimum wage rates.

When the relationship between employer and employee is left undisturbed by legislative enactments or by violent measures on the part of trade unions, the wages paid by the employer for every type of labor are exactly as high as the increment of value that it adds to the materials in production. Wages cannot rise any higher than this because, if they did, the employer could no longer make a profit and hence would be compelled to discontinue a line of production that did not pay. But neither can wages fall any lower, because then the workers would turn to other branches of industry where they would be better rewarded, so that the employer would be forced to discontinue production because of a labor shortage.

There is, therefore, in the economy always a wage rate at which all workers find employment and every entrepreneur who wishes to undertake some enterprise still profitable at that wage finds workers. This wage rate is customarily called by economists the "static" or "natural" wage. It increases if, other things being equal, the number of workers diminishes; it decreases if, other things being equal, the available quantity of capital for which employment in production is sought suffers any diminution. However, one must, at the same time, observe that it is not quite precise to speak simply of "wages" and "labor." Labor services vary greatly in quality and quantity (calculated per unit of time), and so too do the wages of labor.

If the economy never varied from the stationary state, then in a labor market unhampered by interference on the part of the government or by coercion on the part of the labor unions there would be no unemployed. But the stationary state of society is merely an imaginary construction of economic theory, an intellectual expedient indispensable for our thinking, that enables us, by contrast, to form a clear conception of the processes actually taking place in the economy which surrounds us and in which we live. Life—fortunately, we hasten to add—is never at rest. There is never a standstill in the economy, but perpetual changes, movement, innovation, the continual emergence of the unprecedented. There are, accordingly, always branches of production that are being shut down or curtailed because the demand for their products has fallen off, and other branches of production that are being expanded or even embarked upon for the first time. If we think only of the last few decades, we can at once enumerate a great number of new industries that have sprung up: e.g., the automobile industry, the airplane industry, the motion picture industry, the rayon industry, the canned goods industry, and the radio broadcasting industry. These branches of industry today employ millions of workers, only some of whom have been drawn from the increase in population. Some came from branches of production that were shut down, and even more from those that, as a result of technological improvements, are now able to manage with fewer workers.

Occasionally the changes that occur in the relations among individual branches of production take place so slowly that no worker is obliged to shift to a new type of job; only young people, just beginning to earn their livelihood, will enter, in greater proportion, the new or expanding industries. Generally, however, in the capitalist system, with its rapid strides in improving human welfare, progress takes place too swiftly to spare individuals the necessity of adapting themselves to it. When, two hundred years or more ago, a young lad learned a craft, he could count on practicing it his whole life long in the way he had learned it, without any fear of being injured by his conservatism. Things are different today. The worker too must adjust himself to changing conditions, must add to what he has learned, or begin learning anew. He must leave occupations which no longer require the same number of workers as previously and enter one which has just come into being or which now needs more workers than before. But even if he remains in his old job, he must learn new techniques when circumstances demand it.

All this affects the worker in the form of changes in wage rates. If a particular branch of business employs relatively too many workers, it discharges some, and those discharged will not easily find new work in the same branch of business. The pressure on the labor market exercised by the discharged workers depresses wages in this branch of production. This, in turn, induces the worker to look for employment in those branches of production that wish to attract new workers and are therefore prepared to pay higher wages.

From this it becomes quite clear what must be done in order to satisfy the workers' desire for employment and for high wages. Wages in general cannot be pushed above the height that they would normally occupy in a market unhampered either by government interference or other institutional pressures without creating certain side effects that cannot be desirable for the worker. Wages can be driven up in an individual industry or an individual country if the transfer of workers from other industries or their immigration from other countries is prohibited. Such wage increases are effected at the expense of the workers whose entrance is barred. Their wages are now lower than they would have been if their freedom of movement had not been hindered. The rise in wages of one group is thus achieved at the expense of the others. This policy of obstructing the free movement of labor can benefit only the workers in countries and industries suffering from a relative labor shortage. In an industry or a country where this is not the case, there is only *one* thing that can raise wages: a rise in the general productivity of labor, whether by virtue of an increase in the capital available or through an improvement in the technological processes of production.

If, however, the government fixes minimum wages by law above the height of the static or natural wage, then the employers will find that they are no longer in a position to carry on successfully a number of enterprises that were still profitable when wages stood at the lower point. They will consequently curtail production and discharge workers. The effect of an artificial rise in wages, i.e., one imposed upon the market from the outside, is, therefore, the spread of unemployment.

Now, of course, no attempt is being made today to fix minimum wage rates by law on a large scale. But the position of power that the trade unions occupy has enabled them to do so even in the absence of any positive legislation to that effect. The fact that workers form unions for the purpose of bargaining with the employers does not, in and of itself, necessarily provoke disturbances in the operation of the market. Even the fact that they successfully arrogate to themselves the right to break, without notice, contracts duly entered into by them and to lay down their tools would not itself result in any further disturbance in the labor market. What does create a new situation in the labor market is the element of coercion involved in strikes and compulsory union membership that prevails today in most of the industrial countries of Europe. Since the unionized workers deny access to employment to those who are not members of their union, and resort to open violence during strikes to prevent other workers from taking the place of those on strike, the wage demands that the unions present to the employers have precisely the same force as government decrees fixing minimum wage rates. For the employer must, if he does not wish to shut down his whole enterprise, yield to the demands of the union. He must pay wages such that the volume of production has to be restricted, because what costs more to produce cannot find as large a market as what costs less. Thus, the higher wages exacted by the trade unions become a cause of unemployment.

The unemployment originating from this source differs entirely in extent and duration from that which arises from the changes constantly taking place in the kind and quality of the labor demanded in the market. If unemployment had its cause only in the fact that there is constant progress in industrial development, it could neither assume great proportions nor take on the character of a lasting institution.

The workers who can no longer be employed in one branch of production soon find accommodation in others which are expanding or just coming into being. When workers enjoy freedom of movement and the shift from one industry to another is not impeded by legal and other obstacles of a similar kind, adjustment to new conditions takes place without too much difficulty and rather quickly. For the rest, the setting up of labor exchanges would contribute much toward reducing still further the extent of this type of unemployment.

But the unemployment produced by the interference of coercive agencies in the operation of the labor market is no transitory phenomenon continually appearing and disappearing. It is incurable as long as the cause that called it into existence continues to operate, i.e., as long as the law or the violence of the trade unions prevents wages from being reduced, by the pressure of the jobless seeking employment, to the level that they would have reached in the absence of interference on the part of the government or the unions, namely, the rate at which all those eager for work ultimately find it.

For the unemployed to be granted support by the government or by the unions only serves to enlarge the evil. If what is involved is a case of unemployment springing from dynamic changes in the economy, then the unemployment benefits only result in postponing the adjustment of the workers to the new conditions. The jobless worker who is on relief does not consider it necessary to look about for a new occupation if he no longer finds a position in his old one; at least, he allows more time to elapse before he decides to shift to a new occupation or to a new locality or before he reduces the wage rate he demands to that at which he could find work. If unemployment benefits are not set too low, one can say that as long as they are offered, unemployment cannot disappear.

If, however, the unemployment is produced by the artificial raising of the height of wage rates in consequence of the direct intervention of the government or of its toleration of coercive practices on the part of the trade unions, then the only question is who is to bear the costs involved, the employers or the workers. The state, the government, the community never do so; they load them either onto the employer or onto the worker or partially onto each. If the burden falls on the workers, then they are deprived entirely or partially of the fruits of the artificial wage increase they have received; they may even be made to bear more of these costs than the artificial wage increase yielded them. The employer can be saddled with the burden of unemployment benefits to some extent by having to pay a tax proportionate to the total amount of wages paid out by him. In this case, unemployment insurance, by raising the costs of labor, has the same effect as a further increase in wages above the static level: the profitability of the employment of labor is reduced, and the number of workers who still can be profitably engaged is concomitantly decreased. Thus, unemployment spreads even further, in an ever widening spiral. The employers can also be drawn on to pay the costs of the unemployment benefits by means of a tax on their profits or capital, without regard for the number of workers employed. But this too only tends to spread unemployment even further. For when capital is consumed or when the formation of new capital is at least slowed down, the conditions for the employment of labor become, *ceteris paribus,* less favorable.[2]

It is obviously futile to attempt to eliminate unemployment by embarking upon a program of public works that would otherwise not have been undertaken. The necessary resources for such projects must be withdrawn by taxes or loans from the application they would otherwise have found. Unemployment in one industry can, in this way, be mitigated only to the extent that it is increased in another.

From whichever side we consider interventionism, it becomes evident that this system leads to a result that its originators and advocates did not intend and that, even from their standpoint, it must appear as a senseless, self-defeating, absurd policy.

6. Capitalism: The Only Possible System of Social Organization

Every examination of the different conceivable possibilities of organizing society on the basis of the division of labor must always come to the same result: there is only the choice between communal ownership and private ownership of the means of production. All intermediate forms of social organization are unavailing and, in practice, must prove self-defeating. If one further realizes that socialism too is unworkable, then one cannot avoid acknowledging that capitalism is the only feasible system of social organization based on the division of labor. This result of theoretical investigation will not come as a surprise to the historian or the philosopher of history. If capitalism has succeeded in maintaining itself in spite of the enmity it has always encountered from both governments and the masses, if it has not been obliged to make way for other forms of social cooperation that have enjoyed to a much greater extent the sympathies of theoreticians and of practical men of affairs, this is to be attributed only to the fact that no other system of social organization is feasible.

Nor is there any further need to explain why it is impossible for us to return to the forms of social and economic organization characteristic of the Middle Ages. Over the whole area now inhabited by the modern nations of Europe the medieval economic system was able to support only a fraction of the number of people who now dwell in that region, and it placed much less in the way of material goods at the disposal of each individual for the provision of his needs than the capitalist form of production supplies men with today. A return to the Middle Ages is out of the question if one is not prepared to reduce the population to a tenth or a twentieth part of its present number and, even further, to oblige every individual to be satisfied with a modicum so small as to be beyond the imagination of modern man.

All the writers who represent the return to the Middle Ages, or, as they put it, to the "new" Middle Ages, as the only social ideal worth striving for reproach the capitalist era above all for its materialistic attitude and mentality. Yet they themselves are much more deeply committed to materialistic views than they believe. For it is nothing but the crassest materialism to think, as many of these writers do, that after reverting to the forms of political and economic organization characteristic of the Middle Ages, society could still retain all the technological improvements in production created by capitalism and thus preserve the high degree of productivity of human labor that it has attained in the capitalist era. The productivity of the capitalist mode of production is the outcome of the capitalist mentality and of the capitalist approach to man and to the satisfaction of man's wants; it is a result of modern technology only in so far as the development of technology must, of necessity, follow from the capitalist mentality. There is scarcely anything so absurd as the fundamental principle of Marx's materialist interpretation of history: "The hand mill made feudal society; the steam mill, capitalist society." It was precisely capitalist society that was needed to create the necessary conditions for the original conception of the steam mill to be developed and put into effect. It was capitalism that created the technology, and not the other way round. But no less absurd is the notion that the technological and material appurtenances of our economy could be preserved even if the intellectual foundations on which they are based were destroyed. Economic activity can no longer be carried on rationally once the prevailing mentality has reverted to traditionalism and faith in authority. The entrepreneur, the catalytic agent, as it were, of the capitalist economy and, concomitantly, also of modern technology, is inconceivable in an environment in which everyone is intent solely on the contemplative life.

If one characterizes as unfeasible every system other than that based on private ownership of the means of production, it follows necessarily that private property must be maintained as the basis of social cooperation and association and that every attempt to abolish it must be vigorously combatted. It is for this reason that liberalism defends the institution of private property against every attempt to destroy it. When, therefore, people call the liberals apologists for private property, they are completely justified, for the Greek word from which "apologist" is derived means the same as "defender." Of course, it would be better to avoid using the foreign word and to be content to express oneself in plain English. For to many people the expressions "apology" and "apologist" convey the connotation that what is being defended is unjust.

Much more important, however, than the rejection of any pejorative suggestion that may be involved in the use of these expressions is the observation that the institution of private property requires no defense, justification, support, or explanation. The continued existence of society depends upon private property, and since men have need of society, they must hold fast to the institution of private property to avoid injuring their own interests as well as the interests of everyone else. For society can continue to exist only on the foundation of private property. Whoever champions the latter champions by the same token the preservation of the social bond that unites mankind, the preservation of culture and civilization. He is an apologist and defender of society, culture, and civilization, and because he desires them as ends, he must also desire and defend the one means that leads to them, namely, private property.

To advocate private ownership of the means of production is by no means to maintain that the capitalist social system, based on private property, is perfect. There is no such thing as earthly perfection. Even in the capitalist system something or other, many things, or even everything, may not be exactly to the liking of this or that individual. But it is the only possible social system. One may undertake to modify one or another of its features as long as in doing so one does not affect the essence and foundation of the whole social order, viz., private property. But by and large we must reconcile ourselves to this system because there simply cannot be any other.

In Nature too, much may exist that we do not like. But we cannot change the essential character of natural events. If, for example, someone thinks—and there are some who have maintained as much—that the way in which man ingests his food, digests it, and incorporates it into his body is disgusting, one cannot argue the point with him. One must say to him: There is only this way or starvation. There is no third way. The same is true of property; either-or—either private ownership of the means of production, or hunger and misery for everyone.

The opponents of liberalism are wont to call its economic doctrine "optimistic." They intend this epithet either as a reproach or as a derisive characterization of the liberal way of thinking.

If by calling the liberal doctrine "optimistic" one means that liberalism considers the capitalist world as the best of all worlds, then this is nothing but pure nonsense. For an ideology based, like that of liberalism, entirely on scientific grounds, such questions as whether the capitalist system is good or bad, whether or not a better one is conceivable, and whether it ought to be rejected on certain philosophic or metaphysical grounds are entirely irrelevant. Liberalism is derived from the pure sciences of economics and sociology, which make no value judgments within their own spheres and say nothing about what ought to be or about what is good and what is bad, but, on the contrary, only ascertain what is and how it comes to be. When these sciences show us that of all the conceivable alternative ways of organizing society only one, viz., the system based on private ownership of the means of production, is capable of being realized, because all other conceivable systems of social organization are unworkable, there is absolutely nothing in this that can justify the designation "optimistic." That capitalism is practicable and workable is a conclusion that has nothing to do with optimism.

To be sure, the opponents of liberalism are of the opinion that this society is very bad. As far as this assertion contains a value judgment, it is naturally not open to any discussion that intends to go beyond highly subjective and therefore unscientific opinions. As far, however, as it is founded on an incorrect understanding of what takes place within the capitalist system, economics and sociology can rectify it. This too is not optimism. Entirely aside from everything else, even the discovery of a great many deficiencies in the capitalist system would not have the slightest significance for the problems of social policy as long as it has not been shown, not that a different social system would be better, but that it would be capable of being realized at all. But this has not been done. Science has succeeded in showing that every system of social organization that could be conceived as a substitute for the capitalist system is self-contradictory and unavailing, so that it could not bring about the results aimed at by its proponents.

How little one is justified in speaking in this connection of "optimism" and "pessimism" and how much the characterization of liberalism as "optimistic" aims at surrounding it with an unfavorable aura by bringing in extrascientific, emotional considerations is best shown by the fact that one can, with as much justice, call those people "optimists" who are convinced that the construction of a socialist or of an interventionist commonwealth would be practicable.

Most of the writers who concern themselves with economic questions never miss an opportunity to heap senseless and childish abuse on the capitalist system and to praise in enthusiastic terms either socialism or interventionism, or even agrarian socialism and syndicalism, as excellent institutions. On the other hand, there have been a few writers who, even if in much milder terms, have sung the praises of the capitalist system. One may, if one wishes, call these writers "optimists." But if one does so, then one would be a thousand times more justified in calling the antiliberal writers "hyperoptimists" of socialism, interventionism, agraian socialism, and syndicalism. The fact that this does not happen but that, instead, only liberal writers like Bastiat are called optimists, shows clearly that in these cases what we are dealing with is not an attempt at a truly scientific classification, but nothing more than a partisan caricature.

What liberalism maintains is, we repeat, by no means that capitalism is good when considered from some particular point of view. What it says is simply that for the attainment of the ends that men have in mind only the capitalist system is suitable and that every attempt to realize a socialist, interventionist, agrarian socialist, or syndicalist society must necessarily prove unsuccessful. Neurotics who could not bear this truth have called economics a dismal science. But economics and sociology are no more dismal because they show us the world as it really is than the other sciences are—mechanics, for instance, because it teaches the impracticability of perpetual motion, or biology because it teaches us the mortality of all living things.

7. Cartels, Monopolies, and Liberalism

The opponents of liberalism assert that the necessary preconditions for the adoption of the liberal program no longer exist in the contemporary world. Liberalism was still practicable when many concerns of medium size were engaged in keen competition in each industry. Nowadays, since trusts, cartels, and other monopolistic enterprises are in complete control of the market, liberalism is as good as done for in any case. It is not politics that destroyed it, but a tendency inherent in the inexorable evolution of the system of free enterprise.

The division of labor gives a specialized function to each productive unit in the economy. This process never stops as long as economic development continues. We long ago passed the stage at which the same factory produced all types of machines. Today a machine factory that does not limit itself exclusively to the production of certain types of machinery is no longer able to meet competition. With the progress of specialization, the area served by an individual supplier must continue to widen. The market supplied by a textile mill that produces only a few kinds of fabrics must be larger than that served by a weaver who weaves every kind of cloth. Undoubtedly this progressive specialization of production tends toward the development in every field of enterprises that have the whole world for their market. If this development is not opposed by protectionist and other anticapitalist measures, the result will be that in every branch of production there will be a relatively small number of concerns, or even only a single concern, intent on producing with the highest degree of specialization and on supplying the whole world.

Today, of course, we are very far from this state of affairs, since the policy of all governments aims at snipping off from the unity of the world economy small areas in which, under the protection of tariffs and other measures designed to achieve the same result, enterprises that would no longer be able to meet competition on the free world market are artificially preserved or even first called into being. Apart from considerations of commercial policy, measures of this kind, which are directed against the concentration of business, are defended on the ground that they alone have prevented the consumers from being exploited by monopolistic combinations of producers.

In order to assess the validity of this argument, we shall assume that the division of labor throughout the whole world has already advanced so far that the production of every article offered for sale is concentrated in a single concern, so that the consumer, in his capacity as a buyer, is always confronted with only a single seller. Under such conditions, according to an ill-considered economic doctrine, the producers would be in a position to keep prices pegged as high as they wished, to realize exorbitant profits, and thereby to worsen considerably the standard of living of the consumers. It is not difficult to see that this idea is completely mistaken. Monopoly prices, if they are not made possible by certain acts of intervention on the part of the government, can be lastingly exacted only on the basis of control over mineral and other natural resources. An isolated monopoly in manufacturing that yielded greater profits than those yielded elsewhere would stimulate the formation of rival firms whose competition would break the monopoly and restore prices and profits to the general rate. Monopolies in manufacturing industries cannot, however, become general, since at every given level of wealth in an economy the total quantity of capital invested and of available labor employed in production—and consequently also the amount of the social product—is a given magnitude. In any particular branch of production, or in several, the amount of capital and labor employed could be reduced in order to increase the price per unit and the aggregate profit of the monopolist or monopolists by curtailing production.

The capital and labor thereby freed would then flow into another industry. If, however, all industries attempt to curtail production in order to realize higher prices, they forthwith free labor and capital which, because they are offered at lower rates, will provide a strong stimulus to the formation of new enterprises that must again destroy the monopolistic position of the others. The idea of a universal cartel and monopoly of the manufacturing industry is therefore completely untenable.

Genuine monopolies can be established only by control of land or mineral resources. The notion that all the arable land on earth could be consolidated into a single world monopoly needs no further discussion; the only monopolies that we shall consider here are those originating in the control of useful minerals. Monopolies of this kind do, in fact, already exist in the case of a few minerals of minor importance, and it is at any rate conceivable that attempts to monopolize other minerals as well may some day prove successful. This would mean that the owners of such mines and quarries would derive an increased ground rent from them and that the consumers would restrict consumption and look for substitutes for the materials that had become more expensive. A world petroleum monopoly would lead to an increased demand for hydroelectric power, coal, etc. From the standpoint of world economy and *sub specie aeternitatis*, this would mean that we would have to be more sparing than we otherwise would have been in our use of those costly materials that we can only exhaust, but cannot replace, and thus leave more of them for future generations than would have been the case in an economy free of monopolies.

The bugbear of monopoly, which is always conjured up when one speaks of the unhampered development of the economy, need cause us no disquiet. The world monopolies that are really feasible could concern only a few items of primary production. Whether their effect is favorable or unfavorable cannot be so easily decided. In the eyes of those who, in treating economic problems, are unable to free themselves from feelings of envy, these monopolies appear as pernicious from the very fact that they yield their owners increased profits. Whoever approaches the question without prepossessions will find that such monopolies lead to a more sparing use of those mineral resources that are at man's disposal only in a rather limited quantity. If one really envies the monopolist his profit, one can, without danger and without having to expect any harmful economic consequences, have it pass into the public coffers by taxing the income from the mines.

In contradistinction to these world monopolies are the national and international monopolies, which are of practical importance today precisely because they do not originate in any natural evolutionary tendency on the part of the economic system when it is left to itself, but are the product of antiliberal economic policies. Attempts to secure a monopolistic position in regard to certain articles are in almost all cases feasible only because tariffs have divided the world market up into small national markets. Besides these, the only other cartels of any consequence are those which the owners of certain natural resources are able to form because the high cost of transportation protects them against the competition of producers from other areas in the narrow compass of their own locality.

It is a fundamental error, in judging the consequences of trusts, cartels, and enterprises supplying a market with one article alone, to speak of "control" of the market and of "price dictation" by the monopolist. The monopolist does not exercise any control, nor is he in a position to dictate prices. One could speak of control of the market or of price dictation only if the article in question were, in the strictest and most literal sense of the word, necessary for existence and absolutely irreplaceable by any substitute. This is evidently not true of any commodity. There is no economic good whose possession is indispensable to the existence of those prepared to purchase it on the market.

What distinguished the formation of a monopoly price from the formation of a competitive price is the fact that, under certain very special conditions, it is possible for the monopolist to reap a greater profit from the sale of a smaller quantity at a higher price (which we call the monopoly price) than by selling at the price that the market would determine if more sellers were in competition (the competitive price). The special condition required for the emergence of a monopoly price is that the reaction of the consumers to a price increase does not involve a falling off of demand so sharp as to preclude a greater total profit from fewer sales at higher prices. If it is actually possible to achieve a monopolistic position in the market and to use it to realize monopoly prices, then profits higher than average will be yielded in the branch of industry concerned.

It may be that, in spite of these higher profits, new enterprises of the same kind are not undertaken because of the fear that, after reducing the monopoly price to the competitive price, they will not prove correspondingly profitable. One must, nevertheless, take into account the possibility that related industries, which are in a position to enter into production of the cartelized article at a relatively small cost, may appear as competitors; and, in any case, industries producing substitute commodities will be immediately at hand to avail themselves of the favorable circumstances for expanding their own production. All these factors make it extraordinarily rare for a monopoly to arise in a manufacturing industry that is not based on monopolistic control of particular raw materials. Where such monopolies do occur, they are always made possible only by certain legislative measures, such as patents and similar privileges, tariff regulations, tax laws, and the licensing system. A few decades ago people used to speak of a transportation monopoly. To what extent this monopoly was based on the licensing system remains uncertain. Today people generally do not bother much about it. The automobile and the airplane have become dangerous competitors of the railroads. But even before the appearance of these competitors the possibility of using waterways already set a definite limit to the rates that the railroads could venture to charge for their services on several lines.

It is not only a gross exaggeration, but a misunderstanding of the facts, to speak, as one commonly does today, of the formation of monopolies as having eliminated an essential prerequisite for the realization of the liberal ideal of a capitalist society. Twist and turn the monopoly problem as one may, one always comes back to the fact that monopoly prices are possible only where there is control over natural resources of a particular kind or where legislative enactments and their administration create the necessary conditions for the formation of monopolies. In the unhampered development of the economy, with the exception of mining and related branches of production, there is no tendency toward the exclusion of competition. The objection commonly raised against liberalism that the conditions of competition as they existed at the time when classical economics and liberal ideas were first developed no longer prevail is in no way justified. Only a few liberal demands (viz., free trade within and between nations) need to be realized in order to re-establish these conditions.

31

Why the Worst Get on Top

Friedrich A. Hayek

Power tends to corrupt, and absolute power corrupts
absolutely.   —Lord Acton.

We must now examine a belief from which many who
regard the advent of totalitarianism as inevitable derive con-
solation and which seriously weakens the resistance of many
others who would oppose it with all their might if they fully
apprehended its nature. It is the belief that the most repellent features of the totalitarian regimes are due to the historical accident that they were established by groups of
blackguards and thugs. Surely, it is argued, if in Germany
the creation of a totalitarian regime brought the Streichers
and Killingers, the Leys and Heines, the Himmlers and
Heydrichs to power, this may prove the viciousness of the
German character but not that the rise of such people is the
necessary consequence of a totalitarian system. Why should
it not be possible that the same sort of system, if it be necessary to achieve important ends, be run by decent people for
the good of the community as a whole?

We must not deceive ourselves into believing that all
good people must be democrats or will necessarily wish to

Reprinted from *The Road to Serfdom* by Friedrich A. Hayek (Chicago: The University of Chicago Press, 1956).

have a share in the government. Many, no doubt, would rather entrust it to somebody whom they think more competent. Although this might be unwise, there is nothing bad or dishonorable in approving a dictatorship of the good. Totalitarianism, we can already hear it argued, is a powerful system alike for good and evil, and the purpose for which it will be used depends entirely on the dictators. And those who think that it is not the system which we need fear, but the danger that it might be run by bad men, might even be tempted to forestall this danger by seeing that it is established in time by good men.

No doubt an American or English "fascist" system would greatly differ from the Italian or German models; no doubt, if the transition were effected without violence, we might expect to get a better type of leader. And, if I had to live under a fascist system, I have no doubt that I would rather live under one run by Englishmen or Americans than under one run by anybody else. Yet all this does not mean that, judged on our present standards, our fascist system would in the end prove so very different or much less intolerable than its prototypes. There are strong reasons for believing that what to us appear the worst features of the existing totalitarian systems are not accidental by-products but phenomena which totalitarianism is certain sooner or later to produce. Just as the democratic statesman who sets out to plan economic life will soon be confronted with the alternative of either assuming dictatorial powers or abandoning his plans, so the totalitarian dictator would soon have to choose between disregard of ordinary morals and failure. It is for this reason that the unscrupulous and uninhibited are likely to be more successful in a society tending toward totalitarianism. Who does not see this has not yet grasped the full width of the gulf which separates totalitarianism from a liberal regime, the utter difference between the whole moral atmosphere under collectivism and the essentially individualist Western civilization.

The "moral basis of collectivism" has, of course, been much debated in the past; but what concerns us here is not its moral basis but its moral results. The usual discussions of the ethical aspects of collectivism refer to the question whether collectivism is demanded by existing moral convictions; or what moral convictions would be required if collectivism is to produce the hoped-for results. Our question, however, is what moral views will be produced by a collectivist organization of society, or what views are likely to rule it. The interaction between morals and institutions may well have the effect that the ethics produced by collectivism will be altogether different from the moral ideas that lead to the demand for collectivism. While we are likely to think that, since the desire for a collectivist system springs from high moral motives, such a system must be the breeding-ground for the highest virtues, there is, in fact, no reason why any system should necessarily enhance those attitudes which serve the purpose for which it was designed. The ruling moral views will depend partly on the qualities that will lead individuals to success in a collectivist or totalitarian system and partly on the requirements of the totalitarian machinery.

We must here return for a moment to the position which precedes the suppression of democratic institutions and the creation of a totalitarian regime. In this stage it is the general demand for quick and determined government action that is the dominating element in the situation, dissatisfaction with the slow and cumbersome course of democratic procedure which makes action for action's sake the goal. It is then the man or the party who seems strong and resolute enough "to get things done" who exercises the greatest appeal. "Strong" in this sense means not merely a numerical majority—it is the ineffectiveness of parliamentary majorities with which people are dissatisfied. What they will seek is somebody with such solid support as to inspire confidence that he can carry out whatever he wants. It is here that the new type of party, organized on military lines, comes in.

In the Central European countries the socialist parties had familiarized the masses with political organizations of a semi-military character designed to absorb as much as possible of the private life of the members. All that was wanted to give one group overwhelming power was to carry the same principle somewhat further, to seek strength not in the assured votes of huge numbers at occasional elections but in the absolute and unreserved support of a smaller but more thoroughly organized body. The chance of imposing a totalitarian regime on a whole people depends on the leader's first collecting round him a group which is prepared voluntarily to submit to that totalitarian discipline which they are to impose by force upon the rest.

Although the socialist parties had the strength to get anything if they had cared to use force, they were reluctant to do so. They had, without knowing it, set themselves a task which only the ruthless ready to disregard the barriers of accepted morals can execute.

That socialism can be put into practice only by methods which most socialists disapprove is, of course, a lesson learned by many social reformers in the past. The old socialist parties were inhibited by their democratic ideals; they did not possess the ruthlessness required for the performance of their chosen task. It is characteristic that both in Germany and in Italy the success of fascism was preceded by the refusal of the socialist parties to take over the responsibilities of government. They were unwilling wholeheartedly to employ the methods to which they had pointed the way. They still hoped for the miracle of a majority's agreeing on a particular plan for the organization of the whole of society; others had already learned the lesson that in a planned society the question can no longer be on what do a majority of the people agree but what the largest single group is whose members agree sufficiently to make unified direction of all affairs possible; or, if no such group large enough to enforce its views exists, how it can be created and who will succeed in creating it.

There are three main reasons why such a numerous and strong group with fairly homogeneous views is not likely to be formed by the best but rather by the worst elements of any society. By our standards the principles on which such a group would be selected will be almost entirely negative.

In the first instance, it is probably true that, in general, the higher the education and intelligence of individuals become, the more their views and tastes are differentiated and the less likely they are to agree on a particular hierarchy of values. It is a corollary of this that if we wish to find a high degree of uniformity and similarity of outlook, we have to descend to the regions of lower moral and intellectual standards where the more primitive and "common" instincts and tastes prevail. This does not mean that the majority of people have low moral standards; it merely means that the largest group of people whose values are very similar are the people with low standards. It is, as it were, the lowest common denominator which unites the largest number of people. If a numerous group is needed, strong enough to impose their views on the values of life on all the rest, it will never be those with highly differentiated and developed tastes—it will be those who form the "mass" in the derogatory sense of the term, the least original and independent, who will be able to put the weight of their numbers behind their particular ideals.

If, however, a potential dictator had to rely entirely on those whose uncomplicated and primitive instincts happen to be very similar, their number would scarcely give sufficient weight to their endeavors. He will have to increase their numbers by converting more to the same simple creed.

Here comes in the second negative principle of selection: he will be able to obtain the support of all the docile and gullible, who have no strong convictions of their own but are prepared to accept a ready-made system of values if it is only drummed into their ears sufficiently loudly and frequently. It will be those whose vague and imperfectly formed ideas are easily swayed and whose passions and emotions are readily aroused who will thus swell the ranks of the totalitarian party.

It is in connection with the deliberate effort of the skilful demagogue to weld together a closely coherent and homogeneous body of supporters that the third and perhaps most important negative element of selection enters. It seems to be almost a law of human nature that it is easier for people to agree on a negative program—on the hatred of an enemy, on the envy of those better off—than on any positive task. The contrast between the "we" and the "they," the common fight against those outside the group, seems to be an essential ingredient in any creed which will solidly knit together a group for common action. It is consequently always employed by those who seek, not merely support of a policy, but the unreserved allegiance of huge masses. From their point of view it has the great advantage of leaving them greater freedom of action than almost any positive program. The enemy, whether he be internal, like the "Jew" or the "kulak," or external, seems to be an indispensable requisite in the armory of a totalitarian leader.

That in Germany it was the Jew who became the enemy until his place was taken by the "plutocracies" was no less a result of the anticapitalist resentment on which the whole movement was based than the selection of the kulak in Russia. In Germany and Austria the Jew had come to be regarded as the representative of capitalism because a traditional dislike of large classes of the population for commercial pursuits had left these more readily accessible to a group that was practically excluded from the more highly esteemed occupations. It is the old story of the alien race's being admitted only to the less respected trades and then being hated still more for practicing them. The fact that German anti-Semitism and anti-capitalism spring from the same root is of great importance for the understanding of what has happened there, but this is rarely grasped by foreign observers.

To treat the universal tendency of collectivist policy to become nationalistic as due entirely to the necessity for securing unhesitating support would be to neglect another and no less important factor. It may, indeed, be questioned whether anyone can realistically conceive of a collectivist program other than in the service of a limited group, whether collectivism can exist in any form other than that of some kind of particularism, be it nationalism, racialism, or classism. The belief in the community of aims and interests with fellow-men seems to presuppose a greater degree of similarity of outlook and thought than exists between men merely as human beings. If the other members of one's group cannot all be personally known, they must at least be of the same kind as those around us, think and talk in the same way and about the same kind of things, in order that we may identify ourselves with them. Collectivism on a world scale seems to be unthinkable—except in the service of a small ruling élite. It would certainly raise not only technical but, above all, moral problems which none of our socialists is willing to face. If the English proletarian, for instance, is entitled to an equal share of the income now derived from his country's capital resources, and of the control of their use, because they are the result of exploitation, so on the same principle all the Indians would be entitled not only to the income from but also to the use of a proportional share of the British capital.

But what socialists seriously contemplate the equal division of existing capital resources among the people of the world? They all regard the capital as belonging not to humanity but to the nation—though even within the nation few would dare to advocate that the richer regions should be deprived of some of "their" capital equipment in order to help the poorer regions. What socialists proclaim as a duty toward the fellow-members of the existing states they are not prepared to grant to the foreigner. From a consistent collectivist point of view the claims of the "have-not" nations for a new division of the world are entirely justified—though, if consistently applied, those who demand it most loudly would lose by it almost as much as the richest nations. They are, therefore, careful not to base their claims on any equalitarian principles but on their pretended superior capacity to organize other peoples.

One of the inherent contradictions of the collectivist philosophy is that, while basing itself on the humanistic morals which individualism has developed, it is practicable only within a relatively small group. That socialism so long as it remains theoretical is internationalist, while as soon as it is put into practice, whether in Russia or in Germany, it becomes violently nationalist, is one of the reasons why "liberal socialism" as most people in the western world imagine it is purely theoretical, while the practice of socialism is everywhere totalitarian.[1] collectivism has no room for the wide humanitarianism of liberalism but only for the narrow particularism of the totalitarian.

If the "community" or the state are prior to the individual, if they have ends of their own independent of and superior to those of the individuals, only those individuals who work for the same ends can be regarded as members of the community. It is a necessary consequence of this view that a person is respected only as a member of the group, that is, only if and in so far as he works for the recognized common ends, and that he derives his whole dignity only from this membership and not merely from being man. Indeed, the very concepts of humanity and therefore of any form of internationalism are entirely products of the individualist view of man, and there can be no place for them in a collectivist system of thought.[2] Apart from the basic fact that the community of collectivism can extend only as far as the unity of purpose of the individuals exists or can be created, several contributory factors strengthen the tendency of collectivism to become particularist and exclusive. Of these, one of the most important is that the desire of the individual to identify himself with a group is very frequently the result of a feeling of inferiority and that therefore his want will be satisfied only if membership of the group confers some superiority over outsiders. Sometimes, it seems, the very fact that these violent instincts which the individual knows he must curb within the group can be given a free range in the collective action toward the outsider, becomes a further inducement for merging personality in that of the group. There is a profound truth expressed in the title of Reinhold Niebuhr's *Moral Man and Immoral Society*—however little we can follow him in the conclusions he draws from his thesis. There is, indeed, as he says elsewhere, "an increasing tendency among modern men to imagine themselves ethical because they have delegated their vices to larger and larger groups."[3] To act on behalf of a group seems to free people of many of the moral restraints which control their behavior as individuals within the group.

The definitely antagonistic attitude which most planners take toward internationalism is further explained by the fact that in the existing world all outside contacts of a group are obstacles to their effectively planning the sphere in which they can attempt it. It is therefore no accident that, as the editor of one of the most comprehensive collective studies on planning has discovered to his chagrin, "most 'planners' are militant nationalists."[4]

The nationalist and imperialist propensities of socialist planners, much more common than is generally recognized, are not always as flagrant as, for example, in the case of the Webbs and some of the other early Fabians, with whom enthusiasm for planning was characteristically combined with the veneration for the large and powerful political units and a contempt for the small state. The historian Élie Halévy, speaking of the Webbs when he first knew them forty years ago, records that their socialism was profoundly antiliberal. "They did not hate the Tories, indeed they were extraordinarily lenient to them, but they had no mercy for Gladstonian Liberalism. It was the time of the Boer War and both the advanced liberals and the men who were beginning to form the Labour Party had generously sided with the Boers against British Imperialism, in the name of freedom and humanity. But the two Webbs and their friend, Bernard Shaw, stood apart. They were ostentatiously imperialistic. The independence of small nations might mean something to the liberal individualist. It meant nothing to collectivists like themselves. I can still hear Sidney Webb explaining to me that the future belonged to the great administrative nations, where the officials govern and the police keep order." And elsewhere Halévy quotes George Bernard Shaw, arguing, about the same time, that "the world is to the big and powerful states by necessity; and the little ones must come within their border or be crushed out of existence."[5]

I have quoted at length these passages, which would not surprise one in a description of the German ancestors of National Socialism, because they provide so characteristic an example of that glorification of power which easily leads from socialism to nationalism and which profoundly affects the ethical views of all collectivists. So far as the rights of small nations are concerned, Marx and Engels were little better than most other consistent collectivists, and the views occasionally expressed about Czechs or Poles resemble those of contemporary National Socialists.[6]

While to the great individualist social philosophers of the nineteenth century, to a Lord Acton or a Jacob Burckhardt, down to contemporary socialists, like Bertrand Russell, who have inherited the liberal tradition, power itself has always appeared the archevil, to the strict collectivist it is a goal in itself. It is not only, as Russell has so well described, that the desire to organize social life according to a unitary plan itself springs largely from a desire for power.[7] It is even more the outcome of the fact that, in order to achieve their end, collectivists must create power—power over men wielded by other men—of a magnitude never before known, and that their success will depend on the extent to which they achieve such power.

This remains true even though many liberal socialists are guided in their endeavors by the tragic illusion that by depriving private individuals of the power they possess in an individualist system, and by transferring this power to society, they can thereby extinguish power. What all those who argue in this manner overlook is that, by concentrating power so that it can be used in the service of a single plan, it is not merely transferred but infinitely heightened; that, by uniting in the hands of some single body power formerly exercised independently by many, an amount of power is created infinitely greater than any that existed before, so much more far-reaching as almost to be different in kind. It is entirely fallacious when it is sometimes argued that the great power exercised by a central planning board would be "no greater than the power collectively exercised by private boards of directors."[8] There is, in a competitive society, nobody who can exercise even a fraction of the power which a socialist planning board would possess, and if nobody can consciously use the power, it is just an abuse of words to assert that it rests with all the capitalists put together.[9] It is merely a play upon words to speak of the "power collectively exercised by private boards of directors" so long as they do not combine to concerted action—which would, of course, mean the end of competition and the creation of a planned economy. To split or decentralize power is necessarily to reduce the absolute amount of power, and the competitive system is the only system designed to minimize by decentralization the power exercised by man over man.

We have seen before how the separation of economic

and political aims is an essential guaranty of individual freedom and how it is consequently attacked by all collectivists.
To this we must now add that the "substitution of political
for economic power" now so often demanded means necessarily the substitution of power from which there is no escape for a power which is always limited. What is called
economic power, while it can be an instrument of coercion,
is, in the hands of private individuals, never exclusive or
complete power, never power over the whole life of a person. But centralized as an instrument of political power it
creates a degree of dependence scarcely distinguishable
from slavery.

From the two central features of every collectivist system, the need for a commonly accepted system of ends of
the group and the all-overriding desire to give to the group
the maximum of power to achieve these ends, grows a definite system of morals, which on some points coincides and
on other violently contrasts with ours—but differs from it
in one point which makes it doubtful whether we can call it
morals: that it does not leave the individual conscience free
to apply its own rules and does not even know any general
rules which the individual is required or allowed to observe
in all circumstances. This makes collectivist morals so different from what we have known as morals that we find it
difficult to discover any principle in them, which they nevertheless possess.

The difference of principle is very much the same as
that which we have already considered in connection with
the Rule of Law. Like formal law, the rules of individualist
ethics, however unprecise they may be in many respects, are
general and absolute; they prescribe or prohibit a general
type of action irrespective of whether in the particular instance the ultimate purpose is good or bad. To cheat or
steal, to torture or betray a confidence, is held to be bad,
irrespective of whether or not in the particular instance any

harm follows from it. Neither the fact that in a given instance nobody may be the worse for it, nor any high purpose for which such an act may have been committed, can alter the fact that it is bad. Though we may sometimes be forced to choose between different evils, they remain evils.

The principle that the end justifies the means is in individualist ethics regarded as the denial of all morals. In collectivist ethics it becomes necessarily the supreme rule; there is literally nothing which the consistent collectivist must not be prepared to do if it serves "the good of the whole," because the "good of the whole" is to him the only criterion of what ought to be done. The *raison d'état,* in which collectivist ethics has found its most explicit formulation, knows no other limit than that set by expediency—the suitability of the particular act for the end in view. And what the *raison d'état* affirms with respect to the relations between different countries applies equally to the relations between different individuals within the collectivist state. There can be no limit to what its citizen must be prepared to do, no act which his conscience must prevent him from committing, if it is necessary for an end which the community has set itself or which his superiors order him to achieve.

The absence of absolute formal rules in collectivist ethics does not, of course, mean that there are not some useful habits of the individuals which a collectivist community will encourage and others which it will discourage. Quite the reverse; it will take a much greater interest in the individual's habits of life than an individualist community. To be a useful member of a collectivist society requires very definite qualities which must be strengthened by constant practice. The reason why we designate these qualities as "useful habits" and can hardly describe them as moral virtues is that the individual could never be allowed to put these rules above any definite orders or to let them become an obstacle to the achievement of any of the particular aims of his community.

They only serve, as it were, to fill any gaps which direct orders or the designation of particular aims may leave, but they can never justify a conflict with the will of the authority.

The differences between the virtues which will continue to be esteemed under a collectivist system and those which will disappear is well illustrated by a comparison of the virtues which even their worst enemies admit the Germans, or rather the "typical Prussian," to possess, and those of which they are commonly thought lacking and in which the English people, with some justification, used to pride themselves as excelling. Few people will deny that the Germans on the whole are industrious and disciplined, thorough and energetic to the degree of ruthlessness, conscientious and single-minded in any tasks they undertake; that they possess a strong sense of order, duty, and strict obedience to authority; and that they often show great readiness to make personal sacrifices and great courage in physical danger. All these make the German an efficient instrument in carrying out an assigned task, and they have accordingly been carefully nurtured in the old Prussian state and the new Prussian-dominated Reich. What the "typical German" is often thought to lack are the individualist virtues of tolerance and respect for other individuals and their opinions, of independence of mind and that uprightness of character and readiness to defend one's own convictions against a superior which the Germans themselves, usually conscious that they lack it, call *Zivilcourage,* of consideration for the weak and infirm, and of that healthy contempt and dislike of power which only an old tradition of personal liberty creates. Deficient they seem also in most of those little yet so important qualities which facilitate the intercourse between men in a free society: kindliness and a sense of humor, personal modesty, and respect for the privacy and belief in the good intentions of one's neighbor.

After what we have already said it will not cause surprise that these individualist virtues are at the same time eminently social virtues—virtues which smooth social contacts and which make control from above less necessary and at the same time more difficult. They are virtues which flourish wherever the individualist or commercial type of society has prevailed and which are missing according as the collectivist or military type of society predominates—a difference which is, or was, as noticeable between the various regions of Germany as it has now become of the views which rule in Germany and those characteristic of the West. Until recently, at least,in those parts of Germany which have been longest exposed to the civilizing forces of commerce, the old commercial towns of the south and west and the Hanse towns, the general moral concepts were probably much more akin to those of the Western people than to those which have now become dominant all over Germany.

It would, however, be highly unjust to regard the masses of the totalitarian people as devoid of moral fervor because they give unstinted support to a system which to us seems a denial of most moral values. For the great majority of them the opposite is probably true: the intensity of the moral emotions behind a movement like that of National Socialism or communism can probably be compared only to those of the great religious movements of history. Once you admit that the individual is merely a means to serve the ends of the higher entity called society or the nation, most of those features of totalitarian regimes which horrify us follow of necessity. From the collectivist standpoint intolerance and brutal suppression of dissent, the complete disregard of the life and happiness of the individual, are essential and unavoidable consequences of this basic premise, and the collectivist can admit this and at the same time claim that his system is superior to one in which the "selfish" interests of the individual are allowed to obstruct the full realization of the ends the community pursues. When German philosophers again and again represent the striving for personal happiness as itself immoral and only the fulfillment of an imposed duty as praiseworthy, they are perfectly sincere, however difficult this may be to understand for those who have been brought up in a different tradition.

Where there is one common all-overriding end, there is no room for any general morals or rules. To a limited extent we ourselves experience this in wartime. But even war and the greatest peril had led in the democratic countries only to a very moderate approach to totalitarianism, very little setting-aside of all other values in the service of a single purpose. But where a few specific ends dominate the whole of society, it is inevitable that occasionally cruelty may become a duty; that acts which revolt all our feeling, such as the shooting of hostages or the killing of the old or sick, should be treated as mere matters of expediency; that the compulsory uprooting and transportation of hundreds of thousands should become an instrument of policy approved by almost everybody except the victims; or that suggestions like that of a "conscription of woman for breeding purposes" can be seriously contemplated. There is always in the eyes of the collectivist a greater goal which these acts serve and which to him justifies them because the pursuit of the common end of society can know no limits in any rights or values of any individual.

But while for the mass of the citizens of the totalitarian state it is often unselfish devotion to an ideal, although one that is repellent to us, which makes them approve and even perform such deeds, this cannot be pleaded for those who guide its policy. To be a useful assistant in the running of a totalitarian state, it is not enough that a man should be prepared to accept specious justification of vile deeds; he must himself be prepared actively to break every moral rule he has ever known if this seems necessary to achieve the end set for him. Since it is the supreme leader who alone determines the ends, his instruments must have no moral convictions of their own. They must, above all, be unreservedly committed to the person of the leader; but next to this the most important thing is that they should be completely un-principled and literally capable of everything. They must have no ideals of their own which they want to realize; no ideas about right or wrong which might interfere with the intentions of the leader. There is thus in the positions of power little to attract those who hold moral beliefs of the kind which in the past have guided the European peoples, little which could compensate for the distastefulness of many of the particular tasks, and little opportunity to gratify any more idealistic desires, to recompense for the undeni-able risk, the sacrifice of most of the pleasures of private life and of personal independence which the posts of great re-sponsibility involve. The only tastes which are satisfied are the taste for power as such and the pleasure of being obeyed and of being part of a well-functioning and immensely pow-erful machine to which everything else must give way.

Yet while there is little that is likely to induce men who are good by our standards to aspire to leading positions in the totalitarian machine, and much to deter them, there will be special opportunities for the ruthless and unscrupulous. There will be jobs to be done about the badness of which taken by themselves nobody has any doubt, but which have to be done in the service of some higher end, and which have to be executed with the same expertness and efficiency as any others. And as there will be need for actions which are bad in themselves, and which all those still influenced by traditional morals will be reluctant to perform, the readi-ness to do bad things becomes a path to promotion and power. The positions in a totalitarian society in which it is necessary to practice cruelty and intimidation, deliberate de-ception and spying, are numerous. Neither the Gestapo nor the administration of a concentration camp, neither the Ministry of Propaganda nor the S.A. or S.S. (or their Italian or Russian counterparts), are suitable places for the exercise of humanitarian feelings. Yet it is through positions like these that the road to the highest positions in the totalitarian state leads. It is only too true when a distinguished American economist concludes from a similar brief enumeration of the duties of the authorities of a collectivist state that "they would have to do these things whether they wanted to or not: and the probability of the people in power being individuals who would dislike the possession and exercise of power is on a level with the probability that an extremely tender-hearted person would get the job of whipping-master in a slave plantation."[10]

We cannot, however, exhaust this subject here. The problem of the selection of the leaders is closely bound up with the wide problem of selection according to the opinions held, or rather according to the readiness with which a person conforms to an ever changing set of doctrines. And this leads us to one of the most characteristic moral features of totalitarianism: its relation to, and its effect on, all the virtues falling under the general heading of truthfulness.

Notes

1. Cf. now the instructive discussion in Franz Borkenau, *Socialism, National or International?* (1942).
2. It is entirely in the spirit of collectivism when Nietzsche makes his Zarathustra say:
   "A thousand goals have existed hitherto, for a thousand people existed. But the fetter for the thousand necks is still lacking, the one goal is still lacking. Humanity has no goal yet.
   "But tell me, I pray, my brethren: if the goal be lacking to humanity, is not humanity itself lacking?"
3. Quoted from an article of Dr. Niebuhr's by E. H. Carr, *The Twenty Years' Crisis* (1941), p. 203.
4. Findlay Mackenzie, ed., *Planned Society, Yesterday, Today, Tomorrow: A Symposium* (1937), p. xx.
5. Élie Halévy, *L'Ere des tyrannies* (Paris, 1938), p. 217, and *History of the English People*, Epilogue, I, 105–6.

6. Cf. Karl Marx, *Revolution and Counter- revolution,* and Engels's letter to Marx, May 23, 1851.
7. Bertrand Russell, *The Scientific Outlook* (1931), p. 211.
8. B. E. Lippincott, in his Introduction to Oscar Lange and F. M. Taylor, *On the Economic Theory of Socialism* (Minneapolis, 1938), p. 35.
9. We must not allow ourselves to be deceived by the fact that the word "power," apart from the sense in which it is used with respect to human beings, is also used in an impersonal (or rather anthropomorphic) sense for any determining cause. Of course, there will always be something that determines everything that happens, and in this sense the amount of power existing must always be the same. But this is not true of the power consciously wielded by human beings.
10. Frank H. Knight in the *Journal of Political Economy,* December, 1938, p. 869.

32

The Perils of Regulation: A Market-Process Approach

Israel M. Kirzner

Introduction

Economists have for at least two centuries debated the merits of government regulation of the market economy. In recent decades, however, this debate appeared to die down, and for a number of years it seemed that economists, with very few exceptions, subscribed to (and indeed helped propagate) a strongly approving view of extensive government intervention in the marketplace. Only recently has the pendulum of professional opinion begun to swing away from a definitely interventionist position, permitting a renewal of the classic debate about government regulation of the economy.

The position in favor of extensive government regulation of the market, of course, must be sharply distinguished from the views of radical critics of capitalism. The interventionist position, unlike that of radical critics, in general thoroughly appreciates the role of the market system in the efficient allocation of resources. The interventionist position fully accepts the central theorem of welfare economics concerning the Pareto optimality achieved, on appropriate as-

Reprinted from *Discovery and the Capitalist Process* by Israel M. Kirzner (Chicago: The University of Chicago Press, 1985).

sumptions, by the competitive market in general equilibrium. Intervention, however, is said to be required by the
real-world impossibility of fulfilling the assumptions needed
to hold for a perfectly competitive equilibrium to prevail.
Because of chronic "market failure" attributable to the violation of these assumptions, the interventionist position deems
it essential that government actively modify the operation
of the free market by extensive, even massive, doses of intervention and regulation. The interventionist position holds
that the market economy, suitably modified by a judicious
combination of government controls on prices, quality of
outputs, and the organization of industry, can achieve reasonably satisfactory results. This position came to be so en-
trenched in professional opinion that, supported (as it always has been) by the layman's intuition, interventionism
became a virtually unchallenged orthodoxy.

Only recently has this orthodoxy begun to crumble.
Both the layman and the economist have come to suspect
that government interventions, especially those limiting
competition and controlling prices, are consistently responsible for undesirable consequences. Confidence in the ability
of government officials to construct a useful program of
controls that would correct "market failure" without generating new problems attributable to government action itself
has been rather thoroughly shaken. For many members of
the public, and even for many economists, the crumbling
of orthodoxy has come as a sharp surprise, if not a jarring
shock. Economists now must rethink the theory of the market. They have begin to see that the assumption that the
market can approximate a competitive equilibrium is more
robust than hitherto believed. They have argued that government regulation produces its own undesirable distortions in market outcomes. Finally, economists have begun
to understand that the political economy of regulation tends
to ensure that market interventions are far more likely to
be undertaken to further the well-being of special interests

(not excepting those of the regulators themselves) than of the public at large.

This essay, too, draws attention to problems that appear to be the inescapable results of government regulation of the market. However, the approach taken here differs substantially from those just mentioned in that it does not postulate instantaneous or even rapid achievement of a general equilibrium in the free market; nor does it emphasize the undesirable distortions in equilibrium conditions introduced by government regulation. And to simplify matters, the discussion will relate to controls assumed to be deliberately introduced and enforced by legislators and officials intent on nothing but the welfare of the consuming public. The position developed here argues that intervention tends to interfere harmfully in the *entrepreneurial process* upon which the most basic of the market's virtues (conceded in principle by its interventionist critics) must surely depend.

To avoid misunderstanding, it should be emphasized that I do not wish to minimize the impact of those implications of regulation upon which my own argument does *not* rest. There can be little doubt that much regulation has been inspired, consciously or not, by considerations other than the goal of contributing to the public weal.[1] And the propensity of government interventions to generate tendencies toward suboptimal equilibrium configurations has certainly been amply demonstrated by economists from Bastiat to Friedman.[2] I merely contend that, valid though these approaches to a critique of interventionism undoubtedly are, they do not exhaust the phenomena to be explained. To sharpen the presentation of the approach taken here, regulations are assumed to be introduced and enforced with only the public welfare in mind. Many of regulation's undesirable consequences undoubtedly can be attributed to the tendency for regulation to serve the interests of regulators. I maintain that, quite apart from such difficulties, regulation generates economic confusion and inefficiency. This confusion and inefficiency are perceived more clearly by assuming, for the sake of argument, that those *other* difficulties (arising out of the regulators' self-interest) are absent.

Interventionism and Socialism: A Parallel

The surprise and dismay experienced today by so many economists and others at the manifest failure of well-meaning interventionist measures to create anything but inefficiencies of their very own is reminiscent in many ways of the surprise and disquiet experienced some sixty years ago when Mises first demonstrated on theoretical grounds, the inability of a socialized economy to perform the economic calculation needed for social efficiency. It is instructive to pursue this parallel further, for properly understood, Mises's theoretical argument regarding the socialist (that is, nonmarket) economy suggests useful insights into the problems of the hampered (that is, regulated) market economy. It was the earlier failure (by Mises's readers) to understand the operation and function of the market economy that led them to assume uncritically that a socialist society, in principle, need encounter no difficulty in the attainment of social efficiency. The realization that this assumption was far from obviously justified occasioned the surprise and disquiet following Mises's famous article. The now crumbling orthodoxy upon which the interventionist approach until very recently has rested reflects misunderstandings concerning the operation and function of markets. And those misunderstandings bear a remarkable likeness to those pointed out by Mises, and later by Hayek. These deep-rooted misunderstandings, in turn, appear responsible for the surprise and dismay occasioned by the realization that government regulation may itself be the problem rather than the solution it had so obviously seemed to be.

The hampered, regulated market, of course, is not at

all the same thing as the fully socialized economy which Mises and Hayek studied. In the socialized economy there is no market at all, free or otherwise, for the services of material factors. In the socialized economy, therefore, there can be no market prices for such factor services. This absence of market prices is crucial to the Mises-Hayek critique of socialism. The regulated market economy, on the other hand, no matter how hampered it may be, *is* unquestionably a market economy, in which prices emerge through the interplay of profit-seeking market transactions. The Mises-Hayek critique of socialism, therefore, is certainly not applicable, as it stands, to the regulated market.

A brief review of the Mises-Hayek critique of socialism nonetheless proves helpful for a critical appraisal of regulation. For the Mises-Hayek discussion offers an appreciation for the operation of the market process by revealing the enormous difficulties confronting socialist planners trying to emulate the market economy's achievements without a market. This discussion also reveals the hazards besetting the path of regulators seeking to improve on the market's performance. Just as the attempt to seek social efficiency through central planning rather than through the spontaneous market process, in the Mises-Hayek view, must necessarily fail, so too, for essentially similar reasons, most attempts to control the outcomes of the spontaneous market by deliberate, extra-market, regulatory action necessarily tend to generate unexpected and wholly undesired consequences.

I turn, therefore, to a brief review of the debate on socialist economic calculation, drawing particular attention to a widespread failure to appreciate fully certain important elements in the Mises-Hayek critique. It is these important elements, indeed, that will be found to be the basis for this essay's critical analysis of government regulation of the market economy. These elements underlie our perception of the parallel between a critique of the regulated market on the one hand and of socialism, without any market at all, on the other.

Mises and Hayek on Socialism

Mises's demonstration of the economic calculation problem facing the socialist planning authorities was first presented in 1920.[3] The demonstration was subsequently repeated in more or less similar terms (with critical attention paid to the attempts of socialist writers to respond to his challenge) in several of Mises's later works.[4] Hayek first addressed the problem in two essays, which respectively introduced and summed up the debate concerning socialist calculation (in the volume of essays on the subject that he edited in 1935).[5] An important third essay, published in 1940, contains Hayek's most complete appraisal of the issues.[6] Many writers on the Continent, in England, and in the United States attempted to meet Mises's arguments, the best-known socialist contribution being that of Oskar Lange.[7] A thorough survey of the state of literature at the onset of World War II, provided by a Norwegian economist, was made available in English in 1949.[8]

For Mises, the defining element in socialism lies in its collective ownership of the means of production, in particular land and capital. It follows, therefore, that under socialism there exists no market for these factors of production or for their services; without private ownership, there can be no market exchanges between individual owners; and without market exchanges, of course, there can be no ratios of exchange—that is, there can be no market prices. Mises finds in the absence of factor prices the essence of the difficulty. Without prices, socialist decision makers (the central planners and their subordinates, the managers of socialized enterprises) do not have available relevant indicators (prices) of the relative economic importance of the various factor services in their various alternative uses. Socialist planners cannot know whether the allocation of a unit of a particular resource to a specific line of production is more or less desirable than its replacement by some quantity of another resource which is technologically capable of substituting for the first. Planners cannot know in advance where efficiency is likely to be attained, nor do they have any way of assessing ex post whether or to what extent such efficiency may have been achieved.

Professor Armentano illustrates Mises's point by imagining a socialist director choosing between the construction of a power plant that uses fossil fuel and one that uses nuclear fuel. Since the state owns all of the resources, no objective money prices exist for any of the alternative projects' required resources. The socialist planner has no way of knowing which project is cheaper, which promises the greater return on investment, which, in sum, offers the most efficient way to produce electricity. "If and when the power plant is built at a particular point with particular resources, it will represent an 'arbitrary' and not an economic decision."[9]

Hayek's most complete discussion of the problem of socialist calculation appeared in 1940 as a review article analyzing particularly the contributions of two socialist economists, Oskar Lange and H. D. Dickinson.[10] Both Lange and Dickinson conceded that economic calculation is unthinkable without factor prices.[11] They pointed out, however, that a price need not mean merely an exchange ratio established in a market, the notion of price, they maintained, can be understood more broadly as "the terms on which alternatives are offered." Using price in this broader sense, they argued, there is every possibility for setting up a socialist economy in which "prices" are announced by the planning authorities and are used as guides in the decisions of socialist managers (who are instructed to obey specified rules in which these "prices" appear). These writers believed the authorities could handle the adjustment of prices on the basis of trial and error, with the relation between perceived supply and demand indicating to the authorities where adjustments should be made. In this fashion, the socialist writers held, a socialist economy could achieve an efficient allocation of resources without markets in the material factors of production, and without profit-maximizing entrepreneurial decisions.

Hayek's critique of the Lange-Dickinson proposals was long and detailed. He considered their approach to be a vast improvement as compared with the earlier socialist reactions to Mises, in which the nature of the problem was hardly perceived at all. Yet he continued to find the Lange-Dickinson proposals seriously deficient both in their perception of the problem to be solved and of the practical difficulties confronting the suggested solution. The difference, Hayek wrote, between the "system of regimented prices" proposed by the socialist economists "and a system of prices determined by the market seems to be about the same as that between an attacking army in which every unit and every man could move only by special command and by the exact distance ordered by headquarters and an army in which every unit and every man can take advantage of every opportunity offered to them."[12]

Some Thoughts on the Socialist Calculation Literature

Despite Hayek's powerful critique of the Lange-Dickinson proposals, the postwar textbook literature, curiously, came to present the results of the interwar debate as if Mises's original claim (to have demonstrated the impossibility of economic calculation under socialism) had been decisively refuted by Lange, Dickinson, and Lerner.[13] Several writers have noted that this view conveyed by the literature is seriously mistaken.[14] A careful review of the debate surely reveals that the Lange-Dickinson-Lerner solution hardly comes to grips with the difficulties that Mises and Hayek explained. The textbook literature did not so much ignore the arguments of Mises and Hayek *as it failed to understand the view of the market process, which underlies their critique of socialist calculation.* Indeed, the authors of the socialist proposals themselves offered their solution from a perspective on the nature and function of the market economy that differed sharply from the "Austrian" perspective shared by Mises and Hayek. My purpose in drawing attention to this defective view of the market reflected in the Lange-Dickinson literature is not merely to throw light on the socialist calculation debate (an issue only tangentially relevant to our own theme of efficiency in the regulated market economy); for the insights into the market process expressed in the Mises-Hayek view and overlooked in the Lange-Dickinson proposal become crucial to a critique of the economics of regulation.

Lange's response to Mises placed much emphasis on the *"parametric function of prices,* i.e., on the fact that ... each individual separately regards the actual market prices as given data to which he has to adjust himself."[15] For Lange, each person in the market treats prices as if they were equilibrium prices to which he must adjust himself passively. If the market prices happen *not* to be equilibrium prices, then these market prices must somehow change "by a series of successive trials"—prices rising where demand exceeds supply, and so on.[16] Lange does not address the question of *how* market prices actually change if each person at all times considers prices as given data to which he must silently adjust himself.

For Lange, indeed, the function that prices play in the efficiency of markets is simply the function that the equilibrium set of prices would fill. Prices, that is, provide the parameters to guide market participants in engaging in the set of activities that are consistent with equilibrium conditions. Lange understandably held that this function of prices could be simulated in a socialist economy. Socialist managers can be given lists of "prices" to which they can react according to well-defined rules (analogous to, but of course not identical with, the "rule" that capitalist decision makers are assumed to follow: that is, to maximize profits), Lange believed the task of ensuring that the lists of "prices" would be those required to ensure overall efficiency in the socialist economy could be fulfilled by again simulating (what he thought to be) the market trial and error procedure.

But here lies Lange's cardinal misunderstanding: he assumed that there exists in the market a procedure (involving "a series of successive trials") whereby prices are somehow adjusted toward equilibrium *without essentially altering the "parametric" character and function of prices* (that is, without departing from the supposition that each person separately regards market prices as given data, which he is unable to change). The market process through which prices are adjusted toward equilibrium, however, is a process in which prices are *not* treated as given parameters but are themselves hammered out in the course of vigorous and rivalrous bidding.

In emphasizing exclusively the "parametric" function of market prices. Lange misunderstood the central role of the market. The primary function of the market is *not* to offer an arena within which market participants can have their decentralized decisions smoothly coordinated through attention to the appropriate list of given prices. The market's essential function, rather, is to offer an arena in which market participants, by entrepreneurial exploitation of the profit opportunities offered by disequilibrium prices, can nudge prices in the direction of equilibrium. In this entrepreneurial process prices are *not* treated as parameters. Nor, in this process, are prices changed impersonally in response to excess demand or supply. It is one thing for Lange to assume that socialist managers can be motivated to follow rules with respect to centrally promulgated given "prices" (in the way capitalist decision makers can be imagined to treat given equilibrium market prices).[17] It is quite another to assume that the *non*parametric function of price in the market system, the function dependent on entrepreneurial alertness to opportunities for pure profit, can be simulated in a system from which the entrepreneurial function has been wholly excised.

That Lange did not understand this nonparametric function of prices must certainly be attributed to a perception of the market system's operation primarily in terms of perfectly competitive equilibrium. (Indeed, it is this textbook approach to price theory that Lange explicitly presents as his model for socialist pricing.[18]) Within this paradigm, as is now well recognized, the role of the entrepreneurial quest for pure profit, as the key element in bringing about price adjustment, is completely ignored. It is not difficult to see how Lange could conclude that such a (nonentrepreneurial) system might be simulated under socialism.

Mises and Hayek, by contrast, saw the price system under capitalism from a totally different—an Austrian—perspective. For these writers, the essence of the market process lies not in the "parametric" function of price, and not in the perfectly competitive state of equilibrium, but in the rivalrous activity of entrepreneurs taking advantage of disequilibrium conditions. The debate between Lange-Dickinson on the one hand and Mises-Hayek on the other can best be understood as a clash between two conflicting views of the price system. Mises's views on the market as a process have been expounded extensively in a number of his works.[19] The idea of the market as a *dynamic process* is at the very heart of his system. Hayek's perception of the price system was articulated (during the same period in which his critical essays on socialist calculation were written) in a remarkable series of papers on the role of knowledge and discovery in market processes.[20]

That the postwar textbooks incorrectly presented the debate on socialist calculation as having been decisively won by Lange must be attributed not to ideological bias (although this may not have been entirely absent) but to an utter failure to understand the flaws in Lange's discussion (flaws that Hayek indeed had identified). Not recognizing the Austrian background of Hayek's critique, Anglo-American economists saw in Lange a cogent application of standard price theory; Hayek's critique simply was not understood.

The Market Process: An Austrian View[21]

Before returning to the theme of efficiency in the regulated economy, it is useful to review some Austrian lessons to be drawn from the socialist calculation debate. The Austrian understanding of the market as a dynamic process of discovery generated by the entrepreneurial-competitive scramble for pure profit may be spelled out in terms of a brief discussion of several key concepts. A sensitive appreciation of these ideas will alert us to problems raised by government regulation of the market that might otherwise easily be overlooked. It is partly because the terms convenient for the exposition of these concepts also are used in non-Austrian contexts, with rather different meanings, that the ideas developed here are so often misunderstood and therefore require brief elaboration.

Competition. What keeps the market process in motion is competition—*not* competition in the sense of "perfect competition," in which perfect knowledge is combined with very large numbers of buyers and sellers to generate a state of perennial equilibrium—but competition as the rivalrous activities of market participants trying to win profits by offering the market better opportunities than are currently available. The existence of rivalrous competition requires *not* large numbers of buyers and sellers but simply *freedom of entry*. Competition places pressure on market participants to discover where and how better opportunities, as yet un-noticed, *might* be offered to the market. The competitive market process occurs because equilibrium has not yet been attained. This process is thwarted whenever nonmarket barriers are imposed blocking entry to potential competitors.

Knowledge and Discovery. As Hayek has emphasized, the competitive market process is a discovery procedure.[22] If all that needed to be known were already known, then the market would already have attained full equilibrium, the state in which all decisions correctly anticipate all other decisions being made within the market. An institutional device for social organization that mobilizes existing knowledge and brings it to bear upon decision makers is necessary because realistically people never do have command even over all the information that is already known somewhere.[23] Market equilibrium is thinkable only if we can presuppose the full mobilization of existing knowledge, so also centralized economic control would be thinkable (whether by Lange-Dickinson-Lerner proposals or other devices) if we could assume existing knowledge already to be fully mobilized. It is just because, without a market, such prior mobilization is so difficult to assume that a market is seen to be a prerequisite for economic calculation.

The competitive market process is needed not only to mobilize existing knowledge, but also to generate awareness of opportunities whose very existence until now has been known to no one at all.[24] The entrepreneurial process, moreover, disseminates existing information through the market. The process itself is a continual one of the discovery of opportunities. The discoverer of these opportunities himself, at least, has had no inkling whatever of their very existence. The market, in other words, is not merely a process of search for information of the need for which men had previously been aware, it is a discovery procedure that tends to correct ignorance where the discoverers themselves

were totally unaware that they indeed were ignorant. A realization that the market yields knowledge—the sort of
knowledge that people do not at present even know they
need—should engender among would-be social engineers
who seek to replace or to modify the results of the free
market a very definite sense of humility. To announce that
one can improve on the performance of the market, one
must also claim to know in advance what the market will
reveal. This knowledge is clearly impossible in all circumstances. Indeed, where the market process has been
thwarted, in general it will not be possible to point with
certainty to what *might* have been discovered that has now
been lost.

Profit and Incentives. In standard treatments of price theory,
decision makers are assumed to maximize utility or "profit."
The profit for which entrepreneurs are so eager (and which
for Austrians drives the market process) is *not* that "profit"
maximized by the firm in the standard theory of the firm.
The standard theory assumes that the firm confronts definitely known and given cost and revenue possibilities. For
the theory of the firm, therefore, to maximize profits does
not mean *to discover* an opportunity for pure gain; it means
merely to perform the mathematical calculations required
to exhaust the *already fully perceived* opportunity for gain
that the given revenue and cost curves might present. The
urge of would-be entrepreneurs to grasp profit, by contrast,
is the force which *itself reveals* the existence of gaps between
costs and revenues. This distinction is of considerable importance.

It is elementary to the theory of the market that the
market performs its functions by virtue of the *incentives* it
offers to those who make "correct" decisions. For example,
the incentive of the higher wages offered by industries in
which the marginal productivity of labor is greatest attracts
labor to more important uses. Such incentives tend to en-

sure that once a superior use for a given factor (or group of factors) is discovered, it becomes worthwhile for factor owners to forgo alternative ways of putting their factors to work. This is well understood. What is not always understood is that the market also offers incentives for the *discovery* of new opportunities (for the most useful employment of factors), that is, for the exploitation of opportunities that until now have remained unexploited. These opportunities have remained unexploited *not* because of high costs, and not even because of the high cost of searching for them. They have remained unexploited simply because of sheer oversight, possibly including oversight of the opportunity to find them through deliberate search. Pure entrepreneurial profit is the market form in which *this* kind of incentive presents itself. The availability of pure entrepreneurial profit has the function not of outweighing the costs associated with withdrawing inputs from alternative uses, but of alerting decision makers to the present error of committing factors to uses less valuable to the markets than others waiting and able to be served.

Market Prices. Market prices in the Austrian view are not primarily approximations to the set of equilibrium prices. Instead, they are (disequilibrium) exchange ratios worked out between entrepreneurial market participants. On the one hand, these exchange ratios with all their imperfections reflect the discoveries made up until this moment by profit-seeking entrepreneurs. On the other hand, these ratios express entrepreneurial errors currently being made. Market prices, therefore, offer opportunities for pure profit. And we can rely on these opportunities to create a tendency for market prices to be changed through the rivalrous bidding of alert entrepreneurs. The course of market prices, in other words, is closely bound up, in *two* distinct ways, with the incentive system of pure entrepreneurial profit. First, the configuration of market prices at any given moment must be attributed to the pure profit incentives that have until now determined bids and offers. Second, this present configuration of market prices, together with existing and future conditions of supply and demand, is responsible for the opportunities for pure profit. The discovery and exploitation of these opportunities will constitute the course of the market process in the immediate future. From this perspective on market prices it is not difficult to perceive how small must be the resemblance to them of any centrally promulgated set of socialist "prices." The entrepreneurial drive for pure profit plays no role at all in the determination of socialist "prices."

Regulated Market Economy

I shall assume, as noted at the outset of this essay, that government regulation of the market economy is generated by dissatisfaction with market outcomes. Legislators or other government officials (perhaps in response to public outcry, or in anticipation thereof) are disturbed either by the high price that certain would-be purchasers are asked to pay in the market or by the low price (for example, farm prices or the wages of labor) received by certain sellers in the market; or they are disturbed by the quality of goods or services being offered for sale (for example, because of the absence of safety devices) or by the unavailability in the market of goods or services that they believe to be important. They are disturbed by the conditions under which workers are expected to work, or they are disturbed by the pattern of income distribution generated by the market, by unemployment, or by "profiteering," or by the side effects (such as environmental pollution, or spread of disease, or exposure of the young to pornography) generated by uncontrolled market activity.

Hoping to correct what are perceived to be unsatisfactory conditions, the government intervenes in the market. It seeks to replace the outcomes expected to result from unchecked market transactions by a preferred configuration of prices and outputs, to be achieved not, as under socialism, by replacing the market by central ownership of factors, but by imposing appropriate regulations and controls. The laissez-faire market is replaced by the regulated market. Price ceilings and price and wage floors, transfers of incomes, imposed safety standards, child labor laws, zoning laws, prohibited industrial integration, tariff protection, prohibited competition, imposed health warnings, compulsory old age pensions, and prohibited drugs are all examples of the countless controls that well-meaning public officials impose.

In the face of these controls, regulations, and interventions there remains, nonetheless, a genuine market both for factor services and for consumer products. Government controls constrain and constrict; they rearrange and repattern the structure of incentives; they redistribute incomes and wealth and sharply modify both the processes of production and the composition of consumption. Yet within the limits that such controls impose, buying and selling continue, and the constant effort to capture pure entrepreneurial gain keeps the market in perpetual motion. Government regulations drastically alter and disturb opportunities for entrepreneurial gain, but they do not eliminate them. These controls thoroughly influence the prices that emerge from the interplay of entrepreneurial competition. But unless directly mandated prices are involved, exchange ratios still reflect the outcome to date of the entrepreneurial process.

Traditionally, criticism of government intervention involves one or more of several general lines of argument.[25] First, critics may argue that the admitted failure of market outcomes to meet successfully the aspirations of regulators is a result not of market failure to achieve peak efficiency, but of inescapable scarcity. If costs are fully taken into account, efforts to improve outcomes must be found to be doomed to failure or to lead to even less preferable outcomes. Second, critics may agree that from the viewpoint of the value system adopted by the would-be regulators market outcomes might be improved upon. But, these critics maintain that the market faithfully reflects consumers' values. Regulation in such circumstances therefore must violate consumer sovereignty, if not consumer freedom.

Third, critics may argue that the unwished-for market outcomes are to be attributed not to the free market, but to earlier government interventions in the market which have hindered the corrective forces of the market from doing their work. Additional regulation, it is then pointed out, either may be unnecessary (since the earlier interventions can simply be eliminated) or may compound the problems. Fourth, critics may argue that whether or not the undesirable outcomes of the market are (in the sense appropriate to economic science and not necessarily from the viewpoint of the regulators' values) to be regretted, government regulation is simply incapable of achieving improvement. The technology of regulation is such that its full costs outweigh by far any benefits that may be achieved.

The Austrian lessons drawn from the preceding survey of the debate about socialist economic calculation suggest that another set of considerations, until now not sufficiently emphasized in the literature, deserve to be included in the list of causes to which one might attribute the failures of regulation. These considerations constitute a separate line of criticism of government intervention, to be added to the other lines of criticism (where one or more of these may be relevant).[26]

Government Regulation and the
Market Discovery Process

The perils associated with government regulation of the economy addressed here arise out of the *impact that regulation can be expected to have on the discovery process, which the unregulated market tends to generate.* Even if current market outcomes in some sense are judged unsatisfactory, intervention, and even intervention that can successfully achieve its immediate objectives, cannot be considered the obviously correct solution. After all, the very problems apparent in the market might generate processes of discovery and correction superior to those undertaken deliberately by government regulation, deliberate intervention by the state not only might serve as an imperfect substitute for the spontaneous market process of discovery; but also might impede desirable processes of discovery the need for which has *not* been perceived by the government. Again, government regulation itself may generate new (unintended and undesired) processes of market adjustments that produce a final outcome even less preferred than what might have emerged in the free market.

Here I discuss critically the impact of government regulation on the discovery process of the unregulated market at four distinct levels. First, I consider the likelihood that would-be regulators may not correctly assess the course the market might itself take in the absence of regulation. Second, I consider the likelihood that, because of the presumed absence of entrepreneurial incentives operating on government decision makers, government regulatory decisions will fail to exploit opportunities for social betterment waiting to be discovered. Third, I consider the likelihood that government regulation may stifle or inhibit desirable discovery processes which the market might have generated. Finally, I consider the likelihood that government regulation may influence the market by creating opportunities for new, and not necessarily desirable, market discovery processes which would not be relevant in an unregulated market.

The Undiscovered Discovery Process

We assumed earlier that regulation is demanded because of undesirable conditions that emerge in the market in the absence of regulation. But the urge to regulate, to control, to alter these outcomes must presume not only that these undesirable conditions are attributable to the absence of regulation, but also that the speedy removal of such conditions cannot be expected from the future course of unregulated market events. To attribute undesirable conditions to absence of regulation, moreover, also may require the denial of the proposition that were a better state of affairs indeed feasible, the market probably would have already discovered how to achieve it.

More specifically, many demands for government intervention into the market rest on one or both of two possible misunderstandings concerning the market discovery process. Demand for government intervention, on the one hand, might grow out of a failure to realize that the market already may have discovered virtually everything worth discovering (so that what appears to be obvious inefficiency might be able to be explained altogether satisfactorily if government officials had all the information the market has long since discovered and taken advantage of). Demand for regulation, on the other hand, may stem from the belief that unsatisfactory conditions will never be corrected unless by deliberate intervention. Such demands for regulation might be muted, that is, were it understood that genuine inefficiencies can be relied upon in the *future* to generate market processes for their own correction. (This second misunderstanding itself may rest on either of two bases. First, the tendency of markets to discover and eliminate inefficiency simply is not recognized. Second, by contrast, it is assumed, far too sanguinely, that market processes are *so* rapid that our awareness of an unmistakably unsatisfactory condition proves that some kind of market "failure" has occurred and that one cannot rely on future corrective processes.)

These misunderstandings, so often the foundation for demands for intervention, surely derive from an unawareness of several basic principles of the theory of market process. These principles show that, first, were knowledge perfect, it would be inconceivable that unexploited opportunities could yet remain for rearranging the pattern of input utilization or output consumption in such a way as to improve the well-being of all market participants; second, the existence of such unexploited opportunities, reflecting imperfect knowledge throughout the market, expresses itself in the unregulated market in the form of opportunities for pure entrepreneurial profit; and third, the tendency for such pure profit opportunities to be discovered and exploited tends more or less rapidly to eliminate unexploited opportunities for improving the allocation of resources.[27] These principles of the theory of market process suggest that if genuine inefficiency exists, then (perhaps because of a recent sudden change in conditions of resource supply, of technology, or of consumer tastes) the market has not yet discovered *all that it will surely soon tend to discover.*

These principles may be denied either by expressing a lack of confidence in the systematic tendency for imperfect knowledge to be spontaneously improved or by attributing to the market the ability to attain equilibrium instantaneously (that is, by assuming that ignorance is not merely a disequilibrium phenomenon, but that ignorance disappears the very instant it emerges). Both denials may lead to demands for government intervention. The denial based on a lack of confidence about improving knowledge leads to the belief that current inefficiencies will not tend to be corrected spontaneously (and also to the propensity to see inefficiency where the market *already* has made necessary corrections). The denial based on the belief in instantaneous correction of disequilibrium conditions leads to the view that existing inefficiencies somehow are consistent with market equilibrium and that therefore extramarket steps are called for to achieve correction.

The Unsimulated Discovery Process

Government regulation takes the general form of imposed price ceilings and floors, of mandated quality specifications, and of other restraints or requirements imposed in interpersonal market transactions. The hope surrounding such government impositions, I continue to assume, is that they will constrain market activities to desired channels and at desired levels. But what is the likelihood that government officials, with the best of intentions, will *know* what imposed prices, say, might evoke the "correct," desired actions by market participants? This question parallels that raised by Mises and Hayek with respect to "market" socialism.[28] Government officials in the regulated economy do enjoy the advantage (*not* shared by socialist planning officials) of making their decisions within the framework of genuine market prices. But the question remains: How do government officials know what prices to set (or qualities to require and so forth)? Or to press the point further: How do government officials know if their earlier decisions were in error and in what direction to make corrections? In other words, how will government officials *discover* those opportunities for improving the allocation of resources, which one cannot assume to be automatically known to them at the outset of a regulatory endeavor?

The compelling insight underlying these questions rests heavily on the circumstance that officials institutionally are precluded from capturing *pecuniary* profits in the market, in the course of their activities (even though they are as eager as anyone else for entrepreneurial "profit" in the broadest sense of the term). The regulators' estimates of the prices consumers are prepared to pay, or of the prices resource owners are prepared to accept, for example, *are not profit-motivated estimates.* The estimates are not profit motivated at the time of an initial government regulatory action, and they are not profit motivated at each subsequent date when modification of a regulation might be considered. But estimates of market demand conditions or market supply conditions that are not profit motivated cannot reflect the powerful, discovery-inspiring incentives of the entrepreneurial quest for profit.

Nothing in the course of the regulatory process suggests a tendency for as yet unperceived opportunities of resource allocation improvement to be discovered. Nothing ensures that government officials who might perceive market conditions more accurately than others will tend systematically to replace less competent regulators. There is no entrepreneurial profit at work, and there is no proxy for entrepreneurial profit or loss that easily might indicate where errors have been made and how they should be corrected. What regulators know (or believe they know) at a given moment presumably remains only partly correct. No systematic process seems at work through which regulators might come to discover what they have not known, *especially since they have not known that they enjoy less than complete awareness of a particular situation.*

The problem raised here is not quite the same as the one identified in other literature critical of government intervention. It is often noted, for example, that government officials are not motivated to minimize costs, since they will not personally benefit from the resulting economies.[29] The problem raised here differs importantly from such questions of incentives for adopting known efficiencies. For even if one could imagine an official so dedicated to the citizenry that he would ensure the adoption of all known possible measures for cutting costs, one cannot yet imagine him somehow divining *as yet undiscovered* techniques for cutting costs. What the official knows, he knows, and what he knows that he does *not* know, one may imagine him diligently undertaking to find out, through appropriate cost-benefit-calculated search. But one can hardly imagine him discovering, except by the sheerest accident, those opportunities for increasing efficiency of which he is completely unaware. The official is not subject to the entrepreneurial profit incentive, which somehow appears continually and successfully to inspire discovery of hitherto undreamed of possibilities for eliminating unnecessary expenditures. Nothing within the regulatory process seems able to simulate even remotely well the discovery process that is so integral to the unregulated market.

The Stifled Discovery Process

The most serious effect of government regulation on the market discovery process well might be the likelihood that regulation, in a variety of ways, may discourage, hamper, and even completely stifle the discovery process of the unregulated market. Indeed, that much regulation is introduced as a result of unawareness of the market's discovery process already has been noted.

Government regulation plainly might bar exploitation of opportunities for pure entrepreneurial profit. A price ceiling, a price floor, an impeded merger, or an imposed safety requirement might block possibly profitable entrepreneurial actions. Such restraints and requirements may be designed to block *particular* activities. If so, the likelihood is that since the possibility of such activities is so clearly seen and feared, the blocked activity may provide standard rates of return, but *not* particularly profitable ones in the entrepreneurial sense. Regulated restraints and requirements, though, are also likely to block activities that have *not* yet been foreseen by anyone, including the regulatory authorities. Regulatory constraints, that is, are likely *to bar the discovery* of pure profit opportunities.

That government regulation diminishes competition is common knowledge. Tariffs, licensing requirements, labor legislation, airline regulation, and bank regulation reduce the number of potential participants in particular markets. Government regulation, therefore, is responsible for imposing monopoly-like inefficiencies ("deadweight" welfare losses) upon the economy. But such losses by no means constitute the full impact of the countercompetitive measures often embodied in regulatory constraints.

The beneficient aspect of competition in the sense of a rivalrous process, as noted earlier, arises out of *freedom of entry*. What government regulations so often erect are *regulatory barriers to entry*. Freedom of "entry," for the Austrian approach, refers to the freedom of potential competitors to discover and to move to exploit existing opportunities for pure profit. If entry is blocked, such opportunities simply may never be discovered, either by existing firms in the industry, or by regulatory authorities, or for that matter by outside entrepreneurs who *might* have discovered such opportunities were they allowed to be exploited when found.

From *this* perspective on regulation's anticompetitive impact, it follows that much regulation introduced explicitly to *create or maintain* competition is no less hazardous to the competitive-entrepreneurial process than are other forms of regulation that restrict competition. Entry of competitors, in the dynamic sense, need not mean entry of firms of about equal size. For example, entry might imply the *replacement*, by merger or other means, of a number of relatively high-cost producers by a *single* low-cost producer. Antitrust activity designed ostensibly to protect competition might *block* this kind of entry. Such regulatory activity thus blocks the capture of pure profit, obtainable in this case by the discovery and implementation of the possibility of lowering the price to consumers by taking advantage of hitherto unexploited, and perhaps unsuspected, economies of scale.

The literature critical of government regulation often draws attention to the undesirable effects of imposed prices. A price ceiling for a particular product or service (rent control, for example) tends to generate artificial shortages (of housing). A price floor for a particular product or service (minimum wages, for example) tends to generate an artificial surplus (teenage unemployment). These important, well-recognized consequences of imposed prices flow from the efforts of the regulators to legislate prices at other than equilibrium levels.

Quite apart from the discoordination generated by such imposed prices in the markets for *existing* goods and services, price (and also quality) restraints also may well inhibit the discovery of wholly new opportunities. A price ceiling does not merely block the upper reaches of a given supply curve. Such a ceiling also may inhibit the discovery of as yet unsuspected sources of supply (which in the absence of the ceiling would have tended to shift the entire supply curve to the right) or of as yet wholly unknown new products (tending to create supply curves for wholly new graphs).[30] The lure of pure profit tends to uncover such as yet unknown opportunities.

Price and quality restraints and requirements and restrictions on organizational forms operate (in a generally understood but not precisely predictable way) to inhibit entrepreneurial discovery. Price ceilings, for example, not only restrict supply from known sources of natural gas (or from known prospects for search), but also inhibit the discovery of wholly unknown sources. Drug testing regulations, as another example, not only reduce the flow of new pharmaceutical drugs where successful research might have been more or less predictable, but also discourage the entrepreneurial discovery of wholly unknown research procedures. Against whatever benefits might be derived from government regulation and intervention, one is forced to weigh, as one of regulation's intrinsically immeasurable costs, the stifling of the market discovery process.

The Wholly Superfluous Discovery Process

There is yet one more aspect of government regulation's complex impact on the discovery process. Whether intended by the regulatory authorities or not and whether suspected by them or not, the imposition of regulatory restraints and requirements tends to create entirely new, and not necessarily desirable opportunities for entrepreneurial discovery.

That such opportunities may be created follows from the extreme unlikelihood that government-imposed price, quality, or quantity constraints introduce anything approaching an equilibrium configuration. These constraints, on the contrary, introduce pure profit opportunities that would otherwise have been absent, as they simultaneously reduce or possibly eliminate other opportunities for pure profit that might otherwise have existed. This rearrangement of opportunities for pure profits, of course, is unlikely to be the explicit aim of regulation, nor even, indeed, is such rearrangement ever likely to be fully *known* to the authorities. Market ignorance is a fact of economic life. It follows that the replacement of one set of (unregulated) prices by another set of (partly regulated) prices, simply means that regulation has generated a possibly major alteration in the pattern of the discovery process. The now regulated market will tend to pursue the altered discovery process.

This regulation-induced alteration in the pattern of market discovery is closely related to the often noticed circumstance that regulation may result in a different set of *equilibrium* market consequences. Such consequences, moreover, may not have been correctly foretold by the authorities and, indeed, may be wholly undesired by them. regulation often imposes costs not immediately recognized.³¹ Unless, quite fantastically, the regulatory authorities (somehow all acting in completely coordinated fashion) are perfectly informed on all relevant data about the market, they will *not* generally be able to perceive what new profit opportunities they create by their own regulatory actions. Inevitably, therefore, the imposition of a set of regulatory constraints on a market must set in motion a series of entrepreneurial actions that have *not* been anticipated and, therefore, that may well lead to wholly unexpected and even undesired final outcomes.³²

The one kind of new "profit" opportunity created by regulation that is by now well anticipated, though hardly desired of course, involves bribery and corruption of the regulators. There is widespread understanding of the unwholesome channels into which the entrepreneurial quest for pure profit inevitably tends to be attracted if arbitrary restraints on otherwise profitable activities are imposed.³³

The basic insight underlying these conclusions, in sum, is a simple one. The competitive-entrepreneurial process, being a process of discovery of the as yet unknown, can hardly be predicted in any but the broadest terms. The imposition of regulatory constraints necessarily results, therefore, in a pattern of consequences different from and, most plausibly, distinctly less desirable than what would have occurred in the unregulated market. One might therefore refer to this unplanned, undesired pattern of consequences of regulation as the wholly superfluous discovery process.

Discovery, Evidence, and Illustration

The preceding discussion is theoretical and general, providing no hints of possible verification of its conclusions. While this discussion relies on highly plausible insights into the character of human action, a reader may believe himself justified in demanding evidence that might support the discussion's rather strong conclusions. Yet such evidence can hardly be furnished, and it may be instructive to spell out the reasons.

Evidence about Discovery

Econometricians have endeavored to measure the consequences of particular economic policies. Much of their ingenuity and sophistication has been called forth to grapple with the formidable problem of describing *what might have occurred* in the absence of particular policies. The problem of describing concretely what might have happened but did not, it should be noted, exists even in situations in which all the alternatives before relevant decision makers are clearly defined, so that one at least knows the list of options from among which choices would have been forthcoming. The problem derives from the circumstance that it is not possible, without more or less sophisticated conjecture, to be confident as to which of an array of options a particular decision maker *might* have selected in hypothetical circumstances.

This problem becomes infinitely more formidable if one wishes to describe, in specified hypothetical circumstances, *what might have been spontaneously discovered.* Here the problem is not merely that a particular decision maker's preferences are unknown. The problem is that one cannot imagine what specific, now unknown opportunities might have been discovered in the relevant hypothetical circumstances.

One should not be surprised, therefore, that the losses from the regulatory stifling of market discovery processes are difficult to single out. Indeed, one should not be surprised that analysis, too, has tended to overlook such losses. Therefore one can only hope to draw brief attention to studies that perhaps can provide some illustrative flavor of the kinds of losses attributable to regulatory constraints, to which I have sought to direct attention. For purposes of such illustration, I draw on work focusing on the discovery process initiated by the lure of entrepreneurial profit in technological innovation and in corporate entrepreneurial endeavor.

Discoverers: Innovators

Much recent work by economists is devoted to gaining insight into the process of technological innovation. A small part of that work has considered the impact of government regulation on innovative activity at the technological frontiers. Although the authors of these studies are not primarily concerned with the impact of regulation upon entrepreneurial incentives, it is difficult to read their work without noticing its direct relevance to this essay's concerns.

A 1971 Brookings Institution volume, for example, was devoted to a symposium examining technological change in regulated industries (in particular electric power, telecommunications, and air and surface transportation).[34] In the analytical framework within which this examination was conducted, brief attention is paid to the thesis (attributed, perhaps too hastily, to Schumpeter) that it is "the incentive to earn very large profits" which "spurs entrepreneurs to introduce new techniques," so that the limits on possible profits imposed by regulatory commissions may inhibit such innovation.[35]

A similar possible link between regulatory constraints and the possible slowing down of the processes of technological discovery is noted particularly in the context of drug research in the pharmaceutical industry. The classic paper by Professor Peltzman, examining the impact of the 1962 drug amendments upon drug research, together with the work of others, has led to widespread discussion of the possibility that drug research in the United States lags seriously behind that of other countries.[36] Peltzman's results do not prove that regulation inhibits entrepreneurial discovery, which means the discovery of hitherto unknown opportunities, unknown even in the sense that it had not been known that they were there to be discovered. That is, Peltzman's findings would fit in equally well with a theory of search based on the assumption of awareness of discoverable opportunities waiting to be researched if the cost were not too high. Nonetheless, once attention is focused on entrepreneurial discovery, it is difficult to avoid linking Peltzman's results with the postulation of an entrepreneurial discovery process hampered by regulatory constraints.

Discoverers: Insiders

Another important area in which the role of entrepreneurial discovery has been explicitly explored is that of decision making by corporate managers. In his definitive study of the issue, Henry Manne discusses the impact upon the exercise of entrepreneurship in the corporate firm of regulatory restrictions on insider trading.[37] Manne's study thoroughly examines the entrepreneurial role and its expression in a world of corporations. The study identifies the incentives of entrepreneurial profit needed to evoke the entrepreneurial role and the part that insider trading, in the absence of regulatory prohibition, might play to provide profit opportunities to reward entrepreneurial success. Restrictions on insider trading, Manne shows, no matter how plausible the motives underlying the regulatory restrictions may appear, tend to inhibit the exercise of entrepreneurship in corporate firms.[38]

Conclusion

This essay draws attention to some less obvious drawbacks of government regulation of the market. These drawbacks are rooted in the way regulatory restrictions, restraints, and controls interfere with the spontaneous discovery process that the unregulated market tends to generate. These drawbacks are also to be clearly distinguished from other disadvantages that flow from government intervention.

The peculiar character of the perils of regulation identified here closely parallels certain economic problems associated with the operation of the socialist economy. The review of the Mises-Hayek criticisms of the possibility of economic calculation under socialism provides a classic source for an Austrian perspective on the market process, and simultaneously the review provides important lessons for an understanding of the dangers inherent in regulation.

Recognition of these dangers can be most helpful in explaining the inefficiencies and the stagnation that appear so consistently to beset modern interventionist economies. It is in the nature of the subject, however, that the recognition of these perils does not lead easily to the provision of clear-cut examples of such regulatory damage. Nonetheless, in a modest way it is possible to illustrate these perils from contemporary discussions of palpable problems.

An emphasis on the perils of regulation that arises out of concern for the market process does not, in and of itself, justify the absolute condemnation of government regulation of the market process. Such condemnation would require full consideration, in addition, not only of other perils than those discussed here, but also of the hoped-for benefits sought through regulation of the market. Ultimately, public policy must depend on the value judgments of the policymakers or of those they wish to serve. But, no policy decisions with respect to government regulation can be properly arrived at without a full understanding of all the dangers inherent in such regulation. And such a full understanding arises particularly out of studying the market process of entrepreneurial discovery.

Notes

Reprinted with the permission of the Law and Economics Center, University of Miami, Coral Gables, Florida.

1. For the literature on private incentives for public regulation, see George J. Stigler, "The Theory of Economic Regulation," *Bell Journal of Economics and Management Science* 2 (Spring, 1971): 3–21; reprinted in Stigler, *The Citizen and the State* (Chicago: University of Chicago Press, 1975); Richard A. Posner, "Theories of Economic Regulation," *Bell Journal of Economics and Management Science* 5 (Autumn, 1974): 335–58; Sam Peltzman, "Toward a More General Theory of Regulation," *Journal of Law and Economics* 19 (August, 1976): 211–40.
2. The more trenchant recent criticisms of government regulation from this perspective include Ludwig von Mises, *Human Action* (New Haven: Yale University Press, 1949), part 6; Milton Friedman, *Capitalism and Freedom* (Chicago: University of Chicago Press, 1962); Friedman, *An Economist's Protect* (Glen Ridge, NJ: Thomas Horton and Daughters, 1972).
3. Ludwig von Mises, "Die Wirtschaftsrechnung im sozialistischen Gemeinwesen," *Archiv für Sozialwissenschaften und Sozialpolitik* 47 (April, 1920): 86–121; reprinted in *Collectivist Economic Planning*, trans. and ed. Friedrich A. Hayek (London: Routledge & Kegan Paul 1935).
4. Ludwig von Mises, *Socialism: An Economic and Sociological Analysis*, trans. J. Kahane (New Haven: Yale University Press, 1951), part 2, sect. 1; this edition is translated from the second German edition (published 1932) of Mises's *Die Gemeinwirtschaft* (originally published in 1922); see also Mises, *Human Action*, part 5.
5. Hayek, *Collectivist Economic Planning*. 6. Friedrich A. Hayek, "Socialist Calculation: The Competitive 'Solution,'" *Economics* 7 (May, 1940): 125–49; reprinted as "Socialist Calculation III: The Competitive 'Solution,'" in Hayek, *Individualism and Economic Order* (London: Routledge & Kegan Paul, 1949).
7. Oskar Lange, "On the Economic Theory of Socialism," in Oskar Lange and Fred M. Taylor, *On the Economic Theory of*

Socialism, ed. Benjamin E. Lippincot (New York: McGraw-Hill, 1964).

8. Trygve J. B. Hoff, *Economic Calculation in the Socialist Society;* trans. M. A. Michael (London and Edinburg: Hodge, 1949).

9. Dominic T. Armentano, "Resource Allocation Problems under Socialism," in *Theory of Economic Systems: Capitalism, Socialism, Corporatism*, ed. William P. Snavely (Columbus, OH: Merrill, 1969), pp. 133–34.

10. Hayek, "Socialist Calculation III." Reviewed particularly were Lange, "On the Economic Theory of Socialism," and Henry D. Dickinson, *Economics of Socialism* (London: Oxford University Press, 1939).

11. Thus they agreed with Mises and Hayek that efficiency is impossible without indicators of value and that any hope of solving the problem by direct mathematical methods (for example, by solving the Walrasian equation system) is illusory.

12. Hayek, *Individualism and Economic Order*, p. 187.

13. Abba P. Lerner, *The Economics of Control* (New York: Macmillan, 1944).

14. See more recently Murray N. Rothbard, "Ludwig von Mises and Economic Calculation under Socialism," in *Economics of Ludwig von Mises*, ed. Laurence S. Moss (Kansas City: Sheed and Ward, 1976).

15. Lange, "On the Economic Theory of Socialism," p. 70.

16. Ibid., pp. 70–71.

17. This assumption, of course, is vulnerable to serious question. See James M. Buchanan, *Cost and Choice* (Chicago: Markham, 1969), chap. 6; G. Warren Nutter, "Markets without Property: A Grand Illusion," in *Money, the Market, and the State: Essays in Honor of James Muir Waller*, ed. Nicholas A. Beadles and L. Aubrey Drewry, Jr. (Athens: University of Georgia Press, 1968). It is important to note that the argument stated in the text does *not* depend on any doubt concerning managers' ability and motivation to obey rules. Were socialist managers to be given price lists, then we may assume for the purpose of the present discussion that they *could* make decisions *as if* they were intent on maximizing "profits." (Of

course, the profits maximized in equilibrium contexts are not pure entrepreneurial profits. This distinction is discussed later in this essay.)

18. Lange, "On the Economic Theory of Socialism," p. 65–72.
19. Particularly in Mises, *Human Action*, chap. 15.
20. Hayek, "Economics and Knowledge," "The Use of Knowledge in Society," and "The Meaning of Competition," all reprinted in *Individualism and Economic Order*. In this respect the work of Austrian-born Joseph A. Schumpeter is of considerable relevance for the Austrian view of the market; see particularly Schumpeter, *The Theory of Economic Development*, trans. Redvers Opie (New York: Oxford University Press, 1961); this work first appeared in German in 1912 and was first translated by Opie in 1934. See also Schumpeter, *Capitalism, Socialism and Democracy* (New York: Harper and Row, 1950), chap. 7.
21. This section draws freely from my *Competition and Entrepreneurship* (Chicago: University of Chicago Press, 1973), and *Perception, Opportunity, and Profit* (Chicago: University of Chicago Press, 1979).
22. Friedrich A. Hayek, ed., "Competition as a Discovery Procedure," in *New Studies in Philosophy, Politics, Economics and the History of Ideas* (Chicago: University of Chicago Press, 1978).
23. See Hayek, "Economics and Knowledge," "The Use of Knowledge in Society," and "The Meaning of Competition."
24. See Kirzner, *Perception, Opportunity, and Profit*, chaps. 2, 8, 9.
25. Once again, we assume away criticisms based on the view that regulation may be motivated not by the wish to benefit consumers, but by the wish to benefit the regulators and those they regulate.
26. While these considerations support a stance critical of regulation, in and of themselves they do not necessarily declare regulation to be wrong, or even inefficient. Given sufficiently strong value judgments on the part of would-be regulators—whether in favor of environmental purity, of an egalitarian distribution of wealth, of freedom from pornography or disease, of national prestige, of the enrichment of the arts, or of whatever—criticism of intervention, from the perspective

of these value judgments, may (properly) carry little weight. The economist's task, however, is to spell out as fully as possible the consequences of alternative policies, so that policy decisions at least will not be taken on the basis of erroneous assessments of their likely consequences. The discussion in the following pages does not offer an airtight case against intervention but draws attention to possibly grave perils of intervention, perils that seem to have been taken fully and explicitly into account neither by the literature critical of interventionist policies nor, a fortiori, by the uncritical proponents and supporters of government regulation.

27. Here an improvement in the allocation of resources (given the initial pattern of resource distribution) is defined as a change in the pattern of input utilization and/or input consumption that improves the well-being of each member of the economy. Although this definition is close to the norm of Paretian welfare economics, it does *not* invoke the notion of aggregate welfare.

28. "The Austrian finds no detailed explanation in welfare economics of how government is supposed to obtain the information necessary to carry out its assigned tasks. The knowledge required ... is not to be found collected in one place, but rather dispersed throughout the many members of the economy." Stephen C. Littlechild, *The Fallacy of the Mixed Economy: An "Austrian" Critique of Economic Thinking and Policy* (London: Institute of Economic Affairs, 1978), p. 40. See also Gordon Tullock, *The Politics of Bureaucracy* (Washington, D.C.: Public Affairs Press, 1965), p. 124: "Administrative problems ... could be of such complexity that the centralization of information necessary to make decisions effectively in a bureaucracy might not be possible."

29. It is even most cogently pointed out that the very notion of cost, seen from the perspective of the regulator, is unlikely to coincide with any notion of cost that one might wish to consider relevant to the quest for efficiency. See Buchanan, *Cost and Choice*, chaps. 5 and 6.

30. Professor Machlup valuably refers to the "fertility of freedom" in generating discovery of new possibilities. Fritz Ma-

chlup, "Liberalism and the Choice of Freedoms," in *Roads to Freedom: Essays in Honour of Friedrich A. von Hayek*, ed. Erich Streissler (London: Routledge & Kegan Paul, 1969), p. 130.

31. Murray L. Weidenbaum, "The Impact of Government Regulation" (study prepared for the Joint Economic Committee, Subcommittee on Economic Growth and Stabilization, United States Congress, July, 1987). See also Ernest C. Pasour, "Hide and Seek: Hidden Costs of Government Regulation," *World Research INK 2* (December, 1978): 5.

32. "There is ample evidence that imagination and innovation are not stilled by restrictive legislation—only diverted to figuring out ways around it." Freidman, *Economist's Protect*, p. 149.

33. See, for example, Nicholas Sanchez and Alan R. Waters, "Controlling Corruption in Africa and Latin America," in *The Economics of Property Rights*, ed. Eirik Furubotn and Svetozar Pejovich (Cambridge, MA: Ballinger, 1974); Edward C. Banfield, "Corruption as a Feature of Governmental Organization," *Journal of Law and Economics* 18 (December, 1975): 587–605; and Simon Rottenberg, "Comment," *Journal of Law and Economics* 18 (December, 1975): 611–15.

34. William M. Capron et al., eds., *Technological Change in Regulated Industries* (Washington, D.C.: Brookings Institution, 1971).

35. Ibid., p. 8. See also Chap. 2.

36. Sam Peltzman, "An Evaluation of Consumer Protection Legislation: The 1962 Drug Amendments," *Journal of Political Economy* 81 (September-October, 1973): 1049–91. See also David Schwartzman, *Innovation in the Pharmaceutical Industry* (Baltimore: Johns Hopkins Press, 1976).

37. Henry G. Manne, *Insider Trading and the Stock Market* (New York: Free Press, 1966).

38. Although there are many other studies illustrating the hidden distortion generated by regulation, I do not cite them here, since they do not obviously call our attention to the market discovery process and its modification as a result of the regulatory constraints.

33

The Distribution of Effects of Economic Policy

Oskar Morgenstern

The considerations which follow are devoted primarily to the question of whether it is possible to determine the manner in which the effects of interventionist measures are diffused over the economic system. The best way of treating this problem is to start out from the assumption that there is to be a transition from one existing state of the economic system to another state the nature of which has to be worked out anticipatorily on the basis of new data, namely, the proposed measures of intervention. In accordance with our remarks on the freedom from value judgments of scientific concepts, it must be emphasized that it is not a question of stating whether state B is *in general* "better" or "of a higher value" than state A (for that is the postulate), and it follows that it is also unnecessary to show whether a greater or lesser total welfare results. The problem here is rather to show the course of effects. These can be expressed in terms of the maintenance, gain, or loss of economic positions expressed in money, goods or prospects. This is the exclusive task of economic science and not to establish whether the totality of these shifts represents a plus or minus for the *community as a whole*. Whether the effects described by the scientific

Reprinted from *The Limits of Economics* by Oskar Morgenstern, translated by Vera Smith (London: William Hodge and Company, Limited, 1937).

analysis are to be considered good or bad is a matter for general politics to decide.

The fulfillment of the task of determining the effects of measures of economic policy requires the application of economic theory: in *practice* the place of economic theory is likely to be taken by some kind of amateur economics (what is called in German "Vulgärökonomie"), which is a combination of bald assertions and the gleanings of practical experience. The investigation of the distribution of effects is of importance for the added reason that it almost automatically reveals the nature of the sectional interests involved. In general, the reactions of those who are affected by the measure will be such that the man who anticipates a profit from it will be in its favour while the man who believes himself adversely affected by it will be against it. So long as individuals, whether they be private persons, firms, branches of industry or social groups, classes, etc., have a voice in some way or other in determining the composition and aims of economic policy, these factors are of immense importance. It is only in an absolutist State that they can be pushed into the background and, even then, that is possible only as long as the effects are not such as to lead to a violent political upheaval or a general economic collapse. There are examples of this in history from time immemorial and it seems that history is likely to repeat itself in the future.

The effects of the adoption of a measure of economic policy have a place-incidence and a time-incidence. By the former is meant that the effects are felt by various people, and by the latter that the effects are felt by different people at different points of time. Now it depends on the manner of diffusion what the reaction will be, and—what is of primary importance—how visible will be the results of the measure of economic policy. The totality of the measures may be designated economic policy *simpliciter,* and the term "interventionism" may be used to denote an attitude embodying the desire for permanent protection and continuous interference. As was remarked at the beginning, it is always a question of fixing new data of which the effects are not dissimilar in principle from those of the rest of the data. Changed economic data may originate in nature (as, for example, bad harvests and a rise in the price of grain) or may spring from human actions (as, for example, an increase in the price of grain resulting from the formation of a pool). It is all the same to the consumers of the grain which of the two is the cause of the increase in price or whether it is attributable, in the third place, to Government intervention (such as the introduction of a tariff or the prohibition of imports). The interest of the theorist in the matter is, however, quite different: it does not stop at the question as to whether those favorably or unfavorably affected have a share in determining the economic policy and, if so, in what form. It makes a difference whether the influence is transferred in a general way to some place such as Parliament, or whether it is still possible for the individual groups to have a direct voice in the measures directly or indirectly affecting them. The latter may be regarded as the normal case, but for the sake of simplicity we shall leave it out of account for the present and shall assume that the economic politician will wish to form his own opinion quite independently.

Let us start out from a state of equilibrium and assume, by way of example, that the aim of economic policy is to preserve this equilibrium against external disturbances caused, say, by a very rapid advance in the technique of production, achieved by some country abroad, resulting in a substantial reduction in the price of a commodity which is also produced at home. Now, according to our methodological assumptions, it is not possible to demonstrate "scientifically" that something must or must not be done since it is no part of the business of science to make programmes.

Nevertheless, these are the alternatives: (1a) either the

home industry may at once reduce its costs correspondingly by introducing a similar improved or cheaper method of production, or (1*b*) it may not; or (2) the invasion of its market may be prevented by a sufficiently high tariff or a prohibition of the import of the commodity. Hence it follows that in case (1*a*) everything proceeds in the ordinary way: but those incomes which are identical with the prices of the reduced cost elements (for instance, wages) will have suffered a reduction. This will be wholly or partly compensated by the increased demand for the product caused by the fall in price, and it will depend upon the so-called elasticity of demand for this commodity whether the changes balance each other. In (1*b*) there is nothing else to do but to close down the home factories at a rate roughly depending on the extent to which their plant is already depreciated. This means dismissal of workmen and managerial staff, loss of capital, and a fall in the value of the shares of firms in the industry, reduced tax revenue, and a falling-off in consumption on the part of those immediately affected. If, however, alternative (2) is chosen and a tariff imposed, nothing is *apparently* changed in the economic system in question, for the price remains the same, the workers keep their jobs, the foreign product is perhaps entirely pushed out of the home market, and everything seems to be in perfect order.

These are, other things being equal, the three possible courses. Now the economic politician has to decide first of all which one he considers to be technically possible (he has to establish, for instance, whether as required by (1*a*), the wages and other cost factors can in fact be reduced quickly and sufficiently, or whether trade unions and other influences are likely to prevent this); and, secondly, he has to decide which seems to him the desirable course to take by reason of its conforming to what is considered to be a superior objective. It may also happen that, even given the possibility of an immediate adjustment, an import duty will be introduced, because the "general welfare of the community" or the political constellation demands the keeping up of wages. From this it follows that the first fact necessary to realize is that every advantage has to be purchased at the price of a sacrifice. Thus in (1*a*) the price of the cheapening to the consumer of the commodity concerned is the decline in income of the squeezed cost factors, and, inversely, the keeping up of the price of the commodity by the imposition of a tariff is the cost which the consumers have to bear in order that the incomes of the workers in the industry concerned, which would otherwise be reduced [in (1*a*)], may remain the same. These are the chief effects which may tentatively be called "visible" effects; but as there exists a reciprocal interdependence over the whole of the economic system, there will also be present invisible effects which the conscientious economic politician cannot leave out of account. Even in the case of the effects just quoted, it generally happens that anything in the nature of damage or loss makes a deeper impression upon the mind, and so here the decline in wages makes more impression than the satisfaction of the consumers in being able to buy more cheaply, which may even be condemned if the commodity in question falls under the category of a "luxury article."

If—to keep to the example already cited—things are allowed to run their course in accordance with (1*b*), it becomes evident that there is a local and temporal distribution of the so-called favorable and unfavorable effects, which may be regarded as typical and which is of supreme psychological importance. In their place-incidence the unfavorable effects are confined to a narrow, easily assignable area (the closed factories, the unemployed, the machines which have become valueless, etc.); the same is true of the time incidence, as these unfavorable effects usually set in at the moment when the whole situation is at its climax. Now one of the most important empirical principles of human life—one which has therefore come to play an important role in economics—teaches us that any occurrence which belongs to the present, like all present events, is estimated and felt more deeply than one which lies in the future. The more distant things are in the future the less they are taken into account and used as a basis for conduct, until, finally, very remote possibilities no longer enter into the calculations at all, or are considered only by a few isolated individuals. The massing together of the disadvantageous effects within a small area, *and* their characteristic of being concentrated in the present, thus gives them a much greater significance psychologically than would be the case if they were distributed evenly along with the other effects. (Note that "disadvantageous," "unfavorable," etc., are always to be understood in the above-defined sense of a change in money values or incomes, and not, therefore, in any meta-economic sense.) There may, moreover, be unfavorable elements whose effect is postponed; but even if they were more extensive than the immediate effects, the politicians would but seldom accord them proportionate attention.

Now when we come to consider the *advantages* accruing from these events, the opposite becomes evident—and the case is again typical. The favours which the consumers enjoy in the form of the lower price are distributed over a number (often extraordinarily large) of people, who can only in the rarest cases be counted and identified (in sharp contrast to the *concretely* calculable number of factory workers losing their jobs). The consumption of the commodity takes place only gradually over time, for the most part in the future, which is underestimated. Thus, psychologically, the situation is much more unfavorable. This holds good even when, as here, we are thinking primarily only of the possibility of ascertaining and not of appraising the repercussions. Finally, there are psychological factors also entering in. The economic politician who is seeking after knowledge should, of course, be able to overcome impediments of that kind, but even if the spirit is able and willing, the flesh, as we all know, is often weak.

Without making any judgment as to its ultimate value, we may call the course of affairs described above "the 'right' one in the *laissez-faire* sense." In contrast to it there is the "interventionist" economic policy, which—on the basis of the psychological circumstances just outlined and the lack of a precise realization of the more remote effects—proposes to solve the difficulties by means of a tariff. Now this time the typical distribution of advantages and disadvantages is exactly reversed. There is a local-temporal concentration of advantages, as the factories again become busy, and a local-temporal dispersion of the damage to the consumers, who, moreover, apparently suffer no "real" harm, that is, no positive deprivation of something they previously possessed, but merely do not come into the enjoyment of a reduction in price, which would otherwise have accrued to them. It is superfluous to elaborate these effects further, as the result is the exact converse of the state of affairs described above.

So far we have spoken only of the direct, more or less immediately detectable effects. It is, however, the task of economics to go beyond this point and to make a thorough examination of the secondary effects and repercussions, which necessarily also enter into the question. For otherwise it would, of course, be a simple matter to survey the effects and would not require the aid of science. It will shorten the argument, and will at the same time give the right emphasis to the great complications arising out of the investigation even of a quite simple case, if we drop the assumption so far made of equilibrium as a starting point. Up till now it was assumed that the disturbance under discussion was the only one present, so that all movements away from equilibrium in the economic system concerned were attributable to this one known cause. Actually, in the concrete reality to which our propositions must apply, the matter looks essentially different: the idea that one has to do with an equilibrium as a starting point is misleading. We ought rather to assume as starting-point a situation which may, perhaps, be termed a "disequilibrium," that is, one which merely tends towards an equilibrium. But even the word "situation" is not quite appropriate, as what is involved is simply a short phase of a rapidly moving process. Important as the event described in the above example in its relation to economic policy may be, its true significance can only be appreciated if we know in addition, the forces that have brought the process to the phase in which the event occurs. This is extremely difficult. As soon as we have to do with movements of economic quantities which derive from other often unknown causes, it is generally quite impossible to ascertain whether occurrences which may seem to be direct or immediate effects are actually so, or whether they are not due to entirely different circumstances. To make the right choice here requires a very wide knowledge and experience, and a gift for seeing things in their right proportions.

In order to give a further elucidation (unfortunately only of the difficulties) let us go back once more to the example of the introduction of a tariff. A direct loss could not be proved under the given assumptions; but economics must draw the economic politician's attention to the fact that the ousting of the foreign goods from the home market causes a curtailment of the total volume of international trade carried on between the two countries, so that the foreign country is now no longer in a position to import the same amount of some other commodity. Goods must be exchanged for goods; but what commodity, the other country will no longer buy is a *quastio facti*, just as it is likewise a *quastio facti* whether the loss suffered by the export industries of the country introducing the tariff does not cause more workers to become unemployed, and a much greater fall in the value of fixed capital, than would have happened had the line of business originally affected by the foreign competition been closed down. The point, however, with which we have been dealing from the outset, namely, the establishing of the local and temporal distribution of the effects, again comes into the foreground, even though in the nature of things we cannot achieve absolute certainty in ascribing the individual events to others of more remote origin. The detriment to the export industries is not precisely ascertainable. It is distributed over a large number of firms and industries, and stretches out over unknown periods of time. Even those affected by it cannot in the early stages either exactly foresee their own fate or prepare themselves for it.

Economic theory rightly eliminates from its considerations so-called "frictions," that is, its considerations hold good as a rule under the hypothesis that during the period of time which must be allowed for the working out of the various factors influencing the individual processes, no impediments appear which escaped inclusion in the original assumptions. Thus if we say, for instance, that when the wages in an industry are reduced the workers will leave that industry and migrate to other trades, then all the inferences which are based upon this statement assume that these migrations actually do take place. In the domain of economic policy it is not possible to proceed in this way, since it must be taken into account that this high degree of abstraction is not valid, as it becomes apparent that people do not move away immediately, partly because they are ignorant of labor conditions elsewhere, and partly because they are induced to stay, even at much lower wages, by extraeconomic factors (family reasons, for instance), or because they have not at their disposal the means necessary for moving, etc. These circumstances (which must be introduced into the formula of pure theory somewhat in the nature of what is called in modern logic a "quantificator") mean something more than a mere shift in the degree of abstraction. If the degree of abstraction is lowered, the alleged tendencies while being, it is true, limited and slowed down, are *not* completely diverted from their course and, as it were, reversed. As in the above example the forces dealt with by economic theory still operate.

The part played by frictions has not yet been sufficiently investigated by economists. In recent times there has emerged the still very obscure idea that alongside the hitherto prevalent economic theory, which is of the "long-run" type (that is, it deals with such long periods of time that the forces tending to a new equilibrium can work themselves out quite undisturbed by other forces), we must place a second "short-run" theory. And there may be some who desire to treat frictions similarly. One should be vastly skeptical of such an attempt at division, as in its present form it would amount to trying to find two kinds of truth. What is more probably needed is an attempt to fix the *time-element* into its proper place in general theory. If that were done successfully, the difficulties would fall away of themselves. As is well known, the time element has long been regarded as the chief crux in economics. Nevertheless, it may be noted here that it is quite permissible to talk of "frictions" as long as the hindrances or impediments to which we give this name do not become *independent* causes of an economic kind, of the same category and order as those which were taken into account at the outset of our investigations.

In dealing with economic policy as opposed to economic theory, things are, of course, somewhat different. If it is a question of evaluating decisions of economic policy, the period of time to be taken into account generally plays a quite decisive role. It should be clear from what has been said above that it is always a difficult matter to calculate for long periods, not only because the number of coefficients of uncertainty which enter in, and which have to be taken into account at various points, increases with the length of the period, but also because every event which lies in the more distant future is discounted. The concept of the "time period" must, of course, be taken in a purely relative sense depending on the purpose of the measure. The economic politician—let us assume the Government—is often faced with a serious dilemma: a measure may be recognized as correct in principle, but the period necessary to ensure its success may be so long that before that time is passed undesired secondary effects emerge which make it practically impossible to take what is recognized to be the right course. As long as he is dealing only with general theory, the economist is in a much better position, as he does not require to bother about this aspect of the matter. He lets industries pass away, migrate or spring up without having to care what happens to the participants as *individuals*. He is in a position similar to that of any statistician examining mass phenomena, who has perhaps to calculate a percentage of accidents, but would be greatly embarrassed if he had to select a definite group of persons or even definite individuals to whom these accidents were to happen.

A typical illustration is the so-called compensation theory which teaches that the workers who are thrown out of their jobs by technical progress will in the course of time again find employment elsewhere, particularly in the production, directly or indirectly, of the labor-saving machines themselves. Assuming that this thesis is correct, it means, if we act according to it, that we must disregard the *individual* fate of those affected, who become unemployed. This would demand a hard decision, which is, however, generally made impossible by the fact that this process which the theorist may rightly regard as "harmless" and "unimportant" in a higher sense, is precisely the first to call for action and for a definite policy, since it is the individuals affected who arouse the sympathy of the general public. Countless incidents of the kind are known to economic history, from the machine wreckers of the first industrial revolution to the most recent enemies of progress. They bring with them also characteristic popular theories, such, for example, as the current doctrine of "technocracy," which in its absurdity distracts attention from the real questions involved. The nature of the decision, then, will depend solely upon the general conceptions of value upon which the Government bases its general policy. The position will often be such as to make it obvious that some branch of industry is irremediably doomed to extinction—as, for instance, coachbuilding or wharves for sailing ships—and that it would be utterly foolish to prohibit automobiles and steamships. The decision, however, will not always be so simple, because it may happen that there are too many people (who are, what is not least important, very attached to the declining industry, too much sentiment clings to it, or too much capital is invested in it; in short, there are too many "vested interests," so that, in the vague hope that some sort of miracle may happen, no definite stand is taken, or at any rate not at the right time. The reader need only be reminded of the struggle between rail and road which is at present taking place in every country.

The questions touched upon here have an extremely important, general, political aspect. The more unstable is the system of government and the greater the influence of topical problems upon its behavior—the nearer, in fact, it is forced into contact with the changing fortunes of the ups and down of every kind, political and other, in economic activity—the less it will be inclined to pursue a long-term economic policy. In any case it will not often be able to do so, as it is never certain that the succeeding Government will not take up an entirely different attitude, and interfere with the long-term measures introduced by it, an occurrence which would result in the loss of the capital already invested, etc. It is only where a long-term policy is based upon fairly *general opinions* that a certain degree of continuity is guaranteed, as, for instance, in the State management of forests, where it would scarcely occur to a government suddenly to have all the woods cut down. As a rule, financial policy, of course, is much more mobile in character! It may be concluded, quite apart from any political valuation, that the Government, which will be able to make the most use of the propositions laid down by economic theory, will be the Government whose economic decisions are directed by some definite and immutable State purpose. In many countries, therefore, liberal democracy is the form of government most inimicable to the use of economic theory, a state of affairs which is particularly noticeable in times of economic stress. Contemporary history offers a number of striking examples of this. In periods of rising economic prosperity these things do not play anything like such an important role; but still this is true only if one is not obliged to acknowledge the real cause of crises as being the existence of an excessive economic boom, which it may very well be correct to do.

We may now apply this analysis to estimating the importance, for the actual course of economic policy, of the distribution and accumulation, as described above, of effects of interventionist and other measures of economic policy. For, however paradoxical it may seem, it is possible to make pronouncements about the "trend" of economic policy, that is, about the general direction of its development, without dealing at all closely with its concrete details at any particular moment. Such propositions are necessarily of a general nature, but there are plenty of examples to support the observation that the course of economic policy is determined, in the first place, by the nature of the technical opportunities for obtaining representation of the various sectional interests, and, in the second place, by the resultant effective representation of those interests. This also holds good for States with highly autocratic and absolutist Governments. In fact, in such States the experience has frequently been that one or several "pressure groups" have succeeded in exerting a determining influence upon the form of government itself. In general, this is dependent upon whether it is technically possible or not to organize the interests. This possibility is practically nonexistent in the case of the so-called "consumers' interests," which cannot even be precisely defined. The repeated abortive attempts, in various countries, of associations of consumers in the towns to defend themselves, for example, against an increase in the cost of living brought about by an agrarian-protectionist economic policy, are sufficient to illustrate this fundamental point. It is easy (given, of course, the suitable apparatus such as unions) for those interests to make themselves heard which can be clearly distinguished and easily made public, and the injuring of which is followed by a concentration of effects in the present or in the immediate future. As we know, in such circumstances the other interests which would be "favoured" if the natural course of events were unimpeded are in a perceptibly unfavorable position. Their case is considered to be much less deserving, and, owing to the distortion of the estimation of future events, it is almost always impossible for those who believe they can foresee their future detriment, for example, to stir up their fellow-sufferers to a course of action equal in effectiveness to that of their doubly favoured opponents.

It has been shown that the clustering of the effects, and their incidence in the present, always works in favour of a policy of interference. As a consequence of this and of the principle mentioned above relating to the organization of the representation of sectional interests, it follows, in diametrical opposition to the prevailing opinion, that where the forces are allowed free play the economic system tends to become increasingly rigid as a result of continuous protective interference. This condition would remain unaltered even if representation and co-ordination of all the interests in economic boards and councils or permanent corporations were to be in some way forcibly imposed. Once such a condition is created, what generally happens—a point which cannot be discussed in detail within the confines of this essay—is that each group lets itself be bribed by all the others to vote dishonestly for measures not in conformity with its own interests. This is the true interpretation, however much the proceedings may be clothed in beautiful generalities. This observation refers particularly to the domain of commercial policy, but it applies, as experience shows, to all other spheres also. Thus if "consumers" were also represented as an organized group in such a corporation, it would not make the slightest difference to the principle set out above; indeed, it is to be presumed, on the contrary, that the mere mention of the "purchasing-power argument" would ensure the other groups of the upper hand, for there is nothing before which "consumers" stand in greater awe than the threat of a loss of purchasing power. And it has just been shown that this is quite often destroyed *locally*, however fallacious the theory of purchasing power otherwise is.

Therefore a higher court of appeal is required if a stop is to be put to the process of the continuous growth of intervention, which, as must again be repeated, stamps all economic policy with the tendency to create rigidity in the economic system. This court of appeal can only lie in the general government of the State itself, which sets the aims that the measures of economic policy are intended to achieve. But here it becomes a question of the creation of aims and ends, and no longer merely of the problem of the appropriateness of various means to given ends, and of what services economic theory can render in the solving of that problem. The way in which we find ourselves obliged to overstep the original confines of our analysis when investigating these questions is of itself very significant. For it expresses a fact that is almost always completely neglected in discussions of economic policy, namely, that economic policy is *eo ipso* policy in the wider sense. That is to say, that all the interventionist measures of economic policy taken together merge into the whole social framework, and must therefore be regarded from a much wider angle than that of the possible application of a single discipline. We shall have something more to say of this later.

34

The Market Economy and the Distribution of Wealth

Ludwig M. Lachmann

Everywhere today in the free world we find the opponents of the market economy at a loss for plausible arguments. Of late the "case for central planning" has shed
much of its erstwhile luster. We have had too much experience of it. The facts of the last forty years are too eloquent.

Who can now doubt that, as Professor Mises pointed
out thirty years ago, every intervention by a political authority entails a further intervention to prevent the inevitable
economic repercussions of the first step from taking place?
Who will deny that a command economy requires an atmosphere of inflation to operate at all, and who today does not
know the baneful effects of "controlled inflation?" Even
though some economists have now invented the eulogistic
term "secular inflation" in order to describe the permanent
inflation we all know so well, it is unlikely that anyone is
deceived. It did not really require the recent German example to demonstrate to us that a market economy will create
order out of "administratively controlled" chaos even in the
most unfavorable circumstances. A form of economic organization based on voluntary cooperation and the univer-

Reprinted from *Capital, Expectations and the Market Process* by Ludwig M. Lachmann, edited by Walter E. Grinder (Kansas City: Sheed Andrews and McMeel,
Inc., 1976).

sal exchange of knowledge is necessarily superior to any hierarchical structure, even if in the latter a rational test for the qualifications of those who give the word of command could exist. Those who are able to learn from reason and experience knew it before, and those who are not are unlikely to learn it even now.

Confronted with this situation, the opponents of the market economy have shifted their ground; they now oppose it on "social" rather than economic grounds. They accuse it of being unjust rather than inefficient. They now dwell on the "distorting effects" of the ownership of wealth and contend that "the plebiscite of the market is swayed by plural voting." They show that the distribution of wealth affects production and income distribution since the owners of wealth not merely receive an "unfair share" of the social income, but will also influence the composition of the social product: Luxuries are too many and necessities too few. Moreover, since these owners do most of the saving they also determine the rate of capital accumulation and thus of economic progress.

Some of these opponents would not altogether deny that there is a sense in which the distribution of wealth is the cumulative result of the play of economic forces, but would hold that this cumulation operates in such a fashion as to make the present a slave of the past, a bygone an arbitrary factor in the present. Today's income-distribution is shaped by today's distribution of wealth, and even though today's wealth was partly accumulated yesterday, it was accumulated by processes reflecting the influence of the distribution of wealth on the day before yesterday. In the main this argument of the opponents of the market economy is based on the institution of Inheritance to which, even in a progressive society, we are told, a majority of the owners owe their wealth.

This argument appears to be widely accepted today, even by many who are genuinely in favor of economic freedom. Such people have come to believe that a "redistribution of wealth," for instance through death duties, would have socially desirable, but no unfavorable economic results. On the contrary, since such measures would help to free the present from the "dead hand" of the past they would also help to adjust present incomes to present needs. The distribution of wealth is a datum of the market, and by changing data we can change results without interfering with the market mechanism! It follows that only when accompanied by a policy designed continually to redistribute existing wealth, would the market process have "socially tolerable" results.

This view, as we said, is today held by many, even by some economists who understand the superiority of the market economy over the command economy and the frustrations of interventionism, but dislike what they regard as the social consequences of the market economy. They are prepared to accept the market economy only where its operation is accompanied by such a policy of redistribution.

The present paper is devoted to a criticism of the basis of this view.

In the first place, the whole argument rests logically on verbal confusion arising from the ambiguous meaning of the term "datum." In common usage as well as in most sciences, for instance in statistics, the word "datum" means something that is, at a moment of time, "given" to us as observers of the scene. In this sense it is, of course, a truism that the mode of the distribution of wealth is a datum at any given moment of time, simply in the trivial sense that it happens to exist and no other mode does. But in the equilibrium theories which, for better or worse, have come to mean so much for present-day economic thought and have so largely shaped its content, the word "datum" has acquired a second and very different meaning: Here a datum means a necessary condition of equilibrium, an independent variable, and "the data" collectively mean the total sum of necessary and sufficient conditions from which, once we know them all, we without further ado can deduce equilibrium price and quantity. In this second sense the distribution of wealth would thus, together with the other data, be a DE-TERMINANT, though not the only determinant, of the prices and quantities of the various services and products bought and sold.

It will, however, be our main task in the paper to show that the distribution of wealth is not a "datum" in this second sense. Far from being an "independent variable" of the market process, it is, on the contrary, continuously subject to modification by the market forces. Needless to say, this is not to deny that at any moment it is among the forcers which shape the path of the market process in the immediate future, but *it is* to deny that the mode of distribution as such can have any permanent influence. Though wealth is always distributed in some definite way, the mode of this distribution is ever-changing.

Only if the mode of distribution remained the same in period after period, while individual pieces of wealth were being transferred by inheritance, could such a constant mode be said to be a permanent economic force. In reality this is not so. The distribution of wealth is being shaped by the forces of the market as an object, not an agent, and whatever its mode may be today will soon have become an irrelevant bygone.

The distribution of wealth, therefore, has no place among the data of equilibrium. What is, however, of great economic and social interest is not the mode of distribution of wealth at a moment of time, but its mode of change over time. Such change, we shall see, finds its true place among the events that happen on that problematical "path" which may, but rarely in reality does, lead to equilibrium. It is a typically "dynamic" phenomenon. It is a curious fact that at a time when so much is heard of the need for the pursuit and promotion of dynamic studies it should arouse so little interest.

Ownership is a legal concept which refers to concrete material objects. Wealth is an economic concept which refers to scarce resources. All valuable resources are, or reflect, or embody, material objects, but not all material objects are resources: Derelict houses and heaps of scrap are obvious examples, as are any objects which their owners would gladly give away if they could find somebody willing to remove them. Moreover, what is a resource today may cease to be one tomorrow, while what is a valueless object today may become valuable tomorrow. The resource status of material objects is therefore always problematical and depends to some extent on foresight. An object constitutes wealth only if it is a source of an income stream. The value of the object to the owner, actual or potential, reflects at any moment its expected income-yielding capacity. This, in its turn, will depend on the uses to which the object can be turned. The mere ownership of objects, therefore, does not necessarily confer wealth; it is their successful use which confers it. Not ownership but use of resources is the source of income and wealth. An ice-cream factory in New York may mean wealth to its owner; the same ice-cream factory in Greenland would scarcely be a resource.

In a world of unexpected change the maintenance of wealth is always problematical; and in the long run it may be said to be impossible. In order to be able to maintain a given amount of wealth which could be transferred by inheritance from one generation to the next, a family would have to own such resources as will yield a permanent net income stream, i.e., a stream of surplus of output value over the cost of factor services complementary to the resources owned. It seems that this would be possible only *either* in a stationary world, a world in which today is as yesterday and tomorrow like today, and in which thus, day after day, and year after year, the same income will accrue to the same owners or their heirs; *or* if all resource owners had perfect foresight. Since both cases are remote from reality we can safely ignore them. What, then, in reality happens to wealth in a world of unexpected change?

All wealth consists of capital assets which, in one way or another, embody or at least ultimately reflect the material resources of production, the sources of valuable output. All output is produced by human labor with the help of combinations of such resources. For this purpose resources have to be used in certain combinations; complementarity is of the essence of resource use. The modes of this complementarity are in no way "given" to the entrepreneurs who make, initiate, and carry out production plans. There is in reality no such thing as *A* production function. On the contrary, the task of the entrepreneur consists precisely in finding, in a world of perpetual change, which combination of resources will yield, in the conditions of today, a maximum surplus of output over input value, and in guessing which will do so in the probable conditions of tomorrow, when output values, cost of complementary input, and technology all will have changed.

If all capital resources were infinitely versatile the entrepreneurial problem would consist in no more than following the changes of external conditions by turning combinations of resources to a succession of uses made profitable by these changes. As it is, resources have, as a rule, a limited range of versatility, each is specific to a number of uses.[1] Hence, the need for adjustment to change will often entail the need for a change in the composition of the resource group, for "capital regrouping." But each change in the mode of complementarity will affect the value of the component resources by giving rise to capital gains and losses. Entrepreneurs will make higher bids for the services of those resources for which they have found more profitable uses, and lower bids for those which have to be turned to less profitable uses. In the limiting case where no (present or potential future) use can be found for a resource which has so far formed part of a profitable combination, this resource will lose its resource character altogether. But even in less drastic cases capital gains and losses made on durable assets are an inevitable concomitant of a world of unexpected change.

The market process is thus seen to be a leveling process. In a market economy a process of redistribution of wealth is taking place all the time before which those outwardly similar processes which modern politicians are in the habit of instituting, pale into comparative insignificance, if for no other reason than that the market gives wealth to those who can hold it, while politicians give it to their constituents who, as a rule, cannot.

This process of redistribution of wealth is not prompted by a concatenation of hazards. Those who participate in it are not playing a game of chance, but a game of skill. This process, like all real dynamic processes, reflects the transmission of knowledge from mind to mind. It is possible only because some people have knowledge that others have not yet acquired, because knowledge of change and its implications spread gradually and unevenly throughout society.

In this process he is successful who understands earlier than any one else that a certain resource which today can be produced when it is new, or bought, when it is an existing resource, at a certain price *A*, will tomorrow form part of a productive combination as a result of which it will be worth *A'*. Such capital gains or losses prompted by the chance of, or need for, turning resources from one use to another, superior or inferior to the first, form the economic substance of what wealth means in a changing world, and are the chief vehicle of the process of redistribution.

In this process it is most unlikely that the same man will continue to be right in his guesses about possible new uses for existing or potential resources time after time, unless he is really superior. And in the latter case his heirs are unlikely to show similar success—unless they are superior, too. In a world of unexpected change, capital losses are ultimately as inevitable as are capital gains. Competition between capital owners and the specific nature of durable resources, even though it be "multiple specificity," entail that gains are followed by losses as losses are followed by gains.

These economic facts have certain social consequences. As the critics of the market economy nowadays prefer to take their stand on "social" grounds, it may be not inappropriate here to elucidate the true social results of the market process. We have already spoken of it as a leveling process. More aptly, we may now describe these results as an instance of what Pareto called "the circulation of elites." Wealth is unlikely to stay for long in the same hands. It passes from hand to hand as unforeseen change confers value, now on this, now on that specific resource, engendering capital gains and losses. The owners of wealth, we might say with Schumpeter, are like the guests at a hotel or the passengers in a train: They are always there but are never for long the same people.

It may be objected that our argument applies in any case only to a small segment of society and that the circulation of elites does not eliminate social injustice. There may be such circulation among wealth owners, but what about the rest of society? What chance have those without wealth of even participating, let alone winning, in the game? This objection, however, would ignore the part played by managers and entrepreneurs in the market process, a part to which we shall soon have to return.

In a market economy, we have seen, all wealth is of a problematical nature. The more durable assets are and the more specific, the more restricted the range of uses to which they may be turned, the more clearly the problem becomes visible. But in a society with little fixed capital in which most accumulated wealth took the form of stocks of commodities, mainly agricultural and perishable, carried for periods of various lengths, a society in which durable consumer goods, except perhaps for houses and furniture, hardly existed, the problem was not so clearly visible. Such was, by and large, the society in which the classical economists were living and from which they naturally borrowed many traits. In the conditions of their time, therefore, the classical economists were justified, up to a point, in regarding all capital as virtually homogeneous and perfectly versatile, contrasting it with land, the only specific and irreproducible resource. But in our time there is little or no justification for such dichotomy. The more fixed capital there is, and the more durable it is, the greater the probability that such capital resources will, before they wear out, have to be used for purposes other than those for which they were originally designed. This means practically that in a modern market economy there can be no such thing as a source of permanent income. Durability and limited versatility make it impossible.

It may be asked whether in presenting our argument we have not confused the capital owner with the entrepreneur, ascribing to the former functions which properly belong to the latter. Is not the decision about the use of existing resources as well as the decision which specifies the concrete form of new capital resources, viz. the investment decision, a typical entrepreneurial task? Is it not for the entrepreneur to regroup and redeploy combinations of capital goods? Are we not claiming for capital owners the economic functions of the entrepreneur?

We are not primarily concerned with claiming functions for anybody. We are concerned with the effects of unexpected change on asset values and on the distribution of wealth. The effects of such change will fall upon the owners of wealth irrespective of where the change originates. If the distinction between capitalist and entrepreneur could always easily be made, it might be claimed that the continuous redistribution of wealth is the result of entrepreneurial action, a process in which capital owners play a merely passive part. But that the process really occurs, that wealth is being redistributed by the market, cannot be doubted, nor that the process is prompted by the transmission of knowledge from one center of entrepreneurial action to another. Where capital owners and entrepreneurs can be clearly distinguished, it is true that the owners of wealth take no active part in the process themselves, but passively have to accept its results.

Yet there are many cases in which such a clear-cut distinction cannot be made. In the modern world wealth typically takes the form of securities. The owner of wealth is typically a shareholder. Is the shareholder an entrepreneur? Professor Knight asserts that he is, but a succession of authors from Walter Rathenau[2] to Mr. Burnham have denied him that status. The answer depends, of course, on our definition of the entrepreneur. If we define him as an uncertainty-bearer, it is clear that the shareholder is an entrepreneur. But in recent years there seems to be a growing tendency to define the entrepreneur as the planner and decision-maker. If so, directors and managers are entrepreneurs, but shareholders, it seems, are not.

Yet we have to be careful in drawing our conclusions. One of the most important tasks of the entrepreneur is to specify the concrete form of capital resources, to say what buildings are to be erected, what stocks to be kept, etc. If we are clearly to distinguish between capitalist and entrepreneur we must assume that a "pure" entrepreneur, with no wealth of his own, borrows capital in money form, i.e., in a nonspecific form, from "pure" capital owners.[3]

But do the directors and managers at the top of the organizational ladder really make all the specifying decisions? Are not many such decisions made "lower down" by works managers, supervisors, etc.? Is it really at all possible to indicate "the entrepreneur" in a world in which managerial functions are so widely spread?

On the other hand, the decision of a capital owner to buy new shares in company A rather than in company B is also a specifying decision. In fact this is the primary decision on which all the managerial decisions within the firm ultimately depend, since without capital there would be nothing for them to specify. We have to realize, it seems, that the specifying decisions of shareholders, directors, managers, etc., are in the end all mutually dependent upon each other, are but links in a chain. All are specifying decisions distinguished only by the degree of concreteness which increases as we are moving down the organizational ladder. Buying shares in company A is a decision which gives capital a form less concrete than does the decision of the workshop manager as to which tools are to be made, but it is a specifying decision all the same, and one which provides the material basis for the workshop manager's action. In this sense we may say that the capital owner makes the "highest" specifying decision.

The distinction between capital owner and entrepreneur is thus not always easily made. To this extent, then, the contrast between the active entrepreneurs, forming and redeploying combinations of capital resources, and the passive asset owners, who have to accept the verdict of the market forces on the success of "their" entrepreneurs, is much overdrawn. Shareholders, after all, are not quite defenseless in these matters. If they cannot persuade their directors to refrain from a certain step, there is one thing they can do: They can sell!

But what about bondholders? Shareholders may make capital gains and losses; their wealth is visibly affected by market forces. But bondholders seem to be in an altogether different position. Are they not owners of wealth who can claim immunity from the market forces we have described, and thus from the process of redistribution?

In the first place, of course, the difference is merely a matter of degree. Cases are not unknown in which, owing to failure of plans, inefficiency of management, or to external circumstances which had not been foreseen, bondholders had to take over an enterprise and thus became involuntary shareholders. It is true, however, that most bondholders are wealth owners who stand, as it were, at one remove from the scene we have endeavored to describe, from the source of changes which are bound to affect most asset values, though it is not true of all of them. Most of the repercussions, radiating from this source will have been, as it were, intercepted by others before they reach the bondholders. The higher the "gear" of a company's capital, the thinner the protective layer of the equity, the more repercussions will reach the bondholders, and the more strongly they will be affected. It is thus quite wrong to cite the case of the bondholder in order to show that there are wealth owners exempt from the operation of the market forces we have described. Wealth owners as a class can never be so exempt, though some may be relatively more affected than others.

Furthermore, there are two cases of economic forces engendering capital gains and losses from which, in the nature of these cases, the bondholder cannot protect himself, however thick the protective armor of the equity may happen to be: the rate of interest and inflation. A rise in long-term rates of interest will depress bond values where equity holders may still hope to recoup themselves by higher profits, while a fall will have the opposite effect. Inflation transfers wealth from creditors to debtors, whereas deflation has the opposite effect. In both cases we have, of course, instances of that redistribution of wealth with which we have become acquainted. We may say that with a constant long-term rate of interest and with no change in the value of money, the susceptibility of bond holders' wealth to unexpected change will depend on their relative position as against equity holders, their "economic distance" from the center of disturbances; while interest changes and changes in the value of money will modify that relative position.

The holders of government bonds, of course, are exempt from many of the repercussions of unexpected change, but by no means from all of them. To be sure, they do not need the protective armor of the equity to shield them against the market forces which modify prices and costs. But interest changes and inflation are as much of a threat to them as to other bondholders. In the world of permanent inflation in which we are now living, to regard wealth in the form of government securities as not liable to erosion by the forces of change would be ludicrous. But in any case the existence of a government debt is not a result of the operation of market forces. It is the result of the operation of politicians eager to save their constituents from the task of having to pay taxes they would otherwise have had to pay.

The main fact we have stressed in this paper, the redistribution of wealth caused by the forces of the market in a world of unexpected change, is a fact of common observation. Why, then, is it constantly being ignored? We could understand why the politicians choose to ignore it: After all, the large majority of their constituents are unlikely to be directly affected by it, and, as is amply shown in the case of inflation, would scarcely be able to understand it if they were. But why should economists choose to ignore it? That the mode of the distribution of wealth is a result of the operation of economic forces is the kind of proposition which, one would think, would appeal to them. Why, then, do so many economists continue to regard the distribution of wealth as a "datum" in the second sense mentioned above? We submit that the reason has to be sought in an excessive preoccupation with equilibrium problems.

We saw before that the successive modes of the distribution of wealth belong to the world of disequilibrium. Capital gains and losses arise in the main because durable resources have to be used in ways for which they were not planned, and because some men understand better and earlier than other men what the changing needs and resources of a world in motion imply. Equilibrium means consistency of plans, but the redistribution of wealth by the market is typically a result of inconsistent action. To those trained to think in equilibrium terms it is perhaps only natural that such processes as we have described should appear to be not quite "respectable." For them the "real" economic forces are those which tend to establish and maintain equilibrium. Forces only operating in disequilibrium are thus regarded as not really very interesting and are therefore all too often ignored. There may be two reasons for such neglect. No doubt a belief that a tendency towards equilibrium does exist in reality and that, in any conceivable situation, the forces tending towards equilibrium will always be stronger than the forces of resistance, plays a part in it.

But an equally strong reason, we may suspect, is the inability of economists preoccupied with equilibria to cope at all with the forces of disequilibrium. All theory has to make use of coherent models. If one has only one such model at one's disposal a good many phenomena that do not seem to fit into one's scheme are likely to remain unaccounted for. The neglect of the process of redistribution is thus not merely of far-reaching practical importance in political economy since it prevents us from understanding certain features of the world in which we are living. It is also of crucial methodological significance to the central area of economic thought.

We are not saying, of course, that the modern economist, so learned in the grammar of equilibrium, so ignorant of the facts of the market, is unable or unready to cope with economic change; that would be absurd. We are saying that he is well-equipped only to deal with types of change that happen to conform to a fairly rigid pattern. In most of the literature currently in fashion change is conceived as a transition from one equilibrium to another, i.e., in terms of comparative statics. There are even some economists who, having thoroughly misunderstood Cassel's idea of a "uniformly progressive economy," cannot conceive of economic progress in any other way![4] Such smooth transition from one

684   *Austrian Economics: A Reader*

equilibrium (long-run or short-run) to another virtually bars not only discussion of the process in which we are interested here, but of all true economic processes. For such smooth transition will only take place where the new equilibrium position is already generally known and anticipated before it is reached. Where this is not so, a process of trial and error (Walras's *"tâtonnements"*) will start which in the end may or may not lead to a new equilibrium position. But even where it does, the new equilibrium finally reached will not be that which would have been reached immediately had everybody anticipated it at the beginning, since it will be the cumulative result of the events which took place on the "path" leading to it. Among these events changes in the distribution of wealth occupy a prominent place.

Professor Lindahl[5] has recently shown to what extent Keynes's analytical model is vitiated by his apparent determination to squeeze a variety of economic forces into the Procrustean bed of short-period equilibrium analysis. Keynes, while he wished to describe the *modus operandi* of a number of dynamic forces, cast his model in the mold of a system of simultaneous equations, though the various forces studied by him clearly belonged to periods of different length. The lesson to be learned here is that once we allow ourselves to ignore fundamental facts about the market, such as differential knowledge, some people understanding the meaning of an event before others, and in general, the temporal pattern of events, we shall be tempted to express "immediate" effects in short-period equilibrium terms. And all too soon we shall also allow ourselves to forget that what is of real economic interest are not the equilibria, even if they exist, which is in any case doubtful, but what happens between them. "An auxiliary makeshift employed by the logical economists as a limiting notion"[6] can produce rather disastrous results when it is misemployed.

The preoccupation with equilibrium ultimately stems from a confusion between subject and object, between the mind of the observer and the minds of the actors observed. There can, of course, be no systematic science without a coherent frame of reference, but we can hardly expect to find such coherence as our frame of reference requires ready-made for us in the situations we observe. It is, on the contrary, our task to produce it by analytical effort. There are, in the social sciences, many situations which are interesting to us precisely because the human actions in them are inconsistent with each other, and in which coherence, if at all, is ultimately produced by the interplay of mind on mind. The present paper is devoted to the study of one such situation. We have endeavored to show that a social phenomenon of some importance can be understood if presented in terms of a process reflecting the interplay of mind on mind, but not otherwise. The model-builders, econometric and otherwise, naturally have to avoid such themes.

It is very much to be hoped that economists in the future will show themselves less inclined than they have been in the past to look for ready-made, but spurious, coherence, and that they will take a greater interest in the variety of ways in which the human mind in action produces coherence out of an initially incoherent situation.

Notes

Reprinted from Mary Sennholz, ed., *On Freedom and Free Enterprise: Essays in Honor of Ludwig von Mises* (New York: D. Van Nostrand, 1956).

1. The argument presented in what follows owes a good deal to ideas first set forth by Professor Mises in "Das festangelegte Kapital," in *Grundprobleme der Nationalökonomie*, pp. 201–14 [English trans. in *Epistemological Problems of Economics* (New York: D. Van Nostrand, 1960), pp. 217–31.]
2. Vom Aktienwesen, 1917.

3. This definition has, of course, certain social implications. Those who accept it can hardly continue to regard entrepreneurs as a class access to which is impossible for those with no wealth of their own. Whatever degree of the "imperfection of the capital market" we choose to assume will not give us this result.

4. For a most effective criticism of this kind of model building see Joan Robinson, "The Model of an Expanding Economy," *Economic Journal* 62 (March, 1952): 42–53.

5. Erik Lindahl "On Keynes' Economic System," *Economic Record* 30 (May, 1954): 19–32; 30 (November, 1954): 159–71.

6. Ludwig von Mises, *Human Action* (New Haven: Yale University Press, 1949), p. 352.

The Ludwig von Mises Distinguished Lectures in Economics

Ludwig von Mises (1881–1973) was one of this century's most prominent champions of human freedom. His long career as a scholar, teacher, and author was dedicated to defending private property, the importance of the individual, and limited government. His theoretical work conclusively proved that a free society cannot exist without a free economy.

Each year Hillsdale College presents a series of distinguished lecturers on current economic themes. It is appropriate that this series takes place at Hillsdale College for Professor von Mises bequeathed his entire personal library of over 5,000 volumes, pamphlets, and papers to Hillsdale; it is now housed in a special section of the Mossey Learning Resources Center.

These presentations are given permanence and a wider audience through their publication as volumes in the *Champions of Freedom* book series. For more information, contact the Hillsdale College Press, Hillsdale, Michigan 49242; 517/439-1524.

1973–1974
Henry Hazlitt—"The Return to Sound Money"
Benjamin A. Rogge—"Will Capitalism Survive?"
Leonard Read—"The Miracle of the Market"
Israel M. Kirzner—"Capital, Competition, and Capitalism"
Sylvester Petro—"Labor Unions in a Free Society"
Robert M. Bleiberg—"Wage and Price Controls"

1974–1975
John Davenport—"The Market and Human Values"
Arthur Shenfield—"Must We Abolish the State?"
John Exter—"Money in Today's World"
Bertel M. Sparks—"Retreat from Contract to Status"
R. Heath Larry—"Renaissance Man and Post-Renaissance Management"
Robert M. Bleiberg—"Government and Business"

1975–1976
Esmond Wright—"Life, Liberty and the Pursuit of Excellence"
M. Stanton Evans—"The Liberal Twilight"
Benjamin A. Rogge—"Adam Smith: 1776–1976"
Gottfried Dietze—"Hayek's Concept of the Rule of Law"
Anthony G. A. Fisher—"Must History Repeat Itself?"
Shirley R. Letwin—"The Morality of the Free Man"

1976–1977
Rhodes Boyson—"Paternalism: The Good Man's Evil Enemy of Liberty?"
Leonard Read—"The Something-for-Nothing Syndrome"
Philip M. Crane—"$165 Billion in Red Ink: The Eye of the Hurricane"
Anthony H. Harrigan—"Economics and the Future of the Nation"
Henry Hazlitt—"How Inflation Demoralizes"
Roger A. Freeman—"The Growth of American Government"

1977–1978
Earl L. Butz—"The American Food Machine and Private Entrepreneurship"
Friedrich A. Hayek—"Coping with Ignorance"
Ronald Reagan—"Whatever Happened to Free Enterprise?"
W. Philip Gramm—"The Energy Crisis in Perspective"
Jack Kemp—"The Political Relevance of Ludwig von Mises"
Roger Lea MacBride—"The Politics of Ideas"

1978–1979
Dan Quayle—"Von Mises Looks at Congress"
William E. Simon—"Inflation: Made and Manufactured in Washington, D.C."
George Bush—"Is America a Pushover?"
Benjamin A. Rogge—"The Myth of Monopoly"
Alan Reynolds—"Can Government Stabilize the Economy?"

1979–1980
M. Stanton Evans—"Conservatism and Freedom"
Thomas Sowell—"Knowledge and Decisions"
Arthur Shenfield—"Big Government, Big Labor and Big Business: Parallels True and False"
Arthur B. Laffer—"Would a Federal Tax Cut Be Inflationary?"

Christian Watrin—"A Critique of Macroeconomic Planning from a Misesian-Hayekian Viewpoint"
Walter Williams—"The Poor as First Victims of the Welfare State"

1980–1981
George Gilder—"The Moral Sources of Capitalism"
Antonio Martino—"Statism at Work: The Italian Case; Its Relation to the U.S."
Paul Craig Roberts—"America's Self-Denunciatory Ethic and the Problem of Restoration"
Jay Van Andel—"Economic and Social Challenges of the Eighties"
William Rusher—"Media and the First Amendment"

1981–1982
Israel M. Kirzner—"Mises and the Renaissance of Austrian Economics"
Fritz Machlup—"Ludwig von Mises: A Scholar Who Would Not Compromise"
Roger W. Jepsen—"Reagan, Stockman, and Supply-Side Economics"
Tom Bethell—"Austrians vs. Supply-Siders"
Frank E. Fortkamp—"Liberty for Schools, Schools for Liberty"
Jude Wanniski—"Inflation, Deflation, and the Golden Constant"

1982–1983
Bruce R. Bartlett—"The Role of Economic Theory in Economic Policy: Supply Side Economics"
Arthur Shenfield—"A Durable Free Society: Utopian Dream or Realistic Goal?"
Lewis Lehrman—"Economic Monetary Reform: Putting America Back to Work"
Martin Anderson—"The National Economic Policy: Prospects for Reaganomics"
Murray L. Weidenbaum—"The Need for Free Trade"

1983–1984: The International Economic Order
David Laidler—"The 'Monetary Approach' and the International Monetary System"
Leland B. Yeager—"America and a Healthy World Monetary Order"
Melvyn Krauss—"Is Reagan Losing the Battle of Ideas in the Third World?"
Kurt Leube—"Denationalization of Money"
Anthony Harrigan—"International Trade: Is There Such a Thing?"

1984–1985: Antitrust in a Free Society
Frederick M. Scherer—"Antitrust: Past and Present"
Dominick T. Armentano—"Antitrust Policy in a Free Society"
Joseph D. Reed—"A National Priority: Public Policy for the Information Age"
Dave Button—"Public Policy and Oil Industry Mergers"
Yale Brozen—"Merger Mania: Social Disease or Healthy Adaptation?"

1986: The Federal Budget: The Economic, Political, and Moral Implications for a Free Society
James M. Buchanan—"The Deficit and our Obligation to Future Generations"
Thomas J. DiLorenzo—"Destroying Democracy: How Government Funds Partisan Politics"
Catherine England—"Debt Financing and the Banking Community"
Melvyn Krauss—"The Presumed International Implications of the Federal Deficit"
Paul McCracken—"The Meaning of the Budget in the American Political Process"
Martha Seger—"The Federal Reserve and the Budget Dilemma"
Richard Wagner—"Constitutional Remedies for Democratic Budget Tragedies"

1987: The Privatization Revolution
Allan Carlson—"From Matriarchal State to Private Family: The Privatization of Social Policy"
Arthur Shenfield—"Privatization in the Socialist Camp: Problems and Prospects"
Dick Armey—"Privatization: The Road Away from Serfdom"
J. Peter Grace—"The Problem of Big Government"
John C. Goodman—"The Privatization Solution"
Stuart Butler—"The Political Dynamics of Privatization"
George Marotta—"The World Stock Market and Privatization"

1988: The Politics of Hunger
Eric Brodin—"Man-Made Famine Throughout History"
Mark Huber—"Private-Public Partnerships and African Agricultural Failures"
Robert Kaplan—"Putting the Famine in Perspective"
Mickey Leland—"Is There Really Hunger in America?"
Darrow L. Miller—"The Development Ethic"
Frank Vorhies—"The Black Market for Farming in Southern Africa"

1989: The Free Market and the Black Community
Paul L. Pryde, Jr.—"How the Black Community Can Invest in its Own Future"
Walter E.Williams—"How Much Can Discrimination Explain?"
Charles Murray—"Making Good on a 200-Year-Old Promise: Blacks and the Pursuit of Happiness"
Willie D. Davis—"Positioning for Excellence in a Color-Blind Market"
Steve Mariotti—"Generating Entrepreneurial Activity in the Inner City: Hope for the Future"
William Raspberry—"A Journalist's View of Black Economics"

1990: Austrian Economics: Perspectives on the Past and Prospects for the Future
Richard M. Ebeling—"The Significance of Austrian Economics in Twentieth-Century Economic Thought"
Kurt R. Leube—Commentary
Norman Barry—Commentary
Hans-Hermann Hoppe—"Austrian Rationalism in the Age of the Decline of Positivism"
Robert L. Formaini—Commentary: "The Positivist Horse Is Dead, So Why Do Austrians Insist on Beating It?"
J. Patrick Gunning—Commentary: "Praxeology, Economics, and Ethical Philosophy"
Israel M. Kirzner—"The Driving Force of the Market: The Idea of 'Competition' in Contemporary Economic Theory and in the Austrian Theory of the Market Process"
Stephen Littlechild—Commentary
W. Duncan Reekie—Commentary
Peter J. Boettke—"The Austrian Critique and the Demise of Socialism: The Soviet Case"
Aleksandras Shtromas—Commentary: "Russia on the Road to Political and Economic Freedom"
Samuel Bostaph—Commentary
Jack High—"Regulation as a Process: On the Theory, History, and Doctrine of Government Regulation"
Charles D. Van Eaton—Commentary
Sanford Ikeda—Commentary
Roger W. Garrison—"Austrian Capital Theory and the Future of Macro-economics"
Joseph T. Salerno—Commentary: "The Concept of Coordination in Austrian Macroeconomics"
Peter Lewin—Commentary

Mark Skousen—"Austrian Capital Theory and Economic Development in the Third World"
Sudha R. Shenoy—Commentary: "Austrian Capital Theory and the Under-developed Areas: An Overview"
John B. Egger—Commentary
George A. Selgin—"Monetary Equilibrium and the 'Productivity Norm' of Price-Level Policy"
Lawrence H. White—Commentary: "Norms for Monetary Policy"
Richard M. Ebeling—Commentary: "Stable Prices, Falling Prices, and Market-Determined Prices"
Peter Lewin—Commentary

1990: Austrian Economics: A Reader
A companion to Volume 17. Contains classic works by Ludwig von Mises, Friedrich von Hayek, Carl Menger, Eugen von Böhm-Bawerk, L. G. Bostedo, Ludwig M. Lachmann, M. A. Abrams, Oskar Morgenstern, Vernon A. Mund, Leland B. Yeager, Murray N. Rothbard, Mario J. Rizzo, E. C. Pasour, Israel M. Kirzner, Roger W. Garrison, and Richard M. Ebeling.